American Social Thought: Sources and Interpretations

Volume II: Since the Civil War

Editors:

Robert Allen Skotheim
University of Colorado

Michael McGiffert
University of Denver

Addison-Wesley Publishing Company
Reading, Massachusetts
Menlo Park, California · London · Don Mills, Ontario

This book is in the
ADDISON-WESLEY SERIES IN HISTORY

Consulting Editor
ROBIN W. WINKS

Printed in the United States of America. Published simultaneously in Canada. Library of Congress Catalog Card No. 75-140946.

The Contributing Editors

Ronald Berman (Ph.D., English, Yale, 1959)

is a Shakespearean in the Department of Literature at the University of California, San Diego, whose interests in contemporary American radicalism led him to write *America in the Sixties*, published in 1968.

John C. Burnham (Ph.D., History, Stanford, 1958)

teaches the history of medicine and American science at The Ohio State University. He has published extensively in these fields, including *Psychoanalysis and American Medicine, 1894–1918: Medicine, Science and Culture*, in 1967.

David Marcell (Ph.D., American Studies, Yale, 1964)

is chairman of the American Studies department at Skidmore College and is the author of numerous articles concerning modern American social thought.

David Noble (Ph.D., History, Wisconsin, 1952)

is Professor of History at the University of Minnesota. He has written *The Paradox of Progressive Thought* (1958), *Historians Against History* (1965), *The Eternal Adam and the New World Garden* (1968), and *The Progressive Mind* (1970).

Kermit Vanderbilt (Ph.D., English, Minnesota, 1956)

teaches American literature at San Diego State College. A specialist in the literary and cultural history of the late Nineteenth Century, he has published *Charles Eliot Norton: Apostle of Culture in a Democracy* (1959), and *The Achievement of William Dean Howells* (1968).

General Preface to Both Volumes

During recent decades, as the history of thought has been made an integral part of the study and teaching of history, historians have paid close attention to the relations of ideas to the dynamics and patterns of social development. Consistent with this preoccupation with social thought, historians emphasize the points at which ideas affect, or are affected by, political, social, and economic experience. Few other fields of historical inquiry have produced such illuminating results.

Even though the history of social thought is a popular subject, there is neither a single ruling definition of it, nor one universally approved method of studying it. Some scholars and teachers accent the role of elite thinkers while others emphasize a wider range of public sentiment. Some study the "spirit of an age" or governing "climate of opinion," while others investigate particular ideas, or ideational systems, and their ramifications over periods of time. Some examine the impact of ideas upon behavior; others treat ideas as a part, however significant, of the total historical configuration.

These two volumes, comprised of documents and interpretive commentaries assembled by a dozen scholars, each of whom commands authority in his respective field, are intended to introduce the student to the work that is going forward on several fronts of American intellectual history. These readings reflect both the consensus on the importance of the history of social thought and some of the varying definitions, materials, and approaches to the field of study. With the exception that each contributor has been asked to include both primary and secondary source readings, no attempt has been made by the general editors to impose any rigid formula for the contents or structure of each section. The result, in both its common elements and its variety, expresses the state of scholarship in the 1970's on the history of American social ideas. Hopefully, these volumes will stimulate the interest of students in America's intellectual past and present.

Boulder and Denver, Colorado R. A. S.
March 1971 M. McG.

Contents

Introduction

The history of American social thought since the Civil War is customarily related in terms of reform. Do ideas of a given period, explicitly and implicitly, support the status quo or undermine it? On what basis does a particular historical figure justify or criticize the existing social, economic, and political arrangements? These are the most characteristic questions historians of social thought ask of their materials.

The dominant current of social thought in the late Nineteenth Century is interpreted by historians as conservative in that it defended existing social arrangements. Two ideas, or clusters of beliefs, are singled out as being most important to the conservative argument. The first is what historians usually call Conservative Social Darwinism, which was the application to human society of Charles Darwin's "natural selection" hypothesis in biology. Darwin had explained the evolution of species on the basis of a naturally adaptive and selective process. Species were selected or singled out for survival because they could adapt to their environment. Conservative Social Darwinists applied to contemporary life a jungle metaphor of competitive struggle for existence which Darwin had demonstrated biologically. Individuals who survived most successfully, who were wealthy and powerful, had shown their superior fitness in coping with their environment. Through the evolution of "the survival of the fittest" mankind as a whole progressed. Thus it was proved that reformers ought not to interfere with the supposed cruelty, inhumanity, and suffering in society, because above and beyond the apparent harshness was a cosmic process of betterment at work. By implication, the social, economic, and political status quo was justified.

Even allowing for the exaggerated starkness in this summary of Conservative Social Darwinism, it must be said that there is little evidence from the late 1800's to indicate that belief in it was widespread among the general public. It was largely expressed by intellectuals, particularly social philosophers who were interested in explaining the universe as well as their own lives and times. Rare was the businessman, or other man of action, such as Andrew

Carnegie, who actually related his own career directly to the principles of Conservative Social Darwinism. And, like Carnegie, most Americans who did use Darwin as a social guide minimized the naturalistic brutality of the jungle struggle by insisting that morals as well as power, right as well as fitness, evolved upward in the long run.

Conservative Social Darwinism did, however, complement and reinforce the second leading idea of the late nineteenth century singled out by historians. This was the much more popular belief in Self-Help. From the Puritans on, Americans have been taught the moral that any individual can, and should, achieve worldly success through hard work. Those who are not diligent will be indigent. Theological in its seventeenth-century form (the doctrine of calling, which stipulated that God wanted man to work hard and prosper in his vocation), the Self-Help dogma quickly became detached from its religious moorings and since has been profoundly secular in its implications. Negatively, the failure of revolution, the lack of support for socialism, and the difficulties of organizing the labor movement in the late 1800's, have all been partly attributed by historians to the pervasive American conviction that good men who are patient, loyal, thrifty, energetic, practical, punctual, and clean must (with luck and a little help from their friends) inevitably succeed. Positively, the "meaning of life" expressed by millions of Americans has been largely in terms of their own acting out of the "rags-to-riches" story.

It is this second body of thought, the Self-Help myth, which is the theme of Section One. Professor Kermit Vanderbilt has gathered a remarkably wide range of documents illustrating the variety of formulations of the dogma, mainly, but not exclusively, from the late 1800's when it was particularly popular. The documents illustrate the highly moralistic nature of precepts offered in the "how to succeed" literature. And so comprehensive was the moral guidance offered in the literature that much of the social thought of the period can be found in these selections. But even at its height, Professor Vanderbilt suggests, the myth did not escape criticism from some Americans who perceived its limitations as a guide to life. In the later commentaries on the myth, presented by Professor Vanderbilt at the end of the section, the reader can see how more recent historians have interpreted the Self-Help doctrine, including whether they judge it to be in accord with the facts of American life.

Section Two, edited by Professor John Burnham, presents primary and secondary materials for the understanding of the reform mentality which emerged at the end of the Nineteenth Century and became dominant in the beginning of the Twentieth Century. Moving from the jungle metaphor of the Conservative Social Darwinists, who had insisted that man progressed through competition, the new reformers argued that progress had occurred instead through intelligent cooperation. The reformers agreed with the conservatives that man's environment was influential in making him what he was, but they claimed that man could help mold the environment and thus help mold himself. Future social betterment would therefore come most quickly if society consciously and systematically investigated ways of improving the environment in which men live. Science became the model for society's control over, as well as knowledge of, the world. Professor Burnham suggests that it is a mistake to see the progressive reform mentality mainly in terms of politics and economics, as many historians do. He argues that the distinctiveness of the progressive mind was its comprehensive reformism. He provides illustrations of medical, psychological, and social science contributions in the early 1900's, as well as documents from the areas of political and economic thought, and he suggests that the powerful preoccupation of progressive reform shaped them all into a common pattern.

Professor Burnham emphasizes the role of intellectuals, the educated and articulate elite whose writings he selects for expressions of the progressive mind. The intellectuals are also the subject of Section Three, edited by Professor David Noble, but here the focus is upon a different group of intellectuals who did not share the confident assumptions of the pre-war reformers. Professor Noble has selected documents to illustrate the "estrangement of the intellectuals" around the World War I period and during the 1920's.

There were some intellectuals in the years before the Great War who, like the Transcendentalists of the Nineteenth Century, developed a critique of American life which stood outside the mainstream of public debate. As critical of progressive reformers as of their conservative opponents, these alienated intellectuals attacked many of the basic beliefs of their civilization. The tragedy of the First World War accelerated the assault on the progressive temper. Confidence that the world was improving, that man in the mass was rational and good enough to build a better world, was dealt a sharp blow. The assumption of a moral universe was undermined. Science and technology were darkly revealed to be as easily instruments of death and destruction as of social improvement.

The 1920's brought from the intellectuals widespread criticism of traditional American assumptions and hopes, and an unprecedented self-imposed exile to Europe of discontented writers, artists, and bohemians. Professor Noble's contemporary source selections illustrate the criticism by leading intellectuals, after which he offers a sampling of the scholarship of the estranged intellectuals, including the "lost generation" of expatriates. Professor Noble himself suggests that the scholarship has not sufficiently emphasized the extent to which the alienation of the intelligentsia has been a common occurrence throughout the western world in the last two centuries and the degree to which this represents a romantic revolt against Enlightenment rationalism, science, technology, and the modern world.

The preoccupation of estranged intellectuals in the 1920's was not so much political and economic as personal and cultural. The Great Depression focused the attention of almost all Americans upon political and economic problems. Section Four, edited by Professor Robert Allen Skotheim, presents materials concerning the resulting political radicalism and the later re-embracement of a traditional America by the once estranged intellectuals.

Moderate reformers as well as radicals in the 1930's faced economic and political crises with the basic intellectual outlook structured by the progressivism of pre-World War I years. The first selections from contemporaries illustrate how a Socialist, a supporter of Franklin Roosevelt's New Deal, and a Communist, all expressed a common progressive and experimentalist approach to the Depression. No matter how radical many of the intellectuals were during the early 1930's, few could later fail to credit the New Deal with an attempt to move in what they considered the right direction. This realization had the consequence of reducing the antagonism intellectuals felt toward the dominant institutions of American society. Perhaps even more important to the undermining of radicalism and the rapprochement of the intellectual in America was the "discovery" of European totalitarianism in the 1930's. The rejection of traditional America expressed in the estrangement of the intellectuals before and after World War I was accompanied by an attraction for Europe. When the revolutionary dictatorships spread from Russia to Italy to Germany to Spain by the late 1930's, and when, particularly in the Soviet Union, early hopes turned to ashes under a ruthlessly total subjugation of the individual for the glory of the State, America for the first time benefited by comparison. Whatever the limitations of the New Deal, Roosevelt and the political system had managed to cope with economic catastrophe within the democratic constitutional process which protected the traditional rights of individuals. As America's traditions were celebrated at the end of the Depression decade by the intellectuals and former radicals, the social thought of the United States reflected a nation more united than at any time since World War I.

As was anticipated by the late 1930's, the social thought of the 1940's and 1950's revealed a search for national stability and consensus. Against the background of two decades of international conflict, Americans became increasingly affirmative about their heritage and yet, in a sense, at the same time more apprehensive than before concerning future possibilities. Ordinarily proud of their science and technology, with the exception of dissident criticism such as that of the alienated intellectuals in the 1920's, Americans in the post-war years tried to reconcile the wonders of scientific knowledge and domestic technology with the horrors of atomic warfare. Americans customarily assumed that experts in government could be judged and controlled by public men of common sense, and they tried to reconcile popular government with the increasing power of men with scientific, technological, and military expertise which almost no one else could understand. Generally proud of the high standard of living in the United States and the priority given to material affluence, Americans tried to reconcile post-war prosperity with increasing anxiety concerning the spiritual and psychological quality of life. While preaching that America was a dream fulfilled, many Americans were torn by doubt about those individuals who chose not to conform or who, by their color, religion, or economic poverty, were unable to conform to the dream. Professor David Marcell in Section Five has illustrated these dilemmas expressed by post-war Americans as they tried to achieve stability in a world of revolutionary change. Symbolic of the paradoxical nature of the period, in the final selection, an ex-radical confidently announced at the end of the 1950's that a new era of rejection of radicalism had arrived—just as a time of unprecedented radicalism in the 1960's was about to begin.

The final section documents the new radicalism of the 1960's which has moved in growing force into the 1970's. In his choice of selections, Professor Ronald Berman has illustrated both the political activism and the search for a new life style on the part of the preponderantly youthful rebels. Many of the themes of the earlier sections reappear in the last one, as the contemporary radicals act out of a past which they may or may not be aware of. They attack the middle-class values of the venerable Horatio Alger myth, and reaffirm the old progressive argument that man must create a new environment in which he can live a more humane life. Like the expatriates and bohemians of the 1920's, many of today's young are more concerned about psychological and spiritual matters than economics and politics. The attempt to create a new life style in the 1920's resulted not in a counterculture, but rather in the assimilation by the affluent middle class of those aspects of the new life style which were congenial. The breakdown of a Victorian sexual code, for example, and the disbelief in traditional absolutes generally, proved not to lead to revolt or withdrawal from established society but instead were reconciled to life within the status quo. Whether or not America's sponge-like ability to soak up dissent and squeeze it dry of its radicalism will nullify the current attempt of the young to create a truly different life style is an open question. A parallel case is that of the more political Old and New Lefts. Discouraged about effecting meaningful change within the system, a few radicals in the 1920's and many in the 1930's were often willing to sanction violence in the name of a good cause, and the same willingness is found today in the New Left. Some of the old radicals defended revolutionary dictatorship briefly, but most of them later renounced it and embraced democratic constitutionalism. Only time will tell whether today's radicals will move through the same cycle.

In Section Six, as in Section Five, no distinction is made between contemporary sources and scholarly analysis, since all commentators on these recent events are both participants and contemporary chroniclers.

R. A. S.

Section One
The Gospel of Self-Help and Success in the Gilded Age

KERMIT VANDERBILT

Contents

Introduction

The readings collected here suggest the history of a dynamic and formative idea in American experience. Throughout our colonial and national history, we have cherished the image, first captured by the hardy pioneer, John Smith, who, upon surveying the unlimited possibilities of life in a bountiful virgin land, glimpsed a Western utopia where man need rely "only on his merit to advance his fortunes." When frontiers might have appeared later to shift or recede, the self-reliant American cheerfully confronted each renewed challenge to his character and ingenuity. This ideal of self-help did not, of course, originate in our country; but no other nation in the Western world has wedded the Protestant ethic to an environment so responsive to human enterprise. The moral question was posed by the early New England leaders of church and state: was it not the pious man's duty in this new land to work and pray without ceasing, and his destiny, through God's favor, to grow wealthy? The later Puritan, Cotton Mather, repeated these injunctions to a new generation in his *Essays to Do Good.* Among his young audience was Benjamin Franklin who, in turn, bequeathed the economic virtues of Poor Richard to the next century of rural and urban pioneers.

To the age of Jackson and the generation after, orators and writers propounded the ideal of the self-made man and lauded his vigorous acquisitive spirit. William Ellery Channing, Edward Everett, Henry Ward Beecher, Horace Mann, Freeman Hunt, Timothy Shay Arthur, and countless others declaimed the patriotic duty of young men to compete and achieve. In 1832, Hawthorne urged the youthful hero of "My Kinsman, Major Molineux" along the road to self-reliance. Washington Irving in *Astoria* (1836) recounted the achievement of John Jacob Astor, who rose from German immigrant to multimillionaire. In both "The American Scholar" (1837) and "Self-Reliance" (1841), Ralph Waldo Emerson charged his audiences to beware of the enemies of individualism. By 1851, he was pointedly defending the pursuit of wealth in the lectures on "The Conduct of Life." Two years later, an article titled "Success in Life" appeared in *Harper's New Monthly*

Magazine and confirmed that the predominant clue to American character lay in the national obsession with "getting on." But, predictably, through it all a sour or irreverent note occasionally sounded. In "Bartleby the Scrivener," which appeared also in 1853, Herman Melville chose to portray a perverse young man who "prefers not" to get on in the Wall Street law office where his employer worships the memory of John Jacob Astor. The next year, in *Walden*, Henry David Thoreau also denounced, though somewhat ambivalently, the pervasive commercial spirit which had atrophied the creative and spiritual lives of his busy countrymen.

Thoreau did not live beyond the Civil War to witness the rise and the apotheosis of the busy man of commerce. Manuals explaining how to succeed in business now multiplied sixfold to the end of the century and emanated in large numbers from Thoreau's own New England. Other interests, to be sure, were shaping and coloring the national experience in the Gilded Age. Yet one might argue that the doctrine of self-help and success penetrated, in some guise, every major activity of the period: the new immigration, the rise of socialism, the agrarian revolution (and the exodus of country boys and girls to the city), the march of technology, the growth of corporate business and labor unionism, and more. In education, when Garfield praised the Spencerian Business College in 1869, scarcely two dozen such schools existed. By 1894, five hundred were serving one hundred thousand students. Aware of this trend, Charles Francis Adams could ask Professor Charles Eliot Norton to justify Harvard's continuing to offer classical and humanistic courses to the sons of businessmen. Through the final decades of the century, in politics, in science, in religion, in the new sociology and psychology, men were raising vital questions that touched on environmental determinism, moral agency, free opportunity, private corruption, and public reform, all germane to the mystique of the self-made man.

Perhaps in actuality the acquisition of large fortunes in this period issued more often from the vagaries of chance (including fortunate birth) than through the agency of Christian character and clean living. Perhaps rugged individualism coupled with unlimited economic opportunity was, after all, not an attainable condition but the stuff of dreams for the mass population. If myth it was, success through self-help was indubitably valid in the Jungian sense, for it usually rang true in the subconscious chambers of the middle-class mind. The masses fed their hopes by paying willingly with hard-won savings to listen to those who peddled the dream and outlined the formula of achievement through pious industry and perseverance. Millions of Americans, old and young, devoured the fiction of Horatio Alger, the conservatively oriented McGuffey Readers, the inspirational biographies of William Makepeace Thayer, the resounding optimism of Russell H. Conwell's "Acres of Diamonds," and the perennial flood of treatises which often duplicated a familiar store of anecdotes describing poor boys who had risen in the world.

A smaller audience read the more distinguished literature of the new "realism" movement. There the happy myth of success through individual enterprise might have been qualified, but authors such as Mark Twain, Henry James, and William Dean Howells were themselves sufficiently attracted to moneymaking not to dispel the myth. Mark Twain attained the impetus to continue *Huckleberry Finn* (1885) after he conceived the colorful, Barnum-esque figures, the Duke and the King. James's Christopher Newman (*The American*, 1877) and Howells' Silas Lapham (*The Rise of Silas Lapham*, 1885) were slightly comic as rough-hewn new millionaires in the Franklin tradition; but such finely etched portraits also suggested a large measure of sympathy from their creators. Because they shared the role of the hard-working young man from the provinces, Howells could improvise confidently on the country-boy myth in *The Minister's Charge* (1887) and Twain in *A Connecticut Yankee in King Arthur's Court* (1889).

Earlier, in the 1850's, Charles Eliot Norton had labored as a businessman-philanthropist to relieve the already deplorable slum conditions created by the new industrialism in the American city. At the opening of the post-war era, however, he anticipated the defeat of his efforts to humanize the city. Norton privately questioned in 1869 "whether our period of economical enterprise, unlimited competition, and unrestrained individualism is the highest stage of human progress." By the Eighties, such questionings had grown into public rumblings of discontent, punctuated by dynamite, bloodshed, and labor strikes multiplying by the hundreds each year. A growing number of novelists now began to cast doubts on the legend of the self-made man. E. W. Howe in *The Story of a Country Town* (1883), Joseph Kirkland in *Zury* (1887), and Hamlin Garland in "Mrs. Ripley's Trip" (1888) and other tales from his *Main-Travelled Roads* (1891) exposed the cruel facts of rural deprivation in America. Equally grim were the glimpses of urban poverty in Howells' *A Hazard of New Fortunes* (1890) and Stephen Crane's *Maggie* (1893), or in social reformer Jacob Riis's *How the Other Half Lives* (1890). Charles B. Spahr discovered that by 1890, 11 million of America's 12.5 million families lived on an average income of $380 a year. In 1894, Henry D. Lloyd published *Wealth Against Commonwealth* and Ida Tarbell began to write her exposés of American business for *McClure's* magazine.

The undaunted apostles of self-help and success continued to enroll thousands of devotees. To encourage their readers to keep the faith, the *New York Tribune* conducted a poll in 1892 which tallied 4,047 millionaires in America. Vibrant new voices replaced the earlier merchants of the dream. Andrew Carnegie, Russell H. Conwell, Edward Bok, Elbert Hubbard, and Orison Swett Marden urged the young man at the end of the century to Shift for Himself, to Strive and Succeed. The unbelievers who had multiplied in the audience frequently drove these new spokesmen into a rhetorical stance more defensive than before. But the dominant mood remained sanguine.

When Horatio Alger, Jr., died in the summer of 1899, the soil he had worked so many years was by no means depleted.

In the Twentieth Century, the myth has often fallen on evil times. Herbert Hoover's *American Individualism* appeared in 1922, but so also did Sinclair Lewis's clownish, pathetic businessman-hero of *Babbitt* and H. L. Mencken's essays debunking the Protestant ethic and the middle-class boob. When Hoover reaffirmed rugged individualism twelve years later in *The Challenge of Liberty*, a Depression audience was also making acquaintance with the grotesque entrepreneurs in the works of John Dos Passos and the historical robber barons of Matthew Josephson. At the end of the Thirties, Dale Carnegie and John Steinbeck spoke, separately, on success and failure in America. The survivor of this period will recall, however, that these opposite views were received by a common audience of chastened but resilient Americans who had emerged from the darkest night of the Depression. Willing to concede the truth of a Steinbeck, we were also prepared to acquire and achieve anew in the light of updated success maxims issued by a latter-day Carnegie.

Since World War II, the debate over opportunity, motivation, and success has continued, clustered this time around David Reisman's "inner-directed" nineteenth-century individualist and the more complaisant "other-directed" American at midcentury. Despite Reisman's dichotomy, a new conservatism emerged in the Eisenhower Fifties and survived to see Barry Goldwater, whose own fortune was inherited, run his 1964 campaign for president on a Gilded Age philosophy of *laissez-faire* individualism. The crushing defeat notwithstanding, Goldwater's nineteenth-century message cheered the nation's estimated ninety thousand millionaires. And it ignited the secret dreams shared by millions of upwardly mobile Americans of the great middle-class electorate.

The ideal of the self-made man remains alive at midcentury also through scores of how-to-succeed titles available in paperback books at the American corner drugstore. The present collection of documents does not extend to this reaffirmation of attainable success in America. Included here instead are a group of present-day historians who re-examine the nineteenth-century basis of this continuing gospel of self-help and prosperity. Richard Mosier. Irvin Wyllie, and John Cawelti reassess the spirit of McGuffey, Horatio Alger, and other apostles of opportunity and manhood in the last century, while William Miller tries to gauge the distance between the American dream and the performance, to balance the popular myth against the cold statistical evidence of achieved success during the post-Civil War period. By supplementing this scholarship and insight with the distinguished work of Cochran, Kirkland, Wohl, and other writers listed in the bibliography at the end of these commentaries, the reader today can enjoy a wide ranging introduction to the social thought of the Gilded Age—and the present age.

Sources

James Garfield
Elements of Success

(1869)

After the death of Lincoln until the turn of the century, no president surpassed James Garfield in advancing the gospel of self-help and success. Born in a log cabin, Garfield was the poor country boy, fatherless at eighteen months, a hard-working and self-reliant youngster who rose to election to Congress and finally to the White House. Soon after his assassination, Garfield was the subject of inspirational biographies by success cultists William Makepeace Thayer, Horatio Alger, Jr., and Russell Conwell. (Alger rushed his account into print in thirteen days.) During his lifetime, Garfield not only lived but also propounded the success gospel. His memorable public utterance was "Elements of Success" on June 29, 1869, delivered before the students of the Spencerian Business College in Washington, D.C., and later reprinted to reach a national audience. In the following excerpt, his introductory praise of the new American business college as an aid to rising men and women, and several illustrative anecdotes, are omitted.

. . . Now, young gentlemen, let me for a moment address you touching your success in life; and I hope the very brevity of my remarks will increase the chance of their making a lodgement in your minds. Let me beg you, in the outset of your career, to dismiss from your minds all ideas of succeeding by luck. There is no more common thought among young people than that foolish one, that by and by something will turn up by which they will suddenly achieve fame or fortune. No, young gentlemen, things don't turn up in this world unless somebody turns them up. Inertia is one of the indispensable laws of matter; and things lie flat where they are until by some intelligent spirit (for nothing but spirit makes motion in this world) they are endowed with activity and life. Do not dream that some good luck is going to happen to you, and give you a fortune. Luck is an *ignis fatuus*: you may follow it to ruin, but not to

James Garfield, "Elements of Success," in *President Garfield and Education*, B. A. Hindale, ed. (Boston, 1882), pp. 315–34.

success. The great Napoleon, who believed in his destiny, followed it until he saw his star go down in blackest night, when the Old Guard perished around him, and Waterloo was lost. A pound of pluck is worth a ton of luck.

Young men talk of trusting to the spur of the occasion. That trust is vain. Occasions cannot make spurs, young gentlemen. If you expect to wear spurs, you must win them. If you wish to use them, you must buckle them to your own heels before you go into the fight. Any success you may achieve is not worth the having unless you fight for it. Whatever you win in life you must conquer by your own efforts; and then it is yours,—a part of yourself.

Again: in order to have any success in life, or any worthy success, you must resolve to carry into your work a fulness of knowledge,—not merely a sufficiency, but more than a sufficiency. In this respect, follow the rule of the machinists. If they want a machine to do the work of six horses, they give it nine-horse power, so that they may have a reserve of three. To carry on the business of life, you must have surplus power. Be fit for more than the thing you are now doing. Let everyone know that you have a reserve in yourself—that you have more power than you are now using . . . If you are not too large for the place you occupy, you are too small for it. How full our country is of bright examples, not only of those who occupy some proud eminence in public life, but in every place you may find men going on with steady nerve, attracting the attention of their fellow-citizens, and carving out for themselves names and fortunes from small and humble beginnings and in the face of formidable obstacles . . .

Young gentlemen, let not poverty stand as an obstacle in your way. Poverty is uncomfortable, as I can testify; but nine times out of ten the best thing that can happen to a young man is to be tossed overboard, and compelled to sink or swim for himself. In all my acquaintance, I have never known one to be drowned who was worth the saving. This would not be wholly true in any country but one of political equality like ours. The editor of one of the leading magazines of England told me, not many months ago, a fact startling enough in itself, but of great significance to a poor man. He told me that he had never yet known, in all his experience, a single boy of the class of farm-laborers (not those who own farms, but mere farm-laborers) who had ever risen above his class. Boys from the manufacturing and commercial classes had risen frequently, but from the farm-labor class he had never known one.

The reason is this: In the aristocracies of the Old World, wealth and society are built up like the strata of rock which compose the crust of the earth. If a boy be born in the lowest stratum of life, it is almost impossible for him to rise through this hard crust into the higher ranks; but in this country it is not so. The strata of our society resemble rather the ocean, where every drop, even the lowest, is free to mingle with all others, and may shine at last on the crest of the highest wave. This is the glory of our country, young gentlemen; and you need not fear that there are any obstacles which will prove too great for any brave heart. You will recollect what Burns, who knew all meanings of poverty and struggle, has said in homely verse:

"Though losses and crosses
Be lessons right severe,
There's wit there, you'll get there,
You'll find no other where."

One thought more, and I will close. This is almost a sermon, but I cannot help it; for the occasion itself has given rise to the thoughts I am offering you. Let me suggest, that, in giving you being, God locked up in your nature certain forces and capabilities. What will you do with them? Look at the mechanism of a clock. Take off the pendulum and ratchet, and the wheels go rattling down, and all its force is expended in a moment; but properly balanced and regulated it will go on, letting out its force tick by tick, measuring hours and days, and doing faithfully the service for which it was designed. I implore you to cherish and guard and use well the forces that God has given to you. You may let them run down in a year, if you will. Take off the strong curb of discipline and morality, and you will be an old man before your twenties are passed. Preserve these forces. Do not burn them out with brandy, or waste them in idleness and crime. Do not destroy them. Do not use them unworthily. Save and protect them, that they may save for you fortune and fame. Honestly resolve to do this, and you will be an honor to yourself and to your country. I thank you, young friends, for your kind attention.

Horatio Alger, Jr.
Luck and Pluck

(1869)

With *Luck and Pluck; or John Oakley's Inheritance*, Horatio Alger, Jr. (1834–1899), introduced his "Luck and Pluck Series" in 1869. The frontispiece depicted a country boy waving farewell to parents in a distant farmyard as he leaves, presumably to confront the urban challenge of postwar America. In *John Oakley's Inheritance*, Alger created one of his strongest plots. Otherwise it resembles the companion novels in the Ragged Dick and Tattered Tom series. Stilted in narration and dialogue, the story is dominated by Alger's boy-hero, not a ragged street boy this time but a fifteen-year-old village lad exemplary for his initiative, industry, perseverance, loyalty, sobriety, frugality, and respect for established authority. Orphaned, in effect, and dispossessed at his father's recent death, John lives with his devious stepmother Jane

Horatio Alger, Jr., *Luck and Pluck; or John Oakley's Inheritance* (Boston, 1869).

Oakley and his pampered and quarrelsome stepbrother Ben Brayton. The plot turns on the search for a hidden will which will restore John's rightful inheritance.

The two passages given here illustrate the moral and aesthetic qualities which fifty million American readers would come to recognize as the literary voice of Horatio Alger. In the first selection, from Chapter XV, Jane Oakley has tricked John into making a trip to the home of Ephraim Huxter, her shiftless, drunken brother, so that she can be undisturbed to locate and destroy the undiscovered will. In the second excerpt, John returns home after a resourceful escape from the Huxters to his aunt's home fifty miles away (where he has exposed the chicanery of her store-manager and then managed the business himself). The will has been recovered by his stepmother; stolen and then lost by her son Ben; and finally rediscovered by John's best friend, Sam Selwyn.

Mrs. Oakley's Note

John opened the note, little suspecting the nature of its contents. It was as follows:

> "*John Oakley:* I have made an arrangement with my brother to have you board with him for the present. As you and Benjamin find it so difficult to agree, it will be much better that you should live apart. If you had not treated him so brutally I should not be under the necessity of sending you away from home. I hope you will give my brother no trouble, but will follow his directions. He understands what course I wish him to pursue with you. If he reports favorably of you, I will send for you to return at a proper time. *Jane Oakley*
>
> "P.S. I will forward your trunk by express, early next week."

John read this cold and unjust letter with mingled anger and dismay. It was hard to have all the blame of his quarrel with Ben thrown upon him, when Ben had been the aggressor, and he had only contended for his just rights. So he was to be exiled from home on Ben's account. He could not help thinking how happily his father and he used to live together before the present Mrs. Oakley came to the farm as housekeeper. And now she and her son had taken possession, and he was turned adrift. What would his father have thought, could he have forseen what would happen so soon after his death!

These thoughts, and others not less disturbing, passed through John's mind as he read his stepmother's letter. Mr. Huxter's eyes were fixed upon his face in cruel exultation, for he imagined the nature of John's feelings, and enjoyed his sorrow.

"Well, Oakley, what do you say to that?" he demanded.

"I don't know what to say," said John.

"No, I presume not. The fact is, you haven't got anything to say in the matter. My sister is your natural guardian, and she has sent you to me to manage. She says you're rather a tough subject; but I reckon I can manage you. You'll find me a little harder to deal with than a woman, I can tell you that."

John did not reply. Indeed, he hardly knew what Mr. Huxter had been saying. So many thoughts crowded in upon his mind with regard to the sudden change in his position that he paid little attention to what was said.

"Is this the only business on which Mrs. Oakley sent me?" he asked, at length.

"It's enough, isn't it?" demanded Mr. Huxter, with a laugh. "So you hadn't the least idea what was the object of your expedition?"

"No, I had not," said John, indignantly. "I had no suspicion that it was only a trap."

"I knew you hadn't," said Mr. Huxter, laughing with evident enjoyment. "You were pretty well taken in, hey?"

"I was taken in," said John, shortly.

"Sister Jane was pretty cute. She knew you'd be making a fuss, if you knew. I told her that once I got you here there wouldn't be any more trouble. So now you know all about it, and you may as well settle down to staying here."

Mrs. Huxter, to whom all this was news, listened with earnest attention. She was a good-hearted woman, and she couldn't help pitying John. She liked her sister-in-law, now Mrs. Oakley, no better than John did, and was very thankful when, after a two years' residence under her roof, she had obtained a position as housekeeper at a distance. She readily came to the conclusion that John had been harshly and unjustly treated, and she could not forbear expressing her sympathy.

"I did not know you were going to remain with us, Mr. Oakley," she said. "I'll try to make you comfortable as long as you stay."

"Thank you, Mrs. Huxter," said John, gratefully; for he could understand the kindness which led her to speak.

"You needn't mister him," said Mr. Huxter, roughly. "It's ridiculous to call such a boy 'Mr.'; It'll make him put on airs worse than ever."

"I do not know his first name," said Mrs. Huxter.

"My name is John," said our hero.

"Then I will call you so, if you are willing."

"If he is willing! Don't make a fool of yourself, Mrs. Huxter. It makes no difference whether he is willing or not."

"I shall be glad to have you call me John," said our hero, without regarding Mr. Huxter's brutal speech.

John rose from the table. He had not eaten much, for Mr. Huxter's coarseness, and the note from his stepmother, had taken away his appetite.

"Won't you have something more, John?" asked Mrs. Huxter. "You've eaten very little."

"No, thank you. I don't feel much appetite this morning."

He took his hat, and was about to leave the house by the back door which led out of the kitchen.

"Where are you going, Oakley?" demanded Mr. Huxter.

"I am going out for a walk," said John, shortly.

Mr. Huxter hesitated whether to obey the dictates of the petty tyranny which impelled him to forbid John to go out, but finally decided not to interfere at present. He contented himself, therefore, with saying:

"I expect you to return within an hour."

John made no reply, but his manly spirit revolted against such contemptible despotism. He did not recognize Mr. Huxter's authority, and did not mean to. He resolved to take an independent stand at once, and return when he pleased, and no sooner. I wish it to be distinctly understood that John did not expect, at his present age, to enjoy all the privileges of a grown man. He was always respectful to rightful authority, but he considered that Mr. Huxter's authority was not rightful, and that his commands ought to have no weight with him. Mr. Huxter did not know the character with which he had to deal. He did not know that John could be as firm under some circumstances, as he was compliant in others. If he had known him better he might have felt less confident of triumphing over him.

When he left the room Huxter turned to his wife, and said, harshly:

"I've got something to say to you, Mrs. Huxter. You needn't trouble yourself to take that boy's part. He is a proud-spirited young rascal, and he needs taking down."

"He seems to me a very good sort of boy," said his wife.

"That shows what a good judge you are," said Mr. Huxter, with a sneer. "He's a young bully, and was all the time fighting with Ben."

"I always thought Ben inclined to be a bully," said Mrs. Huxter.

"Well, he is a proud young upstart," admitted his uncle, who had not forgiven Ben's disdain. "Got some of the Brayton blood in him. But the other's just as bad. It's six of one and half a dozen of the other. However, wife," pursued Mr. Huxter, with a change of tone, "it's likely to be a good thing for us. We're to have six dollars a week for boarding young Oakley."

"That's very good pay. I really think we ought to make him comfortable."

Conclusion

A letter was at once despatched to John, from Squire Selwyn, requesting his immediate return to Hampton.

Though no reason was assigned for the summons, John of course lost no time in obeying it. On the third day he was set down at the lawyer's house.

"O John, how glad I am to see you!" said Sam, in his delight flinging both arms around John's neck, and giving him a warm embrace.

John's greeting was no less hearty.

"Such news, John!" said Sam.

"It isn't the will?" inquired John, eagerly.

"But it is, though."

"Found?"

"Yes, and I found it. Didn't I tell you so! Don't you remember my dream?"

"But perhaps it's all a dream now."

"Well, if it is, it's a substantial dream, and father's got the document locked up in his safe. You're no longer dependent on Mrs. Oakley, and you can go to college with me, and—you don't know how glad I am."

"Yes, I do, Sam," said John. "You're just as glad as if it had happened to yourself, and that's what I expected of you. But you haven't told me how it was found yet."

"Oh, it was such fun!" said Sam. "Sit down here, and I'll tell you all about it."

It need hardly be said that John was amused by the story of Ben's ludicrous embarrassment; but he was surprised as well.

"How could Ben have got hold of it? I don't understand that."

"Nor I," said Sam. "But as long as we've got it, we won't trouble ourselves about that."

It was decided that the next morning Squire Selwyn, accompanied by John, should call on Mrs. Oakley, and make arrangements founded on the new phase of affairs.

Mrs. Oakley had not received intelligence of John's return, and her surprise was accompanied by a nervous sensation, when Hannah came up to her chamber, and announced that Squire Selwyn was below, and Master John was with him.

"John Oakley?" she demanded, hastily.

"Yes, ma'am."

Mrs. Oakley entered the parlor with her old haughty step, and coldly bade the lawyer "good morning." Of John she took no notice.

"Good-morning, Mrs. Oakley," said John.

"So you have got back, have you?" she said.

"Yes, he has got home to stay," said Squire Selwyn, significantly.

"With or without my permission, I suppose," said Mrs. Oakley.

"I don't know that he needs anybody's permission to live in his own house," said the lawyer.

"His own house!" repeated Mrs. Oakley, in a voice which, despite her efforts, betrayed some nervousness.

"Yes, Mrs. Oakley. My object in calling upon you this morning is to apprise you that the will is found."

"What will?" she demanded.

"Your late husband's last will and testament, in which he bequeaths this estate to his son John, here present."

"Where's the will?"

"Here," said the lawyer, producing it.

"Will you let me see it?"

"Excuse me, but it must remain in my possession till it is publicly read."

"What reason have I for believing this is to be a genuine document?" said Mrs. Oakley, harshly. It was foolish thus to contend, and she knew it; but it angered her that by the document she should be stripped of two-thirds of what she had come to look upon as her own.

"I am prepared to swear that it is the will which I drew up for your husband three months before his death."

"I suppose I am not to ask how it came into your possession?" said Mrs. Oakley. "If it was concealed in this house, some one must have entered illegally, and made a secret search."

Mrs. Oakley fixed her eyes upon John, feeling satisfied that he had entered the house on the day she left her keys out, and opened the drawer.

"If you think I had anything to do with it, Mrs. Oakley," said John, "you are mistaken. I only reached Hampton last evening, summoned by Squire Selwyn."

"I accused you of nothing," said Mrs. Oakley, but she was greatly surprised.

"As to who found the will, Mrs. Oakley," said Squire Selwyn, composedly, "I will only suggest that your son Benjamin can probably throw more light on this matter than any one else."

"Benjamin!" exclaimed Mrs. Oakley, quickly.

"Yes, I have reason to think he can give you all the information you desire."

Mrs. Oakley compressed her lips closely. Was it possible that Ben had found the will and deliberately carried it to Squire Selwyn? Could he have sold her and his own interests to the enemy? No doubt she argued, Squire Selwyn had bribed him at a heavy price to deliver it up.

"I don't understand this," she said. "If Benjamin found the will, he should have brought it to me."

"As, of course, you would have placed it in my hands, there is no harm done," said the lawyer, watching keenly the face that showed some discomposure as he spoke. "But you can settle that with Ben. I will merely read you the provisions of the will informally, previous to presenting it for probate."

To this Mrs. Oakley could make no objection, though she was fully acquainted with the document to be read.

It provided that the home estate, consisting of the family mansion, and lands situated in the town of Hampton, valued together at twenty thousand dollars, should go to John. Of the remaining estate, invested in stocks and bonds, valued at forty thousand dollars, one half was to go to John, and the remaining half to Mrs. Oakley. Squire Selwyn was appointed executor, and guardian of John, until the latter should attain his majority.

"If the will is genuine . . .," commenced Mrs. Oakley.

"You certainly do not question my word to that effect?" said the lawyer, gravely.

"I have no right to stay in this house," continued Mrs. Oakley.

"I am quite sure John would wish you to exercise your own choice in that matter."

"I shall not remain a tenant on sufferance," said Mrs. Oakley, coldly. "Next week Benjamin and I go to the city."

"You will act your own pleasure, of course," said Squire Selwyn, rather glad to hear it, if the truth must be told.

Some other matters were discussed and they rose to go. John received no invitation to remain.

"I am afraid I must burden your hospitality, Squire Selwyn," he said, as they left the house.

"You are a welcome guest, and will always be, John," said the lawyer. "Sam will be delighted at the arrangement."

"I don't know how my aunt will manage without me," said John. "I was her business manager."

"It seem to me, John, that your aunt had better sell out her store, and come and keep house for you. You will have a large house, and you are not quite old enough to marry and go to housekeeping."

"Not quite," said John, laughing.

"Your aunt will thus be relieved from business anxieties, and you are quite rich enough to provide for her and your cousins."

"It is an excellent arrangement," said John. "I'll write to her at once."

John did write, and, as might have been expected his aunt was very glad to accept his offer. It was, of course, impossible to doubt the validity of the will, and its provisions were, as soon as practicable, carried into effect. Mrs. Oakley removed to New York with Ben, and established herself at a boarding-house. On some accounts it was an unwise step. Ben, having nothing useful to do, grew dissipated, and contracted debts on all hands. In five years his mother's twenty thousand dollars had dwindled to a few hundreds, and once more she found herself obliged to exert herself for a support. She opened a boardinghouse, by means of which she managed to make a living. As for Ben, who she fondly hoped would grow up a gentleman, he appears to be sinking deeper and deeper every day into worthlessness and dissipation. He has cost his mother many sorrowful hours.

Mr. Huxter is dead. Probably his excesses in drinking hastened his death. His poor wife was left quite destitute. When John heard of her distress, grateful for her sympathy at a time when he stood in need of it, he asked permission to help her. A certain sum is paid her annually by him, by which, with her earnings as a dress-maker, a trade which she followed before her marriage, she is able to make a comfortable living for herself and her children.

John returned to his studies, and was admitted to college with Sam, where both took a high rank. They graduated at the last commencement, and are now both studying law.

Squire Bradley, of Wilton, who was much impressed by the skill with which

John ferreted out Mr. Hall's rascality, is anxious to have John enter his office; but Sam, who is unwilling to part with one who from boyhood has been his most intimate friend, insists that John shall enter his father's office with him, after completing a course at a celebrated Law School where they now are. Probably this arrangement will best suit John. I have no hesitation in predicting for him a noble manhood and an honorable career. In spite of the gifts of Fortune that he possesses, I consider his warm and generous heart, his personal integrity, and his manly character, to be John Oakley's *most valuable inheritance.*

And now, kind reader, let me hope to meet you soon again with the second volume of the "Luck and Pluck Series,"

Sink or Swim;
or,
Harry Raymond's Resolve.

William Mathews
Getting On in the World

(1873)

William Mathews, professor of rhetoric at the University of Chicago and a financial writer for the *Chicago Tribune*, expanded his journalistic pieces into a book on self-help in the early 1870's. In his prefatory note, Mathews disclaimed having personally experienced the road to success or having written with absolute originality upon "a subject which so many pens have discussed." Even so, he did not hesitate to compile a bulky treatise called *Getting On in the World* (1873). Like various pamphleteers of the Gilded Age, he was clearly hoping to grow rich by assembling the chiefly moral advice which others should follow to grow rich in America. The following excerpt is from Chapter VI, "Self-Reliance."

Of all the elements of success none is more vital than self-reliance, a determination to be one's own helper, and not to look to others for support. It is the secret of all individual growth and vigor, the master-key that unlocks all difficulties in every profession or calling. *Aide toi, et le ciel t'aidera*, as the French have it—help yourself, and Heaven will help you,—should be the motto of every man who would make himself useful in the world or carve his way to riches or honor . . .

William Mathews, *Getting On in the World* (Chicago, 1873).

Read the history of the rich and the poor in all ages and countries, and you will find, almost invariably, that the "lucky dogs," as they are called, began life at the foot of the ladder, without a finger's lift from Hercules; while the "unfortunates," who flit along life's paths more like scarecrows than human beings, attribute the very first declensions in their fortunes to having been bolstered and propped by others. It is a proverb, that rich young men, who begin their fortunes where their fathers left off, leave off where their fathers began. The only money which benefits a man is that which he has himself earned. Inherited wealth, instead of prompting to further acquisition, is "a title-deed to sloth." The ready-made fortune of an ancestor, like his ready-made clothes, rarely fits the man to whom it falls. But why confine ourselves to those who have won distinction in the marts of commerce? Whence come the great lights of the intellectual firmament, the stars that shine with steady radiance through the ages? Have they not, in the vast majority of cases, emerged to eminence from the chilling depths of obscurity, destitution, and want? Who are they that

"Pluck bright glory from the pale-faced moon,
Or dive into the bottom of the deep,
Where fathom-line could never touch the ground,
And drag up drowned honor by the locks?"

The scions of noble blood? The sons of the rich, who were dandled in the lap of luxury, whose path was smoothed for them at every step, who were never for an instant compelled to fight against the armed resistance of misfortune, penury, and wrong? No! they are men of humble parentage, men whose cradles were rocked in lowly cottages, and who have buffeted the billows of fate without dependence, save upon the mercy of God and their own energies, the gentlemen of nature, who have trodden under foot the "painted lizards" of society, and worked out their own distinction with an ardor that could not be quenched, and a perseverance that considered nothing as done while anything yet remained to be done.

There are many persons who are always looking to government, to reform societies, to improved educational institutions, to workingmen's or other associations, to anything and everything but their own hands and brains, to better their condition and make their life-journey easy. But even the best institutions can give a man no active help. Laws, wisely administered, will secure to men the fruits of their industry; but no laws which the wit of man can devise can make the idle industrious, the thriftless provident, or the drunken sober. Nine-tenths of the great social evils which our reformers denounce are but the outgrowth of individual life, and no legislation can extirpate them, unless the axe is also laid at their root. It is said that when Fuseli presided at the Academy of Art in London, he read while his pupils drew, and rarely opened his lips. "I believe he was right," says his great pupil, Leslie, "for those students who are born with powers that will make them eminent, it is sufficient to place works before them. *They* do not want instruction, and those that *do* are not *worth* it. Art may be learned, but cannot be taught." What Leslie affirmed of painting is true of every pursuit under the sun. The world, though rough, is, after all, the best schoolmaster—better than books, better than study—for it makes a man his own teacher, and gives him that practical training which no schools, academies, or colleges can ever impart.

Henry James
The American

(1877)

In *The Gilded Age* (1873), Mark Twain and Charles Dudley Warner satirized the cult of the self-made man in America by creating Colonel Beriah Sellers, a wildly optimistic speculator and would-be millionaire. Four years later, Henry James presented the age a more complex portrait of the self-made millionaire in Christopher Newman, hero of *The American* (1877). The following passage appears early in the novel just after Newman, a shrewd but culturally inexperienced and vulnerable Yankee abroad, has arrived in Paris to buy a portion of high culture in the old world and perhaps also to purchase a cultivated European wife to grace his fortune. Before he falls into a Continental "great and gilded trap," he meets an old American acquaintance, expatriate Tom Tristram, who urges Newman to recount his postwar career from rags to riches.

Newman had pushed his hat back from his forehead, folded his arms, and stretched his legs. He listened to the music, he looked about him at the bustling crowd, at the plashing fountains, at the nurses and the babies. "I have worked!" he answered at last.

Tristram looked at him for some moments, and allowed his placid eyes to measure his friend's generous longitude and rest upon his comfortably contemplative face. "What have you worked at?" he asked.

"Oh, at several things."

"I suppose you're a smart fellow, eh?"

Newman continued to look at the nurses and babies; they imparted to the scene a kind of primordial, pastoral simplicity. "Yes," he said at last, "I suppose I am." And then, in answer to his companion's inquiries, he related briefly his history since their last meeting. It was an intensely Western story, and it dealt with enterprises which it will be needless to introduce to the

---

Henry James, *The American* (Boston, 1877), from Chapter II.

reader in detail. Newman had come out of the war with a brevet of brigadier-general, an honor which in this case—without invidious comparisons—had lighted upon shoulders amply competent to bear it. But though he could manage a fight, when need was, Newman heartily disliked the business; his four years in the army had left him with an angry, bitter sense of the waste of previous things—life and time and money and "smartness" and the early freshness of purpose; and he had addressed himself to the pursuits of peace with passionate zest and energy. He was of course as penniless when he plucked off his shoulder-straps as when he put them on, and the only capital at his disposal was his dogged resolution and his lively perception of ends and means. Exertion and action were as natural to him as respiration; a more completely healthy mortal had never trod the elastic soil of the West. His experience, moreover, was as wide as his capacity; when he was fourteen years old, necessity had taken him by his slim young shoulders and pushed him into the street, to earn that night's supper. He had not earned it, but he had earned the next night's, and afterwards, whenever he had had none, it was because he had gone without it to use the money for something else, a keener pleasure or a finer profit. He had turned his hand, with his brain in it, to many things; he had been enterprising, in an eminent sense of the term; he had been adventurous and even reckless, and he had known bitter failure as well as brilliant success; but he was a born experimentalist, and he had always found something to enjoy in the pressure of necessity, even when it was as irritating as the haircloth shirt of the mediæval monk. At one time failure seemed inexorably his portion; ill luck became his bed-fellow, and whatever he touched he turned, not to gold, but to ashes. His most vivid conception of a supernatural element in the world's affairs had come to him once when this pertinacity of misfortune was at its climax; there seemed to him something stronger in life than his own will. But the mysterious something could only be the devil, and he was accordingly seized with an intense personal enmity to this impertinent force. He had known what it was to have utterly exhausted his credit, to be unable to raise a dollar, and to find himself at nightfall in a strange city, without a penny to mitigate its strangeness. It was under these circumstances that he made his entrance into San Francisco, the scene, subsequently, of his happiest strokes of fortune. If he did not, like Dr. Franklin in Philadelphia, march along the street munching a penny-loaf, it was only because he had not the penny-loaf necessary to the performance. In his darkest days he had had but one simple, practical impulse—the desire, as he would have phrased it, to see the thing through. He did so at last, buffeted his way into smooth waters, and made money largely. It must be admitted, rather nakedly, that Christopher Newman's sole aim in life had been to make money; what he had been placed in the world for was, to his own perception, simply to wrest a fortune, the bigger the better, from defiant opportunity. This idea completely filled his horizon and satisfied his imagination. Upon the uses of money, upon what one might do with a life into which one had succeeded in injecting the golden stream, he had up to his thirty-fifth year very scantily reflected. Life had been for him an open game, and he had played for high stakes. He had won at last and carried off his winnings; and now what was he to do with them? He was a man to whom, sooner or later, the question was sure to present itself, and the answer to it belongs to our story. A vague sense that more answers were possible than his philosophy had hitherto dreamt of had already taken possession of him, and it seemed softly and agreeably to deepen as he lounged in this brilliant corner of Paris with his friend.

"I must confess," he presently went on, "that here I don't feel at all smart. My remarkable talents seem of no use. I feel as simple as a little child, and a little child might take me by the hand and lead me about."

"Oh, I'll be your little child," said Tristram, jovially; "I'll take you by the hand. Trust yourself to me."

"I am a good worker," Newman continued, "but I rather think I am a poor loafer. I have come abroad to amuse myself, but I doubt whether I know how."

"Oh, that's easily learned."

"Well, I may perhaps learn it, but I am afraid I shall never do it by rote. I have the best will in the world about it, but my genius doesn't lie in that direction. As a loafer I shall never be original, as I take it that you are."...

William Holmes McGuffey
McGuffey's Reader

(1879)

William Holmes McGuffey (1800–1873), Ohio educator and college president, produced his *Eclectic First Reader* in 1836. Together with five subsequent collections, all expanded and revised through countless editions, the McGuffey Readers helped to shape a conservative middle-class morality in America throughout the Nineteenth Century and into the Twentieth. By 1920, an estimated 122 million copies had been sold.

The excerpts following are taken from the 1879 revision of the *Fifth Eclectic Reader*. (William's brother Alexander had compiled the first edition of this reader in 1844.) Simply to glance at some of the titles in the table of contents is to anticipate the moral burden of the readings: "Work" and "A Boy on the Farm" (cheerful toil), "The Discontented Pendulum" (persever-

William Holmes McGuffey, *McGuffey's Fifth Eclectic Reader* (New York, 1879).

ance), "Behind Time" (punctuality), "The Art of Discouragement" (positive thinking), "The Venomous Worm" (abstinence), "My Mother's hands" (American momism), "Respect for the Sabbath Rewarded" (financial profit through church attendance), "The Heritage" (the self-help rewards of poverty), and so on. McGuffey's study helps, which reveal a part of the stern effort required from his young readers, have been preserved in the sampling that follows.

A Boy on a Farm

Charles Dudley Warner (b. 1829, ——) was born at Plainfield, Mass. In 1851 he graduated at Hamilton College, and in 1854 was admitted to the bar at Philadelphia, but moved to Chicago to practice his profession. There he remained until 1860, when he became connected with the Press at Hartford, Conn., and has ever since devoted himself to literature. "My Summer in a Garden," "Saunterings," and "Backlog Studies" are his best known works. The following extract is from "Being a Boy."

1. Say what you will about the general usefulness of boys, it is my impression that a farm without a boy would very soon come to grief. What the boy does is the life of the farm. He is the factotum, always in demand, always expected to do the thousand indispensable things that nobody else will do. Upon him fall all the odds and ends, the most difficult things.

2. After everybody else is through, he has to finish up. His work is like a woman's, perpetually waiting on others. Everybody knows how much easier it is to eat a good dinner than it is to wash the dishes afterwards. Consider what a boy on a farm is required to do; things that must be done, or life would actually stop.

3. It is understood, in the first place, that he is to do all the errands, to go to the store, to the postoffice, and to carry all sorts of messages. If he had as many legs as a centiped, they would tire before night. His two short limbs seem to him entirely inadequate to the task. He would like to have as many legs as a wheel has spokes, and rotate about in the same way.

4. This he sometimes tries to do; and the people who have seen him "turning cart-wheels" along the side of the road have supposed that he was amusing himself and idling his time; he was only trying to invent a new mode of locomotion, so that he could economize his legs, and do his errands with greater dispatch.

5. He practices standing on his head, in order to accustom himself to any position. Leap-frog is one of his methods of getting over the ground quickly. He would willingly go an errand any distance if he could leap-frog it with a few other boys.

6. He has a natural genius for combining pleasure with business. This is the reason why, when he is sent to the spring for a pitcher of water, he is absent so long; for he stops to poke the frog that sits on the stone, or, if there is a pen-stock, to put his hand over the spout, and squirt the water a little while.

7. He is the one who spreads the grass when the men have cut it; he mows it away in the barn; he rides the horse, to cultivate the corn, up and down the hot, weary rows; he picks up the potatoes when they are dug; he drives the cows night and morning; he brings wood and water, and splits kindling; he gets up the horse, and puts out the horse; whether he is in the house or out of it, there is always something for him to do.

8. Just before the school in winter he shovels paths; in summer he turns the grindstone. He knows where there are lots of wintergreens and sweet-flags, but, instead of going for them, he is to stay indoors and pare apples, and stone raisins, and pound something in a mortar. And yet, with his mind full of schemes of what he would like to do, and his hands full of occupations, he is an idle boy, who has nothing to busy himself with but school and chores!

9. He would gladly do all the work if somebody else would do the chores, he thinks; and yet I doubt if any boy ever amounted to any thing in the world, or was of much use as a man, who did not enjoy the advantages of a liberal education in the way of chores.

Definitions. 1. Fac-tō'tum, *a person employed to do all kinds of work.* In-dis-pĕn'sa-ble, *absolutely necessary.* 2. Per-pĕt'ū-al-ly, *continually.* 3. Cĕn'ti-pĕd, *an insect with a great number of feet.* 4. E-cŏn'o-mīze, *to save.* Dis-pătch', *diligence, haste.* 6. Pĕn'-stŏck, *a wooden tube for conducting water.* 8. Chōres, *the light work of the household either within or without doors.*

Work

Eliza Cook (b. 1817, d. 1889) was born at London. In 1837 she commenced contributing to periodicals. In 1840 the first collection of her poems was made. In 1849 she became editor of "Eliza Cook's Journal."

1. Work, work, my boy, be not afraid;
   Look labor boldly in the face;
   Take up the hammer or the spade,
   And blush not for your humble place.

2. There's glory in the shuttle's song;
   There's triumph in the anvil's stroke;

There's merit in the brave and strong,
  Who dig the mine or fell the oak.

3. The wind disturbs the sleeping lake,
  And bids it ripple pure and fresh;
It moves the green boughs till they make
  Grand music in their leafy mesh.

4. And so the active breath of life
  Should stir our dull and sluggard wills;
For are we not created rife
  With health, that stagnant torpor kills?

5. I doubt if he who lolls his head
  Where idleness and plenty meet,
Enjoys his pillow or his bread
  As those who earn the meals they eat.

6. And man is never half so blest
  As when the busy day is spent
So as to make his evening rest
  A holiday of glad content.

Definitions. 3. Mĕsh *net-work.* 4. Rīfe, *abounding.* Stăg′-nant, *inactive.* Tôr′por, *laziness, stupidity.* 5. Lolls, *reclines, leans.*

Respect for the Sabbath Rewarded

In the city of Bath, not many years since, lived a barber who made a practice of following his ordinary occupation of the Lord's day. As he was on the way to his morning's employment, he happened to look into some place of worship just as the minister was giving out his text—"Remember the Sabbath day, to keep it holy." He listened long enough to be convinced that he was constantly breaking the laws of God and man by shaving and dressing his customers on the Lord's day. He became uneasy, and went with a heavy heart to his Sabbath task.

At length he took courage, and opened his mind to his minister, who advised him to give up Sabbath work, and worship God. He replied that beggary would be the consequence. He had a flourishing trade, but it would almost all be lost. At length, after many a sleepless night spent in weeping and praying, he was determined to cast all his care upon God, as the more he reflected the more his duty became apparent.

He discontinued his Sabbath work, went constantly and early to the public services of religion, and soon enjoyed that satisfaction of mind which is one of the rewards of doing our duty, and that peace which the world can neither give nor take away. The consequences he foresaw actually followed. His genteel customers left him, and he was nicknamed "Puritan" or

"Methodist." He was obliged to give up his fashionable shop, and, in the course of years, became so reduced as to take a cellar under the old market-house and shave the poorer people.

One Saturday evening, between light and dark, a stranger from one of the coaches, asking for a barber, was directed by the hostler to the cellar opposite. Coming in hastily, he requested to be shaved quickly, while they changed horses, as he did not like to violate the Sabbath. This was touching the barber on a tender chord. He burst into tears; asked the stranger to lend him a half-penny to buy a candle, as it was not light enough to shave him with safety. He did so, revolving in his mind the extreme poverty to which the poor man must be reduced.

When shaved, he said, "There must be something extraordinary in your history, which I have not now time to hear. Here is half a crown for you. When I return, I will call and investigate your case. What is your name?" "William Reed," said the astonished barber. "William Reed?" echoed the stranger: "William Reed? by your dialect you are from the West." "Yes, sir, from Kingston, near Taunton." "William Reed, from Kingston, near Taunton? What was your father's name?" "Thomas." "Had he any brother?" "Yes, sir, one, after whom I was named; but he went to the Indies, and, as we never heard from him, we supposed him to be dead."

"Come along, follow me," said the stranger, "I am going to see a person who says his name is William Reed, of Kingston, near Taunton. Come and confront him. If you prove to be indeed he who you say you are, I have glorious news for you. Your uncle is dead, and has left an immense fortune, which I will put you in possession of when all legal doubts are removed."

They went by the coach; saw the pretended William Reed, and proved him to be an impostor. The stranger, who was a pious attorney, was soon legally satisfied of the barber's identity, and told him that he had advertised him in vain. Providence had now thrown him in his way in a most extraordinary manner, and he had great pleasure in transferring a great many thousand pounds to a worthy man, the rightful heir of the property. Thus was man's extremity God's opportunity. Had the poor barber possessed one half-penny, or even had credit for a candle, he might have remained unknown for years; but he trusted God, who never said, "Seek ye my face," in vain.

The Venomous Worm

John Russell (b. 1793, d. 1863) graduated at Middlebury College, Vt., in 1818. He was at one time editor of the "Backwoodsman," published at Grafton, Ills. [sic.], and later of the "Louisville Advocate." He was the author of many tales of western adventure and of numerous essays, sketches, etc. His language is clear, chaste and classical; his style concise, vigorous, and sometimes highly ornate.

Who has not heard of the rattlesnake or copperhead? An unexpected sight of either of these reptiles will make even the lords of creation recoil; but there is a species of worm, found in various parts of this country, which conveys a poison of a nature so deadly that, compared with it, even the venom of the rattlesnake is harmless. To guard our readers against this foe of human kind is the object of this lesson.

This worm varies much in size. It is frequently an inch in diameter, but, as it is rarely seen except when coiled, its length can hardly be conjectured. It is of a dull lead color, and generally lives near a spring or small stream of water, and bites the unfortunate people who are in the habit of going there to drink. The brute creation it never molests. They avoid it with the same instinct that teaches the animals of India to shun the deadly cobra.

Several of these reptiles have long infested our settlements, to the misery and destruction of many of our fellow-citizens. I have, therefore, had frequent opportunities of being the melancholy spectator of the effects produced by the subtile poison which this worm infuses.

The symptoms of its bite are terrible. The eyes of the patient become red and fiery, his tongue swells to an immoderate size, and obstructs his utterance; and delirium of the most horrid character quickly follows. Sometimes, in his madness, he attempts the destruction of his nearest friends.

If the sufferer has a family, his weeping wife and helpless infants are not unfrequently the objects of his frantic fury. In a word, he exhibits to the life, all the detestable passions that rankle in the bosom of a savage; and such is the spell in which his senses are locked, that no sooner has the unhappy patient recovered from the paroxysm of insanity occasioned by the bite, than he seeks out the destroyer for the sole purpose of being bitten again.

I have seen a good old father, his locks as white as snow, his step slow and trembling, beg in vain of his only son to quit the lurking-place of the worm. My heart bled when he turned away, for I knew the fond hope that his son would be the "staff of his declining years," had supported him through many a sorrow.

Youths of America, would you know the name of this reptile? It is called the *Worm of the Still.*

Definitions. 1. Rĕp'tĭles̱, *animals that crawl, as snakes, lizards, etc.* Recoil', *to start back, to shrink from.* 2. Cō'bra, *a highly venomous reptile inhabiting the East Indies.* In-fĕst'ed, *troubled, annoyed.* 3. Sŭb'tĭle, *acute, piercing.* In-fūs̱'es̱, *introduces.* 4. Ob-strŭcts', *hinders.* De-lĭr'i-ŭm, *a wandering of the mind.* 5. Răṉk'le, *to rage.* Păr'ox-ȳs̱m, *a fit, a convulsion.* 7. Wõrm, *a spiral metallic pipe used in distilling liquors.* Stĭll, *a vessel used in distilling or making liquors.*

The Heritage

James Russell Lowell (b. 1819, d. 1891) was born in Cambridge, Mass., and was graduated from Harvard College. He entered the profession of law; but, in 1848, turned aside to publish "The Pioneer, a Literary and Critical Magazine." In 1855 he was appointed professor of Belles-lettres in Harvard College. From 1877 to 1885 he was U.S. Minister, first to Spain, afterwards to Great Britain. Lowell's powers as a writer were very versatile, and his poems range from the most dreamy and imaginative to the most trenchant and witty. Among his most noted poetical works are "The Biglow Papers," "The Fable for Critics," "The Vision of Sir Launfal," "The Cathedral," and "The Legend of Brittany;" while "Conversations on some of the Old Poets," "Among my Books," and "My Study Windows," place him in the front rank as an essayist.

1. The rich man's son inherits lands,
   And piles of brick, and stone, and gold,
   And he inherits soft white hands,
   And tender flesh that fears the cold,
   Nor dares to wear a garment old;
   A heritage, it seems to me,
   One scarce would wish to hold in fee.

2. The rich man's son inherits cares;
   The bank may break, the factory burn,
   A breath may burst his bubble shares,
   And soft white hands could hardly earn
   A living that would serve his turn;
   A heritage, it seems to me,
   One scarce would wish to hold in fee.

3. The rich man's son inherits wants,
   His stomach craves for dainty fare;
   With sated heart, he hears the pants
   Of toiling hinds with brown arms bare,
   And wearies in his easy-chair;
   A heritage, it seems to me,
   One scarce would wish to hold in fee.

4. What doth the poor man's son inherit?
   Stout muscles and a sinewy heart,
   A hardy frame, a hardier spirit;
   King of two hands, he does his part
   In every useful toil and art;
   A heritage, it seems to me,
   A king might wish to hold in fee.

5. What doth the poor man's son inherit?

Wishes o'erjoyed with humble things,
A rank adjudged by toil-worn merit,
Content that from employment springs,
A heart that in its labor sings;
A heritage, it seems to me,
A king might wish to hold in fee.

6. What doth the poor man's son inherit?
A patience learned of being poor,
Courage, if sorrow come, to bear it,
A fellow-feeling that is sure
To make the outcast bless his door;
A heritage, it seems to me,
A king might wish to hold in fee.

7. O rich man's son! there is a toil
That with all others level stands;
Large charity doth never soil,
But only whiten, soft, white hands,—
This is the best crop from thy lands;
A heritage, it seems to be
Worth being rich to hold in fee.

8. O poor man's son! scorn not thy state;
There is worse weariness than thine
In merely being rich and great:
Toil only gives the soul to shine,
And makes rest fragrant and benign;
A heritage, it seems to me,
Worth being poor to hold in fee.

9. Both, heirs to some six feet of sod,
Are equal in the earth at last;
Both, children of the same dear God,
Prove title to your heirship vast
By record of a well-filled past;
A heritage, it seems to me,
Well worth a life to hold in fee.

Definitions. 1. Hĕr'it-aġe, *that which is inherited, or taken by descent, from an ancestor.* 3. Săt'ed, *surfeited, glutted.* Hinds, *peasants, countrymen.* 5. Ad-jŭdged', *decided, determined.* 8. Be-nīgn' (*pro.* be-nīn'), *having healthful qualities, wholesome.*

Notes. 1. *To hold in fee,* means to have as an inheritance. 9. *Prove title.* That is to prove the right of ownership.

William Dean Howells
The Rise of Silas Lapham

(1885)

Among American novelists of the Eighties and Nineties who depicted the growing crisis of individualism in an urban-industrial society, William Dean Howells (1837–1920) stands preeminent for both the complexity and the range of his literary treatment. He explored the "woman question" in *Dr. Breen's Practice* (1881) and *A Woman's Reason* (1883), the country boy's plight in the alien city in *The Undiscovered Country* (1880) and *The Minister's Charge* (1887), and the aimless career of a Wall Street speculator in *A Hazard of New Fortunes* (1890). In *The Rise of Silas Lapham* (1885), Howells created a protagonist whose rise from back-country yokel to Boston millionaire embraced almost totally the reigning myth of the age. That later scholarship has shown few real-life Silas Laphams ever to have existed among the urban-industrial elite in the Seventies and Eighties merely confirms the hold which the country boy as a mythical hero enjoyed in the popular mind. Howells adopted the legend, not without covert ambivalence and ironic reservation, to write his most popular novel. In the opening pages, he acquaints the reader with the environmental forces which have shaped Silas Lapham. A short segment of Bartley Hubbard's mildly ironic interview with Silas is reproduced here.

When Bartley Hubbard went to interview Silas Lapham for the "Solid Men of Boston" series, which he undertook to finish up in *The Events*, after he replaced their original projector on that newspaper, Lapham received him in his private office by previous appointment.

"Walk right in!" he called out to the journalist, whom he caught sight of through the door of the counting room.

He did not rise from the desk at which he was writing, but he gave Bartley his left hand for welcome, and he rolled his large head in the direction of a vacant chair. "Sit down! I'll be with you in just half a minute."

"Take your time," said Bartley, with the ease he instantly felt. "I'm in no hurry." He took a notebook from his pocket, laid it on his knee, and began to sharpen a pencil.

"There!" Lapham pounded with his great hairy fist on the envelope he had been addressing. "William!" he called out, and he handed the letter to a boy who came to get it. "I want that to go right away. Well, sir," he continued, wheeling round in his leather-cushioned swivel chair, and facing Bartley,

---

William Dean Howells, *The Rise of Silas Lapham* (Boston, 1885), from Chapter I.

seated so near that their knees almost touched, "so you want my life, death, and Christian sufferings, do you, young man?"

"That's what I'm after," said Bartley. "Your money or your life."

"I guess you wouldn't want my life without the money," said Lapham, as if he were willing to prolong these moments of preparation.

"Take 'em both," Bartley suggested. "Don't want your money without your life, if you come to that. But you're just one million times more interesting to the public than if you hadn't a dollar; and you know that as well as I do, Mr. Lapham. There's no use beating about the bush."

"No," said Lapham, somewhat absently. He put out his huge foot and pushed the ground-glass door shut between his little den and the bookkeepers, in their larger den outside.

"In personal appearance," wrote Bartley in the sketch for which he now studied his subject, while he waited patiently for him to continue, "Silas Lapham is a fine type of the successful American. He has a square, bold chin, only partially concealed by the short reddish-grey beard, growing to the edges of his firmly closing lips. His nose is short and straight; his forehead good, but broad rather than high; his eyes blue, and with a light in them that is kindly or sharp according to his mood. He is of medium height, and fills an average armchair with a solid bulk, which on the day of our interview was unpretentiously clad in a business suit of blue serge. His head droops somewhat from a short neck, which does not trouble itself to rise far from a pair of massive shoulders."

"I don't know as I know just where you want me to begin," said Lapham.

"Might begin with your birth; that's where most of us begin," replied Bartley.

A gleam of humorous appreciation shot into Lapham's blue eyes.

"I didn't know whether you wanted me to go quite so far back as that," he said. "But there's no disgrace in having been born, and I was born in the State of Vermont, pretty well up under the Canada line—so well up, in fact, that I came very near being an adoptive citizen; for I was bound to be an American of *some* sort, from the word Go! That was about—well, let me see!—pretty near sixty years ago: this is '75, and that was '20. Well, say I'm fifty-five years old; and I've *lived* 'em, too; not an hour of waste time about *me*, anywheres! I was born on a farm, and . . ."

"Worked in the fields summers and went to school winters: regulation thing?" Bartley cut in.

"Regulation thing," said Lapham, accepting this irreverent version of his history somewhat dryly.

"Parents poor, of course," suggested the journalist. "Any barefoot business? Early deprivations of any kind, that would encourage the youthful reader to go and do likewise? Orphan myself, you know," said Bartley, with a smile of cynical good-comradery.

Lapham looked at him silently, and then said with quiet self-respect, "I guess if you see these things as a joke, my life won't interest you."

"Oh yes, it will," returned Bartley, unabashed. "You'll see; it'll come out all right." And in fact it did so, in the interview which Bartley printed.

"Mr. Lapham," he wrote, "passed rapidly over the story of his early life, its poverty and its hardships, sweetened, however, by the recollections of a devoted mother, and a father who, if somewhat her inferior in education, was no less ambitious for the advancement of his children. They were quiet, unpretentious people, religious, after the fashion of that time, and of sterling morality, and they taught their children the simple virtues of the Old Testament and Poor Richard's Almanac."

Bartley could not deny himself this gibe; but he trusted to Lapham's unliterary habit of mind for his security in making it, and most other people would consider it sincere reporter's rhetoric.

Russell H. Conwell
Acres of Diamonds

(1888)

The long list of clergymen who have propounded the Protestant Ethic of work and wealth in America reaches back to Puritan Cotton Mather and forward to Henry Ward Beecher, Lyman Abbott, William Lawrence, and two famous nineteenth-century Unitarians who abandoned the pulpit—Ralph Waldo Emerson and Horatio Alger, Jr. None worked harder and accumulated more wealth preaching the gospel of Work and Win than did Russell H. Conwell (1843–1925), the Berkshire country boy who became a Baptist minister in Philadelphia where he founded Temple University. "Acres of Diamonds," his famous success sermon, was published first in 1888. Conwell publicly delivered the lesson six thousand times to millions of hearers. His basic message asserted that the diligent American will turn up his acres of diamonds by seizing the opportunity in his own back yard. Conwell embellished the sermon by interpolating remarks to fit the locale and the particular audience, which in a single tour would range from Decorah, Iowa, to Hiawatha, Kansas, to Athens, New York. The passages reprinted here do not include Conwell's sprinkling of anecdotal "proof" from the lives of famous Americans—such perennial standbys as millionaires Stewart and Astor, and log-cabin presidents Lincoln and Garfield.

Russell H. Conwell, *Acres of Diamonds* (New York, 1915), pp. 17–59, *passim.*

. . . Now then, I say again that the opportunity to get rich, to attain unto great wealth, is here in Philadelphia now, within the reach of almost every man and woman who hears me speak tonight, and I mean just what I say. I have not come to this platform even under these circumstances to recite something to you. I have come to tell you what in God's sight I believe to be the truth, and if the years of life have been of any value to me in the attainment of common sense, I know I am right; that the men and women sitting here, who found it difficult perhaps to buy a ticket to this lecture or gathering tonight, have within their reach "acres of diamonds," opportunities to get largely wealthy. There never was a place on earth more adapted than the city of Philadelphia today, and never in the history of the world did a poor man without capital have such an opportunity to get rich quickly and honestly as he has now in our city. I say it is the truth, and I want you to accept it as such; for if you think I have come to simply recite something, then I would better not be here. I have no time to waste in any such talk, but to say the things I believe, and unless some of you get richer for what I am saying tonight my time is wasted.

I say that you ought to get rich, and it is your duty to get rich. How many of my pious brethren say to me, "Do you, a Christian minister, spend your time going up and down the country advising your people to get rich, to get money?" "Yes, of course I do." They say, "Isn't that awful! Why don't you preach the gospel instead of preaching about man's making money?" "Because to make money honestly is to preach the gospel." That is the reason. The men who get rich may be the most honest men you find in the community.

"Oh," but says some young man here tonight, "I have been told all my life that if a person has money he is very dishonest and dishonorable and mean and contemptible." My friend, that is the reason why you have none, because you have that idea of people. The foundation of your faith is altogether false. Let me say here clearly, and say it briefly, though subject to discussion which I have not time for here, ninety eight out of one hundred of the rich men of America are honest. That is why they are rich. That is why they are trusted with money. That is why they carry on great enterprises and find plenty of people to work with them. It is because they are honest men.

Says another young man, "I hear sometimes of men that get millions of dollars dishonestly." Yes, of course you do, and so do I. But they are so rare a thing in fact that the newspapers talk about them all the time as a matter of news until you get the idea that all the other rich men got rich dishonestly.

My friend, you take and drive me—if you furnish the auto—out into the suburbs of Philadelphia, and introduce me to the people who own their homes around this great city, those beautiful homes with gardens and flowers, those magnificent homes so lovely in their art, and I will introduce you to the very best people in character as well as in enterprise in our city, and you know I will. A man is not really a true man until he owns his own home, and they that own their homes are made more honorable and honest and pure, and true and economical and careful, by owning the home.

For a man to have money, even in large sums, is not an inconsistent thing. We preach against covetousness, and you know we do, in the pulpit, and oftentimes preach against it so long and use the terms about "filthy lucre" so extremely that Christians get the idea that when we stand in the pulpit we believe it is wicked for any man to have money—until the collection basket goes around, and then we almost swear at the people because they don't give more money. Oh, the inconsistency of such doctrines as that!

Money is power, and you ought to be reasonably ambitious to have it. You ought because you can do more good with it than you could without it. Money printed your Bible, money builds your churches, money sends your missionaries, and money pays your preachers, and you would not have many of them, either, if you did not pay them. I am always willing that my church should raise my salary, because the church that pays the largest salary always raises it the easiest. You never knew an exception to it in your life. The man who gets the largest salary can do the most good with the power that is furnished to him. Of course he can if his spirit be right to use it for what it is given to him.

I say, then, you ought to have money. If you can honestly attain unto riches in Philadelphia, it is your Christian and godly duty to do so. It is an awful mistake of these pious people to think you must be awfully poor in order to be pious.

Some men say, "Don't you sympathize with the poor people?" Of course I do, or else I would not have been lecturing these years. I won't give in but what I sympathize with the poor, but the number of poor who are to be sympathized with is very small. To sympathize with a man whom God has punished for his sins, thus to help him when God would still continue a just punishment, is to do wrong, no doubt about it, and we do that more than we help those who are deserving. While we should sympathize with God's poor—that is, those who cannot help themselves—let us remember there is not a poor person in the United States who was not made poor by his own shortcomings, or by the shortcomings of some one else. It is all wrong to be poor, anyhow. Let us give in to that argument and pass that to one side. . .

Some old gentleman gets up back there and says, "Mr. Conwell, have you lived in Philadelphia for thirty-one years and don't know that the time has gone by when you can make anything in this city?" "No, I don't think it is." "Yes, it is; I have tried it." "What business are you in?" "I kept a store here for twenty years, and never made over a thousand dollars in the whole twenty years."

"Well, then, you can measure the good you have been to this city by what this city has paid you, because a man can judge very well what he is worth by what he receives; that is, in what he is to the world at this time. If you have not made over a thousand dollars in twenty years in Philadelphia, it would have been better for Philadelphia if they had kicked you out of the city nineteen years and nine months ago. A man has no right to keep a store in Philadelphia twenty years and not make at least five hundred thousand dollars, even though it be a corner grocery uptown." You say, "You cannot make five thousand dollars in a store now." Oh, my friends, if you will just take only four blocks around you, and find out what the people want and what you ought to supply and set them down with your pencil, and figure up the profits you would make if you did supply them, you would very soon see it. There is wealth right within the sound of your voice. . .

But another young man gets up over there and says, "I cannot take up the mercantile business." (While I am talking of trade it applies to every occupation.) "Why can't you go into the mercantile business?" "Because I haven't any capital." Oh, the weak and dudish creature that can't see over its collar! It makes a person weak to see these little dudes standing around the corners and saying, "Oh, if I had plenty of capital, how rich I would get." "Young man, do you think you are going to get rich on capital?" "Certainly." Well, I say, "Certainly not." If your mother has plenty of money, and she will set you up in business, you will "set her up in business," supplying you with capital.

The moment a young man or woman gets more money than he or she has grown to by practical experience, that moment he has gotten a curse. It is no help to a young man or woman to inherit money. It is no help to your children to leave them money, but if you leave them education, if you leave them Christian and noble character, if you leave them a wide circle of friends, if you leave them an honorable name, it is far better than that they should have money. It would be worse for them, worse for the nation, that they should have any money at all. Oh, young man, if you have inherited money, don't regard it as a help. It will curse you through your years, and deprive you of the very best things of human life. There is no class of people to be pitied so much as the inexperienced sons and daughters of the rich of our generation. I pity the rich man's son. He can never know the best things in life.

One of the best things in our life is when a young man has earned his own living, and when he becomes engaged to some lovely young woman, and makes up his mind to have a home of his own. Then with that same love comes also that divine inspiration toward better things, and he begins to save his money. He begins to leave off his bad habits and put money in the bank. When he has a few hundred dollars he goes out in the suburbs to look for a home. He goes to the savings bank, perhaps, for half of the value, and then goes for this wife, and when he takes his bride over the threshold of that door for the first time he says in words of eloquence my voice can never touch: "I have earned this home myself. It is all mine, and I divide with thee." That is the grandest moment a human heart may ever know.

But a rich man's son can never know that. He takes his bride into a finer mansion, it may be, but he is obliged to go all the way through it and say to his wife, "My mother gave me that, my mother gave me that, and my mother gave me this," until his wife wishes she had married his mother. I pity the rich man's son.

The statistics of Massachusetts showed that not one rich man's son out of seventeen ever dies rich. I pity the rich man's sons unless they have the good sense of the elder Vanderbilt, which sometimes happens. He went to his father and said, "Did you earn all your money?" "I did, my son. I began to work on a ferry-boat for twenty-five cents a day." "Then," said his son, "I will have none of your money," and he, too, tried to get employment on a ferry-boat that Saturday night. He could not get on there, but he did get a place for three dollars a week. Of course, if a rich man's son will do that, he will get the discipline of a poor boy that is worth more than a university education to any man. He would then be able to take care of the millions of his father. But as a rule the rich men will not let their sons do the very thing that made them great. As a rule, the rich man will not allow his son to work—and his mother! Why, she would think it was a social disgrace if her poor, weak, little lily-fingered, sissy sort of a boy had to earn his living with honest toil. I have no pity for such rich men's sons . . .

Greatness consists not in the holding of some future office, but really consists in doing great deeds with little means and the accomplishment of vast purposes from the private ranks of life. To be great at all one must be great here, now, in Philadelphia. He who can give to this city better streets and better sidewalks, better schools and more colleges, more happiness and more civilization, more of God, he will be great anywhere. Let every man or woman here, if you never hear me again, remember this, that if you wish to be great at all, you must begin where you are and what you are, in Philadelphia, now. He that can give to his city any blessing, he who can be a good citizen while he lives here, he that can make better homes, he that can be a blessing whether he works in the shop or sits behind the counter or keeps house, whatever be his life, he who would be great anywhere must first be great in his own Philadelphia.

Andrew Carnegie
Wealth

(1889)

Among businessmen and industrialists of the late Nineteenth Century, the literate Andrew Carnegie (1835–1919) was in the vanguard as spokesman of the duty resting with the very rich to administer their wealth for the common good. Such model citizenship, he also noted, would help to ease socialist and anarchist discontent with the imagined inequities of the capitalist order. Like Girard, Stanford, Cornell, Rockefeller, and Vanderbilt, Carnegie eventually endowed an American university. He also built more than 2500 free libraries and established enormous endowments for the advancement of (non-denominational) education in America. In his rise from a Scotch immigrant bobbin-boy to multimillionaire steel tycoon, Carnegie came to distinguish between indiscriminate charity and creative philanthropy. Misappropriated charity appeared in fortunes bequeathed to children of the rich (who are then deprived of the moral rewards of self-help) and in the huge legacies intended for public uses after the donor's death (and usually squandered to the harm of the recipients). On the other hand, philanthropy, as Carnegie viewed it, is dynamic and reproductive, for it serves "the best and most valuable of all that humanity has yet accomplished." This *summum bonum*, for Carnegie, embraced "Individualism, Private Property, the Law of Accumulation of Wealth, and the Law of Competition." To create "the ladder upon which the aspiring can rise," he administered more than three hundred million dollars of Carnegie surplus profit before his death in 1919. His "true Gospel concerning Wealth" appears in the following essay.

The problem of our age is the proper administration of wealth, so that the ties of brotherhood may still bind together the rich and poor in harmonious relationship. The conditions of human life have not only been changed, but revolutionized, within the past few hundred years. In former days there was little difference between the dwelling, dress, food, and environment of the chief and those of his retainers. The Indians are today where civilized man then was. When visiting the Sioux, I was led to the wigwam of the chief. It was just like the others in external appearance, and even within the difference was trifling between it and those of the poorest of his braves. The contrast between the palace of the millionaire and the cottage of the

Andrew Carnegie, "Wealth," *The North American Review*, CXLVIII (June 1889), pp. 653–64.

laborer with us today measures the change which has come with civilization.

This change, however, is not to be deplored, but welcomed as highly beneficial. It is well, nay, essential for the progress of the race, that the houses of some should be homes for all that is highest and best in literature and the arts, and for all the refinements of civilization, rather than that none should be so. Much better this great irregularity than universal squalor. Without wealth there can be no Mæcenas. The "good old times" were not good old times. Neither master nor servant was as well situated then as today. A relapse to old conditions would be disastrous to both—not the least so to him who serves—and would sweep away civilization with it. But whether the change be for good or ill, it is upon us, beyond our power to alter, and therefore to be accepted and made the best of. It is a waste of time to criticise the inevitable.

It is easy to see how the change has come. One illustration will serve for almost every phase of the cause. In the manufacture of products we have the whole story. It applies to all combinations of human industry, as stimulated and enlarged by the inventions of this scientific age. Formerly articles were manufactured at the domestic hearth or in small shops which formed part of the household. The master and his apprentices worked side by side, the latter living with the master, and therefore subject to the same conditions. When these apprentices rose to be masters, there was little or no change in their mode of life, and they, in turn, educated in the same routine succeeding apprentices. There was, substantially, social equality, and even political equality, for those engaged in industrial pursuits had then little or no political voice in the State.

But the inevitable result of such a mode of manufacture was crude articles at high prices. Today the world obtains commodities of excellent quality at prices which even the generation preceding this would have deemed incredible. In the commercial world similar causes have produced similar results, and the race is benefited thereby. The poor enjoy what the rich could not before afford. What were the luxuries have become the necessaries of life. The laborer has now more comforts than the farmer had a few generations ago. The farmer has more luxuries than the landlord had, and is more richly clad and better housed. The landlord has books and pictures rarer, and appointments more artistic, than the King could then obtain.

The price we pay for this salutary change is, no doubt, great. We assemble thousands of operatives in the factory, in the mine, and in the countinghouse, of whom the employer can know little or nothing, and to whom the employer is little better than a myth. All intercourse between them is at an end. Rigid castes are formed, and, as usual, mutual ignorance breeds mutual distrust. Each caste is without sympathy for the other, and ready to credit anything disparaging in regard to it. Under the law of competition, the employer of thousands is forced into the strictest economies, among which the rates paid to labor figure prominently, and often there is friction between the employer and the employed, between capital and labor, between rich and poor. Human society loses homogeneity.

The price which society pays for the law of competition, like the price it pays for cheap comforts and luxuries, is also great; but the advantages of this law are also greater still, for it is to this law that we owe our wonderful material development, which brings improved conditions in its train. But, whether the law be benign or not, we must say of it, as we say of the change in the conditions of men to which we have referred: It is here; we cannot evade it; no substitutes for it have been found; and while the law may be sometimes hard for the individual, it is best for the race, because it insures the survival of the fittest in every department. We accept and welcome, therefore, as conditions to which we must accommodate ourselves, great inequality of environment, the concentration of business, industrial and commercial, in the hands of a few, and the law of competition between these, as being not only beneficial, but essential for the future progress of the race. Having accepted these, it follows that there must be great scope for the exercise of special ability in the merchant and in the manufacturer who has to conduct affairs upon a great scale. That this talent for organization and management is rare among men is proved by the fact that it invariably secures for its possessor enormous rewards, no matter where or under what laws or conditions. The experienced in affairs always rate the MAN whose services can be obtained as a partner as not only the first consideration, but such as to render the question of his capital scarcely worth considering, for such men soon create capital; while, without the special talent required, capital soon takes wings. Such men become interested in firms or corporations using millions; and estimating only simple interest to be made upon the capital invested, it is inevitable that their income must exceed their expenditures, and that they must accumulate wealth. Nor is there any middle ground which such men can occupy, because the great manufacturing or commercial concern which does not earn at least interest upon its capital soon becomes bankrupt. It must either go forward or fall behind: to stand still is impossible. It is a condition essential for its successful operation that it should be thus far profitable, and even that, in addition to interest on capital, it should make profit. It is a law, as certain as any of the others named, that men possessed of this peculiar talent for affairs, under the free play of economic forces, must, of necessity, soon be in receipt of more revenue than can be judiciously expended upon themselves; and this law is as beneficial for the race as the others.

Objections to the foundations upon which society is based are not in order, because the condition of the race is better with these than it has been with any others which have been tried. Of the effect of any new substitutes proposed we cannot be sure. The Socialist or Anarchist who seeks to overturn present conditions is to be regarded as attacking the foundation upon which civilization itself rests, for civilization took its start from the day that the capable, industrious workman said to his incompetent and lazy fellow, "If thou dost not sow, thou shalt not reap," and thus ended primitive Communism by separating the drones from the bees. One who studies this subject will soon be brought face to face with the conclusion that upon the sacredness of property civilization itself depends—the right of the laborer to his hundred dollars in the savings bank, and equally the legal right of the millionaire to his millions. To those who propose to substitute Communism for this intense Individualism the answer, therefore, is: The race has tried that. All progress from that barbarous day to the present time has resulted from its displacement. Not evil, but good, has come to the race from the accumulation of wealth by those who have the ability and energy that produce it. But even if we admit for a moment that it might be better for the race to discard its present foundation, Individualism—that it is a nobler ideal that man should labor, not for himself alone, but in and for a brotherhood of his fellows, and share with them all in common, realizing Swedenborg's idea of Heaven, where, as he says, the angels derive their happiness, not from laboring for self, but for each other—even admit all this, and a sufficient answer is, This is not evolution but revolution. It necessitates the changing of human nature itself—a work of æons, even if it were good to change it, which we cannot know. It is not practicable in our day or in our age. Even if desirable theoretically, it belongs to another and long-succeeding sociological stratum. Our duty is with what is practicable now; with the next step possible in our day and generation. It is criminal to waste our energies in endeavoring to uproot, when all we can profitably or possibly accomplish is to bend the universal tree of humanity a little in the direction most favorable to the production of good fruit under existing circumstances. We might as well urge the destruction of the highest existing type of man because he failed to reach our ideal as to favor the destruction of Individualism, Private Property, the Law of Accumulation of Wealth, and the Law of Competition; for these are the highest results of human experience, the soil in which society so far has produced the best fruit. Unequally or unjustly, perhaps, as these laws sometimes operate, and imperfect as they appear to the Idealist, they are, nevertheless, like the highest type of man, the best and most valuable of all that humanity has yet accomplished.

We start, then, with a condition of affairs under which the best interests of the race are promoted, but which inevitably gives wealth to the few. Thus far, accepting conditions as they exist, the situation can be surveyed and pronounced good. The question then arises—and, if the foregoing be correct, it is the only question with which we have to deal—What is the proper mode of administering wealth after the laws upon which civilization is founded have thrown it into the hands of the few? And it is of this great question that I believe I offer the true solution. It will be understood that *fortunes* are here spoken of, not moderate sums saved by many years of effort, the returns from which are required for the comfortable maintenance and education of families. This is not *wealth*, but only *competence*, which it should be the aim of all to acquire.

There are but three modes in which surplus wealth can be disposed of. It can be left to the families of the decedents; or it can be bequeathed for public purposes; or, finally, it can be administered during their lives by its possessors. Under the first and second modes most of the wealth of the world that has reached the few has hitherto been applied. Let us in turn consider each of these modes. The first is the most injudicious. In monarchical countries, the estates and the greatest portion of the wealth are left to the first son, that the vanity of the parent may be gratified by the thought that his name and title are to descend to succeeding generations unimpaired. The condition of this class in Europe today teaches the futility of such hopes or ambitions. The successors have become impoverished through their follies or from the fall in the value of land. Even in Great Britain the strict law of entail has been found inadequate to maintain the status of an hereditary class. Its soil is rapidly passing into the hands of the stranger. Under republican institutions the division of property among the children is much fairer, but the question which forces itself upon thoughtful men in all lands is: Why should men leave great fortunes to their children? If this is done from affection, is it not misguided affection? Observation teaches that, generally speaking, it is not well for the children that they should be so burdened. Neither is it well for the state. Beyond providing for the wife and daughters moderate sources of income, and very moderate allowances indeed, if any, for the sons, men may well hesitate, for it is no longer questionable that great sums bequeathed oftener work more for the injury than for the good of the recipients. Wise men will soon conclude that, for the best interests of the members of their families and of the state, such bequests are an improper use of their means.

It is not suggested that men who have failed to educate their sons to earn a livelihood shall cast them adrift in poverty. If any man has seen fit to rear his sons with a view to their living idle lives, or, what is highly commendable, has instilled in them the sentiment that they are in a position to labor for public ends without reference to pecuniary considerations, then, of course, the duty of the parent is to see that such are provided for *in moderation*. There are instances of millionaires' sons unspoiled by wealth, who, being rich, still perform great services in the community. Such are the very salt of the earth, as valuable as, unfortunately, they are rare; still it is not the exception, but the rule, that men must regard, and, looking at the usual result of enormous sums conferred upon legatees, the thoughtful man must shortly say, "I would as soon leave to my son a curse as the almighty dollar," and admit to himself that it is not the welfare of the children, but family pride, which inspires these enormous legacies.

As to the second mode, that of leaving wealth at death for public uses, it may be said that this is only a means for the disposal of wealth, provided a man is content to wait until he is dead before it becomes of much good in the world. Knowledge of the results of legacies bequeathed is not calculated to inspire the brightest hopes of much posthumous good being accomplished. The cases are not few in which the real object sought by the testator is not attained, nor are they few in which his real wishes are thwarted. In many cases the bequests are so used as to become only monuments of his folly. It is well to remember that it requires the exercise of not less ability than that which acquired the wealth to use it so as to be really beneficial to the community. Besides this, it may fairly be said that no man is to be extolled for doing what he cannot help doing, nor is he to be thanked by the community to which he only leaves wealth at death. Men who leave vast sums in this way may fairly be thought men who would not have left it at all, had they been able to take it with them. The memories of such cannot be held in grateful remembrance, for there is no grace in their gifts. It is not to be wondered at that such bequests seem so generally to lack the blessing.

The growing disposition to tax more and more heavily large estates left at death is a cheering indication of the growth of a salutary change in public opinion. The State of Pennsylvania now takes—subject to some exceptions—one-tenth off the property left by its citizens. The budget presented in the British Parliament the other day proposes to increase the death duties; and, most significant of all, the new tax is to be a graduated one. Of all forms of taxation, this seems the wisest. Men who continue hoarding great sums all their lives, the proper use of which for public ends would work good to the community, should be made to feel that the community, in the form of the state, cannot thus be deprived of its proper share. By taxing estates heavily at death the state marks its condemnation of the selfish millionaire's unworthy life . . .

There remains, then, only one mode of using great fortunes; but in this we have the true antidote for the temporary unequal distribution of wealth, the reconciliation of the rich and the poor—a reign of harmony—another ideal, differing, indeed, from that of the Communist in requiring only the further evolution of existing conditions, not the total overthrow of our civilization. It is founded upon the present most intense individualism, and the race is prepared to put it in practice by degrees whenever it pleases. Under its sway we shall have an ideal state, in which the surplus wealth of the few will become, in the best sense, the property of the many, because administered for the common good, and this wealth, passing through the hands of the few, can be made a much more potent force for the elevation of our race than if it had been distributed in small sums to the people themselves. Even the poorest can be made to see this, and to agree that great sums gathered by some of their fellow-citizens and spent for public purposes, from which the masses reap the principal benefit, are more valuable to them than if scattered among them through the course of many years in trifling amounts . . .

Poor and restricted are our opportunities in this life, narrow our horizon, our best work most imperfect; but rich men should be thankful for one inestimable boon. They have it in their power during their lives to busy themselves in organizing benefactions from which the masses of their fellows will derive lasting advantage, and thus dignify their own lives. The highest life is probably to be reached, not by such imitation of the life of Christ as Count Tolstoï gives us, but, while animated by Christ's spirit, by recognizing the changed conditions of this age, and adopting modes of expressing this spirit suitable to the changed conditions under which we live; still laboring for the good of our fellows, which was the essence of his life and teaching, but laboring in a different manner.

This, then, is held to be the duty of the man of wealth: First, to set an example of modest unostentatious living, shunning display or extravagance; to provide moderately for the legitimate wants of those dependent upon him; and after doing so to consider all surplus revenues which come to him simply as trust funds, which he is called upon to administer, and strictly bound as a matter of duty to administer in the manner which, in his judgment, is best calculated to produce the most beneficial results for the community—the man of wealth thus becoming the mere agent and trustee for his poorer brethren, bringing to their service his superior wisdom, experience, and ability to administer, doing for them better than they would or could do for themselves.

We are met here with the difficulty of determining what are moderate sums to leave to members of the family; what is modest, unostentatious living; what is the test of extravagance. There must be different standards for different conditions. The answer is that it is as impossible to name exact amounts or actions as it is to define good manners, good taste, or the rules of propriety; but, nevertheless, these are verities, well known although undefinable. Public sentiment is quick to know and to feel what offends these. So in the case of wealth. The rule in regard to good taste in the dress of men or women applies here. Whatever makes one conspicuous offends the canon. If any family be chiefly known for display, for extravagance in home, table, equipage, for enormous sums ostentatiously spent in any form upon itself—if these be its chief distinctions, we have no difficulty in estimating its nature or culture. So likewise in regard to the use or abuse of its surplus wealth, or to generous, freehanded cooperation in good public uses, or to unabated efforts to accumulate and hoard to the last, whether they administer or bequeath. The verdict rests with the best and most enlightened public sentiment. The community will surely judge, and its judgments will not often be wrong.

The best uses to which surplus wealth can be put have already been indicated. Those who would administer wisely must, indeed, be wise, for one of the serious obstacles to the improvement of our race is indiscriminate charity. It were better for mankind that the millions of the rich were thrown into the sea than so spent as to encourage the slothful, the drunken, the unworthy. Of every thousand dollars spent in so called charity today, it is probable that $950 is unwisely spent; so spent, indeed, as to produce the very evils which it proposes to mitigate or cure. A well known writer of philosophic books admitted the other day that he had given a quarter of a dollar to a man who approached him as he was coming to visit the house of his friend. He knew nothing of the habits of this beggar; knew not the use that would be made of this money, although he had every reason to suspect that it would be spent improperly. This man professed to be a disciple of Herbert Spencer; yet the quarter-dollar given that night will probably work more injury than all the money which its thoughtless donor will ever be able to give in true charity will do good. He only gratified his own feelings, saved himself from annoyance—and this was probably one of the most selfish and very worst actions of his life, for in all respects he is most worthy.

In bestowing charity, the main consideration should be to help those who will help themselves; to provide part of the means by which those who desire to improve may do so; to give those who desire to rise the aids by which they may rise; to assist, but rarely or never to do all. Neither the individual nor the race is improved by alms-giving. Those worthy of assistance, except in rare cases, seldom require assistance. The really valuable men of the race never do, except in cases of accident or sudden change. Every one has, of course, cases of individuals brought to his own knowledge where temporary assistance can do genuine good, and these he will not overlook. But the amount which can be wisely given by the individual for individuals is necessarily limited by his lack of knowledge of the circumstances connected with each. He is the only true reformer who is as careful and as anxious not to aid the unworthy as he is to aid the worthy, and, perhaps, even more so, for in alms-giving more injury is probably done by rewarding vice than by relieving virtue.

The rich man is thus almost restricted to following the examples of Peter Cooper, Enoch Pratt of Baltimore, Mr. Pratt of Brooklyn, Senator Stanford, and others, who know that the best means of benefiting the community is to place within its reach the ladders upon which the aspiring can rise—parks, and means of recreation, by which men are helped in body and mind; works of art, certain to give pleasure and improve the public taste, and public institutions of various kinds, which will improve the general condition of the people; in this manner returning their surplus wealth to the mass of their fellows in the forms best calculated to do them lasting good.

Thus is the problem of Rich and Poor to be solved. The laws of accumulation will be left free; the laws of distribution free. Individualism will continue, but the millionaire will be but a trustee for the poor; intrusted for a season with a great part of the increased wealth of the community, but administering it for the community far better than it could or would have done for itself. The best minds will thus have reached a stage in the development of the race in which it is clearly seen that there is no mode of disposing of surplus wealth creditable to thoughtful and earnest men into whose hands it flows save by using it year by year for the general good. This day already dawns. But a little while, and although, without incurring the pity of their fellows, men may die sharers in great business enterprises from which their capital cannot be or has not been withdrawn, and is left chiefly at death for public uses, yet the man who dies leaving behind him millions of available wealth, which was his to administer during life, will pass away "unwept, unhonored, and unsung," no matter to what uses he leaves the dross which he cannot take with him. Of such as these the public verdict will then be: "The man who dies thus rich dies disgraced."

Such, in my opinion, is the true Gospel concerning Wealth, obedience to which is destined some day to solve the problem of the Rich and the Poor, and to bring "Peace on earth, among men Good-Will."

Edward Bok
The Young Man in Business

(1894)

Like Carnegie, Edward Bok (1863–1930) rose from immigrant boy to a position among the famous and wealthy in the Gilded Age. The story of this enterprising Brooklyn street boy who became editor of *Ladies' Home Journal* just after his twenty-sixth birthday is vividly recaptured in his now classic autobiography, *The Americanization of Edward Bok* (1920). After reading the essay printed here, students of the cult of self-help will be amused to know, or recall, that Bok ardently followed his final word of advice, that young men should acquire wife and home to insure a successful business career. Bok married the boss's daughter, wealthy Mary Louise Curtis. The present article appeared in the January, 1894, *Cosmopolitan*. Sharing the same issue, it might be noted, was Howells' satirical counter-statement, *A Traveler from Altruria*.

A well known New York millionaire gave it as his opinion not long since

Edward Bok, "The Young Man in Business," *Cosmopolitan*, XVI (January 1894), pp. 332–39.

that any young man possessing a good constitution and a fair degree of intelligence, might acquire riches. The statement was criticised—literally picked to pieces—and finally adjudged as being wildly extravagant. The figures then came out, gathered by a careful statistician, that of the young men in business in New York City only sixty percent were earning $1000 per year, twelve percent had an income of $2000, and only five percent commanded salaries in excess of the latter figure. The great majority of young men in New York City—that is, between the ages of twenty-three and thirty—were earning less than thirty dollars per week. On the basis, therefore, that a young man must be established in his life profession by his thirtieth year, it can hardly be said that the average New York young man in business is successful. Of course, this is measured entirely from the standpoint of income; yet, after all, is not that point of view a tolerably fair one? A young man may not, in every case, receive the salary his services merit, but as a general rule, his income is a pretty accurate indication of his capacities.

Now, as every young man naturally desires to make a business success, it is plain from the above statement that something is lacking; either the opportunities, or the capabilities in the young men themselves. No one conversant with the business life of any of our large cities can, it seems to me, even for a single moment doubt the existence of the chances for young men. Take New York as a fair example. Here exist more opportunities than there are young men capable of embracing them. The demand is far in excess of the supply. Positions of trust are constantly going begging for the right kind of young men to fill them. But the material doesn't exist, or, if it does, it certainly has a most unfortunate way of hiding its light under a bushel, so much so that businessmen cannot see even a glimmer of its rays. Let a position of any real importance become open, and it is the most difficult kind of problem to find anyone to fill it satisfactorily. Businessmen are constantly passing through this experience.

In order that, in this article, I might deal with facts rather than with theories, I made a personal canvass of a dozen of the largest houses in five different commercial and professional lines of business to see to what extent there existed openings for young men. In only two of the houses approached were the heads of the firms satisfied that the positions of trust in their houses were filled by capable men. And in both of these instances I was told that "of course, if the right sort of a young man came along who could tell us something about our business we did not already know, we should not let him slip through our fingers. Positions can always be created." In the remaining ten cases, one or more opportunities presented itself in each instance; in fact, in four of the houses positions had been open for six months or more, and the sharpest kind of a lookout kept for possible occupants. These positions commanded salaries all the way from two to five thousand dollars per year. Take in that particular profession, the publishing business, with which I am naturally most conversant, I know, personally, of not less than six positions actually yawning for the men to come and fill them—not clerical positions, but positions of executive authority. Young men are desired in these positions because of their progressive ideas and capacity to endure work; in fact, "young blood" as it is called, is preferred in nine positions out of every ten nowadays.

I have dwelt upon this phase of the question because I wished to make it as clear as it is given me to do, that the chances for business success with any young man are not wanting. The opportunities exist, plenty of them. It is simply that the average young man of today is incapable of filling them, or if he be not exactly incapable (I am willing to give him the benefit of the doubt), he is unwilling, which is even worse. That exceptions can be brought up to controvert this statement I know, but in this article I shall deal with the many and not with the few.

The average young man in business today is nothing more or less than a plodder—a mere automatic machine. He comes to his office at nine o'clock in the mornings; is faithful in the duties he performs; goes to lunch at twelve, comes back at one; takes up whatever he is told to do until five, and then goes home. His work for the day is done. One day is the same to him as another; he has a certain routine of duties to do, and he does them day in and day out, month in and month out. His duties are regulated by the clock. As that points, so he points. Verily, it is true of him that he is the same yesterday, today and forever. No special fault can be found with his work. Given a particular piece of work to do, he does it just as a machine would. Such a young man, too, generally considers himself hard-worked—often over-worked and under-paid, wondering all the time why his employer doesn't recognize his value and advance his salary. "I do everything I am told to do," he argues, "and I do it well. What more can I do?"

This is simply a type of a young man which exists in thousands of offices and stores. He comes to his work each day with no definite point or plan in view; he leaves it with nothing accomplished. He is a mere automaton. Let him die, and his position can be filled in twenty-four hours. If he detracts nothing from his employer's business he certainly adds nothing to it. He never advances an idea; is absolutely devoid of creative powers; his position remains the same after he has been in it for five years as when he came to it.

Now, I would not for a moment be understood as belittling the value of faithfulness in an employee. But, after all, faithfulness is nothing more nor less than a negative quality. By faithfulness a man can hold a position a lifetime. He will keep it just where he found it. But by the exercise of this single quality he does not add to the importance of the position any more than he adds to his own value. It is not enough that it should be said of a young man that he is faithful; he must be something more. The willingness and capacity to be faithful to the smallest detail must be there, serving only, however, as a foundation upon which other qualities are built.

Altogether too many young men are content to remain in the positions in which they find themselves. The thought of studying the needs of the next position just above them never seems to enter into their minds. I believe it is possible for every young man to rise above his position, and I care not how humble that position may be, nor under what disadvantages he may be placed. But he must be alert. He must not be afraid of work, and of the hardest kind of work. He must study not only to please, but he must go a step beyond. It is essential, of course, that he should first of all fill the position for which he is engaged. No man can solve the problem of business before he understands the rudiments of the problem itself. Once the requirements of a position are understood and mastered, then its possibilities should be undertaken. It is foolish, as some young men argue, that to go beyond their special position is impossible with their employers. The employer never existed who will prevent the cream of his establishment from rising to the surface. The advance of an employee always means the advance of the employer's interests. Every employer would rather pay a young man five thousand dollars a year than five hundred. What is to the young man's interests is by far greater to the interests of his employer. A five-hundred-dollar clerkship is worth just that amount and nothing more to an employer. But a five-thousand dollar man is fully worth five times that sum to a business. A young man makes of a position exactly what he chooses: a millstone around his neck, or a stepping-stone to larger success. The possibilities lie in every position: seeing and embracing them rests with its occupant. The lowest position can be so filled as to lead up to the next and become a part of it. One position should only be the chrysalis for the development of new strength to master the other just above it . . .

A young man in business nowadays with an ambition to be successful must also be careful of his social life. It is not enough that he should take care of himself during the day. To social dissipations at night can be traced the downfall of hundreds upon hundreds of young men. The idea that an employer has no control over a young man's time away from the office is a dangerous fallacy. An employer has every right to ask that those into whose hands he entrusts responsibilities shall follow social habits which will not endanger his interests upon the morrow. So far as social life is concerned, young men generally run to both extremes. Either they do not go out at all, which is stagnating: or, they go out too much, which is deadly. Only here and there is found one who knows the happy medium. A certain amount of social diversion is essential to everybody, boy, man, girl or woman. And particularly so to a young man with a career to make. To come into contact with the social side of people is broadening: it is educative. "To know people," says a writer "you must see them at play." Social life can be made a study at the same time that it is made a pleasure. To know the wants of people, to learn their softer side, you must come into contact with their social natures. No young man can afford to deny himself certain pleasures, or a reasonable amount of contact with people in the outer world. It is to his advantage that people should know he exists: what his aims and aspirations are. It is well for a young man to keep himself honorably in the eyes of the public. His evening occupations should be as widely different from those which occupy him during the day as possible. The mind needs a change of thought as well as does the body of raiment. "All work and no play makes Jack a dull boy" contains a vast amount of truth.

At the same time, nothing is more injurious to the chances of a young man in business than an over-indulgence in the pleasures of what, for the want of a better word, we call "society." It is a rough but a true saying that "a man cannot drink whisky and be in business." Perhaps a softer and more refined translation of this is that a man cannot be in society and be in business. This is impossible, and nothing that a young man can bear in mind will stand him to such good account as this fact. No mind can be fresh in the morning that has been kept at a tension the night before by late hours, or befogged by indulgence of late suppers. We need more sleep at twenty-five than we do at fifty, and the young man who grants himself less than eight hours' sleep every night just robs himself of so much vitality. The loss may not be felt or noticed at present, but the process of sleeping is only Nature's banking system of principal and interest. A mind capable of the fulfilment of its highest duties should be receptive to ideas, quick to comprehend, instantaneous in its conception of a point. With a fresh mind and a clear brain, a young man has two of the greatest levers of success. These cannot be retained under social indulgences. The dissipation of a night has its invariable influence upon the work of the morrow. I do not preach total abstinence of any habits to which human nature is prone. Every man ought to know what is good for him and what is injurious to his best interests. But an excess of anything is injurious, and a young man on the threshold of a business career cannot afford to be excessive in a single direction. He should husband his resources. He will need them all.

For no success is easily made nowadays. Appearances are tremendously deceptive in this respect. We see men making what we choose to regard and call quick success, because at a comparatively early age they acquire position or means. But one needs only to study the conditions of the business life of today to see how impossible it is to achieve any success except by the very hardest work. No young man need approach a business career with the idea that its achievement is easy. The histories of successful men tell us all too clearly the lessons of the patience and efforts of years. Some men compass a successful career in less time than others. And if the methods employed are necessarily different, the requirements are precisely the same. It is a story of hard work in every case, of close application and of a patient mastery of the problem in hand. Advantages of education will come in at times and push one man ahead of another. But a practical business knowledge is apt to be a greater possession.

I know there are thousands of young men who feel themselves incompetent for a business career because of a lack of early education. And here might come in—if I choose to discuss the subject, which I do not—the oft-mooted question of the exact value of a college education to the young man in business. Far abler pens than mine have treated of this: it is certainly not for me to enter into here. But I will say this: a young man need not feel that the lack of a college education will stand in any respect whatever in the way of his success in the business world. No college on earth ever made a business man. The knowledge acquired in college has fitted thousands of men for professional success, but it has also unfitted other thousands for a practical business career. A college training is never wasted, although I have seen again and again five-thousand-dollar educations spent on five-hundred-dollar men. Where a young man can bring a college education to the requirements of a practical business knowledge, it is an advantage. But before our American colleges become an absolute factor in the business capacities of men, their methods of study and learning will have to be radically changed. I have had associated with me both kinds of young men, collegiate and non-collegiate, and I must confess that the ones who had a better knowledge of the practical part of life have been those who never saw the inside of a college and whose feet never stood upon a campus. College-bred men, and men who never had college advantages, have succeeded in about equal ratios. The men occupying the most important commercial positions in New York today are self-made, whose only education has come to them from contact with that greatest college of all, the business world. Far be it from me to depreciate the value of a college education. I believe in its advantages too firmly. But no young man need feel hampered because of the lack of it. If business qualities are in him they will come to the surface. It is not the college education: it is the young man. Without its possession as great and honorable successes have been made as with it. Men are not accepted in the business world upon their collegiate diplomas, nor on the knowledge these imply.

The young man engaged in business today, in this country, has advantages exceeding those of any generation before him. He lives in a country where every success is possible; where a man can make of himself just what he may choose; where energy and enterprise are appreciated, and a market is always ready for good wares. And he lives at a time when more opportunities are open to him than at any period in the history of our land. Young men have forged to the front wonderfully during the past ten years. Employers are more than ever willing to entrust great responsibilities on their shoulders. Salaries are higher than ever; young men never before earned the incomes which are received by some today. All success is possible. But—and it's a big word in this connection—he must remember a few very essential truths, and these are:

Above all things, before a young man attempts to make a success, he should convince himself that he is in a congenial business. Whether it be a trade or a profession—both are honorable and productive—let him satisfy himself, above everything else, that it enlists his personal interest. If a man shows that he has his work at heart, his success can be relied on. Personal interest in any work will bring other things; but all the other essentials combined cannot create personal interest. That must exist first: then two-thirds of the battle is won. Fully satisfied that he is in the particular line of business in which he feels a stronger, warmer interest than in any other, then he should remember:

First—That, whatever else he may strive to be, he must, first of all be absolutely honest. From honorable principles he can never swerve. A temporary success is often possible on what are not exactly dishonest, but "shady" lines; but such success is only temporary, with a certainty of permanent loss. The surest business success—yes, the only successes worth the making, are built upon honest foundations. There can be no "blinking" at the truth or at honesty, no half-way compromise. There is but one way to be successful, and that is to be absolutely honest. Honesty is not only the foundation, but the cap-stone as well, of business success.

Second—He must be alert, alive to every opportunity. He cannot afford to lose a single point, for that single point might prove the very link that would make complete the whole chain of a business success.

Third—He must ever be willing to learn, never overlooking the fact that others have long ago forgotten what he has still to learn. Firmness of decision is an admirable trait in business. The young man whose opinions can be tossed from one side to the other is poor material. But youth is full of errors, and caution is a strong trait.

Fourth—If he be wise, he will entirely avoid the use of liquors. If the question of harm done by intoxicating liquor is an open one, the question of the actual good derived from it is not.

Fifth—Let him remember that a young man's strongest recommendation is his respectability. Some young men, apparently successful, may be flashy in dress, loud in manner, and disrespectful of women and sacred things. But the young man who is respectable always wears best. The way a young man carries himself in his private life oft-times means much to him in his business career. No matter where he is, or in whose company—respectability, and all that it implies, will always command respect. And if any young man wishes a set of rules even more concise, here it is:

Get into a business you like.

Devote yourself to it.

Be honest in everything.

Employ caution; think out a thing well before you enter upon it.

Sleep eight hours every night.

Do everything that means keeping in good health.

School yourself not to worry; worry kills, work doesn't.

Avoid liquors of all kinds.

If you must smoke, smoke moderately.

Shun discussion on two points—religion and politics.

And lastly, but not least: Marry a true woman, and have your own home.

Elbert Hubbard
A Message to Garcia

(1899)

If one can rely on the flamboyant author, Elbert Hubbard (1856–1915), nine million reprints of his "A Message to Garcia" were distributed within the first ten months after it appeared in his *Philistine* of March 1899. Eventually the figure quadrupled, as copies were distributed by the world's business employers, army generals, and government officials. In the American school, the "Message" challenged the popularity of McGuffey's Readers. As late as the 1940's the "Message" was still being used in schools. Though Hubbard ridiculed at times the readership he sought, he eschewed all irony when preaching the Protestant Ethic of salvation through obedient, cheerful labor. In 1899, he seems to have experienced the defiance growing among the message-carriers and day-laborers of the world. As his biographer, Freeman Champney, reminds us, Hubbard gave his "Message" to the world in the same year that Edwin Markham would also receive international fame for his grim warning in "The Man With the Hoe."

In all this Cuban business there is one man stands out on the horizon of my memory like Mars at perihelion.

When war broke out between Spain and the United States, it was very necessary to communicate quickly with the leader of the Insurgents. Garcia was somewhere in the mountain fastnesses of Cuba—no one knew where.

Elbert Hubbard, "Heart to Heart Talks with Grown-Ups by the Pastor of His Flock," *Philistine*, VIII (March 1899), pp. 109–16.

No mail or telegraph message could reach him. The President must secure his co-operation, and quickly. What to do!

Someone said to the President, "There is a fellow by the name of Rowan will find Garcia for you, if anybody can."

Rowan was sent for and was given a letter to be delivered to Garcia. How "the fellow by the name of Rowan" took the letter, sealed it up in an oilskin pouch, strapped it over his heart, in four days landed by night off the coast of Cuba from an open boat, disappeared into the jungle, and in three weeks came out on the other side of the Island, having traversed a hostile country on foot, and delivered his letter to Garcia—are things I have no special desire now to tell in detail. The point that I wish to make is this: McKinley gave Rowan a letter to be delivered to Garcia; Rowan took the letter and did not ask, "Where is he at?" By the Eternal! there is a man whose form should be cast in deathless bronze and the statue placed in every college of the land. It is not book-learning young men need, nor instruction about this and that, but a stiffening of the vertebrae which will cause them to be loyal to a trust, to act promptly, concentrate their energies: do the thing—"Carry a message to Garcia."

General Garcia is dead now, but there are other Garcias.

No man who has endeavored to carry out an enterprise where many hands were needed, but has been well-nigh appalled at times by the imbecility of the average man—the inability or unwillingness to concentrate on a thing and do it.

Slipshod assistance, foolish inattention, dowdy indifference, and half-hearted work seem the rule; and no man succeeds, unless by hook or crook or threat he forces or bribes other men to assist him; or mayhap, God in His goodness performs a miracle, and sends him an Angel of Light for an assistant. You, reader, put this matter to a test: You are sitting now in your office—six clerks are within call. Summon any one and make this request: "Please look in the encyclopedia and make a brief memorandum for me concerning the life of Correggio."

Will the clerk quietly say, "Yes, sir," and go do the task? On your life he will not. He will look at you out of a fishy eye and ask one or more of the following questions:

Who was he?

Which encyclopedia?

Where is the encyclopedia?

Was I hired for that?

Don't you mean Bismarck?

What's the matter with Charlie doing it?

Is he dead?

Is there any hurry?

Shall I bring you the book and let you look it up yourself?

What do you want to know for?

And I will lay you ten to one that after you have answered the questions, and explained how to find the information, and why you want it, the clerk will go off and get one of the other clerks to help him try to find Garcia—and then come back and tell you there is no such man. Of course I may lose my bet, but according to the Law of Average I will not.

Now, if you are wise, you will not bother to explain to your "assistant" that Correggio is indexed under the C's, not in the K's, but you will smile very sweetly and say, "Never mind," and go look it up yourself.

And this incapacity for independent action, this moral stupidity, this infirmity of the will, this unwillingness to cheerfully catch hold and lift—these are the things that put pure Socialism so far into the future. If men will not act for themselves, what will they do when the benefit of their effort is for all? A first mate with knotted club seems necessary; and the dread of getting "the bounce" Saturday night holds many a worker to his place.

Advertise for a stenographer, and nine out of ten who apply can neither spell nor punctuate—and do not think it necessary to.

Can such a one write a letter to Garcia?

"You see that bookkeeper," said a foreman to me in a large factory.

"Yes; what about him?"

"Well, he's a fine accountant, but if I'd send him up-town on an errand, he might accomplish the errand all right, and on the other hand, might stop at four saloons on the way, and when he got to Main Street would forget what he had been sent for."

Can such a man be entrusted to carry a message to Garcia?

We have recently been hearing much maudlin sympathy expressed for the "downtrodden denizens of the sweat-shop" and the "homeless wanderer searching for honest employment," and with it all often go many hard words for the men in power.

Nothing is said about the employer who grows old before his time in a vain attempt to get frowsy ne'er-do-wells to do intelligent work; and his long, patient striving with "help" that does nothing but loaf when his back is turned. In every store and factory there is a constant weeding-out process going on. The employer is continually sending away "help" that have shown their incapacity to further the interests of the business, and others are being taken on.

No matter how good times are, this sorting continues: only if times are hard and work is scarce, the sorting is done finer—but out and forever out the incompetent and unworthy go. It is the survival of the fittest. Self-interest prompts every employer to keep the best—those who can carry a message to Garcia.

I know one man of really brilliant parts who has not the ability to manage a business of his own, and yet who is absolutely worthless to any one else, because he carries with him constantly the insane suspicion that his employer is oppressing, or intending to oppress, him. He can not give orders; and he will not receive them. Should a message be given him to take to Garcia, his answer would probably be, "Take it yourself!"

Tonight this man walks the streets looking for work, the wind whistling through his threadbare coat. No one who knows him dare employ him, for he is a regular firebrand of discontent. He is impervious to reason, and the only thing that can impress him is the toe of a thick-soled Number Nine boot.

Of course I know that one so morally deformed is no less to be pitied than a physical cripple; but in our pitying let us drop a tear, too, for the men who are striving to carry on a great enterprise, whose working hours are not limited by the whistle, and whose hair is fast turning white through the struggle to hold in line dowdy indifference, slipshod imbecility, and the heartless ingratitude which, but for their enterprise, would be both hungry and homeless.

Have I put the matter too strongly? Possibly I have; but when all the world has gone a-slumming I wish to speak a word of sympathy for the man who succeeds the man who, against great odds, has directed the efforts of others, and having succeeded, finds there's nothing in it: nothing but bare board and clothes. I have carried a dinner-pail and worked for day's wages, and I have also been an employer of labor, and I know there is something to be said on both sides. There is no excellence, per se, in poverty; rags are no recommendation; and all employers are not rapacious and high-handed, any more than all poor men are virtuous.

My heart goes out to the man who does his work when the "boss" is away, as well as when he is at home. And the man who, when given a letter for Garcia, quietly takes the missive, without asking any idiotic questions, and with no lurking intention of chucking it into the nearest sewer, or of doing aught else but deliver it, never gets "laid off," nor has to go on a strike for higher wages. Civilization is one long, anxious search for just such individuals. Anything such a man asks shall be granted. His kind is so rare that no employer can afford to let him go. He is wanted in every city, town and village—in every office, shop, store and factory.

The world cries out for such: he is needed, and needed badly—the man who can carry A MESSAGE TO GARCIA.

Henry Harrison Lewis
Are Young Men's Chances Less?

(1900)

By the turn of the century, the frontiers of opportunity appeared to recede with the advance of industrial consolidation and an impersonal corporate management. In 1900, corporation lawyer James B. Dill argued in *Munsey's Magazine*, however, that the consolidation movement was a boon to rising young men. But they must now unite the older requisite of strong character with a new imperative; a college education. Governor Theodore Roosevelt repeated the formula in "Character and Success" in *Outlook*. The country was enjoying a prosperity unprecedented in its history; yet the droves of young men arriving in New York were searching in vain for the road that should lead them onward and upward. To the question "Are Young Men's Chances Less?" came the hopeful answer from Henry H. Lewis that the bitch-goddess Success had never smiled more beneficently upon the industrious young American. Lewis drew reassuring testimony from industrialists, financiers, and professional men, though he urged the reader to lower his expectations of rising to great wealth. Success should be viewed, rather, in the attainment of "sound character and good deeds."

Are young men's chances of success more hopeful or less today, than they were a generation ago? Are the concentration of business and the growth of great corporations a help or a menace to the youth who faces the world with no other heritage than his brains and his hands? Especially in the large cities is this a vital question. It is estimated that 150 young men from the country and the smaller cities come into New York to seek their fortunes every day in the year. They all hope to win success. But they are often told that the increase of population, the steadily advancing requirements for entering a business career or the professions, and the lessening opportunities for conducting independent enterprises, make the outlook continually darker.

The observation of men of experience is worth more than theoretical study to help toward a clear understanding of such a subject. I have preferred, therefore, directly to ask the opinions of a number of men who are themselves in positions that enable them to open careers for large numbers of young men, and who have been obliged to make a practical study of the present conditions of success. Their opinions are here presented for what they are worth.

Henry Harrison Lewis, "Are Young Men's Chances Less?" *World's Work*, I (December 1900), pp. 170–73.

Perhaps no better evidence could be obtained than the careers of some of these men themselves. Many of them are still young, young enough to have won success under the present industrial conditons.

One such is Mr. Charles M. Schwab of Pittsburg. Twenty years ago he received as wages a dollar a day at the Carnegie Works. Now he is the president of the company and receives a salary twice as large, perhaps, as the President of the United States, and he owns $15,000,000 worth of the company's stock. About 20,000 men are employed under him, and there are forty or more of his subordinates who receive salaries from $15,000 to $50,000 a year. Mr. Schwab began life with no money nor influence. He has risen by his business ability, and because of improvements in the manufacture of steel which he effected by a careful study of metallurgy, carried on in a laboratory which he fitted up in his own house and in which he worked outside of business hours.

There are, as everybody knows, many careers of a similar kind. Mr. Carnegie's own career is one. There is a man in New York who, twenty years ago, was shovelling gravel on a construction train on the Long Island Railroad. Now he is at the head of the consolidated street traction service of the city. He is Mr. Herbert H. Vreeland, who, yet a young man, receives a princely salary and does a great public service.

A list of men could be made of wearisome length who, by the time they have reached middle life, have won important administrative positions, or large fortunes, or both.

High Positions Waiting for Men

Nearly all men who have themselves succeeded maintain that modern business organization has made more opportunities and better ones than before existed.

Mr. Charles R. Flint of New York says, "I have today places for several men to whom I would pay $10,000 a year. But they must be men of all-round business ability."

The president of one of the largest trusts in the country says, "I am anxious at the present time to fill five positions, three of which would yield $15,000 a year, and the other two $10,000 each. If the right man could be found, they could step into these places and these salaries to-morrow."

One of the largest, perhaps the largest, retail merchant in New York said that if he could find a young man who would now train himself, ultimately to succeed the managing partner of his house, he would pay him $50,000 a year.

Bankers, merchants, manufacturers, and railway presidents declare that they are looking for young men capable of directing great business operations.

"But the trusts and the vast industrial combinations," it is said, "which are securing control of almost every product are taking away these opportunities by lessening the number of lucrative positions. They are consolidating opportunities. One successful or lucky man now receives a big salary, whereas formerly half a dozen men had this salary divided among them."

But most of the managers of large enterprises deny this also. For instance, Mr. Flint says:

Combinations Multiply Opportunities

"Highly developed organizations, resulting in an enormous volume of business, have increased the necessity for intelligence; and, since the supply of brains is not equal to the demand, the price of brains has risen. The turning over of individual enterprises to combinations has caused the retirement of old men to the advisory boards, and has made way for young men for the active posts. In our factories, our mines, our railways, in every field of organized industry, there are ten times as many men receiving $3000 a year or more as there were thirty years ago. The population of the country certainly has not increased tenfold in that period; and this increase in the number of good salaries is *prima facie* evidence that there has been an increase in the number of opportunities for men of ability.

"But it is said that they are dependent. Dependence of one individual upon another is, however, the condition of civilization. Complete independence is found only in the wigwam of the Indian. Was Captain Clark less the commander, or Chief Engineer Milligan less the engineer, because they were dependent upon each other in making the historic run and the fine fight of the *Oregon* in the Spanish-American War? Each gave to the other his opportunity.

"While economic evolution is centralizing production in large corporations, decentralization of ownership goes on simultaneously through the rapid distribution of shares.

"Under the old conditions of private ownership the control of many of our industrial enterprises would have been inherited by one individual or family. Now the control is subject to the rule that prevails in the administration of our state—the rule of the majority. It is seldom that the heirs of industrial giants have the capacity to succeed to the management of gigantic enterprises. The majority of stockholders—for, generally speaking, the numerical majority is also the majority in interest—elect as officers aspiring young men who, through years of application to a particular industry, have proved their ability to assume the responsibilities of leadership.

"It is not merely in the highest positions that this rule holds good. The rule in every great corporate business is to divide responsibilities among men fitted by their training to direct special departments. The head of a single department in a great modern concern has more authority and more responsibility than the owner of a private business had twenty-five years ago. I know that great industrial concerns are frequently embarrassed because they cannot find men who can command big salaries, and that the directors of our financial institutions are put to it to find trustworthy men capable of handling great undertakings. This state of affairs does not indicate that the young man of today has no chance, does it?"

A similar opinion is held by Mr. James B. Dill, a prominent corporation lawyer in New York "The corporate tendency of today has created an active demand for, and put a premium upon, college-trained minds, both in business and in professional pursuits. The profession of the law, today, as every other profession, calls not only for men of strong individuality, but for men capable of intelligent, strong team-work. The man who is most in demand and receives the greatest reward, is the man of strong individuality who is capable of the most accurate, energetic, and intelligent combination-work. Individualism is not dead. On the contrary, individualism is still more strongly called for in the development of combinations."

General Francis V. Greene, who has found time, before reaching fifty, to win success as a soldier, a writer, an engineer, and a business man, adds his testimony:

"There are three sorts of men, and for two of these sorts the tendency to industrial consolidation is a distinct advantage, while for the third there is no salvation in any economic system that has yet been devised. These three classes are the thoroughly competent who go to the top and command annual salaries that would once have been fortunes; the half competent who find profitable employment in subordinate positions and are saved from going into business for themselves and failing, as they would have fallen under the old system; and the incompetent who sit on the park benches as they would have done before.

"In the four years ending June 30th, 1900, the exports of the United States were $4,800,000,000. In this same period the imports were $2,900,000,000, leaving a balance in our favor of almost $2,000,000,000. This country is so big, and its trade is becoming so vast that big concerns are needed to handle it. No collection of small manufacturers, without a common purpose except to fight one another, could hope to handle such a business. It requires consolidation, organization, and heads capable of handling armies of men. This is the opportunity of the young man with brains. So far as I know anything about large concerns, they all are looking for good men to take high executive positions. The man who has the advantage of an education in a technical school, and possesses business ability, will be rushed right along to the top. The great combinations can well afford to pay large salaries to men who can manage their expensive machinery and who are trained to high special labor. Every increase in the extent of commercial organization and in the trade of the country widens the range of opportunities. There never has been a time in the history of the world when there have been so many chances for young men as now."

Chances in Banks and Railroads

In banking, consolidation has affected the chances of young men less directly. But Mr. William H. Kimball, president of the Seventh National Bank of New York, says:

"The large banking concerns are the concerns that make the most money and present the best opportunities for young men. The chances for young men in banking today are as good as ever, and the facilities for reaching the top are better. The same capacity, integrity, and ambition are required, and these qualities, with persistence, are bound to win success sooner or later. The outcry that the trusts are taking away the opportunities of young men affords a good excuse for those who do not wish to work."

Another banker, Mr. W. A. Nash, of the New York Corn Exchange Bank, says:

"Our country is filling up rapidly, but new avenues of occupation are continually opened and opportunities for advancement are far more frequent today than when I was a boy. Bankers are on the alert for trustworthy and capable young men. Influence and personal interest may be important in securing a position, but afterwards every man must stand on his own merits."

Conditions in the Professions

Now to turn to the professions. Dr. George F. Shrady, of New York, gives an interesting review of the outlook for young physicians:

"The young man entering upon the practice of medicine today has just as good an opportunity for success as the man of thirty years ago had, perhaps better," he says.

"There has been an equalization of advantages. A young man of today has a better foundation for his medical education than he used to have, thanks to the high schools, the technical schools, and the hospitals. In the early days he went from the plough to read in the doctor's office, thence to an ill-equipped medical college, and thence to practice. He had to learn his profession by practice and hard knocks. A young practitioner's earnings were, I think, comparatively more thirty years ago than they are today; living expenses were not so high, and neither were the office and professional expenses so large. The great development of the country and of the advance in the science of medicine have made new fields for medical men. The specialists receive fewer but larger fees.

"Today the standard required is much higher than it has ever before been, and the rewards of the successful are proportionately greater. I may compare the physician of today with the well-trained and groomed thoroughbred. The track is 'faster' now that it ever was, the thoroughbreds are trained to a finer point, and those who start in the race are more numerous. It is a hard race, and the track is crowded with particularly good runners. The best naturally win. But there is the law of compensation to be considered in medicine as in other callings. If there are more physicians, there are also more patients, and they are richer and better able to pay big fees. There are few fortunes to be made in medicine, to be sure, but there is always a good living for competent men. As in other things, the unequipped go to the bottom. Medicine used to be a limited monarchy with a few uncrowned kings at the head. Now it is a great republic in which every good man is the equal of his fellow. There is only one thing that will bring the young man of today success in medicine, and that is a love for his profession and the hardest kind of hard work. The man who splits his own wood is warmed twice. There is a great field for specialists in the big cities that did not exist thirty years ago. But the country doctor, too, is a well-educated man and vastly superior to his predecessor. He is self-reliant, and a good general practitioner, as a rule. One of the greatest factors in the success of the young doctor is his affability of manner. The day of the frank and brutal practitioner is past. The opportunity for success in the medical profession is greater than it ever was, for the brilliant man; and it is as great for the mediocre man."

Two College Presidents' Opinions

President Schurman, of Cornell University, has a hopeful view:

"Judging from our experience at Cornell University, there never has been a time when there were so many demands for the able and well-trained young men as at present," says President Schurman. "Perhaps the majority of these applications come from concerns supported by large combinations of capital. As the success of this sort of business depends upon the ability with which its affairs are managed, young men of character and brains are indispensable, and wonderfully high salaries await those who can earn them. I think that the opportunities for young men under the present system of large combinations of capital are greater than ever before in the history of the world.

"It is a mistake, however, to suppose that small concerns and competitive undertakings have been eliminated by those great combinations. There are now, and always will be, small factories, small stores, and other similar enterprises. Service in some of these may give a young man more varied responsibility and consequently more varied training. But so far as success is concerned, if one measures success by the financial compensation received, I think young men will have better opportunities in the large institutions than in the small."

The president of a university who prefers that his name should not be made known, lest he should be thought to criticize his associates said, in answer to my inquiry: "I'll tell you frankly, I think about no other subject so much, for two reasons: I can't find the men I want as teachers, and I cannot give the definite advice that I should like to be able to give to many a young man who talks with me about his career.

"Now then, this university wants young men trained to enter its faculty after they have had experience, who can teach, who are men of force, first-class, forthright men—men who *could* do anything, but who prefer this noble labor to any other. But most of the young men who choose academic careers are like the older ones—men of high ideals, men of studious habits, men who love knowledge and are eager in its quest, men with whom it is a joy to live if sometimes a trial to work; but they lack force. The chance is here. There are more opportunities than there are strong men.

"I have concluded, and the conclusion saddens me, that most youth of force prefer commercial careers. The stronger boys go into business or into the active professions. But lawyers and men of affairs tell me that they, too, are looking for the same sort of men that I wish to see in training for teaching. I have concluded, therefore, that there are many more chances for strong men than there are strong men for these chances.

"But all this does not touch the man of mediocre ability and energy—the seventy-five or eighty or ninety or ninety-five out of every hundred. But these commonplace men, if they are industrious and have good habits, do manage to get along well—just as well, I think, as they ever did. I can't believe that a healthful and industrious young fellow has any greater difficulty than his father had.

"But he differs from his father in this—and I think that this is probably the cause of the constant complaints we hear: his father was not so ambitious. More young men nowadays hope for a brilliant success, perhaps a spectacular success, than dared hope for it a generation ago.

"But, after all, there are more successful men in every calling today than ever before—whether a larger proportion, I do not know. I tell the youth that seek my advice one thing that I know is sound doctrine: 'Don't think too much about yourself and about how fast you think you ought to rise. Work! A morbid man wouldn't know a Great Opportunity if he met it in the street every morning.'"

The Chance for doing Good

Most of these opinions turn, not unnaturally, perhaps, about the question of mere material success—money-making and the measure of success given by money. The higher view—the view of success as an all-round normal development of character and mind—implies of course a moderate degree of financial achievement and of personal independence. These acquired, the chance of a good influence in the world, of a widespread effect of sound character and good deeds, is greater than ever before. There can hardly be doubt of this conclusion.

Russell Sage
Ambitious to Rise in Life—Never by Luck

(1901)

These documents on late nineteenth century self-help and success are appropriately concluded with the getting-ahead philosophy of financier-octogenarian Russell Sage (1816–1906). It was promulgated by the worshipful and tireless Orison Swett Marden (1850–1924). Driven to bankruptcy in the Nineties, Marden abandoned the hotel business to join other journalists of the era who built new fortunes after writing countless tracts on how to succeed or after assembling inspirational advice from the already wealthy. Marden's many volumes ultimately reached sales of three million. From his profits, he soon founded the magazine *Success* in 1897. Marden enlisted, among other writers, a struggling young Theodore Dreiser who, like his employer, had nursed his boyhood ambition by reading Samuel Smiles' classic, *Self-Help*. Dreiser interviewed successful authors such as hard-working Howells along with various magnates of the New York business world. The interview-monologue from Russell Sage is a virtual compendium of the rags-to-riches myth in America. Sage delivered his remarks in his New York office amid furnishings preserved from the early Gilded Age. The great banker himself was attired in clothes "fashioned in the style of thirty years ago, but of good material and well kept." The interview (not by Dreiser) appeared in the November 1898 issue of *Success* and was reprinted, with slight changes, in the following version from Marden's *Talks with Great Workers*.

"I have come to ask you to tell me the story of your life," I said, "for I am sure it must be of great interest."

Mr. Sage smiled. "I don't know about its being of interest. It is very simple and commonplace to me. You know I began as a grocery clerk, in a country town. That is a very humble beginning, I'm sure. I received a dollar a week for working from early morning until late at night, but I was well satisfied with my lot, because I knew that it was bound to lead to better things. So I worked my very best, and saved my wages, which were slowly increased as I went along, and finally I had enough money to start a little store for myself. When I was twenty-one years old I had a store of my own, and I made a success of it."

"But how did you happen to come to New York?" I asked.

"Oh, I was ambitious," laughed Mr. Sage. "Like most boys, I thought there

---

Russell Sage, "Ambitious to Rise in Life—Never by Luck: Russell Sage upon Opportunity, Integrity, Physical Vigor," in Orison Swett Marden, *Talks with Great Workers* (New York, 1901), pp. 18–22.

was no other place like a city for success, and I finally sold my country store when I was still very young, and came to New York. I started in as office boy, at very low wages, and from that day on I worked myself up and up, until I finally became a financier on my own account. It took a long time, though. It was not all accomplished in a day; though when I came to New York I expected to be rich in two or three years. I was very much like other boys, you see. They all expect to get rich in a day."

"But some of them never get rich." I said.

"Well, it's their own fault if they do not succeed," said the financier. "Surely, every one has as good a chance as I had. I don't think there could be a poorer opportunity for a boy to rise. The trouble is that most of them are not very anxious to rise. If they find themselves wealthy some morning they are glad, of course; but they are not willing to work, and make themselves rich."

"Some say that it is all luck," I ventured to suggest.

"Oh, pshaw!" said Mr. Sage, with great disgust. "There's no such thing as luck. I'm sure there was none of it about my career. I know just how I earned every penny, and the reason for it, and I never got anything I didn't work for. I never knew any one to obtain lasting wealth without lots of hard work."

"Do you think there are as good opportunities for getting rich today as there were thirty years ago, or when you made your start, Mr. Sage?"

"Undoubtedly. I think there are even greater opportunities, for new industries are being established all the time, and there are broader fields to work in. But then, the old fields of business are not overworked, by any means. I always say that there is room for good men anywhere and at any-time. I don't think there can ever be too many of them. It is true that there are many applicants for every place in New York, but if I were unable to get a place in an Eastern city I should go West, for there are great opportunities there for every one."

"People say, though, that the West is not what it is supposed to be," I remarked.

"Yes, there are always pessimists," said Mr. Sage. "The people who say the West has no opportunities are the same persons who used to call it foolish for any young man to come to New York. When I decided to come here, I was told on every side that I would regret my action; but I never have. Some people never see opportunities in anything, and they never get along. I did not see any very great opportunity ahead of me when I came to New York, but I knew that if I had a chance I could make one. I knew that there are always openings for energetic, hard-working fellows, and I was right."

"Of course, you believe that strict honesty is essential to success, Mr. Sage? I've heard many people say that honesty doesn't pay, especially in Wall street."

"That is a foolish question," said the financier. "It is absurd to imagine that it pays to be dishonest, whatever your business or profession. Do you suppose if I had been dishonest in any dealings when I started out, that I would be worth anything today?"

"What do you think of the chances for country boys in a great city like New York today, Mr. Sage?"

"I think they are as great as ever. Employers are on the lookout for bright young men, and I believe that they would prefer that they come from the country, provided there is no danger of their becoming dissipated. I think that is the only thing men have against country fellows, and there are many things in their favor. I think an earnest, ambitious, hard-working boy from the country has a splendid chance of becoming somebody. There are much greater opportunities for him to exercise his good qualities, and the reward of his enterprise is much larger. The same energetic labor that would make a man worth twenty-five thousand dollars in a small town would be very likely to make him worth a hundred thousand or so in a great city, and all on account of the wider field."

"What, Mr. Sage, are the essentials of success?"

"The essentials of success, in my opinion, are just three: honesty, industry, and economy. Any young man, amid existing opportunities, has a chance of becoming a millionaire."

"To what do you owe your wonderful vitality?" I asked. Mr. Sage smiled, before answering me.

"I never smoke, I never drink any liquors, I retire early, and get up early, and take care of myself in every possible way," he said. "Don't you think I ought to be healthy? I have always taken care of myself, and I think I've proved that hard work is not bad for one's health. In fact, I think that work is the best thing I know of for improving a man's constitution, for it makes a good appetite, and encourages digestion. It is not work that ruins so many men. It's the wine they drink, and the late hours they keep, and their general dissipation. I expect to be at my desk for many years to come, and just because I've taken good care of myself.

"You ask me why I don't stop work. I'll do it if you will answer me one question: 'What else can I do that will do as much good and keep me as well?' Well, you can't answer it; nobody can."

Interpretations

W. C. Crosby
Acres of Diamonds

(1928)

Despite the continuing popularity of Conwell, Hubbard, and Marden, the tradition of the self-made man in America met a formidable challenge in the early Progressive years of the present century. The doubters grew more prominent in the 1920's when a new generation, disillusioned by war and uninspired by the business civilization they had returned to, began to achieve historical perspective on the enterprise and rhetoric of their elders. The selection reprinted here is representative of their cynical reassessments of the Gilded Age.

Before the World War the Rev. Dr. Russell H. Conwell of Philadelphia and his lecture, "Acres of Diamonds," were as standard and staple a part of the American scene as Anheuser-Busch beer, the Odd Fellows, Peruna, or William Jennings Bryan. But the war brought in a new generation, and to its jazzy and godless tastes poor Conwell was flat and insipid, and his Message only gaudy buncombe. When, in March, 1923, a crowd gathered in Philadelphia to see him receive the Edward W. Bok medal as the town's "most valuable citizen," he was already decayed to the estate of a mere legend. The orators of the evening tried heroically to pump the breath of life into him, and make him Somebody. He had, they thundered, delivered "Acres of Diamonds" for a world's record of six thousand times; in fifty years of lecturing he had addressed thirteen millions of people; as a pastor he had built the largest Protestant church in America; and as an educator he had founded Temple University, which enrolled then over ten thousand students. Such record-breaking statistics, of course, are always more or less impressive; Tyrus Raymond Cobb, in twenty-three years of baseball, has not yet played in three thousand games. But the spirit which thumped and roared in Conwell's breast and the Message which used to knock them cold along the Chautauqua

Reprinted by permission of the publisher from W. C. Crosby, "Acres of Diamonds," *American Mercury*, XIV (May 1928), pp. 104–13.

circuit were as alien to that 1923 crowd as leg-of-mutton sleeves or red-flannel underwear. The old man sat on the stage with his hands folded contentedly on his paunch, apparently unaware that his day had passed him by, and still firm in the faith that his gospel of Success contained the ultimate answer to the riddle of existence. But even Bruce Barton, who canonized him as an American saint in 1921 by interviewing him for the celebrated *American Magazine*, had been forced to ignore his fundamental doctrine, and to draw him out on such generalities as Happiness and Immorality in order to make a plausible story. Times had changed indeed.

In the smug days of America's Gilded Age, Russell H. Conwell had been a national figure—the biographer of Presidents, the intimate of celebrities, the inspirer of legions of earnest young men and women, an orator second only to the immortal Bryan himself. In villages and towns throughout the Bible Belt, when the Chautauqua season arrived and the tent auditorium was raised to the hallelujahs of the local clergy, Conwell's was the name that headlined the programme. On the night of his lecture, the crowds of farmers and townsmen would sniff self-righteously by the beer-drinking corner loafers and into the tent, to sit spell-bound while the *maestro* poured forth the Pollyanna economics and saccharine sentiments of his World-Famous inspirational Lecture. Upon its conclusion they would wave him the Chautauqua salute, press forward to shake his hand, and go home to sand the sugar or water the milk, assured that it was the Lord's will that they should succeed in the world and make piles of money. The smug, thrifty, tightly moral American middle-class, rustic and urban, knew precisely what it wanted to hear. Conwell rose to fame and opulence by serving it its own ideas, buttered with the authority of a Baptist pontiff and spiced with illustrative stories from the lives of the great. Thus he ground out the breath-taking message of "Acres of Diamonds" across the continent and even in foreign lands. Everybody can be successful and wealthy, for opportunity lies in your own backyard. "Where can I get rich?" The question rose in volume to the platform, and back Conwell thundered oracularly, "Right where you are. At home. Not somewhere else."

Someone has estimated that if he had saved and invested the money he made from "Acres of Diamonds," instead of building Temple University with it, he would have possessed eight million dollars, not counting his ten thousand dollars a year salary, and the proceeds from his thirty-seven books. Besides delivering the lecture orally six thousand times, he printed it in book form, always with his own picture as frontispiece, at least eleven times. It was also translated into at least one foreign language, and published frequently, in abridged form, in magazines and church papers. As Conwell often announced, however, the biggest profits from the lecture were not in the dollars it earned, but in the lives it inspired and uplifted. Testimonials poured in on him. One young man wrote: "During my college days I heard your wonderful lecture at Waco, Texas, and it has been my ideal and inspiration ever since . . . and now I am the grateful pastor of a congregation of five hundred people and just thirty-six years of age." A Pennsylvania paper contributed this one: "It was the lecture of Doctor Conwell on 'Acres of Diamonds,' delivered fifteen years ago in Reynoldsville, that inspired a group of Reynoldsville men, . . . and ultimately resulted in the founding of the Reynoldsville Brick and Tile Company." Such glowing testimonies could be multiplied indefinitely.

"In 1870 we went down the Tigris river," "Acres of Diamonds" always began. "We hired a guide at Bagdad. . . He was well acquainted with the country, but he was one of those guides who love to entertain their patrons; he was like a barber who tells many stories in order to keep your mind off the scratching and the scraping." One story which the guide related concerned a certain Al Hafed, who lived, contented and wealthy, on a large farm not far from the river Indus. Chancing to hear one time from a visiting priest of the value of diamonds, Al Hafed "went to his bed that night a poor man—not that he had lost anything, but poor because he was discontented and discontented because he thought he was poor. He said: 'I want a mine of diamonds.'" So, selling his farm and collecting money, off he went in search of diamonds. But after he had wandered over the world, and been reduced to poverty and rags, he drowned himself, disappointed and despairing because he had not found diamonds. The man who bought Al Hafed's farm "led his camel out into the garden to drink, and as that camel put its nose down into the clear water of the garden brook Al Hafed's successor noticed a curious flash of light from the sands of the shallow stream. . . . 'And thus,' said the guide to us, 'were discovered the diamond mines of Golconda.' . . . Had Al Hafed remained at home and dug in his own garden, instead of wretchedness, starvation, poverty and death in a strange land, he would have had 'acres of diamonds.'"

There always followed the story about "that man out in California, who in 1847, owned a ranch there. He read that gold had been discovered in Southern California, and he sold his ranch to Colonel Sutter and started off to hunt for gold." Colonel Sutter's little girl was playing with some dried sand from the mill-race, and in that sand "a visitor saw the first shining scales of real gold that were discovered in California; and the man who wanted the gold had sold this ranch and gone away, never to return."

Now under full way, "Acres of Diamonds" wound swiftly from incident to incident, some long, some short, some from the lecturer's own life, most of them from his reading. In the version printed with his biography, there are twenty-five such stories, each one illustrating the message, "Opportunity is in your own backyard."

The tattered tents and thin crowds along the Chautauqua circuit today are pathetic reminders of the flourishing state of that noble institution in the Gilded Age. Charles and Mary Beard have described the outpouring of the pious and hopeful to Lake Chautauqua and to the hundreds of travelling Chautauquas throughout the land as a typically 100 percent American phenomenon, unprecedented in the world's history. Chautauquaing was quite as lucrative and steady a career as acting in "Uncle Tom's Cabin." Even so eminent a philosopher as William James was once inveigled into it, as the Beards record. "It was after lecturing to comfortable and excellent people at Chautauqua," they say, "that James heaved an immense sigh of relief as he escaped into the freight yards at Buffalo, where the noise, grime, and jar of reality broke the monotony of moderation, purity, and median lines of thought." But to Russell H. Conwell the sweet moderations of the American middleclass represented the final wisdom of life. In the close air of the lecture-tent he found his greatest satisfaction.

The note most often harped on before the old-time Chautauqua audiences was that of Success, and Success was measured neatly by the amount of money one had in bank. It was in that Gilded Age that newspaper reporters got into the habit of asking famous men to what they owed their success, and of reporting the invariable answer: to honesty and hard work. The cynical conclusion of the present age that luck is the chief factor would have seemed sacrilege in those innocent days. Horatio Alger wrote inspirational novels for the uplift of the youth of the land. Orison Swett Marden published "Pushing to the Front" and promoted magazines to teach the lower middleclass how to get rich. Hundreds of other gifted soothsayers made their living by writing and lecturing, always on Success. But of them all, Russell H. Conwell was easily the most eminent. He was the real high priest in the temple.

"I have always preached the gospel of worldly success because I have always believed it to be in harmony with the spiritual gospel," he declared in 1916, toward the end of his long life. "Any Christian who has a chance to get rich, and doesn't, is not living up to his full duty," he said to Bruce Barton, when that talented metaphysician was interviewing him for the *American Magazine*. Thus his closing notes were the same he sounded in the first edition of "Acres of Diamonds" in 1888: "To secure wealth is an honorable ambition, and is one great test of a person's usefulness to others... I say, Get rich, get rich! ... Money being power, it ought to be entirely in the hands of good men and women." The germ of Service lurked in those innocent words!

The stodgy *bourgeoisie* who paid for his lectures and bought his books had, in Conwell's eyes, other commendable virtues beside their love of money. He had hated the aristocracy since his days at New Haven, when the young gentlemen of Yale remained blandly indifferent to the presence in their midst of the Massachusetts boy-orator. He knew little about the working classes, although he admitted, in his broadly tolerant way, that there might be good Christians even among this lowly group. But all the ins and outs of *bourgeois* psychology he knew and praised; the middle class was the flowering of God's handicraft and the hope of the nation. "After all, the great government of this country is going to be borne triumphantly through all its difficulties by the even balance of the middle class of people, which is an honor to America and which has maintained so grandly the honor of the American flag."

Every little thing about the middle class was perfect and good. "The place where we find the most health is among the middle class of people. The homes we have in Philadelphia where men are earning from fifteen to fifty dollars a week are the happiest homes in the world. They are the most healthful homes in the world; no class of people live so long, and none enjoy their lives so much, as those who own their own homes, with an income of from fifteen to fifty dollars a week."

A middle-sized family for the middle classes was his ideal in an age when apartments were called flats and still had backyards. "I read the account of that man in Kentucky . . . 130 years old, with nineteen children. I should say that is two or three too many! But, on the other hand, with none, it is two, three, six, or eight too few. There is a middle ground, and for this we are seeking our civilization." . . . "No man can enjoy over fifty thousand dollars . . . Fifty thousand dollars furnishes everything that any healthy man or woman could enjoy, and when a man gets beyond that sum he is going into care; he has passed beyond the place where perfect happiness is found."

Conwell tusselled with the problem of how to get the fifty thousand with all his might. His answer was of the sort that shows the third assistant bookkeeper how to rise to be second assistant: thrift, frugality, hard work, honesty, and all the rest of the shopkeeping morality. All about him in the eighties and nineties the ruthless merchant princes and money barons were exploiting the country for huge gains, stuffing their pockets with the profits of extortion, trickery and corruption, but Conwell never saw it so. Instead, he reached into the grab bag of his memory, pulled out Emerson's old "make a better mousetrap" theory, refurbished it with new words and yelled, "If you have anything the people want, they will pay you for it. The more they need it, the more they will pay you for it. Find out then the world's need and earnestly endeavor to supply that need." Pressed by ambitious clerks and farm hands for more specific advice, he offered the stale suggestion of spare-time study, and soon he had thousands flocking into Y.M.C.A. training classes and enrolling in correspondence schools. He eventually founded his own night-school for the submerged classes of aristocratic Philadelphia, but this expedient was suggested to him, and did not originate in his own head.

But to criticize him for lack of originality is to chastize an elephant for not flitting like a humming-bird. His massive power, his strength as a preacher and lecturer, did not lie in ideas, but in inspiration. When he had emotionalized his hearers into a fine frenzy of determination, his job was done. If the frenzy sizzled out in nothingness, who could blame him? But if it proved the starting point for a career, he got the credit. The technique of inspiration, as he practiced it, began and ended with the success story. By reciting enough stories of how success had been won by homely methods, he convinced every dolt in his audience that he could step out and miraculously achieve fame and wealth. The method was sound, too; the fact that Conwell was called upon to give his lecture six thousand times proved that the people got a real thrill out of it.

In the maw of his incredibly capacious memory he carried literally thousands of success stories—how great men had overcome difficulties, how poor boys had found riches, how inventors had happened upon profitable devices, how iron-willed young men had fought through to success, how pious and charitable acts had brought their return in buttered bread, how hard work had won promotion. His mind worked in terms of stories, and these stories he wove into glittering tales of wealth and fame which hypnotized his listeners into a glassy-eyed determination to go out and do likewise. . .

Since he was an ordained Baptist minister, one question was continually popped at Conwell which did not trouble the layman Marden: how to hitch money-grubbing as the end of life with the teachings of Holy Writ. Conwell answered with large gestures and his usual muddy logic: "We ought to get rich if we can by honorable and Christian methods, *and those are the only methods that sweep us quickly toward the goal of riches.*" Again,

> Money is power, money has powers; and for a man to say, "I do not want money" is to say, "I do not wish to do any good to my fellow-men." It is absurd thus to talk.

Finally,

> And yet this religious prejudice is so great that some people think it is a great honor to be one of God's poor. I am looking in the faces of people who think just that way. I heard a man once say in a prayer-meeting that he was thankful that he was one of God's poor, and then I silently wondered what his wife would say to that speech, as she took in washing to support the man while he sat and smoked on the veranda. I don't want to see any more of that kind of God's poor.

Conwell went further. He demanded that the church itself become businesslike and "show results." "The world is demanding more and better returns from the church for the time and money given it. Real, practical Christian work is what is asked of the church. The sooner it conforms to this demand, the more quickly it will regain its old influence and be prepared to make effective its fight against evil." So says an editorial quoted approvingly in his official biography. He put his own Baptist Temple on a strictly business basis. Regular dues, like those of a club, were exacted of the members, in addition to the voluntary offerings. "One dollar and twenty cents a year for those under eighteen years of age and three dollars for those over that age" were the rates for irregular attendants. He got church trustees who were hard bargainers. "When they wanted lumber they knew where to purchase it and how to obtain discounts. When they needed money they knew where the money was and what securities were good on the market." Attendance on choir rehearsals was checked by a device closely resembling a time-clock.

All the events in Conwell's life seemed to conspire to make him the spokesman of the lower middle class he loved so well. He was born of poor parents on a rocky farm in the Berkshire Hills of Western Massachusetts in 1843. No pride of lineage marred his outlook, although his toe-kissing biographer insists on saying the family could be traced "to the days of William the Conqueror."

On a neighboring farm lived the venerable William Cullen Bryant, a circumstance which enabled young Russell to indulge himself early in that adoration of celebrity which was a marked characteristic of his later life. He and his brother dragged the doddering poet to the stream beside which he had written "Thanatopsis," and demanded that he recite from it for their benefit. The old man obliged with the lines of moralizing which close the poem. Conwell's youth passed like that of many another New England farm boy. He worked hard under the supervision of a dour father, enjoyed the simple pleasures of country life, ran away from home once or twice, and got some schooling at Wilbraham, a Methodist academy. Later he became a student at Yale, working his way through. From his youngest days he had enjoyed the gift of gab. His biographer relates glowingly his prowess as a village debater and orator. When the Civil War broke out he blossomed forth as a recruiting orator, and if the biographer is to be believed, raised whole regiments by the charm of his speeches. His fame as the Boy Orator spread to the edges of the country. . .

Equipped with this magnificent memory and his booming, resonant voice, Conwell went forth at the end of the war to open his oyster, firmly believing that diligence and hard work would bring him success. A tough and recalcitrant oyster it proved to be in those first years; none of the openers worked. His admittance to the bar, his marriage, and his bold removal to the frontier city of Minneapolis in 1865 should, according to all the precepts of the success teachers, have been the opening wedges to a high, wide and handsome career. But though he worked like a dog, glad-handed the local population, and slaved zealously in the pious activities of the Sunday-school and the Y.M.C.A., all that came of the two years in the West was a charity appointment as immigration agent in Germany for the State of Minnesota, obtained on the plea of broken health.

Convinced, now, that his pot of gold, lay at the near end of the rainbow, Conwell, after two years in Germany, formed connections in Boston with that estimable paper, the *Traveller*, and went on special assignments for it and one or two others. In the course of two years or so he did a series of articles called "Revisiting the Battlefields," and another called "Letters From an Around-the-World Tourist." He faithfully saw and reported what he had set out to see, and came home with his fly-paper memory stuck full of impressions of the great people he had interviewed. Of a type are all his reports. After one glimpse, "Victor Hugo impressed him as a stern, reserved man, who hated

Napoleon the Third, and looked upon his ascension to the throne as a great crime."

Back in Boston, Conwell worked harder than ever. A mere list of his activities shows a bewildering versatility, but also points to a corresponding lack of success in any one of them. He wrote editorials for the *Traveller*; corresponded for outside papers; went abroad several times to interview celebrities; continued his lecturing; opened two law offices, one in Somerville, where he lived, the other in Tremont Temple in Boston; managed a campaign for General Nathaniel P. Banks and otherwise fiddled with politics; speculated in Somerville real estate; founded and edited the Somerville *Journal*; began the Young Men's Congress, a debating club which flourished until 1913; organized the Tremont Temple Bible-Class, which he also taught; coöperated in bringing two children into the world; established a free legal clinic for the poor, and jeopardized his professional standing by announcing that he would accept no client of whose righteousness and innocence he was not convinced.

The man seemed to be rattling himself to pieces, like a stalled flivver, when two events gratuitously directed him into the path which led to his eventual success; his first wife died, and he married a wealthy Newton Centre church-worker. Thus relieved of drudgery, he became a preacher in his thirty-seventh year, serving his apprenticeship at Lexington, Mass. This ministry gave him the background which he had lacked as a lawyer-lecturer-politician; it transformed his incessant buzzing and frittering into purposeful activity. He continued to buzz and fritter and spread his shot, but now he began to have significance and meaning. His memory and his booming, persuasive voice became of prime value to him. His solicitude for other people's welfare hung more easily upon him as a preacher than as a lawyer. But of the gifts which counted most toward his success behind the sacred desk, his newspaper training ranked highest. Conwell knew what was news in the elegant eighties and gay nineties, and he saw to it that his church and his preaching made it. The conservative clergy of the day scorned him as a sensationalist and upstart, but the people flocked to him, and eventually many other Protestant sorcerers copied his methods. Conwell's contribution to the progress of Christianity in the United States was the "home-like" church; he transferred the hearty informality of the middle-class fireside into the worship of the Almighty. The Protestants of the Gilded Age, accustomed to worshipping God on hard benches and in high, starched collars and frock coats, accepted the new idea of being jolly and informal about the business with the glad relief of a flapper checking her corset.

After eighteen months in Lexington, Conwell was called to a struggling mission church in Philadelphia in 1883, and here he demonstrated the advertising value of his home-like church idea. The board made Conwell a sporting proposition in regard to salary. The church had paid a salary of eight hundred dollars: every time he doubled the membership they would double his salary. To the man who had worked his way through school peddling Ridpath's [sic] "Life of John Brown" from door to door in New England, the offer was good as a gold mine. His commissions mounted so rapidly that when he reached ten thousand all hands piped a halt, and ten thousand dollars remained his salary for the rest of his days.

"Conwell evenings" became a Philadelphia institution, and other preachers flocked from miles around to observe how the members of his congregation spoke to every stranger at the services. One preacher visitor from Albany records: "A well-dressed lady near me said, 'Good evening' most cheerfully, as a polite usher showed me into a pew. They say that all the members do that. It made me feel welcome. She also gave me a hymn book. I saw others thus kindly greeted. How it did help me to praise the Lord! At home with the people of God! That is just how I felt." Others felt the same way; the church was so crowded that tickets of admission had to be issued. In 1893 the huge new Baptist Temple was dedicated, seating forty-two hundred in the main auditorium, with carpets on the floor, no hard benches, and with an office "equipped with desks, filing cabinets, telephones, speaking-tubes, and everything necessary to conduct the business of the church in a business-like way." Conwell had at last found a job in which he could satisfy every heart's desire.

His lack of success in Minneapolis and Boston had not been due to want of hard work, but rather to the way he scattered his shot. He always worked hard. Everyone who ever met or heard him testifies to his enormous driving energy. Throughout life he continued the habit, learned on the farm, of rising at four or five in the morning, and of considering sixteen hours a fair working day. Commuting between Somerville and Boston on the train, he learned to read five foreign languages. Always there was a book in his pocket, and never was a spare minute allowed to go to waste. When he was forced to work swiftly he could make a newspaper reporter rushing copy two minutes before the deadline look like a sluggard. The speed with which he wrote some of his thirty seven books set records hardly surpassed even in these heroic days.

Many of these books were campaign biographies written at the behest of the Republican National Committee. They "were penned quickly and had a large sale. In this way Doctor Conwell wrote biographies of General U. S. Grant, Rutherford B. Hayes, James A. Garfield, and James G. Blaine." His most successful biography financially was the life of Charles H. Spurgeon. When the great pulpit-thumper checked out, a publishing house wired Conwell an offer; he was on a lecture tour, but by dictating to a secretary during the day on the train, without notes or clippings, he finished the book in twelve days, and saw it reach the gratifying sale of 125,000 copies in four months. He dictated his life of Blaine in three weeks. When news of Bayard Taylor's death in Germany was received in America, he set to work at once and had his "Life of Bayard Taylor" completed before the body arrived. Five thousand copies sold before the funeral. Conwell wound up his biographizing by embalming in print his life long friend. "Philadelphia's great merchant, John Wanamaker," in 1924.

To the earnest, enquiring youths, aflame with ambition after hearing "Acres of Diamonds," who asked for practical hints on how to be successful and rich, Conwell, in his later days, answered, "Study." Education was the open sesame to better jobs and bigger salaries. At first, his advice was simple and direct—carry a book in your pocket and study during your spare moments. "Out of the forty-five hundred millionaires in the United States, more than thirty-nine hundred of them were poor boys . . . The study of their biographies reveals the almost universal fact that they carried a book in their pockets to study in spare moments." In 1884 a young printer came to Conwell. He had the laudable desire of becoming a preacher, but he knew no Greek or Latin; would Conwell help him study in the evenings? Conwell promised the young man three evenings each week. The first night appointed the youth brought six friends with him, since seven could be taught as easily as one. The second night forty showed up. By the end of the first year more than two hundred and fifty students were studying at night, under Conwell and other volunteer teachers. Thus was born Temple University, which has, this present year, over twelve thousand students in day, afternoon and evening classes: "an institution for strong men and women who can labor with both mind and body."

This faith in the efficacy of education was curiously coupled with a hatred of existing educational institutions. They were "aristocratic," and Conwell had hated the aristocracy since the days of his snubbing at Yale. The greatest peril to democracy, he boomed in his old age, was "an institutional aristocracy which shuts the doors of the professions to all who have not loitered in some aristocratic school for a certain number of hours and paid a high tuition fee." The insidious agents of aristocracy were shutting the door of opportunity in the face of the poor by requiring one and two years of collegiate work for entrance to medical schools. The American Medical Association was raising standards so high that the graduates of Conwell's Temple University medical night-school could not get licenses to practice, and so he shouted, "If these obstacles are arbitrarily increased, we will eventually have in this country two classes—a peasant class and an aristocratic class."

Conwell went to his reward in 1925. With the stilling of the booming voice, his name was forgotten, even by his beloved middle class, almost as quickly as that of last year's murderer. The Baptist Temple goes its uneventful way, but it is heard of no more. Only Temple University strives to keep his memory green, and even here one wonders how long the administration will print Conwell's picture as the frontispiece of every bulletin and catalogue, and how long the line "Founded by Russell H. Conwell" will be run under the name of the school. Already his dream for the building of Temple University has been scrapped for a skyscraper Temple of Learning, an idea obviously borrowed from the University of Pittsburgh's plan for a thirty-odd-story

Cathedral of Learning. The tuition fee has been raised to $215; the entrance requirements have been made more rigid. The authorities even boast in public that children of rich parents now come to them for instruction. Conwell's simple educational aim, that every boy in America should learn a trade and work his way through school, has been ditched for the ideal of winning football games.

Nobody knows what magic produced last year's winning team, but the school was not slow in taking advantage of it. The students were pepped up with such posters as this:

FOOTBALL: NOV. 19
Bucknell *vs.* Temple
Franklin Field
Game Called 2 o'clock
This is Temple's greatest opportunity to impress
upon the world that she rightly belongs in the
very front rank of the Great American
Universities
Most people judge a University by the kind of
football team it has. This year Temple has a
GREAT team. It has shown its mettle and
has scored many fine victories. Let us
show the world that Temple also
has a real body of Alumni and
Students back of this
Fine Team.
THIS IS TEMPLE'S REAL OPPORTUNITY

For this did Russell H. Conwell deliver "Acres of Diamonds" six thousand times!

Pare Lorentz
A Young Man Goes to Work

(1931)

This autobiographical account was written in the early Depression years by a young Pare Lorentz who from childhood had admired the American folk heroes of nineteenth-century enterprise—the Garys, Hills, and Edisons.

Pare Lorentz, "A Young Man Goes to Work," *Scribner's Magazine*, LXXXIX (February 1931), pp. 205–208.

Equipping himself with the college education needed to insure success in a new age of corporate business, he ventured forth in the late Twenties to test "the ubiquitous legend of working up from the bottom." In the following pages, Lorentz describes the sobering result. He also re-examines the time-honored principles and rewards that have formed the Horatio Alger myth in the American business world.

Six years ago I left college and went to work for a corporation. Big business sounded like adventure. The minute I stepped into the long corridors of the corporation I was excited. For one thing, it was a man's world. Here was masculinity, power! This sense of power was heightened by the competitive presence of other young men equally eager, ignorant, and assured. We were assembled from various colleges and states. And we felt from the first the omniscient, paternal hand of the company. A lower berth to Detroit? The traffic department brought it to our desk. We couldn't find a place to live? The advertising manager called his club and put us up for a week. Overnight we became members of a small army.

This army spirit became more and more evident. Rookies, we ate together, and our unlearned gaiety was smiled down upon by the weary twenty-seven-year-old veterans. I had a job in the advertising department and we regarded the accountants with the same condescension that an air-squadron man accords a quartermaster. We were the gentlemen of the army.

There were twenty of us that first year. I think we represented a fairly healthy and intelligent group of college men. We had various varsity sweaters, honor society pins, and innumerable stories of our own capacity for liquor and last-minute touchdowns. We had, too, a certain healthy scepticism. We had nibbled at the raw meat of the post-war writers. We had known some ex-service men. We knew that patriotism was the bunk and we joked about the government; that is, our government. But, among other things, we hadn't the slightest conception of the financial structure of the company for which we worked.

It was a fairly gay life. We were trained. The sergeant, a copywriter four years in the service, took us through the factories, explained the big advertising programmes, took us to engravers, printers, typographers, and to the sanctums of great advertising agencies. There was gold in that company, millions and millions of dollars. Men whose names figured in the daily papers fêted our superior officers. It didn't matter that we started to work for twenty-five dollars a week. The company was stretching into every continent of the world. We might end up in China, Russia, South America—what did it matter? We were in the army.

But in time we began to grumble. Each luncheon was a protest meeting, and we talked, unwittingly, as though we were secret agents engaged in actual combat with the financial barons of the country. It is possible that the ignominy of our work subconsciously shamed us. After all, we were writing copy, haranguing dealers, and estimating the number of shoppers who passed given points; none of which things could be called exhilarating or powerful. But I think the actual nature of the work never struck us. We had to "lick this problem," and "clean up this mess," and "bear down on that wholesaler." The subtle feeling of power that had interested us in the company crept through the corridors. Foreign companies, great areas of men and shops were bought and sold in the quiet upper offices. Yet the tempo of our work was so slow and undetermined we smarted in harness. We had ideas—we knew they were good, but we couldn't get loose with them.

What really made us uneasy and discontented was a slow realization of the discipline of a corporation. We had expected anything but discipline. From earliest memory we had absorbed the myths of the land, and if we had any spiritual tradition it was one of individual freedom. The old fathers, the pioneers, the forty-niners and then—the latest folk heroes—the Edisons, Garys, Hills: these legendary heroes were to us as American as pumpkin pie. They had with their own hands built something. While we had not swallowed these myths whole, nevertheless they had been so much with us it was an integral part of our ambitions. We did not look upon ourselves as business men. We were corporation men. This, too, was an important illusion. We had seen social structure crack and change after the war. Prohibition was one of the phenomena but, more important, social life was altered by the pressure of big business. The municipal power plant was absorbed by a utility. Automobiles and hard roads overcame the peculiar barriers of small towns. Chain stores took over ancient mercantile establishments. We saw corporation initials tacked to coal mines, hard ware stores, steel mills. The small town became a subsidiary of the city. And we heard on all sides of the phenomenal growth of corporations, of the eminent mentalities of their directors.

Thus, the legend of starting at the bottom, the world-diffused idea of the American hero, logically directed us to the Armageddon of the world—big business. We didn't know what to expect. That was part of the game. After all, Ford had started with a bicycle shop. And our superior officers furthered this legend. The company was growing; any man might rise from the ranks. Yet the first time one of us acted in the spirit of Frank Merriwell there was trouble. My roommate edited a sales magazine. We covered an engineer's meeting and my partner wrote an amusing piece about Hoover's standardization campaign, incidentally calling attention to some weak points in the schedule. When the advertising manager saw the piece he hit the ceiling. Hoover was "a superpower man"; it was treasonable to disagree with the Secretary of Commerce.

The lad argued the point. He was fired on the spot. Every day we felt the pressure of discipline. It never occurred to us that we were temperamentally unfit to work for corporations. We thought by demanding a few changes in the policies of the company we could capture the power we still felt to be ours for the taking. We still thought we were two-gun men pushing back the frontiers of the world and we serenely wrote advertisements telling the public how our company was pioneering for humanity and tried ourselves to believe we were covered-wagon drivers.

In time we became fearful of each other. We were too far away from our superior officers. If one of our squad lunched with a vice-president we hung around until we found out how much he was "in." It was this under-current of fear that finally drenched our spirits. We saw older men, intelligent, educated men, shunted aside. How did they get that way? We never learned. Politics!

This fear was even deeper rooted than we first knew. A staff of lawyers examined every line of advertising that left the offices. We learned to be careful about boasting of the company's power because some senator might "start an investigation." We must not send copy to South America of a certain nature because of the German competitor. And we must not advertise this because of our Western subsidiary. Day by day, we ran afoul of new taboos.

At the end of the second year there were only three of us left in the office. Four of the original squad went to South America, full of gaiety, to capture the Golden Fleece. Even after two years they did not stop to consider the fact that the fleece was in reality only a silver eagle, and that it was guarded abroad even more closely than at home by a hierarchy of fearful clerks, vice-managers, and far-off directors. The others drifted away.

I hear from these men occasionally. The great day, as Lewis Mumfold calls it, has never materialized. Six years ago they were ready to hike to the four corners of the world, to fight or play at the drop of a hat. And it is not maturity and respectability which have overcome them. It is not that corporate life is impoverishing. Some of them have decent incomes. Chagrin and confusion have overcome them. They discovered a world of highly geared machines, not an open wilderness. In order to supply reasonable demands they have been forced to submit to low living and—this is encouraging—they are ashamed. I think these men are pathetic because by character they are not clerks. (There are more than enough little men in any country who willingly take the yoke.) Six years ago they were potential Jim Hills, ready to fight railroads over the mountains, dive into the cypress swamps of Louisiana, tackle the rapids of the St. Lawrence, but they discovered an involved financial morass hiding the channels to these glorious routes. They had not learned in the academic courses of American colleges how and by whom business is run.

They are not Babbitts. They are victims of an American heritage. In England, Germany, or France any young man who enters the business world with no money or power takes for granted his clerical position. The German probably would play the piccolo on the side and dabble in chemistry. The Englishman probably would content himself with playing a good game of tennis and the feeling that he was doing his bit for the Empire. But we have no social tradition, no class acceptance except the ubiquitous legend of working up from the bottom. Those men who were so hilarious when they went to work for a corporation would have quit on the spot if the personnel man had made an honest speech. These corporation recruiting officers pride themselves on being tough but never once do they get down to the basic position of a great corporation which is, as Mr. Brady remarked, "that no corporation executive is worth a big salary." He is the bankers' clerk, secure as long as the dividends come in.

America is no longer the land of opportunity for a young man of honor and decency. The man who starts at the bottom of a corporation to work his way up is a fool. Amos and Andy make a quarter of a million dollars through the Radio Corporation because they are worth that much, presumably, in sales power, while the young M.I.T. graduate of 1916 whose minor patents improved the radio makes at the most $15,000. And his creations may be pigeonholed, destroyed or promoted, as the company wills. Yet, despite the fact that social life is so sensitively geared, so in the hands of the financiers that corporation earnings affect the whole world, the great American myth is lustily alive.

The myth is a part of the propaganda program of every giant manufacturing concern, every tentacled utility in the country. Great corporations are directed by the most talked of, respected men in the country. (And, with the new sleight-of-hand known as the holding company, they have put their hands on an amazing amount of property.) And where else can the young chemist, engineer, the ambitious prospector, turn?

One of the most honorable old Tories I know, when I spoke with him of corporate practice, said: "A man doesn't have to work for anybody, unless he wants to." However, from schoolbooks to national advertising, the cards are stacked. Where can you get cold facts about business?

From the time a young man enters preparatory school he is lured by the game. This is a land of miracles—big corporations represent our divine power! This belief is fostered on all sides.

And what happens? The young man goes to college. He begins to think about a job and he hears the siren voice. The General Electric Company, the Westinghouse Company, and the A. T. and T., to take three respected companies, each year recruit engineering and academic graduates from the best colleges in the country. They have what amounts to recruiting officers who interview the men—not on a basis of grades, but general appearance, character, and ability. They select a good number of talented young men each year. These students know that the great men of their profession work for corporations. What they do not know is under what conditions these men work. The General Electric Company starts its young engineers off at $30 or $35 a week. These men go into the plants and work from shop to shop. Thus, for $35 a week the company gets men who can qualify as union electricians or mechanics, worth at least $60 a week. No matter. They are being trained for "executive" positions. At the end of the first year about ten percent of the men give up. They have spent at least six years of their lives training to be engineers. They have attended the best schools in the country. And they quit. For them, the myth explodes.

The men who quit are replaced by the recruiting sergeant. At the end of the second year a larger percentage falls away. At the end of the third year the men who have stuck out what they call the "test" are making up to $60 a week. They have performed manual labor worth twice that money to the company. And then they take an examination, *to see whether they are good enough to stay on permanently*. If they leave they can either go to another corporation or give up engineering. I am speaking of electrical engineering, but this practice with variations is true of building engineering, it is true of pharmaceutical corporations, chemical manufacturers.

Every business, every profession has been affected. Even medicine has felt the pressure. The state of medical practice is so serious the government has appointed Ray Lyman Wilbur head of a commission detailed to spend five years studying the cost of medical care, and, incidentally, reward. Lawyers are excited because banks are, in effect, practising law. Doctors are worried because great corporations are subsidizing doctors, setting up clinics as well as legal machinery. Invent a device for a plane, a ship, a railroad engine. Without capital you cannot compete. With capital you are controlled.

From gas to light, heat, power, transportation, banks, groceries, and even churches, small community life is run mainly by corporate agencies. No youngster of any ambition cares to bury himself in the minor activities of a small town when college has given him the urge to go out and battle in the high places. And since the days of Thomas Paine it has been a deep-rooted conviction of the yeoman that this country alone in the world allows a free-for-all; a nation fostering absurd riches and power, open to all comers. While even Paine must have realized that his dream of a "decent" nation was short-lived, that sooner or later the valleys would be gutted and the hills trimmed, it is appalling to see how the machinery of business has in one decade physically exhausted and financially overpowered the country.

When I think of the coming youngsters I think of the post-Civil War Southerners. They were cheated, terribly cheated. And there wasn't much they could do about it. They never recovered their dignity simply because they could not, and cannot today, reconcile the neccessities of life with the traditions of their fathers. The traditions of the founders of America belong with the folk myths, not the folk ways of the country. The young man who can conduct his life today in this country in the ways of the old freeman, who can clothe and feed himself decently and walk free among his neighbors, indeed has to be agile and tough.

All the older men I know think I am either young and ignorant or else uncouth when I show serious concern over the future of nonliterary young men. I could never work for a corporation because I am a writer, they say. Yet my first appreciation of my own generation grew out of those luncheons five years ago. Those men were honorable and they were not literary. They were ashamed of the hypocrisy and fear they discovered. They were pitifully uneducated. They had no knowledge of music or art. They hadn't the vaguest conception of European politics and they had never read one line of Emerson. But they were highly honorable and they had guts enough to fight to preserve their decency, something a great majority of the literati would not understand.

To the youngster, the initials of our great corporations represent the highest American culture. What is he to do when he discovers that intrigue, bootlicking, "good-fellowship," all the mores of clerkship, mean advancement in these ponderous organizations? It is encouraging that a good percentage of the young men who enter these companies sicken and leave. (In fact, personnel men have a laconic phrase they use on these endlessly confused men; "not corporation material," they say.) It is appalling to think that, unless they have a peculiar talent or profession, there are few places for them to go unless they become antisocial, unproductive outlaws.

The great American game of starting from scratch is definitely over.

Richard D. Mosier
The Morality of the Middle Class

(1947)

Since World War Two, a gifted new group of historians has reassessed the legacy of the Gilded Age, including what Vernon Louis Parrington earlier termed "the custodianship of America by the middle class." Richard D. Mosier presented one of the first of these studies in a book about the McGuffey Readers.

Page after page, lesson after lesson, the conviction grows that the virtues of the McGuffey Readers are the virtues of the middle class, and that the McGuffey Readers have so thoroughly integrated Christian and middle class ideals that they can hardly be distinguished. It is clear, for example, that we should not be wasteful, for wastefulness is almost as bad as unholiness. In one of the stories Ben saves the string from his package, while John cuts his. Later Ben uses his on a top and saves the day in an archery contest when his string breaks. "Ben's last arrow won the prize; and when the bow and arrows were handed to him, John said, 'How valuable that whipcord has been to you, Ben,

Richard D. Mosier, *Making the American Mind: Social and Moral Ideas in the McGuffey Readers* (New York, 1947), Chapter IV, pp. 114–23. Reprinted, without footnotes, by permission of the publisher, Columbia University Press.

I'll take care how I waste anything, hereafter.'" Another story teaches the virtue of perserverance. [*sic*] A little boy becomes disgusted when he repeatedly fails to get his kite aloft, although aided by his sister and aunt. His aunt, however, succeeds in making him try again until finally the kite is kept up. "Yes, my dear children, I wish to teach you the value of PERSEVERANCE . . . Whenever you fail in your attempts to do a good thing, let your motto be, TRY AGAIN."

Labor is a great virtue as a means to happiness. Happiness consists in keeping busy. Such is the moral of a story of Mrs. Lord and her two girls. They have a quiet evening by the fireside, but they find that they have all been happier than the previous night when all had a livelier time of playing. The secret is that the work kept them busy and therefore happy. When one of the girls is unable to explain the secret of this happiness, the other, Katie, shouts: "I know! I know! It is because we have all been doing something useful tonight. We feel happy because we have been busy." A lesson on Franklin reveals that the secret of his success has been his industry and temperance:

> His youth had not been wasted in idleness, nor overcast by intemperance. He had been, all his life, a close and deep reader, as well as thinker; and by the force of his own powers, had wrought up the raw materials which he had gathered from books, with such exquisite skill and felicity, that he had added a hundred-fold to their original value, and justly made them his own.

Moreover, honesty is the best policy. One of the lessons advises young men to be honest, not only in financial affairs but also in the sense of being honorable men. According to this lesson, if you seek the road to success, you should:

> Let your first step, then, in that discipline which is to give you decision of character, be the heroic determination to be honest men, and to preserve this character through every vicissitude of fortune, and in every relation which connects you with society.

However, circumstances do alter cases, as one lesson explains. For farmer Derby tells Scrapewell that he would like to borrow his horse and gets the most complete set of excuses on record why the horse is unobtainable. The fact that Derby was going to find out about a deal that would have netted Scrapewell fifty dollars changes the whole situation, and there follows the complete explanation of all the excuses. On the other hand, another story warns us to keep out of the reach of our enemies. It is the story of the fox who tries to convince the cock that he is now his friend. The cock replies that the same thing may not be true of the dogs running down the road in the fox's direction. The fox agrees that perhaps not all the animals have heard about the friendship among former enemies and hurries off to security in the woods. "This story shows us," the lesson concludes, "that when a known enemy wishes to seem a friend, there is most cause for us to keep out of his reach";

and, adds the author, hoping to convert a mere warning into a virtue, "that shame is likely to follow falsehood." One is tempted to conclude that the leaders of the world who are now concerned about the atom bomb have read the story of the cock and the fox and agree with the fox that perhaps not all the animals have heard about the friendship among former enemies.

The contrast between Charlie and Rob illustrates a theme that occurs many times in the lessons. While both boys are splitting wood, Rob tells of his plans to become a bank clerk, starting out by keeping the books for his father's small business. Charlie, however, is skeptical of the value of such a small beginning, and prefers to dream of the time when he may get rich. "I'd like to sleep over the next ten years, and wake up to find myself a young man with a splendid education and plenty of money," Charlie tells Rob. But Rob has other ideas. "I don't care how I get rich, you know," he tells Charlie, "so that it's in an honest and useful way." In concluding the lesson, the author asks, "Now, which of these boys, do you think, grew up to be a rich and useful man, and which of them joined a party of tramps before he was thirty years old?"

Another lesson illustrates the dangers of truancy from school. James Brown became truant and told his mother that he had gone to school. One day some "bad boys" took him on the water in a boat, and they all nearly drowned. That taught him to go to school as he should, and to obey his parents. The situation in which James found himself is worthy of the attention of every prospective truant:

> Think of James Brown, the truant, at this time! He was far from home, known by no one. His parents were ignorant of his danger. He was struggling in the water, on the point of being drowned. Some men, however, saw the boys, and went out to them in a boat. They reached them just in time to save them from a watery grave. . . . James was very sorry for his conduct, and he was never known to be guilty of the same thing again. He became regular at school, learned to attend to his books, and, above all, to obey his parents perfectly.

The importance of a well spent youth is a theme that recurs frequently enough to be noted. One of the lessons on this theme warns of the dangers that befall those who forget the ways of God and spend their early days in idleness and sin. In the dictionary of the middle class idleness and sin are synonymous, and a life of toil is a life that is holy.

> As spring is the most important part of the year, so is youth the most important period of life. Surely, God has a claim to our first and principal attention, and religion demands the morning of our days, and the first season, the spring of our lives: before we are encumbered by cares, distressed by afflictions, or engaged in business, it becomes us to resign our souls to God.

Let us, then, take an example from the industrious bee:

Oh! we may get weary,
And think work dreary;
'Tis harder by far
To have nothing to do.

Typical of the success stories is the lesson of Robert, who is forced to go to the store for a job when another boy who stole their last five cents made his mother cry. The owner of the store is touched, offers Robert a bit of money, but it is refused because the boy's mother would not like to have Robert beg. Then Robert is hired as a cash boy, and runs home with an advance on his salary. By such virtues are the poor rewarded. But for all those who are to become cash boys and workers in the counting houses there stands the lesson of "The Maniac" as a terrible and solemn warning to those who make mistakes in counting revenues. Conrad Lange, a collector of revenues in Berlin, made a mistake in his accounts. He said, "Once one is two." During the investigation he was imprisoned for two days; released, he went insane, repeating always, "once one is two." Accuracy is indeed a virtue prized by the counting houses and the collectors of great revenues.

> This affecting story, whether true or untrue, obviously abounds with lessons of instruction. Alas! how easily is the human mind thrown off its "balance"; especially when it is stayed on *this world* only—and has no experimental knowledge of the meaning of the injunction of Scripture, to cast all our cares upon Him who careth for us, and who heareth the young ravens when they cry.

An interesting story on peaches tells how a father gave his four sons each a peach. He then asked what they had done with them. The first had planted the seed of his. The second had eaten his and also some of his mother's peach. The third had taken the pit of his brothers peach and had eaten the kernel of it, then he sold his own peach. The fourth son had given his peach to a sick friend. To the first the father said, "Provide for the *future* by taking care of the *present*." To the second the father said, "You have acted in a natural and childlike manner, as might be expected. There is still room enough in your life to learn wisdom." To the third the father said, "It was prudent, but it was by no means natural act for children. I pray God, that you may not be a miser." Concerning the fourth? "Charles was silent, but his mother embraced him with a tear in her eye."

In another lesson, which is primarily a dialogue between Mary and Sarah, we learn the virtues of "keeping everything in its place." While little Amy, in another lesson, was figuring out how much she would earn by picking berries for Mr. Thornton at 13 cents a quart, a group of enterprising boys set about the work, so that by the time Amy was ready with her decision the berries had all been picked. "Amy was a dear little girl," the lesson tells us, "but she was too apt to waste time in getting ready to do her tasks, instead of doing them at once as she ought." Still another little girl was careless about her studies and would rather play than learn. When her father learned that she was doing poorly in the business of acquiring knowledge, "instead of smiling at her, he turned away his head with a frown, and put her hand out of his, and turned from her, and went into another part of the garden." Finally, however, Mary learned her lessons; "She was so pleased with the knowledge which she had thus gained, that she loved her father more than she had ever done, for having made her do what had given her, and might still give her so much pleasure." Evidently there are lessons for parents as well as for children.

But many of the lessons turn on the theme of the proper conduct in the acquisition of wealth. One lesson, for example, warns that love of popularity generally leads men to do wrong as easily as right. We are told that we should do right, even if not immediately rewarded. Sudden riches generally leads to sudden ruin. "If it be admitted, then, that strict integrity is not always the shortest way to success; is it not the surest, happiest, and best?" A bit of verse strengthens the virtue of hard labor:

> Little child, now learn of me.
> Let thy youth the seed-time be. And,
> When wintry age shall come, richly
> Bear thy harvest home.

Not only hard work, however, but sticking to one's task is also an ingredient of success:

> So little child, your duty do
> In cheerfullness all day;
> And you, like me, shall soon be blest
> With flowers upon your way.

The story of Casabianca, a boy of thirteen who stood on a burning deck rather than disobey his father, illustrates the virtue of obedience which good Christian children should display. The story is in the form of a poem, but is followed by this prose explanation of its moral: "But no voice of permission could come from the mangled body of his lifeless father; and the boy, not knowing that he was dead, would rather die than disobey." It might be added, in passing that in refusing to disobey and remaining on the deck of the ship the boy was condemned to death in a watery grave. A closely related lesson tells how Mr. Rose took Edgar and Thomas Read out on the lake in a boat, and how, in violation of Mr. Rose's injunction to sit quietly, the children began to play, upsetting the boat. The lesson concludes: "Children should always be careful and quiet when they are in a boat on the water, and should obey what older people tell them."

Even the lessons on intemperance return to the theme of virtuous industry. A lesson entitled "The Whiskey Boy," for example, relates how John's father taught him to drink whisky mixed with water and sugar. Soon he drank it "straight" and would not stop. He grew ugly and sore and was disliked by other boys. He ended up by dying in the poorhouse. "Oh, that there were no such thing as whisky," for whisky is the bringer of evil and destroys the virtue of industry, thrift, and hard labor. Another lesson on intemperance entitled "Don't Take Strong Drink," explains that, "No little boy or girl should ever drink rum or whiskey, unless they want to become drunkards." Moreover, the "Bible says that no drunkard shall inherit the kingdom of heaven." But most important, "Whisky makes the happy miserable and it causes the rich to become poor."

But the theme of idleness and its sinfulness is clearly the most recurrent in the whole series. There is, for example, the story of the idle school boy who, after a badly spent youth in school, "often wishes that he had been more attentive to his books, when young," for "he cannot live over again the time he has spent so badly, and he must be a poor ignorant fellow for the rest of his life." Another lesson tells how John, a little idler, didn't like school or books and had no friends. On one very lonesome day John couldn't even get the animals to play with him because they all had something to do. This made him resolve to change his ways. "I see that all have something to do," concluded the little idler, "while I am idle and good for nothing. I am not fit company even for the animals." And a poem about lazy Ned explains:

> Thus he would never take the pains
> To seek the prize that labor gains,
> Until the time had passed;
> For, all his life, he dreaded still
> The silly bug-bear of up hill,
> And died a dunce at last.

Even the flight of an eagle to its young teaches the lesson of the determined spirit that will brook no obstacles to its path. Joseph, the boy in the lesson, watches an eagle carrying fish to its young. When some cruel men stone the bird to make it drop its catch, the bird returns to the sea to search for more food for its young. "Glorious bird!" shouts Joseph,

> I will learn a lesson from thee today. I will never forget hereafter, that when the spirit is determined, it can do almost anything. Others would have dropped, and hung the head, and mourned over the cruelty of man, and sighed over the wants of the nestlings; but thou, by at once recovering the loss, hast forgotten all.

But none of the tenderer virtues are in contradiction with the vigor, perseverance, and industry with which one pursues one's private goals. This theme is illustrated in the story of Fred, who coolly rescued a young girl from a blazing house. "It was no time for words," the lesson tells us, "but for instant, vigorous action." Moreover, Fred "trusted in an arm stronger than his own, and silently sought help and guidance." This brave deed, carried out with vigor and concern for others illustrates that "true manliness is in harmony with gentleness, kindness, and self-denial." The same theme is illustrated in the case of George, the son of a poor, sick woman, who went to collect firewood for his mother. At dinner time he chanced to find ripe strawberries growing in the woods. He would have eaten them immediately, but he thought of his mother and decided to save them for her. Her gratitude and tears were infinitely more pleasing to him than the whole heap of strawberries. The moral synthesis, then, does not deny the virtues of kindness, tenderness, and love.

The good Christian virtues of kindness, tenderness, and love are displayed by an unusual number of merchants and wealthy men in the stories of the McGuffey Readers. Whether this attempt to present the merchant and the man of wealth as a good steward who is kind to the poor was an attempt to form such a picture of the merchant and man of wealth in the child's mind, or whether it was, on the other hand, an attempt to spur the wealthy with a reminder of the duties to the poor that God has laid upon His stewards, are questions which seem impossible to answer. But in the stories and lessons of the McGuffey Readers the merchants and men of wealth perform their duties as stewards in the most remarkable and sympathetic manner.

One story, for example, explains how Henry is forced to go into the streets of Philadelphia to beg for some money for his poor sick mother. Washington, as it later turns out, notices him, sends him for the doctor for his mother, and goes himself to the poor hovel and comforts the mother, leaving her a draft on his money for a considerable sum. We are given a picture of Henry. "The tears running fast down his cheeks, but nobody seemed to care; for although clean, Henry looked poor and miserable, and it is common for the poor and miserable to cry." In explaining his miserable state to Washington, Henry says, "My father was a rich merchant of this city; but he became a bondsman for a friend, who soon after failed, and he was entirely ruined." Let the children who read this story, concludes the lesson, "when they think of the great and good Washington, that he was not above entering the dwellings of poverty, carrying joy and gladness to the hearts of its inmates."...

The theme of these lessons on stewardship was well stated by another lesson which made the point that one should, "Be thus ever ready to help the poor, and wretched, and distressed, and every year of your life will be to you a happy New Year." The Christian duty of giving money to the poor was abundantly illustrated in the McGuffey Readers, and perhaps they played a role in the great gifts of charity of the last three decades of the nineteenth century. However that may be, it is clear that the buying of books, particularly McGuffey Readers, was likewise a duty laid upon rich and poor alike. The final lesson of one of the first readers contains a farewell note to the children, stressing their progress so far, and emphasizing the point that they are ready now for the second reader of the McGuffey series:

> There are many children whose parents are too poor to send them to school. Do you not pity them? They can not have nice books, and learn to read them, as you do. Are not your parents kind to send you to school, and buy new books for you? Should you not try to please them? You must not waste time in school. Try always to know your lessons. If you are good, and try to learn, your teacher will love you, and you will please your parents. When you go home, you must ask for a New Second Reader.

The morality of the middle class, then, was erected on the theory that the Lord had commanded that all good Christians should labor in the Lord's vineyard. It follows from that theory that those who refuse to labor and to acquire in accordance with the commandments of the middle class refuse the right to stewardship. In attempting to account for those who labored thriftily in the Lord's vineyard but who were unable to attain to God's holy stewardship, it was necessary to have recourse to the older Calvinist notion of the elect. Those who were the elect of God were chosen for stewardship, the Calvinists had warned. It was not difficult to pass from this premise to Peter Oxenbridge Thacher's conviction that, "The diversity of poverty and riches is the order of Providence." Nor, accepting this premise, could one deny Bishop Lawrence's conviction that, "Godliness is in league with riches . . ."

Moreover, one could believe that God had elected some for the responsibilities of holy stewardship, for while many failed, some climbed from the lowest and humblest ranks of society to the highest pinnacle of financial success. John D. Rockefeller climbed from the heartless poverty of the waif to the leadership of a great oil combination. James Farrell forged for himself the virtues which carried him from humble labor to the presidency of the United States Steel Company. Henry Ford climbed from a humble position paying two and a half dollars a week to leadership in the automobile industry; and Julius Rosenwald lifted himself from peddling small wares to the highest position in the mail-order business. Truly God was on the side of the elect, and surely the Christian virtues formed the character which resulted in these amazing successes.

The McGuffey Readers accepted the premise that the Christian virtues of thrift, labor, industry, honesty, punctuality, and good-will carried men to the successes which daily could be witnessed by the humblest man. One must keep these premises in mind in evaluating the amazing bulk of success literature which flooded America in the last three decades of the nineteenth century, and they cannot be overlooked in any explanation of the McGuffey Readers. All the virtues of success were taught in the McGuffey Readers; the stories of success in many of the lessons rivaled those of Horatio Alger; and the middle class virtues stressed in the McGuffey Readers were those stressed by many of the authors of success literature. The nature of these virtues has been admirably summarized by Professor Curti who, writing of William

Thayer, tells how Thayer, author of numerous books on success, in his life of James A. Garfield, *From the Log Cabin to the White House*,

> reminded his readers that Garfield, like Lincoln, had worked hard and improved every moment of leisure by reading, and that he had become known for his industry, tact, perseverance, integrity, courage, economy, thoroughness, punctuality, decision, benevolence, and geniality. Such traits were indispensable for the success which, Thayer never forgot to remind his readers, could be won only through strict regard for morality and religion.

This description of middle class virtues would be as accurate for the McGuffey Readers, with the additional note, perhaps, that the McGuffey Readers completed the middle class and Christian synthesis so thoroughly that the Christian virtues can hardly be separated from those of the middle class. Indeed, this great moral synthesis, though enjoined by the Puritans and Protestants, was the work of generations of Americans who achieved so striking an integration of Christian and middle class virtues as to put the Puritan fathers in the shade. The great achievement of the McGuffey Readers is the complete integration of Christian and middle class ideals; and in that respect, the McGuffey Readers are the great textbook product of American middle class culture.

William Miller
American Historians and the Business Elite

(1949)

The Research Center in Entrepreneurial History at Harvard was founded in 1948. Before its doors were closed in 1958, the members of the Center employed new techniques of social science to lend precision to their investigations of the American business system. Representative of their imaginative and painstaking scholarship is the following essay by William Miller. The issue for Miller is not whether the notions of self-help and unlimited opportunity have become anachronistic in a modern business world. Rather, he questions the degree to which these factors may ever have determined a business elite in America. His provocative final comment on the

---

William Miller, "American Historians and the Business Elite," *The Journal of Economic History*, IX (November 1949), pp, 184–208. (Reprinted in William Miller, *Men in Business* [New York, 1962], pp. 309–28.) Reprinted here, without footnotes, by permission of the author and The Economic History Association.

"poor farm boys" may entice the reader to pursue this subject in the late Richard Wohl's recently published discussion of the "country boy myth" (see Selected Additional Reading).

. . . Some general American historians have made enough casual remarks about the recruitment of modern business leaders to form a rough explanatory model. I want now to point out some of the facets of this model and then to introduce some of my own findings to show how obsolete it had become by the first decade of this century, if, indeed, it ever fitted the facts.

Virtually all the generalizations that go to make up this model are based upon a few remarkable life histories from the "robber baron" period; thus in most of the books that are at all concerned with the recruitment of business leaders one finds accounts of Andrew Carnegie, John D. Rockefeller, J. Pierpont Morgan, James J. Hill, and Edward H. Harriman. In *The Growth of the American People 1865–1940*, Arthur M. Schlesinger, Sr., cites in addition such older heroes as Cornelius Vanderbilt and Gustavus F. Swift but not later ones. Charles A. and Mary R. Beard, in *The Rise of American Civilization*, add to the ubiquitous five Jay Gould, William H. Vanderbilt, Collis P. Huntington, Jay Cooke, William A. Clark, and Philip D. Armour. Few general historians discuss a greater number of men than do the Beards; but much more significant, practically none discusses any *later* men.

The last extended discussion of the "typical" business leader by Samuel Eliot Morison and Henry Steele Commager in *The Growth of the American Republic*—a widely used textbook—follows (italics mine):

> The *most typical figure* of the industrial age was undoubtedly Andrew Carnegie. *A poor immigrant boy* from Scotland, he followed and helped to *perpetuate* the American tradition of rising *from poverty to riches,* and his success he ascribed entirely to the political and economic democracy which obtained in this country. By dint of unflagging industry and unrivalled business acumen and resourcefulness and especially through his extraordinary ability to choose as associates such men as Charles Schwab, Henry Frick, and Henry Phipps, and to command the devotion of his workmen, Carnegie built up the greatest steel business in the world, and retired in 1901 to chant the glories of "Triumphant Democracy" and to give away his enormous fortune of three and a half hundred millions.

Arthur Schlesinger says vaguely of the latest group of business leaders he discusses that they arose "in most cases from obscure origins and unhindered by moral scruples, they were fired by a passionate will to succeed." In the last discussion of business leaders in *The American Nation*, John D. Hicks says: "Typical of the railroad builders was James J. Hill," who, he points out, was an immigrant from Canada. The Beards' analysis of the life histories of American business leaders ends with the eleven men named above, of whom they write:

> Of the group here brought under examination only two, Morgan and Vanderbilt, built their fortunes on the solid basis of family inheritances while only one had what may be called by courtesy a higher education: Morgan spent two years in the University of Göttingen. Carnegie began life as a stationary engineer; Jay Cooke as a clerk in a general store in Sandusky; Jay Gould as a surveyor and tanner; Huntington, Armour, and Clark as husky lads on their fathers' farms; Hill as a clerk for a St. Paul steamboat company; Harriman as an office boy in a New York broker's establishment; Rockefeller as a bookkeeper in Cleveland.

The Beards' inference is that these men, starting from the lowliest jobs as exemplars of the tradition, rose from the most humble origins to the very top. This may actually have been so, not only of these few men but of the large majority of business leaders whom they are taken to represent. But, it may be asked, how many in modern times start much higher than these men did, even among the well-born, college-trained young men who, as *Fortune* put it, spend a few years in "the mummery of 'working in the plant'" before ascending to the highest executive levels? Surely, of itself, an initial low-status job does necessarily imply lowly origins.

It is instructive to note that even the more perspicacious historians, when they err on the origins of business leaders, do so on the side of the tradition. Thus the Beards describe Rockefeller, the son of a "Barnumesque" itinerant entrepreneur, as "the son of a farmer"; and Henry B. Parkes writes of F. Augustus Heinze, the copper magnate who was born in Brooklyn, New York, into a comfortable business family, as a "young German immigrant."

Though most historians say little about it, there has been in the United States for well over a century a sizable and growing working class, propertyless, segregated, often remarkably apathetic to the alleged opportunities of American business and political life. Into this class most immigrants, starting with the Irish in the 1840's, have been channeled. Historians generally imply by the individuals they select as examples that this class and (for so little is said in this connection of rich men's business-bred, college-educated sons) this class alone has supplied our business leaders, that their school, to quote Carnegie himself, was "the sternest of all schools—poverty," that they were graduated from it early in life into apprenticeships as "mechanics" or "poor clerks," and that "against the boy who swept the office, or who begins as a shipping clerk at fourteen," the college graduate "has little chance, starting at twenty."

Yet to read the lives of business leaders, even of those who presumably are the pillars of this traditon, is to look almost in vain for working class or foreign origins, and even poor and unschooled farm boys are not conspicuous among such leaders. Of Rockefeller and Heinze I have already spoken. The historians themselves have accounted for J. Pierpont Morgan and William H. Vanderbilt. Jay Cooke's father, Eleutheros, was "a lawyer who was sent to Congress." Harriman's father, Orlando, was an Episcopal clergyman, "the one exception of his generation in a family of several brothers" who followed the family tradition of successful "trading and commercial pursuits." Harriman himself married the daughter of a banker and railroad president who started him on his railroad career. Even a farm boy such as Elbert H. Gary, who "experienced early in life the arduous regimen of work on a pioneer farm, an experience which endowed him with excellent health and a robust physique," was raised in a settlement named after his forebears and in a house that "was a large one for the time—the largest in the settlement . . . 'the big white house on the hill' it came to be called."

Doubtless examples can be found in the period emphasized by the historians of men whose life histories more fully substantiate the tradition. What of the men in the later period to which the historians tacitly allow their explanations of origins and ascent to apply and which is the subject of this essay?

Had the "typical" American business leader of the first decade of the twentieth century been an immigrant? Was he best represented in manufacturing, for example, by Franz A. Assmann, the German-born president of the American Can Company; or in railroading by Edward T. Jeffery, the English-born president of the Denver and Rio Grande; or in insurance by Alexander E. Orr, the Irish-born president of the New York Life; or in banking by Jacob H. Schiff, the German-born Jew who became senior partner of Kuhn, Loeb and Co.?

Simply to ask the question is to answer it. Of the 187 businessmen studied here whose birthplaces are known, only 18, or less than 10 percent, were born abroad. Surely these men were less "typical" of the top-most business leaders of their time than the 55 percent who were born in the eastern part of the United States, in New England and the middle Atlantic states.

Table 1
American Business and Political Leaders by Region of Birthplace*

Birthplace	*Business Leaders (Percent of)*	*Political Leaders (Percent of)*
New England	18 }55	22
Middle Atlantic	37 }	27
East North Central	22	27
South	9	11
West	4	7
United States	90	94
Foreign	10	6
Total cases (= 100 percent)	187	188

*These are census regions. Combined in "South" are South Atlantic, South Central, West South Central; in "West" West North Central, Mountain, Pacific.

Of the eighteen business leaders who were foreign-born, moreover, scarcely two or three fit the historians' concept of the *poor* immigrant who made good, and even these men had been brought to the United States at such an early age that they may be said to have been bred if not born here. Two of the eighteen men were of rich, colonial American business families who happened to be residing temporarily in Canada when they were born. Four more, rich and highly placed abroad, either settled here as representatives of big foreign business firms or were brought over by fathers who represented such firms. At least two others had letters of introduction from their fathers or other relatives abroad to American bankers and merchants who helped to establish them here. Thus it appears to be unsafe in writing of elites to associate immigrant status, even where that fits, with the idea of poverty.

If not typically poor immigrants, were these business and political leaders the sons of foreigners? More of them were, surely, but the next table shows that the typical leader in each field was born into an American family.

Table 2
American Business and Political Leaders by Region of Father's Birthplace

Father's Birthplace	*Business Leaders (Percent of)*	*Political Leaders (Percent of)*
New England	27	33
Middle Atlantic	31	28
East North Central	4	5
South	12	17
United States, unspecified*	7	4
United States	81	87
Foreign	19	13
Total cases (= 100 percent)	176	176

*Fathers of none of these men were known to have been born in the "West" as defined in Table 2. All those known to have been born in the United States, the exact region being unknown, are counted here.

Moreover, these families themselves had, in most instances, been in America for many generations. Almost three-fourths of the business and political leaders were at least of the fourth generation of their paternal lines to reside in America; many were of the seventh and even the eighth generations. Colonial families were represented by 73 percent of the business leaders and 79 percent of those in politics. Fifty-six percent of the former and 47 percent of the latter were of families that had settled in America in the seventeenth century.

Even were they not of colonial ancestry, most of these leaders could point to British, and many to English, forebears.

Table 3
American Business and Political Leaders by Paternal Family's Origin*

Family Origin	*Business Leaders (Percent of)*	*Political Leaders (Percent of)*
England and Wales	53	56
Ireland	14	13
Scotland	7	8
Canada	3	1
British Empire, other, or unspecified	5	5
British Empire	82	83
Germany	12	8
Other countries	6	9
Total cases (= 100 percent)	162	162

*Or country of leader's own origin if he was the first in the family to settle in America. In either case, *last country* before settlement in America.

They could claim Protestant, and often Episcopal or Presbyterian, backgrounds.

Table 4
American Business and Political Leaders by Religious Background*

Denomination	*Business Leaders (Percent of)*	*Political Leaders (Percent of)*
Episcopal	25	12
Presbyterian	21	17
Methodist	9	13
Baptist	5	7
Other Protestant	14	20
Protestant, unspecified	16	25
Protestant	90	94
Catholic	7	4
Jewish	3	2
Total cases (= 100 percent)	174	165

*In almost all instances this is the religion of the leader himself and most likely of his family as well. In a few instances where a shift in religion is known to have occurred, only the old religion is counted.

If not of recent foreign origin, was the typical American business leader of the early twentieth century a migrant from a farm?

Table 6 shows that the political leaders far more frequently than those in business came from rural areas, that almost 60 percent of the latter were recruited from the larger towns and cities. Indeed, more than 20 percent of them were born in cities that around the middle of the nineteenth century had populations of 100,000 or more. Upon these men rural influences even in a predominantly rural society must have been at a minimum.

Table 5
American Business and Political Leaders by Size of Birthplace*

Size of Birthplace	*Business Leaders (Percent of)*	*Political Leaders (Percent of)*
Rural (under 2,500)	41	75
Town (2,500–8,000)	19 } 59	9
City (over 8,000)	40 }	16
Total cases (= 100 percent)	164	180

*Population is from the census nearest each man's date of birth. In a few instances of men raised in places (that is, moved there before reaching the age of 7) sufficiently larger or smaller than their birthplaces to alter their classification in the scale used in the table, that place, not the birthplace, was used.

Yet more significant in answering the question are the occupations of the fathers of these business leaders. Here we find that even of those born in rural areas fewer than one third (and only 12 percent of the whole group) had fathers who were mainly farmers. Fifty-six percent of all the business leaders, on the other hand, had fathers who had been in business—often big business—before them; eight of ten, indeed, came from business or professional families. (See Table 6 on the opposite page.)

Darwin P. Kingsley, who was president of the New York Life Insurance Company from 1907 to 1931 and chairman of the board from 1931 to his death two years later, once said of his impoverished early years:

> On the 40-acre farm, in Vermont, where I was born, everything we wore and everything we ate was grown on the farm, except a little sugar once in a while in place of maple sugar, which was indigenous, and a little tea. From a dozen sheep came wool which was first spun and then woven by hand into winter clothing. Our garden supplied flax which was made into summer garments . . . I well remember the first time my father took his wool and swapped it for fulled cloth. We all regarded that as an epochal advance into a higher state of civilization.
>
> At Alburg, where I was born, there were not then (1857) enough houses to form even a hamlet. In the summer I attended the old "deestrict" school, a primitive affair innocent of any suggestion of higher education. In our home were very few books. Life there was clean through and

Table 6
American Business and Political Leaders by Father's Occupation*

Occupation	*Business Leaders (Percent of)*		*Political Leaders (Percent of)*
Businessman	56	}79	33
Professional	23		18
Farmer	12		38
Public Official	7		9
Worker	2		2
Total cases (= 100 percent)	167		167

*Some fathers engaged in more than one occupation. The one used here was dominant in the period in which each man was raised. In a few instances this was not clear so a choice was made more or less arbitrarily (considering our lack of knowledge of income and status factors in the early nineteenth century) by which business (including higher company positions as well as company ownership) took precedence over farming and professional or public-official positions over both. This conforms roughly to the ascending order of status used in classifying occupations today. In no instance was there a problem of a father who was a worker (including wage as well as salaried occupations). About one-third of the professionals were lawyers or engineers who might have been called businessmen, given the nature of their professional work; the others were clergymen, doctors, writers, etc. "Public official" includes professional politicians (even if not officeholders) and lawyers who were chiefly public men.

> through, self-respecting, and full of moral and religious discipline. But it was extremely narrow, uninspiring, and unimaginative. There was little or nothing to fire a boy with ambition or enthusiasm or to acquaint him with the world that lay beyond his "cabined, cribbed, and confined" sphere.

Yet it was not this kind of poverty that Carnegie had in mind when he recommended his "sternest of all schools"; this kind of spiritual and intellectual poverty was probably most prevalent among the poor, but this much at least they shared with large segments of the population at all levels, including those born and raised among the very rich. Call Kingsley's family poor in material things as well; but compared with the sons of many urban and rural wage workers even in the 1850's he and other farmers' sons like him were not worst off.

Nevertheless, in the next table, showing the social status of the families of these business and political leaders, Kingsley and a few others with apparently similar or poorer backgrounds were classified as lower class. Men were classified as of the upper class when it was clear that their fathers, like those of August Belmont, Cornelius K. G. Billings, or Charles Deering, were themselves big businessmen, or where their families, like those of Robert Todd Lincoln or Winslow Shelby Pierce, were politically eminent. Generally speaking, those in between—including some businessmen with no special claims to wealth or power or professionals like the average clergyman, doctor, or lawyer—were ranked as of middle-class origins. This does not mean that their fathers were not of help to them. James B. Duke, for example, rose to wealth and power with a company founded by his father; George W. Perkins moved to a partnership in the House of Morgan—probably the acting head of the house at one stage—from a vice-presidency in the New York Life Insurance Company in which his father, a minor executive there, had given him his business start.

Not all the men ranked in the upper class, of course, had fathers as rich and powerful as those of Belmont or Billings, or families as well connected as those of Lincoln or Pierce. Many in the middle bracket, likewise, probably were not as fortunate in their upbringing as Elbert H. Gary, whose family is classified there; probably few so classified were as poor in material things as the Harrimans.

Table 7
American Business and Political Leaders by Family Status

Status	*Business Leaders (Percent of)*	*Political Leaders (Percent of)*
Upper	50	36
Middle	45	50
Lower	5	14
Total cases (= 100 percent)	179	180

Poor boys, as Carnegie rightly said, usually go to work early in life. Clearly few of these business and political leaders were poor boys. And, as the following table shows, few of them went to work at an early age.

Table 8
American Business and Political Leaders by Age on Going to Work*

Age	*Business Leaders (Percent of)*	*Political Leaders (Percent of)*
15 or under	20	13
16–18	35	10
19 and over	45	77
Total cases (= 100 percent)	179	182

*This is age on taking first regular business, professional, or other job (except work on father's or other relative's farm) after leaving school or, in a very few instances, after leaving the Union or Confederate armies.

Only one in five of these business leaders had a job before he was 16; slightly more than half of them had jobs before they were 19. Delaying the business debuts of most of the others—their late start, according to the tradition, being itself a handicap—was the pursuit of higher education, an undertaking that should so have altered their characters as to make them even poorer prospects for business success. The educational levels attained by all the leaders studied here are shown in the following table.

Table 9
American Business and Political Leaders by Highest Education Level Attained*

Education	*Business Leaders (Percent of)*		*Political Leaders (Percent of)*	
Grammar school	22		18	
High school	37		27	
Some college	12	41	11	55
College graduate	29		44	
Total cases (= 100 percent)	183		188	

*I have reduced the many types of older schools to this modern terminology, including in "grammar school" institutions called by that name, as well as district, public, common and similar schools; in "high school," academies and others of similar rank. Counted among grammar-school boys are those who had little or no formal education as well as graduates; among high-school boys, all those who attended whether graduates or not. A few who had private tutors well into their teens but did not attend college are counted with the high-school group.

Of the business leaders who did not go to work until they were 19 or older, 76 percent had gone to college. Four out of five of these, in turn, were of the upper class. No group, if the traditional account of the origins and ascent pattern of the American business elite truly represented the facts, could have been worse off than this one in the competition for business eminence. Yet about 28 percent of the business leaders are found in it. These men shared *all* the alleged handicaps: upper-class upbringing, college education, a late business start; yet, if speed of ascent be taken as the measure of the *greatest* attainment, these men were actually the most successful of all. Not only did they spend less time after starting to work in getting to the top, but, as the following table shows, they go there on the whole earlier in life than those allegedly most favored. This table shows the ages at which the two polar groups attained the high positions that made them eligible for this study.

Still, one has to stretch a point to attribute to more than two or three general American historians *any* discussion of the speed of ascent of the business elite. More of them stress this elite's typically lower-class, foreign or farm *origins* and speculate on the forces that impelled men upward from such insalubrious environs. Yet poor immigrant boys and poor farm boys together actually make up no more than 3 percent of the business leaders who are the subject of this essay. If men with such backgrounds had been in fact representative of the great enterpreneurs of the later nineteenth century, they must have been supplanted with extraordinary rapidity by the higher status, more highly educated bureaucrats of the following generation. More likely, poor immigrant and poor farm boys who become business leaders have always been more conspicuous in American history books than in American history.

Table 10
American Business Leaders by Age on Becoming President or Partner of Major Company*

Age	*Late-Starting, Upper-Class, College Men (Percent of)*	*Early-Starting, Middle- and Lower-Class Noncollege Men (Percent of)*
Under 45	43 } 66	26 } 48
45–49	23 }	22 }
50 and over	34	52
Total cases (= 100 percent)	40	53

*Board chairmen are a special case in regard to age on attaining the position and were omitted from this table.

Irvin G. Wyllie
As the Twig is Bent

(1954)

In 1954, Irvin G. Wyllie published his stimulating and compact survey of the orators and pamphleteers who propagandized the self-help doctrines of the last century. A delightful book to read, Wyllie's *The Self-Made Man in America: The Myth of Rags to Riches*, is also distinguished for its invaluable bibliography.

Irwin G. Wyllie, *The Self-Made Man in America: The Myth of Rags to Riches* (New Brunswick, 1954), Chap. II, pp. 21–33. Reprinted without footnotes by permission of the publisher, Rutgers University Press.

What makes the man? Is he shaped by conditions that surround him, or by forces inherent in himself? Through the long history of American thinking on the subject of success no questions have been more central, and none have been answered more confidently. To the generation that sired Andrew Carnegie and John D. Rockefeller the relation of a favorable economic environment to personal fortune should have been obvious. And sometimes it was. P. T. Barnum, for example, admitted that "In a new country, where we have more land than people, it is not at all difficult for persons in good health to make money." But most prophets of success refused to tell their tales in terms of the favorable ratio of men to resources, preferring instead to talk about how character could triumph over circumstance. "The things which are really essential for a successful life are not circumstances, but qualities," one spokesman said, "not the things which surround a man, but the things which are in him; not the adjuncts of his position, but the attributes of his character." This had to be the emphasis, of course, for otherwise there could be no such social being as a self-made man.

In minimizing the role of the economic environment advocates of self-help did not, however, dismiss it entirely. They simply insisted that American opportunities were so plentiful, and so open to all, that each and every man could make as much of himself as he desired. "The road to fortune, like the public turnpike, is open alike to the children of the beggar, and the descendant of kings," one adviser declared. "There are tolls to be paid by all, yet all have rights, and it only remains for us to avail ourselves of these." It was a matter of common agreement that never in the history of the world had chances for success been greater than in post-Civil War America. As Horace Greeley told an audience of young hopefuls at the Cooper Union in 1867, "There is in this land of ours larger opportunities, more just and well grounded hopes, than any other land whereon the sun ever shone." In less fortunate lands men might behold success from afar and worship it, but few could dream of achieving it. Here on the other hand the attainment of fame and fortune was a common expectation.

How could this be? In America was there not inequality in the land, and more poverty than wealth? True, the apostles of self-help admitted, but this condition forced the young to struggle against adversity and thus furnished the very means by which they might develop the qualities necessary for success. "It is the struggle which develops," said an authority on self-help, "—the effort to redeem one's self from iron surroundings,— which calls out manhood and unfolds womanhood to the highest possibilities." In the religion of success poverty became the equivalent of sin in Calvinist theology, an evil to be struggled against and overcome. The greater the poverty out of which a man climbed, the greater the testimony to the force of his character. According to this reasoning, those who would be least likely to succeed would be the children of the rich, for without struggle against adversity they would be deprived of the means of developing the necessary strength of character. This was what Henry Ward Beecher tried to convey to the wealthy merchants of Brooklyn's Plymouth Church when he told them that their financial losses might be their children's gain. "How blessed, then, is the stroke of disaster which sets the children free, and gives them over to the hard but kind bosom of Poverty, who says to them, 'Work!' and, working, makes them men."

Among business enterprisers the stoutest defender of the advantages of poverty was Andrew Carnegie, who insisted that practically all the titans of his generation has been trained in poverty's stern but efficient school. "They appear upon the stage, athletes trained for the contest, with sinews braced, indomitable wills, resolved to do or die. Such boys always have marched, and always will march, straight to the front and lead the world; they are the epochmakers." Society could ill afford to be without poverty, Carnegie argued, for without poverty there would be no extraordinary men, and without extraordinary men there could be no social progress. "Abolish luxury, if you please," he said, "but leave us the soil, upon which alone the virtues and all that is precious in human character grow; poverty—honest poverty."

In defending poverty Carnegie was not simply justifying maldistribution of wealth under a capitalist economy. He was also romanticizing the circumstances which had surrounded his own childhood and that of many of these wealthy men of the nineteenth century. Just how many other business leaders of his generation actually did rise from poverty we shall probably never know, but there have been some informed guesses. In his study of deceased American millionaires, mostly men of the last century, Pitirim Sorokin, for example, discovered that 38.8 percent of them started life poor. Another statistical study of the American business elite showed that 43 percent of those leaders who came to maturity around the year 1870 originated in the lower classes; they encountered fewer difficulties on their road from rags to riches than earlier or later generations. From a strictly statistical point of view, around 1835 appears to have been the most propitious birth year for a poor boy who hoped to rise into the business elite. Carnegie hit it right on the mark, for he was born in 1835 and came to his business maturity after the Civil War. With the evidence around him, it is not surprising that he should have sensed that in his generation, more than ever before, poor boys were on the march. And what was more natural than his attempts and those of other self-made men to discover in the poverty of their youth the source of their later strength?

Along with the glorification of poverty in the success cult's ideology went the glorification of rural childhood. Throughout the last century self-help propagandists insisted that rural origins foretold success and urban origins failure. It is not difficult to understand the basis for such assertions for it is an historic fact that the great cities of the nineteenth century were built up, in part at least, by migrations from rural areas, and that the country boy sometimes did rise into the ranks of the urban business elite. Philip D. Armour, James J. Hill, Collis P. Huntington, Cornelius Vanderbilt, Daniel

Drew, and Jay Gould all came from the farm. Self-help publicists needed only a hasty glance at the rolls of wealth to convince themselves that there must be some cause and effect relationship between country origins and the qualities that enabled a man to conquer fortune. As Orison Marden noted, "The sturdy, vigorous, hardy qualities, the stamina, the brawn, the grit which characterize men who do great things in this world, are, as a rule, country bred."

One of the favorite migrations of ambitious country boys was from New England to the urban centers of New York and Pennsylvania. Because of its accessibility New York City was especially attractive to boys from back-country New England. In the years after 1820 they swarmed into the rising metropolis, captured it, and dominated its business life until after the Civil War. "All do not succeed," a contemporary reported, "but some do, and this is quite sufficient to keep the ambition to get a clerkship in New York alive." Joseph A. Scoville, who knew as much as any man about the New York business community at mid-century, thought there was no mystery about the country boy's rise to positions of leadership. "He needs but a foothold," said Scoville. "He asks no more . . . wherever this boy strikes, he fastens." According to Scoville New York merchants preferred to hire country boys, on the theory that they worked harder, and were more resolute, obedient, and cheerful than native New Yorkers. Too often city boys objected to menial tasks, complaining that they were intended for better things. Nothing, not even the blackening of the employer's boots, was beneath the dignity of the New Englander. Presumably this attitude went far towards explaining his rapid rise.

It would be difficult to say how many farmers' sons thus won fame and fortune but there is little doubt that contemporaries exaggerated their number. In 1883 a Brooklyn clergyman, Wilbur F. Crafts, published the results of his investigations of the lives of five hundred successful Americans representing all lines of endeavor. According to his data 57 percent of the successful men of his day were born in the country, and only 17 percent in the city. "The first conclusion from these facts," said Crafts, "is that a man who wishes to succeed should select a country farm for his birthplace . . ." Another study, published in 1909, showed that out of 47 railroad presidents who answered questions about their origins, 55.4 percent came from farms or villages. Three more recent surveys, however, point toward the opposite direction. Farm boys accounted for only 24.6 percent of the deceased American millionaires investigated by Sorokin; only 23.8 percent of the elite businessmen whose origins were checked by C. Wright Mills; and only 12 percent of the twentieth-century leaders studied by William Miller. Even so, as a group, farmers' sons ranked second only to the sons of businessmen in the achievement of outstanding success. This and the fact that farm boys started with fewer advantages made them the favorite candidates for heroes in the cult of the self-made man.

The alleged advantages of rural beginnings concerned mostly health and morals. Fresh air and good food kept the country boy in good physical condition, and his daily round of work left him little time for the mischief that distracted his less busy city cousin. Whereas city boys wasted their lives and their substance in saloons, gambling dens, and houses of prostitution, country boys supposedly led a Spartan life that prepared them for the hard struggle of the business world. "Our successful men did not feed themselves on boyhood cigarettes and late suppers, with loafing as their only labor, and midnight parties for their regular evening dissipation," a clergyman declared in 1883. "Such city-trained bodies often give out when the strain comes in business, while the sound body and mind and morals of the man from the country hold on and hold out." In 1909 President Louis W. Hill of the Great Northern Railway testified that, despite the personal inconvenience involved, he had chosen to live on a farm rather than in the city in order to give his three boys the best possible start in life. "I believe," said Hill, "there is no end of arguments that living on the farm gives the best chance for a growing boy."

In only one respect, and that a crucial one, did philosophers of success concede that cities offered advantages which rural villages could not match. Opportunities for making money, they agreed, were better in the city. If the farm boy expected to become a millionaire he had to migrate to a metropolis. Even the most insensitive observers seemed to understand that the road to fortune must pass through the city. Many self-help handbooks therefore encouraged farm boys to leave home. "A boy at home seldom has a chance," said one blunt adviser. "Nobody believes in him—least of all his relations." Out of deference to parents most writers tried to be more subtle; instead of telling boys to leave home they advised them indirectly to do so by talking about the importance of setting up in the right location. "No man can expect to become distinguished in any sphere unless he has the amplest field for the exercise of his powers," one handbook declared. "A. T. Stewart located anywhere out of New York City, would not be what he is, and many a clergyman or lawyer, fixed in a small village, would not have reached the eminence which the world freely accords them." It was sad, but true, that if a country boy desired fortune he had to leave home to achieve it. If there was any consolation in this uprooting, it was in the conviction that his chance of failure was slight so long as he remained faithful to the virtues that formed his country character.

When the boy ventured into the world his memories of home and mother were supposed to be a source of powerful influence on his future. Poverty and rural surroundings might school him in virtue, but the schooling was often harsh. Not so with the lessons learned at a mother's knee. Of all the external influences leading young men into the byways of success, none had greater honor in the cult of self-help than that of mother. "The testimony of great men in acknowledgment of the boundless debt they owe to their mothers would make a record stretching from the dawn of history to to-day," said a high priest of the cult. "Few men indeed, become great who do not owe their greatness to a mother's love and inspiration." In the case of successful moneymakers, mothers deserved credit not because of any instruction in the ways of business, but because of their role of molding the character on which business achievement was supposed to depend. As Albert J. Beveridge remarked, American mothers trained their sons in honor rather than success, but success was the inevitable by-product. Granting this power of mothers, it was fortunate that there were no irresponsibles among those described in the literature of success. "I can not imagine a better woman than my mother," said Philip D. Armour in typical testimony. "My childhood was ideal. God did not overlook me."

According to most self-help advocates a young man who moved away from his parental home was not doomed thereby to lose forever the blessings of female comfort and counsel, for they assumed that a young man with ambition would marry. "Marry a true woman, and have your own home," was an oft-repeated exhortation. The young businessman who desired a good name, they cautioned, would do well to marry, because a good wife would be the means of saving him from loose women, gambling, drink, and other vices which damaged reputation. In addition, they argued, the married man was morally superior to the bachelor, and therefore preferred by both creditors and employers.

It should be noted, however, that the young businessman who married in order to improve his success did not choose his wife on the basis of her material possessions. In the theory of success money was to be earned, not married, and he who married for money was engaging in dangerous speculation, for the heiress was quite likely to be indolent and extravagant. "With the very best of purposes she does not know how to adapt herself to a mode of life less expensive than that which obtained in her father's house, and her inheritance alone is rarely ever sufficient for that."

The good wife enriched her husband by bringing profitable qualities of character, not money, into the home. She was economical, hard working, orderly, neat, steady, and firm in disposition. She was never extravagant, because "An extravagant wife is an injury to a merchant's credit." She was cheerful, especially in hard times, and never addicted to nagging. The nagging wife was a millstone about her husband's neck, making him useless to himself, his employer, and to the world. "I have seen more men fail in business through the attitude taken by their wives . . . than from all the vices put together," Charles M. Schwab testified. "A nagging wife . . . is one of the worst handicaps he could have." The wife who gave her husband kindness and affection enriched him also with wealth:

> I came to the desk where old Commerce grew grey,
> And asked him what helped him this many a day,
> In his old smokey room with his ledger to stay?
> And it all was the beauty,
> The comfort and duty,
> That cheered him at home.

In point of fact, successful moneymakers were married men more often than not. Almost 97 percent of the millionaires of the nineteenth century were married, and 94 percent of those of the twentieth century. In each of these eras wealthy men ranked well above the average for adult males in the matter of taking vows. Undoubtedly the millionaire's financial status contributed much of his eligibility, but this was a point that prophets of success were reluctant to concede. "They are not married men because they are better off than their fellows," said one authority, "but are better off because they are married men." This bordered on doctrinal heresy, of course, for if it were admitted that a wife held the key to her husband's success, what then became of the self-made man?

Whenever self-help theorists touched on the roles played by the economic environment, by rural upbringing, or by wives and mothers, they always had to be wary lest they attribute too much to these external influences. Sound doctrine demanded that explanations for success be found within the man and not outside him. As Emerson remarked, "the reason why this or that man is fortunate is not to be told. It lies in the man; that is all anybody can tell you about it." Long after Emerson's passing a more practical philosopher, Henry Ford, reiterated the same point. "The law of success is in the person himself," said Ford. "What is the law by which the apple becomes an apple? Well, it's the same way with success."

By the same token the causes of failure lay within the man. Every year after 1890 the firm of Dun and Bradstreet analyzed the business failures of the preceding year in terms of the personal and impersonal factors involved. Invariably the greater number of failures were explained by such categories as incompetence, inexperience, extravagance, fraud, and neglect. Only infrequently were failures charged against depressed business conditions or other causes beyond the control of the individual. After surveying the causes of failure thus reported for the period 1902–1910, one self-help theorist concluded that "Long years of experience have demonstrated to the seekers after the underlying causes of business failure the fact that, generally speaking four-fifths of all failures are due to faults inherent in the person, while about one-fifth are due to causes outside and beyond his control . . . In other words, the cool, disinterested judgment of thousands of investigators shows that success or failure largely lies within the person himself rather than with outside conditions." In all times and places this was the doctrine which identified true prophets of the cult of the self-made man.

John G. Cawelti
From Rags to Respectability: Horatio Alger

(1965)

John G. Cawelti sampled literary materials different from Irvin Wyllie's and interpreted the shifting ideal of the self-made man in America. In the following excerpt from Chapter IV of his *Apostles of the Self-Made Man*, Cawelti explains that the usual success of Alger's poor-boy hero involved not a meteoric rise to great wealth and social power, but, rather, a modest rise to take possession of the solid middle-class attainments which Alger's respectable Protestant-bourgeois American reader easily understood and admired.

... Alger's contemporary position as a symbol of individualistic free enterprise has obscured the actual characteristics of his stories. A number of misconceptions must be cleared away before we can get to the heart of the Alger version of what constitutes success. Here, for example, is a typical interpretation of the Alger hero in a recent book:

> Alone, unaided, the ragged boy is plunged into the maelstrom of city life, but by his own pluck and luck he capitalizes on one of the myriad opportunities available to him and rises to the top of the economic heap. Here, in a nutshell, is the plot of every novel Alger ever wrote; here, too, is the quintessence of the myth. Like many simple formulations which nevertheless convey a heavy intellectual and emotional charge to vast numbers of people, the Alger hero represents a triumphant combination—and reduction to the lowest common denominator—of the most widely accepted concepts in nineteenth-century American society. The belief in the potential greatness of the common man, the glorification of individual effort and accomplishment, the equation of the pursuit of money with the pursuit of happiness and of business success with spiritual grace: simply to mention these concepts is to comprehend the brilliance of Alger's synthesis.

This passage illustrates several important misconceptions concerning Alger's books. In the first place, Alger's heroes are rarely "alone and unaided," and do not win their success entirely through individual effort and accomplishment. From the very beginning of his career, the Alger boy demonstrates an astounding propensity for chance encounters with benevolent and useful friends, and his success is largely due to their patronage and assistance. In

---

John G. Cawelti, *Apostles of the Self-Made Man* (Chicago, 1965), Chapter IV, pp. 108–20. Reprinted, without footnotes, by permission of the author and the publisher, The University of Chicago Press.

the course of his duties Fred Fenton, the hero of *The Erie Train Boy*, meets a wealthy young girl named Isabel Archer—presumably named in homage to Alger's literary idol, Henry James—who gives him money to pay his mother's rent. In addition, he encounters an eccentric miner, who later helps him sell some land belonging to his late father, and the uncle of a wealthy broker, who gives young Fred his chance in business. Alger's heroes are well aware of their indebtedness to these patrons, and modestly make no pretense of success through their own efforts, although Alger assures his readers that they deserve their advancement. Ragged Dick, congratulated on his achievement by one of the innumerable wealthy men who befriended him, replies: "'I was lucky,' said Dick, modestly. 'I found some good friends who helped me along.'"

Nor did the Alger hero rise "to the top of the economic heap." Some years ago a writer for *Time*, in a mathematical mood, calculated that the average Alger hero's fortune is only $10,000. Usually the hero is established in a secure white-collar position, either as a clerk with the promise of a junior partnership or as a junior member of a successful mercantile establishment. None achieve anything resembling economic or political prominence. Moderate economic security would best summarize the pecuniary achievements of the typical Alger hero, in spite of such tantalizing titles as *Fame and Fortune*, *Striving for Fortune*, and *From Farm to Fortune*. For example, at the end of *Fame and Fortune*, the hero is in possession of a magnificent income of $1,400 a year, plus the interest on about $2,000 in savings. In Alger's mind, this was "fame and fortune."

We may admit that Alger's representation of economic reality was highly sentimentalized, but it is unfair to call him an uninhibited adulator of wealth who equated spiritual grace with business success. The true aim of the Alger hero is respectability, a happy state only partially defined by economic repute. Nor was Alger unaware that many men were successful as the result of questionable practices. He may have lacked knowledge of these practices, but Alger frequently reminded his readers that many wealthy and successful men were undeserving of their fortunes. One of his favorite villains is the wealthy, unscrupulous banker who accumulates wealth by cheating widows and orphans. On the whole, Alger's formula is more accurately stated as middle-class respectability equals spiritual grace.

Alger was no more an unrestrained advocate of the "potential greatness" of the common man than he was of the uninhibited pursuit of financial success. His heroes are ordinary boys only in the sense of their lowly origin. In ability and personal character they are far above average. Many boys in the Alger books are unable, in spite of their earnest efforts, to rise above a lowly position. Micky McGuire, a young slum boy who is a secondary character in the *Ragged Dick* series, is reformed at last through the efforts of Dick and his patron Mr. Rockwell. But the old maxim "No Irish Need Apply" still held for Alger.

Micky has already turned out much better than was expected, but he is hardly likely to rise much higher than the subordinate position he now occupies. In capacity and education he is far inferior to his old associate, Richard Hunter, who is destined to rise much higher than at present.

Who, then, is the Alger hero, and what is the nature of the adventures in which he is involved? Alger has two types of heroes. The first, and probably the more popular, is the poor, uneducated street boy—sometimes an orphan, more frequently the son of a widowed mother—who rises to moderate affluence. The second is a well-born and well-educated middle-class youth whose father dies, leaving the son to fend for himself. In some cases a villainous squire or distant relative attempts to cheat the hero out of his rightful legacy, but, in the end, the hero is restored to his inheritance or succeeds in rising to his proper place.

Alger made desultory attempts to vary the character of his hero in each story, but such an achievement was beyond his skill, and the reader could be certain that, whatever the situation, and whether the hero smokes or uses slangy language, the same solid core of virtue is present. Alger's heroes, who range in age from around twelve to eighteen, are in the tradition of the didactic novels of self-improvement. One must give Alger some credit for making his young paragons a little less earnest and more lively than the placid prigs of T. S. Arthur. The Alger hero might begin as an intemperate spendthrift like Ragged Dick, but soon he becomes a master of the traditional virtues of industry, economy, integrity, and piety. He is manly and self-reliant—two of Alger's favorite words—and, in addition, kind and generous. Never a genius, he is usually a boy of above-average intelligence, particularly in the area of mathematics, and is also a strenuous devotee of self-culture. The Alger hero is never snobbish or condescending; indeed, he is the veritable apotheosis of modesty. Thoroughly democratic in his tastes, he befriends other poor boys and is uniformly courteous to people of all classes. The Alger hero demonstrates to a high degree those traits that might be called the employee virtues: fidelity, punctuality, and courteous deference. It is upon these latter traits that Alger places the greatest stress.

Against his hero, Alger sets three types of boys who serve as foils to the hero's sterling qualities. One of these may be called the lesser hero. He is usually a slightly younger and less vigorous edition of the major figure. The lesser hero often has greater advantages than his friend, but he lacks the enterprise, the courage, and the self-reliance of the hero, and frequently depends on him for protection against the harsh urban world, enabling the hero to demonstrate his courage and generosity. Another boy who appears in almost all the Alger books is the snob. Insisting that he is a gentleman's son, the snob looks down his nose at the hero's willingness to work at such lowly trades as that of bootblack or newsboy. Sometimes the snob is the son of a rich but grasping relative of the hero's, envious of his greater capabilities and endeavoring to get him into trouble. The young snob shows the obverse of all the hero's virtues: he is lazy, ignorant, arrogant, and unwilling to work because he considers it beneath his station. He is overtly contemptuous and secretly envious of the hero's successes. Alger delights in foiling this little monster, usually by arranging for his father to fail in business, thereby forcing the snob to go to work at a salary lower than the hero's.

Another type appearing somewhat less frequently in the Alger books is the poor boy who lacks the intelligence and ability of the hero and is more susceptible to the corruption of his environment. Often he becomes involved in plots against the hero, but is usually won over when he recognizes his true manliness and forgiving character. Although sometimes reformed through the hero's efforts, the Micky McGuire type is doomed to remain in a subordinate but respectable position by his lack of intelligence and enterprise. Curiously enough, these dim-minded characters are Alger's most interesting and vivid creations, and foreshadow the "bad boy" heroes of later juvenile books. In addition, they frequently represent immigrant groups—Irish, Italians, Germans—who, not all bad, play a distinctly inferior role in Alger's version of America.

The adult characters vary no more than the boys in the typical Alger book. The central adult figure is the benevolent businessman whose chance encounter with the hero gives him his big opportunity. Like all adults in Alger, this figure is thinly characterized, his major traits being the ability to recognize and reward the hero's potentialities. He is called upon to deliver long homilies on the virtues requisite to success. Generally, he is a merchant or a highly reputable stockbroker. In his business dealings he is honest and upright, scorning all but the most elevated commercial practices. In effect his role is to serve as an ideal adoptive father for the hero.

The second most important male adult in the Alger books is the villain, who usually has some important hold over the hero. Sometimes he is a mean stepfather, more often a grasping uncle or cousin who becomes the hero's guardian, and frequently a cruel, miserly squire who holds a mortgage on the family property. Whatever his mask, he invariably attempts to assert his tyrannical authority over the hero, and fails. One is tempted to describe him in Freudian terms as the overbearing father-figure whose authority the adolescent hero rejects and overthrows.

Few of the Alger heroes are orphans; the majority have a widowed mother dependent upon them for support. Here Alger differs appreciably from his predecessors. The Alger mother stands in a very different relationship to her doughty young offspring than do the mothers in T. S. Arthur's novels. The "Arthurian" mother is pre-eminently a source of moral authority, an instructor and preceptor, whose gentle commands the young hero is expected to obey. In Alger, the mother rarely commands or instructs; although she presumably has some hand in her son's development, her authoritative function is mentioned only rarely. On the contrary, she is both a dependent and an admiring on-looker. Always gentle and supremely confident in her son's ability, she never criticizes or disciplines. Indeed, occasionally she is weak and indecisive, qualities which might lead the family into difficulty were it not for the manly self-reliance of her son. Characteristic of the Alger version of maternity is this interchange between Paul the peddler and his mother:

> "You see, mother, Phil would be sure of a beating if he went home without his fiddle. Now he doesn't like to be beaten, and the padrone gives harder beatings than you do, mother."
>
> "I presume so," said Mrs. Hoffman, smiling. "I do not think I am very severe."
>
> "No, you spoil the rod and spare the child."

The benevolent merchant, the villainous father-figure, and the gentle and appreciative mother are at the center of most Alger books. They are joined by a variety of minor figures, all of whom can be traced to the traditional stereotypes of the sentimental novel: the warm-hearted Irish woman, poor and crude, kind and generous, who helps the hero escape from the villain; the snobbish female with aristocratic pretensions; the "stage Yankee" who appears in an occasional novel as a friend of the hero; and a variety of minor villains, such as the miserly moneylender, the petty swindler, and, in the Western stories, the stagecoach robber.

From such material, together with carefully accumulated local color—the books are filled with detailed descriptions of New York City—Alger constructed his tales. Almost invariably, they follow the same formula: by an amazing series of coincidences, and a few acts of personal heroism and generosity, the hero escapes from the plots laid by his enemies—usually an unholy alliance between the snobbish boy and the villainous father-figure—and attains the patronage of the benevolent merchant. In generating the action, chance and luck play a dominant role. Alger was apparently aware that the unbelievable tissue of coincidences which ran through his stories put some strain on the tolerance of his youthful readers. In *Struggling Upward*, for example, Linton Tomkins, the lesser hero, chances upon practically every other character in the book in the course of a twenty-minute promenade. Somewhat amazed at this feat, Alger can only remark that "Linton was destined to meet plenty of acquaintances." At the book's conclusion he confesses:

> So closes an eventful passage in the life of Luke Larkin. He has struggled upward from a boyhood of privation and self-denial into a youth and manhood of prosperity and honor. There has been some luck about it, I admit, but after all he is indebted for most of his good fortune to his own good qualities.

However much the hero's good qualities may have been involved, and they often seem incidental, Alger is obsessed with luck. The chapter which contains the crucial turning point of the book is invariably entitled———'s luck, and every accession to the hero's fortunes stems from a coincidence: the land thought to be worthless suddenly becomes valuable because a town has been built around it; the strongbox which the hero saves from thieves turns out to belong to an eccentric and wealthy old man who rewards the hero; the dead father's seemingly worthless speculation in mining stock is in fact a bonanza.

Alger's emphasis on luck resembles that found in the stories of T. S. Arthur and other apostles of the self-made man in the pre-Civil War era. Like them, he represents American society as an environment in which sudden and unaccountable prosperity frequently comes to the deserving like manna from heaven. To some extent, this reliance on luck or Providence is a literary shortcoming. Both Alger and Arthur turned out books at a tremendous rate; sloppiness and inadequacies in plotting and motivation could be concealed in part by defending coincidence. Furthermore, accident, luck, and chance have always played a large role in folk and popular literature, for they allow for exciting plot manipulation and the maintenance of suspense. It is equally true that the form which the accidental takes in a given work is some indication of the beliefs of an author and his intended audience.

In the case of Arthur and his contemporaries, the accidental assumes the form of the more or less direct intervention of Divine Providence. God acts to reward the deserving, punish the evil, and convert the doubting to a faith in his powers. Alger ignores the religious implications of the accidental. In his stories, luck is seemingly independent of the divine, inhering in the particular social environment of America, with its absence of hereditary class distinctions and the freedom it allows. Because most of the great merchants had been poor boys themselves, they were always on the lookout for deserving young men to assist. If the hero has the daring and self-assurance to seize one of his many opportunities to come to the attention of a benevolent patron, and is also blessed with the virtues of industry, fidelity, and good manners, he is certain to get ahead.

Religion itself does not play a major role in the life of the Alger hero. His heroes pray and go to Sunday School willingly enough, but Alger places greater stress on their obligations to others—loyalty to family and employer, and personal assistance to the less fortunate. His books encourage humanitarianism in their emphasis on practical good works and frequent insistence that Americans extend opportunities for worldly success to the juvenile proletariat of the cities. Although, like most writers in the tradition of self-improvement, Alger attributes success and failure to qualities within the individual, he occasionally points out to his young readers that a stifling and corrupting environment can be a major cause of vice and failure. An important factor in the rise of his streetboy heroes is their removal from the streets, where, if they remain, moral decay and poverty are certain. Alger can hardly be granted a profound understanding of the contemporary scene, but sympathy for the underprivileged is strong in his books. Judging from the prominence of his themes, there is as much evidence that Alger was an important influence on future reformers as a popular model for incipient robber barons.

Luck is not the only element in the success of the Alger hero. He has to deserve his luck by manifesting certain important traits which show him to be a fit candidate for a higher place in society. He carries the full complement of middle-class virtues, but these are not solely industry, frugality, and piety. Far more important are those qualities of character and intellect which make the hero a good employee and a reputable member of middle-class society. To his hero's cultivation of these qualities Alger devotes much of his attention. The hero has to learn how to dress neatly and modestly, to eliminate slang and colloquialisms from his speech, and to develop a facility with the stilted and pretentious language that Alger took to be the proper medium of verbal intercourse among respectable Americans. In addition, he has to educate himself. Alger's conception of the liberally educated man is also closely tied to social respectability. It is particularly desirable for the hero to have a neat hand and mathematical ability, but it is also important that he show a smattering of traditional culture. A foreign language is usually the prescribed curriculum. Ragged Dick studies French, for example. Since a foreign language plays no part in the hero's economic life, it is apparently intended by Alger as a certificate of a certain kind of respectability. The ability to learn French or Latin, although he might never have an opportunity to use such a skill, shows that the hero has a respect for learning as an end in itself and is no mere materialist. Thus, the Alger hero is a pale reflection of the ideal of self-culture as well as a devotee of rising in society.

Inner attainments are marked by characteristic external signs. The most crucial event in the hero's life is his acquisition of a good suit. The good suit, which is usually presented to the hero by his patron, marks the initial step in his advancement, his escape from the dirty and ragged classes and his entry upon respectability. It immediately differentiates the hero from the other bootblacks, and often leads to a quarrel with such dedicated proletarians as Micky McGuire. A second important event follows on the first: he is given a watch. The new watch marks the hero's attainment of a more elevated position, and is a symbol of punctuality and his respect for time as well as a sign of the attainment of young manhood. Alger makes much of the scene in which his hero receives from his patron a pocket watch suitably engraved.

Perhaps the most important group of qualities which operate in the hero's favor are those which make him the ideal employee: fidelity, dependability, and a burning desire to make himself useful. In a common Algerine situation, the hero, entrusted with some of his employer's money, is confronted by a villainous robber. At great risk to his own life, he defends his employer's property, preferring to lose his own money, or even his life, rather than betray his patron's trust. Under lesser stress, the hero demonstrates his superiority over the snobs by showing his willingness to perform any duties useful to his employer, and by going out of his way to give cheerful and uncomplaining service without haggling over wages. In *Fame and Fortune*, Roswell Crawford, a snob, is fired from his position as errand boy in a dry goods store when he not only complains of being required to carry packages—work too low for a "gentleman's son"—but has the additional temerity to ask for a raise. Ragged Dick, on the other hand, generously offers to carry Roswell's packages for him. Needless to say, Dick receives a raise without asking for it, because his patron recognizes his fidelity and insists on a suitable reward.

Emphasis on fidelity to the employer's interests is perhaps the worst advice Alger could have given his young readers if financial success was of major interest to them. Contrast the Alger hero's relations with his employers and Benjamin Franklin's as described in the *Memoirs*. Franklin keeps his eyes on his own interests when he works for his brother, and for the Philadelphia printers, Bradford and Keimer; indeed, he shows considerable satisfaction at his ability to turn Keimer's faults to his own benefit. By studying the inadequacies of his former employer he is able to make his own business a success. The Alger hero would never resort to such a self-serving device.

Placed against Emerson and his philosophy of self-reliance, Alger is simply another exponent of the idealized version of the self-made man found in the novels of T. S. Arthur, Sylvester Judd, and other sentimentalists of the 1840's and 1850's. His understanding of social mobility is on the same level of abstraction and idealization. Emerson, in comparison, has a much more profound understanding of the implications of social mobility and the actual characteristics likely to lead to economic and social advancement, as well as a broader ideal of self-culture. It is as true of Alger as of Arthur that he presents the mobile society through the rose-colored glasses of the middle-class ethical tradition of industry, frugality, and integrity, and the sentimental Christian version of a benevolent Providence.

The great attainment of Alger's hero is to leave the ranks of the "working class" and become an owner or partner in a business of his own. Yet few of Alger's heroes have any connection with such enterprises as mining, manufacturing, or construction, the industries in which most of the large fortunes of the late nineteenth century were made. Alger's favorite reward is a junior partnership in a respectable mercantile house. This emphasis is a throwback to the economic life of an earlier period, when American business was still dominated by merchants whose economic behavior in retrospect seemed refined and benevolent in comparison to the devastating strategies of transcontinental railroad builders, iron and steel manufacturers, and other corporate giants. Alger's version of success is, in effect, a reassertion of the values of a bygone era in an age of dramatic change and expansion.

Selected Additional Reading

Documents of the Gilded Age

Abbott, Lyman, ed. *How to Succeed in Public Life.* (New York: Putnam, 1882.)

Barnum, Phineas T. *The Art of Money Getting.* (New York: Ogilvie, 1882.)

Barnum, Phineas T. *How I Made Millions.* (Chicago: G. W. Dillingham, 1888.)

Bok, Edward W. *Successward: Young Man's Book for Young Men.* (New York: Revell, 1895.)

Bolton, Sarah K. *Lives of Poor Boys Who Became Famous.* (New York: Crowell, 1885.)

Carnegie, Andrew. *The Gospel of Wealth, and Other Timely Essays.* Edited by Edward C. Kirkland. (Cambridge, Mass. Harvard Univ. Press, 1962.)

Dill, James B. "The College Man and the Corporate Proposition," *Munsey's Magazine*, XXIV (October 1900), pp. 148–52.

Drysdale, William. *Helps for Ambitious Boys.* (New York: Crowell, 1899.)

Eddy, Mary Baker. *Science and Health.* (Boston: Christian Science Publishing Co., 1875.)

Greeley, Horace. *An Address on Success in Business.* (New York: S. N. Packard, 1868.)

Hubbard, Elbert. *Little Journeys to the Homes of Great Businessmen.* (East Aurora, N.Y.: Roycrofters, 1909.)

Marden, Orison S. *How They Succeeded: Life Stories of Successful Men Told by Themselves.* (Boston: Lothrop, 1901.)

Marden, Orison S. *Pushing to the Front.* (Boston: Houghton Mifflin, 1894.)

Rockefeller, John D. "John D. Rockefeller on Opportunity in America," *Cosmopolitan*, XLIII (August 1907), pp. 368–72.

Rockefeller, John D. *Random Reminiscences of Men and Events.* (New York: Doubleday, 1909.)

Roosevelt, Theodore. "Character and Success," *Outlook*, LXIV (March 31, 1900), pp. 725–27.

Smiles, Samuel. *Self-Help.* (New York: Harper, 1860.)

Thayer, William Makepeace. *From Log Cabin to the White House: The Life of James A. Garfield.* Enlarged and revised edition. (Norwich, Conn.: Henry Bill Publishing Co., 1882.)

Secondary Sources on the Gilded Age

Barmash, Isadore. *The Self-Made Man.* (New York: Macmillan, 1969.)

Boller, Paul, Jr., *American Thought in Transition: The Impact of Evolutionary Naturalism, 1865–1900.* (Chicago: Rand McNally, 1969.)

Cochran, Thomas C., and William Miller. *The Age of Enterprise: A Social History of Industrial America.* (New York: Macmillan, 1949.)
Commager, Henry Steele. *The American Mind: An Interpretation of American Thought and Character Since the 1880's*, Part I (New Haven: Yale Press, 1950.)
Curti, Merle. *The Growth of American Thought*, Part VI (New York: Harper, 1943.)
Dietrickson, Jan. *The Image of Money in the American Novel of the Gilded Age.* (Oslo and New York: Humanities, 1969.)
Dorfman, Joseph. *The Economic Mind in American Civilization*, Vol. III (New York: Viking, 1949.)
Elson, Ruth M. *Guardians of Tradition: American Schoolbooks of the Nineteenth Century.* (Lincoln, Neb.: University of Nebraska, 1964.)
Falk, Robert. "Notes on the 'Higher Criticism' of Horatio Alger, Jr.," *Arizona Quarterly*, XIX (Summer 1963), pp. 151–67.
Hays, Samuel P. *The Response to Industrialism: 1885–1914.* (Chicago: University of Chicago, 1957.)
Josephson, Matthew. *The Robber Barons: The Great American Capitalists, 1861–1901.* (New York: Harcourt Brace, 1934.)
Kirkland, Edward C. *Dream and Thought in the Business Community, 1860–1900.* (Ithaca, N.Y.: Cornell Univ. Press, 1956.)
Lynn, Kenneth. *The Dream of Success.* (Boston: Little, Brown, 1955.)
Meyer, Donald B. *The Positive Thinkers: A Study of the American Quest for Health, Wealth and Personal Power from Mary Baker Eddy to Norman Vincent Peale.* (Garden City, N.Y.: Doubleday, 1965.)
Morgan, H. Wayne, ed. *The Gilded Age: A Reappraisal.* (Syracuse: Syracuse Univ. Press, 1963.)
Parrington, Vernon L. *Main Currents in American Thought*, Vol. III (New York: Harcourt Brace, 1930.)
Riesman, David, *et al. The Lonely Crowd.* (New Haven: Yale Press, 1950.)
Seelye, John. "Who Was Horatio? The Alger Myth and American Scholarship," *American Quarterly*, XVII (Winter 1965–1966), pp. 749–56.
Smith, Henry N. *Virgin Land: The American West as Symbol and Myth.* (Cambridge, Mass.: Harvard Univ. Press, 1950.)
Taylor, Walter. *The Economic Novel in America.* (Chapel Hill, N.C.: University of No. Carolina Press, 1942.)
Tebbel, John. *From Rags to Riches: Horatio Alger, Jr., and the American Dream.* (New York: Macmillan, 1963.)
Vanderbilt, Kermit. *The Achievement of William Dean Howells: A Reinterpretation.* (Princeton: Princeton Univ. Press, 1968.)
Vanderbilt, Kermit. *Charles Eliot Norton: Apostle of Culture in a Democracy.* (Cambridge, Mass.: Harvard Univ. Press, 1959.)
Vanderbilt, Kermit. "James, Fitzgerald, and the American Self-Image," *Massachusetts Review*, VI (Winter-Spring 1965), pp. 289–304.

Weiss, Richard. *The American Myth of Success: From Horatio Alger to Norman Vincent Peale.* (New York: Basic Books, 1969.)

Wohl, R. Richard. "The 'Country Boy' Myth and Its Place in American Urban Culture," *Perspectives in American History.* Edited by Moses Rischin (Charles Warren Center for Studies in American History, Harvard), III (1969), pp. 77–156.

Wright, Louis B. "Franklin's Legacy to the Gilded Age," *Virginia Quarterly Review*, XXII (Spring 1946), pp. 268–79.

Section Two
Intellectuals and Progressivism, 1900–1918

JOHN C. BURNHAM

Contents

Introduction

During the first years of the Twentieth Century, one of the great American reform movements, Progressivism, grew and flourished. Unlike earlier reform efforts, Progressivism was not primarily political and economic in nature. Presidential candidates, trust-busting, municipal reform, and social legislation such as workmen's compensation laws, it is true, were all claimed by the Progressives. But the basic contribution of Progressivism was the resolution of a moral and intellectual crisis by attempting actions in nongovernmental areas that were more significant and lasting than the well-known political residues from the period before and during World War I.

The Progressive crisis grew out of the social, economic, and general power displacements that accompanied the second industrial revolution and the growth in scale and area of operations of business and industry. For many years morally sensitive Americans had been aware of the social injustices and social corruption that followed and festered in the wake of industrial progress. For some time, an influential minority of intellectuals had claimed that social change was inevitable and, like economic depression, unpreventable, and, further, that in the end progress would follow social inequality and rottenness. Those Americans who were inveterate reformers tried to improve specifics in society through such devices as civil service reform or personal uplift work among the poor.

Progressivism was born from a combination of the moral fervor bequeathed by the Victorian Era, on the one hand, and, on the other hand, the discovery that man could change not only himself but his destiny and his society. The passion for righteousness noticeable in the early years of the Twentieth Century grew directly out of the moral training of two generations of Americans in the late Nineteenth Century. While this sensitivity to good and evil was nurtured by the churches, Progressivism was nonsectarian and, indeed, the churches tended to follow and adopt rather than to initiate the reform impulse.

What was new in Progressivism was a fresh version of the idea that man can deliberately engineer fundamental changes. Many influential Americans came to believe that for the first time they had the power to obliterate poverty, disease, and unhappiness. Nor was their faith merely theoretical; in a single lifetime many of them had seen fatal diseases such as diphtheria cured, had watched technical innovations such as electric light and power transform everyday life, and had talked openly about machines that performed such theretofore impossible feats as flying. Science and applied science provided models for the way in which human effort might manage not only material but social and moral miracles.

The reformers included many intellectuals, and they in turn helped intellectualize a surprisingly large portion of the population. The personnel of the leadership were upper middle- or upper-class people, already closely connected with intellectuals or already within that group. Not only were the Progressives close to the intellectual community, but the chief means that they advocated to effect control and change was fundamentally intellectual: education. The Progressive goal, radically democratizing society, likewise required extensive rationalization and intellectual exploration. No other great reform movement in American history has ever been as essentially intellectual as was Progressivism.

Despite their democratic commitments, the intellectuals and leaders of the Progressive Movement viewed themselves as a natural elite sent to enlighten and guide their fellow citizens. The reformers avowed that their idealism was practical and realistic, and they worked at every level possible through whatever institutions were at hand: government, pre-existing professional organizations and agencies, specially formed voluntary groups, or any social structure through which the elite could shape lives and customs. Clearly one of the fundamental practical conclusions of these consciously pragmatic crusaders was that the promise of American life could be realized only through social means, in society at large. When they spoke of the brotherhood of man, it had concrete meaning to them in terms of both means and ends.

Sources

Progressivism as Ideal and Ideology

William James
Noblesse Oblige and a New Noblesse

(1908)

The idea that the most moral and able members of society ought to look after their weaker brothers can be traced back to the idea of the stewardship of the elect in puritan times. William James (1842–1910), psychologist and philosopher at Harvard and exponent of pragmatism, in 1908 discussed the responsibility of the intellectual to improve his own society in the new world of the Twentieth Century.

Of what use is a college training? We who have had it seldom hear the question raised—we might be a little nonplussed to answer it offhand. A certain amount of meditation has brought me to this as the pithiest reply which I myself can give: The best claim that a college education can possibly make on your respect, the best thing it can aspire to accomplish for you, is this: that it should *help you to know a good man when you see him.* This is as true of women's as of men's colleges; but that it is neither a joke nor a one-sided abstraction I shall now endeavor to show.

What talk do we commonly hear about the contrast between college education and the education which business or technical or professional schools confer? The college education is called higher because it is supposed to be so general and so disinterested. At the "schools" you get a relatively narrow practical skill, you are told, whereas the "colleges" give you the more liberal culture, the broader outlook, the historical perspective, the philosophic atmosphere, or something which phrases of that sort try to express. You are made into an efficient instrument for doing a definite thing, you hear, at the schools; but, apart from that, you may remain a crude and smoky kind of petroleum, incapable of spreading light. The universities and colleges, on the other hand, although they may leave you less efficient for this or that practical task, suffuse your whole mentality with something more

William James, "The Social Value of the College-Bred," *McClure's Magazine*, 30 (February 1908), pp. 419–22.

important than skill. They redeem you, make you well-bred; they make "good company" of you mentally. If they find you with a naturally boorish or caddish mind, they cannot leave you so, as a technical school may leave you. This, at least, is pretended; this is what we hear among college-trained people when they compare their education with every other sort. Now, exactly how much does this signify?

It is certain, to begin with, that the narrowest trade or professional training does something more for a man than to make a skillful practical tool of him—it makes him also a judge of other men's skill. Whether his trade be pleading at the bar or surgery or plastering or plumbing, it develops a critical sense in him for that sort of occupation. He understands the difference between second-rate and first-rate work in his whole branch of industry; he gets to know a good job in his own line as soon as he sees it; and getting to know this in his own line, he gets a faint sense of what good work may mean anyhow, that may, if circumstances favor, spread into his judgments elsewhere. Sound work, clean work, finished work: feeble work, slack work, sham work—these words express an identical contrast in many different departments of activity. In so far forth, then, even the humblest manual trade may beget in one a certain small degree of power to judge of good work generally.

Now, what is supposed to be the line of us who have the higher college training? Is there any broader line—since our education claims primarily not to be "narrow"—in which we also are made good judges between what is first-rate and what is second-rate only? What is especially taught in the colleges has long been known by the name of the "humanities," and these are often identified with Greek and Latin. But it is only as literatures, not as languages, that Greek and Latin have any general humanity-value; so that in a broad sense the humanities mean literature primarily, and in a still broader sense the study of masterpieces in almost any field of human endeavor. Literature keeps the primacy; for it not only *consists* of masterpieces, but is largely *about* masterpieces, being little more than an appreciative chronicle of human master-strokes, so far as it takes the form of criticism and history. You can give humanistic value to almost anything by teaching it historically. Geology, economics, mechanics, are humanities when taught with reference to the successive achievements of the geniuses to which these sciences owe their being. Not taught thus, literature remains grammar, art a catalogue, history a list of dates, and natural science a sheet of formulas and weights and measures.

The sifting of human creations!—nothing less than this is what we ought to mean by the humanities. Essentially this means biography; what our colleges should teach is, therefore, biographical history, that not of politics merely, but of anything and everything so far as human efforts and conquests are factors that have played their part. Studying in this way, we learn what types of activity have stood the test of time; we acquire standards of the excellent and durable. All our arts and sciences and institutions are but so many quests of perfection on the part of men; and when we see how diverse the types of excellence may be, how various the tests, how flexible the adaptations, we gain a richer sense of what the terms "better" and "worse" may signify in general. Our critical sensibilities grow both more acute and less fanatical. We sympathize with men's mistakes even in the act of penetrating them; we feel the pathos of lost causes and misguided epochs even while we applaud what overcame them.

Such words are vague and such ideas are inadequate, but their meaning is unmistakable. What the colleges—teaching humanities by examples which may be special, but which must be typical and pregnant—should at least try to give us, is a general sense of what, under various disguises, *superiority* has always signified and may still signify. The feeling for a good human job anywhere, the admiration of the really admirable, the disesteem of what is cheap and trashy and impermanent—this is what we call the critical sense, the sense for ideal values. It is the better part of what men know as wisdom. Some of us are wise in this way naturally and by genius; some of us never become so. But to have spent one's youth at college, in contact with the choice and rare and precious, and yet still to be a blind prig or vulgarian, unable to scent out human excellence or to divine it amid its accidents, to know it only when ticketed and labeled and forced on us by others, this indeed should be accounted the very calamity and shipwreck of a higher education.

The sense for human superiority ought, then, to be considered our line, as boring subways is the engineer's line and the surgeon's is appendicitis. Our colleges ought to have lit up in us a lasting relish for the better kind of man, a loss of appetite for mediocrities, and a disgust for cheapjacks. We ought to smell, as it were, the difference of quality in men and their proposals when we enter the world of affairs about us. Expertness in this might well atone for some of our awkwardness at accounts, for some of our ignorance of dynamos. The best claim we can make for the higher education, the best single phrase in which we can tell what it ought to do for us, is, then, exactly what I said: it should enable us to *know a good man when we see him.*

That the phrase is anything but an empty epigram follows from the fact that if you ask in what line it is most important that a democracy like ours should have its sons and daughters skillful, you see that it is this line more than any other. "The people in their Wisdom"—this is the kind of wisdom most needed by the people. Democracy is on its trial, and no one knows how it will stand the ordeal. Abounding about us are pessimistic prophets. Fickleness and violence used to be, but are no longer, the vices which they charge to democracy. What its critics now affiirm is that its preferences are inveterately for the inferior. So it was in the beginning, they say, and so it will be world without end. Vulgarity enthroned and institutionalized, elbowing everything superior from the highway, this, they tell us, is our irremediable destiny; and the picture-papers of the European continent are already drawing Uncle Sam with the hog instead of the eagle for his heraldic emblem. The privileged aristocracies of the foretime, with all their iniquities, did at least preserve some taste for higher human quality and honor certain forms of refinement by their enduring traditions. But when democracy is sovereign, its doubters say, nobility will form a sort of invisible church, and sincerity and refinement, stripped of honor, precedence, and favor, will have to vegetate on sufferance in private corners. They will have no general influence. They will be harmless eccentricities.

Now, who can be absolutely certain that this may not be the career of democracy? Nothing future is quite secure; states enough have inwardly rotted; and democracy as a whole may undergo self-poisoning. But, on the other hand, democracy is a kind of religion, and we are bound not to admit its failure. Faiths and utopias are the noblest exercise of human reason, and no one with a spark of reason in him will sit down fatalistically before the croaker's picture. The best of us are filled with the contrary vision of a democracy stumbling through every error till its institutions glow with justice and its customs shine with beauty. Our better men *shall* show the way and we *shall* follow them; so we are brought round again to the mission of the higher education in helping us to know the better kind of man whenever we see him.

The notion that a people can run itself and its affairs anonymously is now well known to be the silliest of absurdities. Mankind does nothing save through initiatives on the part of inventors, great or small, and imitation by the rest of us—these are the sole factors active in human progress. Individuals of genius show the way, and set the patterns, which common people then adopt and follow. *The rivalry of the patterns is the history of the world.* Our democratic problem thus is statable in ultra-simple terms: Who are the kind of men from whom our majorities shall take their cue? Whom shall they treat as rightful leaders? We and our leaders are the *x* and the *y* of the equation here; all other historic circumstances, be they economical, political, or intellectual, are only the background of occasion on which the living drama works itself out between us.

In this very simple way does the value of our educated class define itself: we more than others should be able to divine the worthier and better leaders. The terms here are monstrously simplified, of course, but such a bird's-eye view lets us immediately take our bearings. In our democracy, where everything else is so shifting, we alumni and alumnae of the colleges are the only permanent presence that corresponds to the aristocracy in older countries. We have continuous traditions, as they have; our motto, too, is *noblesse oblige*; and, unlike them, we stand for ideal interests solely, for we have no corporate selfishness and wield no powers of corruption. We ought to have our own class-consciousness. "Les intellectuels"! What prouder club-name could there be than this one, used ironically by the party of "red blood," the party of every stupid prejudice and passion, during the anti-Dreyfus craze, to satirize the men in France who still retained some critical sense and judgment! Critical sense, it has to be confessed, is not an exciting term, hardly a banner to carry in processions. Affections for old habit, currents of self-interest, and gales of passion are the forces that keep the human ship moving; and the pressure of the judicious pilot's hand upon the tiller is a relatively insignificant energy. But the affections, passions, and interests are shifting, successive, and distraught; they blow in alternation while the pilot's hand is steadfast. He knows the compass, and, with all the leeways he is obliged to tack toward, he always makes some headway. A small force, if it never lets up, will accumulate effects more considerable than those of much greater forces if these work inconsistently. The ceaseless whisper of the more permanent ideals, the steady tug of truth and justice, give them but time, *must* warp the world in their direction.

This bird's-eye view of the general steering function of the college-bred amid the driftings of democracy ought to help us to a wider vision of what our colleges themselves should aim at. If we are to be the yeast-cake for democracy's dough, if we are to make it rise with culture's preferences, we must see to it that culture spreads broad sails. We must shake the old double reefs out of the canvas into the wind and sunshine, and let in every modern subject, sure that any subject will prove humanistic, if its setting be kept only wide enough.

Stevenson says somewhere to his reader: "You think you are just making this bargain, but you are really laying down a link in the policy of mankind." Well, your technical school should enable you to make your bargain splendidly; but your college should show you just the place of that kind of bargain—a pretty poor place, possibly—in the whole policy of mankind. That is the kind of liberal outlook, of perspective, of atmosphere, which should surround every subject as a college deals with it.

We of the colleges must eradicate a curious notion which numbers of good people have about such ancient seats of learning as Harvard. To many ignorant outsiders, that name suggests little more than a kind of sterilized conceit and incapacity for being pleased. In Edith Wyatt's exquisite book of Chicago sketches called "Every One his Own Way" there is a couple who stand for culture in the sense of exclusiveness, Richard Elliot and his feminine counterpart—feeble caricatures of mankind, unable to know any good thing when they see it, incapable of enjoyment unless a printed label gives them leave. Possibly this type of culture may exist near Cambridge and Boston, there may be specimens there, for priggishness is just like painter's colic or any other trade-disease. But every good college makes its students immune against this malady, of which the microbe haunts the neighborhood-printed pages. It does so by its general tone being too hearty for the microbe's life. Real culture lives by sympathies and admirations, not by dislikes and disdains—under all misleading wrappings it pounces unerringly upon the human core. If a college, through the inferior human influences that have grown regnant there, fails to catch the robuster tone, its failure is colossal, for its social function stops: democracy gives it a wide berth, turns toward it a deaf ear.

"Tone," to be sure, is a terribly vague word to use, but there is no other, and this whole meditation is over questions of tone. By their tone are all things human either lost or saved. If democracy is to be saved it must catch the higher, healthier tone. If we are to impress it with our preferences, we ourselves must use the proper tone, which we, in turn, must have caught from our own teachers. It all reverts in the end to the action of innumerable imitative individuals upon each other and to the question of whose tone has the highest spreading power. As a class, we college graduates should look to it that *ours* has spreading power. It ought to have the highest spreading power.

In our essential function of indicating the better men, we now have formidable competitors outside. *McClure's Magazine*, the *American Magazine*, *Collier's Weekly*, and, in its fashion, the *World's Work*, constitute together a real popular university along this very line. It would be a pity if any future historian were to have to write words like these: "By the middle of the twentieth century the higher institutions of learning had lost all influence over public opinion in the United States. But the mission of raising the tone of democracy, which they had proved themselves so lamentably unfitted to exert, was assumed with rare enthusiasm and prosecuted with extraordinary skill and success by a new educational power; and for the clarification of their human sympathies and elevation of their human preferences, the people at large acquired the habit of resorting exclusively to the guidance of certain private literary adventures, commonly designated in the market by the affectionate name of ten-cent magazines."

Must not we of the colleges see to it that no historian shall ever say anything like this? Vague as the phrase of knowing a good man when you see him may be, diffuse and indefinite as one must leave its application, is there any other formula that describes so well the result at which our institutions *ought* to aim? If they do that, they do the best thing conceivable. If they fail to do it, they fail in very deed. It surely is a fine synthetic formula. If our faculties and graduates could once collectively come to realize it as the great underlying purpose toward which they have always been more or less obscurely groping, a great clearness would be shed over many of their problems and, as for their influence in the midst of our social system, it would embark upon a new career of strength.

Walter E. Weyl
The Disenchantment of America and Hope for a Modest Step Forward

(1912)

Many Americans had been concerned for some time about the conditions prevailing in American society. The nuckrakers of the first decade of the new century expressed in a sensational way some of these feelings. Here economist Walter E. Weyl (1873–1919), one of the intellectual spokesmen for Progressivism, describes some of the underlying ideas and feelings that surfaced in concern, muckraking, and the whole reform endeavor.

America today is in a somber, soul-questioning mood. We are in a period of clamor, of bewilderment, of an almost tremulous unrest. We are hastily revising all our social conceptions. We are hastily testing all our political ideals. We are profoundly disenchanted with the fruits of a century of independence.

Our visitors from Europe in the early days of independence were obsessed by the unique significance of our democracy. To liberty or to its excesses they ascribed all American qualities, customs, and accidents. Our native apologists laid equal emphasis upon democracy. In half-ludicrous, half-tragic orations, they acclaimed the rule of the people as the essence and import of the new Republic. America was to be the eternal land of liberty, the refuge of the world's oppressed, the mentor of Europe. The chosen people of the West were to teach the true creed of democracy, in obedience to a divine command, as explicit as that laid upon the ancient folk of Israel.

Four generations have passed since Cornwallis surrendered at Yorktown. We have survived the early days of poverty and interstate bickering. We have grown in wealth, power, and prestige. We have issued triumphantly from a great civil war, which put an end forever to chattel slavery. Our institutions have not become less popular; our patriotism, though less fervid, is perhaps deeper; our hope of equality is not quite dead.

Nevertheless, to millions of men there has come a deep and bitter disillusionment. We are no longer the sole guardians of the Ark of the Covenant. Europe does not learn at our feet the facile lessons of democracy, but in some respects has become our teacher. Foreign observers describe our institutions with a galling lack of enthusiasm, and visitors from monarchical lands applaud their native liberty, while condoling with us over our political

---

Walter E. Weyl, *The New Democracy, An Essay on Certain Political and Economic Tendencies in the United States* (New York, 1912), pp. 1–6, 354–55.

"bosses," our railroad "kings," and our Senate "oligarchies." A swelling tide of native criticism overtops each foreign detraction.

The shrill political cries which today fill the air are in vivid contrast with the stately, sounding phrases of the Declaration of Independence. Men speak (with an exaggeration which is as symptomatic as are the evils it describes) of sensational inequalities of wealth, insane extravagances, strident ostentations; and, in the same breath, of vast, boss-ridden cities, with wretched slums peopled by all the world, with pauperism, vice, crime, insanity, and degeneration rampant. We disregard, it is claimed, the lives of our workmen. We muster women into dangerous factories. We enroll in our industrial army, by an infinitely cruel conscription, the anæmic children of the poor. We create hosts of unemployed men, whose sullen tramp ominously echoes through the streets of our relentless cities. Daily we read of the premature death of American babies; of the ravages of consumption and other "poor men's diseases"; of the scrapping of aged workingmen; of the jostling of blindly competing races in factory towns; of the breakdown of municipal government; of the collusion of politicians, petty thieves, and "malefactors of great wealth"; of the sharpening of an irreconcilable class conflict; of the spread of a hunger-born degradation, voicing itself in unpunished crimes of violence; of the spread of a social vice, due in numerous instances (according to the Committee of Fourteen) not to passion or to corrupt inclination, but to "the force of actual physical want." According to some critics—among whom are conservative men with a statistical bent—American democracy is in process of decay.

If we are now scourged with whips, we are, it is claimed, soon to be scourged with scorpions. Our evils, if uncorrected, must grow with the country's growth. If in a century we have increased from seven to ninety millions, we may well increase, in the coming century, to two or three hundreds of millions. In the life time of babes already born, the United States may be a titanic commonwealth bestriding the world; a nation as superior in power to England or Germany as those countries are to Holland or Denmark. It may be a nation spreading northward to the Polar Seas, southward to the Isthmus, or beyond, and westward to Australia. It may be the greatest single factor, for good or evil, in the destinies of the world.

It is this very vastness of our future that gives us pause. It is because in America we are about to play the game of life with such unprecedentedly enormous stakes that we are at last taking thought of the fearful chances of ill skill or ill luck. If today we have individual fortunes of four or five hundreds of millions, whereas in Washington's day we had not a single millionaire, how overwhelming may not be our fortunes in the year 2000, how overbearing may not be the pressure of poverty upon our hundreds of millions of citizens. Already our free lands are gone, our cheap food is in danger. Soon our high wages may be threatened. It is possible to conceive of a progressive deterioration accompanying an increase in population. We have no guarantee that prosperity, intelligence, discontent, and democracy will be our portion.

Today, more than ever before in American history, dire prophecies gain credence. Some foretell the dissolution of the Republic and the rise under democratic forms of an absolutist empire, of a malevolent or "benevolent feudalism" of business princes. Others predict a day of "civil war, immense bloodshed, and eventually military discipline of the severest type." Grave men hope or fear a sudden destructive cataclysm, in which the ponderous pillars of our society will fall upon a blind and wretched people. Revolutionary and reactionary agitators are alike disillusioned. They no longer place their faith upon our traditional democracy.

Even the mass of men—that experimental, inventive but curiously conservative group of average Americans—though voting instinctively, is beginning to feel that in essential respects the nation "conceived in liberty" has not borne its expected fruits. No one believes after this century of progress that the children of America are endowed with equal opportunities of life, health, education, and fructifying leisure, nor that success depends solely upon individual deserts. The "unalienable rights" have not availed against unemployment or the competition of the strongest. Our liberty is not yet absolute nor universally beneficent; our right to bear arms, our right to trial by jury, our right of free speech and free assembly have been sensibly abridged. The slums are here; they cannot be conjured away by any spell of our old democracy. Disenchanted with the glorious large promises of '76, we are even, like our early European visitors, beginning to ascribe all evils to political institutions, and occasionally the unacknowledged thought arises: "Is democracy after all a failure? Is not the bureaucratic efficiency of Prussia as good as the democratic laxness and corruption of Pennsylvania? Are not progress, honesty, security better than the deceptive 'unalienable rights'? Does democracy pay?"

It is in this moment of misgiving, when men are beginning to doubt the all-efficiency of our old-time democracy, that a new democracy is born. It is a new spirit, critical, concrete, insurgent. A clear-eyed discontent is abroad in the land. There is a low-voiced, earnest questioning. There is a not unreverential breaking of the tablets of tradition.

It is not merely the specific insurgent movement in Congress which occupies men's minds. That is but a symptom, but one of a hundred symptoms, of a far broader, subtler, and more general movement of revolt. Men in the Middle West, in the Far West, in the East and South; men in the factory and on the farm; men, and also women—are looking at America with new eyes, as though it were the morning of the first day. They are using old words in strange, new senses; they are appealing to old moralities in behalf of strange, new doctrines. It is not all "talk" of congressmen, for the man who is represented is more insurgent than the man who represents him. There are millions of insurgents who have never been to Washington.

The new spirit is not yet self-conscious. It does not understand its own implications, its own alignments, or its own oppositions. It does not quite know whether to look backward or forward. It is still inchoate. It is still negative.

Protestantism, too, was at first protesting, insurgent, negative, but Protestantism today is positive, plenary, and protested against. So our nascent, insurgent, still unfolded democracy, which unites many men in a common hostility to certain broad economic and political developments, is now passing over to a definite constructive program. It is becoming positive through force and circumscription of its own negations.

As it becomes positive the new spirit seeks to explain itself, and in so doing to understand itself. It seeks to test its motives and ideals in their relation to American history and conditions. Is our new democracy merely the old democracy in a new coat? Is it a return to the past or a turning from the past? Is it an imported creed or a belief of native growth? Is it a high-hung Utopia or an attainable end? Is it a destruction, or a fulfillment, of the fundamental law of American development? Whence does it come? Whither does it lead? What is it and what is it to be? What does it mean, for better or worse, to the common run of us? . . .

We have never had a Utopia, though we have often dreamed that we were on the verge of one. Mankind "never is, but always to be, blest." A perfect state of terrestrial bliss, a lying down together of the human lion and the human lamb, is as remote from our racial experience as is the collision of sun and moon.

The mortal defect of Utopias is that they are too static. The kingdom of heaven on earth is always a permanent, unchanging, perfect, and unutterably stupid place, than which our present society, with all its imperfections, is vastly superior. Utopias break down because they represent attainment, fulfillment. But society does not strive towards fulfillment, but only towards striving. It seeks not a goal, but a higher starting point from which to seek a goal.

Opposed to such Utopias our present ideal of a socialized democratic civilization is dynamic. It is not an idyllic state in which all men are good and wise and insufferably contented. It is not a state at all, but a mere direction.

Were we to move into a democratic, socialized civilization, where misery had become as unknown as witchcraft today; where the people, educated and in process of education, ruled in their own interest both in industry and politics; where the common wisdom of a nation was united to solve common problems and work out a common destiny, we should still be faced by problems new and old. We should carry into the new civilization the tenacious appetites of today. We should struggle along with human frailties, with a residual ignorance, perverseness, meanness of outlook, exaggerated egotism. With the raising of the standard of life we should awaken new appetites and stimulate present ones. Our racial hatreds, our inveterate race animosities, would give way but slowly, so that even in a society advanced in civilization, lynchings and other horrible reversions to barbarism might occasionally occur. We may not hug the illusion of an instantaneous change in the old clinging evils. Drunkenness, prostitution, and a whole series of vices which are but pathological social forms of normal human instincts will but slowly give way. "Virtue cannot so inoculate our old stock but we shall relish of it."

With all these evils we need not now concern ourselves. It will be a wonderful advance in society when our crimes and vices will be crimes and vices of prosperity instead of those of poverty. We may confidently face the new, unknown dangers of prosperity with the powers and knowledge which that prosperity will bring. For this century we need but take this century's forward step. If we can extirpate misery, that will be progress enough.

Herbert Croly
Social Idealism

(1914)

Herbert Croly (1869–1930), author of *The Promise of American Life*, was the prophet of intellectual Progressivism. At the time he wrote the selection below, he had become an editor of the *New Republic*, a journal through which many of the Progressive intellectuals spoke. Croly's idealism and the way in which he proposed to reconcile individual good with the welfare of society are presented in this excerpt.

Genuine individuality is . . . essentially an ideal which does not become of great value to men and women except in a society which has already begun to abstract and to cherish a social ideal. The sacred individual and the sacred community were born of a similar process of abstraction and grow in response to a similar sentiment of loyalty to ideal values.

As the words individual and society, however, are ordinarily used, the value which can be legitimately attributed to individuality and sociality as ideals is constantly being attributed to the merely incipient individuals and societies which are actually participating in the struggle for existence. Both the individual and society are tacitly assumed to be finished achievements instead of formative ideals; and the attempt to define their relation is falsified as a consequence of this initial misconception. The relation between

Herbert Croly, *Progressive Democracy* (New York: Macmillan, 1914), pp. 198–200.

an individual who is only in the process of being individualized and a society which is only in the process of being socialized, is entirely different from the relation between the individual and society conceived as finished products. If both or one be conceived as finished products, the result is a tendency either to sacrifice the individual to society or society to the individual. The interdependence of the two can be conceived only in terms of dependence one upon the other. But if the individual and society are both conceived as formative ideals, which are creating centres of genuine individual and social life out of the materials offered by human nature, then a relation of interdependence can be established between the two, which does not involve the sacrifice either of the individual to society or of society to the individual.

If, then, the progressive democratic faith is to have any meaning, society is not merely a result of the harmony or the conflict of individual interests or wills. It is an end in itself, as is the individual, and correlative with the individual. The individual and the social welfare must both be willed and won from a reluctant world, which, if left to its own action, would go ahead regardless of one as of the other. The individual has the best chance of giving integrity to his life in a society which is being informed by the social ideal. The social ideal cannot mould society to its own needs, unless individuals are seeking to give ascendancy to their own lives. But their interdependence does not carry with it any necessary harmony between the individualizing and the socializing process. Although individuals can obtain a higher integrity of life in a formative social medium, they will never be saved merely as a result of social salvation. Although an advance towards social salvation will be accelerated by increasing individual integrity, society will never be saved as a consequence of the regeneration of individuals. The two ideals cannot become sufficiently interdependent without retaining a large measure of independence.

The faith which a progressive democracy needs does not become effective, consequently, through the agency of individual ideals. It becomes effective through the agency of a social ideal which differs from and is independent of any collection of individual ideals. The existence of an effective social ideal is none the less real because it has no specific habitation as concrete and as visible as the individual body. A habitation it has in the whole group of political and social institutions which have been wrought as the instruments of its purposes; but in spite of this residence, it always requires an effort of the imagination to conceive the social mind and will as possessed of just as much reality as individual minds and wills. The social will is creating an increasing and an ascendant society out of the material afforded by human nature, just as the individual will creates individuals out of similar material.

David Graham Phillips
Education

(1905)

In their efforts to improve the world, Progressives typically advocated education and particularly education of the masses. How could one thus set about changing his fellow man without infringing upon self-reliance and individuality? In 1905 in one of the earlier documents of Progressive belief, David Graham Phillips (1867–1911), a novelist and writer, tried to solve this fundamental problem of democratic reform.

So long as the training of children centred around the slipper and the switch, an ignorant mother was not at a great disadvantage—the best educated mothers knew little. But now-a-days the child of the highly educated mother has an enormous advantage, other things being equal, because such a mother applies science to the conduct of her home as her husband applies it to the conduct of his profession or business.

No education in the mother will compensate for lack of character. Character without education is infinitely better than education without character. But character plus education is the true ideal—and it is attainable.

If we are speedily to enter more fully into the rich promised land which Democracy opens to us, we must have not only the man who knows but the woman who knows. After all, is not our ultimate excuse for being alive that we are the parents of the next generation? And there the woman, with practically absolute control over the next generation at its vital, formative age, has the better of the man. If anything, does she not need the higher education more than does the man?

Education for the men; education for the women. But it must be *enlightened and enlightening* education.

Our national ideal is not a powerful state, famed and feared for bluster and appetite, not a people welded by unthinking passion for military glory into an instrument to the greed and vanity of the few; but manhood and womanhood, a citizenship ever wiser and stronger and more civilized, with ever more and more individual units that cannot be controlled in the mass—the democratic man and the democratic woman—alert, enlightened, self-reliant, free.

Now, there can be no difference of opinion as to the way to this ideal, the way to make the individual capable to work out his own salvation without hindrance from the aggressiveness of the neighbor or neighbors, without

---

David Graham Phillips, *The Reign of Gilt* (New York, 1905), pp. 190–96.

hindrance from the prejudices begotten in and of the darkness of his own ignorance.

Against all these foes, those without, those within, there is just one effective weapon—education.

It is impossible for an ignorant man to be free. No matter what constitutions you establish, no matter what laws you pass, no matter how assiduously you safeguard individual rights and liberties, the ignorant man will still be a slave. He rejoices in his chains, his prejudices and his superstitions. He clings to them. He beats off those who seek to deliver. He welcomes those who seek to bind. He shouts for chains, he votes for chains—chains for himself, chains for others. If he is ever in the right it is because he is mistaken. And you may be certain that a demagogue or other slave-hunter will soon recapture him and restore him to his beloved bondage of error.

This is why the man who aspires to freedom instinctively reaches for the weapon of education. This is why the American people always have had as their dominant passion the passion for education. This is why on the frontier the schoolhouse is finished before the home is furnished; why the washerwoman and the drayman toil to keep their children in school and to send at least one son to college; why our self-made men pour out their wealth in educational endowments; why there are all these colossal public appropriations for schools, academies, colleges, universities.

What is an ignorant man?

Of course there are the illiterates and the almost illiterate. But, numerous though they are, they do not count for much in this republic. They do not decide elections. They do not select candidates. They do not propose and compel legislation. The so-called ignorant vote is not a national or a local peril. It is not a national, rarely even a local factor.

The ignorance that counts in a Democracy is educated ignorance. Sometimes it has only been part of the way through the common schools. Sometimes it has one or more university degrees. Sometimes it struts and preens itself as "the scholar in politics." Only too often it writes books, especially histories, and in the magazines and in the newspapers tells how and for whom we ought to vote. More often than not the very conspicuous members of this ignorant class are full to the overflowing with knowledge, knowledge from books, knowledge from experience, knowledge from travel.

No, education—democratic education—is not knowledge. It is not even experience. Profound, deadly, dangerous ignorance is compatible with both.

What, then, is ignorance?

All its shades and kinds can be so classified as to exclude none who ought to be included, include none who has the right to go free. Is not the dangerous, ignorant man of the Democracy the man who cannot reason, cannot think for himself?

What does it mean to think for one's self?

Fortunately, it does not mean original thinking. If that were so there would instantly arise in the world the most contracted and exclusive aristocracy it has ever known. To think for one's self does not even mean correctly to reason out one's own conclusions from given premises. That would involve an amount of mental labor from which many brains might shrink. It merely means to be able to follow reasoning that is laid before one; to hear both sides and suspend judgment until both are heard; to recognize which is sound and which fallacious, and upon that independent and clear judgment to accept the true, or rather, to reject the false.

A Democracy must breed citizens who think for themselves. Without them it cannot live. With them it cannot die. Hence it follows that in a Democracy education means to cultivate the ability to think for one's self. Democracy means the right of private judgment. Education in and for a Democracy means development of the capacity to form private judgment.

So far as the Democracy is concerned, so far as the equable distribution of rights and liberties is concerned, no education that does not increase reasonableness is of the slightest value.

The education that has for its chief aims, its only real aims, culture, refinement, knowledge, learning, may be useful to an aristocracy like Great Britain, to an empire like Germany, to an autocracy like Russia. But it is not only not helpful to but actually hostile to democratic ideas and ideals. It breeds contempt on the one hand, fear and suspicion and hate on the other—the few looking down upon the many, the many looking up at the few. It makes the powerful supercilious. It makes the weak, whether educated or uneducated, helpless. It fills the brain; it does not necessarily strengthen the brain. It *gives* a man something; it does not compel him to make something of himself.

The truth about democratic education is indirectly recognized in practice more and more as science and its rigidly logical methods have grown in educational importance. All our modern systems of education are based perforce, rather than by design, in part upon teaching the brain to reason. But do we realize fully as yet that for us, for our democratic purposes of self-development and self-government, teaching the brain to think is not only the whole foundation of education, but also the sustaining part of the superstructure?

Irving Fisher
National Vitality

(1908)

Irving Fisher (1867–1947) taught at Yale and was an aggressive advocate of eugenics, prohibition, and other Progressive causes. The concern of the National Conservation Commission, from whose report the following is excerpted, was with efficiency, and Fisher, as a political economist, was a natural person to express this concern. But beyond efficiency, Fisher shows that for Progressives, many of whose campaigns he cites, social improvement involved the idea of a vital and vigorous population.

At the conclusion of his White House address on the "Conservation of Natural Resources," President Roosevelt said:

> Finally, let us remember that the conservation of our natural resources, though the gravest problem of today, is yet but part of another and greater problem to which this nation is not yet awake, but to which it will awake in time, and with which it must hereafter grapple if it is to live—the problem of national efficiency.

The conditions on which national efficiency depend may be classified under three heads: Those relating to physical environment, those relating to social environment, and those relating to human nature. Under the first head comes the problem of the conservation of land, forests, minerals, and water. The second comprises social questions, whether political, economic, or religious. The third covers the study of the characteristics of man himself—physical, mental, and moral.

This report falls under the third head, concerning as it does vitality, the measure of life itself, and the basis of all human qualities. The object is to review briefly the condition of American vitality, contrasted with the vitality of other nations; to show the extent to which it may be increased; and to point out the value of such an increase in years of life, enjoyment of life, and economic earnings.

The world is gradually awakening to the fact of its own improvability. Political economy is no longer the "dismal science," teaching that starvation wages are inevitable from the Malthusian growth of population, but is now seriously and hopefully grappling with the problem of abolition of poverty. In like manner hygiene, the youngest of the biological studies, has repudiated the outworn doctrine that mortality is fatality, and must exact a regular and

---

Irving Fisher, "National Vitality: Its Waste and Conservation," extract from *Report of the National Conservation Commission* (Senate Document No. 676, 60th Congress, second session, Vol. III), pp. 636–37.

inevitable sacrifice at its present rate year after year. Instead of this fatalistic creed we now have the assurance of Pasteur that "It is within the power of man to rid himself of every parasitic disease," as well as the optimistic writings of Metchnikoff and others.

Many evidences of a world-wide awakening to the importance of improving human vitality can be given. Among them are the recent English parliamentary report of the interdepartmental committee on physical degeneration (prompted by the fact that the English army recruits were decreasing in stature); in America, the many societies and congresses to prevent and control tuberculosis, insanity, alcoholism, social diseases and vice, and infant mortality; the growth of preventive sanatoria, dispensaries, and similar institutions; the establishment of numerous journals of preventive medicine, both technical and popular; the increased attention to the subject of health in the public press; the spread of athletics and the physical training movement; the growth of the custom among city people to organize country clubs, and the increasing popularity of golf and similar recreations; the constant agitation and legislation in reference to child labor, slaughterhouses, impure foods, milk supply, and water contamination; the increased vigilance of health boards; the growth of sick-benefit associations and insurance among working men; the efforts toward improving the sanitary surroundings and hours of labor of workmen, and especially of women and children, and, finally, the movement to secure a national organization of health at Washington.

A number of universities are supporting special investigations in physiology, hygiene, and preventive medicine. Some schools also have placed the allied subjects of domestic science and dietetics on their curricula, while physical education is receiving constantly increasing attention. Within a generation every important college, school, and branch of the Young Men's Christian Association has come to have a gymnasium and classes in gymnastics. Research institutions are being established, such as the Rockefeller Institute for Medical Research, the fund established by Mrs. Sage to study diseases of old age, and the Memorial Institute for Infectious Diseases. The home-economics movement is rapidly growing and seems destined to improve greatly the management of American homes.

The practice of medicine, which for ages has been known as the "healing art," is undergoing a gradual but radical revolution. The change is based on the conviction that an ounce of prevention is worth a pound of cure. As teachers and writers on hygiene, as trainers for athletes, as advisers for the welfare departments of large industrial plants, and in many other directions, physicians are finding fields for practicing preventive medicine. There is a still higher stage of medical science than that of fighting or preventing disease in individuals—the stage which has been called "biological engineering," i.e., the study of the conditions under which the individual may reach his highest efficiency. In the development of this science physicians are turning from private practice to public service and are acting as health officers in federal, state, and city governments, as heads of sanatoria and as medical inspectors of schools, factories, mines, and shops. Even the family physician is in some cases being asked by his patients to keep them well instead of curing them after they have fallen sick.

Finally, we have also the suggestion by Sir Francis Galton of the new science of eugenics, which seeks to study the hereditary conditions of human vitality. He has established a research fellowship on the subject at the University of London. Already Karl Pearson and others have made valuable contributions to the study of human degeneration, the effect of tuberculosis on the race, the comparative number of offspring of various classes, and the extent to which mating is "assortative," so that like marries like.

With all these facts in view it requires no great prophetic vision to see that among the rising generation there will be a great movement to conserve human life and health. The power and success of this movement will depend upon the realization of its stupendous importance.

Walter Lippmann
Mastery of One's Fate

(1914)

The most articulate of the really sophisticated Progressive intellectuals, journalist Walter Lippmann (1889–), here synthesizes what political and social reformers learned from the inspiration of science and the teachings of the new psychology of their day. With this authority, Lippmann attacked attitudes of passivity and tragic acceptance of life. Seldom has change or social control been so persuasively advocated.

The Dyaks of Borneo, it is said, were not accustomed to chopping down a tree, as white men do, by notching out V-shaped cuts. "Hence," says Mr. Marett in telling the story, "any Dyak caught imitating the European fashion was punished by a fine. And yet so well aware were they that this method was an improvement on their own that, when they could trust each other not to tell, they would surreptitiously use it."

If you went to an elder of the Dyak race and asked him why the newer method was forbidden, he would probably have told you that it was wrong.

Walter Lippmann, *Drift and Mastery; An Attempt to Diagnose the Current Unrest* (New York, 1914), pp. 264–76.

The answer would not have satisfied you, but the Dyak would have inquired no further. What was wrong was filled with impending calamity. Now, of course, there is no end of conservatism today which is just as instinctive, just as dumbly irrational as the Dyaks'. I have heard a middle-aged woman say "It isn't done" as if the voice of the universe spoke through her. But there is a rationalized conservatism. If you go to an elder of the Boston race and ask why new projects are so unexceptionally bad, he will tell you that without reverence for tradition life becomes unsettled, and a nation loses itself for lack of cohesion.

These essays are based upon that observation, but added to it is the observation, just as important, that tradition will not work in the complexity of modern life. For if you ask Americans to remain true to the traditions of all their Fathers, there would be a pretty confusion if they followed your advice. There is great confusion, as it is, due in large measure to the persistence with which men follow tradition in a world unsuited to it. They modify a bit, however, they apply "the rule of reason" to their old loyalties, and so a little adjustment is possible. But there can be no real cohesion for America in following scrupulously in the inherited ideals of our people. Between the Sons of the Revolution, the Ancient Order of Hibernians, the Orangemen, the plantation life of the South, the refugees from Russia, the Balkan Slavs, there is in their traditions a conflict of prejudice and custom that would make all America as clamorous as the Stock Exchange on a busy day. Nor is there going to be lasting inspiration for Bulgarian immigrants in the legend of the Mayflower.

The only possible cohesion now is a loyalty that looks forward. America is preeminently the country where there is practical substance in Nietzsche's advice that we should live not for our fatherland but for our children's land.

To do this men have to substitute purpose for tradition: and that is, I believe, the profoundest change that has ever taken place in human history. We can no longer treat life as something that has trickled down to us. We have to deal with it deliberately, devise its social organization, alter its tools, formulate its method, educate and control it. In endless ways we put intention where custom has reigned. We break up routines, make decisions, choose our ends, select means.

The massive part of man's life has always been, and still is, subconscious. The influence of his intelligence seems insignificant in comparison with attachments and desires, brute forces, and natural catastrophes. Our life is managed from behind the scenes: we are actors in dramas that we cannot interpret. Of almost no decisive event can we say: this was our own choosing. We happen upon careers, necessity pushing, blind inclination pulling. If we stop to think we are amazed that we should be what we are. And so we have come to call mysterious everything that counts, and the more mysterious the better some of us pretend to think it is. We drift into our work, we fall in love, and our lives seem like the intermittent flicker of an obstinate lamp. War panics, and financial panics, revivals, fads sweep us before them. Men go to war not knowing why, hurl themselves at cannon as if they were bags of flour, seek impossible goals, submit to senseless wrongs, for mankind lives today only in the intervals of a fitful sleep.

There is indeed a dreaming quality in life: moved as it is from within by unconscious desires and habits, and from without by the brute forces of climate and soil and wind and tide. There are stretches in every day when we have no sense of ourselves at all, and men often wake up with a start: "Have I lived as long as I'm supposed to have lived? . . . Here I am, this kind of person who has passed through these experiences—well, I didn't quite know it."

That, I think, is the beginning of what we call reflection: a desire to realize the drama in which we are acting, to be awake during our own lifetime. When we cultivate reflection by watching ourselves and the world outside, the thing we call science begins. We draw the hidden into the light of consciousness, record it, compare phases of it, note its history, experiment, reflect on error, and we find that our conscious life is no longer a trivial iridescence, but a progressively powerful way of domesticating the brute.

This is what mastery means: the substitution of conscious intention for unconscious striving. Civilization, it seems to me, is just this constant effort to introduce plan where there has been clash, and purpose into the jungles of disordered growth. But to shape the world nearer to the heart's desire requires a knowledge of the heart's desire and of the world. You cannot throw yourself blindly against unknown facts and trust to luck that the result will be satisfactory.

Yet from the way many businessmen, minor artists, and modern philosophers talk you would think that the best world can be created by the mere conflict of economic egotisms, the mere eruption of fantasy, and the mere surge of blind instinct. There is today a widespread attempt to show the futility of ideas. Now in so far as this movement represents a critical insight into the emotional basis of ideas, it is a fundamental contribution to human power. But when it seeks to fall back upon the unconscious, when the return to nature is the ideal of a deliberate vegetable, this movement is like the effort of the animal that tried to eat itself: the tail could be managed and the hind legs, but the head was an insurmountable difficulty. You can have misleading ideas, but you cannot escape ideas. To give up theory, to cease formulating your desire is not to reach back, as some people imagine, to profounder sources of inspiration. It is to put yourself at the mercy of stray ideas, of ancient impositions or trumped-up fads. Accident becomes the master, the accident largely of your own training, and you become the plaything of whatever happens to have accumulated at the bottom of your mind, or to find itself sanctified in the newspaper you read and the suburb that suited your income.

There have been fine things produced in the world without intention. Most of our happiness has come to us, I imagine, by the fortunate meeting of events. But happiness has always been a precarious incident, elusive and shifting in an unaccountable world. In love, especially, men rejoice and suffer through what are to them mysterious ways. Yet when it is suggested that the intelligence must invade our unconscious life, men shrink from it as from dangerous and clumsy meddling. It is dangerous and clumsy now, but it is the path we shall have to follow. We have to penetrate the dreaming brute in ourselves, and make him answerable to our waking life.

It is a long and difficult process, one for which we are just beginning to find a method. But there is no other way that offers any hope. To shove out impulses underground by the taboo is to force them to virulent and uncontrolled expression. To follow impulse wherever it leads means the satisfaction of one impulse at the expense of all the others. The glutton and the rake can satisfy only their gluttonous and rakish impulses, and that isn't enough for happiness. What civilized men aim at is neither whim nor taboo, but a frank recognition of desire, disciplined by a knowledge of what is possible, and ordered by the conscious purpose of their lives.

There is a story that experimental psychology grew from the discovery that two astronomers trying to time the movement of the same heavenly body reached different results. It became necessary then to time the astronomers themselves in order to discount the differences in the speed of their reactions. Now whether the story is literally true or not, it is very significant. For it symbolizes the essential quality of modern science—its growing self-consciousness. There have been scientific discoveries all through the ages. Heron of Alexandria invented a steam-turbine about 200 B.C. They had gunpowder in Ancient China. But these discoveries lay dormant, and they appear to us now as interesting accidents. What we have learned is to organize invention deliberately, to create a record for it and preserve its continuity, to subsidize it, and surround it with criticism. We have not only scientific work, but a philosophy of science, and that philosophy is the source of fruitful scientific work. We have become conscious about scientific method; we have set about studying the minds of scientists. This gives us an infinitely greater control of human invention, for we are learning to control the inventor. We are able already to discount some of the limitations of those engaged in research: we should not, for example, send a man who was color blind to report on the protective coloring of animals; we begin to see how much it matters in many investigations whether the student is an auditory or a visualizing type. Well, psychology opens up greater possibilities than this for the conscious control of scientific progress. It has begun to penetrate emotional prejudice, to show why some men are so deeply attached to authority, why philosophers have such unphilosophical likes and dislikes. We ask now of an economist, who his friends are, what his ambitions, his class bias. When one thinker exalts absolute freedom, another violent repression, we have ceased to take such ideas at their face value, and modern psychology, especially the school of Freud, has begun to work out a technique for cutting under the surface of our thoughts.

The power of criticizing the scientific mind is, I believe, our best guarantee for the progress of scientific discovery. This is the inner sanctuary of civilized power. For when science becomes its own critic it assures its own future. It is able, then, to attack the source of error itself; to forestall its own timidities, and control its own bias.

If the scientific temper were as much a part of us as the faltering ethics we now absorb in our childhood, then we might hope to face our problems with something like assurance. A mere emotion of futurity, that sense of "vital urge" which is so common today, will fritter itself away unless it comes under the scientific discipline, where men use language accurately, know fact from fancy, search out their own prejudice, are willing to learn failures, and do not shrink from the long process of close observation. Then only shall we have a substitute for authority. Rightly understood science is the culture under which people can live forward in the midst of complexity, and treat life not as something given but as something to be shaped. Custom and authority will work in a simple and unchanging civilization, but in our world only those will conquer who can understand.

There is nothing accidental then in the fact that democracy in politics is the twin-brother of scientific thinking. They had to come together. As absolutism falls, science arises. It *is* self-government. For when the impulse which overthrows kings and priests and unquestioned creeds becomes self-conscious we call it science.

Inventions and laboratories, Greek words, mathematical formulæ, fat books, are only the outward sign of an attitude toward life, an attitude which is self-governing, and most adequately named humanistic. Science is the irreconcilable foe of bogeys, and therefore, a method of laying [bare] the conflicts of the soul. It is the unfrightened, masterful and humble approach to reality—the needs of our natures and the possibilities of the world. The scientific spirit is the discipline of democracy, the escape from drift, the outlook of a free man. Its direction is to distinguish fact from fancy; its "enthusiasm is for the possible"; its promise is the shaping of fact to a chastened and honest dream.

James Oppenheim
A New System of Values

(1916)

In 1916 James Oppenheim (1882–1932), a social worker turned poet, summarized the way in which Progressive thinking had transformed traditional values.

AND THE GREATEST OF THESE?

Understanding—not faith.
Will—not hope.
Service—not charity.

James Oppenheim, *War and Laughter* (New York, 1916), p. 176.

■ Progressivism in Action

Arthur B. Reeve
Poverty is Treatable

(1908)

Most of the practical effects of the Progressive movement grew out of the discovery that one aspect or another of human unhappiness and misery was not necessary, that preventive or curative measures would be effective. In 1908 Arthur B. Reeve (1880–1936) summarized the inspiring record of what organized charity had actually been able to accomplish.

A poor woman, suffering terribly from consumption, with an anæmic, unkempt child, living in a tumbled-down lodging, was discovered in Philadelphia a couple of years ago. The brotherly love of a relief society furnished her with rent and groceries for many months, but the society at length appealed to organized charity for aid in taking care of the case. Her present needs having been provided for, the charity society began to look up the woman's references. Every one of them proved to be false and the relief society's officers then became disgusted.

"Wait until the investigation is over," cautioned the trained charity worker. A few days afterwards, a chance remark by the little boy led to the discovery of the real story that had been hidden for two years. The feeble-minded mother had wandered from a well-to-do home in another city, taking with her the only child. The family had searched for them in vain. Within forty-eight hours after this clue had been disclosed the woman was back in her own home with a trained nurse, and the child was back at school. Which was the better neighbor, organized or unorganized charity?

There was once a poor wayfarer who fell among thieves on the road to Jericho. Charity, then in its childhood, bound up his wounds and carried him to an inn. Today charity, in its maturity, does the same—and more. It polices and lights the Jericho road so that the wayfarer need not fall among thieves at all; it goes even deeper and seeks to find out and remedy the causes that make men thieves.

Arthur B. Reeve, "The Prevention of Poverty," *World's Work*, 15 (1908), pp. 9872–76.

This is the so-called "new view" of charity. A new spirit of hopefulness has come into it. "Poverty," said a leader of charity recently, "is now believed to be a preventable disease—at least, in a large measure. The poor we have with us yet, millions of them; but there are those of us who believe that we have at last found a way which in the future will reduce poverty to its lowest terms; will perhaps even minimize the personal causes of poverty, such as thriftlessness, drunkenness, ignorance, and the like; will certainly minimize industrial causes such as lack of work, bad housing, disease, low standards of living. It is important to remedy the effects of poverty; but there is vastly more promise for the future in remedying the causes." This is the optimism at the close of the first quarter of a century of organized charity—back to the causes.

The Federation of Charities

Twenty-five years ago a small group of earnest men and women met together in New York to consider why it was that, with the hundreds and thousands of relief measures in the city, so little headway was made. They were asking themselves the same question that business men were asking at the same time, that laboring men had been asking for a couple of generations. The answer at which they arrived was the same as that of the business man and the laboring man. In place of waste and overlapping and destructive competition there must be economy, organization, and coöperation. The result of this and similar meetings elsewhere has been that there are today nearly 200 charity organization societies in the United States—to be exact, 197 in North America and 189 in foreign countries. Each is a sort of clearing-house in its own city for the various allied charitable societies, differing possibly in name but one in spirit and principles; [it] is a veritable "trust to abolish poverty."

What has charity organization actually accomplished? Has a quarter of a century of social service justified its existence? To quote its individual successes would make an interesting but interminable series of human documents. The great, concrete, quickly grasped successes, however, have been of prevention, not of palliation. Let us take some of the more striking, more human achievements.

Poverty a Curable Condition

Twenty-five years ago it was the current belief that poverty was permanent. Today, in spite of all the social misery—perhaps increased social misery—that one sees on every hand, it is the belief that poverty is, to a great extent, curable. The old charity, charity that meant a dole to the poor by a sort of Lady Bountiful, has passed away. Today the new charity is ushered in, charity that is nothing short of ultimate justice to the poor. As preventive medicine is today recognized as more important than pounds of curative medicine, so in charity the new view is that prevention far outranks palliation—always remembering that adequate relief is to poverty exactly what curative medicine is to disease.

A quarter of a century ago thousands of charitable societies were blindly endeavoring to cope single-handed with the poverty evil, each in its own little way. Today they are uniting, strong in the new-found powers of organization and coöperation. From the same platforms, in a recent series of charity organization meetings, spoke Protestants, Roman Catholics, and Jews; Democrats and Republicans; representatives of every race and color; delegates from scores of associations, local, state, and national; expounders of every social theory, from individualism to socialism. The audience was composed of lawyers and physicians, clergymen and bankers, business men and scholars—nearly every conceivable occupation and profession. And not a jarring note was struck. Such a gathering would have been impossible a generation ago. Now, in the face of a common enemy, differences are obliterated.

For tangible achievements let us take New York as the best example—New York whose population in the Borough of Manhattan alone has doubled in a generation, while the greater city has more than doubled the area of the original city. Seven years ago New York was full of "old law" tenements with "air shafts" perhaps eighteen inches wide and closed at the bottom—dark, filthy, malodorous breeders of disease and vice. Today, as a result of the tenement-house reform, begun and kept alive by the Charity Organization Society, one million people are housed in "new law" tenements; they are far from perfect as yet, but they have courts measuring feet where air-shafts measured inches, are open at the bottom as well as the top, with more air, more light, and better sanitation. The battle has only begun; congestion is fast crowding on the heels of reform, but the course is plain and there will be no retreat.

Ten years ago there was in New York no municipal lodging-house; homeless men and women slept on the floors and benches of police stations, or wherever they could. Today, owing to the campaign of the Charity Organization Society, which maintained for years a privately supported free lodging-house, rather to demonstrate the need than to claim to satisfy it, the city has a clean, sanitary municipal lodging-house, the first of its kind in the United States, and a larger one is being erected.

In 1891 the first public bathhouse was erected in New York, in answer to the insistent demand of the Association for Improving the Condition of the Poor, a society closely allied in joint work with organized charity. Today there are eighteen public baths built or building by the city and various charitable societies. So with parks, playgrounds, recreation piers, all of which movements organized charity has helped along by means of committees or by the strong support of its individual members.

Five years ago tuberculosis was increasing throughout the country with ominous speed, and little organized effort was being made to check it. Today the original Charity Organization Society's tuberculosis committee of New York has been duplicated by local committees in almost every city of the Union, with a great national organization sprung directly from it, national and local campaigns of education, popular lectures, traveling exhibits, instruction, and literature distributed by the million pieces. At last tuberculosis is "fluctuating" instead of showing uniform increase. As in the case of tenement houses, the way is plain; and as in the case of the lodging-house, the city has taken action to provide free sanatoria.

A dozen years ago there was but one savings bank in the whole of New York City that would accept a deposit of less than a dollar. Today many do so; several department stores have taken up the idea, and the Penny Provident Fund, a charity organization activity which started this new trend in thrift, has annual deposits of $100,000, in small amounts, at its 300 branches. Every year it is graduating its pupils in provident habits into the larger field of substantial deposits in regular savings institutions.

During the hard times of 1893 there was no place where the poor could borrow money except from the pawnbrokers, where the maximum legal rate of interest of 3 percent a month was the rule rather than the exception. If this winter proves to be the poor man's "hard times," there is the Provident Loan Association, an outgrowth of organized charity, which charges no more than 10 percent a year and is limited by its charter to 1 percent a month. Last year it loaned some ten million dollars to the poor of New York. Best of all, it has by competition forced the pawnbrokers to reduce their rates.

The list of results could be expanded indefinitely, not only for New York but for every city where the charity organization idea has obtained a foothold and enables social work to assume proportions that make it really effective.

How Organized Charity Does its Work

Quite as interesting as the results obtained are the methods and machinery by which an organized charity does its work. Let us take, for example, the homeless man wandering the streets. Suppose he is directed to the Joint Application Bureau of the Charity Organization and the Society for Improving the Condition of the Poor. His story is the old one of a lost grip on life. His present distress must be relieved—but, more than that, he must get a new grip on things. First he is sent to the wood-yard. (The homeless woman is sent to the laundry.) After a "day's" work, which consists of three hours, he receives tickets for two meals and clean lodging for the night. Not long ago one of the critics of this method complained that the wood-yard blistered his hands, but after a few questions he added: "Of course, you see that I am not used to working." If the man is not homeless he receives fifty cents instead of tickets. Later, in either case, he is given the addresses of a number of good employment agencies or of several employees of labor who happen to need men at that particular time. Naturally there are no sinecures given out—sinecures never get as far as employment agencies or application bureaus. The trouble with most homeless men is that they are unskilled laborers—and therein lies the tale of the great need of industrial education in America. But if a man makes an honest effort to find work, he can depend on the charity society to stick by him.

Sometimes, however, a man is unfit for ordinary work; he may be the victim of a dangerous trade, return to which means for him certain death. He may be a man physically or socially "handicapped." For him a Special Employment Bureau for the Handicapped is maintained, to add him as a fraction, if not as a unit, to the sum total of productive labor, instead of allowing him to become a zero or perhaps a minus quantity.

Thousands of cases, of course, do not come to the central bureaus but are taken up at the ten district offices in the city, each having a section under its charge with a population as great as the city of New Orleans. All cases are investigated and registered in a registration bureau. This, as well as the same work among the homeless, is the so-called. "case work." It has been harshly criticized by its enemies and as warmly defended by its friends. Perhaps a better way to express it would be to soften the word "investigation"—it is merely the work of finding out the truth, as in the case of the woman suffering from consumption. "Case work" is absolutely necessary, for relief given in ignorance may be the worst possible thing. Then there is the statistical bureau, in which the experience in a hundred thousand cases in the past is made to contribute to the solution of the millions of the future. It is a sort of social clinic, as necessary to the charity worker as the medical clinic is to the doctor.

The most recent charity development in New York is the Department for the Improving of Social Conditions, which includes the three important committees on tenement houses, tuberculosis, and mendicancy. The work of the tenement-house committee has already been touched on. One of its greatest achievements last year was the killing of several bills in the state legislature that were surreptitiously introduced to nullify the advance of the last decade. The committee has already pointed out the graft into which the city's tenement-house department fell and has helped to reorganize the department.

Though Koch discovered the tubercle bacillus in 1882 and the city of New York did much to check the progress of consumption during the following years, it was not until 1902 that the really effectual way was found to educate the people to the dangers of the "great white plague." That was when the tuberculosis committee was formed. Last year its popular exhibit was shown before 70,000 persons, and in the past five years lectures have been given to 150,000. About 60,000 of its famous "Don't" cards (beginning: "Don't give consumption to others! Don't let others give it to you!") were distributed, and the Board of Health is now engaged in distributing 400,000 more. Similar warnings go to each of the 600,000 school children of the city. By the courtesy of a large department store, which has the advertising rights, the backs of the street-car transfers are used on Sundays for tuberculosis warnings, thus reaching more than a million people once a week. Besides this preventive work, a great deal of actual relief work is being done for poor tuberculous patients. Among other things, the old Staten Island ferry-boat *Southfield* has been transformed into a free day-camp for consumptives who cannot afford to leave the city—the treatment being given at the surprisingly low cost of only thirty-seven cents a day for each patient that can be accommodated—an object lesson in the possibilities of such relief.

The mendicancy committee, one of the first activities of the society, was in a fair way to suppress street-begging when the present police commissioner, two years ago, saw fit to withdraw the detail of police from it. At once New York became again infested with "pan-handlers," ingenious letter-writers, and mendicants of all sorts. But the city has already been educated in a great degree to the knowledge that the stray dime given in ignorance perpetuates the condition that it seeks to cure. The 8,000 records accumulated have also become an invaluable storehouse of information, and the work is now to educate the people to the evil of indiscriminate giving, rather than to suppress the mendicant himself.

It is not enough to better the living environment of the poor, nor to afford relief, nor even to secure work. Habits of thrift must also be inculcated, and this is the work of the committee on provident habits, with its Penny Provident Fund, already described, working through a stamp savings-card system. Moreover, crises in the lives of the poor must be tided over, and this is the work of the Provident Loan, now a separate institution.

It must have become evident to the reader by this time that organized charity has created a demand for an entirely new kind of skilled worker with the poor. Indeed, within the past decade, a new profession has come into existence—a large body of specialists thoroughly trained in the latest methods of coping with the problems of poverty. In 1898 the first course of summer-school training in "applied philanthropy" was begun in New York. Since then this temporary school has been endowed into a permanent undertaking with both winter and summer courses, and the idea has spread to other cities. Hundreds of young men and women have thus been educated for this new calling of social work in the New York School of Philanthropy, the Boston School for Social Workers, the Chicago Institute of Social Service, and the St. Louis School of Philanthropy. Here is a unique development of charity work. New York alone has turned out 600 trained workers.

There is also a library where social problems can be studied by the public, by the students in the schools, and by the volunteer workers, where the records of the past guide the future. One of the most recent additions to the New York school is a bureau of social research, which has been organized among the students for the express purpose of special study at first hand of social questions which have scarcely been dealt with before.

Moreover, a national publication committee has been formed and a weekly magazine is published—*Charities and the Commons.* Into this magazine have been merged several charity periodicals, making now a strong paper which goes to those interested in charity all over the country. Better than that, it is frequently quoted at length as an authority by newspapers and magazines, and thus widely extends its field. It is becoming the great American organ of social service movements, for scarcely a leader in such work can be named who is not a regular, and free, contributor to its success. Last year was added a regular press service to which the most noted social workers of the country also contributed articles, which are syndicated in newspapers throughout the United States—reaching two million readers every week. In every conceivable way effort is made to arouse the social conscience of America to its duties.

One of the great ideas contributed by New York has been the idea of a United Charities Building, where, under one roof, the headquarters of all these activities are centred. The result is that in improving social conditions all are working in harmony and in close touch. So much has Berlin thought of the idea that it has adopted it from America and will soon house all its charitable activities under one roof.

An entirely new field is opened for organized charity in relief following disasters such as the *Slocum* disaster and the San Francisco earthquake and fire. It has been calculated that in the past thirty-six years in twenty-seven such great calamities—fires, earthquakes, floods, yellow-fever epidemics, droughts, hurricanes, cyclones, tidal waves, and ship-wrecks—at least $25,000,000 has been contributed for relief. In every one of these cases, had organized charity been on the spot, the adequate machinery of relief and a small force would have been ready, while behind the local society would have stood the united societies of the country—a sort of first aid in case of disaster. Such was actually the case in the Park Place disaster in New York in 1891, the hard times of 1893, the coal scarcity of 1902, the Kansas, Missouri, and Oregon floods of 1903, the *Slocum* disaster of 1904, the Baltimore fire of the same year, and the San Francisco disaster of 1906. And, in the present winter, should hard times again strike the poor as they did in 1893, here is a powerful agency to meet them.

The Men Who Lead the Work

There are scores of great personalities in the movement. Although Buffalo antedated New York by a few years in organized charity, it has been the latter city which has led the way, and in it many great names stand forth. Above all should be mentioned Mrs. Josephine Shaw Lowell, more than any one else the founder of the society, and for twenty-three years, up to the week of her death, its constant servant—wise, sympathetic, ever eager to uplift humanity by patient labor. She died in 1905, leaving her work as her monument.

In all but five of the years of its history, one man has headed the New York Charity Organization Society—Mr. Robert W. de Forest. He it is of whom Dr. Emil Münsterberg, director of the Berlin public charities, said: "I have come to believe that Mr. de Forest is the true incarnation of American charity." As Tenement-House Commissioner in 1900, and chairman of the executive committee of the Sage foundation and its vice-president in 1907, as president recently of the National Conference of Charities and Correction and of the New York state conference, in scores of ways Mr. de Forest has indelibly stamped his impress on social service.

Dr. Edward T. Devine, the general secretary of the New York Charity Organization Society, the first director of the school of philanthropy, holds the chair of Social Economy at Columbia, endowed by Mr. Jacob H. Schiff, and was also the representative appointed by President Roosevelt to aid in the relief and rehabilitation of San Francisco. The present director of the school, Dr. Samuel McCune Lindsay, formerly of the University of Pennsylvania and secretary of the National Child Labor Committee, now holds the chair of Social Legislation at Columbia.

Outside of New York there are so many leaders that one scarcely knows where to end—Mr. Robert Treat Paine of Boston, who originated the famous phrase, "Not alms but a friend"; Dr. Jeffrey R. Brackett and Miss Zilpha D. Smith, of the Boston School for Social Workers; Miss Mary E. Richmond, the head and heart of the Philadelphia society; Mrs. John M. Glenn of Baltimore and Mr. John M. Glenn, formerly in the same city, who is now the director of the Sage Foundation; in Buffalo, Mr. Frederic Almy; in Chicago, Mr. Ernest P. Bicknell; Professor Graham Taylor, famous for his settlement, the "Commons"; Miss Jane Addams, famous for her work at Hull House; Professor Charles R. Henderson of the University of Chicago; and a host almost as large as that in New York.

Here we have, compressed, the record of a generation of achievement in social service. But more important than achievement, or machinery, or personalities, is the outcropping of the "new spirit" behind all. No one has "glimpsed" it better than Professor Simon N. Patten:

> Our children's children may learn with amazement how we thought it a natural social phenomenon that men should die in their prime, leaving wives and children in terror of want; that accidents should make an army of maimed dependents, that there should not be enough houses for workers, and that epidemics should sweep away multitudes as autumn frosts sweep away summer insects . . . And they will be unable to put themselves in our places, because the new social philosophy, which we are this moment framing, will have so moulded their minds that they can not return to the philosophy that moulds ours."

Ernest Poole
Disease is Preventable and Curable

(1903)

Once thought to be a hereditary disease (it "ran in families"), tuberculosis constituted one of the major social as well as medical problems of turn-of-the-century America. The knowledge that firm programs of control and environmental manipulation could relieve society of the burden of tuberculosis (or consumption, as it was commonly known) was one of the major inspirations of the Progressive Movement. Ernest Poole (1880–1950) in 1903 furnished a typical statement of the specific way in which new medical knowledge inspired social reformers.

The Greatest of Plagues: An Unnecessary Evil

This Plague Consumption is to be stamped out once for all. It has hung upon the earth for thousands of years. It has killed not millions but billions of men, women, and children: more than all wars and plagues the world over. And now of the seventy millions in our country, seven millions must inevitably die of this scourge unless the present ratio be brought down. Each year it kills over a hundred thousand of our men and women, and most of these are cut off in the very prime of life. To women between twenty and forty-five it brings one-third of all deaths; to men between thirty and forty-five it brings thirty-two percent. Most startling of all—to young men between twenty and twenty-nine it brings no less than thirty-six percent of deaths from all causes. It is a Plague in disguise. Its ravages are insidious, slow. They have never yet roused a people to great, sweeping action. The Black Plague in London is ever remembered with horror. It lived one year; it killed fifty thousand. The Plague Consumption kills this year in Europe over a million; and this has been going on not for one year but for centuries. It is the Plague of all plagues—both in age and in power—insidious, steady, unceasing.

It can be stamped out. Its workings are no longer hidden. We know now that consumption is not produced by direct heredity—the tendency alone is inherited. It is produced by infection from living germs, coughed up, millions in a day. Ignorance lets these millions live, spat out on walls and floors and pavements, to float later in the air and so spread the infection. Darkness, foul air, and filth keep these millions alive. Sunlight has killed them in fifteen minutes; in dark tenement halls they are known to have lived two years. Darkness, foul air, ignorance, drink—these weaken men, women,

Committee on the Prevention of Tuberculosis, *A Handbook on the Prevention of Tuberculosis* (New York, 1903), pp. 306–309, 321, 326–28.

and children, and so make them ready for infection. Then the germs, if breathed in, may bring pulmonary tuberculosis—consumption; or if swallowed, tuberculosis of the stomach or the intestines; or if brought in contact with a wound, tuberculosis of the skin or of the joints. These latter forms are most common in little children. They bring but one-fourth of all deaths from the Plague. Tuberculosis of the lungs is the one great form of the Plague to be fought above all others. It can be stamped out.

In New York City a strong beginning has already been made. While the population has vastly increased in the last twenty years, the number of deaths from this cause has remained about the same. Far greater effort, however, is now called for. Dr. Hermann M. Biggs, Medical Officer of the Department of Health, has recently said: "The measures now in force are quite inadequate as compared to the importance and magnitude of the problem. The sanitary authorities, however enthusiastic and efficient, and the medical profession, however influential and numerous, cannot grapple with this problem unless they have the hearty support of the people." And he adds: "I believe that tuberculosis may be practically stamped out." This is said from years of wide experience. It is supported by science the world over. Experience everywhere has shown just what must be done. The time is ripe for the people to act on a tremendous scale. Not hundreds, not thousands, but tens of thousands are to be saved for New York City alone in these next ten years. They are to be saved by attacking this Plague in its stronghold.

The Stronghold of the Plague

Its stronghold is the tenement. Statistics prove this the world over. They show in New York State that in cities of over twenty-five thousand—now swiftly absorbing young men from the country, so making the problem still more appalling—the death-rate from consumption is over twice the rate in smaller towns and villages. In the city it is worst of all in the tenements. In New York City today there are at least twenty thousand in the tenements who are suffering in some stage of this disease. It is here among the crowded poor that the Plague feeds fat on ignorance and poverty, in dark halls, foul rooms, dark closets. It is here that it shatters the home as it has shattered homes among us all. Here it fastens on the bread-winner, eating up the small savings, lingering on for months and even years, so making the greatest of human powers—Love—only a means of infection and death. It is from here that sweat-shop garments and wares of all kinds go out infected to all classes of people. It is here that unceasing danger lies for the whole community.

"The Lung Block"

"The Lung Block" has well earned its name. It is bounded by the streets Cherry, Catherine, Hamilton, Market. It is close to the East River—to open air. It should be wholesome. For a month I worked through it with the help of those who know it best. I went through with health and tenement inspectors, as a settlement visitor one week, as a "fresh-air man" the next. I use this one block as a center, not to prove, but to image what has already been proved all through the civilized world, to image the three great evils we must fight in the tenement. These evils are Congestion, Dissipation, Infection.

That the Plague spreads with congestion has long been proved beyond the shadow of a doubt. It spreads even faster than the crowd pours in. So it is in the block we have taken. It stands in one of the most congested wards of the most crowded city in the world, and this Seventh Ward is steadily, swiftly packing closer. Between 1890 and 1900, the density of its already crowded population increased no less than sixty-five percent. Now it holds four hundred and seventy-eight humans to an acre. The Lung Block alone holds nearly four thousand, not to mention dogs, cats, parrots and one weakened old monkey. Of the humans, some four hundred are babies.

It is a block packed close with huge grimy tenements; these tenements are honeycombed with rooms; these rooms are homes for people. To squeeze in more homes, light and air are slowly shut out. Halls, courts, air-shafts, are all left cramped and deep and sunless . . .

The Warfare Against the Plague

Congestion, Dissipation, Infection! The war against them will be fought on two lines, Prevention and Cure.

Prevention is slow. Foul air, darkness, and ignorance—these must be steadily changed for fresh air, cleanliness, knowledge, and light. It means years of unceasing work ahead: unceasing work by the new Tenement House Department which in one year has made such a splendid beginning; unceasing support of this work by the people of New York; unceasing appropriations; unceasing belief that to save thousands of human lives is cheap at any cost. It means millions of dollars to be spent in new parks, in playgrounds, in public baths. It means big-hearted brotherhood. It means self-defence.

Cure need not be slow. Those sick of the Plague must now be treated "at the right time, in the right place, in the right way, till they're cured"—not as before, "at the wrong time in the wrong place, in the wrong way, till they're dead.". . .

What the Situation Demands

The right time, the right place, the right way, are all demanded. The sick will never report at the right time until they believe they can be healed; until they know we have the right ways and the right places to cure them. These right places must now be made.

Millions must be spent—because thousands of human lives will not be saved for less. Most doctors agree that every consumptive should be taken outside the city to sanatoria. All doctors agree that there are thousands in the most wretched of our tenements who cannot possibly be cured in their present foul surroundings. As one has said: "It is open air, and open air all the time, that counts." He adds: "The Plague is not cured by quacks, by patent medicines, nostrums, or other secret remedies; but solely and exclusively by scientific and judicial use of fresh air, sunshine, water, abundant and good food; milk, eggs, meat, vegetables, fruit; and by the help of certain medical substances when these hygienic and dietetic means do not suffice in themselves to combat the disease."...

Millions must be spent because it is sound common-sense, because these few millions will save to the city countless millions more. Dr. Biggs of the Health Department has estimated that the total loss to New York City alone from this Plague is at least twenty-three millions of dollars a year, and that the loss to the United States must be over three hundred and thirty millions. Why? The Plague attacks young men most of all. The average cost to society of a man's bringing up is fifteen hundred dollars. This loan he returns by the labor of his manhood. Multiply this by the thousands of young men who die each year of the Plague in New York alone. To this loss you must add millions more for the care and expense they require from families or friends or the city, in their lingering illness. It costs each patient several hundred dollars to die. And add still more. For, as was recently said, the Plague, because so lingering and hence so costly, because it attacks most often the breadwinner of the family, is "a cause of poverty out of all proportion to its importance as a cause of death." Wives and children are forced on charity lists.

And so each year the expense rolls up into the millions. We are told that five millions wisely used now for great sanatoria, for more dispensaries and diet stations, for more inspectors, would save countless millions to be lost year after year in the future.

What has been spent before has been mostly useless. Four percent of the tenement consumptives have gone to hospitals—most of them to die, and for lack of room many have gone into the wards with other patients. This four percent has cost the city five hundred thousand a year without proportionate result. "Treble this sum," says Dr. Knopf, "and thousands of lives may be saved annually." Not only will these lives be saved; they will cease to be a menace to others.

Philip S. Moxom
Morals Can Be Reformed: The Children

(1910)

By 1910, when this article was written, reformers were stating clearly their basic belief that deliberate environmental change would improve the world. Here a well-known Congregational clergyman of Springfield, Massachusetts, Philip Stafford Moxom (1848–1923), expressed the relatively timid and conventional view that bringing all children up right would effect social reform.

In all work for the moralization of human life, the workers are confronted by the disturbing fact of large and continuous waste. In the midst of the broad stream of general development there is a persistent counter-current of degeneration. The waste of life is represented, but not wholly comprehended, by what has been picturesquely called "the submerged tenth." With all the good work carried on in the world by Churches, Missions, Rescue Homes, Schools, Temperance, and other reform societies—an innumerable multitude of remedial agencies—there is a constant production of "the bad." I use this term, not in the sense made familiar to us by narrow sympathies and ill-instructed moral judgment, but as one would use it who judges castings: some are defective and go into the old-iron heap to be broken up for remelting. There are the shiftless, the incompetent, the confirmed drunkards, the tramps, the vicious, the unproductive and the criminals of all grades. Not all of these are among the poor; wealth is no sure preventive of waste, and the wealthy furnish their quota for the old-iron heap.

In every center of population, and even in many rural districts, specimens of this motley class are to be found. To some extent, the Church works upon it, and not entirely in vain, but with very limited success. The various enterprises for reform accomplish somewhat, but only a very little and in a very costly way. Society is like a leaking ship. The Church and kindred organizations are at the pumps, but the hold is not cleared. It would seem as if the most important task in which benevolent people can engage is that of stopping the leak. Of course the question will rise, "Can it be done?" Many say, "No." Others doubtfully ask, "How can it be done?" The problem of stopping the waste should be attacked on its least difficult side, and it has such a side. The saying, "The best way to do anything is to do it," is often pertinent, because almost any right endeavor is better than doing nothing while discussing the question of ways and means.

Philip S. Moxom, "The Child and Social Reform," *The North American Review*, 192 (December 1910), pp. 789–98.

Is the submerged tenth a necessary and inevitable feature of society? That is a question which earnest and thoughtful men and women are asking more insistently every day. Whence come "the bad?" They are recruited from the ranks of childhood. Are they the product of heredity? Perhaps to a very limited extent, though that is a word with which we hide our ignorance while flattering ourselves with a feeling of important knowledge. Much more are they the product of environment.

Modern psychology is confirming the empirical teaching of experience that comparatively little change in moral bent, in one direction or the other, takes place after adolescence. The waste begins before that period, though it may not appear until later. Somewhat, but not very much, can be done for the moral improvement of the present adult generation. Nothing is more disappointing than work for the reform of depraved adults. The success of Mrs. Booth in her work among State prisoners is due largely to the fact that a considerable number of these prisoners are not criminals by bent of nature, but through misfortune or even accident. Others have recuperative energy still dormant in their natures, the germ of which was implanted in childhood. Besides, the waste of life is not defined by prison walls.

I am persuaded that, while the reform of an adult criminal or degenerate—who has become such in childhood—is not impossible, it seldom is accomplished. At any rate, every consideration of economy and effectiveness would lead us to approach the problem of reform at the point of least resistance, and especially to turn the belated endeavors for reform into efforts for prevention.

Childhood is the time of extreme plasticity—physically, mentally and morally. Children born in a certain environment, unless they are early removed or reached by positively counteracting influences, are foredoomed it is not putting it too strongly to say foredamned. There is the real grim fact of predestination which, apart from all theories, we are compelled to face. There is a kind of Calvinism deep in nature and human life. That fact indicates pretty clearly what our aim and endeavor should be.

What is the true, comprehensive and entirely wise enterprise—shall I say of the Church?—of society? *Effective moral care for all children from the cradle.* Let no waif escape a wisely sympathetic and sufficiently authoritative ministry. What forms this ministry may take will be considered somewhat at length later. At present I wish to insist on this: that every child in the community should be, and can be, reached by moralizing influences.

There are difficulties in the way of such an enterprise, but none that is insuperable; and such difficulties as exist are less among the poor than among the rich. That is, the sources of waste are more accessible among the former than among the latter.

An adequate and practically universal care for the moral health and education of childhood involves many things, but pre-eminently it involves a method which shall persistently seek out and follow up every child for its good. Such a method will require work—patient, tireless and tactful—and a great deal of it and for a long time. But that is what the Church and all other philanthropic and reformative societies are for, not for play or self-indulgence or even mutual admiration. Besides, all these are working now, and the efforts which they put forth in but very moderately successful enterprises of reform would accomplish vastly more if they were directed to the end of prevention. Formation is less arduous than reformation and it is much more profitable in results.

But such work is expensive. All good work is expensive—of time and labor and money and life. Men will give thousands of dollars for a scheme to extract gold from sea water; there are investments which pay much better in real values.

Let us conceive, then, an enterprise which should enlist all the churches, all the women's clubs, all reform organizations—all that large part of society which is well disposed toward mankind and is engaged in some sort of endeavor to improve life and lessen its waste. Conceive that this enterprise has for its end an adequate care for all children from birth to the beginning of adolescence; that is, to the age of fourteen years. Indeed, this period may be lessened. Many psychologists hold that the bent of a child is determined before the age of seven years. It is now a commonplace of psychology that the problem of moral development and the formation of habits which are the secure basis of sound character can be successfully handled only in early childhood. The mother who neglects the first years of her child's life imperils its whole character and career. All efficacious reforms in society must go back to the cradle and the nursery.

The two great forces which act within or on the child in its growth are heredity and environment. Of the former, with respect to moral traits, we know as yet but little. That there is a physical inheritance is obvious. To some extent, still very ill-defined, there appears to be what may be called a moral inheritance. But *character* is the one thing which every one must create for himself, since it is the product of choices and determinations. If we say that character is the sum total of one's habits, it is still true that one's habits are determined both by his environment and by his own more or less deliberate choice. We do know that bad parents prejudice their children's future. Heredity is so far a positive force in human life that men and women have no right to become parents without regard for the influence of their own condition and habits on their offspring. The progress of the race is continually handicapped by the morally and physically unfit recruits to its number brought in by wholly unfit parents.

Of the second force, namely, environment, we know much more than we do of heredity. It includes all those influences which act upon the child from without—material, mental, and moral. Under the head of environment falls the entire enterprise of education, and this is so large that at last we are beginning to appreciate the truth of Lessing's prophetic words, "*Die Erziehung ist Offenbarung*" ("Education is revelation"). Education has a much larger place even in the animal world than many suppose; for it is now recognized that a good part of what we have called instinct is really the result of an educational process carried on by parents among wild animals. The play of many animals proves to be a schooling of the young in attack or defence or escape from enemies.

We have not stated the whole problem when we say *heredity* and *environment*. There is the element of individuality—a force which sometimes overcomes both heredity and environment. Every child is something new in the world. In that baby just born is coiled up a force which is unmeasured and unpredictable, which will sooner or later confound all the maxims of the father and baffle all the persuasions of the mother. Humanity never gets beyond the possibility of surprises in the form of revelations of what lies germinant in its nature individualized in children.

But the main influence in shaping a life is that of environment. A good environment will overcome the worst, as a bad environment will often defeat the best—heredity. Of environment the chief elements are, *first, the home*. The importance of making a good home need scarcely be argued here. Those who have good homes realize their importance. But thousands of our fellow beings have not and, without some marked social and economic changes, cannot have good homes. Among the working-classes—that is, operatives in mills, factories and the like—certain economic or industrial conditions tend to prevent the making of good homes. In many places operatives are discouraged from getting homes by the uncertainty of permanent employment.

The concentration of people of the same economic condition in cities, where high rents and poverty are in combination, prevents the creation of good homes. In the tenement districts of New York or Boston, how many real homes are there? Or rather, how few? In such districts there exists and increases a powerful instinctive attachment to the crowd. Hence the failure of attempts to ruralize urban people by moving them to the country individually or in groups. They will not stay in the country. The development of the electric railway and various other means of locomotion is opening up new possibilities in dealing with this condition; but the extreme attachment to the crowd must be reduced without lessening the element of good, which, after all, is its root.

The first essential of a good home is cleanliness. This is as necessary to moral as it is to physical health. To this must be added some degree of skill in domestic economy, so that there shall be the greatest attainable comfort. But the general atmosphere and spirit of the home are still more important. Cheerfulness, obedience, respect for elders and regard for the rights of others, are essential elements. Furthermore, it is difficult to conceive of a good home without the restraints and inspirations of religion. Where there is no reverence for God there will be little controlling respect for parents and regard for law.

The homes of a nation are the fountains of its life. In these are made the laws by which it is ruled. Out of these rise the forces which shape its character and determine its destiny. How shall good homes be created? This question leads us back at once to the consideration of individual men and women and the formation of individual character. We are forced to reason in a circle. The child must be rightly moulded so that when he founds a home, it shall be such as will furnish a favorable environment for young life.

But the main point now is, that the home is the first important element in the environment of the child, and therefore the creation of good homes demands the thought and endeavor of all who would work effectively to stop the waste of life and to moralize human society. It is said sometimes that the mother makes the home and that the primary need is of good mothers. This is true, but it is not the whole truth. American homes are suffering today because of a lack of good fathers. Many fathers have abdicated their privilege and abandoned their duty as fathers. They leave the entire responsibility for the care of the home and the training of children to the mothers. However willing the mothers may be to assume the responsibility, they cannot supply the lack of the masculine element in the administration of the home. Children need the father as certainly if not as continuously as they need the mother. "Mother," said a child in a suburban home of New York, "who is that man that comes here to stay over Sundays? I don't like him, and I wish he would stay away." The man was the child's father and the supposed head of that family. If there is truth in Professor Münsterberg's criticism of American schools because of a deficiency of the masculine element in the teaching force, there is more poignant truth in the criticism of some foreign observers, notably English, that there is a deficiency of the paternal influence in American homes.

The second element in the proper environment of the child is a *good school.* By this I mean a school good not only in equipment, teachers and method, but good also in atmosphere and surroundings. The importance of this can scarcely be exaggerated. Here is a point at which an intelligent ministry to childhood can make great gain. Why should our schools, especially primary and grammar schools, always be situated as they are now in the midst of the population which they are meant to serve? Said a headmaster of a leading high school to me: "I would have a circle of kindergartens around the city away from its traffic and noise." Mr. McNutt suggests a scheme which, now that means for transportation are so greatly increased, grows feasible. His scheme is: Put all the kindergarten, primary and even grammar schools outside of the city—away from it—out in the country. Carry the children out every morning and back every evening six days in the week. Give them air and light. Bring them into contact with nature—with the soil and grass and flowers and trees and birds. Teach them the meaning of nature by such contact with it. Get them out of the wilderness of brick and stone and waken the stifled or never-developed interest in growing things and animals. Produce a generation in which the inbred attachment to the crowd shall be changed from a mere gregarious instinct into an intelligent human interest in fellow man and purified into a true altruism.

How much such a scheme would mean for the physical, intellectual and moral improvement of life in Boston, New York, Chicago and other great cities if it were liberally and persistently carried out. The main difficulties to be overcome are the inertia of ignorance and long-established custom and the opposition of unenlightened selfishness.

Equally important with the good school, but more difficult to attain, is *the good city*; that is, a social environment which would tend to elevate young life; at least, would not depress and degrade it. What have we now? A vast amount of unthinking as well as vicious profanity, coarseness, obsenity, and brutality on the part of men in the presence of children. The children hear and learn that which pollutes their minds and makes moral training difficult.

But the effluent force of our coarseness is everywhere. Our walls are disfigured by vulgar and often evilly suggestive advertisements. Our streets are picketed with saloons, and in the larger cities it is even difficult to enforce the law requiring a saloon not to be nearer to a schoolhouse than four hundred feet.

There is so much in ordinary social surroundings which is coarsening and even positively corrupting that the wonder is that life improves from generation to generation as much as it does.

The fourth element of primary importance in the environment of child life is *the good Church*. We are not concerned now with theology or ecclesiastical policy, but with the Church as the institution upon which, next to the home, rests the duty of caring for the religious and moral training of the young. It is immaterial now whether it be called church or synagogue, whether it be Protestant, Roman Catholic or Hebrew, Unitarian or Trinitarian; it is that institution which stands for the inspirations and sanctions of religion.

Today most of the churches are organized and conducted with a view to the needs and tastes of adults. The children have an entirely subordinate place. They are drawn more or less successfully into an annex called the Sunday-school, where they are held in a sort of probation for future adult membership in the Church. If we stop to reflect we shall recognize the truth that the Church cannot do much toward changing the moral bent of adults. It can do much to change and improve the next generation of adults by working rationally upon the children. Why should not the Church change its line of approach to its enterprise of saving the world? Why not for a time let the adult sinner go his way, if he will, to whatever perdition may await him; and spend all our money in a prolonged, intelligent and devoted ministry to the children? Let us not persecute them with exhortations to a piety which they do not understand and would not like if they could; but seek to provide for them that culture in moral habits and wholesome activities and pure interests which will make them good men and women, reverent toward God, docile to the real teaching of experience, and in love with everything beautiful and true, beginning at a time when right habits can be formed even though right principles cannot yet be understood.

These, then, are elements of environment which being good shall mould the children and with them humanity into forms of health and beauty and intelligence and righteousness: the *home*, the *school*, the *city* and the *Church*.

Now let us return for a few minutes to the question of expense. One thing men are perpetually forgetting, namely, that *society must take care of the bad and bear the burden of the cost whether it will or no*. There is no alternative save temporary neglect, and that is more expensive than care. Just as a city, if it will not pay for wise and adequate sanitation, must pay for disease and death; so in the moral and economic realm, society, if it will not pay for prevention, must suffer loss and pay much for very imperfect cure.

It is becoming almost a truism that prevention is economical of money as well as of life. What mean our innumerable Charity organizations and Bethels, Houses of Correction, Reformatories, Jails, Penitentiaries, Police, Sheriffs, Courts, and executions and all the machinery of criminal law? These only partly represent the cost of neglecting to mould and train childhood. Add to this the economic loss in the unproductiveness of "the bad" and those who must guard them. The cost of all these remedial, restraining and punitive agencies is enormous, quite equal to the cost of caring for the primary education and nurture of every needy child in the country. Indeed, the estimate is made that every child in a community not otherwise properly cared for could be saved at a cost in money and labor less by one-fourth than that which is now required to protect society very imperfectly from the consequences of its own neglect.

It is cheaper to take care of the bad at the beginning. It would cost less to stop the leaks than it does to work the pumps. In fact, the cost is already provided for in the money, energy and labor which we now misdirect in numerous and for the most part fruitless enterprises for reform.

But if the cost of a complete preventive system were even more than we now pay for restraint there could be no rational hesitation, in view of value received, in adopting it. The restraint is grotesquely inadequate. Our reforms are only just a little less than dismal failures. A child saved is surely more valuable than a man hanged or a woman imprisoned. Besides, every waif saved becomes a productive worker, increasing the wealth which as an incompetent or a criminal he would waste or destroy.

Let us look once more for a moment at the field. There is today a stratum of society which practically is untouched by any reformative agency. The Church does not reach it. The Young Men's Christian Association does not. To a limited extent, the Volunteers and the Salvation Army and some of the city missions do. The mission Sunday-school, with its day nurseries and free kindergartens, does more. Certain enterprises, like those of the late

Charles Loring Brace in New York and of Dr. Bernardo in London, have been so successful as to point out unerringly the general direction in which we must go. But what has been occasional and sporadic must be organized and developed into an enterprise covering the whole field.

At the risk of wounding adult susceptibilities I must repeat that not much can be done for this generation in the way of changing the moral bent of "grown-up" persons. For good or ill, the moral character of most is already determined for this world. What shall be done? For one thing let the Church concentrate its energies on the children. Today its mission and even its right to exist are sharply challenged. A new crusade for the moralization and salvation of childhood would give it a new lease of life and a stronger power than ever.

The Church stands for the magnificent undertaking of the salvation of the world. Let it save one whole generation and its task will be enormously reduced and simplified. Can it be done? Dr. Bernardo, the founder of homes for waifs in London, out of 9,556 children in a given time lost only 1.84 percent. That is, out of every hundred all but a fraction less than two were saved. What does this mean? The Church prays for the coming of God's kingdom on the earth, and the logic of experience is teaching it that the kingdom of God will come on earth only through the gateway of childhood.

The fate of the world is determined by the influences which prevail with the child from birth to seven years of age, certainly from birth to fourteen years of age. Such is substantially the unanimous judgment of living psychologists. All our problems go back to the child—corrupt politics, dishonesty and greed in commerce, war, anarchism, drunkenness, incompetence and criminality. We know now that much of our labor for the radical betterment of society is costly and fruitless. It is because we are working against nature. We take the twig after it is bent and has stiffened into a tree. We take the brook after it has become a torrent. We take the fire after it has become a conflagration. God is teaching us, in ways made costly by our ineptitude, to *begin at the beginning* and to meet the demands of the situation by conforming to fundamental principles.

George W. Jacoby
Character Can Be Changed: The Adults

(1912)

When psychotherapy, a new area of medicine, was developed, the physicians who practiced it were aware at once of the social implications of their work: they were changing human mental habits, the structures of which character is made. Such a medical practitioner was George W. Jacoby (1856–1940) of New York, whose relatively conservative views are set forth below.

What is to be understood by "psychotherapy" can easily be deduced... Etymologically the word admits of a double interpretation, cure of the mind (ἡ ψυχή, ἡ θεραπεία), as well as cure through the mind.

Psychotherapy differs from psychiatry in that it concerns itself above all with functional disorders, or, more correctly expressed, with functional symptoms and their removal. That these disorders or symptoms, psychically caused and dependent not on organic changes but essentially on erroneous ideas, may be influenced psychically—that is, by the awakening of correct ideas—has already been demonstrated and will be made clearer... Inasmuch, therefore, as psychotherapy removes false ideas and the dependent functional disorders or symptoms, it is actually a "cure of the mind."

It can hardly be necessary again to recall that by "mind," in the medico-scientific sense, we understand those manifestations of the central nervous system which find their expression in apperception, association of ideas, and conscious activity of the will. Just as diseases are nothing else than manifestations of life under abnormal conditions, so, insofar as functional disorders and symptoms are concerned, abnormal conditions are represented by certain false ideas, the removal of which is the task of psychotherapy.

If, furthermore, we remember how intimate are the relations which exist between body and mind, especially between the higher psychic functions and their bodily organs, the brain and the nervous system, then we need but recall the law of psychophysical parallelism to appreciate at once that a beneficial reaction of psychotherapy upon the physical condition cannot be wanting. This does not alone mean that, with the passing of erroneous ideas, the dependent functional disorders must disappear, but it also signifies that purely physical diseases, associated with organic changes as well, may be beneficially influenced by psychotherapy—of course, not directly, but by the devious

---

George W. Jacoby, M.D., *Suggestion and Psychotherapy* (New York, 1912), pp. 209–21, 312–14.

channel of enhancing the confidence of the patient in the therapeutic power of medicinal remedies or any other curative factor which may be employed. Psychotherapy, therefore, is "cure of the mind" insofar as false ideas are removed, and, on the other hand, is "cure through the mind" insofar as purely physical states may indirectly be ameliorated by means of suggestive influence.

After all that has been said, it may seem superfluous even to discuss the question of psychotherapy's inherent right to intervene in relieving human suffering. Nevertheless, we must not forget that there exists a constantly increasing number of learned, half-learned, and unlearned individuals who are of the opinion that the efforts of medicine and hygiene, hence also those of psychotherapy, cannot be made to harmonize with the aims of nature. Applying the law of evolution unrestrictedly to human society, these people say that nature, by means of the struggle for existence, strives to cause a survival of the fittest, but that it cannot attain this aim in human beings as it can in plants and animals, because the science of medicine is steadily opposing its purpose . . .

All of this may be answered by the recognized fact that civilization has completely changed the natural conditions of life, and that, for this reason, the law of development as affecting human society must be materially restricted in its application. The number of accidents occurring as a result of industrial conditions has been augmented proportionately with the progress in the development of technical appliances; nor, despite our vaunted civilization, has the number of those injured on the field of battle been diminished. . .

Material conditions have been so altered by civilization that today life is less a question of bodily than of mental fitness. For people living in a rough and uncultivated land, not yet influenced by cultural development, and for those who pass their lives in a primeval forest or on a lonesome prairie, the natural requirements are entirely different, of course, from those of dwellers in a densely inhabited community. Where the people are isolated and dependent on themselves, they require, in their struggle for existence, well-developed muscles and impregnable health, but where pioneer work is no longer needed other qualifications are essential.

Civilization causes a survival of the fittest in quite another sense than does nature. Our civilization could not persist and could not develop if pestilence, disease, and accident, through which the best cultural elements are often swept away, were allowed full sway. Nor should we lose from sight for a moment the fact that civilization has been the cause of numberless evils which originally did not exist and against which nature has supplied no means of defence. We ourselves can and must provide for such defence by scientific insight into the origin of these evils and the methods of combating them.

It cannot but be considered fortunate that the very same civilization which, through interference with natural laws of life, has been the cause of so many new ills to man, should at the same time place in his hands, through the achievements of medicine and hygiene, the weapons with which these afflictions may be combated . . .

Since, therefore, it is personal interest which bids the human race to preserve the sick and the feeble, insofar as they constitute valuable cultural elements, considerations of an ethical and altruistic kind demand that the same be done for those of inferior worth.

The endeavors of medicine and hygiene are rooted in a soil of altruistic sentiment, which looks beyond the mere question of benefit. Yet medical science does not desire artificially to prolong the lives of degenerated and incurable weaklings. Its aim is to make the weak strong, the sick well, to restore to them the joy of living and of usefulness so they may again fulfill their missions in life. It aims at the recognition and the avoidance of those noxious influences which threaten human health and well-being at every step, and which modern cultural development has called into existence in the shape of new dangers and diseases in no wise ordained by nature.

It aims also, however, to protect the healthy against any injury which might be caused through the physically or mentally diseased. To stand passively by while the helplessly degenerate transmit noxious germs to healthy individuals would no longer be compassion but would be criminal weakness. All that has been achieved by medical science through prophylaxis and therapeutics is the outcome of laborious investigations the justifiability of which can be questioned only by visionary fanatics. . .

It will be unnecessary to do more than refer to the fact that a belief in the miraculous is sure to be a hindrance to progress of all kind, in that it causes a passivity which allows every misfortune unopposedly to take its course . . . we must learn that progress is essentially a question of our own endeavors, and that the impulse which is innate in the human race, to defend itself against evils, whether dependent on our own misdeeds or not, has been implanted in us so we may learn to recognize the laws of nature and adapt ourselves to them.

What can be accomplished by such persistent endeavor is nowhere more strikingly shown than in the remarkable achievements of medical science and hygiene. That we are no longer impotent against pestilence and disease which formerly depopulated entire countries, that infant mortality has been reduced extraordinarily, that the average duration of human life has increased notwithstanding the exhausting struggle for existence, that we are able to trace most processes of disease from their first causes to their final stages and to influence their course prophylactically as well as therapeutically, are facts which of themselves must silence all objections to the legitimacy of the science of medicine, whether they be raised by fanatics on the subject of nature's manner and purpose of selection or by religious enthusiasts. Many an unsolved and apparently insoluble enigma still confronts us; our discernment of the course of disease and of its remedies is by no means perfect, and we still must allow people to die without ascertainable cause; but not even those facts constitute valid arguments for the opponents of medical science.

The weakling alone is discouraged by failure. The physician never is apathetically resigned, but ceaselessly strives onward along the road which his desire to triumph over disease and suffering bids him take . . .

Child-training, however, is not the sole task of psycho-prophylactic treatment. Adults, too, require training—frequently more so than children. Consider, for example, those drones of wealth whose entire lives are filled with outward form and trivialites, whose lack of serious purpose makes them easy victims to the unbridled play of their imaginations. Constituting, as they do, so large a proportion of sufferers from neurasthenia and other psycho-neuroses, they teach us particularly that inordinate relaxation leads to imaginary disorder, ideational diseases, quite as much as does over-taxation through work.

Let us here emphasize the principle that health cannot, as Hoffmann expresses it, be absorbed in comfortable repose with the aid of a drug, but must be acquired and maintained through useful work. When races or individuals, enervated through luxurious living, unwilling to accept further cares or obligations, tend toward "race-suicide" through their need for repose, and, worshipping a morbid feminism, look on hard work as a disgrace, they represent the dead twigs of humanity which have fallen and must be replaced by fresh shoots; they have become useless and must give place to those who, through earnest work, have remained young, strong, and active.

May these few allusions suffice to indicate the unlimited field open to psycho-prophylaxis. These times of relentless, brutal competition in all fields of culture require, above all, combative characters, men of action with wills of force and purpose. Psychotherapy will have an important influence in the production of such characters, in counteracting excessive effeminateness and sensitiveness, since the positive ideas which it arouses exert not only a curative, but also an inherent preventive action. Imagination kept within proper bounds by trained habit enables us to protect ourselves more or less against detrimental influences; it not only guards us from that fear which increases actual suffering or even produces disease, but it also augments our capacity for the enjoyment of all that is good and beautiful. This occurs in conformity with natural laws. Observation of them keeps us strong bodily and mentally; neglect of them inevitably leads to degeneration of the race. This degeneration, manifesting itself in an alarming increase in nervous troubles, as well as in other ways, can be combated only by training the brain to adapt itself to the conditions of life furnished by the intensity of work and progressive culture.

Cui bono? Why put ourselves to all this trouble? Who can be helped by such means? If such questions can still be asked, the nature of psychotherapy has not been grasped. Psychotherapy must stand or fall together with the right of existence of the entire science of medicine.

Randolph S. Bourne
What Practical Course of Action Can a Young Reformer Follow?

(1913)

Those Progressives who became involved in the movement not so much because of professional involvement as because they were touched by the values and ideology of the movement faced a difficult question: how could they act practically and effectively to bring about social reform? One of the younger and more radical Progressives, Randolph S. Bourne (1886–1918), in 1913 explored the life alternatives open to "young radicals."

The great social movement of yesterday and today and tomorrow has hit us of the younger generation hard. Many of us were early converted to a belief in the possibilities of a regenerated social order, and to a passionate desire to do something in aid of that regeneration. The appeal is not only to our sympathy for the weak and exploited, but also to our delight in a healthy, free, social life, to an artistic longing for a society where the treasures of civilization may be open to all, and to our desire for an environment where we ourselves will be able to exercise our capacities, and exert the untrammeled influences which we believe might be ours and our fellows'. All these good things the social movement seems to demand and seems to offer, and its appeal is irresistible. Before the age of machinery was developed, or before the structure of our social system and the relations between classes and individuals was revealed, the appeal might have been merely sentimental. But it is no longer so. The aims of the social movement today seem to have all the tremendous power of a practicable ideal. To the satisfactions which its separate ideals give to all the finer instincts of men is added the overwhelming conviction that those satisfactions are most of them realizable here and now by concerted methods which are already partly in operation and partly successful. It is this union of the idealistic and the efficient that gives the movement its hold on the disinterested and serious youth of today.

With that conversion has necessarily come the transvaluation of many of our social values. No longer can we pay the conventional respect to success or join in the common opinions of men and causes. The mighty have been pulled down from their seats, and those of low degree exalted. We feel only contempt for college presidents, editors, and statesmen who stultify their talents and pervert their logical and historical knowledge in defending outworn political philosophies and economic codes. We can no longer wholly

Randolph S. Bourne, *Youth and Life* (Boston and New York, 1913), pp. 291–306.

believe in the usefulness or significance of those teachers and writers who show themselves serenely oblivious to the social problems. We become keen analysts of the society around us; we put uncomfortable questions to our sleek and successful elders. We criticise the activities in which they engage, the hitherto sacred professions and businesses, and learn to distinguish carefully between actual productive work for society, work which makes for the material and spiritual well-being of the people for whom it is done, and parasitic or wasteful work, which simply extends the friction of competition, or lives on the labor or profits of others. We distinguish, too, between the instruction and writing that consists in handing down unexamined and uncriticized moral and political ideas, and ideas that let in the fresh air and sunlight to the thick prejudices of men. We come to test the papers we read, the teachers we learn from, the professional men we come into contact with, by these new standards. Various and surprising are the new interweavings we discover, and the contrasts and ironies of the modern intellectual life. The childlike innocence in which so many seem still to slumber is almost incredible to those whose vision is so clear. The mechanical way in which educated men tend to absorb and repeat whole systems of formulas is a constant surprise to those whose ideas hum and clash and react against each other. But the minds of so many of these men of position seem to run in automatic channels, such that, given one set of opinions, one could predict with accuracy their whole philosophy of life. Our distrust of their whole spiritual fabric thus becomes fundamental. We can no longer take most of them seriously. It is true that they are doing the serious work of the world, while we do nothing as yet except criticize, and perhaps are doomed to fail altogether when we try. To be sure, it is exactly their way of doing that serious work that we object to, but still we are the dreamers, they the doers; we are the theorists, they the practical achievers. Yet the precision of our view will not down; we can see in their boasted activity little but a resolute sitting on the lid, a sort of glorified routine of keeping the desk clear. And we would rather remain dreamers, we feel, than do much of their work. Other values we find are changed. We become hopelessly perverted by democracy. We no longer make the careful distinctions between the fit and the unfit, the successful and the unsuccessful, the effective and the ineffective, the presentable and the unpresentable. We are more interested in the influences that have produced these seeming differences than in the fact of the differences themselves. We classify people by new categories. We look for personality, for sincerity, for social sympathy, for democratic feeling for social productiveness, and we interpret success in terms of these attainments.

The young radical, then, in such a situation and in possession of these new social values, stands on the verge of his career in a mood of great perplexity. Two questions he must answer—"What is to be done?" and "What must I do?" If he has had an education and is given a real opportunity for the choice of a vocation, his position is crucial. For his education, if it has been in one of the advanced universities, will have only tended to confirm his radicalism and render more vivid the contrast between the new philosophy which is being crystallized there out of modern science and philosophy and the new interpretations of history and ethics, and the obscurantist attitude of so many of our intellectual guardians. The youth, ambitious and aggressive, desires an effective and serviceable career, yet every career open to him seems a compromise with the old order. If he has come to see the law as an attempt to fit immutable principles of social action on a dynamic and ever-growing society; if he has come to see the church as an organization working along the lines of greatest spiritual resistance, preaching a personal where the world is crying for a social gospel; if he has come to see higher education as an esoteric institution of savants, only casually reaching down to touch the mass of people with their knowledge and ideas; if he has come to see business as a clever way of distributing unearned wealth, and the levying of a refined tribute on the propertyless workers; if he has come to see the press as devoted to bolstering up all these institutions in their inefficiency and inertia; if he has caught this radical vision of the social institutions about him, he will find it hard to fit neatly into any of them and let it set its brand upon him. It would seem to be a treason not only to society but to his own best self. He would seem to have become one of the vast conspiracy to keep things as they are. He has spent his youth, perhaps, in studying things as they are in order to help in changing them into things as they ought to be, but he is now confronted with the question how the change can be accomplished, and how he can help in that accomplishment.

The attempt to answer these questions seems at first to bring him to a deadlock and to inhibit all his powers. He desires self-development and self-expression, and the only opportunities offered him seem to be ways of life and training that will only mock the best social ideals that he has. This is the dilemma of latter-day youth, and it is a dilemma which is new and original to our own age. Earnest men and women have always had before them the task of adjusting themselves to this world, of "overcoming the world," but the proper method has always been found in withdrawing from it altogether, or in passing through it with as little spot and blemish as possible, not in plunging into its activity and attempting to subjugate it to one's ideals. Yet this is the task that the young radical sets for himself. Subjugation without compromise! But so many young men and women feel that this is impossible. Confident of their sincerity, yet distrustful of their strength, eager yet timorous, they stand on the brink, longing to serve, but not knowing how, and too likely, through their distrust and fears, to make a wreck of their whole lives. They feel somehow that they have no right to seek their own welfare or the training of their own talents until they have paid that service to society which they have learned is its due.

It does not do to tell them that one of their best services will be that training. They demand some more direct way of influencing their fellows, some short road to radical activity. It would be good for them to know that they cannot hope to accomplish very much in radiating their ideals without the skill and personality which gives impetus to that radiation. Goodwill alone has little efficacy. For centuries well-wishers of men have shown a touching faith in the power of pure ideals to propagate themselves. The tragic failures of the beginnings of the social movement itself were largely due to this belief. Great efforts ended only in sentimentality. But we have no intention now that the fund of intellectual and spiritual energy liberated by radical thought in the younger generation shall die away in such ineffective efforts. To radiate influence, one's light must shine before men, and it must glow, moreover, with a steady and resolute flame, or men will neither see nor believe the good works that are being done.

It would be an easy way out of the dilemma if we could all adopt the solution of Kropotkin, the Russian radical writer, and engage in radical journalism. This seems to be the most direct means of bringing one's ideals to the people, to be a real fighter on the firing line. It is well to remember, however, that a weak propagandist is a hindrance rather than an assistance, and that the social movement needs the best of talent, and the skill. This is a challenge to genius, but it is also a reminder that those who fight in other ranks than the front may do as valiant and worthy service. One of the first lessons the young radical has to learn is that influence can be indirect as well as direct, and will be strongest when backed by the most glowing personality. So that self-cultivation becomes almost a duty, if one wants to be effective towards the great end. And not only personality but prestige; for the prestige of the person from whom ideals come is one of the strongest factors in driving home those ideas to the mind of the hearer and making them a motive force in his life. Vested interests do not hesitate to make use of the services of college presidents and other men of intellectual prestige to give their practices a philosophic support; neither should radicals disdain, as many seem to disdain, the use of prestige as a vantage-ground from which to hurl their dogmas. Even though Kropotkin himself deprecated his useless learning, his scientific reputation has been a great factor in spreading his radical ideas.

It is the fashion among some radicals to despise the applause of the conventional, unthinking mass, and scorn any success which has that appreciation as an ingredient. But this is not the way to influence that same crass, unthinking mass or convert it to one's doctrines. It is to alienate at the beginning the heathen to whom the gospel is being brought. And even the radical has the right to be wise as a serpent and harmless as a dove. He must see merely that his distinctiveness is based on real merit and not, as many reputations are, on conformity to an established code. Scientific research, engineering, medicine, and any honest craft, are vocations where it is hard to win prestige without being socially productive; their only disadvantage lies in the fact that their activity does not give opportunity for the influence of the kind the radical wishes to exert. Art, literature, and teaching are perilous; the pressures to conform are deadly, but the triumphs of individuality splendid. For one's daily work lies there directly in the line of impressing other minds. The genius can almost swing the lash over men's spirits, and form their ideas for them; he combines enormous prestige with enormous direct influence. Law, the ministry, and business seem to be peculiarly deadly; it is hard to see how eminence can be attained in those professions except at the cost of many of one's social ideals.

The radical can thus choose his career with full knowledge of the social possibilities. Where he is forced by economic necessity to engage in distasteful and unsocial work, he may still leave no doubt, in the small realm he does illuminate, as to his attitude and his purpose, his enthusiasm and his hope. For all his powers and talents can be found to contribute something; fusing together they form his personality and create his prestige, and it is these that give the real impetus and the vital impulse that drive one's beliefs and ideals into the hearts of other men. If he speaks, he will be listened to, for it is faith and not doubt that men strain their ears to hear. It is the believing word that they are eager to hear. Let the social faith be in a youth, and it will leak out in every activity of his life, it will permeate his words and color his deeds. The belief and the vision are the essentials; these given, there is little need for him to worry how he may count in society. He will count in spite of himself. He may never know just how he is counting, he may never hear the reverberations of his own personality in others, but reverberate it will, and the timbre and resonance will be in proportion to the quality and power of that vision.

The first concrete duty of every youth to whom social idealism is more than a phrase is to see that he is giving back to society as much as or more than he receives, and, moreover, that he is a nourisher of the common life and not a drain upon its resources. This was Tolstoy's problem, and his solution to the question—"What is to be done?"—was—"Get off the other fellow's back!" His duty, he found, was to arrange his life so that the satisfaction of his needs did not involve the servitude or the servility of any of his fellow men; to do away with personal servants, and with the articles of useless luxury whose production meant the labor of thousands who might otherwise have been engaged in some productive and life-bringing work; to make his own living either directly from the soil, or by the cooperative exchange of services, in professional, intellectual, artistic, or handicraft labor. Splendidly sound as this solution is, both ethically and economically, the tragic fact remains that so inextricably are we woven into the social web that we cannot live except in some degree at the expense of somebody else, and that somebody is too often a man, woman, or even little child who gives grudgingly, painfully, a stint of labor that we may enjoy. We do not see the labor and the pain, and with easy hearts and quiet consciences we enjoy what we can of the good things of life; or, if we see the truth, as Tolstoy saw it, we still fancy, like him, that we have it in our power to escape the curse by simple living and our own labor. But the very food we eat, the clothes we wear, the simplest necessities of life with which we provide ourselves, have their roots somewhere, somehow, in exploitation and injustice. It is a cardinal necessity of the social system under which we live that this should be so, where the bulk of the work of the world is done, not for human use and happiness, but primarily and directly for the profits of masters and owners. We are all tainted with the original sin; we cannot escape our guilt. And we can be saved out of it only by the skill and enthusiasm which we show in our efforts to change things. We cannot help the poisonous soil from which our sustenance springs, but we can be laboring mightily at agitating that soil, ploughing it, turning it, and sweetening it, against the day when new seed will be planted and a fairer fruitage be produced.

The solution of these dilemmas of radical youth will, therefore, not come from a renunciation of the personality or a refusal to participate actively in life. Granted the indignation at our world as it is, and the vision of the world as it might and ought to be, both the heightening of all the powers of the personality and a firm grappling with some definite work-activity of life are necessary to make that indignation powerful and purging, and to transmute that vision into actual satisfaction for our own souls and those of our fellows. It is a fallacy of radical youth to demand all or nothing, and to view every partial activity as compromise. Either engage in something that will bring revolution and transformation all at one blow, or do nothing, it seems to say. But compromise is really only a desperate attempt to reconcile the irreconcilable. It is not compromise to study to understand the world in which one lives, to seek expression for one's inner life, to work to harmonize it and make it an integer, nor is it compromise to work in some small sphere for the harmonization of social life and the relations between men who work together, a harmonization that will bring democracy into every sphere of life, industrial and social.

Radical youth is apt to long for some supreme sacrifice and feels that a lesser surrender is worth nothing. But better than sacrifice is efficiency! It is absurd to stand perplexedly waiting for the great occasion, unwilling to make the little efforts and test the little occasions, and unwilling to work at developing the power that would make those occasions great. Of all the roads of activity that lie before the youth at the threshold of life, one paramount road must be taken. This fear that one sees so often in young people, that, if they choose one of their talents or interests or opportunities of influence and make themselves in it "competent ones of their generation," they must slaughter all the others, is irrational. It is true that the stern present demands singleness of purpose and attention. A worthy success is impossible today if the labor is divided among many interests. In a more leisurely time, the soul could encompass many fields, and even today the genius may conquer and hold at once many spiritual kingdoms. But this is simply a stern challenge to us all to make ourselves geniuses. For serious and sincere as the desire of radical youth may be to lead the many-sided life, a life without a permanent core of active and productive interest, of efficient work in the world, leads to dilettantism and triviality. Such efficient work, instead of killing the other interests of life, rather fertilizes them and makes them in turn enrich the central activity. Instead of feeding on their time, it actually creates time for the play of the other interests, which is all the sweeter for its preciousness.

Interpretations

The Levels of Progressive Thought

The following selections represent a second look at Progressivism by scholars of a later period. Because the movement did involve both intellectuals and intellectual arguments about how to carry out social reforms without diminishing the maintenance of other values, historians have taken a special interest in Progressivism. Here Vernon L. Parrington, a classic literary historian who lived through the Progressive era, suggests in posthumously published lecture notes that the movement, expressed through novels dealing with social problems, represented a surprising deviation in development. Three historians from the 1960's then discuss the types of thinking that contributed to the development of the Progressive impulse. Each writer attempts to place the basis of Progressive thought in the society from which it sprang.

Vernon L. Parrington
Progressivism an Unexpected Twist

(1930)

No sooner was naturalism fairly under way than it was well-nigh submerged under a wave of social speculation and inquiry. The years 1903–1917 were a distinctive period—a time of extraordinary ferment, when America was seeking to readjust her ideals and institutions to a revolutionary economic order that had come upon her. The popular phase was revealed in the muck-

---

Vernon Louis Parrington, *Main Currents in American Thought*, Volume III, pp. 346–51,

raking movement, a movement which instructed the American middle class in certain elements of economics—particularly the close connection between economics and politics. But underneath, an intellectual revolution was in progress, setting steadily towards a new social philosophy. The old America had been intensely conservative, naïvely provincial and self-satisfied, compassed by a complacence founded on optimism—the gospel of the business man. The new America was eager and hopeful, impatient to square institutions to the new conditions. The total movement was profoundly democratic—a new Jacksonianism rising in protest against a menacing plutocracy.

1. *The Movement of Criticism.* The work of a vigorous social idealism. Passed through three broad phases:

a) Political. The movement of Progressivism, 1903–1912. An attempt to democratize the machinery of government to the end that the will of the majority shall prevail. Its impulse and much of its program came from Populism; and it resulted in a clarification of the issue between republicanism and democracy. An attack on the representative system and the checks and balances of the Fathers. It gave rise to a critical examination of the spirit and purpose of the Constitution.

b) Economic. A growing conviction that talk of political democracy is futile except in so far as it leads to economic democracy. That power is economic in origin and that those who control the economics will control the government. The gospel of economic determinism. Certain conclusions emerged:

1) That capitalism is no longer competitive but monopolistic.
2) That *laissez-faire*ism no longer suffices.
3) That centralization has submerged the individual citizen; that he is impotent before the leviathan corporation; and that henceforth the struggle is to be between organized groups for the control of the state.

c) Literary. An examination and rejection of traditional literary and cultural ideas. An attack upon:

1) Puritan reticence and smug respectability.
2) Middle-class optimism and sentimentality.

Led by H. L. Mencken, Ludwig Lewisohn, and the younger intellectuals. The bias aristocratic.

2. *The Incoming of Old-World Thought.* The breaking-down of the older provincialism and the reception of new ideas.

a) The philosophy of collectivism. Derived chiefly from Germany and England; largely Marxian and Fabian. The conviction that the state must absorb the trust. Later the appearance of syndicalism and guild socialism, based on a distrust of the bureaucratic, omnicompetent state. Anarchism has remained alien in spirit.

b) The new aristocracy. A reversion from an easy-going Jacksonianism based on the doctrine of equalitarianism. A direct denial of that doctrine and the theory of leadership. In business the doctrine of the expert and the rule of efficiency. In philosophy the doctrine of the intellectual aristocrat—a suggestion of Nietzsche and the will to power. Thus Mencken joins hands with Judge Gary in upholding the ethics of the strong. The total result an effective denial of our traditional ideal of democracy.

c) The problem novel. All this ferment entered into literature, tyrannizing in its insistence. Old forms became old-fashioned overnight. The novel was so useful that it was drafted by the new crusading enthusiasm. Romance and naturalism alike were swept away; the political novel and the economic novel took their place to arouse public opinion to action. It was the glorification of propaganda. Except for James Branch Cabell and Edith Wharton not a writer escaped. There is something pathetic in the way the harmless bleating romantics were dragged at the chariot wheels of social problems. Booth Tarkington, Mary Johnston, Winston Churchill, William Allen White, were sacrificed equally with potential naturalists like Robert Herrick, Upton Sinclair, and Ernest Poole. Their careers may be seen from Churchill, Poole, and Herrick.

1) Winston Churchill. [The most representative of the spirit of Progressivism.] A conscientious middle-class romantic. Churchill was a faithful reflector of middle-class movements. His work falls into three phases:

(a) *Romantic historical tales. Richard Carvel* (1899) the type of Cavalier romance. A blend of Thackeray's *Henry Esmond* and *The Virginians*, John Paul Jones added for extra historical flavor. A double background: (1) the old South of the Revolution with a Loyalist villain and a patriot hero; (2) the London of Brooks Club and a gaming aristocracy, with Charles Fox. The heroine another edition of Beatrix Esmond the hero another Henry Esmond. *The Crisis* (1910) a romance of the borderland of the Civil War: a fire-eating Southern heroine and a sober Yankee-Puritan hero. *The Crossing* (1904) a romance of the settlement of the Inland Empire. A theme not yet adequately dealt with in American fiction. The story breaks in two: the first half Churchill's best work in romance; the last half his worst.

(b) *Political novels.* Coincided with the rise of the Progressive movement. *Coniston* (1906) a study of the legislative boss in New Hampshire. A reflection of his experience in the state legislature. How the "interests," and in particular the railroads, manage to put their bills through. Jethro Boss sells political control to the highest bidder.

Mr. Crewe's Career (1908): the same theme a generation later. Consolidation of the railroads has brought about absentee dictatorship of state politics. The boss has removed to New York and manages the legislature through his local lawyer. The philosophy of big-business prosperity rests on property rights, held in trusteeship by the corporations that fill the empty dinner pails, make and unmake business confidence. The revolt of the younger generation —Austen Vane and Victoria Flint, in whom stirs a new social conscience.

(c) *Economic novels.* Began with *The Inside of the Cup* (1913), a venture in higher criticism and social interpretation. So compare *Robert Elsmere* (1888). An attack on old dogmas and an attempt to discovery the democratic springs of Christianity. The clash between the reborn Son of God and an unregenerate society, and the need to establish the Kingdom of God in this world. The church today controlled by business subscriptions. The solution to be sought in a free pulpit, supported by the common people, preaching a new social Christianity.

A Far Country (1915), a study in the emptiness of the profit motive. A background of banking—J. P. Morgan and Company. The dissatisfaction of the prodigal son who has wasted his intellectual and moral patrimony—the lawyer who sells his brain to rise and loses the things that make life worth while. His conversion brings the call to self-education.

The Dwelling Place of Light (1917), a study of the blighting effect of industrialism on the native Yankee stock that has failed to rise into the exploiting class. The restlessness of modern life due to the failure of normal instincts to find satisfaction in daily existence—an emptiness due to loss of beauty, freedom, creative craftsmanship. The search for compensation brings death and not life. A background of the Lawrence strike and syndicalism.

2) *Robert Herrick.* The most promising of the potential naturalists. An intellectual fascinated by the crude materialism of Chicago in the late nineties. Suffered from the inhibitions of a Puritan idealism; the problems of this raw world cried aloud for solution—the woman question, the labor question, the problem of the professions—and warped him away from naturalism, making him an easy victim of the new social enthusiasm. The key to his thought—economic determinism.

The Memoirs of an American Citizen (1905). His best work and the nearest approach to naturalism. A detailed study of the American business man—the captain of industry who rises in a competitive society by his own will. The competitive order, he perceives, requires an ethics different from the Christian ideal. The survival of the fittest means the survival of the strongest, the most cunning and unscrupulous. The realist who deals with facts discovers that he lives in a world of pigs—little pigs of the village, larger hogs of the city. To get in the trough a man must have fingers and toes and use them. The world belongs to the strong. That which gives dignity is bigness: the larger the hog, the more imposing. Little business is dirty and petty, but big business may become poetic. To grind a mess of sausages is messy, but to provide sausages for every breakfast table in America is grandiose. To realize his ambition Van Harrington plays fast and loose with conventional ethics, but unlike Frank Cowperwood he seeks a new ethics. As a superman his work will be justified by its creativeness, by its service to humanity.

A Life for a Life (1910). In certain other of his work Herrick betrays naturalistic tendencies, notably in *The Web of Life* (1900), where he considers the problem of social complexity and how it binds the life of men and women and determines their fate. But in *A Life for a Life* he surrenders wholly to the problem. His theme is how the predatory egoism of the profit struggle may be cured, and he presents alternative solutions: syndicalism and Christianity. The cure lies in individual self-conquest—breaking through the web of "things as they are" and choosing life instead of power.

Herrick was on the threshold of naturalism. He felt the complexity of life and the determining force of that complexity; but he failed to achieve the attitude of objectivity.

3) Ernest Poole. *The Harbor* (1915). The culmination of the novel of naturalistic propaganda and the most widely read. A dramatic record of a changing industrial order, traced through three stages: (1) The old world of small competitive business that is dead; (2) The present world of corporation control; (3) The world of syndicalistic control that struggles to be born.

Against this changing world stands the young idealist troubled in his loyalties, who sets up different gods to worship: (1) The idol of art—aloofness from the mass struggle; (2) The idol of efficiency by the supermen who rule in trusteeship; (3) The idol of mass solidarity and workers' control—the conclusion that is on the dawn of realization: "The world for all the workers." *Conclusion.* The ferment of social thought, shot through with Marxianism, familiarized the American novelists with one doctrine important for the naturalist—the doctrine of economic determinism. In none of them did it pass over into a larger conception of philosophical determinism, and this sets the limitation to their naturalism. The common zeal for reform or revolution, moreover, kept them from objectivity. In none is there the calm detachment and the amoral presentation of material without which naturalism sinks into propaganda. Their position presupposes a large confidence in individual initiative—a confidence in the power of men to alter the world they live in. It is admirable, but it is not the way of the naturalists, who do not seek to change what they regard as an essentially unresponsive world that changes only after its own way.

John C. Burnham
The Paradigm of Progressive Thinking

(1960)

Recent interpretations have made the progressive movement of the pre-1917 era one of the most interesting topics in American history. Much of this new scholarship represents the search of modern liberals for their own political identity. Currently a more thoroughgoing reinterpretation is being undertaken by a group of historians who are studying *social control* as the Progressives visualized it and put it into action.[1] This latest research on Progressivism ranges far beyond what is essentially political history.

A study of the two professions dealing with the human psyche, psychiatry and psychology, before World War I, contributes to a broader view of Progressivism by suggesting the hypothesis that the Progressive movement was not limited to politics, economics and social philosophy, but pervaded all of the endeavors of middle-class Americans. If the physicians and scientists of the mind were prototypical, an examination of the rest of national life—as it is ordinarily subdivided—will also show that early twentieth-century Americans in their occupations and other social capacities operated on "Progressive" assumptions or at least were aware of the relevance of their activities to "Progressive" ends.[2] The basis for the hypothesis is the striking fact that

---

John C., Burnham, "Psychiatry, Psychology, and the Progressive Movement," *American Quarterly*, XII, No. 4, pp. 457–65 (Winter, 1960), by permission of the University of Pennsylvania, publisher, and the author.

[1] For a partial treatment of social control, see Stow Persons, *American Minds, A History of Ideas* (New York: Henry Holt & Co., 1958), chap. XXV, and Henry F. May, *The End of American Innocence, A Study of the First Years of Our Own Time, 1912–1917* (New York: Alfred A. Knopf, 1959), pp. 154–58.

[2] Each area also had its conservatives analogous to Aldrich and Taft.

reformers in psychiatry and psychology shared with reformers in politics and economics a set of social assumptions that indentified them all as Progressives.

From the more traditional research on the subject we already know the suppositions of Progressivism. The essence of the movement was the "firm belief that to a considerable degree man could make and remake his own world."[3] Although the Progressives did not all believe that man is inherently good, they agreed at least that the human being is malleable. The responsibility for the ills of the world rested, therefore, largely or entirely upon the social environment in which the individual lived.[4] Although modern environmentalism grew out of Darwinian thinking, the Progressives believed that man could change his own environment and so reconstruct both societies and individuals.[5]

The most elusive element in the basic social thinking of the Progressives was—who should tamper with the environment and so foreordain the fates of his fellow men? It turned out, inevitably, that the Progressives themselves were to be the self-appointed arbiters of man's destiny. They were able, literate and largely professional groups, accustomed to the role of leadership and, like Theodore Roosevelt, unafraid of it.[6]

The Progressives were consciously motivated by altruism. Direction was to come from the Man of Good Will who had transcended his own interests; he governed by right of his moral superiority.[7] The Calvinistic background of

[3] George E. Mowry, *The Era of Theodore Roosevelt, 1900–1912* (New York: Harper & Bros., 1958), pp. 17–18, 37.

[4] *Ibid.*, pp. 49–51. David W. Noble, *The Paradox of Progressive Thought* (Minneapolis: University of Minnesota Press, 1958), summarizes the views of the high priest of Progressivism, Herbert Croly, on the subject, p. 62.

[5] Eric F. Goldman, *Rendezvous with Destiny, A History of Modern American Reform* (New York: Alfred A. Knopf, 1952), p. 94; Mowry, *Era of Theodore Roosevelt*, p. 50. Such thinking was not far distant from other doctrines of the times, such as an economic interpretation of history.

[6] Richard Hofstadter, *The Age of Reform, From Bryan to F. D. R.* (New York: Alfred A. Knopf, 1955), has been pre-eminent in suggesting as a major factor in Progressivism the changing status of certain middle-class groups, chap. iv; and Mowry, *Era of Theodore Roosevelt*, has documented the middle-class nature of Progressive leadership, pp. 85 ff. (Psychiatrists and psychologists in general belonged to this dominant part of the middle class.) The Progressive reliance on the executive and the cult of the strong man were notable contemporaneous developments; *ibid.*, p. 88; Goldman, *Rendezvous with Destiny*, p. 80; Noble, *Paradox of Progressive Thought*, p. 74. Even the Progressives' faith in democracy was dependent upon their providing a proper environment for that democracy. See the sophisticated discussion of Progressivism in May, *End of American Innocence*, pp. 21–29.

[7] Hofstadter, *Age of Reform*, p. 258; compare the summary in Mowry, *Era of Theodore Roosevelt*, pp. 104–5.

many Progressives indicated a direct relationship as well as an analogy between Progressive leadership and the stewardship of the elect. Social responsibility inspired in many Progressives a feeling of guilt for all of the evil that a faulty society had caused, and the sophisticated with New England consciences equated righteousness with social reform.[8]

These, then, were the elements of Progressivism—optimism, environmentalism, moral fervor and leadership by an enlightened elite. None of them was new in American thought, but at the time they took on a special meaning because of the frequency with which they appeared and because of their application to social control. Although most obvious in political and social thinking, they also characterized, first, the psychotherapy movement in the psychiatry of that day and, second, the revolt of the behaviorists in contemporaneous psychology. In each case it turned out that an autonomous historical development within a science contained the same elements as a new political and social movement.

Psychiatry (which at that time included neurology) provides a nice example. In the late nineteenth century, physicians who dealt with the mentally ill usually were "organicists" who adhered strictly to scientific materialism. They believed that behavior and thinking were but the expression of the functioning of the nervous system and that physical defects or diseases were at the bottom of all mental diseases. The organicists performed autopsies on the brains of deceased mental patients, searching for evidence of lesions or brain damage. The work of this group was vindicated by the discovery that a common type of insanity was caused by syphilis. Yet nothing is quite as depressing as the literature of psychiatry-neurology around the turn of the century—endless reports of post-mortem examinations of demented brains and discussions of the problems of keeping and managing the insane. The psychiatrist was expected to do little more than deliver a prognosis of the melancholy course of the disease and then supervise the housing, feeding and restraining of the patient.[9] Well into the twentieth century the three main causes of insanity were thought to be heredity, alcohol and syphilis.[10]

By the 1890's a great deal of discussion of hysteria (disease symptoms occurring in the absence of physical disease), hypnotism and faith healing, plus a rebellion against the dreary routine of prognosis and commitment, led to a revival of attention to so-called "moral treatment." Every experienced physician knew the importance of the patient's state of mind for the treatment of illness, and early in the first decade of the century, following developments in continental Europe, American medical prac-

[8] *Ibid.*, p. 87; Hofstadter, *Age of Reform*, pp. 204–6, 208–12.

[9] The cure rate was about twenty percent; A. I. Noble, "The Curability of Insanity," *American Journal of Insanity*, LXIX (1913), 715–17.

[10] E.g., H. M. Swift, "Insanity and Race," *American Journal of Insanity*, LXX (1913), 154.

titioners took up the fad of psychotherapy. In large part the psychotherapy movement was a formal recognition of the medical value of a constructive intellectual and emotional environment, especially in the treatment of what we would now call neurotic diseases.[11]

Strict organicists who believed that insanity was caused by heredity, alcohol and syphilis were not necessarily outside of the Progressive movement. There were reform groups dedicated to the elimination of the baneful effects of all three. The eugenics movement, advocating the sterilization of insane, defective and criminal persons in order to improve the race, represented the Progressive attempt to deal with that part of man which was not malleable.[12] Many psychiatrists supported the efforts of the prohibitionists to remove from commerce what they regarded as social poison. And one of the lasting reforms of Progressivism was effected by the crusaders (many of them physicians) who opposed both prostitution and promiscuity with the powerful argument that only prevention could control venereal diseases.[13] These were typical Progressive reform movements, but Progressive psychiatrists fought their finest—and most fundamental—battles in the name of psychotherapy.

Basically the physicians who employed or advocated psychotherapy in any of its many forms were unwilling to accept the pessimistic attitude of current psychiatry and neurology. Under the competitive pressure of Christian Science and other faith cures that were demonstrably effective, these physicians ignored materialism and undertook to cure patients by whatever method worked. Effective psychotherapy required hope—indeed, faith in the patient's ability to cure himself. C. P. Oberndorf, one of the first psychoanalytic psychotherapists in the United States, later attributed his early successes in treatment to his enthusiasm and to his confidence in the new tools with which he worked. Others using quite different methods of psychotherapy likewise showed an optimism that set them apart from conservatives in the psychiatric profession.[14]

[11] See Walter Bromberg, *Man Above Humanity, A History of Psychotherapy* (Philadelphia: J. B. Lippincott Co., 1954), chap. viii.

[12] Mark Hughlin Haller, "American Eugenics: Heredity and Social Thought, 1870-1930" (Ann Arbor: University Microfilms, 1960), especially pp. 4, 157–58, shows how Progressives' assumptions of environmentalism did not deter them from supporting the eugenics movement.

[13] For somewhat different views, see Louis Filler, *Crusaders for American Liberalism* (2d ed., Yellow Springs, Ohio: Antioch Press, 1950), chap. xxii, and Harold Underwood Faulkner, *The Quest for Social Justice, 1898–1914* (New York: The Macmillan Co., 1931), pp. 159–62.

[14] C. P. Oberndorf, *A History of Psychoanalysis in America* (New York: Grune & Stratton, 1953), p. 152. E.g., see the revealing paper, Charles W. Burr, "The Prevention of Insanity and Degeneracy," *American Journal of Insanity*, LXXIV (1917), 409–24, and especially the discussion, 422–23.

The basis for the new hope was the conviction that an individual's behavior was determined—to a large extent—by his environment. A Boston physician in 1909 defined psychoneurotics "as people who, for one reason or another, are not well adapted to their environment." The conclusion was obvious; as one psychiatrist observed in 1911, "If the mental habits and the surroundings of an individual are largely responsible for the onset of a psychosis, we can look forward to accomplishments which may rival the success achieved in the crusade against tuberculosis."[15]

The psychotherapists' primary objective became, then, to re-educate the patient so that he adapted himself to his environment, adjusted himself to the reality that surrounded him. Thoughtful physicians quickly perceived that the largest part of the environment that required the patient to change his conduct was the society in which he lived, including his family. A New York asylum superintendent reported in 1913 that "The patient is no longer regarded simply as a separate individual, but also as a social unit, whose cure cannot be considered complete until he has been restored to social adaptability and efficiency."[16] At the same time physicians saw the possibility of altering not just the patient but also his environment. Since the important environment was social, the forward-looking psychiatrists found themselves committed to social meliorism, and therefore were Progressives indeed.[17]

The environment of children was especially a target for the social-reformer psychiatrists. Under the influence of early Freudian ideas, they asserted that childhood experiences were of overwhelming importance in later life. The most influential of these psychiatrists was William Healy, a conventionally trained specialist in nervous and mental diseases, who gave up his practice (at considerable sacrifice) in 1909 to work with juvenile delinquents in Chicago. Through his own experience with the motivations of youthful lawbreakers, Healy came to a strongly psychoanalytic point of view. His works (richly illustrated with interesting case histories) persuaded untold numbers of persons that favorable changes in the social environ-

[15] Richard C. Cabot, "The Analysis and Modification of Environment," *Psychotherapy*, III, No. 3 (1909), 5. James V. May, "The Modern Trend of Psychiatry," *Interstate Medical Journal,* XVIII (1911), 1098.

[16] *E.g.*, see the systematic work of Morton Price, "The Subconscious Setting of Ideas in Relation to the Pathology of the Psychoneuroses," *The Journal of Abnormal Psychology*, XI (1916), 1–18. William L. Russell, "The Widening Field of Practical Psychiatry," *American Journal of Insanity*, LXX (1913), 460, *E.g.*, William A. White, *The Principles of Mental Hygiene* (New York: The Macmillan Co., 1917), p. 316.

[17] *E.g.*, C. C. Wholey, in *The Journal of the American Medical Association*, LXII (1914), 1036. Thomas W. Salmon, "Some New Fields in Neurology and Psychiatry," *The Journal of Nervous and Mental Disease*, XLVI (1917), 90–99.

ments of youngsters could prevent delinquency and promote not only mental health but social progress.[18]

The presumptuousness of psychiatrists in deciding how the world should be run was not different from that of other Progressives. Like Dr. George Van Ness Dearborn of Boston, physicians appealed to "the sound principle of *noblesse oblige.*" Moreover, as doctors they dealt with matters of life and death, and as psychotherapists in daily practice they undertook to interfere in and change the attitudes and ways of life of their patients. They were, therefore, accustomed to the responsibilities of leadership. As early as 1907 E. W. Taylor of Boston pointed out that the role of the physician was expanding and that he had to look after the social as well as the physical welfare of his patients. He was becoming, said Lewellys Barker of Johns Hopkins, the "moral director" of his patients.[19]

A number of theories were used by the psychotherapists in rationalizing their attempts to recast the world. A New York neurologist who advocated a type of psychotherapy called suggestion proposed in 1912 that physicians combat the psychic infections of civilization—noxious suggestion with psychotherapy, that is, with suggestion that would foster what he believed to be the better cultural elements (surely an ambiguous goal for social control).[20] Most Americans were not strong on systematics, and hope sufficed to nourish many of their opinions; only those who used the most radical of the psychotherapies, psychoanalysis, invoked a fairly consistent theory to justify their reformism.[21]

[18] *E.g.*, William Healy, *The Individual Delinquent: A Text-Book of Diagnosis and Prognosis for All Concerned in Understanding Offenders* (Boston: Little, Brown & Co., 1915); William Healy, *Mental Conflicts and Misconduct* (Boston: Little, Brown & Co., 1917), especially chap. xvii. Healy's case affords evidence of a situation in which political Progressives had a direct influence on the development of psychiatry. In an interview with the writer Dr. Healy remarked that the method of studying children (integrating medical, social, psychometric and psychiatric studies of a single individual) which yielded him such rich results was suggested in large part by a group of social reformers associated with Hull House and led by Jane Addams and Julia Lathrop, two of the best-known Progressives. The Hull House reformers found financial support for the work and invited Healy to undertake it.

[19] George Van Ness Dearborn, *The Influence of Joy* (Boston: Little, Brown & Co., 1916), p. 35. E. W. Taylor, "The Attitude of the Medical Profession Toward the Psychotherapeutic Movement," *Boston Medical and Surgical Journal*, CLVII (1907), 845–46. Lewellys F. Barker, "On the Psychic Treatment of Some of the Functional Neuroses," *International Clinics*, I (17th ser., 1907), 13, 15, 17.

[20] George W. Jacoby, *Suggestion and Psychotherapy* (New York: Charles Scribner's Sons, 1912), chap. ii, especially pp. 207, 218–19.

[21] *E.g.*, J. T. W. Rowe, "Is Dementia Praecox the 'New Peril' in Psychiatry?" *American Journal of Insanity*, LXIII (1907), 389, 393, Even most American psychoanalysts in this early period, it must be admitted, had less regard for theoretical consistency than their European counterparts.

The psychoanalysts, whose alleged commitment to a so-called "sexual" view of the world was notorious, illustrated most strikingly the intense moralism of the Progressive psychiatrists. By means of sublimation man's evil would be turned into good, they asserted; even the grossest sexual perversions would become artistic creations and love for fellow man. James Jackson Putnam, scion of the Puritans, married to a Cabot, and professor of neurology at Harvard, wrote: "It may well be urged that psychoanalysis does not take the cultivation of social ideals as an end for which it should directly strive. Technically, this is true. But psychoanalysts know well the evils that attend the over-assertion of personal desires, cultivated too exclusively in and for themselves, and the importance of the opposite course follows by inference." In their long, conventional textbook on nervous and mental diseases, two of the leading psychiatrists of the country, Smith Ely Jelliffe and William A. White, reminded their readers of the "socially useful ends" of psychotherapy. As sophisticated about right and wrong as the most advanced intellectual rebels of the time, Progressive psychiatrists found altruism medically justifiable.[22]

Some of the psychotherapists were psychologists who had abandoned strictly experimental psychology. Like the psychiatrists, these men tended to be lay preachers who sought to reform the world by means of re-education and retraining. The scholarly psychologist of Boston, L. E. Emerson, for example, repeatedly pointed out the ethical and reform possibilities of Freudianism. More orthodox psychologists were likewise led, when dealing with matters outside of experimental psychology, to dilate on the possibilities of fostering the "higher aspirations" of men through psychotherapy and psychoanalysis.[23] The best example of the foregoing is the famous book of E. B. Holt of Harvard on *The Freudian Wish and Its Place in Ethics*.[24] Holt asserted that Freudian psychology justified the ancient belief that knowledge is virtue, with the implication that evil need not be always with us. Holt saw man as an individual interacting with his environment and, significantly, utilized not only psychoanalytic psychology but also behaviorism. For

[22] James J. Putnam, "The Psychoanalytic Movement," *Scientific American Supplement*, LXXVIII (1914), 391, 402. Freud commented regretfully on Putnam's inclination to make psychoanalysis "the servant of moral aims." Sigmund Freud, *An Autobiographical Study*, trans. by James Strachey (2d ed., London: Hogarth Press, 1946), p. 94. Smith Ely Jelliffe and William A. White, *Diseases of the Nervous System, A Text-Book of Neurology and Psychiatry* (2d ed., Philadelphia: Lee & Febiger, 1917), p. 98. James J. Putnam, "On Some of the Broader Issues of the Psychoanalytic Movement," *The American Journal of the Medical Sciences*, CXLVII (1914), 397–402.

[23] *E.g.*, Ernest K. Lindley, in *The Journal of the Indiana State Medical Association*, IX (1916), 7; Stephen S. Colvin, "What Dreams Mean," *The Independent*, LXXII (1912), 847.

[24] Edwin B. Holt, *The Freudian Wish and Its Place in Ethics* (New York: Henry Holt & Co., 1915).

within orthodox experimental psychology the Progressives were those who adhered to behaviorism.[25]

For years psychologists had been aware of ferment and discontent in their profession. Most of the criticism centered around the fact that dry, descriptive academic psychology was not useful. Then John B. Watson took leadership of the revolt of the behavioristic psychologists. They dispensed with consciousness and introspective methods and studied the human organism in its environment, using the methods of animal psychology. Watson began his behaviorist manifesto in 1913 by making the purpose of the revolt clear: "Psychology as the behaviorist views it is a purely objective experimental branch of natural science. Its theoretical goal is the *prediction and control of behavior.*"[26] Here was usefulness with a vengeance.

The behaviorists had observed that animals' innate patterns of action could be modified by training, and the young Turks soon tended to embrace a radical environmentalism. Most psychologists more or less covertly subscribed to an instinct psychology such as that of William James or William McDougall. Now out of the laboratory itself came a challenge to essentially conservative nativism.[27] One would misunderstand behaviorism if he overlooked the explicit meliorism involved in the movement. Watson himself took pains to clarify the relation of behaviorism to social control, and the more alert members of the profession also realized what was involved.[28] The goal of behaviorism was, after all, merely a restatement of the classical purpose of any science including psychology: to predict. And prediction, to the Progressive behaviorists as to other scientists, involved control.[29]

The elements of Progressivism thus appeared as conspicuous features of reform movements within psychology and psychiatry. The mass of material in both sciences remained, as before, primarily descriptive. But the social attitudes of some of the practitioners of the two disciplines led to profound changes in the very nature of psychiatry and psychology, just as Progressivism left its mark on American political and social institutions.

[25] The social psychologies of men such as G. H. Mead and J. Mark Baldwin were too close to social philosophy to be properly included here. A case might be made, however, for including G. Stanley Hall and the genetic psychology of that time.

[26] John B. Watson, "Psychology as the Behaviorist Views It," *The Psychological Review*, XX (1913), 158; see also 168–69, 177. Italics added. For an interesting variation with Freudian elements, see John B. Watson and J. J. B. Morgan, "Emotional Reactions and Psychological Experimentation," *The American Journal of Psychology*, XXVIII (1917), 163–74.

[27] *E.g.*, see M. E. Haggerty, "The Laws of Learning," *The Psychological Review*, XX (1913), 411; Howard C. Warren, "The Mental and the Physical," *ibid.*, XXI (1914), 99.

[28] *E.g.*, see John B. Watson, "An Attempted Formulation of the Scope of Behavior Psychology," *ibid.*, XXIV (1917), 329–52; A. P. Weiss, "Relation Between Functional and Behavior Psychology," *ibid.*, pp. 353–68.

[29] See John Dewey, "The Need for Social Psychology," *ibid.*, pp. 274–75.

Progressive psychiatry and Progressive psychology were uniquely American phenomena. The European professional literature was devoid of the optimistic social reformism of the New World versions of these disciplines. Psychologist Carl Rahn shrewdly epitomized the situation in his observation about psychoanalysis: "Where the European follower of Freud emphasizes the point that the formulation of the symbol is indicative of a 'renunciation of reality,'" wrote Rahn, "the American disciple sees it as a 'carrier of energy' exquisitely fitted for increasing man's control over his environment . . ."[30]

One can easily account for the rise of psychotherapy and the rise of behaviorism in terms of the internal histories of psychiatry and psychology. But the fact that these movements coincided in time with the Progressive social reform movement, and the fact that social control was an aim of reformers in both politics and science, can be accounted for only by treating the developments in psychiatry and psychology and in all other middle-class endeavors as part and parcel of the Progressive movement itself.[31] The historian will discover the full dynamics of Progressivism only when he examines not just politics, economics and social philosophy, but all aspects of American life.[32]

James R. McGovern
Dynamic Underlying Attitudes of the Progressive Leaders

(1966)

Even such an important movement as Progressivism has not been analyzed from the standpoint of personality types though it has been brilliantly treated in conventional, "situational" terms in the form of political, socio-economic,

[30] See Edwin G. Boring, *A History of Experimental Psychology* (2d ed., New York: Appleton-Century-Crofts, Inc., 1950), pp. 642–43. Carl Rahn, in a review of W. A. White, *Mechanisms of Character Formation*, in *The Psychological Bulletin*, XIV (1917), 327. The absence of a British counterpart is especially striking in view of the nearly contemporaneous reform movement there.

[31] The intellectual spokesmen for Progressivism were well aware of the possibilities of the new movements in psychiatry and psychology; e.g., see Walter Lippmann, *A Preface to Politics* (New York: M. Kennerley, 1913).

[32] Even though not focusing on Progressivism, May, *End of American Innocence*, gives an idea of the light that can be shed on the movement by an approach such as the one suggested here.

James R. McGovern, "David Graham Phillips and the Virility Impulse of Progressives," *New England Quarterly* (Sept. 1966), pp. 334–55. Reprinted with permission of the publisher, and the author. Abridged.

and intellectual interpretations. The dominant Mowry-Hofstadter school has demonstrated a relationship between Progressivism and its socio-economic environment. However, any explanation of the correlation of group membership and ideology requires more than a simplistic model of environmental challenge and socio-economic response. Their "status revolution" thesis does not, for example, explain why some Anglo-Saxon, Protestant, middle-class townsmen and urbanites failed to support the movement and why many outside these categories did.[1] Nor is it as certain as these authors assume that the socio-economic factor dominates the thought of its socio-economic group. After all, ideologies also reflect personal needs, hence psychological affinities as well as economic interests together with conscious rational and moral imperatives.[2] This is not to say that ideology has its exclusive or even its major sources in the irrational, much less that politics is neuroses to the left and right of an ambivalent center. Rather it is to assert that distinct personality types are particulary receptive to certain ideologies and help to promote them, and that they make significant contributions to historical change.

One of the most interesting and least examined features of the Progressive period is the emergence of a "virility impulse." This may be described as an exaggerated concern with manliness and its conventional concomitants—power and activity. Social Darwinism is usually called upon to explain the phenomenon without inquiring why, in personal terms, it was so attractive to its supporters. Symbolically, the period begins with Roosevelt's charge up San Juan Hill and ends with his loathing of cowardly officials for refusing his offer to lead a cavalry charge across No-Man's land.[3] It was marked by

[1] Both George E. Mowry's *The Era of Theodore Roosevelt, 1900–1912* (New York, 1958), and Richard Hofstadter's *The Age of Reform* (New York, 1955), view Progressivism as a response by middle-class, Anglo-Saxon, Protestant groups in the period around 1900 to the concentrations of economic power which threatened their status and values. But objections to the thesis have arisen. On the powerful, non-reform wing of the Republican party in New York state, derived from these same traditional elements in the population, see Herbert H. Rosenthal, "The Progressive Movement in New York State, 1906–1914." Unpublished Ph.D. dissertation, Harvard University, 1953. J. Joseph Huthmacher, "Urban Liberalism in the Age of Reform," *Mississippi Valley Historical Review*, XLIX, 234 (Sept., 1962), holds that Yankee groups in Massachusetts were often less interested in reform than immigrants.

[2] For a sophisticated discussion of these relationships see T. W. Adorno, *et al.*, *The Authoritarian Personality* (New York, 1951), 1–11.

[3] Roosevelt's letters are classic revelations of the highly virile type. They resound with such comments from the camp as "I must be off, now, down the river; so goodbye." Theodore Roosevelt to Henry C. Lodge, April 20, 1887 in Elting Morison, *Letters of Theodore Roosevelt*, I, 127 (Cambridge, Mass., 1951). Again, "I took three cattle thieves into Mandan for trial." Theodore Roosevelt to Frances T. S. Dana, Oct. 21, 1886, *Letters*, I, 113. He also pokes fun at effete society in England and the East. See for example *Letters*, I, 390, 510.

"super-presidents" and robust statesmen like Beveridge and Lodge who advanced the "rough and ready" philosophy of Mahan.[4] Fears for our manly vigor were openly expressed by T. R. and Brooks Adams, Roosevelt dynamically coping with the problem through lectures to women's organizations and gymnastics.[5] While national foreign policy was ambitious, firm, and even belligerent, contemporary novelists like Dreiser and London exalted the Nietzchean hero and others like David Graham Phillips and Winston Churchill took hope in the Great Man.[6] It was a time when the Big Stick and the Bull Moose captured the public fancy. Above all, however, the period was marked by activity—strenuous, dedicated efforts to alter America and the world.

To illustrate the psychological dimension of Progressivism, David Graham Phillips, who belonged both to the socio-economic background conventionally assigned Progressives and the "virility impulse,"[7] is a revealing figure. Phillips was born in 1867 in Madison, Indiana, an Ohio river community

[4] Albert J. Beveridge, like Roosevelt made his ritualistic trip to the western bad-lands where he too proved robust. See Claude G. Bowers, *Beveridge and the Progressive Era* (Cambridge, Mass., 1932), 28–29. He also searched for the hero. See Albert J. Beveridge, *Work and Habits* (Philadelphia, 1907), 69. The words "might," "build," "fearlessly," "firmly," "vigorously," "powerful," and "tremendous" are among his favorites. He introduces *Work and Habits* with the statement, "Every man's problem is how to be effective. Consciously or unconsciously, the question you are asking yourself is, 'How shall I make my strength count for most in this world of effort,'" *Work and Habits*, 9. Henry C. Lodge collaborated with Roosevelt in *Hero Tales from American History* (New York, 1902), which stressed the fighting virtues. He belittled the flabbiness of his age and its non-virile man remarking that "The athlete does not win the race by sitting in an armchair." John A. Garraty, *Henry Cabot Lodge* (New York, 1953), 206.

[5] Brooks Adams was concerned about "race suicide" and the "failure of the sexual instinct." Arthur F. Beringause, *Brooks Adams* (New York, 1955), 361. See also Thornton Anderson, *Brooks Adams, Constructive Conservative* (Ithaca, 1951), 179–180, 200.

[6] Richard and Beatrice Hofstadter, "Winston Churchill: a Study in the Popular Novel," *American Quarterly*, II, 15 (Spring, 1950). Phillips' admiration for the hero is a major characteristic of his novels *George Helm* (New York, 1912) and *The Fashionable Adventures of Joshua Craig* (New York, 1909).

[7] The best study of Phillips, though with a literary rather than historical emphasis, is Paul C. Rodgers' "David Graham Phillips: a Critical Study." Unpublished doctoral dissertation, Columbia University, 1955. Although the author does not attempt a psychological interpretation, he uses correspondence with Phillips' living relatives which details Phillips' family life. Rodgers' bibliography on Phillips is the most complete available. Isaac F. Marcosson, *David Graham Phillips and His Times* (New York, 1932), is informative but not analytical. George Mowry provides a good brief description of Phillips' life and writing in his introduction to Phillips, *The Treason of the Senate* (Chicago, 1964). Kenneth S. Lynn, *The Dream of Success* (Boston, 1955), includes a chapter analyzing Phillips' writing, concluding that he was a "dream panderer" for the middle-class and his literature therefore mirrored its aspirations.

which had declined in wealth after the Civil War. A close college friend of Beveridge at DePauw which he attended for three years, he was graduated from Princeton in 1887. After a successful newspaper career on the *New York Sun* and as a foreign correspondent for Pulitzer's *New York World*, he became in the early years of the twentieth century one of America's most adept "pioneer realists" in fiction and a leading muckraker. He completed by 1911, the year of his death, twenty-six books, most of them novels with Progressive themes which sold in the hundreds of thousands. Six of his novels appeared serially in the *Saturday Evening Post*; he also wrote over one hundred articles for popular magazines many of them in a muckraking vein, including the famous series for *Cosmopolitan*, "The Treason of the Senate." His revelations undoubtedly caused Theodore Roosevelt to coin the angry term "muckraker."

Phillips was raised in an educated, middle-class, solid-citizen type of Protestant family[8] which probably lost some status in the period, 1870 to 1900, and thus conformed to the major tenets of the Mowry-Hofstadter "situational" position. A reading of his vast literature with this in mind, however, proves interpretively unconvincing. His Progressivism was probably influenced by the Protestant code of free enterprise and abstemious living and the status problems of his class at a time of relative affluence, yet the vehemence, tenacity, and rigidity with which he presents his views suggests that he was influenced primarily by personal, non-objective purposes. And since he is sociologically representative, a revelation of his deep personality interests in Progressivism indicates that the current typing of the Progressives has been overestimated . . .

Phillips feared his tendencies towards passivity, [and] he compelled himself to achieve an incredible burden of work as compensation. He commented anxiously about his "inert disposition"[9] and feared that relaxation "would mean only disaster to me." He declared openly, "I could not trust myself in luxurious surroundings for fear they would soon eat all of the manhood out of me."[10] He became therefore a "glutton for work,"[11] instructing a friend who sought to emulate Phillips' literary successes that he wrote "every night, seven days a week" because "I think it's fatal to give way to moods.

[8] Phillips' father was college educated, a respected local figure, and prosperous enough to provide a college education for his daughters as well as his sons. I. F. Marcosson, *David Graham Phillips and His Times*, 11–25.

[9] Convinced that he would make no progress as a journalist if he remained in England where living was too comfortable, Phillips wrote Joseph Pulitzer that he would welcome a new assignment, declaring, "Being of an inert disposition, I do not wish to struggle against any greater odds than I must." Marcosson, 167.

[10] *The New York Times*, May 21, 1905, III, 1.

[11] Marcosson, 70.

Travailler, toujours travailler, encore travailler."[12] To another gentleman who marveled at his capacity for work, he replied that "everyman is as lazy as he dares to be."[13]

Even this abundant productivity did not silence his fearful, self-punishing and self-accusing characteristics, still other signs of passivity.[14] Though a successful novelist, he did not enjoy writing which seemed something like a penance for him. "I'm still sweating away," he wrote about an impending novel. "I feel like the devil. But the crazy thing inside of me won't let me stop. And only one life too!"[15] Moreover, he actually wrote standing up for eight- to ten-hour stretches without relief.[16] Similarly he lashed himself with doubts about his career despite his literary successes, having "no notion how the game's going to turn out" and being "in despair" because "the more I write, the farther I seem to be from the goal . . ."[17]

But the most telling sign of Phillips' passivity was his pseudo-aggression. With a pen for a sword, he fought paper wars against fancied enemies showing a safe type of literary indignation against distant foes.[18] While charming and kind though aloof and formal in his personal relations[19] where normal aggressions find release, Phillips' writing is filled with invective.[20] He described the typical "cultured person" as one "whose mind is a sort of unlined crazy quilt," a "flabby non-entity, fit only to be a professor . . ."[21] And ladies of

[12] Marcosson, 226–227. Freud identified conscientiousness of this type as a primary defense system against obsessive neurosis. Sigmund Freud, *The Origins of Psychoanalysis, Letters to Wilhelm Fliess, Drafts and Notes: 1887–1902* (New York, 1954), 150. See also T. W. Adorno, 480. Phillips' frequent use of the word "must" also reflects his compulsiveness. See, for example, the chapter "Democracy's Dynamo" in his essays in *Reign of Gilt* (New York, 1905), 183–201.

[13] Marcosson, 280.

[14] Sigmund Freud, *New Introductory Lectures on Psychoanalysis and Other Works* in *The Complete Psychological Works of Sigmund Freud*, XXII, 116 (London, 1964).

[15] Anonymous, "Phillips' Methods," *Bookman*, XXXVII, 13 (March, 1911).

[16] Rodgers, 41.

[17] Marcosson, 206, 227.

[18] Edmund Bergler, *The Counterfeit Sex* (New York, 1960), 70, 159–160. This type of "pseudo-aggression" is described by Bergler as a "defense against passivity."

[19] Marcosson, 70, 80–81, 172, 292. Adorno, 478–480, sees this manner as role-playing in which warmth is avoided as it represents weakness.

[20] Bergler believes that writers who are accused by their "inner conscience" of masochism reply with aggression which is actually "pseudo-aggression" as it is directed at "fantasied enemies." Edmund Bergler, *The Writer and Psychoanalysis*, 237.

[21] D. G. Phillips, "Restless Husbands," *Cosmopolitan*, LI, 424 (Aug., 1911).

leisure had bodies "overlaid with carriage fat and automobile fat and street car fat and theatre fat or home-chair fat and skins disordered from lounging and eating candy."[22] He belittled the stay-at-home woman who enjoyed the "silly and shallow twaddle about 'woman and the home'..."[23] Senator Chauncey Depew of New York was reviled by Phillips as the "sly courtier agent [of the Vanderbilts] with the greasy conscience and the greasy tongue and the greasy backbone and the greasy hinges of the knees."[24] But if the Senate was immoral as he argued in the prosecuting style of his "The Treason of the Senate,"[25] the people were lazy and got what they deserved. Actually, "The Treason of the Senate" represented a departure from Phillips' typical literary attacks on impersonal enemies. In this work he named actual people. Although at first, he preferred not to write such pointed articles,[26] once having decided upon them, he launched a series of verbal assaults. These, in turn, provoked counter-attacks[27] from offended persons.[28] Phillips then became visibly depressed over these rebuffs, the typical reaction of mythical compensatory type of aggression.

Phillips was concerned over the "wrong values" undermining the Republic which honored wealth before character, leisure before work, and externals before self-respect.[29] His upset might be regarded as a lingering remnant of Reisman's "inner-directed" personality or as the reaction of a displaced son who had suffered from the "status revolution," but it also conveys a sense of a victim who parades his distress.[30] Such a mentality is ever ready to withhold satisfaction for the joy of being thought proper. Its advocate admonishes that work is not for the positive fruits of work, but for the pleasure of working itself, that while others have money, he has the pleasure of self-respect, which Phillips, in fact, equated with manhood.[31]

That Phillips should conceal his personality through defenses of exag-

[22] D. G. Phillips, "The Passion for as Good as," *Delineator*, LXXVII, 354 (Nov., 1910).

[23] D. G. Phillips, *The Reign of Gilt*, 272.

[24] D. G. Phillips, "The Treason of the Senate," *Cosmopolitan*, XL, 496 (March, 1906).

[25] The many articles comprising "The Treason of the Senate" have been collected in D. G. Phillips, *The Treason of the Senate* (Chicago, 1964).

[26] Rodgers, 159–60.

[27] Harold D. Lasswell, *The Psychopathology of Politics* (Chicago, 1931), 78–126, discusses the self-punishing traits of the agitator.

[28] Rodgers, 167–69.

[29] Phillips, *The Reign of Gilt*, 20–31, *passim.*

[30] Theodore Reik, *Of Love and Lust* (New York, 1959), 235–48.

[31] Phillips, *The Reign of Gilt*, 63.

gerated tough-mindedness and literary virility is not surprising.[32] These qualities, in turn, shaped his Progressive ideology. He rejected, therefore, what he construed to be affected, leisurely, and "aristocratic" behavior observed particularly among the *nouveaux riches* and their descendants. Those few industrialists who worked hard passed inspection,[33] but many were becoming soft and therefore threatening to Phillips' own precarious equilibrium.[34] Thus he wrote, "Wealth possessed means ease and power without effort . . . It means the mind at rest, tending to sloth and slumber . . . Above all, it means an atmosphere of self-complacency and satiety and langour that insensibly relaxes the strongest fibre."[35] He viewed "high society" indignantly and saw fit to punish its members in full view of his middle-class reading audience in an article for the *Post* entitled "The Penalties of Plutocracy."[36] "Snobbism," the manner of the effeminate, "should be exterminated, just as, more and more scientifically, bodily disease is being stamped out."[37] Personal identification is also suggested by such a statement as "The world has room for idlers—it has room for all sorts of people. But America has no room for them. That great workshop wants no idlers . . . hindering the toilers at their tasks."[38] His concern over the enervating effects of the automobile describes a psychological rather than economic posture.[39] His pronounced hostility to private charity, "cheap and nasty schemes of so-called philanthropy,"[40] which merely deprived the recipient of the opportunity to be self-reliant, seems to have been a projection of

[32] Phillips shows most of the characteristics of the authoritarian personality. Adorno's research indicated that "an underlying need for dependence (passivity, sympathy, comfort) in conflict with the desire to maintain masculine pride and self-respect could give rise to an exaggerated value for independence. . . " Adorno, 53. This type is inclined not to be tough, rather tough-minded. Melanie Klein, "Early Stages of the Oedipus Conflict," *International Journal of Psychoanalysis*, IX, 167–172 (March, 1928). Miss Klein states that exaggerated maleness represents a "femininity complex." Edmund Bergler "Two Forms of Aggression in Obsessional Neurosis," *Psychoanalytic Review*, XXIX, 188–196 (April, 1942), holds that hyper-aggression is a defense against passivity and inertia. Karl Abraham while noting that passivity and inertia, hyper-sensitivity and unwillingness to assume the initiative in sex typify the feminine male, observes that sadistic aggression is also prominent as a disguise for passivity. See Karl Abraham, *Selected Papers of Karl Abraham* (New York, 1953), 283–91.

[33] D. G. Phillips, "Money to Give Away," *Saturday Evening Post*, 175, 9 (June 27, 1903).

[34] Phillips, *The Reign of Gilt*, 52–55. See also Adorno, 237.

[35] Phillips, *The Reign of Gilt*, 103.

[36] D. G. Phillips, "The Penalties of Plutocracy," *Saturday Evening Post*, 178, 10–11 (July 8, 1905).

[37] Phillips, *The Reign of Gilt*, 148.

[38] Phillips, *The Reign of Gilt*, 127.

[39] D. G. Phillips, *Delineator*, LXXVI, 354 (Nov., 1910).

[40] Phillips, *The Reign of Gilt*, 211.

Phillips' own needs and fears. Culture was to be avoided under the direct compulsion because it might produce effeminacy. He admonished, "If any symptoms of the artistic temperament appear, fight them to the death. Work, work whether you want to or not."[41] Phillips feared that "pretentious culture" imported from Europe might undermine the simplicity of a vigorous democracy.[42] In fact, one of Phillips' favorite fantasy images is that of a masculine America as against decadent Europe, the principal danger for America being seduction by European ideas of leisure.[43] But Phillips could not permit this to happen to Americans any more than to himself. He thought we would not succumb for we would rid ourselves of false ideals, and would eventually reform Europe and make her as energetic and productive as America itself would become.

Since Phillips' preoccupation with virility caused him to view dependency and weakness contemptuously, his dismay at the encroachments of the organization upon the individual stemmed from psychological, not economic motivation. Only the virile reformer whom Phillips admired could rectify such unhealthy conditions and prepare the way for a revitalization of American life.[44] . . .

Phillips' heroes are rigidly defined and highly conventionalized supermales.[45] They studiously avoid self-indulgence and, with a curious twist, are at times so masculine that they are above sex and cannot let marital responsibilities get in the way of manly independence.[46] Such men announce themselves with a herald's call. "The coming of a man makes us suddenly aware how few real men there are—real live men . . ."[47] Such a man has the "look of power—sad, stern, inexorable—the look of men whose wills and passions hurl them on and on to the conquest of the world."[48] The reader soon learns that the hero has a "magnetic and masterful will," and a quality of "inevitableness,"[49] has "magnetic eyes,"[50] and personality with

[41] D. G. Phillips, *Cosmopolitan*, LI, 424 (Aug., 1911).

[42] Phillips, *The Reign of Gilt*, 136.

[43] Phillips, *The Reign of Gilt*, 137, 238.

[44] Phillips' fiction best displays his admiration for the "he-man" reformer. Marcosson, 32–45, describes Phillips' fond feelings for Beveridge.

[45] Phillips like the insecure males of Adorno's study holds a highly conventionalized sense of maleness. Adorno, 476–77.

[46] D. G. Phillips, *Light Fingered Gentry*, 328; D. G. Phillips, *George Helm* (New York, 1912), 63.

[47] Phillips, *George Helm*, 17.

[48] Phillips, *George Helm*, 21.

[49] D. G. Phillips, *The Fashionable Adventures of Joshua Craig* (New York, 1909), 266. Victor Dorn, another typical hero has a walk which illustrated that "steady, forward advance." See D. G. Phillips, *The Conflict* (New York, 1911), 131.

[50] Phillips, *George Helm*, 106.

"steel, inflexible determination."[51] He never makes excuses nor accepts defeats nor does he admit to weaknesses without remorse.[52] ... A second, major male type in Phillips' fiction is the man who hasn't measured up and so, in consequence, is necessarily female in this conventionalized framework. A "soft" male voice in a Phillips novel was "suggestive of hidden dangers," and the character who can admit some personal weaknesses to a woman attacks himself with "I ought to have been the woman and you the man. Weak-weak-weak!"[53] Ineffective, subject to their environments, such figures could not, as Phillips' heroes must, reform both business and politics.[54]

If Phillips found pleasure and vicarious security in playing roles of his fictionalized heroes, their masculinity was ever threatened just as his own. They too might succumb to inertia[55], or dependency and thus lose their identities. Even so masterful a figure as Horace Armstrong might lose his character in the world of corporate business because "with the thought he was in another man's power, had come a physical sensation of actual chains ... In another man's power! ... Dependent on the nod of a fellow man" Armstrong became so distressed that when he saw the owner again he felt "he would spring at him and sink his fingers in his throat and wring the life out of him."[56] Another hero is concerned lest he may have to "bow the knee" to another man.[57] He was alarmed about "any man or any enterprise that menaced my self-ownership."[58] Such figures were also on guard against the dependency involved in securing money through inheritance. "'John,' asked Hiram, 'can you think of a single instance in which inherited wealth has been a benefit, a single case where a man has become more of a man than he would if he hadn't had it?'"[59] Occasionally, a dependent male figure who is treated as an effete person can recover virility by going to work,[60] but it is

[51] D. G. Phillips, *Light Fingered Gentry*, 432, 434.

[52] D. G. Phillips, *Joshua Craig*, 242, 277.

[53] D. G. Phillips, *Susan Lenox*, II, 390, 207.

[54] Harvey Saylor, a powerful Senator and political boss combats "the interests." See *The Plum Tree*, 169–76, 194–97. Horace Armstrong turned the tables on a corrupt insurance company. See *Light Fingered Gentry*, 269–91, 303–07. Other highly virile figures who reform society include Victor Dorn in *The Conflict*, George Helm in *George Helm*, Joshua Craig in *The Fashionable Adventures of Joshua Craig* and Hampdon Scarborough in *The Cost* (Indianapolis, 1904).

[55] D. G. Phillips, *Susan Lenox*, II 243–44.

[56] D. G. Phillips, *Light Fingered Gentry*, 41–42.

[57] D. G. Phillips, *The Plum Tree*, 295.

[58] Phillips, *The Plum Tree*, 41.

[59] D. G. Phillips, *The Second Generation* (New York, 1907), 76.

[60] Phillips, *The Second Generation.* Compare Arthur Ranger's personality on page 3 with that on pages 189–91.

better, of course, to avoid soft environments from the first. Phillips' taboos were numerous: autos made men fat[61] and eastern colleges were certain to deman[62] as were marriages to wealthy women.[63] Wealth was not the gauge of manly success most people assumed for although the hard-working manufacturer was a fine type,[64] others fell prey to their affluent surroundings and they or their sons lost character.[65]...

The foregoing discussion of the personality of Phillips from the standpoint of his behavior and writing, both fictional and non-fictional, reveals his high readiness of response to Progressivism. The wealthy class, in general, was unacceptable to Phillips because it projected his fears of indolence and passivity. The reformer was acceptable because Phillips' insecure masculine feelings could be reinforced through identification; he hoped that vigorous reform would eradicate those signs of effeminacy in American life which disturbed him. His feminist sympathies represented a deep, unconscious association best shown in fantasy which demonstrated his desire to receive aggression from women. In all this, Phillips transferred his highly personal feelings to politics and society, rationalizing them into a Progressive ideology which facilitated real socio-economic problems.[66] While ideological influences such as the Protestant Ethic and Social Darwinism[67] impinged on Phillips, these appear to have been influential only in so far as they coincided with his personal needs. Situational, socio-economic factors such as his family's fallen status and its consequent inferiority to the powerful new classes in America may also have influenced him; yet these frustrating experiences, which must incidentally be inferred as they are not directly stated, now appear to have been part of his preoccupation with virility. Phillips' life and thought suggests that the "status revolution" thesis should be seen in much deeper psychological terms than the elementary compensation mechanism which up to now has done so much of its work.

[61] D. G. Phillips, *Susan Lenox*, II, 335.

[62] D. G. Phillips, *Old Wives for New*, 347; *Second Generation*, 3, 29–32, 155.

[63] D. G. Phillips, *Light Fingered Gentry,* 380–94.

[64] D. G. Phillips, *The Second Generation*, 2.

[65] Phillips, *The Second Generation*, 249–56 and *George Helm*, 210–38, 300, describe the evil effects of wealth on character and self-respect just as *Old Wives for New*, 347–49, and *The Second Generation*, 3–5, illustrate the enervating effects of wealth on the sons of the rich.

[66] Lasswell, *The Psychopathology of Politics*, 74–105, describes a similar process of displacement. Erik Erikson has observed that "at certain stages of individual development and at certain periods in history, ideological polarization, conflict, and commitment correspond to an inescapable inner need." Erik Erikson, "The Problem of Ego Identity," 81.

[67] There are a lot of fangs, tusks, claws, and paws as against rabbits and hens in Phillips' fiction. For example, see *The Cost*, 170, 266–67, 362, 372, 375, *The Deluge* (New York, 1907), 292, 300, 333, 337, 366 and *Light Fingered Gentry,* 37, 67, 114, 235, 285, and 289.

An important question remains. Why was American society susceptible at this time to the leadership and influence of this activist personality type? Unquestionably real rational objectives, the preservation of traditional American values, middle-class fears and immigrant hopes explain a great deal, but the fervor and dynamism of Progressivism suggest some irrational content among its followers as well as its leaders.

Part of the explanation may be found in the fact that the "active mastery" over life which typified middle-class work patterns was threatened in this period. As entrepreneurial and self-employment opportunities declined sharply after 1900,[68] and since white collar management had not yet become an acceptable image of American self-reliance, anxiety about roles were common. College men at the University of Chicago in convocation learned in 1907, for example, about "the crushing out of opportunities for young men through the growth of capitalistic combinations . . ."[69] The same speaker noted the "considerable anxiety by reason of the disappearance of traditional landmarks," and reminded his audience that "new meanings must be written into such terms as 'success' and getting on in the world." Little wonder this speaker stressed the importance of being "well-equipped, highly trained men" so as "to develop into a manhood of discipline, capacity, and power."[70] While at the same time the enterpreneurial freedom of American men was being undermined, their economic future being made uncertain, and their working patterns being altered, the test of manliness remained in large measure what it had been—the man's ability as a breadwinner. Although singly responsible for the economic welfare of his middle-class family in the past, he enjoyed the assurance at that earlier time, at least, of an autonomous economic sphere in the race for life and so some personal control over his status. But now, by the turn of the century, all anxieties were reinforced.

Contemporaneously, leisure became a significant fact for large numbers of men who were thereby diverted, as one commentator on the recreation of the period observed, from "active aggressiveness for a time in a passive receptivity . . ."[71] The estimated work week for non-agricultural workers declined from 57.1 hours in 1890 to 50.3 in 1910 to 45.5 in 1920.[72] Money spent for recreation comprised 3.6 percent of the national income in 1909, a figure which compares closely with the 5.8 percent expended as recently as 1950[73]

[68] Willford I. King, *The Wealth and Income of the People of the United States* (New York, 1915), 264.

[69] Albert Shaw, *The Outlook for the Average Man* (New York, 1907), 12.

[70] Shaw, *The Outlook for the Average Man*, 12, 17.

[71] Helen C. Crew, "The Matter of Idling," *Outlook*, CIV, 381 (June, 1913).

[72] W. S. and E. S. Woytinsky, *World Population and Production: Trend and Outlook* (New York, 1953), 280–81.

[73] J. Frederic Dewhurst, *America's Needs and Resources: A New Survey* (New York, 1955), 1073.

and which represents nearly as high a percentage of expenditures to disposable income as prevailed in 1925.[74] The total of theater, opera, and motion picture expenditures had already reached a plateau in 1909 which held throughout the booming twenties. Statistics on alcoholic consumption, foreign travel, and transportation for 1909 are impressive even by comparison with those of 1950.[75] That this situation produced uneasy and even guilty feelings may be surmised not merely from Phillips' concern, but also from the numerous magazine articles with such reassuring titles as "The Right Use of Leisure," and "The Lawful Business of the Loiterer," and still others with a justifying tone as "The Matter of Idling," and "The Ethics of Leisure."[76] Undoubtedly the initial experience shared by the bulk of middle-class men of entrepreneuring less and consuming more, and of spending more of their time in a woman's world involved problems of role change and of sexual identification which might demand some public demonstration of activism such as Progressivism.

Concomitantly, while men were bound to be more passive, women were free to be more active. The increase of feminine employment in business and the professions was very marked between 1880 and 1920.[77] This enlarged sphere of women's activity, the more disturbing because it was disrupting traditional roles, may have contributed a situational base for the psychological element in Progressivism. One needs hardly speculate that the allusions in fiction and non-fiction of the period to women refusing to bear children describes a fact which contributed considerable anxieties to the sex roles of the period.[78] The instances in popular literature of near or actual role reversals with women consciously wishing to be like men or becoming like them in personality are also suggestive of basic tensions.[79] All in all, there are several psychological conditions which probably shaped the nature and direction of the Progressive Movement.

Although it is impossible to measure exactly the emotional element in Progressivism, the movement had a significant irrational component. Psy-

[74] Julius Weinberger, "Economic Aspects of Recreation," *Harvard Business Review* XV, 458 (Summer, 1937).

[75] W. S. Woytinsky, 280–81. See also W. H. Horwill, "Leisurely America," *Living Age*, CCLIII, 333 (May, 1907).

[76] Temple Scott, "The Right Use of Leisure," *Forum*, XLVI, 77–93 (July, 1911); "The Lawful Business of the Loiterer," *Living Age*, CCLVII, 813–15 (June, 1908); Helen C. Crew, 381; H. L. Stuart, "The Ethics of Luxury and Leisure," *American Journal of Sociology* XXV, 254–59 (Nov., 1918).

[77] Joseph A. Hill, *Women in Gainful Occupations, 1870 to 1920* (Washington, 1929), 42.

[78] Robert Herrick, *Together* (New York, 1908), 156–58. See Arthur Beringause, 361, for the observations of Brooks Adams on the subject.

[79] Woman's wish to be a man or like a man is a major theme in Phillips' fiction. Winston Churchill's heroines express similar desires. See Richard and Beatrice Hofstadter, *American Quarterly*, II, 26, and Robert Herrick, *Together*, 219.

chological and social psychological elements intertwined with socio-economic and abstract considerations to produce its decidedly popular successes. In a sense, Robert Frost was a historian when he wrote that it was only when one's inner wants combine with one's external needs that the job was ever done for heaven or the future's sake. Perhaps the already burdened historian will agree that the fullest description of any historical period awaits a consideration of psychology as well as the many other tools which he has used so confidently. Because, even if allowance is made for contemporary popular imagery, when the Progressive Party held its convention in 1912 and called its song book *Progressive Battle Hymns* enjoining on its front page, "We stand at the Armageddon and we battle for the Lord," and instructing delegates to sing with "vivacity and force" such songs as "Ro-o-se-velt O Ro-o-se-velt . . . thy gleaming sword shall never rust" to the strains of "Maryland, My Maryland," no other interpretation is fully satisfying.

Paul F. Bourke
The Implications of the Progressive Movement

(1969)

Shortly before America's involvement in the First World War there appeared a series of works of social and cultural criticism remarkable for their range and sophistication. The familiar list includes Herbert Croly's *The Promise of American Life* (1909) and *Progressive Democracy* (1914), Walter Weyl's *The New Democracy* (1912), Walter Lippmann's *Preface to Politics* (1913) and *Drift and Mastery* (1914), Van Wyck Brooks's *The Wine of the Puritans* (1909), *America's Coming of Age* (1915), and *H. G. Wells* (1915), and Randolph Bourne's *Youth and Life* (1913), *The Gary Schools* (1916) and *Education and Living* (1917). The authors of these books were involved as well in the development of vehicles for social criticism such as The *New Republic* and *The Seven Arts* which continued and institutionalized the preoccupations of their books.

These facts of creativity and speculative ferment are obvious; what has proved more difficult is an assessment of the character and purpose of this body of social theory. While we are justified in thinking of these men as constituting a fairly coherent group—they knew and were influenced by each other and they joined in the creation of journals devoted to agreed ends—we have yet to clarify precisely what they were about. Most commonly these

---

Paul F. Bourke, "The Social Critics and the End of American Innocence: 1907–1921," *American Studies*, 3. I (July 1969), pp. 57–72. Reprinted with permission of the publisher, Cambridge University Press, and the author.

men are viewed as the theoretical wing of Progressivism, so that they are explained by whatever broad hypothesis is offered about the movement as a whole. Among the questions raised about them, accordingly, are those that one always asks of theoreticians in a political movement: were their formulations influential, did they shape policy, were they close to the sources of power? We have had, for example, a minor controversy about the precise influence of Croly's *The Promise of American Life* on Theodore Roosevelt's New Nationalism. Charles Forcey has settled this point in the course of writing a book largely concerned with the relationship of the editors of the *New Republic* to the centers of political power.[1]

Even where considerations of effectiveness have not been the main concern, it is still true to say that the writings of these men are generally assimilated to the rubric of Progressivism, either as direct reflections of it, or as part of the spirit of the times which is ultimately defined by the fact of political reform. Eric Goldman's summary exemplifies the first of these attitudes:

> The New Freedom spawned a hundred other shimmering escapes from the past—the New Poetry, the New History, the New Democracy, the New Art, the New Woman. . .[2].

Alfred Kazin's judgments on Brooks and Bourne illustrate, on the other hand, the appeal to a *Zeitgeist*. He finds Brooks's *America's Coming of Age* an expression of the "ardor and uplift so characteristic of the Progressive period", and writes of Brooks's criticism "against the background of that brave new world of Progressivism"; while Bourne is held to be a personification of "a certain literary idealism in the Progressive Period." Kazin is not writing political history, but where he feels the need for a generalization about the period as a whole he sounds very much as if he is.[3]

All of these approaches are illuminating. Croly and his colleagues on the *New Republic* were undoubtedly preoccupied by the hope of influencing the politics of Progressivism, just as they did articulate and reflect many of its qualities: the moral optimism, the concern for efficiency, the desire to rationalize the power of industrialism. It is equally true that a man like Van Wyck Brooks shared many of these social values, even though institutional politics was far from the center of his thought. But it is also clear that an account such as Goldman's which makes political Progressivism the organiz-

[1] Charles Forcey, *The Crossroads of Liberalism* (New York, 1961). Forcey cites and discusses other works which have raised the question of Croly's influence on Roosevelt. For other treatments of the social critics as Progressives writing books rather than working in politics or reform institutions, see George Mowry, *The Era of Theodore Roosevelt* (New York, 1958); Arthur Link, *Woodrow Wilson and the Progressive Era* (New York, 1954) and Richard Hofstadter, *The Age of Reform* (New York, 1955).

[2] Eric Goldman, *Rendezvous with Destiny* (New York, 1952), p. 244.

[3] Alfred Kazin, *On Native Grou..ds* (New York, 1942), pp. 142, 144, 145.

ing principle, and which defines social and cultural theory in terms of it, cannot explain the extraordinary range of the literature. Kazin's account, which does explore this range but which relies ultimately on the political categories, leaving unstated the connections between political and intellectual innovation, is equally limited. Above all, these accounts make it difficult to understand why the politics of Progressivism were one of the principal targets for all of these men. It is the achievement of Henry May's *The End of American Innocence* that it has made us aware of the need for a different approach to the intellectual history of the period.

May's approach is to define the "philosophy" of the period, by which he means general beliefs and attitudes rather than a technical discipline. He finds American Victorianism, which is defined by its commitment to morality, culture and progress, surviving more or less intact into the first decade of this century. This trinity of beliefs, he argues, was the basis of a general consensus that shaped late nineteenth century attitudes. It found expression in the values of politicians, critics and creative writers, and represents the irreducible minimum defining the American popular and academic mind. There was questioning of and dissent from this common faith before 1912 in the work of late Victorians like Beard, Dewey, James and Veblen, but their efforts were only intimations of a full-scale assault on the nineteenth century led by a younger generation—men such as Lippmann, Bourne and Brooks. The early politics of Progressivism before 1912 did not seriously challenge the fundamental cultural consensus and much of the political innovation that followed 1912 was not affected directly by the intellectual rebellion that accompanied it. One of May's most emphatic points is that to seek the key to the intellectual innovation of the period through politics is to miss much of the essential character of the rebellion: that it was in revolt against a middle-class politics of morality and uplift—a politics that did not disappear. The strategic value of May's book is that it has provided a bridge between a reading which is severely political and one which is concerned to explore explicitly non-political writing but finds no other contextual or chronological model available except Progressivism[4] . . .

[4] Henry May, *The End of American Innocence* (New York, 1959) Part I. For an approach somewhat similar to May's see Daniel Aaron, *Writers on the Left* (New York, 1961). The above paragraphs are not intended as a full-scale analysis of the historiography of the intellectual history of the period; they are concerned only to illustrate the force of May's restatement of the problem raised by the intellectual ferment of the prewar years. In any wider discussion of the literature, important works such as David Noble, *The Paradox of Progressive Thought* (Minneapolis, 1958), and Morton White, *Social Thought in America* (New York, 1949), which do not bear specifically on the explanatory question, would have to be included. Such a discussion would also include, of course, Christopher Lasch, *The New Radicalism in America* 1889–1963 (New York, 1965), which stands now as the essential argument to be explored for understanding many aspects

There is no possibility of arguing away the evidence that in intellectual style the years after the first decade were different. Two kinds of evidence reinforce and even demand such a view: the autobiographies of the participants and their contemporary writings. The first kind of evidence has been extraordinarily important in fixing our view of the period—the people whose careers spanned these years before the Great War were remarkably prolific in autobiography and to a large degree they have written their own history. It is from these writings—the memoirs of Mabel Dodge, Lincoln Steffens, Van Wyck Brooks, Joseph Freeman, Floyd Dell, Hutchins Hapgood, Max Eastman, to list only a few—that the characteristic generalizations about rebellion have come; it is from the second body of evidence—the works of social criticism, primarily—that the formal ideas of the rebellion have been reconstructed.[5]

The recollection of novelty and innovation is clear in these examples from Mabel Dodge and Floyd Dell:

> Looking back on it now, it seems as though everywhere, in that year of 1913, barriers went down and people reached each other who had never been in touch before; there were all sorts of new ways to communicate as

---

of the period. Lasch's book does not speak distinctively, however, to the problem raised by May: what to make of the impressive body of evidence pointing towards the few years before 1917 as a period of significant change in the history of American values in this century. Lasch's argument can be read as offering implicit qualification to May's case by emphasizing that crucial social shifts producing "the new radicalism" can be detected at least a generation before the war. This could remain true without conflicting with May's proposal that significant alterations in conceptual language occurred around the end of the first decade of this century. The argument of my essay does return briefly to some issues raised in Lasch's richly suggestive book but these require detailed elaboration in another context. The questions posed by May for intellectual historians remain no less pressing.

[5] Mabel Dodge, *Movers and Shakers* (New York, 1936). Lincoln Steffens, *The Autobiography of Lincoln Steffens* (New York, 1931). Van Wyck Brooks, *Scenes and Portraits* (New York, 1954). Joseph Freeman, *An American Testament* (New York, 1936). Floyd Dell, *Homecoming* (New York, 1933). Hutchins Hapgood, *A Victorian in the Modern World* (New York, 1939). Max Eastman, *Enjoyment of Living* (New York, 1939). Harold Stearns, *The Street I Know* (New York, 1935). Louis Untermeyer, *From Another World* (New York, 1939), Alyse Gregory, *The Day is Gone* (New York, 1948). Ample testimony to the impact of this literature is offered by Kazin, *On Native Grounds*, p. 134: "Who does not know the now routine legend in which the world of 1910–1917 is Washington Square turned Arcadia, in which the barriers are always down, the magazines always promising, the workers always marching, geniuses sprouting in every Village bed-room, Isadora Duncan always dancing—that world of which John Reed was the Byronic hero, Mabel Dodge the hostess, Randolph Bourne the martyr, Van Wyck Brooks the oracle? No other generation in America ever seemed to have so radiant a youth, or has remembered it in so many winsome autobiographies written at forty". The gently sceptical tone of this passage is, curiously enough, generally absent from Kazin's account of these years which is largely in terms of the legend.

> well as new communications. The new spirit was abroad and swept us all together. My own part in it was involuntary. The share I had in bringing people together was inspired not at all by any conscious realisation in me, for I was at that time really more essentially an instrument of the times than ever before. (Dodge)[6]
>
> The year 1912 was really an extraordinary year in America as well as in Europe. It was the year of the election of Wilson, a symptom of immense political discontent. It was a year of intense woman-suffragist activity. In the arts it marked a new era. Color was everywhere—even in neckties. *The Lyric Year* published in New York contained Edna St. Vincent Millay's "Renascence." In Chicago Harriet Monroe founded *Poetry*. Vachel Lindsay suddenly came into his own with "General Booth Enters Heaven", and commenced to give back to his land in magnificent chanted poetry its own barbaric music. *Hindle Wakes* startled New York, as it was later to startle Chicago. The Irish Players came to America. It was then that plans were made for the Post-Impressionist Show which revolutionized American ideas of art. In Chicago Maurice Brown started the Little Theatre. One could go on with the evidence of a New Spirit suddenly come to birth in America. (Dell)...[7]

The significance of 1912 and what follows—at least in terms of the autobiographical evidence—need not be understood primarily as the beginnings of an intellectual revolution, although the formal or theoretical dimension is important. These years should be defined as well in the terms in which they were remembered by Mrs. Dodge and so many others: that is, as years in which a pattern of revolt and innovation which was well established found wider expression and was, at the same time, extended and altered by a younger generation.

To turn to the more formal evidence for intellectual change after 1910—the writings of the social critics—is to be impressed again by the novelty of what these men were doing, as much as by the novelty of what they were saying, What is unusual about the writings of Croly, Lippmann, Bourne and Brooks is the high level of abstraction and eclecticism, the marked self-consciousness of performing a novel function in assessing a whole culture, the concern to repudiate old style dissent, the concern for effectiveness and public identity

[6] Dodge, *Movers and Shakers*, p. 39.

[7] Dell, *Homecoming*, p. 218. Dell's litany of achievements not only shaped later assessments, it also offered considerable assistance to his contemporaries when they came to write their own memoirs. Compare Freeman, *An American Testament*, p. 37, which reproduces Dell's account almost verbatim adding a few new symptoms of "the new spirit" for good measure. The habit of inferring a new *Zeitgeist* from evidence of creative ferment has stuck.

as critics, and finally the consistent preoccupation with establishing a group consciousness for men like themselves.

The point of these observations is strengthened if we ask the question which these men often asked: what precedents for social criticism existed?[8] Their answer takes us back to that group which May calls Questioners: those late Victorians who anticipated, in his view, the political and social ideas of the Rebellion. The list includes John Dewey, William James, Charles Beard, James Harvey Robinson, Lester Frank Ward and E. A. Ross.[9] Simple generalizations about the complex intellectual concerns of these men are worthless, but certain things may be said to suggest that the substantive shift from their writings to those of the generation of 1912 was not striking. May's strategy is to show how this older group of scholars in their attacks on nineteenth century formalism in philosophy, law, economics, and history anticipated "the more devastating questions" of the intellectual Liberation from Europe.[10]

They were more than forerunners, however; they were the teachers of the young rebels . . .

It is useful in this connection to return to the one safe generalization which can be offered about the older generation of social theorists—James, Dewey, Veblen, Beard, Ross and Ward. There is one social and institutional fact which was common to them and which had important consequences for the style and form of their writing: they were all academic men. This meant that there were limits to the level of abstraction and generalization they attained in their work. They spoke within disciplines: philosophy, economics, history, political science and sociology and to that extent the very style of their formulations was predetermined; the moves, so to speak, were familiar.

The key books produced by the academics—for example, *Ethics*, *The Theory of the Leisure Class*, *School and Society*, *Social Control*—reflect the efforts of these men to gain leverage on society through a redefinition of scholarly or academic discourse. They reflect as well an implicit confidence that such leverage could be gained by operating within the institution of the

[8] See, for example, the address of Herbert Croly delivered shortly before the first appearance of *The New Republic* in November 1914 in which he asks this question and answers it in the course of outlining the intentions of the new journal. The address is in the *Willard Straight Papers*, Cornell University Library. I am indebted to David Levy of the University of Oklahoma for drawing it to my attention.

[9] See the estimates of some key figures in this group offered by Lippmann, "An Open Mind: William James", *Everybody's Magazine*, 23 (1910), 800–801 and "The Hope of Democracy", *The New Republic*, 7 (1916), 231. Randolph Bourne, "John Dewey's Philosophy", *The New Republic*, 2 (1914), 145–46. Frequent reference to others listed here occur in the writings of the younger men.

[10] Although May in fact claims relatively little for this shift he makes no attempt to reconcile the fact of clear intellectual affiliation between the two generations and the belief in the novelty of their enterprise expressed by the younger men. May, *The End of American Innocence*, pp. 140–66, 219.

university. For the generation that came to maturity in the late 1880's and 1890's the university offered an institutional connection and a promise of identity which was quite distinctive in the sense that it had not existed before the last quarter of the nineteenth century and it was not to continue to perform precisely this function for very long after 1900.[11]

What is most interesting about this group is how very quickly their central role as the bearers and articulators of critical values is at first complemented and then supplanted by the work of young men who were often their students but whose mature social role was markedly different. The force of this is reflected in the fact that the history of modern American liberal theory after about 1910 can be written without attending to the academic community as the prime *source* of critical attitudes. In 1900 it could be said that the test for a liberal theory was the degree to which one approached the position of certain academics; within two decades the test had changed.

Evidence of the institutional aspect of this shift was provided by William James in his famous Radcliffe address of 1907, "The Social Value of the College Bred." This was one of James's most widely reprinted essays despite the fact that its moral was far from clear. He began by arguing that the highest end of college education was "to enable us to know a good man when we see him." A democracy, he continued, is notoriously incapable of establishing these high preferences without leadership . . .

James offered here an early American use of the noun "intellectual" and it is illuminating to notice how closely he tied it to the fact of college education. James was clear that membership of the club was a function of experience in the only institution which could dedicate itself to the task of "raising the tone of democracy." The aim of the university was to produce people with this sense of common purpose, with this vocational commitment to "indicating the better man." It was precisely at this point however, that James's message became obscured. He concluded by warning about the rise of certain novel institutions dedicated to performing the same task:

> In our essential function of indicating the better man, we now have formidable competitors outside. *McClure's Magazine*, the *American Magazine*, *Collier's Weekly*, and in its fashion, the *World's Work* constitute together a real popular university along this very line.[12]

[11] There has been little work on the university as a social institution. The best suggestions are contained in such works as Richard Hofstadter and Walter Metzger, *The Development of Academic Freedom in the United States* (New York, 1955); Frederick Rudolph *The American College and University* (New York, 1961); Merle Curti and Vernon Carstensen, *The University of Wisconsin* (Madison, 1949); Lawrence Veysey, *The Emergence of the American University* (Chicago, 1965), and R. Jackson Wilson, *In Quest of Community*, 1860–1920 (New York, 1968).

[12] James, *Memories and Studies*, 323–24.

If James was speaking to college graduates who had found their careers throughout the entire spectrum of occupations, why speak of the magazines as rivals, and why use the odd word "outside," since this was presumably where most of his audience already were? . . .

We might conclude that James had difficulty in accepting the possibility that other agencies of disinterested public criticism might seem important and might indeed take on the quality of public institutions. In fact, something very like this was to occur and long before the middle of the twentieth century.

Within three years of the James address one of his most gifted pupils who had recently spent a year assisting George Santayana at Harvard indicated the possibility of a different kind of assessment of these new institutions for "raising the tone of democracy." Writing to the man whose career symbolized the rise of critical journalism, Walter Lippmann declared:

> What I have dreamed of doing is to work under you. Can you use me in your work? There is no position I should go at with such eagerness, because there is no kind of work that appeals to me as much as yours does. Money does not happen to be an important consideration for me at the present time. Opportunity to work and to learn is the thing I am looking for.[13]

Lippmann's appeal to Lincoln Steffens illustrates the important fact that the spectrum of possible social action for young men of intellectual sophistication and radical temper had widened significantly within a generation. If we compare Lippmann's confident and unequivocal choice of a non-academic career with the almost accidental fashion in which his mentor, Steffens, made his way into journalism we may sense the degree of the shift. Steffens returned from years of wandering through European universities with the vague intention of finding an academic career—thinking, as did Herbert Croly and Walter Weyl, that his interests could best be served in this way.[14] Accidents of one sort or another diverted each of these men from what would have been the conventional pattern in the late nineteenth century. They were available accordingly to make contact with a group of young men after 1910 for whom it was no accident that their careers lay outside the walls of the academy.

An important distinction between the two groups of social theorists represented by Dewey on the one hand and Lippman on the other lies, then, in the area of social role. There is a social program to be inferred from the writings of Dewey, James, Ross, Beard, Veblen and others but it is contained within a known disciplinary framework and it is expressed within an estab-

[13] Walter Lippmann to Lincoln Steffens, 18 May 1910, *Lincoln Steffens Papers*, Columbia University Library.

[14] Steffens, *The Autobiography*, p. 169. Forcey, *Crossroads of Liberalism* has the most convenient summary of the careers of Croly and Weyl.

lished institution. The younger men were all attempting to bring the insights of academic scholarship into more direct relation with American society and they were doing it outside the institution of the university and outside the pattern of specific disciplines. They were attempting to establish a new social role—that of independent social criticism—which demanded a new intellectual style—that of synthesizing the insights which had previously been the property of different specialisms. It is primarily for this reason that, of the older generation, James and Dewey appealed most directly to men like Lippmann and Bourne, since both James and Dewey offered the nearest American model for the kind of generalizing language they required. Both James and Dewey had the same appeal in one sense as Freud, Bergson and other representatives of the European "Liberation" after 1910: that is, the capacity to offer formulations which transcended the scope of technical intellectual pursuits and which had relevance for all fields of social inquiry. It is the pressure to find such a language in the second decade of this century which is especially interesting, a pressure which is inextricably tied to the emergence of a new social role.

When we come to ask, finally, about the wider context in which these shifts occurred, we are forced back inevitably to the fact of the Progressive Movement. From this perspective, however, the relevance of the Progressive Movement to an understanding of the literature of social criticism is not as the source of a new *Zeitgeist* which is reflected in the literature, nor is it as the political movement which the critics attempted to influence. If we view the social criticism of these years as a social phenomenon and as an innovation in itself, the importance of Progressivism is in the way it established novel careers open to a king of talent which had previously been channeled in other directions. Withdrawal—either into the academy or into a world of private rebellion—was not inevitable. For men whose temperaments required some kind of identity as critics, Progressivism helped to create another alternative. This does not refer simply to the well-known Progressive anticipations of the New Deal "Brains Trust" where members of the faculty of the University of Wisconsin, for example, drafted legislation and advised the state of Wisconsin on a wide range of public matters. The widened spectrum of opportunity operated in less immediate ways. It is important that by 1910 even the relatively simple-minded phenomenon of muckraking had enjoyed its vogue, that Theodore Roosevelt had emerged as a systematic reformer, that there were numbers of state administrations dotted around the country which talked the same way, that the churches had assumed a social responsibility, and that such institutions as settlement houses were common. In all the writings of the younger men, this context is assumed and the pressing task these men set themselves was caught in Bourne's phrase, "to know what to do with your freedom once you have got it." Bourne's early essays continually remind his fellow radicals of the gulf between their social ideals and the traditional institutions, but at the same time he counsels them to abandon an easy fatalism and take heart from what had become available:

> The radical can thus choose his career with full knowledge of the social possibilities. Where he is forced by economic necessity to engage in distasteful and unsocial work, he does illuminate, as to his attitude and purpose, his enthusiasm and hope. For all his powers and talents can be found to contribute to something; fusing together they form his personality and create his prestige and it is these that give the real impetus and the vital impulse that drive one's belief and ideals into the hearts of other men. If he speaks he will be listened to for it is faith and not doubt that men strain their ears to hear. It is the believing word that they are eager to hear.[15]

This faith did not necessarily lead to any specific career but it widened the area of speculation on what might be done. In fact for most of these men critical journalism occupied their days and provided a living. It was an unusual kind of journalism however which bridged the gap between a professional and a part-time concern for social ideas. Where a man like Hutchins Hapgood saved his rebellion for private parties and wrote for most of his early career conventional "news," Walter Lippmann and Randolph Bourne moved a little closer to resolving this tension.

Progressivism as a cast of mind did not create anything like a *Zeitgeist* for these men. It simply extended the habit of inspecting institutions and of demanding from them a public concern. In this sense, however, criticism became respectable, so that extraordinarily conventional people like the Willard Straights or Mrs. Rankine could find it in themselves to provide money for the establishment of vehicles of expression such as the *New Republic* and *The Seven Arts*. In so doing they brought to prominence an unusual group of men whose attempts to establish an appropriate model for social criticism undermined the simple moralisms of much that passed for reform and middle class Progressivism.

For a more precise definition of this group we can do no better than to adopt William James's word—intellectuals. We noticed how closely his sense of the word was tied to institutional affiliation with the university. In the years which followed his speech the word acquired a wider reference. Harold Stearns's attempt in 1921 to assess this altered usage offers interesting evidence for the social history of the period, separating James's Radcliffe address from *America and the Young Intellectual*. Stearns excluded from his definition college and university professors, allowing as an exception an occasional man of genius like William James who was able to "rise above his professional identifications." Similarly, in the world of science,

[15] Randolph Bourne, "For Radicals", in *Youth and Life* (New York, 1913), p. 308.

only a man like Huxley or Agassiz retained a capacity to "transcend his special sphere."

> No, the term intellectuals has come to mean something both broader and narrower: publicists, editors of nontrade magazines, pamphleteers, writers on general topics. In France they are represented by such men as Henri Barbusse, Anatole France and Romain Rolland; in England, say, by Shaw, Wells, Chesterton, Angell, Massingham, Scott, Brailsford, Wallas and Cole; in America—by such as the reader may nominate.[16]

The possibility of generalizing the word in this way was an essential part of the changed conditions in American intellectual life which became apparent in the years between James and Stearns.

Selected Additional Reading

Aaron, Daniel. *Man of Good Hope, A Story of American Progressives.* (New York: Oxford, 1961.)

Bremner, Robert H. *From the Depths, The Discovery of Poverty in the United States.* (New York: N.Y. Univ. Press, 1956.)

Commager, Henry Steele. *The American Mind, An Interpretation of American Thought and Character Since the 1880's.* (New Haven: Yale Press, 1950.)

Cremin, Lawrence A. *The Transformation of the School, Progressivism in American Education, 1876–1957.* (New York: Knopf, 1961.)

Faulkner, Harold Underwood. *The Quest for Social Justice, 1898–1914.* (New York: Macmillan, 1931.)

Forcey, Charles. *The Crossroads of Liberalism; Croly, Weyl, Lippmann, and the Progressive Era.* (New York: Oxford, 1961.)

Goldman, Eric F. *Rendezvous with Destiny: A History of Modern American Reform.* (New York: Knopf, 1952.)

Haber, Samuel. *Efficiency and Uplift, Scientific Management in the Progressive Era, 1890–1920.* (Chicago: University of Chicago, 1964.)

Hofstadter, Richard. *The Age of Reform: From Bryan to F.D.R.* (New York: Knopf, 1955.)

Lasch, Christopher. *The New Radicalism in America (1889–1963): The Intellectual as a Social Type.* (New York: Knopf, 1965.)

[16] Harold Stearns, "Where are our Intellectuals", in *America and the Young Intellectuals* (New York, 1921), pp. 46–7.

Levine, Daniel. *Varieties of Reform Thought.* (Madison, Wisc.: University of Wisc., 1964.)

Lubove, Roy. *The Professional Altruist, The Emergence of Social Work as a Career.* (Cambridge, Mass.: Harvard University Press, 1965.)

May, Henry F. *The End of American Innocence, A Study of the First Years of Our Time, 1912–1917.* (New York: Knopf, 1959.)

Noble, David W. *The Paradox of Progressive Thought.* (Minneapolis: University of Minn., 1958.)

Schneider, Robert W. *Five Novelists of the Progressive Era.* (New York: Columbia, 1965.)

White, Morton G. *Social Thought in America: The Revolt Against Formalism.* (New York: Viking, 1949.)

Wiebe, Robert H. *The Search For Order, 1877–1920.* (New York: Hill and Wang, 1967.)

Section Three
Alienation and the Lost Generation

DAVID W. NOBLE

Contents

Introduction

The 1920's is the decade of the Lost Generation, the decade of the most dramatic alienation of American intellectuals from the mainstream of their society. No consensus has emerged as yet among scholars to explain this alienation. And too often the explanations have focused only on the events of the 1920's themselves, or on the immediately preceding years of the Progressive Movement. American cultural historians have not shown great interest in using general theories about the existence of alienation in modern civilization, which have been developed by Marxists or by European conservative philosophers speaking from a neo-medieval perspective.

One reason that recent scholars have ignored general theories of alienation is to be found in the following selection of readings from the 1920's. Men like Van Wyck Brooks and Lewis Mumford and Randolph Bourne write from an extremely nationalistic perspective. They attribute the alienation of American intellectuals largely to the absence of an American national culture. They believe that dependence upon Europe has been responsible for the superficiality of American culture. And the scholars of the 1950's and 1960's have to a great extent continued this nationalistic tradition without asking whether American alienation is related to a pattern of alienation within modern civilization.

But there is a remarkable parallel between Van Wyck Brooks' analysis of the conflict between the materialism of the general society and the spirituality of the artist, and the similar analysis developed by Ralph Waldo Emerson in the 1830's. Our scholars have not noticed that Emerson's belief that the artist must free himself from bondage to a society dominated by business ethics and relate to a culture with aesthetic and spiritual values paralleled the appearance in Western Europe of the artistic rebel as romantic hero.

Throughout Western Europe, England, and the United States in the early Nineteenth Century, artists and intellectuals were rejecting the rational, universal principles of Enlightenment science and capitalism as materialistic and therefore destructive to the human soul. Throughout the entire Nineteenth Century, therefore, romantic artists were looking for an alternative spiritual environment, and to a considerable extent, they defined national culture, in contrast to international civilization, as capable of providing such a spiritual environment. Capitalism, technology, science were defined as parts of the international civilization to be rejected. Since Marx divided capitalism from technology and science, and ascribed alienation to capitalism but related human fulfillment to technology and science, the American intellectuals working in the romantic tradition would not work with Marxian ideas.

Many American intellectuals, like Henry Adams, were in cultural despair by the late Nineteenth Century because they saw the forces of science and technology and capitalism overwhelming the romantic protest. But the extreme alienation of the 1920's, the dramatic appearance of a Lost Generation, is to be explained by the growing optimism of the years of Progressivism, 1900–1917, for it was the pre-war progressive confidence that decadence was being overcome, that a more human culture was being constructed, that patterns of fragmentation were being overcome, that materialism was being restrained, that a spiritual awakening was occurring.

The extreme bleakness of vision of many young people in 1920, therefore, came from the failure of the progressive movement that threw them back into an already existing despair. Ernest Hemingway, born in 1898, was as pessimistic in 1920 as the elderly Mark Twain had become by 1890. The promise of the Progressive Movement was the creation of a national culture with a spiritual orientation and the promise had failed.

The alienation of the 1920's, therefore, is to be seen as a continuation of an intellectual pattern which had emerged in Europe and the United States in the early Nineteenth Century. But it is also to be seen as a reaction to the loss of the hope that Progressivism had discovered the means to end the Nineteenth-century alienation of the intellectual in the first years of the Twentieth Century.

Sources

Randolph S. Bourne
Disillusionment with Progressivism

(1917)

Randolph S. Bourne (1886–1918) was one of the most intelligent and perceptive of the young intellectuals who had hoped that with the development of John Dewey's philosophy of pragmatism the fragmentation and materialism of American society was being overcome during the Progressive Era. Writing for the *New Republic* magazine and other new journals of opinion that had been created in the early 20th Century to further the revolutionary construction of an organic national culture, Bourne was bitterly disillusioned by the way in which these liberal intellectuals apparently had regressed into a defense of the nineteenth-century patterns of civilization by justifying American participation in World War I. This essay expresses that disillusionment as it analyzes the regression of Bourne's intellectual fathers.

To those of us who still retain an irreconcilable animus against war, it has been a bitter experience to see the unanimity with which the American intellectuals have thrown their support to the use of war-technique in the crisis in which America found herself. Socialists, college professors, publicists, new-republicans, practitioners of literature, have vied with each other in confirming with their intellectual faith the collapse of neutrality and the riveting of the war-mind on a hundred million more of the world's people. And the intellectuals are not content with confirming our belligerent gesture. They are now complacently asserting that it was they who effectively willed it, against the hesitation and dim perceptions of the American democratic masses. A war made deliberately by the intellectuals! A calm moral verdict, arrived at after a penetrating study of inexorable facts! Sluggish masses, too remote from the world-conflict to be stirred, too lacking in intellect to perceive their danger! An alert intellectual class, saving the people in spite of themselves, biding their time with Fabian strategy until the nation could be

---

Randolph Bourne, "The War and the Intellectuals," *The Seven Arts*, II (June 1917), pp. 133–46. Reprinted with permission of AMS Press, Inc., New York.

moved into war without serious resistance! An intellectual class, gently guiding a nation through sheer force of ideas into what the other nations entered only through predatory craft or popular hysteria or militarist madness! A war free from any taint of self-seeking, a war that will secure the triumph of democracy and internationalize the world! This is the picture which the more self-conscious intellectuals have formed of themselves, and which they are slowly impressing upon a population which is being led no man knows whither by an indubitably intellectualized President. And they are right, in that the war certainly did not spring from either the ideals or the prejudices, from the national ambitions or hysterias, of the American people, however acquiescent the masses prove to be, and however clearly the intellectuals prove their putative intuition.

Those intellectuals who have felt themselves totally out of sympathy with this drag toward war will seek some explanation for this joyful leadership. They will want to understand this willingness of the American intellect to open the sluices and flood us with the sewage of the war spirit. We cannot forget the virtuous horror and stupefaction which filled our college professors when they read the famous manifesto of their ninety-three German colleagues in defence of their war. To the American academic mind of 1914 defence of war was inconceivable. From Bernhardi it recoiled as from a blasphemy, little dreaming that two years later would find it creating its own cleanly reasons for imposing military service on the country and for talking of the rough rude currents of health and regeneration that war would send through the American body politic. They would have thought anyone mad who talked of shipping American men by the hundreds of thousands—conscripts—to die on the fields of France. Such a spiritual change seems catastrophic when we shoot our minds back to those days when neutrality was a proud thing. But the intellectual progress has been so gradual that the country retains little sense of the irony. The war sentiment, begun so gradually but so perseveringly by the preparedness advocates who came from the ranks of big business, caught hold of one after another of the intellectual groups. With the aid of Roosevelt, the murmurs became a monotonous chant, and finally a chorus so mighty that to be out of it was at first to be disreputable and finally almost obscene. And slowly a strident rant was worked up against Germany which compared very creditably with the German fulminations against the greedy power of England. The nerve of the war-feeling centered, of course, in the richer and older classes of the Atlantic seaboard, and was keenest where there were French or English business and particularly social connections. The sentiment then spread over the country as a class-phenomenon, touching everywhere those upper-class elements in each section who identified themselves with this Eastern ruling group. It must never be forgotten that in every community it was the least liberal and least democratic elements among whom the preparedness and later the war sentiment was found. The farmers were apathetic, the small business men and workingmen are still apathetic towards the war. The election was a vote of confidence of these latter classes in a President who would keep the faith of neutrality. The intellectuals, in other words, have identified themselves with the least democratic forces in American life. They have assumed the leadership for war of those very classes whom the American democracy has been immemorially fighting. Only in a world where irony was dead could an intellectual class enter war at the head of such illiberal cohorts in the avowed cause of world-liberalism and world-democracy. No one is left to point out the undemocratic nature of this war-liberalism. In a time of faith, skepticism is the most intolerable of all insults.

Our intellectual class might have been occupied, during the last two years of war, in studying and clarifying the ideals and aspirations of the American democracy, in discovering a true Americanism which would not have been merely nebulous but might have federated the different ethnic groups and traditions. They might have spent the time in endeavoring to clear the public mind of the cant of war, to get rid of old mystical notions that clog our thinking. We might have used the time for a great wave of education, for setting our house in spiritual order. We could at least have set the problem before ourselves. If our intellectuals were going to lead the administration, they might conceivably have tried to find some way of securing peace by making neutrality effective. They might have turned their intellectual energy not to the problem of jockeying the nation into war, but to the problem of using our vast neutral power to attain democratic ends for the rest of the world and ourselves without the use of the malevolent technique of war. They might have failed. The point is that they scarcely tried. The time was spent not in clarification and education, but in a mulling over of nebulous ideals of democracy and liberalism and civilization which had never meant anything fruitful to those ruling classes who now so glibly used them, and in giving free rein to the elementary instinct of self-defence. The whole era has been spiritually wasted. The outstanding feature has been not its Americanism but its intense colonialism. The offence of our intellectuals was not so much that they were colonial—for what could we expect of a nation composed of so many national elements?—but that it was so one-sidedly and partisanly colonial. The official, reputable expression of the intellectual class has been that of the English colonial. Certain portions of it have been even more loyalist than the King, more British even than Australia. Other colonial attitudes have been vulgar. The colonialism of the other American stocks was denied a hearing from the start. America might have been made a meeting-ground for the different national attitudes. An intellectual class, cultural colonists of the different European nations, might have threshed out the issues here as they could not be threshed out in Europe. Instead of this, the English colonials in university and press took command at the start, and we became an intellectual Hungary where thought was subject to an effective process of Magyarization.

The reputable opinion of the American intellectuals became more and more either what could be read pleasantly in London, or what was written in an earnest effort to put Englishmen straight on their war-aims and war-technique. This Magyarization of thought produced as a counter-reaction a peculiarly offensive and inept German apologetic, and the two partisans divided the field between them. The great masses, the other ethnic groups, were inarticulate. American public opinion was almost as little prepared for war in 1917 as it was in 1914 . . .

We have had to watch, therefore, in this country the same process which so shocked us abroad—the coalescence of the intellectual classes in support of the military programme. In this country, indeed, the socialist intellectuals did not even have the grace of their German brothers and wait for the declaration of war before they broke for cover. And when they declared for war they showed how thin was the intellectual veneer of their socialism. For they called us in terms that might have emanated from any bourgeois journal to defend democracy and civilization, just as if it was not exactly against those very bourgeois democracies and capitalist civilizations that socialists had been fighting for decades. But so subtle is the spiritual chemistry of the "inside" that all this intellectual cohesion—herd-instinct become herd-intellect—which seemed abroad so hysterical and so servile, comes to us here in highly rational terms. We go to war to save the world from subjugation! But the German intellectuals went to war to save their culture from barbarization! And the French went to war to save their beautiful France! And the English to save international honor! And Russia, most altruistic and self-sacrificing of all, to save a small State from destruction! Whence is our miraculous intuition of our moral spotlessness? Whence our confidence that history will not unravel huge economic and imperialist forces upon which our rationalizations float like bubbles? The Jew often marvels that his race alone should have been chosen as the true people of the cosmic God. Are not our intellectuals equally fatuous when they tell us that our war of all wars is stainless and thrillingly achieving for good?

An intellectual class that was wholly rational would have called insistently for peace and not for war. For months the crying need has been for a negotiated peace, in order to avoid the ruin of a deadlock. Would not the same amount of resolute statesmanship thrown into intervention have secured a peace that would have been a subjugation for neither side? Was the terrific bargaining power of a great neutral ever really used? Our war followed, as all wars follow, a monstrous failure of diplomacy. Shamefacedness should now be our intellectuals' attitude, because the American play for peace was made so little more than a polite play. The intellectuals have still to explain why, willing as they now are to use force to continue the war to absolute exhaustion, they were not willing to use force to coerce the world to a speedy peace . . .

The case of the intellectuals seems, therefore, only very speciously rational. They could have used their energy to force a just peace or at least to devise other means than war for carrying through American policy. They could have used their intellectual energy to ensure that our participation in the war meant the international order which they wish. Intellect was not so used. It was used to lead an apathetic nation into an irresponsible war, without guarantees from those belligerents whose cause we were saving. The American intellectual, therefore, has been rational neither in his hindsight nor his foresight. To explain him we must look beneath the intellectual reasons to the emotional disposition. It is not so much what they thought as how they felt that explains our intellectual class. Allowing for colonial sympathy, there was still the personal shock in a world-war which outraged all our preconceived notions of the way the world was tending. It reduced to rubbish most of the humanitarian internationalism and democratic nationalism which had been the emotional thread of our intellectuals' life. We had suddenly to make a new orientation. There were mental conflicts. Our latent colonialism strove with our longing for American unity. Our desire for peace strove with our desire for national responsibility in the world. That first lofty and remote and not altogether unsound feeling of our spiritual isolation from the conflict could not last. There was the itch to be in the great experience which the rest of the world was having. Numbers of intelligent people who had never been stirred by the horrors of capitalistic peace at home were shaken out of their slumber by the horrors of war in Belgium. Never having felt responsibility for labor wars and oppressed masses and excluded races at home, they had a large fund of idle emotional capital to invest in the oppressed nationalities and ravaged villages of Europe. Hearts that had felt only ugly contempt for democratic strivings at home beat in tune with the struggle for freedom abroad. All this was natural, but it tended to over-emphasize our responsibility. And it threw our thinking out of gear. The task of making our own country detailedly fit for peace was abandoned in favor of a feverish concern for the management of the war, advice to the fighting governments on all matters, military, social, and political, and a gradual working up of the conviction that we were ordained as a nation to lead all erring brothers towards the light of liberty and democracy. The failure of the American intellectual class to erect a creative attitude toward the war can be explained by these sterile mental conflicts which the shock to our ideals sent raging through us.

Mental conflicts end either in a new and higher synthesis or adjustment, or else in a reversion to more primitive ideas which have been outgrown but to which we drop when jolted out of our attained position. The war caused in America a recrudescence of nebulous ideals which a younger generation was fast outgrowing because it had passed the wistful stage and was discovering concrete ways of getting them incarnated in actual institutions. The shock of the war threw us back from this pragmatic work into an emotional bath of these old ideals. There was even a somewhat rarefied revival of our primitive Yankee boastfulness, the reversion of senility to that republican childhood when we expected the whole world to copy our republican institutions. We amusingly ignored the fact that it was just that Imperial German regime, to whom we are to teach the art of self-government, which our own Federal structure, with its executive irresponsible in foreign policy and with its absence of parliamentary control, most resembles. And we are missing the exquisite irony of the unaffected homage paid by the American democratic intellectuals to the last and most detested of Britain's tory premiers as the representative of a "liberal" ally, as well as the irony of the selection of the best hated of America's bourbon "old guard" as the missionary of American democracy to Russia.

The intellectual state that could produce such things is one where reversion has taken place to more primitive ways of thinking. Simple syllogisms are substituted for analysis, things are known by their labels, our heart's desire dictates what we shall see. The American intellectual class, having failed to make the higher syntheses, regresses to ideas that can issue in quick, simplified action. Thought becomes any easy rationalization of what is actually going on or what is to happen inevitably tomorrow. It is true that certain groups did rationalize their colonialism and attach the doctrine of the inviolability of British sea-power to the doctrine of a League of Peace. But this agile resolution of the mental conflict did not become a higher synthesis, to be creatively developed. It gradually merged into a justification for our going to war. It petrified into a dogma to be propagated. Criticism flagged and emotional propaganda began. Most of the socialists, the college professors and the practitioners of literature, however, have not even reached this high-water mark of synthesis. Their mental conflicts have been resolved much more simply. War in the interests of democracy! This was almost the sum of their philosophy. The primitive idea to which they regressed became almost insensibly translated into a craving for action. War was seen as the crowning relief of their indecision. At last action, irresponsibility, the end of anxious and torturing attempts to reconcile peace-ideals with the drag of the world towards Hell. An end to the pain of trying to adjust the facts to what they ought to be! Let us consecrate the facts as ideal! Let us join the greased slide towards war! The momentum increased. Hesitations, ironies, consciences, considerations—all were drowned in the elemental blare of doing something aggressive, colossal. The new-found Sabbath "peacefulness of being at war"! The thankfulness with which so many intellectuals lay down and floated with the current betrays the hesitation and suspense through which they had been. The American university is a brisk and happy place these days. Simple, unquestioning action has superseded the knots of thought. The thinker dances with reality.

With how many of the acceptors of war has it been mostly a dread of intellectual suspense? It is a mistake to suppose that intellectuality necessarily makes for suspended judgments. The intellect craves certitude. It takes effort to keep it supple and pliable. In a time of danger and disaster we jump desperately for some dogma to cling to. The time comes, if we try to hold out, when our nerves are sick with fatigue, and we seize in a great healing wave of release some doctrine that can be immediately translated into action. Neutrality meant suspense, and so it became the object of loathing to frayed nerves. The vital myth of the League of Peace provides a dogma to jump to. With war the world becomes motor again and speculation is brushed aside like cobwebs. The blessed emotion of self-defense intervenes too, which focused millions in Europe. A few keep up a critical pose after war is begun, but since they usually advise action which is in one-to-one correspondence with what the mass is already doing, their criticism is little more than a rationalization of the common emotional drive.

The results of war on the intellectual class are already apparent. Their thought becomes little more than a description and justification of what is going on. They turn upon any rash one who continues idly to speculate. Once the war is on, the conviction spreads that individual thought is helpless, that the only way one can count is as a cog in the great wheel. There is no good holding back. We are told to dry our unnoticed and ineffective tears and plunge into the great work. Not only is everyone forced into line, but the new certitude becomes idealized. It is a noble realism which opposes itself to futile obstruction and the cowardly refusal to face facts. This realistic boast is so loud and sonorous that one wonders whether realism is always a stern and intelligent grappling with realities. May it not be sometimes a mere surrender to the actual, an abdication of the ideal through a sheer fatigue from intellectual suspense? The pacifist is roundly scolded for refusing to face the facts, and for retiring into his own world of sentimental desire. But is the realist, who refuses to challenge or criticise facts, entitled to any more credit than that which comes from following the line of least resistance? The realist thinks he at least can control events by linking himself to the forces that are moving. Perhaps he can. But if it is a question of controlling war, it is difficult to see how the child on the back of a mad elephant is to be any more effective in stopping the beast than is the child who tries to stop him from the ground. The ex-humanitarian, turned realist, sneers at the snobbish neutrality, colossal conceit, crooked thinking, dazed sensibilities, of those who are still unable to find any balm of consolation for this war. We manufacture consolations here in America while there are probably not a dozen men fighting in Europe who did not long ago give up every reason for their being there except that nobody knew how to get them away.

But the intellectuals whom the crisis has crystallized into an acceptance of war have put themselves into a terrifyingly strategic position. It is only on the craft, in the stream, they say, that one has any chance of controlling the current forces for liberal purposes. If we obstruct, we surrender all power for influence. If we responsibly approve, we then retain our power for guiding. We will be listened to as responsible thinkers, while those who obstructed the coming of war have committed intellectual suicide and shall be cast into outer darkness. Criticism by the ruling powers will only be accepted from those intellectuals who are in sympathy with the general tendency of the war. Well, it is true that they may guide, but if their stream leads to disaster and the frustration of national life, is their guiding any more than a preference whether they shall go over the right-hand or the left-hand side of the precipice? Meanwhile, however, there is comfort on board. Be with us, they call, or be negligible, irrelevant. Dissenters are already excommunicated. Irreconcilable radicals, wringing their hands among the debris, become the most despicable and impotent of men. There seems no choice for the intellectual but to join the mass of acceptance. But again the terrible dilemma arises—either support what is going on, in which case you count for nothing because you are swallowed in the mass and great incalculable forces bear you on; or remain aloof, passively resistant, in which case you count for nothing because you are outside the machinery of reality.

Is there no place left, then, for the intellectual who cannot yet crystallize, who does not dread suspense, and is not yet drugged with fatigue? The American intellectuals, in their preoccupation with reality, seem to have forgotten that the real enemy is War rather than imperial Germany. There is work to be done to prevent this war of ours from passing into popular mythology as a holy crusade. What shall we do with leaders who tell us that we go to war in moral spotlessness, or who make "democracy" synonymous with a republican form of government? There is work to be done in still shouting that all the revolutionary by-products will not justify the war, or make war anything else than the most noxious complex of all the evils that afflict men. There must be some to find no consolation whatever, and some to sneer at those who buy the cheap emotion of sacrifice. There must be some irreconcilables left who will not even accept the war with walrus tears. There must be some to call unceasingly for peace, and some to insist that the terms of settlement shall be not only liberal but democratic. There must be some intellectuals who are not willing to use the old discredited counters again and to support a peace which would leave all the old inflammable materials of armament lying about the world. There must still be opposition to any contemplated "liberal" world-order founded on military coalitions. The "irreconcilable" need not be disloyal. He need not even be "impossibilist." His apathy towards war should take the form of a heightened energy and enthusiasm for the education, the art, the interpretation that make for life in the midst of the world of death. The intellectual who retains his animus against war will push out more boldly than ever to make his case solid against it. The old ideals crumble; new ideals must be forged. His mind will continue to roam widely and ceaselessly. The thing he will fear most is premature crystallization. If the American intellectual class rivets itself to a "liberal" philosophy that perpetuates the old errors, there will then be need for "democrats" whose task will be to divide, confuse, disturb, keep the intellectual waters constantly in motion to prevent any such ice from ever forming.

H. L. Mencken
Disillusionment with the People

(1922)

In escaping the growing despair of the late Nineteenth Century, the Progressive Movement had placed great emphasis on the people as the source of national rejuvenation. Both in explicit political theory and in the educational philosophy of John Dewey, the argument was that the upper classes had been corrupted by European ideas but that the common people remained pure and untainted. By tapping that purity, therefore, American politics could be made organically democratic. All through the early years of the Twentieth Century, H. L. Mencken (1880–1956) had been attacking this faith in the political wisdom of the people. Now, in the 1920's, because of disillusionment with the failure of Progressivism, more and more young intellectuals listened to Mencken and some, like Walter Lippmann, joined him in undermining the belief that constructive political reform could come from the general public.

> No person shall be a Representative who . . . shall not, when elected, be an inhabitant of that State in which he shall be chosen . . . No person shall be a Senator who . . . shall not, when elected, be an inhabitant of that State for which he shall be chosen.

Specialists in political archæology will recognize these sentences; they are from Article I, Sections 2, and 3, of the constitution of the United States. I have heard and forgotten how they got there; no doubt the cause lay in the fierce jealousy of the States. But whatever the fact, I have a notion that there are few provisions of the constitution that have had a more profound effect upon the character of practical politics in the Republic, or, indirectly, upon the general colour of American thinking in the political department. They have made steadily for parochialism in legislation, for the security and prosperity of petty local bosses and machines, for the multiplication of pocket and rotten boroughs of the worst sort, and, above all, for the pro-

H. L. Mencken, "Politics," from *Civilization in the United States*, Harold E. Stearns, Ed. (New York, 1922), pp. 21–27.

gressive degeneration of the honesty and honour of representatives. They have greased the ways for the trashy and ignoble fellow who aspires to get into Congress, and they have blocked them for the man of sense, dignity, and self-respect. More, perhaps, than any other single influence they have been responsible for the present debauched and degraded condition of the two houses, and particularly of the lower one. Find me the worst ass in Congress, and I'll show you a man they have helped to get there and to stay there. Find me the most shameless scoundrel, and I'll show you another.

No such centripedal mandate, as far as I have been able to discover, is in the fundamental law of any other country practising the representative system. An Englishman, if ambition heads him toward St. Stephen's, may go hunting for a willing constituency wherever the hunting looks best, and if he fails in the Midlands he may try again in the South, or in the North, or in Scotland or Wales. A Frenchman of like dreams has the same privilege; the only condition, added after nineteen years of the Third Republic, is that he may not be a candidate in two or more *arrondissements* at once. And so with a German, an Italian, or a Spaniard. But not so with an American. He must be an actual inhabitant of the State he aspires to represent at Washington. More, he must be, in all save extraordinary cases, an actual inhabitant of the congressional district—for here, by a characteristic American process, the fundamental law is sharpened by custom. True enough, this last requirement is not laid down by the constitution. It would be perfectly legal for the thirty-fifth New York district, centering at Syracuse, to seek its congressman in Manhattan, or even at Sing Sing. In various iconoclastic States, in fact, the thing has been occasionally done. But not often; not often enough to produce any appreciable effect. The typical congressman remains a purely local magnifico, the gaudy cock of some small and usually far from appetizing barnyard. His rank and dignity as a man are measured by provincial standards of the most puerile sort, and his capacity to discharge the various and onerous duties of his office is reckoned almost exclusively in terms of his ability to hold his grip upon the local party machine.

If he has genuine ability, it is a sort of accident. If he is thoroughly honest, it is next door to a miracle. Of the 430-odd representatives who carry on so diligently and obscenely at Washington, making laws and determining policies for the largest free nation ever seen in the world, there are not two dozen whose views upon any subject under the sun carry any weight whatsoever outside their own bailiwicks, and there are not a dozen who rise to anything approaching unmistakable force and originality. They are, in the overwhelming main, shallow fellows, ignorant of the grave matters they deal with and too stupid to learn. If, as is often proposed, the United States should adopt the plan of parliamentary responsibility and the ministry should be recruited from the lower house, then it would be difficult, without a radical change in election methods, to fetch up even such pale talents and modest decencies as were assembled for their cabinets by Messrs. Wilson and Harding. The better sort of congressmen, to be sure, acquire after long service a good deal of technical proficiency. They know the traditions and precedents of the two houses; they can find their way in and out of every rathole in the Capitol; they may be trusted to carry on the legislative routine in a more or less shipshape manner. Of such sort are the specialists paraded in the newspapers—on the tariff, on military affairs, on foreign relations, and so on. They come to know, in time, almost as much as a Washington correspondent, or one of their own committee clerks. But the average congressman lifts himself to no such heights of sagacity. He is content to be led by the fuglemen and bellwethers. Examine him at leisure, and you will find that he is incompetent and imbecile, and not only incompetent and imbecile, but also incurably dishonest. The first principles of civilized law-making are quite beyond him; he ends, as he began, a local politician, interested only in jobs. His knowledge is that of a third-rate country lawyer—which he often is in fact. His intelligence is that of a country newspaper editor, or evangelical divine. His standards of honour are those of a country banker—which he also often is. To demand sense of such a man, or wide and accurate information, or a delicate feeling for the public and private proprieties, is to strain his parts beyond endurance.

The constitution, of course, stops with Congress, but its influence is naturally powerful within the States, and one finds proofs of the fact on all sides. It is taking an herculean effort everywhere to break down even the worst effects of this influence; the prevailing tendency is still to discover a mysterious virtue in the office-holder who was born and raised in the State, or county, or city, or ward. The judge must come from the bar of the court he is to adorn; the mayor must be part and parcel of the local machine; even technical officers, such as engineers and health commissioners, lie under the constitutional blight. The thing began as a belief in local self-government, the oldest of all the sure cures for despotism. But it has gradually taken on the character of government by local politicians, which is to say, by persons quite unable to comprehend the most elemental problems of State and nation, and unfitted by nature to deal with them honestly and patriotically, even if they could comprehend them. Just as prohibition was forced upon the civilized minorities collected in the great cities against their most vigorous and persistent opposition, so the same minorities, when it comes to intrastate affairs, are constantly at the mercy of predatory bands of rural politicians. If there is any large American city whose peculiar problems are dealt with competently and justly by its State legislature, then I must confess that twenty years in journalism have left me ignorant of it. An unending struggle for fairer dealing goes on in every State that has large cities, and every concession to their welfare is won only at the cost of gigantic effort. The State legislature is never intelligent; it represents only the average mind of the county bosses, whose sole concern is with jobs. The machines that they represent are wholly political, but they have no political principles in any rational sense. Their one purpose and function is to maintain their adherents in the public offices, or to obtain for them in some other way a share of the State funds. They are quite willing to embrace any new doctrine, however fantastic, or to abandon any old one, however long supported, if only the business will promote their trade and so secure their power.

This concentration of the ultimate governmental authority in the hands of small groups of narrow, ignorant, and unconscionable manipulators tends inevitably to degrade the actual office-holder, or, what is the same thing, to make office-holding prohibitive to all men not already degraded. It is almost impossible to imagine a man of genuine self-respect and dignity offering himself as a candidate for the lower house—or, since the direct primary and direct elections brought it down to the common level, for the upper house—in the average American constituency. His necessary dealings with the electors themselves, and with the idiots who try more or less honestly to lead them, would be revolting enough, but even worse would be his need of making his terms with the professional politicians of his party—the bosses of the local machine. These bosses naturally make the most of the constitutional limitation; it works powerfully in their favour. A local notable, in open revolt against them, may occasionally beat them by appealing directly to the voters, but nine times out of ten, when there is any sign of such a catastrophe, they are prompt to perfume the ticket by bringing forth another local notable who is safe and sane, which is to say, subservient and reliable. The thing is done constantly; it is a matter of routine; it accounts for most of the country bankers, newspaper owners, railroad lawyers, proprietors of cement works, and other such village bigwigs in the lower house. Here everything runs to the advantage of the bosses. It is not often that the notable in rebellion is gaudy enough to blind the plain people to the high merits of his more docile opponent. They see him too closely and know him too well. He shows none of that exotic charm which accounts, on a different plane, for exogamy. There is no strangeness, no mysteriousness, above all, no novelty about him.

It is my contention that this strangle-hold of the local machines would be vastly less firm if it could be challenged, not only by rebels within the constituency, but also by salient men from outside. The presidential campaigns, indeed, offer plenty of direct proof of it. In these campaigns it is a commonplace for strange doctrines and strange men to force themselves upon the practical politicians in whole sections of the country, despite their constant effort to keep their followers faithful to the known. All changes, of whatever sort, whether in leaders or in ideas, are opposed by such politicians at the start, but time after time they are compelled to acquiesce and to hurrah. Bryan, as every one knows, forced himself upon the Democratic party by appealing directly to the people; the politicians, in the main, were bitterly against him until further resistance was seen to be useless, and they attacked him again the moment he began to weaken, and finally disposed of him. So with Wilson. It would be absurd to say that the politicians of his party—and especially the bosses of the old machines in the congressional districts—were in favour of him in 1912. They were actually against him almost unanimously. He got past their guard and broke down their resolution to nominate some more trustworthy candidate by operating directly upon the emotions of the voters. For some reason never sufficiently explained he became the heir of the spirit of rebellion raised by Bryan sixteen years before, and was given direct and very effective aid by Bryan himself. Roosevelt saddled himself upon the Republican party in exactly the same way. The bosses made heroic efforts to sidetrack him, to shelve him, to get rid of him by any means short of homicide, but his bold enterprises and picturesque personality enchanted the people, and if it had not been for the extravagant liberties that he took with his popularity in later years he might have retained it until his death.

The same possibility of unhorsing the machine politicians, I believe, exists in even the smallest electoral unit. All that is needed is the chance to bring in the man. Podunk cannot produce him herself, save by a sort of miracle. If she has actually hatched him, he is far away by the time he has come to his full stature and glitter—in the nearest big city, in Chicago or New York. Podunk is proud of him, and many other Podunks, perhaps, are stirred by his ideas, his attitudes, his fine phrases—but he lives, say, in some Manhattan congressional district which has the Hon. Patrick Googan as its representative by divine right, and so there is no way to get him into the halls of Congress. In his place goes the Hon. John P. Balderdash, State's attorney for five years, State senator for two terms, and county judge for a brief space—and always a snide and petty fellow, always on the best of terms with the local bosses, always eager for a job on any terms they lay down. The yokels vote for the Hon. Mr. Balderdash, not because they admire him, but because their only choice is between him and the Hon. James Bosh. If anything even remotely resembling a first-rate man could come into the contest, if it were lawful for them to rid themselves of their recurrent dilemma by soliciting the interest of such a man, then they would often enough rise in their might and compel their parish overlords, as the English put it, to adopt him. But the constitution protects these overlords in their business, and in the long run the voters resign all thought of deliverance. Thus the combat remains one between small men, and interest in it dies out. Most of the men who go to the lower house are third-raters, even in their own narrow bailiwicks. In my own congressional district, part of a large city, there has never been a candidate of any party, during the twenty years that I have voted, who was above the intellectual level of a corner grocer. No successful candidate of that district has ever made a speech in Congress (or out of it) worth hearing, or contributed a single sound idea otherwise to the solution of any public problem. One and all, they have confined themselves exclusively to the trade in jobs. One and all, they have been ciphers in the house and before the country.

Well, perhaps I labour my point too much. It is, after all, not important. The main thing is the simple fact that the average representative from my district is typical of Congress—that, if anything, he is superior to the normal congressman of these, our days. That normal congressman, as year chases year, tends to descend to such depths of puerility, to such abysses of petty shysterism, that he becomes offensive alike to the intelligence and to the nose. His outlook, when it is honest, is commonly childish—and it is very seldom honest. The product of a political system which puts all stress upon the rewards of public office, he is willing to make any sacrifice, of dignity, of principle, of honor, to hold and have those rewards. He has no courage, no intellectual *amour propre*, no ardent belief in anything save his job, and the jobs of his friends. It was easy for Wilson to beat him into line on the war issue; it was easy for the prohibitionists to intimidate and stampede him; it is easy for any resolute man or group of men to do likewise. I read the *Congressional Record* faithfully, and have done so for years. In the Senate debates, amid oceans of tosh, I occasionally encounter a flash of wit or a gleam of sense; direct elections have not yet done their work. But in the lower house there is seldom anything save a garrulous and intolerable imbecility. The discussion of measures of the utmost importance—bills upon which the security and prosperity of the whole nation depend—is carried on in the manner of the Chautauqua and the rural stump.

Van Wyck Brooks
The Need for Artistic Heroism

(1922)

In this essay by Van Wyck Brooks (1886–1963), one finds the classic expression of the alienation of the literary artist from the American business society and also a complete expression of the century-old tradition of the artist as a romantic hero capable not only of transcending materialism but of providing inspiration to the general public to follow the artistic hero to salvation. Brooks, one of the major literary critics of his time, represents the paradoxical attitude of many of the older progressives who had faith in the people but also believed in the need of heroic leadership to awaken the people to the fact that they had been misled into a world of false and corrupt values by evil leaders.

Van Wyck Brooks, "The Literary Life," from *Civilization in the United States*, Harold E. Stearns, Ed. (New York, 1922), pp. 179–83, 186–89, 194–97.

Among all the figures which, in Mrs. Wharton's "The Age of Innocence," make up the pallid little social foreground, the still more pallid middle distance, of the New York of forty years ago, there is none more pallid than the figure of Ned Winsett, the "man of letters untimely born in a world that had no need of letters." Winsett, we are told, "had published one volume of brief and exquisite literary appreciations," of which one hundred and twenty copies had been sold, and had then abandoned his calling and taken an obscure post on a women's weekly. "On the subject of *Hearth-fires* (as the paper was called) he was inexhaustibly entertaining," says Mrs. Wharton; "but beneath his fun lurked the sterile bitterness of the still young man who has tried and given up." Sterile bitterness, a bright futility, a beginning without a future: that is the story of Ned Winsett.

One feels, as one turns Mrs. Wharton's pages, how symbolic this is of the literary life in America. I shall say nothing of the other arts, though the vital conditions of all the arts have surely much in common; I shall say nothing of America before the Civil War, for the America that New England dominated was a different nation from ours. But what immediately strikes one, as one surveys the history of our literature during the last half century, is the singular impotence of its creative spirit. That we have and have always had an abundance of talent is, I think, no less evident: what I mean is that so little of this talent succeeds in effectuating itself. Of how many of our modern writers can it be said that their work reveals a continuous growth, or indeed any growth, that they hold their ground tenaciously and preserve their sap from one decade to another? Where, to speak relatively, the characteristic evolution of the European writer is one of an ever-increasing differentiation, a progress toward the creation, the possession of a world absolutely his own (the world of Shaw, the world of Hardy, the world of Hamsun, of Gorky, of Anatole France), the American writer, having struck out with his new note, becomes—how often!—progressively less and less himself. The blighted career, the arrested career, the diverted career are, with us, the rule. The chronic state of our literature is that of a youthful promise which is never redeemed . . .

There are those who will deny this characterization of our literature, pointing to what they consider the robust and wholesome corpus of our "normal" fiction. But this fiction, in its way, precisely corroborates my point. What is the quality of the spirit behind it? How much does it contain of that creative element the character of which consists in dominating life instead of being dominated by it? Have these novelists of ours any world of their own as distinguished from the world they observe and reflect, the world they share with their neighbors? Is it a personal vision that informs them, or a mob-vision? The Danish writer, Johannes V. Jensen, has described their work as "journalism under exceptionally fortunate conditions." Journalism, on the whole, it assuredly is, and the chief of these fortunate conditions (fortunate for journalism!) has been the general failure of the writers in question to establish and develop themselves as individuals; as they have rendered unto Caesar what was intended for God, is it any wonder the Caesar has waxed so fat? "The unfortunate thing," writes Mr. Montrose J. Moses, "is that the American drama"—but the observation is equally true of this fiction of ours—"has had many brilliant promises which have finally thinned out and never materialized." And again: "The American dramatist has always taken his logic second-hand; he has always allowed his theatrical sense to be a slave to managerial circumstance." The two statements are complementary, and they apply, as I say, to the whole of this "normal" literature of ours. Managerial circumstance? Let us call it local patriotism, the spirit of the times, the hunger of the public for this, that, or the other: to some one of these demands, these promptings from without, the "normal" American writer always allows himself to become a slave. It is the fact, indeed, of his being a slave to some demand from without that makes him "normal"—and something else than an artist.

The flourishing exterior of the main body of our contemporary literature, in short, represents anything but the integrity of an inner well-being. But even aside from this, one can count on one's two hands the American writers who are able to carry on the development and unfolding of their individualities, year in, year out, as every competent man of affairs carries on his business. What fate overtakes the rest? Shall I begin to run over some of those names, familiar to us all, names that have signified so much promise and are lost in what Gautier calls "the limbo where moan (in the company of babes) still-born vocations, abortive attempts, larvæ of ideas that have won neither wings nor shapes"? Shall I mention the writers—but they are countless!—who have lapsed into silence, or have involved themselves in barren eccentricities, or have been turned into machines? The poets who, at the very outset of their careers, find themselves extinguished like so many candles? The novelists who have been unable to grow up, and remain withered boys of seventeen? The critics who find themselves overtaken in mid-career by a hardening of the spiritual arteries? Our writers all but universally lack the power of growth, the endurance that enables one to continue to produce personal work after the freshness of youth has gone. Weeds and wild flowers! Weeds without beauty or fragrance, and wild flowers that cannot survive the heat of the day.

Such is the aspect of our contemporary literature; beside that of almost any European country, it is indeed one long list of spiritual casualties. For it is not that the talent is wanting, but that somehow this talent fails to fulfil itself.

This being so, how much one would like to assume, with certain of our critics, that the American writer is a sort of Samson bound with the brass fetters of the Philistines and requiring only to have those fetters cast off in order to be able to conquer the world! That, as I understand it, is the position of Mr. Dreiser, who recently remarked of certain of our novelists: "They succeeded in writing but one book before the iron hand of convention took hold of them." There is this to be said for the argument, that if the American writer as a type shows less resistance than the European writer, it is plainly because he has been insufficiently equipped, stimulated, nourished by the society into which he has been born. In this sense the American environment is answerable for the literature it has produced. But what is significant is that the American writer *does* show less resistance; as literature is nothing but the expression of power, of the creative will, of "free will," in short, is it not more accurate to say, not that the "iron hand of convention" takes hold of our writers, but that our writers yield to the "iron hand of convention"? Samson had lost his virility before the Philistines bound him; it was because he had lost his virility that the Philistines were able to bind him. The American writer who "goes wrong" is in a similar case. "I have read," says Mr. Dreiser, of Jack London, "several short stories which proved what he could do. But he did not feel that he cared for want and public indifference. Hence his many excellent romances." *He did not feel that he cared for want and public indifference.* Even Mr. Dreiser, as we observe, determinist that he is, admits a margin of free will, for he represents Jack London as having made a choice. What concerns us now, however, is not a theoretical but a practical question, the fact, namely, that the American writer as a rule is actuated not by faith but by fear, that he cannot meet the obstacles of "want and public indifference" as the European writer meets them, that he is, indeed, and as if by nature, a journeyman and a hireling.

As we see, then, the creative will in this country is a very weak and sickly plant. Of the innumerable talents that are always emerging about us there are few that come to any sort of fruition: the rest wither early; they are transformed into those neuroses that flourish on our soil as orchids flourish in the green jungle. The sense of this failure is written all over our literature. Do we not know what depths of disappointment underlay the cynicism of Mark Twain and Henry Adams and Ambrose Bierce? Have we failed to recognize, in the surly contempt with which the author of "The Story of a Country Town" habitually speaks of writers and writing, the unconscious cry of sour grapes of a man whose creative life was arrested in youth? Are we unaware of the bitterness with which, in certain letters of his later years, Jack London regretted the miscarriage of his gift? There is no denying that for half a century the American writer as a type has gone down in defeat.

Now why is this so? Why does the American writer, relatively speaking, show less resistance than the European writer? Plainly, as I have just said, because he has been insufficiently equipped, stimulated, nourished by the society into which he has been born. If our creative spirits are unable to grow and mature, it is a sign that there is something wanting in the soil from which they spring and in the conditions that surround them. Is it not, for that matter, a sign of some more general failure in our life? . . .

Here, of course, I touch upon the main fact of American history. That traditional drag, if one may so express it, in the direction of the practical, which has been the law of our civilization, would alone explain why our literature and art have never been more than half-hearted. To abandon the unpopular and unremunerative career of painting for the useful and lucrative career of invention must have seemed natural and inevitable to Robert Fulton and Samuel Morse. So strong is this racial compulsion, so feeble is the hold which Americans have upon ultimate values, that one can scarcely find today a scientist or a scholar who, for the sake of science or scholarship, will refuse an opportunity to become the money-gathering president of some insignificant university. Thus our intellectual life has always been ancillary to the life of business and organization: have we forgotten that the good Washington Irving himself, the father of American letters, thought it by no means beneath his dignity to serve as a sort of glorified press-agent for John Jacob Astor?

It is certainly true that none of these unfavourable factors of American life could have had such a baleful effect upon our literature if there had been others to counteract them. An aristocratic tradition, if we had ever had it, would have kept open among us the right of way of the free individual, would have preserved the claims of mere living. "It is curious to observe," writes Nietzsche in one of his letters, "how any one who soon leaves the traditional highway in order to travel on his own proper path always has more or less the sense of being an exile, a condemned criminal, a fugitive from mankind." If that is true in the old world, where society is so much more complex and offers the individual so much more latitude, how few could ever have had the strength in a society like ours, which has always placed such an enormous premium on conformity, to become and to remain themselves? Is it fanciful indeed to see in the famous "remorse" of Poe the traces left by this dereliction of the tribal law upon the unconscious mind of an artist of unique force and courage? Similarly, a tradition of voluntary poverty would have provided us with an escape from the importunities of bourgeois custom. But aside from the fact that even so simple a principle as this depends largely for its life on precedent (Whitman and the painter Ryder are almost alone among latter-day Americans in having discovered it for themselves), aside from the fact that to secede from the bourgeois system is, in America, to subject oneself to peculiar penalties (did it ever occur to Mark Twain that he *could* be honourably poor?)—aside from all this, poverty in the new world is by no means the same thing as poverty in the old: one has only to think of Charles Lamb and all the riches that London freely gave him, all the public resources he had at his disposal, to appreciate the difference. With us poverty means in the end an almost inevitable intellectual starvation. Consider such a plaint as Sidney Lanier's: "I could never describe to you" (he writes to Bayard Taylor) "what a mere drought and famine my life has been, as regards that multitude of matters which I fancy one absorbs when one is in an atmosphere of art, or when one is in conversational relationship with men of letters, with travelers, with persons who have either seen, or written, or done large things. Perhaps you know that, with us of the younger generation in the South since the war, pretty much the whole of life has been merely not dying." That is what poverty means in America, poverty and isolation, for Lanier, whose talent, as we can see today, was hopelessly crippled by it, was mistaken if he supposed that there was anything peculiar to the South in that plight of his: it has been the plight of the sensitive man everywhere in America and at all times. Add to poverty the want of a society devoted to intellectual things and we have such a fate as Herman Melville's in New York. "What he lacked," wrote Mr. Frank Jewett Mather the other day, explaining the singular evaporation of Melville's talent, "was possibly only health and nerve, but perhaps even more, companionship of a friendly, critical, understanding sort. In London, where he must have been hounded out of his corner, I can imagine Melville carrying the reflective vein to literary completion." Truly Samuel Butler was right when he jotted down the following observation in his notebook: "America will have her geniuses, as every other country has, in fact she has already had one in Walt Whitman, but I do not think America is a good place in which to be a genius. A genius can never expect to have a good time anywhere, if he is a genuine article, but America is about the last place in which life will be endurable at all for an inspired writer of any kind."

To such circumstances as these, I say, the weakness of our literary life is due. If we had lacked nothing else indeed, the lack of great leaders, of a strong and self-respecting literary guild, even of an enlightened publishing system would have sufficed to account for much of it. To consider the last point first: in the philosophy of American publishing, popularity has been regarded not only as a practical advantage but as a virtue as well. Thanks to the peculiar character of our democracy, our publishers have been able to persuade themselves that a book which fails to appeal to the ordinary citizen cannot be good on other grounds. Thus, if we had had to depend on the established system, the present revival in our letters, tentative as it is, would have been still more sadly handicapped. The history of Mr. Dreiser's "Sister Carrie" is enough to suggest what may well have been the fate of many an incipient author less persistent than he. It is certain, in any case, that many other, at a critical moment, has drifted away from literature because of the lack in our publishing world of those opportunities for a semi-creative hack-work which have provided countless European writers with a foothold and even a guideway. The Grub Street of London and Paris is a purgatory, but as long as it exists, with its humble instrumentalities, translating, editing, reviewing, one can at least survive until one has either lost or found oneself: it scarcely needs to be pointed out that the American magazine, with its mechanical exactions, which levy such a terrible toll upon one's individuality, is anything but an advantageous substitute. Till one has found oneself, the less one is subjected to such powerful, such essentially depolarizing influences, the better; the most mediocre institutions, if they enable one at the same time to maintain one's contact with literature and to keep body and soul together, are as life is to death beside them. How many English writers owe their ultimate salvation to such trivial agencies as *T. P.'s Weekly?* In America, where nothing of the kind has existed until lately, or nothing adequate to the number of those who might have benefited by it, the literary aspirant is lost unless his powers mature at once . . .

Certainly if our contemporary literature is not respected, if it has not been able to rally to its support the sensitive public that already exists in this country, it is partly because this literature has not respected itself. That there has been every reason for it makes no difference; that it has begun to respect itself again makes no difference either, for when a people has lost confidence in its literature, and has had grounds for losing confidence in it, one cannot be surprised if it insists a little cynically upon being "shown." The public supported Mark Twain and Howells and the men of their generation, it admired them for what was admirable in them, but it was aware, if only unconsciously, that there was a difference between them and the men of the generation before them; and in consequence of this the whole stock of American literature fell. But those who insist in our day that America prefers European writers to its own, because America is still a colony of Europe, cannot ignore the significant fact that at a time when America was still more truly colonial than it is now American writers had all the prestige in this country that European writers have at present; and it is not entirely because at that time the country was more homogeneous. Poe and Thoreau found little support in the generation of which I speak, as Whitman found little support in the generation that followed it. On the other hand, there were no European writers (and it was an age of great writers in Europe) who were held in higher esteem in this country than Hawthorne, Emerson, Motley, and one or two others almost equally distinguished, as well from a European as from an American point of view; there were few, if any, European writers, in fact, who were esteemed in this country as highly as they. How can one explain it? How can one explain why, at a time when America, in every other department of life, was more distinctly colonial than it is now, American literature commanded the full respect of Americans, while today, when the colonial tradition is vanishing all about us, it so little commands their respect that they go after any strange god from England? The problem is not a simple one, but among the many explanations of it one can hardly deny that there were in that period a number of writers of unusual power, who made the most (who were able to make the most) of their power, who followed their artistic conscience (who were able to follow it) and who by this fact built up a public confidence in themselves and in the literature they represented. Does it matter at all whether today we enjoy these writers or not? They were men of spiritual force, three or four of them: that is the important point. If the emerging writers of our epoch find themselves handicapped by the scepticism of the public, which has ceased to believe that any good thing can come out of Nazareth, let them remember not only that they are themselves for the most part in the formative stage, but that they have to live down the recent past of their profession.

Meanwhile, what constitutes a literature is the spiritual force of the individuals who compose it. If our literature is ever to be regenerated, therefore, it can only be through the development of a sense of "free will" (and of the responsibility that this entails) on the part of our writers themselves. To be, to feel oneself, a "victim" is in itself not to be an artist, for it is the nature of the artist to live, not in the world of which he is an effect, but in the world of which he is the cause, the world of his own creation. For this reason, the pessimistic determinism of the present age is, from the point of view of literature, of a piece with the optimistic determinism of the age that is passing. What this pessimistic determinism reveals, however, is a *consciousness of the situation*: to that extent it represents a gain, and one may even say that to be conscious of the situation is half the battle. If we owed nothing else to Mr. Dreiser, for instance, we should owe him enough for the tragic sense of the waste and futility of American life, as we know it, which his books communicate. It remains true that in so far as we resent this life it is a sign of our own weakness, of the harm not only that our civilization has done us but that we have permitted it to do us, of our own imperfectly realized freedom; for to the creative spirit in its free state the external world is merely an impersonal point of departure. Thus it is certain that as long as the American writer shares what James Bryce calls the "mass fatalism" of the American people, our literature will remain the sterile, supine, and inferior phenomenon which, on the whole, it is.

"What we want," wrote Henry Adams in 1862 to his brother Charles, "is a *school*. We want a national set of young men like ourselves or better, to start new influences not only in politics, but in literature, in law, in society, and throughout the whole social organism of the country—a national school of our own generation. And that is what America has no power to create . . . It's all random, insulated work, for special and temporary and personal purposes. And we have no means, power or hope of combined action for any unselfish end." *That is what America has no power to create*. But can it be said that any nation has ever created a school? Here we have the perfect illustration of that mass fatalism of which I have spoken, and Henry Adams himself, in his passivity, is the type of it. Secure as he was, uniquely secure, why did he refuse to accept the responsibility of those novels in which he expressed the contempt of a powerful and cultivated mind for the meanness, the baseness, the vulgarity of the guiding element in American society? In the darkest and most chaotic hours of our spiritual history the individual has possessed a measure of free will only to renounce it: if Henry Adams had merely signed his work and accepted the consequences of it, he might by that very fact have become the founder, the center, of the school that he desired. But it is true that in that generation the impulses of youth were, with an extraordinary unanimity, focused upon a single end, the exploitation of the continent; the material opportunities that American life offered were too great and too all-engrossing, and it is unlikely that any considerable minority could have been rallied for any non-utilitarian cause. Sixty years later this school remains, and quite particularly as regards our literature, the one thing necessary; the reforestation of our spiritual territory depends on it. And in more than one sense the times are favourable. The closing of the frontier seems to promise for this country an intenser life than it has known before; a large element of the younger generation, estranged from the present order, exists in a state of ferment that renders it highly susceptible to new ideas; the country literally swarms with half-artists, as one may call them, men and women, that is to say, who have ceased to conform to the law of the tribe but who have not accepted the discipline of their own individual spirits. "What I chiefly desire for you," wrote Ibsen to Brandes at the outset of his career, "is a genuine, full-blooded egoism, which shall force you for a time to regard what concerns you yourself as the only thing of any consequence, and everything else as non-existent... There is no way in which you can benefit society more than by coining the metal you have in yourself." The second half of this rather blunt counsel of perfection is implied in the first, and it connotes a world of things merely to name which would be to throw into relief the essential infantility of the American writer as we know the type. By what prodigies of alert self-adaptation, of discriminating self-scrutiny, of conscious effort does the creative will come into its own! As for us, weak as too many of us are, ignorant, isolated, all too easily satisfied, and scarcely as yet immune from the solicitations of the mob, we still have this advantage, that an age of reaction is an age that stirs the few into a consciousness of themselves.

Lewis Mumford
The Fragmented City

(1922)

Lewis Mumford (1895–) emerged as one of the major architectural critics and social philosophers in America during the 1920's and 1930's. In this essay, a powerful analysis of urban alienation, Mumford is aware that technological growth is not necessarily progress. To a considerable extent, the older philosophers of the Progressive Movement had not associated cultural fragmentation with technology but only with business enterprise. Separating capitalism from technology, men like Thorstein Veblen had argued that pure technology necessarily led away from social fragmentation toward organic cultural unity. In 1920 young men like Mumford could no longer separate so easily capitalism and technology and no longer could believe so easily in the inevitability of progress as had their intellectual fathers.

Around us, in the city, each epoch in America has been concentrated and crystallized. In building our cities we deflowered a wilderness. Today more than one-half the population of the United States lives in an environment which the jerry-builder, the real estate speculator, the paving contractor, and the industrialist have largely created. Have we begotten a civilization? That is a question which a survey of the American city will help us to answer.

If American history is viewed from the standpoint of the student of cities, it divides itself roughtly into three parts. The first was a provincial period, which lasted from the foundation of Manhattan down to the opening up of ocean commerce after the War of 1812. This was followed by a commercial period, which began with the cutting of canals and ended with the extension of the railroad system across the continent, and an industrial period, that gathered force on the Atlantic seaboard in the 'thirties and is still the dominant economic phase of our civilization. These periods must not be looked upon as strictly successive or exclusive: the names merely express in a crude way the main aspect of each era. It is possible to telescope the story of America's colonial expansion and industrial exploitation by following the material growth and the cultural impoverishment of the American city during its transformations.

The momentum of the provincial city lasted well on to the Civil War. The economic basis of this period was agriculture and petty trade: its civic expression was, typically, the small New England town, with a central com-

---

Lewis Mumford, "The City," from *Civilization in the United States*, Harold E. Stearns, Ed. (New York, 1922), pp. 3–11, 16–20.

mon around which were grouped a church—appropriately called a meeting-house—a school, and perhaps a town hall. Its main street would be lined with tall suave elms and bordered by reticent white houses of much the same design as those that dotted the countryside. In the growing towns of the seaboard this culture was overthrown, before it had a chance to express itself adequately in either institutions or men, and it bloomed rather tardily, therefore, in the little towns of Concord and Cambridge, between 1820 and the Civil War. We know it today through a largely anonymous architecture, and through a literature created by the school of writers that bears the name of the chief city. Unfortunately for the further development of what we might call the Concord culture, the agricultural basis of this civilization shifted to the wheat-growing West; and therewith channels of trade were diverted from Boston to ports that tapped a richer, more imperial hinterland. What remained of the provincial town in New England was a mummy-case.

The civilization of the New England town spent itself in the settlement of the Ohio Valley and the great tracts beyond. None of the new centers had, *qua* provincial towns, any fresh contribution to make. It had taken the culture of New England more than three centuries before it had borne its Concord fruit, and the story of the Western movement is somehow summed up in the legend of Johnny Appleseed, who planted dry apple seeds, instead of slips from the living tree, and hedged the roads he travelled with wild apples, harsh and puny and inedible. Cincinnati and Pittsburgh jumped from a frustrate provincialism into the midst of the machine era; and so for a long time they remained destitute of the institutions that are necessary to carry on the processes of civilization.

West of the Alleghenies, the common, with its church and school, was not destined to dominate the urban landscape: the railroad station and the commercial hotel had come to take their place. This was indeed the universal mark of the new industrialism, as obvious in nineteenth-century Oxford as in Hoboken. The pioneer American city, however, had none of the cultural institutions that had been accumulated in Europe during the great outbursts of the Middle Age and the Renaissance, and as a result its destitution was naked and apparent. It is true that every town which was developed mainly during the nineteenth century—Manchester as well as Milwaukee—suffered from the absence of civic institutes. The peculiarity of the New World was that the facilities for borrowing from the older centers were considerably more limited. London could export Madox Brown to Manchester to do the murals in the Town Hall; New York had still to create its schools of art before it had any Madox Browns that could be exported.

With the beginning of the nineteenth century, market centers which had at first tapped only their immediate region began to reach further back into the hinterland, and to stretch outward, not merely for freight but for immigrants, across the ocean. The silly game of counting heads became the fashion, and in the literature of the 'thirties one discovers that every commercial city had its statistical lawyer who was bold enough to predict its leadership in "population and wealth" before the century was out. The chief boast of the American city was its prospective size.

Now the New England town was a genuine community. In so far as the New England community had a common social and political and religious life, the town expressed it. The city which was representative of the second period, on the other hand, was in origin a trading fort, and the supreme occupation of its founders was with the goods life rather than the good life. New York, Pittsburgh, Chicago, and St. Louis have this common basis. They were not composed of corporate organizations on the march, as it were, towards a New Jerusalem: they were simply a rabble of individuals "on the make." With such a tradition to give it momentum it is small wonder that the adventurousness of the commercial period was exhausted on the fortuities and temptations of trade. A state of intellectual anæsthesia prevailed. One has only to compare Cist's *Cincinnati Miscellany* with Emerson's *Dial* to see at what a low level the towns of the Middle West were carrying on.

Since there was neither fellowship nor social stability nor security in the scramble of the inchoate commercial city, it remained for a particular institution to devote itself to the gospel of the "glad hand." Thus an historian of Pittsburgh records the foundation of a Masonic lodge as early as 1785, shortly after the building of the church, and in every American city, small or big, Odd Fellows, Mystic Shriners, Woodmen, Elks, Knights of Columbus, and other orders without number in the course of time found for themselves a prominent place. (Their feminine counterparts were the D.A.R. and the W.C.T.U., their juniors, the college Greek letter fraternities.) Whereas one will search American cities in vain for the labour temples one discovers today in Europe from Belgium to Italy, one finds that the fraternal lodge generally occupies a site of dignity and importance. There were doubtless many excellent reasons for the strange proliferation of professional fraternity in the American city, but perhaps the strongest reason was the absence of any other kind of fraternity. The social center and the community center, which in a singularly hard and consciously beatific way have sought to organize fellowship and mutual aid on different terms, are products of the last decade.

Perhaps the only other civic institution of importance that the commercial towns fostered was the lyceum: forerunner of the elephantine Chautauqua. The lyceum lecture, however, was taken as a soporific rather than a stimulant, and if it aroused any appetite for art, philosophy, or science there was nothing in the environment of the commercial city that could satisfy it. Just as church-going became a substitute for religion, so automatic lyceum attendance became a substitute for thought. These were the prayer wheels of a preoccupied commercialism.

The contrast between the provincial and the commercial city in America was well summed up in their plans. Consider the differences between Cambridge and New York. Up to the beginning of the nineteenth century New York, at the tip of Manhattan Island, had the same diffident, rambling town plan that characterizes Cambridge. In this old type of city layout the streets lead nowhere, except to the buildings that give onto them: outside the main roads the provisions for traffic are so inadequate as to seem almost a provision against traffic. Quiet streets, a pleasant aspect, ample domestic facilities were the desiderata of the provincial town; traffic, realty speculation, and expansion were those of the newer era. This became evident as soon as the Empire City started to realize its "manifest destiny" by laying down, in 1808, a plan for its future development.

New York's city plan commissioners went about their work with a scarcely concealed purpose to increase traffic and raise realty values. The amenities of city life counted for little in their scheme of things: debating "whether they should confine themselves to rectilinear and rectangular streets, or whether they should adopt some of those supposed improvements, by circles, ovals, and stars," they decided, on grounds of economy, against any departure from the gridiron design. It was under the same stimulus that these admirable philistines had the complacency to plan the city's development up to 155th Street. Here we are concerned, however, with the results of the rectangular plan rather than with the motives that lay behind its adoption throughout the country.

The principal effect of the gridiron plan is that every street becomes a thoroughfare, and that every thoroughfare is potentially a commercial street. The tendency toward movement in such a city vastly outweighs the tendency towards settlement. As a result of progressive shifts in population, due to the changes to which commercial competition subjects the use of land, the main institutions of the city, instead of cohering naturally—as the museums, galleries, theaters, clubs, and public offices group themselves in the heart of Westminster—are dispersed in every direction. Neither Columbia University, New York University, the Astor Library, nor the National Academy of Design—to seize but a few examples—is on its original site. Yet had Columbia remained at Fiftieth Street it might have had some effective working relation with the great storehouse of books that now occupies part of Bryant Park at Forty-second Street; or, alternatively, had the Astor Library remained on its old site it might have had some connection with New York University—had that institution not in turn moved!

What was called the growth of the commercial city was really a manifestation of the absence of design in the gridiron plan. The rectangular parcelling of ground promoted speculation in land-units and the ready interchange of real property: it had no relation whatever to the essential purposes for which a city exists. It is not a little significant that Chicago, Cincinnati, and St. Louis, each of which had space set aside for public purposes in their original plans, had given up these civic holdings to the realty gambler before half of the nineteenth century was over. The common was not the center of a well-rounded community life, as in New England, but the center of land-speculation—which was at once the business, the recreation, and the religion of the commercial city. Under the influence of New York the Scadders whom Martin Chuzzlewit encountered were laying down their New Edens throughout the country.

It was during the commercial period that the evolution of the Promenade, such as existed in New York at Battery Park took place. The new promenade was no longer a park but a shop-lined thoroughfare, Broadway. Shopping became for the more domesticated half of the community an exciting, bewildering amusement; and out of a combination of Yankee "notions," Barnum-like advertisement, and magisterial organization arose that *omnium gatherum* of commerce, the department store. It is scarcely possible to exaggerate the part that Broadway—I use the term generically—has played in the American town. It is not merely the Agora but the Acropolis. When the factory whistle closes the week, and the factory hands of Camden, or Pittsburgh, or Bridgeport pour out of the buildings and stockades in which they spend the more exhausting half of their lives, it is through Broadway that the greater part of their repressions seek an outlet. Both the name and the institution extend across the continent from New York to Los Angeles. Up and down these second-hand Broadways, from one in the afternoon until past ten at night, drifts a more or less aimless mass of human beings, bent upon extracting such joy as is possible from the sights in the windows, the contacts with other human beings, the occasional or systematic flirtations, and the risks and adventures of purchase.

In the early development of Broadway the amusements were adventitious. Even at present, in spite of the ubiquitous movie, the crowded street itself, at least in the smaller communities, is the main source of entertainment. Now, under normal conditions, for a great part of the population in a factory town one of the chief instincts to be repressed is that of acquisition (collection). It is not merely that the average factory worker cannot afford the luxuries of life: the worst is that he must think twice before purchasing the necessities. Out of this situation one of Broadway's happiest achievements has arisen: the five and ten cent store. In the five and ten cent store it is possible for the circumscribed factory operative to obtain the illusion of unmoderated expenditure—and even extravagance—without actually inflicting any irreparable rent in his purse. Broadway is thus, in more than one sense, the great compensatory device of the American city. The dazzle of white lights, the colour of electric signs, the alabaster architecture of the moving-picture palaces, the æsthetic appeals of the shop windows—these stand for elements that are left out of the drab perspectives of the industrial city. People who do not know how to spend their time must take what satisfaction they can in spending their money. That is why, although the five and ten cent store itself is perhaps mainly an institution for the proletariat, the habits and dispositions it encourages are universal. The chief amusement of Atlantic City, that opulent hostelry-annex of New York and Philadelphia, lies not in the beach and the ocean but in the shops which line the interminable Broadway known as the Boardwalk.

Broadway, in sum, is the façade of the American city: a false front. The highest achievements of our material civilization—and at their best our hotels, our department stores, and our Woolworth towers are achievements—count as so many symptoms of its spiritual failure. In order to cover up the vacancy of getting and spending in our cities, we have invented a thousand fresh devices for getting and spending. As a consequence our life is externalized. The principal institutions of the American city are merely distractions that take our eyes off the environment, instead of instruments which would help us to mould it creatively a little nearer to humane hopes and desires.

The birth of industrialism in America is announced in the opening of the Crystal Palace in Bryant Park, Manhattan, in 1853. Between the Crystal Palace Exhibition and the Chicago World's Fair in 1893 lies a period whose defects were partly accentuated by the exhaustion that followed the Civil War. The debasement of the American city during this period can be read in almost every building that was erected. The influence of colonial architecture had waned to extinction during the first half of the century. There followed a period of eclectic experiment, in which all sorts of Egyptian, Byzantine, Gothic, and Arabesque ineptitudes were committed—a period whose absurdities we have only in recent years begun to escape. The domestic style, as the century progressed, became more limited. Little touches about the doors, mouldings, fanlights, and balustrades disappeared, and finally craftsmanship went out of style altogether and a pretentious architectural puffery took its place. The "era of good feeling" was an era of bad taste.

Pittsburgh, St. Louis, and Chicago give perhaps the most naked revelation of the industrial city's characteristics. There were two institutions that set their mark upon the early part of this period. One of them was the Mechanics' Hall. This was usually a building of red brick, structural iron, and glass, whose unique hideousness marks it as a typical product of the age of coal-industrialism, to be put alongside the "smoke-halls" of the railroad termini. The other institution was the German beer-garden—the one bright spot on the edge of an urban landscape that was steadily becoming more dingy, more dull, and more depressing. The cities that came to life in this period had scarcely any other civic apparatus to boast of. Conceive of Pittsburgh without Schenley Park, without the Carnegie Institute, without the Library or the Museum or the Concert Hall, and without the institutions that have grown up during the last generation around its sub-Acropolis—and one has a picture of Progress and Poverty that Henry George might have drawn on for illustration. The industrial city did not represent the creative values in civilization: it stood for a new form of human barbarism. In the coal towns of Pennsylvania, the steel towns of the Ohio and its tributaries, and the factory towns of Long Island Sound and Narragansett Bay was an environment much more harsh, antagonistic, and brutal than anything the pioneers had encountered. Even the fake exhilaration of the commercial city was lacking.

The reaction against the industrial city was expressed in various ways. The defect of these reactions was that they were formulated in terms of an escape from the environment rather than in a reconstruction of it. Symptomatic of this escape, along one particular alley, was the architecture of Richardson, and of his apprentices, McKim and White. No one who has an eye for the fine incidence of beautiful architecture can avoid a shock at discovering a monumental Romanesque building at the foot of Pittsburgh's dingy "Hump," or the hardly less monstrous beauty of Trinity Church, Boston, as one approaches it from a waste of railroad yards that lie on one side of it. It was no accident, one is inclined to believe, that Richardson should have returned to the Romanesque only a little time before Henry Adams was exploring Mont St. Michel and Chartres. Both men were searching for a specific against the fever of industrialism, and architects like Richardson were taking to archaic beauty as a man who was vaguely ill might have recourse to quinine, in the hope that his disease had sufficient similarity to malaria to be cured by it . . .

It is the peculiarity of our metropolitan civilization, then, that in spite of vast resources drawn from the ends of the earth, it has an insufficient civic equipment, and what it does possess it uses only transiently. Those cities that have the beginnings of an adequate equipment, like New York—to choose no more invidious example—offer them chiefly to those engaged in travelling. As a traveller's city New York is near perfection. An association of cigar salesmen or an international congress of social scientists, meeting in one of the auditoriums of a big hotel, dining together, mixing in the lounge, and finding recreation in the theaters hard by, discovers an environment that is ordered, within its limits, to a nicety. It is this hotel and theater district that we must charitably think of when we are tempted to speak about the triumphs of the American city. Despite manifold defects that arise from want of planning, this is the real civic center of America's Metropolis. What we must overlook in this characterization are the long miles of slum that stretch in front and behind and on each side of this district—neighborhoods where, in spite of the redoubtable efforts of settlement workers, block organizers, and neighborhood associations, there is no permanent institution, other than the public school or the sectarian church, to remind the inhabitants that they have a common life and a common destiny.

Civic life, in fine, the life of intelligent association and common action, a life whose faded pattern still lingers in the old New England town, is not something that we daily enjoy, as we work in an office or a factory. It is rather a temporary state that we occasionally achieve with a great deal of time, bother, and expense. The city is not around us, in our little town, suburb, or neighborhood: it lies beyond us, at the end of a subway ride or a railway journey. We are citizens occasionally: we are suburbanites (*denizens, idiots*) by regular routine. Small wonder that bathtubs and heating systems and similar apparatus play such a large part in our conception of the good life.

Metropolitanism in America represents, from the cultural angle, a reaction against the uncouth and barren countryside that was skinned, rather than cultivated, by the restless, individualistic, self-assertive American pioneer. The perpetual drag to New York, and the endeavor of less favorably situated cities to imitate the virtues and defects of New York, is explicable as nothing other than the desire to participate in some measure in the benefits of city life. Since we have failed up to the present to develop genuine regional cultures, those who do not wish to remain barbarians must become metropolitans. That means they must come to New York, or ape the ways that are fashionable in New York. Here opens the breach that has begun to widen between the metropolis and the countryside in America. The countryman, who cannot enjoy the advantages of the metropolis, who has no center of his own to which he can point with pride, resents the privileges that the metropolitan enjoys. Hence the periodical crusades of our State Legislatures, largely packed with rural representatives, against the vices, corruptions, and follies which the countryman enviously looks upon as the peculiar property of the big city. Perhaps the envy and resentment of the farming population is due to a genuine economic grievance against the big cities—especially against their banks, insurance companies, and speculative middlemen. Should the concentration of power, glory, and privilege in the metropolis continue, it is possible that the city will find itself subject to an economic siege. If our cities cannot justify their existence by their creative achievements, by their demonstration of the efficacy and grace of corporate life, it is doubtful whether they will be able to persuade the country to support them, once the purely conventional arrangements by means of which the city browbeats the countryside are upset. This, however, brings us to the realm of social speculation; and he who would enter it must abondon everything but hope.

Metropolitanism is of two orders. At its partial best it is exhibited in New York, the literal mother city of America. In its worst aspect it shows itself in the sub-metropolises which have been spawning so prolifically since the 'eighties. If we are to understand the capacities and limitations of the other great cities in America, we must first weigh the significance of New York.

The forces that have made New York dominant are inherent in our financial and industrial system; elsewhere those same forces, working in slightly different ways, created London, Rome, Paris, Berlin, Vienna, Petrograd, and Moscow. What happened in the industrial towns of America was that the increments derived from land, capital, and association went, not to the enrichment of the local community, but to those who had a legal title to the land and the productive machinery. In other words, the gains that were made in Pittsburgh, Springfield, Dayton, and a score of other towns that became important in the industrial era were realized largely in New York, whose position had been established, before the turn of the century, as the locus of trade and finance. (New York passed the 500,000 mark in the 1850 census.) This is why, perhaps during the 'seventies and 'eighties, decades of miserable depression throughout the industrial centers, there were signs of hope and promise in New York: the Museums of Art and Natural History were built: *Life* and *Puck* and a batch of newspapers were founded: the Metropolitan Opera House and Carnegie Hall were established: and a dozen other evidences of a vigorous civic life appeared. In a short time New York became the glass of fashion and the mould of form, and through the standardization, specialization, and centralization which accompany the machine process the Metropolis became at length the center of advertising, the lender of farm mortgages, the distributor of boiler-plate news, the headquarters of the popular magazine, the publishing center, and finally the chief disseminator of plays and motion pictures in America . . .

The future of our cities depends upon how permanent are the forces which drain money, energy, and brains from the various regions in America into the twelve great cities that now dominate the countryside, and in turn drain the best that is in these sub-metropolises to New York. Today our cities are at a crossing of the ways. Since the 1910 census a new tendency has begun to manifest itself, and the cities that have grown the fastest are those of a population from 25,000 to 100,000. Quantitatively, that is perhaps a good sign. It may indicate the drift to Suburbia is on the wane. One finds it much harder, however, to gauge the qualitative capacities of the new regime; much more difficult to estimate the likelihood of building up, within the next generation or two, genuine regional cultures to take the place of pseudo-national culture which now mechanically emanates from New York. So far our provincial culture has been inbred and sterile: our provincial cities have substituted boosting for achievement, fanciful speculation for intelligent planning, and a zaniacal optimism for constructive thought. These habits have made them an easy prey to the metropolis, for at its lowest ebb there has always been a certain amount of organized intelligence and cultivated imagination in New York—if only because it is the chief point of contact between Europe and America. Gopher Prairie has yet to take to heart the fable about the frog that tried to inflate himself to the size of a bull. When Gopher Prairie learns its lessons from Bergen and Augsburg and Montpellier and Grenoble, the question of "metropolitanism versus regionalism" may become as active in America as it is now in Europe.

Those of us who are metropolitans may be tempted to think that the hope for civilization in America is bound up with the continuance of metropolitanism. That is essentially a cockney view of culture and society, however, and our survey of the development of the city in America should have done something to weaken its self-confident complacence. Our metropolitan civilization is not a success. It is a different kind of wilderness from that which we have deflowered—but the feral rather than the humane quality is dominant: it is still a wilderness. The cities of America must learn to remould our mechanical and financial regime; for if metropolitanism continues they are probably destined to fall by its weight.

Joseph Wood Krutch
The Alienation from Scientific Certainty

(1929)

During the first decade of the Twentieth Century, philosophers such as John Dewey had made a synthesis between the Nineteenth-Century romantic emphasis on will and the Eighteenth-Century emphasis on science and empiricism. Once again, therefore, the developing philosophical pessimism of the Nineteenth Century which had increasingly cut the intellectual off from the rational certainties of the Enlightenment and had led in the direction of existentialism seemed to be overcome and an optimistic rebirth of the Enlightenment seemed to be at hand. Pre-war progressive reform thought was marked by this optimism. But after the war the pessimism returned to permeate the thought of many intellectuals. And what young philosophically-minded Americans like Joseph Wood Krutch (1893–1970) were rediscovering in the 1920's was the existence of the same dark Nineteenth-Century tradition that Hemingway and other literary artists were rediscovering.

We do not, we cannot, actually doubt even the most fantastic of the verities which the scientist announces, since his boasted power to foretell and control upon the basis of his hypotheses has been too often vindicated to permit a skepticism, and when he tells us that soon we shall be doing this or that we know from experience that we had best believe him. Yet our belief is without enthusiasm—even, perhaps, a little perfunctory or impatient—because all his successes seem to achieve and to promise less than once they did.

Doubtless this disillusion is due in part to a clearer and clearer penetration of the ancient fallacy which consists in basing an estimate of our welfare upon the extent to which our material surroundings have been elaborated. This fallacy, born at the same moment with scientific method itself, runs all through the *New Atlantis* of Bacon, where it leads him to accept without question the assumption that we shall be wise and happy in proportion to the ingenuity of the machinery which surrounds us, and it is still the very foundation stone in the faith of the more naïve of contemporary materialists who assume that we have, for example, indubitably bettered ourselves when we have learned, first to say things over wires, and then to dispense even with them. A wider and wider experience with inventions has, however, convinced the more thoughtful that a man is not, as once was said, twice as happy when moving

---

at the rate of fifty miles an hour as he would be if he were proceeding at only half that speed, and we no longer believe that the millennium presents merely a problem in engineering. Science has always promised two things not necessarily related—an increase first in our powers, second in our happiness or wisdom, and we have come to realize that it is the first and less important of the two promises which it has kept most abundantly . . .

First man's body and then his soul were dragged into the laboratory to be measured, tested, and made the subject of experiment. His desires, his beliefs, and his impulses were tracked down, catalogued, and mapped. The history of morals was written, the physiology of love was described, and the functions of faith were analyzed. A vast mountain of data, much of it accurate and incontrovertible, upon every activity of the human spirit, was gathered, and always we were promised the great illumination which was to follow its absorption. Knowledge, we had learned, was power. When one had come to understand the laws of physics one was able intelligently to arrange for one's physical well-being, and so when one had learned the laws of the mental world one would be able in the same way to assure one's spiritual state. Once we had come to grasp the principles of art, we should know how to produce it; once we had unraveled the complexities involved in the history of morals, we should be able to devise and practice a really intelligent moral code; and once we thoroughly understood the functions of religion, we should be able to embrace one capable of perfectly fulfilling those functions.

And yet, for some reason not easy at first to comprehend, the analogy has failed to hold, and a laboratory knowledge of what, for want of better terms, we must still speak of as the solid and its activities does not result in any greater mastery of them. Though the "I" in each one of us is the thing of whose reality we seem to have the directest possible evidence, yet in the laboratory it dissolves into an unstable agglomeration of sensations and impulses which we cannot recognize as ourselves, while the will, which seems to us to inform this nonexistent entity, is revealed as a pure illusion. And if science thus illuminates the problems of the soul by assuring us that it cannot find any of the things we are talking about, its efforts are not much more satisfactory when applied to the study of ethics . . .

We went to science in search of light, not merely upon the nature of matter, but upon the nature of man as well, and though that which we have received may be light of a sort, it is not adapted to our eyes and is not anything by which we can see. Since thought began we have groped in the dark among shadowy shapes, doubtfully aware of landmarks looming uncertainly here and there—of moral principles, human values, aims, and ideals. We hoped for an illumination in which they would at last stand clearly and unmistakably forth, but instead they appear even less certain and less substantial than before—mere fancies and illusions generated by nerve actions that seem terribly remote from anything . . .

We had been assured that many troublesome shadows would flee away, that superstitious fears, irrational repugnances, and all manner of bad dreams would disappear. And so in truth very many have. But we never supposed that most of the things we cherished would prove equally unsubstantial, that all the aims we thought we vaguely perceived, all the values we pursued, and all the principles we clung to were but similar shadows, and that either the light of science is somehow deceptive or the universe, emotionally and spiritually, a vast emptiness . . .

What we have come to realize, then, is that the scientific optimism of which Huxley may be taken as a typical exponent was merely a new variety of faith, resting upon certain premises which are no more unassailable than those which have supported other vanished religions of the past. It had as its central dogma the assumption that truths (of correspondence) were necessarily useful, and that the human spirit flowered best in the midst of realities clearly perceived. After the manner of all religions, it instinctively refrained from any criticism of this essential dogma, and it was left to us in an age troubled by a new agnosticism to perceive how far this first article of the scientific creed is from being self-evidently true. Experience has taught us that the method of the laboratory has its limitation, and that the accumulation of scientific data is not, in the case of all subjects, useful. We have learned how certain truths—intimate revelations concerning the origin and mechanism of our deepest impulses—can stagger our souls, and how a clear perception of our lonely isolation in the midst of a universe which knows nothing of us and our aspirations paralyzes our will. We are aware, too, of the fact that art and ethics have not flowered anew in the light, that we have not won a newer and more joyous acceptance of the universe, and we have come to realize that the more we learn of the laws of that universe—in which we constitute a strange incongruity—the less we shall feel at home in it.

Each new revelation fascinates us. We would not, even it we dared, remain ignorant of anything which we can learn, but with each new revelation we perceive so much the more clearly that half—perhaps the most important half—of all we are and desire to be can find no comfort or support in such knowledge, that it is useless to seek for correspondences between our inner world and the outer one when we know that no such correspondences exist. Many of the things which we value most have a relation to external nature no more intimate than the relation of purple to vibrations of the ether, and the existence of such a relation can never be to us more than an academic fact. We are disillusioned with the laboratory, not because we have lost faith in the truth of its findings, but because we have lost faith in the power of those findings to help us as generally as we had once hoped they might help.

Langston Hughes
The Black Intellectual

(1926)

When the progressive movement had failed to revitalize America, the young intellectuals of the 1920's expressed their alienation in metaphors and imagery of fatigue. The heroes of Hemingway's and Fitzgerald's novels in the 1920's are lacking in vitality; they are old before their time; they know that nothing can be accomplished by acting in a vigorous manner. Increasingly, therefore, white intellectuals have looked to Black America for strength and vitality. This dramatic shift in white attitudes of indifference or hostility toward the black was paralleled by the emergence of a Negro Renaissance centered in Harlem during the 1920's. Negro novelists, playwriters, composers, and poets made significant impact on the white imagination for the first time. The black intellectual, like his white contemporary, reacted against the sterility of white culture. But unlike his white contemporaries, he could believe as Langston Hughes (1886–1954) expresses in the following essay, that there was a separate black national culture, distinct from the materialism and repression of the white middle-class world, which contained the cultural values for vital intellectual expression only if the Negro artist rejected the pressures to conform to the white society.

One of the most promising of the young Negro poets said to me once, "I want to be a poet—not a Negro poet," meaning, I believe, "I want to write like a white poet"; meaning subconsciously, "I would like to be a white poet"; meaning behind that, "I would like to be white." And I was sorry the young man said that, for no great poet has ever been afraid of being himself. And I doubted then that, with his desire to run away spiritually from his race, this boy would ever be a great poet. But this is the mountain standing in the way of any true Negro art in America—this urge within the race toward whiteness, the desire to pour racial individuality into the mold of American standardization, and to be as little Negro and as much American as possible.

But let us look at the immediate background of this young poet. His family is of what I suppose one would call the Negro middle class: people who are by no means rich yet never uncomfortable nor hungry—smug, contented, respectable folk, members of the Baptist church. The father goes to work every morning. He is a chief steward at a large white club. The mother

Langston Hughes, "The Negro Artist and the Racial Mountain." *The Nation* 122 (June 23, 1926), pp. 692–94.

sometimes does fancy sewing or supervises parties for the rich families of the town. The children go to a mixed school. In the home they read white papers and magazines. And the mother often says "Don't be like niggers" when the children are bad. A frequent phrase from the father is, "Look how well a white man does things." And so the word white comes to be unconsciously a symbol of all the virtues. It holds for the children beauty, morality, and money. The whisper of "I want to be white" runs silently through their minds. This young poet's home is, I believe, a fairly typical home of the colored middle class. One sees immediately how difficult it would be for an artist born in such a home to interest himself in interpreting the beauty of his own people. He is never taught to see that beauty. He is taught rather not to see it, or if he does, to be ashamed of it when it is not according to Caucasian patterns.

For racial culture the home of a self-styled "high-class" Negro has nothing better to offer. Instead there will perhaps be more aping of things white than in a less cultured or less wealthy home. The father is perhaps a doctor, lawyer, landowner, or politician. The mother may be a social worker, or a teacher, or she may do nothing and have a maid. Father is often dark but he has usually married the lightest woman he could find. The family attend a fashionable church where few really colored faces are to be found. And they themselves draw a color line. In the North they go to white theaters and white movies. And in the South they have at least two cars and a house "like white folks." Nordic manners, Nordic faces, Nordic hair, Nordic art (if any), and an Episcopal heaven. A very high mountain indeed for the would-be racial artist to climb in order to discover himself and his people.

But then there are the low-down folks, the so-called common element, and they are the majority—may the Lord be praised! The people who have their nip of gin on Saturday nights and are not too important to themselves or the community, or too well fed, or too learned to watch the lazy world go round. They live on Seventh Street in Washington or State Street in Chicago and they do not particularly care whether they are like white folks or anybody else. Their joy runs, bang! into ecstasy. Their religion soars to a shout. Work maybe a little today, rest a little tomorrow. Play awhile. Sing awhile. O, let's dance! These common people are not afraid of spirituals, as for a long time their more intellectual brethren were, and jazz is their child. They furnish a wealth of colorful, distinctive material for any artist because they still hold their own individuality in the face of American standardizations. And perhaps these common people will give to the world its truly great Negro artist, the one who is not afraid to be himself. Whereas the better-class Negro would tell the artist what to do, the people at least let him alone when he does appear. And they are not ashamed of him—if they know he exists at all. And they accept what beauty is their own without question.

Certainly there is, for the American Negro artist who can escape the restrictions the more advanced among his own group would put upon him, a great field of unused material ready for his art. Without going outside his race, and even among the better classes with their "white" culture and conscious American manners, but still Negro enough to be different, there is sufficient matter to furnish a black artist with a lifetime of creative work. And when he chooses to touch on the relations between Negroes and whites in this country with their innumerable overtones and undertones, surely, and especially for literature and the drama, there is an inexaustible supply of themes at hand. To these the Negro artist can give his racial individuality, his heritage of rhythm and warmth, and his incongruous humor that so often, as in the Blues, becomes ironic laughter mixed with tears. But let us look again at the mountain.

A prominent Negro clubwoman in Philadelphia paid eleven dollars to hear Raquel Meller sing Andalusian popular songs. But she told me a few weeks before she would not think of going to hear "that woman," Clara Smith, a great black artist, sing Negro folksongs. And many an upper-class Negro church, even now, would not dream of employing a spiritual in its services. The drab melodies in white folks' hymnbooks are much to be preferred. "We want to worship the Lord correctly and quietly. We don't believe in 'shouting.' Let's be dull like the Nordics," they say, in effect.

The road for the serious black artist, then, who would produce a racial art is most certainly rocky and the mountain is high. Until recently he received almost no encouragement for his work from either white or colored people. The fine novels of Chestnutt go out of print with neither race noticing their passing. The quaint charm and humor of Dunbar's dialect verse brought to him, in his day, largely the same kind of encouragement one would give a side-show freak (A colored man writing poetry! How odd!) or a clown (How amusing!).

The present vogue in things Negro, although it may do as much harm as good for the budding colored artist, has at least done this: it has brought him forcibly to the attention of his own people among whom for so long, unless the other race had noticed him beforehand, he was a prophet with little honor. I understand that Charles Gilpin acted for years in Negro theaters without any special acclaim from his own, but when Broadway gave him eight curtain calls, Negroes, too, began to beat a tin pan in his honor. I know a young colored writer, a manual worker by day, who had been writing well for the colored magazines for some years, but it was not until he recently broke into the white publications and his first book was accepted by a prominent New York publisher that the "best" Negroes in his city took the trouble to discover that he lived there. Then almost immediately they decided to give a grand dinner for him. But the society ladies were careful to whisper to his mother that perhaps she'd better not come. They were not sure she would have an evening gown.

The Negro artist works against an undertow of sharp criticism and misunderstanding from his own group and unintentional bribes from the whites. "O, be respectable, write about nice people, show how good we are," say the Negroes. "Be stereotyped, don't go too far, don't shatter our illusions about you, don't amuse us too seriously. We will pay you," say the whites. Both would have told Jean Toomer not to write "Cane." The colored people did not praise it. The white people did not buy it. Most of the colored people who did read "Cane" hate it. They are afraid of it. Although the critics gave it good reviews the public remained indifferent. Yet (excepting the work of DuBois) "Cane" contains the finest prose written by a Negro in America. And like the singing of Robeson, it is truly racial.

But in spite of the Nordicized Negro intelligentsia and the desires of some white editors we have an honest American Negro literature already with us. Now I await the rise of the Negro theater. Our folk music, having achieved world-wide fame, offers itself to the genius of the great individual American Negro composer who is to come. And within the next decade I expect to see the work of a growing school of colored artists who paint and model the beauty of dark faces and create with new technique the expressions of their own soul-world. And the Negro dancers who will dance like flame and the singers who will continue to carry our songs to all who listen—they will be with us in even greater numbers tomorrow.

Most of my own poems are racial in theme and treatment, derived from the life I know. In many of them I try to grasp and hold some of the meanings and rhythms of jazz. I am sincere as I know how to be in these poems and yet after every reading I answer questions like these from my own people: Do you think Negroes should always write about Negroes? I wish you wouldn't read some of your poems to white folks. How do you find anything interesting in a place like a cabaret? Why do you write about black people? You aren't black. What makes you do so many jazz poems?

But jazz to me is one of the inherent expressions of Negro life in America: the eternal tom-tom beating in the Negro soul—the tom-tom of revolt against weariness in a white world, a world of subway trains, and work, work, work; the tom-tom of joy and laughter, and pain swallowed in a smile. Yet the Philadelphia clubwoman is ashamed to say that her race created it and she does not like to write about it. The old subconscious "white is best" runs through her mind. Years of study under white teachers, a lifetime of white books, pictures, and papers, and white manners, morals, and Puritan standards made her dislike the spirituals. And now she turns up her nose at jazz and all its manifestations—likewise almost everything else distinctly racial. She doesn't care for the Winold Reiss portraits of Negroes because they are "too Negro." She does not want a true picture of herself from anybody. She wants the artist to flatter her, to make the white world believe that all Negroes are as smug and as near white in soul as she wants to be. But, to my mind, it is the duty of the younger Negro artist, if he accepts any duties at all from outsiders, to change through the force of his art that old whispering "I want to be white," hidden in the aspirations of his people, to "Why should I want to be white? I am a Negro—and beautiful!"

So I am ashamed for the black poet who says, "I want to be a poet, not a Negro poet," as though his own racial world were not as interesting as any other world. I am ashamed, too, for the colored artist who runs from the painting of Negro faces to the painting of sunsets after the manner of the academicians because he fears the strange un-whiteness of his own features. An artist must be free to choose what he does, certainly, but he must also never be afraid to do what he might choose.

Let the blare of Negro jazz bands and the bellowing voice of Bessie Smith singing blues penetrate the closed ears of the colored near-intellectuals until they listen and perhaps understand. Let Paul Robeson singing "Water Boy," and Rudolph Fisher writing about the streets of Harlem, and Jean Toomer holding the heart of Georgia in his hands, and Aaron Douglas drawing strange black fantasies cause the smug Negro middle class to turn from their white, respectable, ordinary books and papers to catch a glimmer of their own beauty. We younger Negro artists who create now intend to express our individual dark-skinned selves without fear or shame. If white people are pleased we are glad. If they are not, it doesn't matter. We know we are beautiful. And ugly too. The tom-tom cries and the tom-tom laughs. If colored people are pleased we are glad. If they are not, their displeasure doesn't matter either. We build our temples for tomorrow, strong as we know how, and we stand on top of the mountain, free within ourselves.

Interpretations

The following three essays by recent scholars describe and analyze the alienation of intellectuals in the 1920's. The first by Henry May rightly finds that alienation occurring before 1920. Professor May, however, like many American scholars, exaggerates the influence of European thought in the first decade of the Twentieth Century and minimizes the continuity of an American romantic tradition that began with Emerson and had paralleled European thought throughout the entire Nineteenth Century. The selection by Frederick Hoffman focuses attention on the rejection of the Midwest in the 1920's. To understand this metaphor, it is important to know that many intellectuals of the Progressive Movement had looked to the Midwest for the vitality to overcome the sense of decadence in the 1890's which was associated with the East Coast. To a considerable degree, intellectuals of the 1890–1914 period had believed that Chicago would replace New York as the cultural capitol of the nation. The rejection of the Midwest then in the 1920's is related to the failure of Progressivism to end Nineteenth-Century patterns of alienation through a national revitalization centered on the Midwest. In the third essay, Warren Susman analyzes the attitudes toward French culture which explains the expatriation of so many American intellectuals in Paris before and after World War I. By describing what Americans hoped to find in France, we can better understand what they were alienated from at home.

Henry F. May
Alienation before 1920

(1956)

As the nineteen-twenties move from memory into history, a standard picture of the decade emerges from reminiscence and research into the textbooks. This picture is a puzzling one. The decade is still, as it was in the thirties, the last island of normalcy and isolation between wars and crises. Yet it is also, clearly, a period of major cultural revolution. Both the "revolt of the highbrows" and the "rebellion of youth," first sketched by F. L. Allen, are a standard part of our semiofficial self-picture. In response to current historical fashions and perhaps also to their own changing worries about their country, historians are giving more attention to the revolutionary aspect of this conservative decade.

Having dealt with other revolutions, historians should be able to appreciate both the importance and complexity of this one. For instance, they should be able to avoid taking to task the rebellious intellectuals of the twenties in the manner of some critics of the forties. The spokesmen of a revolution are not, after all, its sole cause, and a healthy regime is seldom overthrown. Yet anybody, today, must recognize that revolutions are expensive. They may release, as this one certainly did, a burst of creative vigor; but they inevitably leave behind division, hatred, and shock. In the twenties, for instance, beliefs and customs that still commanded the deepest loyalties of one part of the population became to another group a dead and repressive Genteel Tradition, to be ceremonially flouted whenever possible. Suspicions dating from this cultural cleavage still poison the air. The historian must hope that analysis of the revolution and its causes can eventually help a little to clear away some of the resentment.

Starting backward, as historians must, we arrive immediately at the First World War, and there many have stopped. It is obvious that America's first major venture into world tragedy, with its rapid cycle of national exaltation, exhaustion, and revulsion played a very large part in the emotional life of the postwar rebels. By contrast with 1918 or 1919 or even 1925, hundreds of autobiographies paint the prewar period as a time of unity, moderation, progress, and sheltered childhood.

Yet we all know that postwar reminiscence, whether of the old plantation or the old literary culture, is a dubious guide for history. Those who

---

Henry F. May, "The Rebellion of the Intellectuals, 1912–1917," *American Quarterly*, XIII, No. 2, pp. 114–26 (1956).

have looked even briefly at the social and literary criticism of the prewar years know that the period 1912–1917 was itself, for some, a time of doubt and fragmentation, of upheaval in ideas, of the disintegration of tradition— in other words it was a pre-revolutionary or early revolutionary period. Nearly every phenomenon of the twenties from Freudianism to expatriation or the abandonment of politics was present before the war, on a smaller scale and with certain differences. If we can recapture any of the meaning or content of this prewar ferment, we may be able to understand better in what sense the revolution of the twenties was and was not postwar. In this way we may even get a few suggestions as to the perennially baffling problem of the relation between ideas and events . . .

Those who were sensitive to Atlantic breezes felt most keenly the swelling winds of antirationalism, which had been gathering force for a long time. Nietzsche, for long known vaguely by the American public as an Anti-christ, was becoming a major prophet. The most vigorous, though not the most accurate, of his American interpreters was H. L. Mencken, who in a widely read and widely praised book published first in 1908 and again in 1913 used the German prophet to belabor religion, women, and, most roughly of all, democracy in his already familiar manner. But the most fashionable of Europeans was the still living and lecturing Henri Bergson, who pushed the current tendency to an extreme, contending that reality, being in constant flux and change, is only distorted by efforts to think about it and must be apprehended through intuition. His was not the only, but it was probably the dominant direction in which philosophy was moving in 1913, and there is plenty of evidence that he was extraordinarily attractive to up-to-date American intellectuals. Irving Babbitt, already an alarmed defender of traditional values, saw the rise of Bergsonism as the culmination of a long, deplorable irrationalist trend, and found it in 1912 "allied with all that is violent and extreme in contemporary life from syndicalism to 'futurist' painting."

Psychology, as well as philosophy, was dealing heavy blows to dominant assumptions and beliefs. From the time of Freud's famous trip to Clark University in 1908, the Viennese theories cropped up in popular magazines and political treatises as well as learned journals. Whether or not, as his supporters claim, Freud is to be regarded as himself a brave and determined champion of reason, the first impact of his doctrines in the United States seemed to confirm and deepen the hedonism, emotionalism, and egocentricity that were beginning to spread so widely. On the other hand, Behaviorism, a movement launched in its most dogmatic form by John B. Watson in 1912, had to wait for its vogue until after the war. Its extreme practicalism, its rejection not only of reason but of consciousness, its suspicion of emotion, did not fit the tastes of the prewar rebels.

It does not need demonstrating that restless and vigorous innovation in the graphic arts got its American start before the war. Two major tendencies already dazzled the intellectuals and startled the public. One was apparently native, the harsh and sometimes violent Ash Can realism of Sloan, Bellows and the *Masses* cartoons. The other was imported from Paris, and consisted of a kaleidoscopic series of schools of experiment in form and technique. Commenting on "Current Impressionism," a term already well out of date but helpful as a catch-all, Louis Weinberg extended his observations from and beyond contemporary art:

> Impressionism as a technique is a means of recording the transitory nature of phenomena and the fluidity of motion. As a principle it is based on a philosophy of change . . .
> But this is not alone a description of the art of our times. It is the very essence of our lives.

Wherever the impressionist or vitalist tendency arose, it was expressed most frequently and characteristically not in painting or philosophy, but in politics and literature. These are the forms in which most American cultural change has been recorded, and it is to them that we must turn for a slightly closer look at prewar tendencies. Santayana's brilliant summary suggests that in politics alone the current drift toward fragmentation and chaos may have reversed itself in the constructive and integrating (though to Santayana most uncongenial) movement towards collectivism. In this one opinion, regarding an area which concerned him little, I think Santayana missed the current drift and underrated the force of his own generalization. It is true that progressivism optimistic, gradual, and in some forms mildly collectivist, was the officially dominant ideology; and that socialism was a swelling movement on the left that seemed to many sober Americans to possess the future. Yet both these political tendencies were in the early teens already under devastating attack, and from much the same irrationalist quarter.

Progressivism in all its varieties took for granted one or both of the two fundamental assumptions which had so far underlain the whole American political tradition. One of these was that we possess secure criteria by which we can judge our political achievement, the other that human beings are able consciously to remold their environment. Now both of these basic assumptions were being seriously shaken by new doctrines that had penetrated the house of progressivism itself.

Recent studies have shown that moral standards of a highly traditional sort motivated a great many of the prewar progressives. Truth and falsehood, good and evil, stand out in nearly all the speeches of Theodore Roosevelt and Wilson and good men threw out bad in most American cities. These venerable distinctions were the first to go; the younger progressive intellectuals, nourished on Dewey and H. G. Wells, were quite willing to throw out moral categories and rely on the shaping intelligence. On a popular level Lincoln Steffens spread the picture of the good boss and the honest crook. James Harvey Robinson, speaking for the main organ of the pragmatic progressives, lumped together as obsolete the ideals of "sound doctrine, consistency, fidelity to conscience, eternal verities, immutable human nature, and the imprescriptable rights of man."

With these went the state and law, the traditional locus and method of American reform. Many of the ablest political theorists of various schools, led by the brilliant Harold Laski, were redefining the state almost out of existence. To some it was a congeries of associations, to others the tool of a class, to still others the expression of the wish of those at present in authority. Its acts were no more final and deserved no greater obedience than those of other human groups, and it was less likely than many to be rationally motivated. Similarly, law, to the followers of the French positivist Leon Duguit or the American Roscoe Pound was no longer either the embodiment of a principle nor the command of a sovereign, but the complex resultant of social forces, prevailing opinion, and judicial will.

There remained the conscious intelligence, remolding the goals of action together with its methods. This was a moving conception, and a sufficient loyalty for many in this generation. Yet this too was seriously menaced by ideas that were attractive to the youngest generation of progressives. From the new and flourishing disciplines of sociology, anthropology and social psychology came an increasingly fashionable emphasis on custom and group emotion. It was sometimes hard to see what function this newest tendency left for intelligence and purpose.

Walter Lippmann's two prewar studies, *A Preface to Politics* (1913) and *Drift and Mastery* (1914) bring together the pragmatist attack on tradition and the implicit Freudian attack on pragmatism. Appealing for a radically instrumental state, he denounces the "routineers" who rely on political machinery, law, and conventional morality. His fellow progressives seem to draw most of his fire for their naïve adherence to literal numerical democracy and narrow utilitarian goals. What is needed in politics is passion and creative emotion, still of course somehow constructively channeled and used by the far-seeing for purposes which will transcend woman suffrage or the eight-hour day.

> . . . the goal of action is in its final analysis aesthetic and not moral—a quality of feeling instead of conformity to rule.

This formulation seems to me far closer to the view of postwar literary intellectuals than to that of the progressive standard-bearers. And the sources are explicit. Lippmann's friend Graham Wallas, the British author of *Human Nature in Politics* had opened the eyes of his Harvard seminar to political psychology. Steffens had helped to guide Lippmann and so, in a negative direction, had his brief experience with municipal socialism in Schenectady. But beyond these immediate guides one finds recurring references to James,

Nietzsche and Bergson and frequent, specific acknowledgment of the work of Freud.

All these new insights enriched the social sciences, and for many they doubtless furnished in practice new sources of power and freedom. Traditional progressivism, with its facile assumptions and sometimes shallow purposes needed—and for that matter still needs—rethinking. Yet much had been accomplished under the auspices of ideas that were beginning to seem stale and boring. And the new beliefs that buzzed and swarmed through the immediate postwar years were not easy to introduce into the progressive hive. To combine Lippmann or Laski with Wilson was, and soon proved to be, as difficult as to match Bergson and Nietzsche with Lyman Abbott . . .

More spectacularly than anywhere else, the new spirit of 1910 or 1912 to 1917 was reflected in a literary renaissance. The story of this sudden creative outburst has often been told, and only two points need making for our present purpose. One of these is that literary departures in the prewar years were closely related to contemporary movements in other fields of thought, the other that prewar writing contains in embryo nearly all the developments of the twenties.

Here too the stimulus came in large part from abroad. Young Americans, brought up on Matthew Arnold and Thackeray, were following before he gave it the advice of Yeats at the *Poetry* dinner in 1912 to forget London and look to Paris for all that was excellent. In Kroch's bookstore in Chicago, in the translation issued by a series of daring new publishers, in the eager if undiscriminating reviews by the young critics, this generation of rebels was nourished on a whole series of movements extending over the last generation in Europe. All the writers that had for so long been belaboring the European bourgeoisie—French symbolists and decadents and naturalists, Scandinavian pessimists and social critics, Russian apostles of mysticism and emotion; even from England D. H. Lawrence as well as Shaw, suddenly began to penetrate the American barrier. What this series of reagents produced was a series of explosions, and what exploded was more than the genteel tradition in literature, more than conventional moral categories. With the conventions of literary form and language went the underlying assumptions about thought and communication. Randolph Bourne perhaps described this grand explosion better than he realized in June, 1917:

> What becomes more and more apparent to the readers of Dostoevsky, however, is his superb modern healthiness. He is healthy because he has no sense of any dividing line between the normal and the abnormal, or even between the sane and the insane.

When Harriet Monroe, full of civic feeling as well as poetic zeal, founded *Poetry* in 1912 she seemed to tap immediately a rich underground gusher of poetic impulse. Soon the flood of experiment became too thick and varied even for *Poetry* to contain and overflowed into *Others* and the *Little Review.* As in the visual arts, a rapid series of schools succeeded each other, but perhaps the literary movement most characteristic of the period, and most obviously related to its philosophic tendencies was that of the Imagists, with its manifestoes in favor of complete freedom, concentration on the fleeting and immediate image for its own sake, and refusal to assign an image any "external" meaning or reference. Already before the war the revolution in the use of language was under way toward its ultimate destinations, Joyce was being published in the London *Egoist* and Gertrude Stein, settled in Paris, had developed her opinions and her characteristic style.

It would be misleading to divide this literary outpouring into precise categories, yet one can find suggestions of two emergent ways of thinking and feeling among writers. One group demanded freedom from European forms, confidence in emotion and spontaneity, and in general preached democratic optimism in the Whitman tradition. The other, more disciplined but also more deeply rebellious against American culture, called for concentration, rejection of irrelevant moral and political purposes, and the development of conscious intellectual aristocracy.

Obviously the former, democratic and optimist group is more distant than the other from postwar directions. This is the tendency one associates particularly with the sudden and brief Chicago Renaissance, with Sandburg and Lindsay and Miss Monroe, though it is found also in other areas, for instance in the organized and vigorous character of what Francis Hackett labeled and dated forever as Miss Amy Lowell's "Votes for Poetry movement." Yet even the most exuberant of the Chicago poets were, like contemporary political radicals, destroying for the sake of redemption, like Sandburg's personified city "Shovelling, wrecking, planning, building, breaking, rebuilding."

And even in Chicago pessimistic and sceptical tendencies were also, and had long been, at work. Dreiser's not exactly rosy picture of American city life was finally finding its audience; and the small town, from E. A. Robinson's New England Tilbury town to Masters' Middlewestern Spoon River, was preparing the way for Winesburg and Gopher Prairie. In the bosom of *Poetry* magazine, at the official heart of the Chicago movement, Ezra Pound, the magazine's foreign editor, was chafing at its cover slogan, the statement of Whitman that "to have great poets there must be great audiences too." Pound preferred Dante's pronouncement that the wisest in the city is "He whom the fools hate worst" and denied that poets have any need for the rabble.

> It is true that the great artist has always a great audience, even in his lifetime; but it is not the *vulgo* but the spirits of irony and of destiny and of humor, sitting with him.

In that sentence lies the germ of a dozen ponderous manifestoes of the post-war Young Intellectuals. Pound stayed on *Poetry* long enough to persuade Miss Monroe to publish Eliot's "Prufrock" in 1915 and then found a refuge from uplift and Whitmanism in the *Little Review.*

In the Eastern centers of the new literary movement the mixture of optimism and nihilism, of reform and rejection was somewhat different. Harvard, which was incubating an extraordinary number of ideas. The dominant note in its teaching of literature was aestheticism, worship of Europe, and contempt for the native production. Irving Babbitt's vigorous attack on democratic sentimentality was already a major influence. Yet Walter Lippmann, for one, managed to combine presidency of the Harvard Socialist Club with assisting Professor Santayana. A certain survival of Emersonian and Puritan responsibility seems to have been a part of the prevalent passionate concern for literature. America might be vulgar and materialistic and nearly hopeless; if so one's duty was to search the harder for seeds of literary springtime, and literary revival would bring social regeneration as well. Like so many writers after the war, Van Wyck Brooks went to Europe to look for these seeds. He found in London in 1913–1914 Ezra Pound, T. S. Eliot, John Gould Fletcher, Conrad Aiken, Elinor Wylie, Robert Frost and Walter Lippmann. Across the channel he could already have run into an equally significant group of fellow-countrymen. It was in London that Brooks began to struggle seriously with the typical problem of the expatriate of the next decade: the love of European tradition and the nostalgic turning toward American vitality. He solved this problem by writing, in London in 1914, the book that most influenced the writers of the next decade, an attack on the Genteel Tradition and an appeal for a literary renaissance that seemed then, as its title implies, to mark an arrival and not just a beginning: *America's Coming-of-Age.*

From here we can see, even more clearly than Santayana could in 1913, the unrest, the disintegration of old standards, the search for vitality and movement that already was under way at that time. We know, too, that what was then unrest later became cultural revolution and angry intellectual civil war. This brings us to the compelling question, what started it all? Why did this search for novelty, this gay destruction of traditional standards, occur at just this moment in the midst of an apparently placid and contented period?

This is hardly a question that can be answered with certainty. All that we know for sure is that a movement so general and noticeable in the prewar years was not started by the war. Perhaps the most obvious forces at work in early twentieth-century civilization were technological change and urban growth, but these had been at work reshaping American culture for several generations and do not afford a direct and simple explanation for the sudden restlessness of 1912–1917. Moreover, an increase of mechanistic materialism rather than a new vitalism would seem a more easily understandable product of machine civilization. It may be that the prewar rebellion was in part a protest against such a long-run tendency; in 1915 the *Nation* suggested that the rising "Bergsonian school . . . owes not a little of its popularity to its expression of revolt from the dreary materialistic determinism of the closing years of the last century."

One is tempted to wonder whether the new physics was at work already disintegrating the comparatively simple universe of nineteenth-century science. It seems, however, that although the Einstein revolution was being discussed before the war by American scientists and reported in the serious periodical press, it did not directly affect as yet the literary and political intellectuals to any great extent, and it was not, as it became after the war, a newspaper sensation.

In part the American intellectual rebellion may be considered merely a belated phase of an European antirationalist tendency. Yet it remains puzzling that Nietzsche and Dostoevsky and Baudelaire waited for their most telling American impact until they competed with Freud and Joyce. Part of the violence of the American literary and intellectual battles of the next decade arises from the fact that influences that had gradually permeated European thought presented themselves to many Americans all at once and in their extreme forms.

The time and special character of the prewar rebellion were, I believe, determined in part by the very surface placidity of the Progressive Era. Traditional American beliefs in moral certainty and inevitable progress had for some time been subjected to inner strain and external attack, yet in the prewar decade, for the last time, the official custodians of culture were able to maintain and defend a common front. Yet these almost hereditary leaders—Roosevelt and Royce and Howells in their several spheres—were growing weaker. A new generation, full of confidence and provided with leisure and libraries, was fairly literally looking for trouble. What attracts us about the standard culture of America in the early years of the century is its confident consensus, its lack of passion and violence. Passion and violence were exactly the demand of the young intellectuals of 1913 and 1914, of Lippmann and Brooks and Bourne and Pound. This was what they wanted, and this was what they got.

The war, then, was not the cause of the cultural revolution of the twenties. It played, however, the immense part that the Civil War played in the economic and political revolution of the mid-nineteenth century, speeding, widening and altering in kind a movement already under way.

The experiences of 1917–1919 darkened and soured the mood of the rebels. Even at its most iconoclastic and even in those spokesmen who adopted the most pessimistic doctrines, the prewar renaissance was always exuberant. Pound, amid his fierce negations, still found it possible to make his famous and somewhat rash prophecy that the coming American Risorgimento would "make the Italian Renaissance look like a tempest in a teapot!"

The rejection of easy rationalism, the spurning of dull politics were to make America better and brighter. In the war and its aftermath however the rebellious generation learned something of the price of destruction and experienced personally both tragedy and (in 1919) failure. Many who had been rebellious optimists became despairing nihilists and those who had already been preaching the futility of conscious effort preached it with different emotional corollaries.

The other effect of the war was that the disintegration of traditional ideas spread far more widely among the population. Most of the prewar rebellion was confined to a small and isolated, though articulate and potentially influential, group of intellectuals. As yet the overwhelming bulk of the people took for granted the truth of the old political and moral slogans. As long as this was so rebels could be ignored or patronized; they did not have to be feared and fought. Without the political events of 1917–1919 traditional beliefs might perhaps have been slowly adapted to new realities. Without the currents of doubt and disintegration already abroad, these political events themselves might have lacked their willing and ready Cassandras.

In 1913 *Sons and Lovers*, *A Preface to Politics*, and *Winds of Doctrine* were published, but *Pollyanna* and *Laddie* were the best-sellers. In 1925 the best-seller list itself had to find place for *An American Tragedy*.

Frederick J. Hoffman
Alienation from the Midwest

(1965)

Most literary portraits of the middle class were drawn by disinherited sons and daughters from that class. The intelligentsia for the most part belonged economically to the middle class; culturally they took pride in repudiating it. Their criticism was an all-out attack upon the customs and manners, the native cultural disposition, of the bourgeoisie. The vigor of anti-bourgeois criticism in the 1920's came, not from the proletarian critics, but from the middle-class men and women who were disgusted with their cultural heritage and viewed the guardians of middle-class morality and culture as hopelessly stupid and comical parodies of human nature. For the most part this reaction was not economic or political in its nature; it was cultural and moral. The burghers offended in a thousand ways and made countless errors of taste.

Frederick J. Hoffmann, *The Twenties* (New York: Viking Press, 1965) pp. 359–60, 368–71. Reprinted without footnotes, by permission of the publisher.

What distressed their critics more than anything else was the religious intensity with which they exploited what had originally been chiefly an economic convenience. The bourgeoisie were condemned, not for having made money, but for having turned the making of it into a religion and a morality. Out of this concept of the conventional man grew the portrait of conventional virtues. The cardinal virtues ascribed to the class were dullness, stupidity, aggressiveness in commerce, conformity to the remnants of traditional morality, and a moral opportunism, linked with certain blind convictions about the economic *status quo.* Their critics felt that money was not an adequate determinant of other values, that money was a value of a kind so totally different from these others that it was bound to kill them or distort them beyond recognition. Convention corrupts taste; and absolute adherence to convention corrupts absolutely.

This criticism of the middle class was almost wholly an urban thing; the critics were augmented from time to time by numbers of refugees from the Midwest. And, though they scattered to various parts of the world, they seemed agreed about the broad outlines of their attack. These outlines, whether they were presented in caricature or satire or polemic, were unified under the characterizations of two terms, each of them applicable to its separate sphere of interest: the cultural bourgeoisie were termed Philistine, the moral were dubbed Puritan. The predominating motif was not so much the consequences of their actions as the *manner* in which they acted. Thus the errors of narrowness and stupidity were condemned in the Puritan; he was a moral Philistine whose sins of taste were the product of his cultural helplessness, his refusal to consider the arts as having values independent of the moral setting in which they were considered . . .

Never in our history was the power of the middle class so strongly entrenched; never did its rituals seem so convincing; and never were its heretics, the anti-bourgeois intellectuals, so loud in disclaiming its virtues. The portrait of the middle-class man, in the dark gray of his moral business suit, humbly worshiping the golden calf, gave the impression of having come from the most improbable of fantasies. Money is the symbol of value, said Richard Roberts in discussing two books by priests of the new religion, "and value is created by the expenditure of the priceless stuff of life. A coin is so much minted life, a holy thing, neither common nor unclean; a sacramental thing like the bread and wine of the Communion, the symbol of life fruitfully expended. That is why the banker should be as a priest, and a bank a holy place." Merchandise is "so much congealed life," continued Roberts; anyone involved in a crooked trade is therefore "defiling the Temple no less than the hucksters and money changers in Jerusalem long ago" (*Nation*, February 16, 1921). And in philosophic terms, Harold Loeb spoke of "the mysticism of money," which is replacing the theology of the past. It may prove to be "like the Christian religion in the early centuries, a revitalizing force to most aesthetic expressions" (*Broom*, September 1922).

What pained most anti-bourgeois writers was not the apparent economic efficiency of the middle class, but its arrogance in assuming that economic success gave it cultural privilege and moral immunity from criticism. It was this smugness, this complete and self-contained satisfaction, that Mencken underscored in his "Americana" and Sinclair Lewis pointed out in his middle-class extravaganza, *The Man Who Knew Coolidge*. The great, complacent, practical man of Mencken's "Americana," for example, is sure of himself, and he laughs at the feeble efforts to find chinks in the armor of his self-confidence. On Park Avenue lives his successful brother of the faith. "Here the American dollar reaches its dizziest point," said Stuart Chase in one of his portraits of the false economic man. "To the towering and relentless rectangles of the street, the richest nation which the world has ever seen consecrates its cash balance, develops its personality in ten easy lessons, reads the confessions of those who have climbed to the stars from one suspender, improves its table manners, consolidates button factories, makes the sign of the cross with Mr. Bruce Barton, buys for a raise, and dedicates its life" (*New Republic*, May 25, 1927).

Ford Madox Ford, in his Preface to *Transatlantic Stories* (1926), spoke of "Middle Westishness," which, he said, was "in fact a world movement, the symptom of an enormous disillusionment . . . and an enormous awakening." It was as prevalent in Cardiff, Wales, as in Lincoln, Nebraska, in Birmingham, England, as in the outskirts of Indianapolis. In the United States it was produced by "a sudden conviction that the world—even the world as seen in the central western states of North America—is a humdrum affair, and bound to be a humdrum affair for all humanity in *saeculum saeculorum*." This conclusion was forced upon him when he realized that the Midwest had taken over Paris in the 1920's, in the final stage of a restless, nomadic move.

Why did so many of these young men and women write so many manuscripts on the same subject? The progress of the American had now apparently been reversed; the long journey across to New England, then to the "Western Reserve" and beyond, had in a half-century or less been turned about. The Middle West had become a metaphor of abuse; it was on the one hand a rural metaphor, of farms, villages, and small towns; on the other, a middle-class metaphor, of conventions, piety and hypocrisy, tastelessness and spiritual poverty. The young man or woman had to go east instead of west: in search of freedom (Floyd Dell), a "style" (Glenway Wescott), culture and sophistication (Willa Cather, Carl Van Vechten, Ruth Suckow), or moral maturity (Wescott, Sherwood Anderson).

Evidence, large and small, of the strength of the metaphor abounds in the novels and the short stories: the hero grows up ("is reared") on a farm, in a village, in a colorless, monotonous small town of merchants and ministers, or, at best, in a small commercial city, a provincial metropolis. In one way or another he discovers his parents, realizes them as an alien, elder generation, who have been taught to adhere firmly to a code that seems inappropriate to the circumstances of their living. The hero proceeds along two lines of education; his parents (or so he thinks) have had only one. He is forced to obey the tradition of the fathers; he searches for another tradition. Books, music, the arts, become valuable sources of the new—the real—education; but good literature and good art are hard to come by. There are "sympathetic souls": a school teacher perhaps, an aging or defeated musician or sculptor; an "intellectual" (often a lawyer, a doctor, a professional of some sort, rarely a minister); or a girl who is vaguely dissatisfied with the choices available to her.

As the second education grows in importance, the young man sharpens his talent for moral classification; he rejects the pattern of the community—as tedious, hypocritically moral, without taste or love of beauty, life-defeating, timid and resentful; he chooses instead an imaginary world (a pattern of fictions made out of what he has read, heard, imagined of a non-Midwestern society), and his growth consists chiefly of his effort to translate this second world into an actual occasion. At this point there are several possibilities: the hero may be frustrated in his efforts to break away, may suffer the fate of a "trapped sensibility"; he *may* try to sustain the second world within the first; he may simply lose his awareness of the second, or forget his earlier zeal for it, become the second-rate citizen he despised in others; or he may (and frequently does) get away—in which case, he begins his journey east. A little money, carefully saved by a loving mother, a will or an insurance policy from an unexpected source, an accommodating countess, a scholarship: the means of escape are various, but the impulse to leave is invariable.

For various reasons the image of the middle class was most appropriately identified with the Midwest as metaphor. All the criticisms of the middle class seemed especially adaptable to the geographical and cultural facts of the "middle border" provincial life. There was a gray dull tone of uniform dreariness: the happy, vital life of the farm was stifled in moral prohibitions and commercial greed; the townsfolk were either without a spark of insight and understanding or viciously hypocritical in the conduct of their affairs; the landscape was not beautiful, the townscape was tediously uniform or hideously vulgar, the social life was timid and ludicrous. Men went to Cleveland or Chicago or Omaha for their "affairs," returning to resume their moral lives. A traveling salesman, a carnival sideshow, a broken-down stock company (playing *Topsy and Eva* or *East Lynne*), the annual "elocutionary" competition—these were the cultural opportunities available to the young in what Fitzgerald called "the bored, sprawling, swollen towns beyond the Ohio . . ." (*The Great Gatsby*)

Warren I. Susman
France and the Alienated American

(1961)

The signal fact about American expatriation in the 1920's is the fact of place: the young intellectuals who discovered they could not live in the United States generally made France and more specifically Paris the center of their expatriate adventures. The movement to Paris and to France represented a major shift of expatriate interest from the prewar center, London and England, a migration which heightens the significance of place in expatriation. There were expatriate groups in other countries during the 1920's, indeed important groups in Italy, England, and Germany. And of course before the war there were also American expatriates in France. Nevertheless, the cultural importance of London before the war and Paris after it cannot be denied. Any attempt to analyze the movement of the 1920's, then, must come to grips with this central fact.

Expatriation is essentially a cultural mechanism available to the intellectual whereby he can attempt to turn his personal problems into public issues. Specifically, expatriation usually involves at least two separate but related acts: the rejection of the homeland and the embracing of another country. But put in this way the specific issues involved in any particular act of expatriation lack clarity. For what precisely does it mean to reject one's country and to embrace another? Exactly *what* is being rejected, *what* embraced? For expatriation to serve its function of creating public issues from private problems, the expatriate must have reference to a particular set of images—of his homeland, of his second country—which will effectively aid in sharpening his own position and in giving significance to his expatriation as part of a larger cultural phenomenon.

France as a second country for Americans was not a new idea in the 1920's. In the eighteenth century Jefferson had suggested that all Americans had two countries, their own and France. In the nineteenth century, T. G. Appleton had become famous for his *bon mot*, "All good Americans, when they die, go to Paris." Yet it is obvious that Jefferson's image of France—republican, revolutionary, the moral and intellectual capital of the Enlightenment—was vastly different from the image Appleton held of the social center that was his France—imperial, reactionary, the capital of high society and the arbiter of high fashion. Both of these images of France as a second country

---

Warren I. Susman, "A Second Country: The Expatriate Image," *Texas Studies in Literature and Language*, III (Summer 1961), pp. 171–83.

were held, furthermore, by individuals who were not themselves part of any expatriate movement.

Thus place alone—or even a significant shift of locus—tells the cultural historian only a little about expatriation. The particular image or vision of place, the particular use to which a place is put are also essential to any full understanding. The cultural historian must discover the set of images developed of the second country which best reveals its nature and meaning. He must see these special attitudes toward place against the background of current images of that place held by others not a part of the movement, if he is to note its peculiar qualities as well as its essential difference from previous expatriate developments and from dissident movements at home. The investigator must assess the consequences for culture generally of these images and uses of place.

France for most American intellectuals during the nineteenth century—and on into the early twentieth century as well—meant the France of history. For the intellectuals of Protestant America the Catholic countries of Europe held a special fascination. But it was not the Europe of their own day which most intrigued them. Rather, their images of Europe were primarily historical, generally medieval ones. Willa Cather's primary interests during her first visit to Europe in 1902 seem to have been the villages, cathedrals, and cemeteries. She had a special fondness for the cathedral at Rouen where Claude, the hero of her war novel *One of Ours* (1922), also has his greatest moment, a fact which stands in striking contrast to the inability of a Hemingway hero like Jake Barnes to bring himself to go into old churches. It was the France that best served as the outstanding representative of the world order of the twelfth and thirteenth centuries that most attracted American interest in the prewar years. The great cathedral at Chartres became for individuals who were as different as Henry Adams, Willa Cather, and Sherwood Anderson the symbol of culture, tradition, and unified social and moral order which seemed most lacking in the modern world. On their voyages to France they came as pilgrims seeking the past, frequently discovering that the France of the present hindered their search. The France of the village—untouched by the passing of centuries—appealed more strongly than more modern Paris, the countryside more than the city. . . .

In the decade preceding America's entrance into the First World War, a group of dissident young American intellectuals sought to create a national American culture. These young publicists and critics, Herbert Croly, Van Wyck Brooks, Harold Stearns, Waldo Frank, Randolph Bourne among others, almost all rejected America's subservience to Anglo-Saxondom because, in part, it suggested cultural dependence on Great Britain at the very time these men sought to create a consciousness of American cultural distinctiveness. For each of these figures, French culture and society—organic, homogeneous, full—provided a model of the general kind of national culture they would create in America. "Our civilization . . . can learn more from

France than from almost any other country," one of the most self-conscious of the younger intellectuals insisted. Frequently, it was their own experience of French ways that taught them exactly what a truly national culture might be like. France seemed to have solved the major problems of the dissociation of the intellectual from society and even of the dissociation of sensibility itself—which appeared to many an intellectual the key cultural problem of his time. Bourne, for example, repudiated England and the English tradition and discovered in France "an intellectual vitality, a sincerity and candor, a tendency to think emotions and feel ideas, that integrated the spiritual world" as he knew it. "In fact, the distinction between the 'intellectual' and the non-intellectual seems to have quite broken down in France. . . It was a new world, where the values and the issues of life got reinstated for me into something of their proper emphasis."

France, and especially some of her young intellectuals, admired and respected many of the products of American cultural development with a fervor and an interest seldom shown by older American intellectuals. They felt France could use with profit an understanding of these Americans in their own development as artists and as Frenchmen. Even more significantly, these young students in France were playing a vital role in their own society in "perpetuating, rejuvenating, vivifying, and if need be, creating the national consciousness." The young Americans in similar positions in the United States might learn how to do this for their own country by frequent interchanges with their French counterparts.

Even before the war intensified the interrelationship, a fruitful exchange of opinions between young American and French intellectuals had developed. They saw their basic problem as similar: the creating and maintaining of a worthwhile national culture in an era of international industrialism. The Americans welcomed such a volume as Pierre de Lanux's *Young France and New America* as a way of learning how each people might develop "the fullest and freest expression . . . along the lines of its own genius." Lanux had suggested in 1917 an image of France that must have seemed especially appealing: "France means . . . among other things, the land of free invention, discussion and experiment for social progress . . . a living laboratory, where every principle was tried . . . before being spread over the world." This image of France stood in chiaroscuro contrast to the image of America frequently held by the young intellectuals of the 1920's. The cultural nationalists did not become expatriates, even to France. They frequently attacked the expatriate position, preferring to find in a study of the American past the grounds for a richer American culture in the future. But they could understand the pull of France; they continued to encourage the interchange between the intellectuals of the two nations; they realized the need for American support and even participation in the cultural activities of Paris.

The movement of Ezra Pound from London to Paris in 1920 gives the historian a symbolic instance on which to build an analysis. Pound's move was made against a background of more than a decade's devotion to the study of the problems of modern culture. He was the link between two expatriate generations, for he knew intimately many of the expatriates of the London era and served later as friend, teacher, and counselor for many of the younger expatriate groups in Paris. Pound was clearly interested in the cause of the arts in America. He shared, in his unique way, many of the aims of the younger cultural nationalists at home. But his analysis of cultural history had left him dedicated to what he called the "comparative method" in the study of literature and culture. He appealed for greater knowledge of the world and its literature in part because he considered such knowledge essential for the creation of a truly American culture: the study of something simply called "American literature" was as misleading for a writer as a course in something called "American chemistry" would be for those wishing to become better chemists.

The question of expatriation itself took on new meaning in Pound's analysis. He defined for himself—and in large measure for many who followed him abroad—a new, self-conscious function for expatriation. The expatriate was essentially an agent for American culture abroad; letters were a "nation's foreign office" and the expatriate a liaison between cultures with a sacred obligation of keeping his own country informed about cultural developments in other lands. In his own career he carefully attempted to fulfill all of these special functions and this tradition was continued by many of the younger Americans in France during the 1920's. Fuller knowledge and appreciation of both literature and life abroad did not make anyone less American; rather it better enabled him to achieve his full American potential.

Pound's position always stemmed from his interest in furthering a cultural renaissance in America. Writing in that prewar decade of the cultural nationalist in America, but from the vantage point of London, he undertook an analysis of the particular conditions necessary to achieve the desired cultural rebirth at home. The greatest deficiency he discovered was quite simply the lack in America of a natural capital. "America, my country, is almost a continent and hardly yet a nation, for no nation can be considered historically as such until it has achieved within itself a city to which all roads lead, and from which there goes out an authority." Such a center should provide real artists with permanent comfort and support to do the kind of work they wish to do, regardless of the public's demands. Great libraries, galleries, studios should offer at such a center the opportunity to see and study the great models for painting, sculpture, or writing by importing and collecting the great works of the present as well as the past. Such a capital should make possible the artist's devotion to his own intellectual development and give him a chance to learn from his fellow artists. It should be a place for the fullest communication—between intellectuals of the day and those of the past. The establishment of such a capital, Pound insisted, had historically preceded all the great renaissances of the past.

Over and over again in his articles before and during the war, Pound called for the creation of these conditions, for the establishment in America of such a capital. Meanwhile, until America was able to provide the circumstances for her renaissance at home, Americans might well have to find some other capital abroad. Even during his London days, Paris stood as a proper model for such a center. Pound knew that the really important things done in the arts for decades had been done in Paris. "There are just two things in the world," he could write in 1913, "two great and interesting phenomena: the intellectual life of Paris and the curious teething promise of my own vast occidental nation." It is not surprising, then, that he should in 1920 discover a way of combining the "two great and interesting phenomena" by making Paris, in the absence of such a capital in the United States, the center of his activities in behalf of an American Renaissance.

But too frequently the discussion of American expatriation is taken out of a larger historical context; too infrequently do students remember that much of what we consider the finest in modern culture—in the arts generally—has been the product of expatriate figures; too seldom do we recall that most of these figures made Paris their capital in the first several decades of our century. Not only did Americans flock to Paris, but also Poles, Russians, Spaniards, Germans, Englishmen, Italians, Irishmen, Latin Americans. Paris was *the* international capital; Pound and the younger Americans who came after him were joining a great international movement.

Paris existed as a comfortable place, a place where the artist was more than tolerated, a place where one could work and learn. This was especially true in the 1920's, when the very opportunities and liberties Paris offered were clearly being denied in America. It remained, as Pound suggested, a center where an individual's peculiarities and eccentricities were forgiven, where there was a sense of leniency, a symptom of "some instinct against vested interest" which recognized that "indiscipline is perhaps in this aspect the only basis of culture." But above all, Paris remained in 1920 "the laboratory of ideas; it is there poisons can be tested, new modes of sanity discovered. It is there that the antiseptic conditions of the laboratory exist. That is the function of Paris." . . .

No matter what the traditional images of France might have been for the young American expatriates, they came clearly not in search of the past; we hear little of pilgrimages to Chartres in expatriate memoirs. They sought instead the great international capital of the present, the laboratory of ideas, the social laboratory as well, where the young Americans, in an environment and with facilities unavailable in the United States, could devote themselves to the present and its problems. John Peale Bishop, writing in 1941, has provided us with the best short analysis, from the point of view of one of these young men himself; it is in these culture capitals that "in each art, the tradition can best be acquired and with it an intenser consciousness of one's own time. The contacts of a capital can mean many things to a young man, but none more important than this. Twenty years ago there were many capitals in the world, but in only one was it possible to know the extreme moment of time. And that was Paris." But in the process itself the French experience also taught the young American a new respect for his own culture and its possibilities, for his own century, while at the same time providing a richer and more cogent understanding of the nature of culture itself. And significantly the movement marked a final break of the main body of our intellectual and artistic effort with the Anglo-Saxon dominance which had ruled for so long.

Thus the new images and uses of place in expatriation mark a positive contribution to American civilization rather than simply a negative rejection of America. While these images clearly drew attention to many of the weaknesses of America, the expatriates sought more frequently, through that French education Henry Adams so scornfully rejected, to fulfill their own potential as intellectuals and in the course of this development the expatriate learned important lessons about the nature of culture which could and did contribute to the new American Renaissance Pound had called for in 1914. It is the importance of Paris as a cultural capital which best sums up the significance of place in the expatriation of the 1920's and which emphasizes the values of such centers for cultural growth. Here the expatriate lived among the problems, the techniques, the activities of the present; yet here, too, he learned how best to use the past.

Selected Additional Reading

Aaron, Daniel. *Writers on the Left*. (New York: Harcourt Brace Jovanovich, 1961.)

Cargill, Oscar. *Intellectual America*. (New York: Macmillan, 1941.)

Goldman, Eric. *Rendezvous with Destiny*. (New York: Knopf, 1952.)

Klapp Orrin. *Collective Search for Identity*. (New York: Holt, 1969.)

Lasch, Christopher. *The New Radicalism in America*. (New York: Knopf, 1965.)

Lowenthal, Leo. *Literature and the Image of Man*. (Boston: Beacon, 1957.)

May, Henry F. *The End of American Innocence*. (New York: Knopf, 1959.)

Nash. Roderick. *The Nervous Generation: American Thought, 1917–1930*. (Chicago: Rand-McNally, 1970.)

Noble, David W. *The Progressive Mind*. (Chicago: Rand McNally, 1970.)

Pappenheim, Fritz. *The Alienation of Modern Man*. (New York: Modern Reader, 1968.)

Rideout, Walter B. *The Radical Novel in the United States*. (New York: Hill and Wang, 1966.)

Watt, Ian. *The Rise of the Novel*. (Berkeley: University of California, 1965.)

Section Four
Radicalism and the Intellectuals' Rapprochement in the 1930's

ROBERT ALLEN SKOTHEIM

Contents

Introduction

No decade in modern American history is so popularly characterized by its preoccupation with reform and radicalism as is the Great Depression of the 1930's. It was the "red decade," the time of the Soviet Union's greatest attraction for Americans, and the high point of the Communist Party's influence among the intelligentsia. It was the time when the Socialist Party saw much of its platform enacted by the national administration in Washington. It was the time of the emergence of the welfare state, increased regulation of business, support for organized labor, and the creation of aid programs for the aged and unemployed. Politically, the Depression offered another chance for planned change, the first since before the Great War.

Intellectually, as well as politically, the 1930's brought a mood much like that which prevailed during the years prior to World War I. Associated with the progressive movement in politics in the earlier Twentieth Century was a reform-oriented intellectual temper. With a faith in the upward evolution of mankind, an optimistic assessment of human nature, and a belief that society would best improve by bringing its principles into accord with the environmental conditions, this pre-World War I intellectual temper can be characterized as progressive and pragmatic. It was progressive in its faith in the future, in its belief that change would signify progress. It was pragmatic in its mode of analysis, in its demand that ideas and institutions be understood in terms of their practical consequences. Progressive intellectuals argued that outworn and irrelevant policies and practices would be exposed for what they were under the penetrating pragmatic analysis. Laws, schools, political and economic policies, beliefs and institutions generally would have to be defended on the basis of their practical consequences rather than merely because of their age or respectability. Reformers thus saw pragmatic analysis as an aid in putting the status quo on the defensive.

This pre-war progressive and pragmatic mentality did not disappear in the post-war years. It remained to characterize much of the intellectual life of the 1920's, but it was no longer accompanied by a national political reform movement. The Depression caused a renewed juxtaposition of political activity in the 1930's with progressive and pragmatic ideas which were still in the air. The result was intellectual and political activity ranging from the moderate reformism of Roosevelt's New Deal to the extreme radicalism of the Communist Party.

Nevertheless, despite the importance of the preoccupation with reform and radicalism in the 1930's, the significance of the history of American social thought during the decade—as seen from the vantage point of the 1970's—lies elsewhere. Less noticed at the time, and still not fully appreciated, was the fact that the social thought of the late 1930's expressed ideas which prefigured the more conservative climate of opinion of the 1940's and 1950's. Indeed, it may be said that what happened after World War II was a mere popularization of streams of social thought created by many intellectuals in the late 1930's. By the time the United States entered the war in 1941, the outlines of the post-war climate of opinion were complete.

One aspect of the increasing conservatism in the social thought of the 1940's and 1950's was the end of the estrangement of the intellectuals from conventional American society. Since the years before World War I, considerable numbers of prominent intellectuals had in various ways proclaimed their alienation from the mores, values, and government of the United States. Despite the fact that during FDR's first term the New Deal was typically criticized by the intellectual community for being too conservative, the New Deal itself significantly contributed to the rapprochement of the intellectuals. By FDR's second term, partly as a result of what Roosevelt had done, and partly because of the enemies he made among Americans more conservative than he, intellectuals became New Dealers. While this embracement reflects FDR's move to the political Left, it also reveals on the part of intellectuals a conservative renunciation of radical alternatives outside the two-party system.

This mood was further evidenced as the intellectuals began to praise the New Deal for coping with the Depression within traditional democratic constitutional limits. This new and basically conservative appreciation for traditional constitutional restraint mirrored the increasing disillusionment felt toward the Soviet Union. Early sympathy with the Bolsheviks and, briefly in the 1920's, with Mussolini's Italy, was grounded in a faith in revolutionary experimentation. It was thought that any social experiment would bring about the change necessary to progress. But, as the 1930's advanced, European dictatorships of all kinds were increasingly condemned as "totalitarian" for their evil subjugation of the individual. As admiration for revolutionary dictatorships diminished, as hope faded for good results from revolutionary change, the American status quo was viewed with greater sympathy. Intellectuals were ready to praise the United States for not being revolutionary, for avoiding the terrors of contemporary Europe, for maintaining continuity with its own past. Preoccupation with radicalism ceased as it was revealed that change of any kind did not necessarily bring about progress for the human condition, and a new conservative mood marked the country's social thought as the intellectuals began to reembrace American traditions. The new mood would become dominant in the 1940's and remain largely unchallenged until a young generation in the 1960's brought forth another form of radicalism.

Sources

The Radical Spectrum

John Dewey
Progressive Pragmatism: The Common Element

(1935)

Common to New Dealers, Socialists, Communists and most others preoccupied with reform in the 1930's was a belief in the possibility of progress through pragmatic adjustment of old policies to new circumstances. Dewey refers to this as the use of the "experimental method." In the following selection, written in 1935, John Dewey (1859–1952) clearly expressed this progressive and pragmatic view. He related the development of Nineteenth-Century liberalism to specific social and economic conditions in the past, and characterized it as absolutistic. He insisted that Twentieth-Century conditions demanded a new liberalism, one which would eliminate absolutism. An experimental approach was essential, Dewey continued, in order to discover which policies—perhaps radical ones—would work best. It was symptomatic of the critical stance that many intellectuals took toward the early New Deal that Dewey, who voted for the Socialist Norman Thomas in 1932 and 1936, specifically distinguished between the experimental method and "just messing around" or "doing a little of this and a little of that in the hope that things will improve"—obvious unfavorable references to the early New Deal.

This absolutism, this ignoring and denial of temporal relativity, is one great reason why the earlier liberalism degenerated so easily into pseudo-liberalism. For the sake of saving time, I shall identify what I mean by this spurious liberalism, the kind of social ideas represented by the "Liberty League" and ex-President Hoover. I call it a pseudo-liberalism because it ossified and narrowed generous ideas and aspirations. Even when words remain the same, they mean something very different when they are uttered by a minority struggling against repressive measures and when expressed by a group that, having attained power, then uses ideas that were once weapons of emancipation as instruments for keeping the power and wealth it has obtained. Ideas

---

John Dewey, "The Future of Liberalism," *The Journal of Philosophy*, XXXII, No, 9 (April 25, 1935), pp. 255–30. Reprinted by permission of the publisher.

that at one time are means of producing social change assume another guise when they are used as means of preventing further social change. This fact is itself an illustration of historical relativity, and an evidence of the evil that lay in the assertion by earlier liberalism of the immutable and eternal character of their ideas. Because of this latter fact, the *laissez-faire* doctrine was held by the degenerate school of liberals to express the very order of nature itself. The outcome was the degradation of the idea of individuality, until in the minds of many who are themselves struggling for a wider and fuller development of individuality, individualism has become a term of hissing and reproach, while many can see no remedy for the evils that have come from the use of socially unrestrained liberty in business enterprise, save change produced by violence. The historic tendency to conceive the whole question of liberty as a matter in which individual and government are opposed parties has borne bitter fruit. Born of despotic government, it has continued to influence thinking and action after government had become popular and *in theory* the servant of the people.

I pass now to what the social philosophy of liberalism becomes when its inheritance of absolutism is eliminated. In the first place such liberalism knows that an individual is nothing fixed, given ready-made. It is something achieved, and achieved not in isolation, but with the aid and support of conditions, cultural and physical, including in "cultural" economic, legal, and political institutions as well as science and art. Liberalism knows that social conditions may restrict, distort, and almost prevent the development of individuality. It therefore takes an active interest in the working of social institutions that have a bearing, positive or negative, upon the growth of individuals who shall be rugged in fact and not merely in abstract theory. It is as much interested in the positive construction of favorable institutions, legal, political, and economic, as it is in the work of removing abuses and overt oppressions.

In the second place, liberalism is committed to the idea of historic relativity. It knows that the content of the individual and freedom change with time; that this is as true of social change as it is of individual development from infancy to maturity. The positive counterpart of opposition to doctrinal absolutism is experimentalism. The connection between historic relativity and experimental method is intrinsic. Time signifies change. The significance of individuality with respect to social policies alters with change of the conditions in which individuals live. The earlier liberalism in being absolute was also un-historic. Underlying it there was a philosophy of history which assumed that history, like time in the Newtonian scheme, means only modification of external relations; that it is quantitative, not qualitative and internal. The same thing is true of any theory that assumes, like the one usually attributed to Marx, that temporal changes in society are inevitable—that is to say, are governed by a law that is not itself historical. The fact is that the historicism and the evolutionism of nineteenth-century doctrine were only half-way doctrines. They assumed that historical and developmental processes were subject to some law or formula outside temporal processes.

The commitment of liberalism to experimental procedure carries with it the idea of continuous reconstruction of the ideas of individuality and of liberty in intimate connection with changes in social relations. It is enough to refer to the changes in productivity and distribution since the time when the earlier liberalism was formulated, and the effect of these transformations, due to science and technology, upon the terms of which men associate together. An experimental method is the recognition of this temporal change in ideas and policies so that the latter shall coordinate with the facts instead of being opposed to them. Any other view maintains a rigid conceptualism and implies that facts should conform to concepts that are framed independently of temporal or historical change.

The two things essential, then, to thoroughgoing social liberalism are, first, realistic study of existing conditions in their movement, and, secondly, leading ideas, in the form of policies for dealing with these conditions in the interest of development of increased individuality and liberty. The first requirement is so obviously implied that I shall not elaborate it. The second point needs some amplification. Experimental method is not just messing around nor doing a little of this and a little of that in the hope that things will improve. Just as in the physical sciences, it implies a coherent body of ideas, a theory, that gives direction to effort. What is implied, in contrast to every form of absolutism, is that the ideas and theory be taken as methods of action tested and continuously revised by the consequences they produce in actual social conditions. Since they are operational in nature, they modify conditions, while the first requirement, that of basing them upon realistic study of actual conditions, brings about their continuous reconstruction.

It follows finally that there is no opposition in principle between liberalism as social philosophy and radicalism in action, if by radicalism is signified the adoption of policies that bring about drastic instead of piece-meal social changes. It is all a question of what kind of procedures the intelligent study of changing conditions discloses. These changes have been so tremendous in the last century, yes, in the last forty years, that it looks to me as if radical methods were now necessary. But all that the argument here requires is recognition of the fact that there is nothing in the nature of liberalism that makes it a milk-water doctrine, committed to compromise and minor "reforms." It is worth noting that the earlier liberals were regarded in their day as subversive radicals.

Thurman Arnold
The Emphasis Upon Experimentation

(1937)

The progressive side of reform thought supplied its optimism, its faith in the future, and its positive goals. The pragmatic side of reform thought supplied its mode of analysis which was so destructive to conservative ideas and institutions. For over half a century John Dewey articulated both these aspects of modern American reform thought.

Thurman Arnold (1891–), more than anyone else in the 1930's, enunciated a pragmatic critique of beliefs and practices which he thought were no longer suited to contemporary conditions. Writing in a witty and cynical style, Arnold scoffed at the outworn ideas and allegiances which prevented contemporary Americans from solving their problems in a practical way. Arnold was thus supporting Dewey's argument for public application of the experimental, or pragmatic, method. Presumably because it seemed to Arnold that all right-thinking men would agree on goals or ends, he dwelt almost exclusively upon means or methods. And because Arnold was a lawyer in various New Deal agencies when he did his writing, some historians have imputed Arnold's pragmatism to Franklin Roosevelt's New Deal as a whole.

And thus the holy war between Capitalism, Communism, and Fascism is one of the greatest obstacles to practical treatment of the actual day-to-day needs of the American people. Even agricultural credit and soil conservation become tainted with Communism. All sorts of sensible suggestions are drowned in the din of battle. It is a fixed idea that any society has a free-will choice to make between these systems. Capitalism is a good system, in which the individual has freedom. Communism and Fascism destroy the freedom of the individual. The whole political campaign of 1936 consisted in ringing the changes on these naïve ideas. Every practical scheme for social betterment had to be tested for tendencies leading to one or the other of these systems. If it led to Communism or Fascism, it was thought better to humiliate the unemployed or to waste natural resources rather than take steps which would change the "capitalistic system."

To this way of thinking about government may be attributed the failure of such schemes as governmental housing and the control of agriculture. Waste and want were present on a large scale in a land of plenty. Yet people with no conceivable material interest at stake preferred that they continue because the practical steps to alleviate them led to another system of govern-

---

Thurman Arnold, *The Folklore of Capitalism* (New Haven: Yale University Press, 1959), pp. 14–15, 21, 61, 79, 389–90. Reprinted by permission of the publisher.

ment. Coupled with this naïve belief that Germany and Russia had actually chosen the erroneous political theories that now threatened America was an astonishing ignorance as to just how the changes in Germany and Russia had come about and how the present governments in those countries operate. For a long time our editorial writers solemnly proved that these governments could not survive, because they were flouting every sound political principle. When their survival began to be recognized as an accomplished fact, these same editorial writers were equally convinced that America was about to become like Germany on the one hand, or Russia on the other, and to imitate both their culture and their institutions. It was thought that the safest insurance against such terrors consisted in stripping the Federal Government of all power of social control . . .

The preceding . . . is only an introduction to an analysis of the part that creeds play in social organization. Its purpose is to show that wherever men become absorbed in a medieval search for the magic formula of universal truth the creeds of government grow in importance and the practical activities of government are mismanaged. Holy wars are fought, orators and priests thrive, but technicians perish. Color and romance abound in such an era, as in all times of conflict, but practical distribution of available comfort and efficient organization is impossible . . .

It was a complicated business, this preservation of the capitalistic system in 1937 against the other "isms" and alien ideals. There was first the task of defining what Capitalism really was. This was a constant process. It had to be done every day and each new restatement led only to the necessity of further definition. The preservation of Capitalism also required that practical plans be tested by expert economic theorists who looked at each practical measure through the spectacles of economic abstractions, in order not to be confused by immediate objectives. Thus child labor had to be debated, not on the basis of whether it was desirable for children to work, but in the light of its effect on the American home in ten years, if it were followed to its logical conclusion. Measures for the conservation of oil, or regulation of agriculture, had to be considered without relation to immediate benefits either to oil or agriculture. Tendencies were regarded as far more important than immediate effects, and the danger to posterity actually seemed more real than the danger to existing persons . . .

The deep hold which this highly religious folklore had upon the small business or professional man, a majority of our industrial leaders, and our press is evidenced by the fact that in 1936 the Constitution became for them a sort of abracadabra which would cure all disease. Copies of the Constitution, bound together with the Declaration of Independence and Lincoln's Gettysburg Address, were distributed in cigar stores; essays on the Constitution were written by high-school students; incomprehensible speeches on the Constitution were made from every public platform to reverent audiences which knew approximately as much about the history and dialectic of that document as the masses in the Middle Ages knew about the Bible—in those days when people were not permitted to read the Bible. The American Liberty League was dedicated to Constitution worship. Like the Bible, the Constitution became the altar whenever our best people met together for tearful solemn purposes, regardless of the kind of organization. Teachers in many states were compelled to swear to support the Constitution. No attempt was made to attach a particular meaning to this phrase, yet people thought that it had deep and mystical significance, and that the saying of the oath constituted a charm against evil spirits. The opponents of such oaths became equally excited, and equally theological about the great harm the ceremony might do . . .

A governmental creed which enables men to face the facts about social organization without disillusionment and with positive enthusiasm for the opportunity presented is a prerequisite to the use of scientific method in government. This is something more than the traditional "realistic" approach. There is plenty of "realism" in this country today, but it is the realism that leads to cynicism. In other words, modern realists are still so emotionally bound by the mythology that the facts which their honesty compels them to admit only make them sad because the human race is not different.

Yet all the signs today point to the fact that a new creed, which can reconcile itself to the facts of human organization, is about to be born. It as yet has no formulas. It is represented vaguely by the personality of Roosevelt who has become a symbol for a political attitude which cannot yet be put into words.

Granville Hicks
Communism as Americanism

(1938)

The most sensational aspect of the social thought in the 1930's was the love affair many intellectuals carried on with Communism. Although the Communist Party membership figures do not tell the whole story of the appeal of the Soviet Union and of the influence of the Party among American intellectuals generally, they do suggest the relative increase in popularity and prestige of Communism in the later 1930's. Whereas dues-paying Communist Party members were only slightly more numerous than Socialists as late as 1934 (approximately 24,000 to 23,000), by 1938 estimates of Party membership

---

Granville Hicks, *I Like America* (New York: Modern Age Books, 1938), pp. 136–37, 138–40, 141–47. Reprinted by permission of the author.

ranged from 75,000 to 100,000 (while Socialist Party figures dropped to 7,000).

Between the late 1920's and 1935 the Moscow-directed policy of Communist Parties around the world was not to cooperate with liberal, socialist, reform parties in each country, but instead to oppose them as being as bad as Fascist parties. Moscow's assumption during this period was that world-wide revolution was sufficiently imminent that Communists did not need allies. In 1935, in reaction to Fascism's increasing strength, Moscow announced a policy of international Communist Party cooperation with liberal, socialist, and reform parties, known collectively as the Popular Front. In the United States this meant that Franklin Roosevelt was no longer to be called a "social fascist," and that Communists were to join in the Popular Front with New Dealers. "Communism is twentieth-century Americanism," announced Party leader Earl Browder in this spirit of cooperation.

Granville Hicks (1901–   ) was raised in an old-stock New England Protestant family, educated at Harvard, and intended to become a minister, but instead became a student of literature and a college teacher of English. Hicks supported the Communist candidate for President, William Z. Foster, in 1932, but did not join the Party until just before the Popular Front policy was announced in 1935. Hicks left the Party when the Nazi-Soviet Pact was announced in August, 1939. In the following selection, written in 1938 at the height of Communist Party membership, he explains his conversion to Communism in a characteristic Popular Front fashion.

One night in 1930 I was visiting friends of mine in New York, and one of their guests was some sort of Wall Street specialist. He told us that capitalists had really learned their lesson. They hadn't been able to prevent this depression, but they would prevent the next one. "The younger men," he said with a sweeping gesture, "the younger men understand what is happening. They know that finance capitalism—that was his phrase—has got to clean house. And they're going to do it! Give us another chance! Give us time! Give us twenty-five more years!"

"And if you fail?" somebody asked.

"Then you can string us up from the lampposts." And he finished his drink.

It made a great impression upon me. For months certain of my friends had been asking, "Why not Communism? Capitalism has failed. Why not Communism?"

I didn't know why not, and I wanted to, badly. I didn't like the idea of being a Communist, and I wanted to find some good reason for not being one. This Wall Street gentleman seemed to have the perfect answer. Capitalists, he assured us, were growing wiser. They knew they had to learn how to distribute the abundance that they were able to produce. They could and they would abolish poverty and depressions. They would learn how to plan. Why not give them their chance? Let them have their twenty-five years and then, if they failed, it was time enough to start worrying about Communism.

I went home in a rather exalted frame of mind: I had at last found the right attitude to take toward the facts of the depression. But my exaltation did not last long. The idea of a capitalism wise enough to plan for abundance appealed to me so much that I began to read what had been written on the subject. I found that many persons had considered the matter. One careful student had even worked out a detailed description of what the capitalists would have to do in order to bring about the era of plenty.

It was this prospectus that shook my faith. I could see that it was perfectly sound, that capitalists would have to do the things he said, and I knew damn well they wouldn't do them. Even the very decent businessmen of my acquaintance wouldn't. Sadly I shook my head; it wouldn't work.

I did not have to wait long to have my doubts confirmed. Their actions showed me that businessmen hadn't learned a thing from the depression. Every advocate of a planned capitalism agreed that the cutting of wages, for instance, would only make the depression worse. Yet most employers were slashing pay, even when it wasn't necessary to save their skins. They were, in fact, up to all their old tricks, taking full advantage of unemployment not only to lower wage rates but also to break unions. If there were any such "new" capitalists as my Wall Street friend has talked about, they were obviously a powerless minority . . .

The businessmen won't bring in the era of abundance. We'll have to do it, and we'll have to start now.

Part of our job, of course, is to convince people that they don't have to be poor—not any more. But we need action as well as argument. Right now we can use our knowledge that abundance is possible. For example, we can work for an adequate wages and hours bill. Today low wages are not merely cruel; they are bad policy. By increasing the ability to consume we can help put our industrial machinery to work.

The same thing is true of relief. Higher relief standards and really effective legislation for social security are sound from an economic as well as a humanitarian point of view. They are absolutely essential at the present stage of our industrial development.

We can fight against every attempt to cut down production, for the only intelligent thing to do, when there are apparent surpluses, is to create new customers, not to produce less.

We can act, in short, as if we lived in a highly advanced industrial civilization, not in some primitive society where people had to starve.

And because we are dealing with matters that directly concern us and all other workers, we will insist upon the full right to organize. We will count upon our government to help us in this fight for abundance, but we will rely primarily on our own strength.

Of course there will be resistance to such measures as I have suggested. We have seen how public opinion can be manipulated to oppose legislation that businessmen are afraid of. We know of the lobbies that great industries maintain and the laws they have contrived to kill. We know, also, how laws can be twisted to defeat the ends they were intended to serve. Resistance, we may expect, will be vigorous, unceasing, and subtle.

But we need not be afraid of this resistance. If we—hand workers and brain workers alike—are organized, we can meet either economic or political attacks.

What, however, if there should be attacks of another kind? Such measures would undoubtedly diminish the profits of big business. They might, moreover, make it clear to millions of Americans that profits ought to be abolished altogether. Businessmen, I'm afraid, wouldn't like that. They might be tempted to abandon their present methods of resistance to change and resort to more desperate measures. For when the masses of the people have learned to use their government for their purposes, big business might decide to take power into its own hands.

Let us imagine that, among the many demagogues that are always plaguing the country, one has emerged as a national figure, a powerful orator, a man quick to play upon prejudices and unrestrained with promises. Suppose that big business decides that this man can be useful. Consequently he finds himself with unlimited means at his disposal. He arms his followers—paid thugs, bums eager for square meals and a chance to loot, young fellows who have never had a job and are restlessly seeking adventure and opportunity. And, with the blessings and the money of big business, he marches on Washington to take over the government.

We have a name for that sort of thing—Fascism . . .

But whatever it is called, it will have to be stopped. Not only because Fascism stirs up race prejudice, crushes labor unions, persecutes religious groups, tortures political opponents, and destroys culture; not only because it thrives upon nationalism and leads inevitably to war; but also because it is a plan for scarcity instead of a plan for abundance. Through Fascism big business, for the sake of profit, abandons any attempt to use our productive capacity and condemns the people to bare subsistence. Glory Fascism offers on every hand, but not the plenty that has become our birthright.

If the people realize this, they will crush the uprising. Then what? Can we tell the businessmen that, if they will promise to be good little boys, all will be forgiven. I shouldn't think so. It is not a question of punishing the leaders, but of taking from them the power that makes it possible for them to start a rebellion. We will have to do the owning of the means of production.

But this, you say, is Socialism. You are quite right. Socialists and Communists do believe that the people should own industry. They say that the profit system stands in the way of abundance for all, and the profit system must be abolished. They say that we are ready to produce enough for everybody, and we ought to do it. They say we have the managerial skill, the labor, the raw materials, and the machines. Let the workers work, the managers manage, and the people own.

I happen to be a Communist. I wasn't born a Communist, nor did I learn Communism in some foreign country, nor am I paid by Moscow. I became a Communist because, after I had discovered that capitalism wouldn't plan, I made up my mind that I would find out just what had to be done. I looked around, and it seemed to me quite clear that the Communists not only had the clearest conception of how a society of abundance was to be brought about but were doing the most effective work toward that end. I decided that that was the group I wanted to work with.

I became a Communist by a process that can be retraced in this book. My own situation was pleasant enough for one of fairly moderate tastes, but I could not help seeing that I was enjoying privileges of which the majority of my fellow-citizens were deprived. I didn't want to see it, and all through the twenties—though it was also true then—I refused to see it. But the depression made me admit that there was a good deal in America that no decent person could afford to like. I looked at housing and diet and wages and unemployment and relief and lack of relief, and all the time I knew there could be enough for everybody.

Some of my friends, I have already pointed out, were saying, "Why not Communism?" But, as I have confessed, I was good at snatching at straws. It wasn't only that, with no excuse whatsoever, I had some of the usual misconceptions of Communism. It was largely that I didn't want to do anything. I wanted to be left alone with my particular job and let someone else do the dirty work of bringing plenty to the American people.

But in time—and I hate to admit how much time—I realized that either I had to stop thinking of myself as a reasonably honest person or else get to work. And for me that meant only one thing. It may not mean the same thing to you. I don't say that the Communists are the only people who are working for a society of abundance. But for me getting to work meant cooperating with the Communists and, eventually, joining the Communist Party.

At this point, inevitably, somebody asks about Russia. The other night I was listening to a radio symposium on democracy. One of the speakers was a Communist, and most of the other speakers and all the questioners in the audience devoted their time to talking about the Soviet Union. That seemed to me a pity. There are plenty of questions to be asked about democracy in the United States, and that, after all, is our problem. Let us by all means discuss democracy in other countries, but not to such an extent that we ignore the tasks that face us as Americans.

Still, since I have said I am a Communist, I have invited arguments about the Soviet Union, and I have no desire to dodge them, so long as we can keep a sense of proportion.

The Russians have put Socialism into practice. When the capitalist system broke down in Russia during the war, a group of determined men, who called themselves Communists to distinguish them from other Socialists who were less determined, offered the people a program to prevent the country from falling into a state of complete collapse. To do this, they had to act quickly. They had to nationalize industries and get them running somehow. Soon the capitalists of other nations, frightened because Socialism was actually being tried, gave aid to the ex-capitalists of Russia. There was a counter-revolution, a long and bloody civil war. But the Communists had the majority of the Russian people back of them, and at last they won. There were several years in which it was almost all they could do to hold their own, but in time they began to repair the damage done by world war and civil war, and finally they were ready to build a new social order from the ground up. Even the most anti-Communist observer has to admit that they have done a remarkable job. No country in the world has ever developed so fast in so short a time. Most workers in other countries are worse off than they were in 1913. Soviet workers, though their standards are still low when compared with those of our higher-paid workmen, are infinitely better off than they were before the war.

The great argument against the Soviet Union used to be that Socialism had failed, but that argument is seldom offered today. In spite of the backwardness of the country, in spite of the devastation wrought by war, in spite of opposition from without and from within, in spite of the ever-present need to prepare for attack from hostile nations, the Soviet Union has proved that Socialism will work. It has shown that unemployment can be abolished, that vast programs of construction can be undertaken, that the general living standard can be raised.

Today the principal argument raised against the Soviet Union is not that Socialism has failed but that it has succeeded through the sacrifice of individualism and liberty.

Perhaps the first thing to remember is that it is not safe to believe all you read. In the early days of the revolution it was reported every week or so that Lenin had been killed. Every two or three months since I can remember somebody has proven conclusively that capitalism has been restored. Enough persons have been reported shot or starved, at one time or another, to depopulate the entire country. Yet Socialism survives, and the population increases faster than that of any other nation in Europe.

It is true that certain liberties have been denied the people of the Soviet Union—the right to advocate the return of capitalism, the right to preach counter-revolution. These are not rights that many people want, but the Soviets have had to be careful, both because the old ruling classes have been their implacable enemies and because they are surrounded by foes. During our participation in the World War we suspended all the rights that have ever been suspended in Soviet Russia, which has been under attack or in immediate danger of attack ever since 1917.

It is unpleasant to know that you might at some time be suspected of being a spy, but the explanation is not that the government is tyrannous but that spies are plentiful and dangerous. It is unpleasant to have to be careful what you say, lest your remarks be interpreted as treason, but the explanation is that there are traitors.

The majority of the people in the Soviet Union have more freedom than they have ever had before, and in certain ways more freedom than has ever been enjoyed by the masses of any other land. It is a pity, no doubt, that they cannot have the right to advocate the restoration of capitalism, even though they do not want it back. But they have other rights, rights that directly concern their daily lives, and these may be more important.

I want to make it perfectly clear, even at the risk of antagonizing some readers, that I regard the Soviet Union as a great achievement in itself, as the only real hope for peace in the world today, and as a powerful force for worldwide Socialism.

But it is not necessary therefore to assume that the introduction of Socialism in the United States would follow the same course as it has in Russia. Our productive system is so much more advanced than Russia's was in 1917 that most of the hardships suffered by the Russian people could be avoided, and control of the productive machinery is so much more centralized that socialization would meet with fewer obstacles. Moreover, much of the preliminary experimentation has already been done—in the Soviet Union—and we could benefit by that experience.

No, the principal reason for talking about the Soviet Union is that persons who misunderstand or deliberately misrepresent what has happened try to find in what they conceive to be the situation there arguments against a planned economy for America. I say that there has been nothing in the history of the Soviet Union to frighten or discourage us; on the contrary, the twenty years of Socialism in Russia ought to give us tremendous hope and enthusiasm. But, whether this is true or not, we ought to be able to stand on our own feet.

After all, the important thing to realize is how close we are—right now—to having a society of abundance. Not only have we the machinery for production; we have the machinery for distribution—railroads, trucks, networks of stores.

History, looking back on the year 1938, is likely to feel that by that time the difficult part of the job was really done. All that remained then, historians will say, was to clear a few obstacles out of the way. And they will wonder why we made such a bother about getting rid of them.

There is no sense in being frightened by the word "collectivism" when you're not frightened by the reality. There is no sense in refusing to look at the logical next step for civilization to take—which happens to be Socialism. There is no sense in being panicky about Communists, merely because they sincerely believe in Socialism and work for it.

I am a Communist, and you are, I hope, a person who believes that we can and ought to give everybody in America a decent income. I believe, as I have said, that this can be done only if we get rid of the profit system, and I am afraid we may have our troubles with the profit-makers. But I do not propose to do away with capitalism right now and all of a sudden. Instead, I merely advocate that we do what we can, within the capitalist framework, to get our productive machinery working and to distribute its output to those who need it.

You are interested in exactly the same measures—wages and hours bills, social security legislation, protection of civil liberties and especially the right to organize. You think, however, that these measures may be enough, that through reforms of this kind we can seize the opportunity for abundance without getting rid of profits.

All right. We agree on these measures. Let us work together for them. If you prove to be right, that settles the matter, for it would be quite impossible to do away with capitalism if the masses of people were prosperous. If you're wrong—well, I don't believe you will stand by and let Fascism stamp its economy of scarcity upon us.

The Nature of the Rapprochement: Sources

"New Republic"
The New Deal as an Integrative Factor

(1932–1940)

The following sample of *New Republic* editorials concerning Franklin Roosevelt and the New Deal between 1932 and 1940 is representative of the attitudes of the liberal-left intellectual community.

Founded on the eve of World War I, the *New Republic* immediately became and remained, along with the *Nation*, America's leading liberal intellectual periodical. In 1932 *New Republic* supported Socialist Norman Thomas for the Presidency, but was sympathetic to Roosevelt in 1933 as the New Deal began. In the spring of 1934, the *New Republic* began to break with the New Deal to go Left (or, as the *New Republic* says, when F.D.R. began to go Right) and in 1935 spoke out in favor of what is called "democratic collectivism," which might be implemented by a party composed of Communists, Socialists, and Left-Wing New Dealers. In the election of 1936, the *New Republic* advised readers to vote for Socialist Norman Thomas or Communist Earl Browder except in states where Republican Alf Landon might win, in which case a vote for F.D.R. was justified.

In other words, during Roosevelt's first term when most of the New Deal program was passed, the *New Republic* was usually critical on the grounds that New Deal reforms were not radical enough.

Only during and after F.D.R.'s second term, when the New Deal was waning but also when criticism from the Right was increasing, did the *New Republic* move toward a position of support for the New Deal. Roosevelt's attempt to force the Supreme Court to approve the constitutionality of New Deal legislation, the so-called "court-packing" bill, which enraged conservative opponents and even alienated some previously disposed to the New Deal, simultaneously drew the *New Republic* editors behind Roosevelt. As

---

From *New Republic* editorials: (Aug. 17, 1932), pp. 4–6; (April 18, 1934), pp. 256–58; (Sept. 23, 1936), pp. 207–8; (Feb. 17, 1937), pp. 31–32; (Sept. 29, 1937), pp. 201–2; (Aug: 31, 1938), pp. 87–88; (May 20, 1940), pp. 706–8. Reprinted by permission of the publisher.

opposition to the New Deal mounted, they became consistent supporters. When F.D.R. tried to defeat Democrats in the primaries of the 1938 Congressional elections, and opponents called Roosevelt's attempt a "purge," the *New Republic* enthusiastically backed him. By the eve of the election of 1940, the *New Republic* could be called solidly pro-New Deal. Thus, the final effect of Roosevelt's administration was to pull many intellectuals from a stance of radical protest outside the two-party system to a position of support for one of the two major parties.

August 17, 1932.

How shall we vote?

. . . We cannot imagine anything which could make us favor either the Republican party or Mr. Hoover. The party now pursues, and has pursued ever since the birth of the paper, policies which in every important respect are diametrically contrary to ours. Anyone who is satisfied with the way the country has been governed since 1920 and with the present results can logically vote for Mr. Hoover, but we obviously are not of that number.

There is more to be said for the Democrats, but not much more. The party is, as it always has been, a sprawling and disjointed affair combining some of the most reactionary elements in the country with some of the progressive ones. It is incapable of pursuing any unified set of policies, whether good or bad, except under a strong leader like Wilson who knows what he wants and is able to carry the voters with him. In the recent convention the more progressive forces won the control from the more reactionary ones; it is frequently said that the West is now at the Democratic wheel. The nomination of Roosevelt proves at least that the power interests do not control the party.

Nevertheless, the element which won represents a liberalism which is more appropriate to 1912 than to 1932, and the platform is a mass of inconsistencies, a puny answer to the challenge of the times. It is uncertain whether Roosevelt himself will hammer out a really significant program of his own, though some of his tendencies are hopeful. It is still more uncertain whether he has the character and the intellectual power to effectuate whatever he may propose. Roosevelt is an untried jockey on a very lame horse. Perhaps his victory would further a slightly better tendency than that of Hoover. On the other hand it is entirely possible that a rigorous and conservative capitalist government like that of the Republicans would be preferable. At least it would tend to sharpen the issues and place the responsibility for what happens clearly on the American capitalist tradition and the persons who now embody it.

The natural conclusion would therefore seem to favor Thomas and the Socialists. If there can be no gain from either Democratic or Republican victory sufficient to outweigh long-term considerations of policy, you do not "throw away your vote" by casting it for a party which, though it cannot win this time, may win in the future—provided you believe the party can win some day, and provided you approve its principles. The Socialist party's proposals for governing the country, if it should ever take power, are deficient in detail but represent a tendency which appears to lie in the main line of social evolution. Capitalism as we have known it will certainly not persist forever, and the coming order is sure to be, as a matter of broad description, a socialistic one. The Socialist platform is closer in almost every respect to what the *New Republic* has been advocating than any of the others. This is, for instance, the only party which supports national economic planning in the interest of the common man. Even if one were much further from agreeing with the Socialist planks than we are, it is a weighty consideration that the larger the Socialist vote is, the more circumspect will be the behavior of the party which wins . . .

There remains the Communist party. The obvious comment is that to vote for a Communist President is to act a contradiction. The Communists do not believe they ever will elect a President; they do not believe in the possibility of doing anything to change a capitalist state by political action. A Communist vote is therefore merely a registration of belief in a future violent revolution, as well as of confidence in the Communist tactics for organizing the class struggle. For reasons unnecessary to enter upon here, the Communists do not appear to be having much more success at this task than do the Socialists. Their legitimacy will appear only if the revolutionary situation which they predict arises, and then only if they grasp the leadership of the revolutionary forces. All this may happen, but we are far from certain that it will. As a mere moral warning to the other parties, a Communist vote—if it were counted—would doubtless have somewhat more effect than a Socialist one.

April 18, 1934
Roosevelt drifts right

Almost from the first months of Roosevelt's administration the statement has been made that he was confronted with a choice between turning to the right or to the left. In crisis after crisis it has been predicted that now at last he must choose. But, apparently, he never has chosen. He has aimed at conciliating everybody, at keeping well nigh unanimous support. No sooner did he say or do something that seemed like facing in one direction than he said or did something else that seemed like facing in the other. As a politician, he is adept at the art of compromise and at making everyone feel happy about it. No doubt he believes he has thus been able to ride the wild horses and make some progress. But the circumstances were such that a middle course was impossible. Having failed resolutely to turn left, he has steadily drifted toward the right. If his action were charted, it would describe a curve with a large number of minor variations, but with a decided trend, over the months, back to old-style capitalism.

A listing of the issues on which he has given way supplies evidence of the manner in which he has gradually been pushed toward the conservative position. He began by failing to demand legislation for drastic reorganization of the banking system immediately after the crisis of a year ago; nothing more is heard now of fundamental banking legislation. Neither in the last session of Congress nor in this has he backed any thoroughgoing revision of the taxes on incomes and corporate profits; he has tried to stop some of the leaks in part, but a complete program of tax revision is still postponed. Without a struggle he allowed the Senate to defeat the St. Lawrence waterway; whatever may be thought of the project, he was driven from his former vigorous support of it by a powerful lobby consisting chiefly of railroad and utility interests. Frightened by the propaganda consequent upon cancellation of the air-mail contracts, he is about to give the subsidies back to private companies. After expressing, directly or indirectly, much concern over the injury to consumers by price-raising provisions in the N.R.A. codes, and after hearings in Washington that brought forth damning evidence on this score, he has done nothing at all to impose any real control over organized business in the interest of the consumers.

Having backed the National Labor Board in its somewhat belated and ineffectual attempts to outlaw company unions, and having given tacit support to the original Wagner Industrial Disputes Bill, he negotiated a compromise with the automobile makers giving company unions—regardless of the degree of employer control—an equal status with genuine unions. He has yielded to the Wall Street outcries by assenting to modification of the Securities Act, and the chances are that the bill to control the Stock Exchange will be so emasculated before passage as to be of little effect. The so-called Tugwell Bill introduced by Senator Copeland to strengthen the Pure Food and Drugs Act has been so altered in committee as a result of objections by protesting interests that it is hardly better than the existing law, and no objection has come from him. The chances are that the bill giving him power to reduce tariffs on a reciprocal basis will be killed by amendments in the Senate, fostered by protective interests, and the chances are that he will swallow it as amended. The C.W.A. has been abandoned; public works are to be allowed to peter out; no really adequate housing program is in sight. These are but the larger items of his surrender.

After each retreat, his enemies on the right have grown bolder. They have sensed in him the reluctance to pick a quarrel that might endanger his support by any powerful group, and have consequently exacted higher and higher prices for the continuance of peace. They have already run away with the first fruits of his program by raising prices and boosting profits as rapidly as relief and other expenditures have supplied any market at all. Increased profits have given them confidence, and have oiled the wheels of the old propaganda machinery. This runs true to form by attempting to squelch every progressive measure, by centering its fire upon all individuals who may influence the President in a direction considered hostile by the large interests, by reviving Red scares. If the New Deal in the end retains anything they dislike, they will not hesitate to attack it on all fronts and to attempt to unseat the President himself. He will find that the only way to retain their toleration is to become wholly their man.

But of course Roosevelt cannot do this except by forfeiting the support on the left, which he began to mobilize at the beginning of his term. Labor is already distrustful and dissatisfied, the farmers are restive, consumers in general complain about prices rising faster than their incomes. If the revival of profits continues at the expense of labor, farmers and consumers, if anything like inflation comes and stimulates a real clamor about the high cost of living, the President will have lost most of his popularity. Then he will have conciliated neither the right nor the left. His strength will wither in the cross-fire.

There is even a good chance that the propaganda of the moneyed interests will cause popular discontent to maintain them in power, though the two sorts of complaints are logically opposite. Workers and farmers cheated by the promises of the administration, consumers suffering from high prices created by artificial scarcity, can be led by the nose to support the very capitalist interests that have brought about the scarcity and the high prices. This sort of thing has happened many times before, and can happen again. The chief safeguard against it would be an intelligent, fighting leadership on the left. Mr. Roosevelt missed the psychological moment to place himself at the head of such a movement. Many of his words and some of his acts implied that he would do so, but he did not follow through to produce the results he promised. No political tragedy is greater than that of the David who faces Goliath without any stones for his slingshot. He discredits not only himself but all other potential generals of his army who would make similar promises. He delivers the people to their enemies. If the leader of a popular movement for change, who speaks loudly but does little, can be called a Kerensky, it does not always follow that he is succeeded by a Lenin. He may just as readily be succeeded by a leader of the old regime, by a vengeful reaction.

Old-style capitalism is getting on its feet again and is preparing to repeat its habitual performance. It is defeating, one by one, the attempts at reform, in the interest of the only kind of recovery that it knows how to manage. This is a recovery in profits which leaves millions in poverty, a recovery that can end, not in general, secure prosperity, but only in a boom of smaller or larger proportions, to be followed by another collapse.

September 23, 1936
The Editors' Choice

Our basic assumptions are as follows. The era of capitalism is past its zenith. Wars, revolutions and counter-revolutions continually are in the offing in this period of crisis. We believe the only ultimate solution compatible with human dignity, and with the basic faith of the American republic in democracy, equality and liberty, lies in the direction of a socialized organization of production and distribution, an order that will be capable of maintaining secure abundance and raising the material and cultural well-being of the people. It is important to make a transition to such an order as quickly as may be. It is also important to make the transition with as little pain and shock to living generations as possible, and particularly without regressing temporarily into war or fascism.

There is only one way to serve both these ends—the way that a democratic republic has left open for us. It is to organize political power by the use of freedom of speech, press and association, to gain popular support for an advance to a humane social order, and to establish it by means of democratic government. We are not so naïve as to suppose this method will not encounter immense difficulties, or so badly informed as to be ignorant of the danger that violent resistance from reactionaries may interrupt it on the way. Nevertheless it is the one chance we have to make intelligent progress, and to make it peaceably. The stronger the democratic movement, the better the chance, no matter what happens.

There is at present no reliable political instrument in the United States for carrying out this purpose. The Republican Party automatically crosses itself out. The Democratic Party, under pressure from the recent economic collapse, has vaguely experimented in the direction of social control, but it has no consistent program and its whole tendency appears to depend largely on the accident of leadership. It wants chiefly to remain in power, to do so by combining the best of two worlds, by pleasing everybody at once. The Socialist and Communist Parties, avowedly dedicated to a new order, have no chance of winning or even of becoming important political influences in the present campaign. The Union Party includes so much demagoguery that, if it were stronger, it would actually be dangerous. It is the nearest thing to embryo fascism we have in this country.

What is needed is of course a party that is at once collectivist in tendency and finds its sinews of support in organized labor and farmers, a party that can be stable, that can grow; and that can win the adherence of the masses—including, naturally, white-collar and professional workers. Labor parties of this kind exist in all other democratic nations. There have been stirrings in the same direction here in 1920, in 1924, and since then in some states and many localities. The idea of such a party is widely understood and favored. The movement is merely waiting to be crystallized. It is awaiting, particularly, the leadership of progressive sections of organized labor. Progressive laborites, in turn, are moving in the direction of such a party through the C.I.O. and Labor's Non-Partisan League, which is under C.I.O. influence.

If there were a labor or a farmer-labor party of this kind now in existence, there would be no question of our choice. However we might differ with it in details of program or personnel, it would represent the aggregation of people and the social tendency that would command our loyalty. Since it is not in existence, the question becomes how best to hold the door open for it. At this point there will be a divergence of judgment among those who have so far followed us with substantial agreement.

The simplest decision is to vote on principle by casting one's ballot for the Socialist or the Communist candidate. It is said that unless enough people eventually do this, regardless of the immediate practical result, we shall never have the party we want. If one continues to choose the lesser of two evils every time there is an election, there will never be anything but evils to choose between. We respect this attitude, and are glad that there will be many who will act in accordance with it. At the same time we believe that this is not the way things happen, or can happen, in American politics. There never will be enough people who vote on principle, regardless of practical result, to build an effective political party. There must be the enthusiasm of a broad movement, which really has a chance in the calculable future, in order to enlist enough votes so that a party can influence governmental policy.

Another argument for voting one of these tickets seems to us more compelling. It is that if the Left parties grow, the pressure for a real labor party will be increased. Not only that, but a large Socialist and Communist vote will exert a leftward influence on the next administration. All this is undoubtedly true.

A few persons argue that the election of Landon would be desirable because his administration would produce resentment among the masses; it would thus hasten independent political action on the part of labor. This doctrine of opposites does not appeal to us. Who knows what form a reaction against Republicanism would take? If it were strong enough, the Democrats might win with H. L. Mencken's Chinaman. They won last time with Roosevelt, who is condemned as a misleader and confuser of labor by those who argue in this way. Still worse, it might open the way for Father Coughlin or the Reverend Gerald L. K. Smith. The doctrine of progress through spasm sometimes works, but it is a dangerous one, and when a deliberate choice can be made, we much prefer a more healthy and normal progression. The miscalculation that may be involved in the support of your chief enemy, on the ground that he is better than those who agree with you more nearly but not nearly enough, was illustrated most strikingly of all by the Communists' aid to Hitler in Germany, before he came to power.

Finally, there is the argument that one should vote for President Roosevelt because either he or Landon will be elected and, after all, he represents in general by far the more progressive tendency. This attitude we respect, but we fear it is based on a miscalculation. Will Mr. Roosevelt act in revival and prosperity as he acted in depression? Does he ever act except as social pressures lead him? Does he really know where he is going? Or does he follow the last advice he has heard, no matter from which side it may come? If it were merely a question of the two leading candidates and their parties, we should be inclined to choose, not the lesser evil, but an increased pressure from the left by an enlarged vote for the minor candidates.

But there is a special argument, more closely connected with our principal assumptions, that impresses us more. The next few years will be critical ones for organized labor. The growth and prestige of the labor movement, both in industry and politics, is fundamentally important. Landon, in spite of his attempt to express a liberal attitude toward labor, will clearly be more favorable to reactionary employers than will Roosevelt. He has adopted their formula that in organization and collective bargaining the workers should be "free from interference from any source." This means, at the least, that governmental power would not be exerted to protect the right of organization from interference by the employer. The Roosevelt doctrine is the one favored by organized labor itself—that the right of labor to organize and bargain through representatives of its choice should be protected by government. Fully as important as this difference in announced policy is the fact that in a close election such as this will probably be, workers' votes in the big industrial states may readily turn the scales. The President must be conscious of the dependence he will owe, if he is elected, to the more progressive cohorts of labor. Here is a social force that is bound to influence his and others' action.

Finally, the very centers of influence in labor that are necessary for leadership in a new labor party are organized, independently of the Democratic Party, in support of Mr. Roosevelt. In New York and other localities they have adopted a new party designation (the American Labor Party) and will support independent candidates of their own, at least below President and Governor. To strengthen the prestige of this movement is essential. To encourage its leaders by a large vote is highly desirable. This group is the nucleus of that larger movement which, when it is formed, will command our loyalty. We ought to be with it from the beginning. To vote for Labor or Socialist candidates in local, state and congressional elections, and for President Roosevelt nationally, will, most of the editors believe, be the clearest possible demonstration of the simultaneous demands for a national labor party in 1940, and for a progressive attitude toward labor in the next administration.

A further refinement of voting policy is possible. Straw votes indicate a close election; if it were not uncertain, there would be little point in amassing an independent vote for Roosevelt. But it will not be equally close in all states. If those who agree with us, but live in states sure to go either for

Landon or for Roosevelt, will vote Socialist or Communist according to their convictions, while those who live in doubtful states cast their ballots for Democratic presidential electors, the double strategy we favor will be furthered . . .

February 17, 1937

Curbing the supreme court

President Roosevelt's message calling for legislation to reform the federal judiciary contains a number of recommendations concerning the lower courts which meet with general approval—such as that injunctions involving the federal government shall not be granted until the Attorney General has had a chance to be heard, that constitutional questions shall have precedence in going to the Supreme Court, and that various other measures shall be taken to expedite business. A bitter controversy rages, however, about his proposal to enlarge the Supreme Court to a possible fifteen members by new appointments—this proposal taking the technical form that when a Justice who has reached the age of seventy does not retire, an additional one may be appointed. (Six out of the nine Justices have now attained this age.) Opposition comes not only from the Right, as would be expected, but from the Left as well. In order to get our bearings in this argument, it would be well to begin by stating the major premises from which we proceed.

During recent years—and not only since the New Deal began—the Supreme Court has invalidated on constitutional grounds an increasing number of progressive measures involving social or economic issues. Their votes in so doing have been, more often than not, narrow majorities. In almost all cases competent authorities, including some of the learned Justices themselves, have believed it both possible and logical to take the opposite view. There is nothing in the words of the Constitution itself that would have necessitated the action taken. The result has proceeded rather from the views of individual Justices, conditioned as they are by varying traditions, environments and prejudices. It is undeniable that if the Court had been differently constituted, different decisions would have flowed from it. The Court is therefore not an infallible and wholly independent agency of government dispensing absolute justice, but a body which, according to its lights, frequently makes political decisions. However concealed may be the political motive, it is almost invariably there, the political consequences of its constitutional judgments are obvious to all. It is furthermore obvious that the general trend of these decisions is conservative; that taken all in all they prevent the other branches of government from acting to alleviate social and economic ills.

So drastic and far-reaching have been a number of these recent decisions that most informed persons are hopeless that government will be able to cope with the task thrust upon it in the modern world so long as we have the same Supreme Court as now or so long as we have the same Constitution. A crisis of some sort is upon us. Something has to be done about the Court or the Constitution or both. This is essentially a political job, in the sense that it must spring from and emphasize the will of the people.

These premises automatically cancel the objections to the President's proposal from the Right, from those who believe that the Supreme Court has been the embodiment of wisdom and has saved us from the perils of democratic institutions. They also cancel the objections of those who believe that there is no correct way of interpreting the Constitution except the way in which the Court has interpreted it, and who hold that the Court has acted in a wholly technical, impartial capacity rather than in a political one. (Let it be noted in passing that although these opinions are often expressed by the same persons, they contradict each other: the Court cannot at the same time be the instrument of wise policy and an automatic interpreter.) Objections from the Left grant that something must be done, but charge that this is not the right way to do it. It is an undignified subterfuge to "pack the Court." If a liberal can do it, a conservative could also. In view of the difficulty of predicting how Justices will decide, packing may be ineffectual in any case (*vide* McReynolds, reactionary, appointed by Wilson, and Stone, liberal, appointed by Coolidge). An age limit will not do the trick, since many conservatives are young and many liberals remain flexible in older years (*vide* Holmes and Brandeis). It would be better to limit the powers of the Court by legislation or constitutional amendment or to extend the powers of government by amendment.

We believe these objections have not taken into consideration the full significance of the premises above set forth. There is no way to safeguard eternal progressivism in government, whether by President Roosevelt's method or by any other. If there is no guarantee of obtaining a progressive Court, there is surely no guarantee that new words in the law or the Constitution would be much differently interpreted than the old ones. The essence of the matter is not thematic or logical, but political. Some effective way or ways must be found of registering a national desire that the Court act differently at the present time. "Packing" the Court is as good a way to do this as any. It is not undignified to seek to add to it new members who will have different opinions about the Constitution and about policy from those of the present majority. There is just as much good logic in the dissents of Justices Brandeis, Stone and Cardozo as in the majority opinions. Able new Justices may be found who disagree in these matters with Justices Butler, McReynolds and Sutherland. Nor is there any betrayal of the existing constitutional system in acknowledging that the issue is and must be political in the deepest sense and that the tendency of an overwhelming majority of citizens has a right to representation in the Supreme Court as in the other branches of the government. To reject this measure in favor of a constitutional amendment is to reject a means of pressure immediately feasible for one that might take years to effectuate and might be blocked by one more than a fourth of the states, containing a small minority of the electorate.

It is true that new appointees by the President may be less good than is desirable, and that they may think in unpredictable ways. It is true that an age limit is not an assurance of liberality or flexibility. But these are not reasons for refraining from exercising possible political pressure on the Court through an indubitably constitutional measure that can surely be passed if it is supported by the progressives in Congress. Rather they are reasons for not stopping with this measure, but for attacking the Court conservatives on all fronts at once. There is no necessity for an exclusive choice between this proposal and others. There is no necessity for making the best an enemy of the good. The political strategy of the situation is to register by all possible means the people's desire for freedom to move in a progressive direction. Let us have also a resolution embodying a well considered constitutional amendment—or a set of them. Let us have also any well considered legislative action, other than this.

There is no question that the Court must be given a new lead, and that most of those who voted for Mr. Roosevelt desire that to happen. The sole danger is that those who are agreed about this will so fall out about the means that their pressure will be ineffective. That would be lamentable, in view of the fact that the nature of the specific means is less important than the pressure itself. The very fact that a series of reactionary decisions led to a strongly supported proposal to pack the Court will of itself, no matter what happens as a result of this bill, exert a potent influence on the Court in the future. The learned Justices are bound to be a little more careful not to clothe their private prejudices in the Constitution, or to veto in the name of that broad document measures that the nation has decided it needs.

September 29, 1937

The President's Fighting Speech

Not in many months has President Roosevelt made a more challenging address than his speech on Constitution Day. He paid his respects to the dictatorships abroad, "both plutocratic and proletarian," with such vigor that the press in Germany was forbidden to present his views; he renewed the pledge to keep America out of war; but most of his time was devoted to things nearer home.

He left no doubt that he will continue to fight for his entire program, including removal of the Supreme Court barrier to the betterment of conditions for the masses of the people. He is convinced, he indicated, that a majority of the people are behind him in his demand for improved economic and social conditions. Particularly, he believes, they want shorter hours, higher wages, stable income for farmers, an end to disruptive trade practices and the abolition of conditions which permit a small minority to profiteer at the expense of a majority.

He reminded his hearers that the Constitution was written not only to protect the few against the tyranny of the many, but the many against the few. He spoke eloquently of the cost of the "twenty-year lag" between the necessity for change and the recognition of that necessity by the Supreme Court. He also mentioned the fundamental absurdity of five-to-four decisions where the odd man on the Court rules. He is determined during his present tenure of office to have the Supreme Court become part of the government of the United States instead of an alternative and superior power.

No one who knows anything of the color of the President's mind need have been surprised by the attitude displayed in this speech. Even his bitterest enemies recognize that he is not a quitter. In the past session of Congress he acted with less than his usual political skill, chiefly because he overestimated his own strength. A compromise was offered under which he could have increased the size of the Court to eleven and established the principle of retirement for age. The President rejected the compromise and was defeated on his proposal. Since then, he has been further embarrassed as to his relation to the Court by the charges that his appointee, Mr. Justice Black, is a member of the Ku Klux Klan.

But while Mr. Roosevelt has lost a salient or two, he has not lost his battle. It remains true that a third—at least—of all Americans are ill housed, ill fed and ill clad. It remains true also that we have made more progress toward a socialized economy in the past four and a half years than in the two previous decades. While support of the President throughout the country may have lessened somewhat since his overwhelming victory at the polls eleven months ago, a large majority still stands behind him. There are scores of men in both houses of Congress who were elected by the people for the express purpose of helping Mr. Roosevelt to carry out the aims of the New Deal. The chief criticism that can now be made of the President is that he does not work closely enough with these congressional supporters, take them into his confidence, rely upon their excellent collective judgment as to what the country wants and how to get it. His tactics are sometimes open to question; but his main objectives must, in our opinion, be endorsed by every American who believes that peace, happiness and security for all are possible within our borders.

August 31, 1938

Roosevelt Forges a Party

In the primary battles which the New Deal is waging within the Democratic Party against Senator Tydings of Maryland, Senator George of Georgia and Representative O'Connor of New York, more is at stake than appears on the surface. The issue between the President and these gentlemen is not a personal one; it does not concern dictatorship vs. independence; it is not an attempt by Washington to control local opinion. Rather it is a symptom of the struggle going on within the party between those who want to make it a reliable instrument of progressivism and those who want to recapture it for a conservative and quietistic policy.

For years it has been said, and with a considerable degree of truth, that there was very little difference between the two great parties; that they did not represent competing philosophies and programs. They were rivals for political patronage more than organizations representing divergent views of the state. The hoary principles to which they referred in campaigns seemed to have little relationship to what they actually did when in office, and in congressional votes the Representatives and Senators often divided without much regard to party lines. The Democratic Party in particular was an illogical combination. Conservative Southerners who, if they had happened to come from the North, would certainly have been stand-pat Republicans, were allied with spoilsmen from the Democratic machines in the Northern cities and with a sprinkling of reformers from all over the country. Occasionally a Democrat like Woodrow Wilson might win the presidency by appealing to independent voters, temporarily imposing the stamp of his thought on the gelatinous mass of party professionals, but to hope for anything of permanent value from such a coalition was naïve. It was analysis of this sort that gave rise to the desire for a reshuffling of political forces or the rise of a successful third party.

Franklin D. Roosevelt, coming in a year of crisis and embracing the tendency known as the New Deal, temporarily at least was able to give the party a progressive direction. But the party was the same old mixture underneath. As time has passed, the question has become more insistent whether the Democratic organization is to relapse into its old character of Tweedledum. The innate conservatism of many prominent Democrats began to reassert itself in the form of congressional obstruction, and in spite of an overwhelming party majority the President began to have serious difficulty in obtaining the passage of important legislation on his program. This time a new force increased the difficulty. The successive routs of the Republican Party made the economic royalists wonder whether they could ever ride back to power in the good old way on the back of the elephant, and so they used every possible device to express their will through renegade Democrats. So far has their infiltration gone that it has become really doubtful whether a progressive successor to the President—if he does not seek a third term—can be nominated or whether such a successor could command effective support in Congress.

In this camouflaged struggle the conservatives have little to lose and everything to gain. If they get control of the Democratic organization, well and good. If they merely keep enough power within it to set laborites and progressives back on their heels, the effort is not wasted. If the progressive forces resist with enough determination to split the party, the Republicans may after all have another chance.

If Mr. Roosevelt expects to change the old character of his party permanently, he will first of all have to stop the guerilla tactics of the conservatives within it. That he can do if he can bring them out into the open and force them to oppose him and the policies he stands for in order to be reelected. There is a net gain for his major objectives in this strategy, whether they are reelected or not. For it is better to have a small and reliable majority than a large and unwieldy one. It is better to have an outspoken and recognized opponent in front than an enemy lurking in the tall grass in the rear. There is no sense whatever in allowing candidates who have seriously sabotaged the Democratic program in Washington to go back home and seek the favor of the voters on the assumption that the White House approves of them. This is so, no matter what one's attitude concerning the specific measures in question.

Mr. Roosevelt has an immense popular following, and within his own party an overwhelming one. It expects him to make good on his promises. Political responsibility is furthered if he tells them frankly who will help him make good and who will not. It is good for the Democratic Party, and good for the nation, that these primary struggles should be conducted on the basis of political principles rather than on the basis of a meaningless party harmony. This may be the last chance for a long while to make the Democratic Party a reliable instrument for progressive-minded citizens. For the President to accept the chance is not for him to try to set up a personal dictatorship or to coerce local opinion. In most cases large majorities of local opinion already want what he wants. He is merely giving them an opportunity to say again whether they do or not and, if they do, to forge a party organization which is more responsive to their will.

May 20, 1940.
Looking Backward

Collectively we have a short memory. The American people face the present, with a slight glance ahead; they are little interested in history, even that of their own yesterday. Only eight years later it is hard for us to recall what life was like in the last year under Hoover.

Banks were closing in 1932—not a dozen a day, as they were a little later, but one every dozen days. People nervously broke up their accounts and divided their money among three banks, or four or five. Without government guarantee of any sort, no institution was wholly safe from the fetid breath of rumor.

As the business index kept going down, the number of the unemployed steadily mounted. Nobody knew how many there were; government statistics on this point were even more inadequate than they are today. People knew, however, that on every street corner there were beggars who showed by face and manner that they were not the glib professionals of happier days. Poor people knew, because families had to double up until tenements were unendurably overcrowded and the money for food got more and more scanty. Charitable organizations, swamped with new needs, appealed desperately for donations but met a steadily dwindling response; before long, they were meeting only 10 percent of the burden. On hundreds of city streets appeared apple-sellers who managed to take away a few cents' worth of business from the grocery stores and just barely keep soul and body contiguous. In every city there sprang up those ironically named Hoover-villes, settlements made of old packing boxes where homeless men lived by thousands, doing odd jobs when they could, or if not, begging at back doors, or rummaging through garbage pails and trash boxes. In New York, the lucky ones with a nickel rode the subways all night in cold weather, or put down newspapers over a grating where exhaust heat came from a building. In Chicago, they slept on the ground under double-decked Wacker Drive. Thousands and thousands of people took to the road including large numbers of young men and boys and some young women.

In the farm regions, misery was universal. Thousands of farmers who had worked hard and lived frugally all their lives but had made the mistake of buying land on mortgage, lost their property. When they could, they went to work as hired hands or sought odd jobs from door to door in nearby small towns. In more than one area, spontaneous action of neighborhood men prevented auctioning off property; a menacing crowd would surround the sheriff and his few deputies, bid $1 for the property and give it back to the owner.

The depression was cruelly hard on boys and girls of high-school and college age who were met by blank refusals whenever they sought employment. If there was money enough for decent clothing and books and supplies, some of them went on in school because there was nothing else to do; but in thousands of cases their families could not afford even these slight expenses and the young people stayed home in complete idleness. Family morale deteriorated when the unemployed father, sitting around the house all day, could no longer maintain any authority. . .

One need only recall what conditions were in 1932 to realize the amazing change in our national thinking that has taken place in eight years. While there is still complaint about paternalism and centralized government (from the Republicans who were the great exponents of these ideas, applied under special circumstances, for the first seventy-five years of their party's life) it is obvious that even the critics are only half-hearted in what they say.

As a nation we have agreed, once and forever, that the individual must not bear the sole responsibility for his failure to cope with economic problems of unemployment or old age which are, quite obviously, beyond his powers, and that society as a whole must take over a substantial part of the burden.

We have at last learned that laissez-faire has been dead for years; that the unguided lust of the business man for profit does not infallibly produce Utopia.

And finally, we have reaffirmed in these past eight years an early American doctrine that had been all but forgotten in preceding decades: that the country exists for the welfare and happiness of all its inhabitants; and that when this condition is not met, reformation is in order no matter how drastic it may be or how much it may be disliked by existing privileged minorities.

What It All Means

The new deal, even in its second term, has clearly done far more for the general welfare of the country and its citizens than any administration in the previous history of the nation. Its relief for underprivileged producers in city and country, though inadequate to the need, has been indispensable. Without this relief an appalling amount of misery would have resulted, and a dangerous political upheaval might have occurred. Since the expenditure of money for relief—even the insufficient amounts recently appropriated—has been the principal target of the administration's conservative enemies, this accomplishment alone would be sufficient reason for support of the New Deal. The assertion of the reactionaries that if the federal budget were balanced by cutting expenses, business would revive sharply enough to absorb the unemployed and make relief expenditures unnecessary, is incapable of proof and seems highly improbable.

In addition, the New Deal in this second period has accomplished much of permanent benefit to the nation. Perhaps its most important achievement was the National Labor Relations Act, the result of which was to inhibit employers' opposition to union organization and true collective bargaining, so that trade-union membership was more than doubled. This was not a mere act of justice; it was the laying of a solid foundation for our society in the future. Without a strong, alert and independent labor movement a modern industrial nation is in constant danger from the enemies of political and social democracy. Second only to the strengthening of unions is the establishment of minimum labor standards. The fury with which reactionaries have attacked these two labor measures is an index of their importance.

Other permanent improvements are the impetus given to conservation of soil and forests, the many-sided TVA, a great road-building program, flood control, a good beginning at slum clearance and adequate housing for those not provided for by private construction, great hydro-electric projects, extension of electricity at reasonable rates through the Rural Electrification Administration, and the inauguration of insurance against unemployment and the other forms of social security.

The government as an instrument of democratic action in the future has also been strengthened and renovated. This is not merely a matter of the addition of many new agencies, but of the more efficient organization of the whole executive department—including a planning board under the President which so far has been relatively unimportant but is capable of future development. The Courts, too, have been revivified, partly by legislation, but principally by excellent new appointment, so that we now have a Supreme Court which is abreast of the times.

It is improbable that these more permanent changes will be or even can be destroyed by any new administration. . .

William Henry Chamberlin
The American "Discovery" of European Totalitarianism

(1934, 1935)

As the selection from Granville Hicks indicates, the Soviet Union was invoked as a model of socialist planning by those critical of the United States for its inability to reduce unemployment and suffering. Because of the curiosity concerning the Bolsheviks, American correspondents in Russia played an important role. William Henry Chamberlin (1897–1969), Moscow correspondent for the *Christian Science Monitor* during the 1920's and early 1930's, was representative of those journalists whose articles contributed to a sympathetic picture of the Soviet Union.

In the following selection, written in 1934–1935, Chamberlin relates his initial admiration for the Bolsheviks and his later disillusionment. He concluded that despite the nobility of the Soviet goals of a classless society, the ruthlessness of Soviet means to reach the goals was little different from that of the Nazis, whom he had also witnessed. The ruthless subjugation of the human personality by the authoritarian state was, Chamberlin concluded, a totalitarianism common to both Communism and Fascism.

Farewell to Russia

When I first came to Moscow in 1922, my attitude toward the Soviet regime was more than friendly; it was enthusiastic. I sometimes look back with a shade of amusement to the rhetorical articles in praise of the Bolshevik Revolution which I published in radical newspapers and magazines at that time, animated, as I can see in retrospect, by little knowledge and much faith. And, if I am sometimes tempted to laugh at the outburst of enthusiastic tourists, I must remember that in 1919 and 1920 my own attitude was very similar to theirs. How ready I was in those years to believe the most fantastic yarns of the well-disposed visitor returning from the Red Mecca of Moscow! And how I was inclined to denounce the mildest and most reasoned critic as a base traitor and defamer! Proceeding from the belief, which I still hold, that the World War was the supreme crime and folly of the century, I jumped to the conclusion, which I have long abandoned, that revolution on the Bolshevik model is the panacea for war and for all social injustice.

William Henry Chamberlin, "Farewell to Russia," *The Atlantic Monthly*, 154 (Nov. 1934), pp. 565–73; "Russia and Germany—Parallels and Contrasts," *Ibid.*, 156 (Sept. 1935), pp. 359–69. Reprinted by permission of *The Atlantic Monthly* and the Estate of William Henry Chamberlin.

Not that I have completed the absolute psychological somersault which I have witnessed in some acquaintances who came to Russia avowed Communists and left the country expressing hopes for the complete overthrow of the Soviet regime. For some achievements of the Revolution I have the sincerest respect, especially for its spread of education among the masses, for its policy of absolute non-discrimination among the races and nationalities of the country, for its exaltation of labor, for its promotion of health and recreation. I always come away from a workers' rest home or from a workers' club, situated perhaps in a former slum district, with a conviction that a vast amount of useful social and educational work has been and is being done under the auspices of the ruling Communist Party...

And yet, when one sums up all that can fairly be said about the constructive sides of the Soviet regime, there remains a formidable burden of facts on the other side. There is the permanent and odious system of terrorism and espionage. There is the decimation of the intelligentsia through secret convincing "sabotage" trials. There is the subjection of the peasantry to wholesale deportations and to a "military feudal exploitation" that reached its terrible and inevitable climax in the great famine of 1932–1933—all for the sake of imposing on the peasants an alien and unfamiliar system which certainly has yet to prove its productive advantages.

How can one reconcile such apparent contradictions: establishment of children's nurseries and sending of some children, with their kulak parents, to Arctic wastes; setting up of technical research institutes and application of inquisitorial methods to scientists of world eminence? It is my personal belief that the Bolshevik Revolution and the Soviet regime which grew out of it can only be understood as an example of historical tragedy of the deepest and truest type, a tragedy of cruelty, of the crushing out of innumerable individual lives, not from sheer wanton selfishness, but from perverted, fanatical idealism—always the surest source of absolute ruthlessness. And behind this tragedy lie several conceptions which are implicit in Communist philosophy; and the longer I have seen these in practice, the more I have come to regard them as sentimental fallacies.

The first, the oldest, and the most demonstrable fallacy is the conviction that the end justifies the means. I think the overwhelming weight of historical evidence is to the effect that the means determine the end, and that an idealistic goal, pursued by brutal methods, has a tendency to disappear from view. Such major atrocities as the liquidation of the kulaks as a class, the state-organized famine, and the persecution of the intelligentsia have harmful results that go far beyond their immediate victims. They brutalize the society that is taught or forced to look on them with indifference or even with applause. More terrible than the commission of these atrocities was the fact that no voice could be publicly raised against them in the Soviet Union...

A second sentimental fallacy of Communism is its virtual ignoring of the grave problems involved when the few men who must inevitably guide the whole political and economic life of the country, under the system of the so-called dictatorship of the proletariat, are granted enormous power with no kind of effective check or control. Lenin was so obsessed with the idea that 'capitalism,' the private ownership of the means of production, was the root of all human ills that he never seems to have foreseen the abuses, equally serious, if of a different kind, which might emerge when all power, political and economic, would be in the hands of a dictatorial state. . .

The materialistic conception of history is a Communist dogma with which I am in vigorous disagreement. This effort to explain all human activity in terms of the play of economic forces seems narrow, inadequate, and unconvincing. It becomes positively ridiculous when there is an effort to explain a jolly overture by Glinka as "Russian trade capitalism expanding" or a melancholy song by Tchaikovsky as "Russian landed aristocracy in decay." More serious than these amateurish experiments in artistic misinterpretation is the tendency to regard the individual merely as a member of this or that class. This impersonal approach is an easy road to pitiless hardness.

Then the practice of "the dictatorship of the proletariat" in the Soviet Union has in it a large element of inverted snobbishness. Reasonable people would generally agree that labor with hand or brain gives one a title to respect. But I am quite unable to comprehend why work in a factory is intrinsically more ennobling than work in an office, or on a farm, or in a research laboratory. By its avowed and systematic discrimination against "nonproletarians"—that is, against nonfactory laborers—in educational opportunity and in promotion in the state service, the Soviet Union is handicapping itself just as much as any state which resorted to some of the more familiar forms of class or race discrimination.

One among many points of faith common to apologists of Communism and of Fascism is an overweening contempt for civil liberties, which are represented as unnecessary and inconvenient barnacles on the ship of progress. The longer I have lived in the Soviet Union, where civil liberties—freedom of speech, press, assembly, and election—are most conspicuously lacking, the more I have become convinced that they are of vital and tremendous importance, and that their existence or absence is as good a test as any of the quality of a nation's civilization. The Communist (or the Fascist—their trend of thought in this question is striking similar) talks of civil liberties as of the outworn fetish of a handful of disgruntled intellectuals who are unable to rise to the necessary vision of the high and noble character and purpose of the Communist (or Fascist) state. But my own observation in Russia has led me to believe that a great deal more is at stake than the freedom of thought of the educated classes, although it seems rather obvious that culture becomes impoverished when the historian must alter his record of the past, the author must give a prescribed coloring to his characters, and free research in any field can be cut off, at the will of an all-powerful state.

It was during my trip through the famine regions of Ukraina and the North Caucasus that I became utterly and definitely convinced that democracy, with all its faults, weaknesses, and imperfections, is enormously superior to dictatorship as a method of government, simply from the point of view of the common man. Is there any recorded case in history where famine—not poverty or hardship or destitution, but stark famine, with a toll of millions of lives—has occurred in a democratically governed country? Is it conceivable that the famine of 1932–1933 could have taken place if civil liberties had prevailed in the Soviet Union, if newspapers had been free to report the facts, if speakers could have appealed for relief, if the government in power had been obliged to submit its policy of letting vast numbers of the peasants starve to death to the verdict of a free election? The countless graves of the humble and obscure famine victims, the peasants of Ukraina and the North Caucasus, of the Volga and Central Asia, are to me the final grim, unanswerable refutation of the specious Communist contention that freedom of speech and press and political agitation is only humbug by which the bourgeoisie tries to delude the masses. . .

Russia and Germany

Soviet Russia and Nazi Germany are usually thought of as complete antipodes. The type of mind that sympathizes with Hitler's regime almost invariably views Communism with utter aversion; the radical who is inclined to justify or at least to condone arbitrary arrests and executions in Russia habitually professes horror and indignation when the same methods of administration are applied in the Third Reich.

But a detached observer who, like the present writer, has lived for fairly long periods of time under both regimes can scarcely fail to see the numerous parallels, as well as the striking contrasts, between Stalin's Russia and Hitler's Germany. The similarities are most vivid and most obvious in such matters as political technique, administrative practice, and ruling-class psychology. The contrasts are most pronounced as regards theoretical philosophy, ultimate goals, and sources of class support.

One of the most important points of similarity is that both Russia and Germany are ruled by dictatorial parties, which avowedly tolerate no other political organizations. . .

At the head of the two tightly disciplined parties one finds leaders whose authority is absolute and whose decisions are accepted as infallible. Indeed, such an absolute and infallible leader is an indispensable element in a system that provides for no democracy in the ruling party, much less in the country as a whole. . .

The infallible leader is not the only common feature of Communist and

National Socialist Party organization. Both parties have found themselves confronted and perplexed by the problem of the careerist, of the man who wishes to join for the sake of the loaves and fishes that are associated with the possession of dictatorial power. And Nazi and Communist leaders alike, with varying degrees of success, have endeavored to preserve idealism within the ranks by means of periodic purges of unworthy members, by erecting bars against a too hasty and indiscriminate admission of new "party comrades," by giving preference to the party "old guard" in appointments to posts of responsibility...

To one who comes, as I did, to Berlin with a background of Moscow experience, many features of life in the German capital seem strikingly, even boringly familiar. It is not novel or surprising, for instance, to find that Germans with even the mildest taint of political oppositionism are often unwilling to come into contact with foreigners, and are always naturally and pathetically eager to be certain that their views will not be quoted...

Both in the new Russia and in the new Germany one finds much more genuine and unquestioning enthusiasm for the new order among the young than among the middle-aged. Russia now has a young generation that has grown up under the Soviet regime, that has been subjected to an unremitting stream of propaganda on its behalf since the cradle, and that naturally, with some unavoidable exceptions, sings Communist songs, thinks along Communist lines, repeats Communist phrases and slogans. The Hitler regime has not had time to train a similar generation in Germany, although it is taking vigorous steps in this direction by training the young teachers along one-hundred-percent National Socialist lines. But in Germany the youth was mostly caught up with the frenzy of nationalist faith that swept Hitler into power; and there are unmistakably more genuine Nazi enthusiasts under thirty than over that age...

Both Communism and National Socialism possess many psychological traits of fanatical religious faith, notably the reassuring conviction that the end justifies the means and the firm will to believe in spite of the most convincing evidence to the contrary. They are often eminently successful in communicating these traits to foreign admirers. The admiring tourist in Russia who spends two days in Leningrad, four days in Moscow, and comes away convinced that all stories of hunger and forced labor are lies, has a worthy companion in the occasional pilgrim to Germany who sees that the German towns are clean and orderly, that the German countryside is well kept and smiling, and uncritically infers that all tales of ugly happenings in concentration camps, general poverty, and espionage are mere inventions of non-Aryan malice.

Propaganda is a very important element in cementing the structure of both the Russian and the German dictatorial regimes. And the organization of propaganda in Moscow, Leningrad, and Kharkov, in Berlin, Cologne, and Munich, falls into very familiar and very similar patterns. With all critical opposition effectively gagged, it is a simple matter for the Communist or the Nazi agitator to magnify successes, to gloss over failures, to exaggerate the distresses of countries under other systems, to stir up mob hatred against minorities which are large enough to be identified and too small to defend themselves, such as the Jews in Germany and the more loosely defined 'kulaks' and 'bourgeoisie' in Russia...

The technique of repression in the two countries is so similar that one is tempted to wonder whether the Nazis have been taking lessons from the Communists, or vice versa. The entire setup of the mysterious Reichstag Fire Case, especially Goering's assertion that it was to be the signal for a general Communist uprising, no sign of which ever materialized, was in the best tradition of the notorious Soviet sabotage trials, where, on at least one occasion, two men who had been dead several years were solemnly mentioned in a bill of indictment as participants in a formidable conspiracy against the Soviet regime. The killings in Russia after the assassination of Kirov last December, which, according to official statements, took 117 lives, were a remarkably faithful imitation of the June 30 'purge' in Germany. The procedure in the two cases was virtually identical: summary wholesale executions without open trial, followed by ambiguously worded official and semi-official statements accusing of all sorts of terrorist schemes, and of treasonable association with the agents of hostile foreign powers, the persons who had already been conveniently put out of the way...

Where the element of parallel and the element of contrast begin to blend is in the attitude of the Russian and German regimes toward the unlucky groups which are singled out for discrimination and persecution. Such groups exist, both in Russia and in Germany. But the basis of selection is different, although the treatment, in some respects, is strikingly similar. Russia is dominated by class fanaticism, Germany by race fanaticism. Those Jews who came off worst under the Hitler dispensation are in much the same position of social ostracism, personal insecurity, and deprivation of almost all means of making a living as were the class victims of the Soviet system—priests and ministers of religion, former aristocrats and merchants, kulaks, and the like. If, as press reports foreshadow, Germany disfranchises the Jews and forbids them to serve in the army, she will be copying exactly the Soviet method of discriminating against Russia's pariah classes.

The idea of a kulak being appointed to manage a state farm in Russia would arouse in good Communists just the same automatic reaction of horror that the discovery of a Jew in a responsible state post would excite in good Nazis. The question of the personal qualifications of the kulak or of the Jew simply would not enter into consideration.

A shelf of the nonsensical books which have been written in Russia since the Revolution seeking to interpret literature, art, philosophy, even science and mathematics, on a "class basis" could be usefully placed side by side with a shelf of equally nonsensical books which have appeared in

Germany since 1933, seeking to impart an Aryan certificate to every manifestation of German culture. Russia boasts of its "class justice," as Germany boasts of its "race justice"; an outsider often finds it uncommonly difficult to discover any cause for pride in either...

On some points the ideals of the two systems are diametrically opposed. National Socialism wishes to put woman back in the home; Bolshevism tries to push her into factory or office. National Socialism exalts Old Germany as unreasonably and as extravagantly as Bolshevism denounces Old Russia. Bolshevism is militantly atheistic; National Socialism started out by professing allegiance to "positive Christianity," although the recent fostering of a kind of romantic paganism in Germany and the sharp conflicts which have arisen between the state and representatives of both of the major Christian communions may raise some doubt as to the substance of this "positive Christianity." The extreme claims of any totalitarian state, whether it be Communist or Fascist in character, tend to come into conflict with those of any religion that lays stress on individual conscience and judgment...

Peter Viereck
The Emergence of a New American Conservatism

(1940)

By the late 1930's a new intellectual temper was discernible. During the early years of the decade there was sympathy for the Soviet Union; support among intellectuals at home for Socialists and Communists rather than for Franklin Roosevelt; and pervasive talk of the bankruptcy of America's political and economic system. The end of the decade brought disillusionment with Russia, increasing support for the New Deal, pervasive talk of America's virtues.

In 1940 this new intellectual temper was captured in a prescient essay by a twenty-three-year old Harvard graduate student, Peter Viereck. He articulated a "new conservatism" remarkably anticipating (even more so in view of the fact that the essay was first written in 1937) the mood of the 1940's and 1950's. Viereck was himself to contribute to the "new conservative" strain in post-war intellectual history.

Why should any young man want to be a conservative, on a globe where so much needs changing? I can best answer in a roundabout way with a few facts

Peter Viereck, from "But—I'm a Conservative!" *The Atlantic Monthly*, 165 (April 1940), pp. 538–43. See also Reading List, p. 356, for other books reflecting seasoned views of this author.

about myself. I am twenty-three years of age, unemployed, short of cash. For six years I have studied at Harvard and at Christ Church, Oxford, as a Fellowship holder, getting my bachelor and graduate degrees in history and literature. At the same time, my work for magazines has given me some practical experience in that less rarefied atmosphere of American journalism. In both spheres I have watched the convention of revolt harden into a dogmatic ritual.

Revolt now has its hierarchy of saints, including such divergent apostles of Progress as the editors of the *Nation* and of the *New Masses*. It has its elaborate, formalized incantations, its holy slogans. Behind much of it today lies the smug convention that our only alternative of fascist terror is Marxism. Marxism means many things. I revolt against its "revolt" primarily for its materialistic assault on all our non-economic values of the spirit. Economic values alone make life possible, but the moral, æsthetic, and intellectual values alone make it worth living.

The Hitler-Stalin pact and Russia's invasion of Finland have laid bare the incompetence of our "fellow travelers" as analysts, prophets, and leaders. By Stalin's non-communist fellow travelers I specifically mean those liberals whose attitude was best summarized by the following manifesto in the *Nation* of August 26, 1939:

> Reactionaries . . . have encouraged the fantastic falsehood . . . that the fascist state and Soviet Russia equally menace the democratic way of life. Soviet and fascist policies are diametrically opposed. The Soviet Union continues as always to be a bulwark against war and aggression, and works unceasingly for a peaceful international order.

This manifesto had four hundred prominent signers. They were the "Four Hundred" of liberalism's Social Register. Being men of integrity, many disillusioned signers should become ardent recruits for a saner movement to conserve civil liberties from the communazi method of "direct action." Among those signers for whom dictator Stalin is suddenly no longer the Sir Gallahad of "true" democracy (mighty handy word, "true"!) are Vincent Sheean, Max Lerner, Frederick Schuman, Louis Fischer, and (just before his death) Heywood Broun. In the interest of all democratic readers, I sincerely petition the *Nation* to publish another poll of these four hundred influential writers to inquire how many still uphold that cocksure manifesto.

Last year the fellow travelers were still the bosses of Student Unions and the American Youth Congress. I was dismissed as an unenlightened reactionary for my "fantastic" notion that the German and Russian state-socialisms are basically alike in economics and in ruthless methods. Similarly, the leftists were the "respectable" people in the world of letters. They were the fashionable folk who "counted"; and the fact cannot be disguised that it paid and still pays, in certain pressure groups, to be a "persecuted" Marxist.

We are witnessing strange and terrible events. It is the deluge time, the time of the breaking of nations. How few at those swanky cocktail parties for Loyalist Spain foresaw that the O.G.P.U.'s sacred Party Line might be what lost democracy to Hitler, Franco, Stalin! Today all those young disciples of revolt's fashionable Four Hundred must reexamine their premises from a fresh perspective. I write from the point of view of millions of ordinary young college graduates trying sincerely to answer two questions: What values are enduring enough to survive all these crashing panaceas? What means must we use to save these precious values?

With these two questions in mind, let me begin by asking: What do I mean by "conservative'? Conservatism must include what Thomas Mann calls humanism: the conservation of our cultural, spiritual, and individualist heritage. Common sense is notoriously the oracle of conservatism. But, at its best, common sense means no mere unimaginative shrewdness. It means the common and universal sense of mankind, the common values basic to every civilized society and creed. These human values are the traffic lights which all (even "mass movements") must obey in order that all may be free. The *New Masses* would dismiss this common-sense conservatism as bigoted and "reactionary." Very well, then, but against what am I reactionary?

Even during the height of Russia's pretensions to "peace and democracy" I have consistently reacted against the self-styled liberalism of the fellow travelers. Today I would make no exception in favor of any of communism's rival versions, so long as communists, like the brilliant Mr. Granville Hicks, merely repudiate Stalin's foreign policy and fail to repudiate Lenin's formulæ of class war and proletarian dictatorship.

Equally, I react against the self-styled Liberty Leaguers. The latter give us only the negative liberty to starve and be unemployed. They accept our American concept of democratic equality, but in the following negative sense: America's impartial Liberty League democracy forbids the Sixty Families equally with the California share-croppers to steal bread. It punishes the coupon-clipping millionaire as well as the unemployed mechanic for sleeping on a park bench or begging in the subway. It gives us the equal right and complete liberty to buy America's plentiful wheat crop—much of which is burnt because we lack the money to buy it. Let us frankly grant that Europe's dictators and revolutions remedy many of these evils. However, my conservatism includes my faith that America can and must remedy these evils *within* our constitutional framework of Law and civil liberties.

The conservative's principle of principles is the necessity and supremacy of Law and of absolute standards of conduct. I capitalize "Law," and I mean it. Suppose it were proved that the eternal absolutes do not really exist. Instinctively we should say: So much the worse for them. But now we must learn to say: So much the worse for existence! We have learned that from sad experience of centuries. Paradoxically, we have learned that man can only maintain his material existence by guiding it by the materially nonexistent: by the absolute moral laws of the spirit.

In America, we try to prove that 'It can't happen here' by citing the vast extent of our compulsory education. Truly, we are almost as well educated a people as the pre-Hitler Germans, and, like the Soviets, we are constantly increasing our educational institutes. What matters more, however, is that never was our system so inadequate as today in teaching discrimination and absolutes of conduct.

We teach a child to read and are surprised at the enormous circulation of the Yellow Press and the Father Coughlins. We are bred as little evolutionary Progressives, but we don't discriminate in what direction we breathlessly rush 'forward.' The explanation is that we are no longer given the standards for discriminating. Fertile soil for freedom and for mutual tolerance is never in human nature to start with, but must be painstakingly ploughed over for centuries. The history of mass movements affords vastly more evidence for original sin than for any natural goodness of man. Education's job is austerely to restrict, not fulfill, the child's 'glorious self-expression.'

Freedom of thought we must never restrict in America. Conduct and action we can and must restrict. Instead of "progressive education" our democratic school system must instill, from kindergarten on, the necessity of limiting all human conduct and instinct by objective Law. Only so can we learn the decent rules of the game as an unbreakable habit. By "Law" I do not mean all existing laws. All are not necessarily good. By "Law" I mean the legal way as a way to whatever goals we may seek; I mean it as a way of living. This way is necessarily freedom's prerequisite. In this sense, Law must tread pitilessly upon individuals, nations, classes. It must trample with callous and sublime indifference upon their economic interests—yes, even their economic interests—and their "healthy instincts of the race."

Soft-hearted liberals are too ready to say that a lawbreaker "means well," that his corruption is due to his social environment and bad companions; they talk too much about his honest fanaticism, his honest non-awareness of Law. Today such qualification leads to overemphasis of the more irrelevant side of the question: the personal side. Too often it is assumed that the "have-not" is automatically exempt from all eternal laws of humanity, whether it be a "have-not" nation or economic class or individual. We who are old-fashioned enough to call a crime a crime are labeled as warmongers or hypocrites or dupes of propaganda. Obviously the more relevant question is simply whether or not the legal way is being violated. In fact, those few groups strong enough to carry off a violent revolution successfully are also (almost invariably) strong enough to change the rules legally to fit their new game.

The "instinctive, unwritten sense of justice" we hear so much about is basically, and always will be, mere glorified lynch law. In instinct, every new 1940 baby is still born a caveman. Law and tradition are the slow accumulation of civilized habits, the few thousand years' habits which alone prevent the

1940 baby from remaining a caveman. Since this accumulation is haphazard, it includes—as radicals correctly accuse—much evil as well as good. But the good and the bad in tradition are often interwoven *inextricably* by the past. And the past cannot be changed—not even by radicals with a Harvard accent.

You weaken the magic of all good laws every time you break a bad one, every time you allow mob lynching of even the guiltiest criminal. I said "magic" deliberately. Social stability rests to some extent on the aura surrounding our basic institutions. Such aura-wreathed pillars of tradition in various modern nations are the United States Supreme Court, an established Church, monarchy, a nonpartisan civil service and the aristocracy trained from birth to fill it. This social cement of tradition is too essential for every well-meaning, humanitarian Tom, Dick, and Harry to tinker with. It keeps us from relapsing into the barbarism inherent in our simian nature and in all mob "awakenings."

As menacing as open anarchists are those who discredit traditional institutions, not by attack, but by excess exploitation. The man who uses our institutions and Law as a barrier to, instead of a vehicle for, democratic reform is the real anarchist. I don't care a hoot whether any country, including ours, decides to use capitalism or socialism or any other material -ism, so long as it is attained through the vehicle of the traditional framework; so long as it is orthodoxly baptized and knighted by the magic wand of tradition; so long as it does not live "without the Law." I repeat: if moral absolutes do not exist, it is not so much the worse for them, but so much the worse for existence.

During the nineteenth century, all external standards and absolutes were one by one sacrificed at the altar of dynamic "Life." A pseudo-Darwinian war of all against all, for survival of the most ferocious or most lucky, becomes exalted as a healthy expression of dynamic Life-force. I suggest coining "dynamism" as the label for this new, unchristian religion, this cult of power, instinct, blind change, blind Life. Dynamism means energy and change for their own sake. It means playing the grand man-of-action merely for action's sake, the deification of such men-of-action as *Führers.* Among dynamism's current incarnations is the unrestrained egoism of persons, nations, and classes. Gangsterism becomes a heroic romantic duty.

Society, as I would conserve it, would rest on five great self-disciplines: rule of reason in the individual, Christian ethics between individuals, Law in the state, free parliamentary negotiation among political parties, peace by negotiations among nations. Dynamism smashes all five of these great self-disciplines. Today the Nazis most radically incarnate dynamism. No wonder a current best seller refers to their "Revolution of Nihilism"!

Dynamism, I believe, will some day be recognized as the most destructive and "radical" revolution of modern times. It strikes at the root. Its modern rival, Marxism, retains at least the traditional respect for reason. The basis of the western world is the disciplining of life's energies and instincts by the supremacy of rational and ethical Law. Here our Christianity combines and conserves the legalistic heritage of the Jews and of the Græco-Roman Empire. In contrast, dynamism glories in the revolt of expansive Life-force against Law's "dead shackles." Transferred from individual to nation, such dynamism becomes lynch law: the "healthy" and natural mob instincts of what Nazis call "the *Volk*" and Reds call "the masses."

With the most passionate intensity, I resent the no-third-way sophistry of forcing American students to choose only from the alternatives of fascists and Marxists. Dynamic fascism, as it is sweeping Europe, is idealism diabolized. Economism, its opposite, whether of capitalist or Marxist brand, is materialism deified. Dynamism is immoral, economic materialism is unmoral; take your choice! Both are present to some degree in all societies. Either in excess explodes the civilization we conservatives would conserve. Our fight as young Americans is twofold: against our established cult of economism and mammon worship, and against all attempts to import fascism in its place.

In one aspect, the challenge of frank and open Bolshevik church burning is almost less dangerous to us than the more subtly masked Nazi challenge. This mask is anti-Semitism. Those ostrich conservatives miss its whole point who whistle in the dark, thinking "What concern of ours are racial persecutions so long as we're not persecuted?" Political anti-Semitism is no isolated program. It is the first step in an ever-widening revolt of mob instinct against all restraints and liberties. It is the thin opening wedge for the subversion of democracy, Christianity, and tolerance in general.

I said our civilization is based on a blend of legalism, reason, and the Christian discipline (Protestant or Catholic or the closely related Jewish). I stated this as a simple objective fact. Whether belief in them is "true" is quite another matter, which each individual must decide for himself. Their truth will always be disputable, in so far as they deal with the nonmaterial and invisible, but their necessity is indisputable.

What are the immediate political duties today of a common-sense conservative? I think a conservative should patriotically join in our country's cautious groping toward a planned economy. Despite party slogans, this groping will in practice steadily continue, whether under Republicans or New Dealers. Leftists try to discredit the conservative attitude by linking it in the public mind with laissez-faire economics. But how on earth can we conserve what's dead and what probably never existed? Purchasing power must be so distributed that every citizen is himself a free and stable property owner and an economically articulate consumer. Necessities (such as wheat) must no longer be burned or ploughed under, but sold, even without profit or below cost, to all citizens who lack them.

Accepting vigilance as the price of liberty, the conservative will be alert equally against all illegalities from all sides, whether from flag-waving Americans or "aliens" or capitalists or labor unions. He will everywhere answer illegal force with force-in-law, returning words for words and bullets for bullets, until Law is respected again. He will answer fascist attacks, from within the United States or without, with the policeman's club and not the Chamberlain umbrella.

Suppose the Communist Party calls itself the 'Paul Reveres of 1936,' and the Nazi Bund pays lip service to George Washington. No matter how democratic their phrases or how American their ancestry, our conservative will judge solely by their methods and actions. Anti-fascist lip service is not enough of a criterion. If fascism ever comes to America, it will assuredly be some homespun, native brand, riding into power on militaristic anti-fascist (i.e. anti-"alien") phrases. The same is true of any native American communist dictatorship; it would vociferously repudiate any openly labeled "communist" party. So we have only one safe criterion, no matter what are men's professed aims and programs. That criterion is whether they pursue those aims within or without the great American constitutional framework.

Our conservative will never admit that the state as a whole is greater than the sum of its separate individuals. All power he will distrust and hence limit. He will fight every extension of government authority, no matter in whose hands, whenever it seems more dangerous than the genuine wrong it would remedy. But he will insist equally on forestalling mass discontent with thoroughgoing social legislation, with the proviso that such new governmental power be as decentralized as possible.

He believes in majority rule for America, but never majority dictatorship. Instead, he believes in the absolute constitutional and human rights of minorities, whether share-croppers or millionaires, whether economic, religious, or racial. He will stubbornly insist that corrupt means betray even the worthiest ends. Karl Marx's disciples would discredit our constitutional and judicial checks merely because irresponsible finance can abuse them. That is drinking poison and then blaming the abused glass; it tackles the wrong cause of the evil. The fact that wealthy Wall Street or radical Norman Thomas or anybody else happens to benefit from free speech does not automatically make free speech vicious.

This year all "ideology" is in flux. Soon, justified by Russian events, conservatives will no longer seem disgracefully unfashionable in intellectual spheres. But let's not gloat over honest disillusionment. Instead, let us conservatives humbly admit that we have equally erred. Our error was our tardiness in realizing the economic lesson of our 1929 crash.

Current Congressional investigations go too far in smearing duped fellow travelers with the communist brush. It is bad morals and bad strategy to allow red-baiting to pass into liberal-baiting and labor-baiting. That only drives labor and the uncrushable mass of liberal voters into a revolutionary camp. Instead, we must offer them our own camp as freedom's refuge from the communism with which they flirted so disastrously. For both decency and strategy, conservatives should repudiate our liberal-baiting rabble rousers unambiguously, be they eloquent Senators or cheap sensational journalists.

To sum up: my great dream, perhaps young and naïve, is for American youth to synthesize cultural, spiritual, and political conservatism with economic reform. Such a movement must simultaneously be broad enough to include some economic ends of the radicals and narrow enough to exclude the means of the communazis. Our generation's New Conservatism must appeal not only to independent-minded conservatives but also to those disillusioned "fellow travellers." The former must accept further economic planning and honestly repudiate their pre-1929 cant. The latter must honestly repudiate despotic Russia and Marxist materialism and the stirring up of a lawless mob movement: their pre-1939 cant.

Only such concessions from both sides can make harmonious synthesis possible within our free representative system. In all democracies, men of good will from right and left must today unite to conserve their free habits of centuries. Conserve from what? From the extreme reaction of what I call the "capitalist anarchists" and from the extreme radicalism of the dynamists.

The success of literal "National Socialists," whether Hitler or Stalin, is in their vote-getting synthesis of romantic expansive nationalism with a planned economy. In contrast, we conservatives must synthesize the good in the latter, not with despotism, but with freedom—that is, with all our ancient civil liberties, tolerance of minorities, and a peaceful internationalism of Law. Our job is to prove right here in America that democracy means, not destructive wrangling, but effective cooperation in solving our spiritual and economic problems. Can this be too much to hope for from American youth? It is not yet too late.

Radicalism and the Intellectuals' Rapprochement: Interpretations

The following three selections are not writings by participants in the controversies of the 1930's, but are attempts by scholars in the 1960's to give historical perspective to the social thought of the Depression Decade.

In the first selection, an excerpt from Daniel Aaron's excellent study of Left-Wing writers between the two world wars, the popularity of literary radicalism is made clear. In the second selection, Howard Zinn delineates the limits of the pragmatic approach in the New Deal and indicates the fundamental conservatism which hemmed in the many real achievements of Roosevelt's administration. The final selection explains the significance of the early sympathetic interpretations of revolutionary dictatorships in Europe, particularly in the Soviet Union, and the later "discovery" of European totalitarianism.

Daniel Aaron
The Case of the Literary Radicals

(1961)

Discussing the militancy of American writers in the summer of 1932, Edwin Seaver compared "this new temper" with the spirit of defeat and despair in 1927. Liberals fought hard to save Sacco and Vanzetti, but "they were handicapped by a terrible sense of inertia, and found themselves unprepared and incompetent to do anything in a crisis whose significance was rapidly achieving world dimensions, even within their own limited sphere of literary

Abridged from *Writers on the Left*, © 1961, by Daniel Aaron, pp. 173–74, 354–56, 196–98, 356–58, 362–63, 390–93, 395–96. Reprinted by permission of Harcourt, Brace, Jovanovich, Inc.

activity." In the space of five years, Seaver said, the writer had changed from a passive and defeated observer of society to an active participant. If the "early twenties were a period of self-discovery and self-expression," the early thirties pointed "to a period of social discovery and social expression." No longer was it fashionable to scoff at Main Street; now, writers like Edmund Wilson were trying to understand it. Menckenian "boob-thumping" was yielding to "serious interrogation," and writers, instead of "crying for freedom," were searching for responsibility. What had happened to them to produce this change? . . .

The trouble with Dos Passos, Granville Hicks decided in 1938, was his excessive detachment or inability "to write about the revolution from the inside." That was why he remained primarily an observer, a writer who used his eyes but not his mind; and that was why he shied away from conclusions and commitments. He came close to Communism for a few years without ever daring to study Marxism closely; he "only partly subdued his passion for aloofness." Politically, as his talk with Dreiser so painfully showed, he was "capable of any kind of preposterous vagary."

If Dos Passos could not make up his mind, Hicks could and did, although he did not actually join the Communist Party until 1935. Before 1930, Hicks considered himself a nominal socialist (he voted for Al Smith in 1928, however) and he knew little about the Communist movement until 1931. The group to which he belonged, for the most part young teachers and writers scattered around New England, regarded the *Nation* and the *New Republic* as their organs, not *The New Masses.* But the Depression quickened their interest in politics and in Communism, which they discovered largely through their reading rather than through direct contact with the party. That came later.

Like his close friends Newton Arvin and Robert Gorham Davis, Hicks came from middle-class, old-stock America, the child of frugal hard-working parents who cheerfully scrimped to assure his Harvard education. After taking his degree in 1923, he spent two years at Harvard Theological School, taught for three years in the Bible and the English departments at Smith College, and returned to Harvard in 1928 to obtain a master's degree in English. From there he went to Rensselaer Polytechnic Institute as a member of the English Department and remained until he was "dropped" in 1935. During this interim, he had undergone certain experiences that produced "the phenomenon known as the alienation of the intellectuals."

In Northampton, Massachusetts, an audience of hostile townsmen packed a mass meeting held in behalf of Sacco and Vanzetti and shouted down a resolution he proposed to send to Governor Fuller. That was two years before the Depression caught him and his friends intellectually and morally unprepared, for they, also, had been enjoying their own kind of spiritual self-indulgence even though it had not taken the form of money-chasing. Observing the effects of the economic earthquake, he recalled his feelings in

Northampton "when my diplomatic little resolution—so tactfully, so politely, so meechingly worded—had been roared down." Dos Passos was right. There were "two nations," and the "other nation" could not be fooled "with careful words" and "noble sentiments." He was ready now to substitute a headier brew for the "near-beer" doled out by the Socialist Party.

Hicks later observed that in his case, as well as with others, "conversion" did not "come overnight" or through a process of "pure logic." He was influenced by John Reed and Lincoln Steffens, impressed by the articles of George Soule in the *New Republic* which analyzed a collapsing capitalism, and attracted to the amiable Communists like Gold, Freeman, and Calverton who wrote him flattering letters and asked for literary contributions. Hicks and Arvin nosed around the party in 1931 "a little furtively, a little frightened of what we were letting ourselves in for," but they still distinguished Communism from the Communist Party and approved of Edmund Wilson's recommendation to take Communism away from the Communists. They pictured party members as spending their time passing out leaflets on the water front or standing outside of subway entrances. Hicks and his friends did not intend to stop being intellectuals; for a short time they were content to operate as an independent cadre on the fringe of the party . . .

In September 1932 [Granville Hicks] and fifty-two other artists and intellectuals, some of them veterans of the two Kentucky expeditions and self-proclaimed converts to Communism and others who would soon become prominent in the Left movement, published an "open letter" to writers, artists, intellectuals, and professional men. The statement denounced the two major parties as "hopelessly corrupt," rejected the Socialists as a do-nothing party, and declared their support for the Communist Party, which also sought to defend the dispossessed classes and establish an equitable society. A month later they organized the League of Professional Writers for Foster and Ford, the Presidential candidates of the Communist Party, and expanded their original declaration into a pamphlet entitled *Culture and Crisis*.

The burden of the pamphlet contained nothing new. Here was the same story of capitalism's fatal contradictions, the lunacy of the administration, the futility of the Socialist Party's "reformist" planning, the threat of fascism, and the fighting program of the Communists, the only party capable of wringing concessions from the ruling class. Its author or authors resorted throughout to the language and imagery of decay, rottenness, breakdown. Roosevelt's election would only prop up the "machine of government" by stuffing the boiler with cotton waste and mending the broken bolts with haywire. "The United States under capitalism" was "like a house rotting away; the roof leaks, the sills and rafters are crumbling." America's plunge into imperialism portended "deep decay." Hoovervilles of tin and paper, the dwellings of the unemployed, were springing up "along the fringes of civilization," part of the wreckage "or nature, of obsolete social patterns and institutions, of human blood and nerve" left by the receding tidal wave of history.

But if the picture of cultural dissolution conjured up by the pamphlet was hardly novel in 1932, the fact that fifty-three writers and artists, many of them well known, were prepared to renounce their bourgeois allegiances, to affiliate as "brain workers" with the only other class they deemed worthy of respect—"the muscle workers"—this was indeed unprecedented in American history. Although speaking for all unemployed America, they addressed themselves specifically to a group most likely to be impressed by the paradox of potential plenty and mass privation, the waste of talent in a country that had "never yet been able to provide its population with a sufficiently large body of trained intellectuals to satisfy its cultural needs." Their Veblenian diagnosis ended with a call to vote Communist:

> Very well, we strike hands with our true comrades. We claim our own and we reject the disorder, the lunacy spawned by grabbers, advertisers, traders, speculators, salesmen, the much-adulated, immensely stupid and irresponsible "business men." We claim the right to live and function. It is our business to think and we shall not permit business men to teach us our business. It is also, in the end, our business to act.
>
> We have acted. As responsible intellectual workers we have aligned ourselves with the frankly revolutionary Communist Party, the party of the workers. In this letter, we speak to you of our own class—to the workers—telling you as best we can why we have made this decision and why we think that you too should support the Communist Party or the political campaign now under way.

The signatories of the *Culture and Crisis* pamphlet were, for the most part, independents, not Communists, and a number of them very quickly withdrew from any affiliation with the party. Probably a good many voted Communist, not because they expected or even wanted the Communists to win, but out of protest. This, at any rate, was the reason that Dos Passos subsequently gave. It certainly wasn't that I wanted the Communists to conduct the revolution in American government which I felt was needed." Yet others, as the Depression deepened, moved closer to the party, uncritically accepted its diagnosis of national and international affairs, battled its intellectual and cultural enemies, and wooed its potential friends . . .

. . . Hicks moved closer to the party.

A letter he wrote to *International Literature* in January 1933 reveals his state of mind at this time. "Literary conditions" in America, he begins, are "in something of a mess." He detects a falling off of interest in Communism since the manifesto of the League of Professional Groups. "Edmund Wilson's articles on Trotsky in the *New Republic* . . . reveal not only a rather lamentable tendency, but an extraordinary naïvete." Apparently Wilson does not realize he is taking a "definitely anti-C.P. stand." Clifton Fadiman "is also wavering," and it seems to Hicks "that Malcolm Cowley and Waldo Frank, though loyal enough to the party, have not carefully enough thought out their position.

Newton Arvin is all right but not doing much work." Finally he complains of "the dogmatism of certain party members and associates of the John Reed type, who cannot disagree with a man's ideas without denouncing him as a social fascist. This dogmatism not only repels sympathizers but also gives ammunition to their enemies among the bourgeois critics."

Despite these misgivings, Hicks became an editor of *The New Masses* in 1934 and finally a party member in 1935, the year the Seventh World Congress of the Communist International met in August of 1935 and inaugurated the Popular Front.

Since 1935 Hicks had regarded fascism as the quintessence of barbarism and decadent capitalism. The party's crusade against Socialist "social fascists," exemplified so unpleasantly by the Madison Square Garden riot, had made him "heartsick," even though he sternly disapproved of the public protestations of the Dos Passos group, some of whom, he felt, were hostile or indifferent to the party. "Public criticism, then, could only aid those whose faults seemed to me worse than the party's, and I had to content myself with private protest." The new line, he believed, brought the strategy of the party closer to American realities and lessened the intellectual and emotional strain generated by the sectarianism of the old Bolshevik fundamentalists. It made fascism the "chief enemy," and it permitted the Communists "to cooperate with the insurgent forces in the labor movement and with the progressives in the New Deal." Hicks, in the role of the Yankee Protestant American, could serve the party as a classic illustration of Browder's Popular Front maxim, "Communism is twentieth-century Americanism."

I like America (1938), the only one of his books the party made a serious effort to circulate, indicates how easily he took to the "new vocabulary" of moderation and patriotism. Read today, with a few of the pro-Russian passages excised, it seems about as revolutionary as Bellamy's *Looking Backward.* Clear, persuasive, undogmatic, it contains not a trace of sectarian jargon or logic. Businessmen are not excoriated as exploiters but shown as decent people forced by an unfeeling and obsolescent economic system to engage in practices personally offensive to them. Communism, far from crushing individualism, is the only system that guarantees "the majority of individuals" the opportunity to develop. "I am a Communist," he tells the reader, "and I want the same things you do."

> Let us work together for them. If you prove to be right, that settles the matter, for it would be quite impossible to do away with capitalism if the masses of the people were prosperous. If you're wrong—well, I don't believe you will stand by and let Fascism stamp its economy of scarcity upon us.

Here is no manifesto demanding a "dictatorship of the proletariat" for the "toiling masses," no declaration of war against a "ruthless capitalist class," no program to establish "soviets" and "Red Guards" and a Negro state in the

South. *I Like America*, instead, is a soft-spoken and amiable declaration of independence in the old reformist vein; it is grass-roots Marxism, an argument for the progressive verities: justice, equality, opportunity.

The subdued evangelical tone pervading *I Like America*, particularly in the pages where Hicks described the reasons why he became a Communist, suggests his prior religious orientation. Behind the perfectly rational reasons for preferring what seemed to be a workable economy over an unworkable one lay the serene faith in the inevitability of socialism. "There is nothing more comforting," Hicks wrote some years after, "especially for minorities, than the belief that God is on your side, and, sensitive as we were to the cruelties both of capitalism and revolution, we needed comfort." One of the participants in Hicks's first book, a fictional symposium called *Eight Ways of Looking at Christianity* (1926), spoke of Christianity as "good news." A little more than a decade later, Hicks testified from his *New Masses* pulpit:

> Communism is good news. Once understood, once believed in, it holds out hope to all but capitalism's pampered few. If one accepts the Marxist analysis of history, one believes that the establishment of a classless society is not only possible but inevitable.

To be sure, Communists did not claim Utopia would be ushered in without pain, that perfection automatically followed from revolution, but a faith in Communism, if it worked no miracles, "inspired a confidence that is capable of changing human lives."

> I have seen among intellectuals, confusion and weakness yield to clarity and strength. I have seen a baffled and desperate day laborer transformed into a militant, capable leader of labor. I have seen men and women, working together for their class, transcend the pettiness and frailty observable in the conduct of each as an individual. There is nothing miraculous about this; it results quite simply from an insight that is confirmed alike by logic and action.

If to be "confused," a word current in Left circles during the thirties, meant among other things a loss of faith in the Communist millennium, then Hicks was never confused; he knew exactly where he stood. His faith was strong enough, at any rate, to carry him over the "hurdle of the trials" and to prevent his private suspicion that they might be complete frame-ups" from undermining his belief in the righteousness of the antifascist crusade . . .

Hicks, living in the comparative isolation of Grafton, New York, and preoccupied with his own work as a publisher's reader and *New Masses* editor, did not belong to the party's inner circle. But he conscientiously and ably carried out his duties as a Communist intellectual in a bourgeois world, whether at Harvard University, where he spent the 1938–1939 term as Counsellor in American Civilization, or in the columns of the radical and liberal press, or on public lecture platforms speaking to indifferent and hostile as well as friendly audiences. His Marxist survey of American literature, *The Great Tradition*, published in 1933 and revised in 1935, received wide if not always friendly attention, and his fine biography of John Reed became the definitive book on this Communist saint. His growing literary reputation, his engaging and un-Bolshevik-like demeanor, and his earnestness and candor made him much sought after as a lecturer. The party considered him one of its most trustworthy spokesmen and particularly valuable as a plausible interpreter of the revolutionary movement to the liberal wing of the middle class. In 1939 he was speaking three or four times a week.

Yet in the spring of that year, one half of him yearned to get out of the movement. He turned down the assignment of educational director for the party, because he did not want to depend upon it for his livelihood. And despite Folsom's urging, he did not bother to attend the third writers' congress June 2–4; the party's policy of keeping its own followers in the background antagonized him (Freeman, already in disgrace, was the one exception, and the "ninth floor" regarded his inclusion as a blunder). As yet, however, he had no overt quarrel with the League or the party. It cost him no more qualms to back F.D.R., support the white-collar unions, boycott Japan, and advocate collective security. The doubts and misgivings he had suppressed only welled up after the announcement of the nonaggression and trade pacts between the Soviet Union and the German Government on August 23, 1939. Sickened by the news, Hicks hesitated for a few weeks and talked with party leaders before he decided to resign. Browder urged him to take his time but warned him that he would have to defend the pact on the party's terms. "If you do stay," he added, "you'd better be prepared for worse shocks to come."

Hicks offered a reasoned and even-tempered explanation for his departure from the Communist Party in a letter he sent to the *New Republic*. It betrayed no anguish; it was not eloquent or denunciatory. Hicks was not even prepared at this time "to condemn the pact and its consequences." History, he said, might ultimately justify the Soviet strategy, and although he could understand "those who have been made bitter by a sense of betrayal," he himself felt "no impulse to denounce the Soviet Union." Even socialist commonwealths could err. Apparently in October, Hicks still adhered to at least portions of the statement he and some 400 writers and artists signed on August 10, repudiating the aspersion that the U.S.S.R. resembled every other totalitarian state.

But the pact disclosed the incompetence and disingenuousness of the American Communist Party, whose leaders were totally unprepared for the announcement. Their apologetics, "completely devoid of clarity and logic," pointed to only one conclusion: "If the party leaders could not defend the Soviet Union intelligently, they would defend it stupidly." Had they been less ignorant, they might have prepared the American people for the new development. Their failure to do so not only destroyed "the democratic-front line" but also convinced many of its defenders, Hicks included, not to "accept a change that is dictated by the exigencies of Soviet foreign policy." Hicks still considered it imperative to aid Russia, but no longer as a party member. He had joined the party because he thought it was effective; "I am resigning," he said, "because it is no longer an organization in which I can be effective." . . .

The Communists longingly looked back to the thirties as the time when Left literature counted for something, when writers and artists willingly collaborated with the party and the working class. They predicted with more vehemence than conviction another proletarian renaissance after the conclusion of the war. Most of their former allies, however, had renounced the old dreams of revolution and by 1940 were already beginning to take stock of themselves and the revolutionary cause they had resolutely or tentatively supported. What happened to American intellectual life in the thirties, Granville Hicks wrote in 1943, "already seems mysterious, even to many who were party members."

Between "Black Thursday," 1929, and the Russian-German pact almost ten years later, the mood of the literary Left had passed from angry elation to disillusionment. Writers who once had marched in May Day parades, picketed department stores, and bled inwardly (and sometimes outwardly) for Spain now wondered why they had given themselves so impetuously to an idea. How could they have been so certain of capitalism's doom? Why had they rapturously identified themselves with the "toiling masses" and thrilled when they met real "workers"? What had led them to expect a dazzling explosion of proletarian culture? Why had Russia become for so many of them the holy land?

Some of those who disparaged their recent enthusiasm or who publicly lamented their gullibility at being "taken in" by the Communists or led astray by ideological chimeras either forgot or chose to ignore the by no means reprehensible motives which first attracted most of them to the party. They did not come into the movement because they were broke or because publishing houses were failing. They became radicals because they thought the economic system had gone kaput, because they saw too many hungry and desperate people, and because men and ideas they detested seemed in the ascendant. Marxism offered a convincing explanation why these conditions obtained as well as a program for changing the world; the party satisfied their latent religiosity and made them feel useful.

The writer who joined the Communist Party, who believed in its doctrines, or who associated in some manner with Communist-controlled organizations was not necessarily simple-minded, easily beguiled, or unworldly. Not every radical writer was neurotic or hungering for a secular religion or on the make. Obviously, many of the intellectuals who went left did so out of some deep-seated personal need; happy, "adjusted" people usually don't join political parties whose acknowledged purpose is the destruction of the old social system and the formation of a new one. But not all literary Communists or fellow travelers were maladjusted by any means, nor did they regard the support of the Left as a violent or a desperate act.

To see the Communist movement "simply as the sum total of the pathologies of its members," or to call the intellectuals' "real revulsion from real lacks in our life a flight from reality," Leslie Fiedler has rightly observed, "is utterly misleading."

The Depression *and* the Communist Party, it has been argued, gave focus to the unformulated radicalism of the 1930's and influenced, directly or indirectly, almost every American writer of any importance. And according to Lionel Trilling, the Left literary movement gave "a large and important part of the intellectual middle class . . . 'something to live for,' a point of view, an object for contempt, a direction for anger, a code of excited humanitarianism" which could not be "wholly reprobated." Influence of this kind is hard to measure, but even if the literary impress of Communism was not so extensive or so labyrinthine as some former Communists would have it, it was certainly considerable.

The Communist Party cannot take sole credit for the W.P.A. writers' projects, although Communists undoubtedly had a great deal to do with the tone and content of some of the writing published under the W.P.A. auspices. If it was not alone responsible for the vigorous Left Wing theater which stirred New York audiences in the thirties, it is hard to imagine this theater apart from such names as Clifford Odets, Alfred Hayes, Albert Maltz, George Sklar, Irwin Shaw, Paul Peters, John Howard Lawson, Harold Clurman, Herbert Biberman, Michael Blankfort, Mark Blitzstein, Sidney Howard, and others, all friends or members of the party at one time or another. By no means all of the realistic novels published during the thirties were inspired by Communism, yet its doctrines contributed to the prevailing radical spirit which lifted many writers out of their small and mean preoccupations and lent some dignity to even the most amateurish of literary productions.

But if politics and social questions agitated the literary mind in a wholesome sense and "drew the literary imagination closer to social reality," they tended under party influence to become ends in themselves and to distract the younger writers in particular from equally important aesthetic considerations. What started out as a liberating doctrine developed into a constricting one as dream hardened into dogma and the new and the idiosyncratic into ritual. Politics in itself, as Philip Rahv wrote in 1939, is neither good nor bad for the writer. "The real question is more specific: what is the artist actually doing in politics? What is he *doing with it* and what is it *doing to him*? How does his political faith affect him as a craftsman, what influence does it exercise on the moral qualities and on the sensibility of his work?"

The strongest writers of the thirties used politics and were not used by it. The party could not have dictated to a Dos Passos, a Hemingway, a Lewis, a Dreiser, a Steinbeck, a Wolfe even if it had tried to do so. But the Left writer, in and out of the party, faced something more insidious than party pressure: his own compulsion to subordinate the problems of his craft and deeply felt intellectual concerns to political policy. He willingly enrolled or inadvertently found himself in the corps of literary shock troops. He attended conventions and wrote resounding manifestoes and signed petitions and protests. He became a spokesman or a partisan in the literary wars, and he accommodated himself too easily to the Philistinism of the party . . .

During and after the war years, the thirties came to be looked upon by many men and women who had lived through them as a time of "smelly orthodoxies" when the intellectuals took refuge in closed systems of belief. The "irresponsible" twenties looked much better after ten years of intense social consciousness, and, as Granville Hicks predicted, the abandoned ivory towers began to be reclaimed. With the cold war and the crusade of Senator McCarthy, the books and issues of the thirties were considered dangerous as well as dated. The official exhumations of the Red Decade and the memoirs of former Communists (some of them as doctrinaire in their anti-Communism as they had been when they ferreted out class enemies for the party) bathed the decade in a lurid light.

In their excavations of the radical past, the historians have dug up little but fragments and ruins. Yet surely a movement which involved so many intelligent and generous men and women cannot be barren of significance. Communism, it has been said, contributed nothing of permanent value to American literature; but even if the poems, plays, novels, criticism, and reportage composed under party sponsorship or written by writers whose social sympathies had been quickened by party agitation were worthless (which is simply not true), no writer who lived through the revolutionary interlude either as advocate or critic remained unaffected. If his agonizing over the working class, his debates over the nature of art and politics, his temptations, his doubts, despairs, ecstasies, meant little to Browder or Foster (one influential trade-union leader was worth more to them than five dozen writers), they were of immense importance to the writer himself. The strong impact of Communism's program upon even those writers who opposed it must be reckoned with. So must the vitalizing influence of the Left Wing intellectuals who stirred up controversies, discovered new novelists and playwrights, opened up hitherto neglected areas of American life, and broke down the barriers that had isolated many writers from the great issues of their times.

We who precariously survive . . . can regret their inadequacies and failures, their romanticism, their capacity for self-deception, their shrillness, their self-righteousness. It is less easy to scorn their efforts, however blundering and ineffective, to change the world.

Howard Zinn

The Limits of Radical Thought in the New Deal

(1966)

The word "pragmatic" has been used, more often perhaps than any other, to describe the thinking of the New Dealers. It refers to the experimental method of the Roosevelt administration, the improvisation from one step to the next, the lack of system or long-range program or theoretical commitment. Richard Hofstadter, in fact, says that the only important contribution to political theory to come out of the Roosevelt administration was made by Thurman Arnold, particularly in his two books, *The Symbols of Government* and *The Folklore of Capitalism.* Hofstadter describes Arnold's writing as "the theoretical equivalent of F.D.R.'s opportunistic virtuousity in practical politics—a theory that attacks theories." As the chief expression of Roosevelt's "ideology," Arnold's work deserves some attention.

All through both his books, in a style of cool irony, Arnold cuts away at "preconceived faiths," "preconceived principles," "theories and symbols of government," "high-sounding prejudices," "traditional ideals," "moral ideals," "permanent cures." In the last paragraphs of *The Symbols of Government*, he writes:

> So long as the public hold preconceived faiths about the fundamental principles of government, they will persecute and denounce new ideas in that science, and orators will prevail over technicians. So long as preconceived principles are considered more important than practical results, the practical alleviation of human distress and the distribution of available comforts will be paralyzed ... The writer has faith that a new public attitude toward the ideals of law and economics is slowly appearing to create an atmosphere where the fanatical alignments between opposing political principles may disappear and a competent, practical, opportunistic governing class may rise to power ...

Because the Roosevelt administration did, in fact, experiment and improvise without a total plan, F.D.R.'s "pragmatism" has come, for many, to be the most important statement about the thinking of the New Dealers. This emphasis on the method rather than on the substance of that thinking tends to obscure what may be its greatest significance.

Most statesmen experiment: Tsar Nicholas instituted a Duma, Lenin encouraged private enterprise for several years, Bismarck sponsored social

---

welfare measures, Mao Tse-tung introduced back-yard steel furnaces, and George Washington supported a national bank. These examples show that experimentation can be linked to a variety of social ideals. Some statesmen engage in more experiments than others, and in a time of crisis one who is willing to undertake a vast number of them deserves commendation, as Roosevelt does. The truly important question that can be asked about the thinking of any government is: in what direction, and how far, is it willing to experiment? What goals, what ideals, what expectations direct that experimentation?

Thurman Arnold himself contributed to this misplaced emphasis on method rather than substance. He was so anxious to demolish old myths that stood in the way of the welfare measures of the New Deal that mythology itself became his chief concern. He was so intent on sweeping away old debris, that he became obsessed, ironically, with a folklore of his own, in which the idea of debris-clearing crowded out the concept of what he wanted to plant in the cleared area.

Examining Arnold's *The Symbols of Government*, one sees that what started him on a crusade against myths was that he sought to expose the symbolism that stood in the way of bringing cheap electric power to people and of instituting relief, public works, social security. His strongest expression on social justice was his statement that: "Those who rule our great industrial feudalism still believe inalterably the old axioms that man works efficiently only for personal profit; that humanitarian ideals are unworkable as the principal aim of government or business organization; that control of national resources, elimination of waste, and a planned distribution of goods would destroy both freedom and efficiency."

As was true of his associate, Thurman Arnold, F.D.R.'s experimentalism and iconoclasm were not devoid of standards and ideals. They had a certain direction, which was toward governmental intervention in the economy to prevent depression, to help the poor, and to curb ruthless practices in big business. Roosevelt's speeches had the flavor of a moral crusade. Accepting the nomination at the Democratic Convention of 1932, he said that "the Federal Government has always had and still has a continuing responsibility for the broader public welfare," and pledged "a new deal for the American people." In a campaign speech that year at the Commonwealth Club in San Francisco, he said: "Our government . . . owes to every one an avenue to possess himself of a portion of that plenty sufficient for his needs, through his own work." In his 1936 speech accepting the nomination, he spoke of the power of the "economic royalists" and said: "Our allegiance to American institutions requires the overthrow of this kind of power."

But F.D.R.'s ideas did not have enough clarity to avoid stumbling from one approach to another: from constant promises to balance the budget, to large-scale spending in emergencies; from an attempt to reconcile big business interests and labor interests (as in the National Recovery Act), to belated support for a pro-labor National Labor Relations Act; from special concern for the tenant farmer (in the Resettlement Administration), to a stress on generous price supports for the large commercial farmer (in the Agricultural Adjustment Act of 1938).

His ideas on political leadership showed the same indecision, the same constriction of boundaries, as did his ideas about economic reform. Roosevelt was cautious about supporting the kind of candidates in 1934 (Socialist Upton Sinclair in California, Progressive Gifford Pinchot in Pennsylvania) who represented bold approaches to economic and social change; and when he did decide to take vigorous action against conservative Congressional candidates in 1938, he did so too late and too timorously. He often attempted to lead Congress in a forceful way to support his economic program; yet his leadership was confined to working with the existing Congressional leadership, including many Southern conservatives who ruled important committees. Roosevelt's political daring did not extend to building new political forces among the poor, the unemployed, the tenant farmers, and other disadvantaged groups, with whose support he might have given the country a bolder economic program.

The circle of men around Roosevelt, the cabinet members and administrators, was an odd mixture of liberals and conservatives who often worked at cross-purposes. Rexford Guy Tugwell, a bold advocate of national planning to help the lower-income groups, was close to Roosevelt for several years; but so was Raymond Moley, who believed in a kind of planning more beneficial to business interests. Even the liberal New Dealers, with rare exceptions, hesitated to carry their general concern for the underprivileged too far. Frances Perkins, the Secretary of Labor, had the humanitarian instincts of a first-rate social worker, but she seemed often to be trailing behind the labor movement, rather than helping to give it direction. (The most advanced piece of New Deal labor legislation was the Wagner Act, but Secretary Perkins wrote later: "I myself, had very little sympathy with the bill.") Progressive Secretary of the Interior Harold Ickes was offset by conservative Secretary of Commerce Daniel Roper. And although Roper was succeeded in 1939 by Harry Hopkins, there remained in the cabinet a powerful force for fiscal conservatism and budget-balancing—Secretary of the Treasury Henry Morgenthau.

The experimentalism of the New Deal, in short, had its limits: up to these limits, Roosevelt's social concern was genuinely warm, his political courage huge, his humanitarian spirit unfailing; beyond them, his driving force weakened. Thus, by 1938, with the nation out of the worst of the depression, with a skeletal structure of social reform in the statute books, and with that year's Congressional elections showing a sudden waning of political approbation, the Roosevelt program began to bog down. As it slid to its close, it left behind a mountain of accomplishment, and ahead, mountains still unclimbed. Many millions—businessmen, professionals, unionized workingmen, commercial farmers—had been given substantial help. Many millions more—sharecroppers, slum-dwellers, Negroes of North and South, the unemployed—still awaited a genuine "new deal."

Why did the New Deal sputter out around 1938–1939? One important factor seems to be that the urgency of 1933–1935 was gone. By 1939, although there were still nine million unemployed, the sense of panic was over. After all, unemployment was normal in America. Harry Hopkins had said in 1937 that even in prosperity it was "reasonable to expect a probable minimum of 4,000,000 to 5,000,000 unemployed." The American nation had developed over the years a set of expectations as to what constituted "normal" times; and by 1938 it was approaching these.

Hopkins' statement and the administration's inaction indicate that the ideals of the New Dealers did not extend very far beyond the traditional structure of the American economy. They had wanted to get out of the terrible economic despair of 1932 and 1933 and to establish certain moderate reforms. These aims had been accomplished. True, some of the New Dealers, including F.D.R. himself, did speak of what still remained to be done. But once the nation was restored to close to the old balance—even if income was still distributed with gross inequality, even if rural and urban slums crisscrossed the land, even if most workingmen were still unorganized and underpaid, and a third of the nation still, in F.D.R.'s words, "ill-nourished, ill-clad, ill-housed"—the driving force of the New Deal was gone.

Why were the expectations and ideals of the New Deal (its folklore, its symbols, according to Thurman Arnold) so limited? Why did the New Dealers not declare that the government would continue spending, experimenting, and expanding governmental enterprises—until no one was unemployed, and all slums were gone from the cities, until no family received below-subsistence incomes and adequate medical care was available to everyone, until anyone who wanted a college education could get one? True, there were political obstacles to realizing such objectives, but to state them as *goals* would itself have constituted the first step toward overcoming those obstacles. For this might have enabled F.D.R. to do what political scientist James MacGregor Burns asserts was not done: to build "a solid, organized mass base" among labor and other underprivileged groups.

Humanitarianism pure and simple can go only so far, and self-interest must carry it further. Beyond the solicitude felt by the new Dealers for the distressed, beyond the occasionally bold rhetoric, there was not enough motive power to create a radically new economic equilibrium; this would have to be supplied by the groups concerned themselves; by the tenant farmers, the aged, the unemployed, the lowest-paid workers in the economy. Those who *did* organize—the larger farm operators, the several million industrial workers who joined the C.I.O.—improved their position significantly. But as Paul Douglas, then an economics professor at the University of Chicago and later a United States Senator, wrote in 1933:

> Along with the Rooseveltian program must go . . . the organization of those who are at present weak and who need to acquire that which the world respects, namely, power . . . Unless these things are done, we are likely to find the permanent benefits of Rooseveltian liberalism to be as illusory as were those of the Wilsonian era.

Many organized movements sprang up in the 1930's, spurred by need and encouraged by the new atmosphere of innovation. The Townsend Movement sought $200 a month pensions for the aged. Father Charles Coughlin's panacea of "Social Justice" was heard by millions of radio listeners. Huey Long, the Louisiana Senator, excited many others with his "Share the Wealth" plan. The National Negro Congress, the Farmers Union, and the American Youth Congress all represented special needs and all hurled their energies into the boiling political pot in Washington.

But there was no political program around which these disparate groups could effectively unite. And many of them began to lose their thrust when their demands were partially met. Even the Congress of Industrial Organizations, the largest and most successful of those mass movements born in the depression, and stimulated by New Deal legislation, came eventually to represent a special interest of its own.

The Madisonian argument that political stability would be assured in a federal republic of many states, because an uprising in one would die for lack of support, applied also in the economic sphere, where no single economic interest, fierce as it might be in its own domain, ever developed a concern wide enough to embrace society at large. Perhaps one reason is that in the United States every little rebellion, every crisis, has been met with enough concessions to keep general resentment below the combustible level, while isolated aggrieved groups fought their way up to the point of complacency.

But if—as Paul Douglas forecasts—the underprivileged are the only ones who can supply the driving force for a sharp change in their condition, then it is probably the intellectuals of society who will furnish the theories, state the ideals, define the expectations. And so it is from those thinkers who clustered, half-friendly, half-reproachful, around the New Deal, their ideological reach less restrained, perhaps, by the holding of power, that our generation may find suggestions.

Part of Roosevelt's "pragmatism" was his rejection of doctrinaire ideas of the left. Marxism was in the air all around him. Many intellectuals were enthusiastic about the Five Year Plans of Soviet Russia. British Marxists were influential: Harold J. Laski lectured and wrote extensively in the United States; John Strachey popularized the concepts of socialism in *The Nature of Capitalist Crisis* (1935) and other works. Some in depression-ridden America were attracted to Marxism's claims that society could be analyzed "scientifically": that economic crisis was inevitable where production was complex and gigantic, yet unplanned; that exploitation of working people was built in a system where private profit was the chief motive; that the state was not neutral but an instrument of those who held economic power; that only the working class could be depended on to take over society and move it towards a classless, strifeless commonwealth. A true pragmatist might at least have explored some of the suggestions of Marxist thought. Roosevelt's thinking, however, remained in a kind of airtight chamber that allowed him to regulate what currents he would permit inside—and Marxism was not one of them.

Nevertheless, to steer clear of the theories of the Marxists, as of the Hooverian folklore of "free enterprise," "thrift," and "laissez-faire," left a vast middle ground of which Roosevelt explored only one sector. Edmund Wilson, for instance, a social critic and essayist, also rejected Marxian dialectics; yet he tried to extract from it some truths. He wrote with apparent warmth of the idea that (as he put it, in an imaginary restatement of a more acceptable Marxism): ". . . if society is to survive at all, it must be reorganized on new principles of equality." Others, not Marxists, but more demanding in their notion of reform than was the New Deal, reconnoitered beyond its ideological fences.

Reinhold Niebuhr, a theologian and social philosopher who carried the Social Gospel to new borders in the 1930's, urged that "private ownership of the productive processes" be abandoned, yet he hoped that through an alliance among farmers, industrial workers, and the lower income classes, the transition to a new order could be accomplished without violence. Stuart Chase, an economist who wrote a series of widely selling books in the 1930's, suggested that old alternatives had been swept aside by the onrush of technology, that the choice was no longer between capitalism and socialism; there was a need, he said, for some uncategorizable collectivist society whose "general objective will be the distribution of the surplus, rather than a wrangling over the ownership of a productive plant which has lost its scarcity position."

William Ernest Hocking, a Harvard philosopher, asked for "collectivism of a sort," but neither the collectivism of a "headless Liberalism" or of a "heady" Communism or Fascism. He wrote: "What the State has to do with production is to drive into economic practice the truth that there is little or no capital whose use is not 'affected by a public interest.'" Hocking said: "Economic processes constitute a single and healthy organism only when the totality of persons in a community who have a right to consume *determine what is produced* . . ." Hocking was setting goals quite beyond the Rooseveltian ones.

Upton Sinclair, a muckraker since the early part of the century, preached a non-Marxist, home-grown socialism that attracted enough adherents to bring him very close to winning the gubernatorial election in California in 1934. Sinclair prophesied that "in a cooperative society every man, woman, and child would have the equivalent of $5000 a year income from labor of the able-bodied young men for three or four hours per day." This prophesy was certainly utopian in 1933, but such vision, even if it were going to be bent and modified in practice, might carry a program of social reform much further—and perhaps win more powerful blocs of electoral support—than did the more moderate goals of the New Deal.

A program may be pragmatic in its willingness to explore various means, yet be certain of its goals; it may be limited in how far it is willing to go, and yet be clear about the direction of its thrust. There is a difference between experimentation and vacillation. Robert MacIver, a distinguished social scientist, was impressed in 1934 by the variety of new institutions created under Roosevelt, but wondered if they meant "the inauguration of a period of social and cultural reformation." He asked: "The new institutions are here, but the essential point is—Who shall control them?" There was uncertainty about the New Deal, particularly in its first two years, when the National Recovery Act set out to create large planning organizations for industry in which big business seemed to be making the important decisions. It led some liberals and radicals to see in it possible Fascist aims, led some important businessmen to support it, and kept political loyalties crisscrossed in a happy chaos.

After 1935 (although ambiguity remained in specific areas like trust-busting), the over-all direction of the New Deal became clear: it was sympathetic to the underprivileged, and to organized labor, and it was pervaded by a general spirit of liberal, humanitarian reform. But also the scope of the New Deal became clear. This limitation is shown in a number of issues that the New Deal faced, or sometimes tried to avoid facing, between 1933 and 1939: the problem of planning; the question of how to deal with monopolistic business; the controversy over deficit financing and the extension of public enterprise; the creation of an adequate system of social security.

Robert Allen Skotheim
The Idea of Totalitarianism

(1968)

The 1960's have brought publication of several excellent studies of American reactions to European dictatorships between the two world wars. Valuable merely as surveys of attitudes on an important subject, these studies are even

From Robert Allen Skotheim, Essay Review, *American Quarterly*, XX, no. 1, pp. 119–29 (1968). Reprinted, without footnotes, with permission of the publisher. Copyright, 1968, Trustees of the University of Pennsylvania. Books referred to in this essay are Peter G. Filene, *Americans and the Soviet Experiment, 1917–1933*, (Cambridge, Mass., 1967) and Frank Warren III, *Liberals and Communism*, (Bloomington, 1966). Still in the process of completion is a survey of American reactions to Mussolini's Italy, by John Diggins. Among his published articles is "Flirtation with Fascism: American Pragmatic

better because of the sophisticated way in which they relate the nature of the views to the wishes and needs of those who did the viewing. Most significant in this scholarship is the fact that it reveals certain common patterns of American thought relevant to our understanding of the chronology of climate of opinion in the twentieth century. Specifically, these various independent researches into American opinions on European dictatorships between the wars jointly reveal evidence showing the continuation of aspects of the pre-World War I progressive-pragmatic intellectual climate into the postwar years. Further, and moving ahead chronologically, they suggest the nature of confrontation during the later 1930's between the older progressive-pragmatic temper and the newer climate of social thought which was already widespread by 1940 and which became dominant after World War II.

The characteristic feature of the dominant intellectual temper in the United States during the years prior to the Great War was a blend of pragmatic analysis and progressive idealism, and a version of the same blend has been found in postwar attitudes toward European dictators. Students of the prewar progressive mind have made it increasingly clear that the appeal of the pragmatic method, with its demand that explicit value judgments be postponed until the practical consequences of a policy or an idea were projected or ascertained, was related to the assumption that progressive change was possible if not probable. That is to say, one was willing to suspend immediate judgment (which might otherwise have been unfavorable) precisely because one tended to equate proposed alternatives with change and with betterment. If, by contrast, one had feared alternatives, and change, and had doubted that betterment was possible, the replacement of immediate (unfavorable) judgment by a pragmatic discussion of projected consequences would have seemed academic at best and irresponsibly relativistic at worst.

The work of Aaron, Diggins, Feuer, Filene, Lasch, and Warren reveals that Americans when sympathetic to European dictatorships usually invoked a pragmatic rationale as a defense for letting the dictatorship work itself out; that the pragmatic defense did not itself determine one's sympathy, but rather was invoked because of one's sympathy for change, or the avowed goals of the dictatorship; finally, that Americans when unsympathetic to dictatorships did not invoke a pragmatic analysis but instead made explicit moral judgments against them. In other words, the pragmatic method, which meant that one could not know the meaning of a policy until one knew how it

Liberals and Mussolini's Italy," *American Historical Review*, LXXI (Jan. 1966), pp. 487–506. His unpublished doctoral dissertation is "Mussolini's Italy: The View from America, 1922–1941" (University of Southern California, 1964). Studies published in the earlier 1960's are Daniel Aaron, *Writers on the Left* (New York, 1961); Lewis Feuer, "Travelers to the Soviet Union, 1917–1932: The Formation of a Component of New Deal Ideology," *American Quarterly*, XIV (Summer 1962), pp. 119–49; Christopher Lasch, *The American Liberals and the Russian Revolution* (New York, 1962).

worked out in practice, was a weapon only of friends of revolutionary dictatorship, not of opponents; just as before the war, the pragmatic analysis was generally used by friends of change, not by opponents to change. (To note that there was nothing in the pragmatic method itself to prevent its use by opponents of change as well as by friends would be to make a point of logic rather than of intellectual history.)

A few illustrations from some of this scholarship must suffice. Christopher Lasch, in his study of liberal thought during the Russian revolutionary era, concludes that "the central fact" of the 1917–1920 period was the refusal of American liberals "to give up the optimism on which liberalism rested"; although there was disillusionment following the war, there was "no real questioning of basic assumptions, no real loss of illusions." Lasch traces the optimism of liberals to their continued belief in progress, and he describes those liberals who were sympathetic to the Bolshevik revolution as pragmatically allowing the revolution to continue, withholding (unfavorable) judgment which they asserted would be irrevelent to the Russian environment. Political democracy, they claimed, was not significant relative to Russian history, as it was by contrast to American history. At the same time, according to Lasch, these liberals "expected democracy eventually to take root in Russia—but in strange new forms." Here, in the case of the liberals who were sympathetic to the Bolsheviks, was the blend of pragmatic rationale and progressive hope. For liberals who were unsympathetic to the revolution, it was enough simply to pass an unfavorable moral judgment. There was no need to express an explicit pragmatic rationale.

Lewis Feuer, in his survey of writings of travelers to the Soviet Union after 1917, declares that by 1932 part of the meaning of "pragmatism" was to view Russia sympathetically: "To be a pragmatist henceforth was, according to the leaders in pragmatic thought, to regard the Soviet Union as a model of the experimental method in social practice." But though Feuer's travelers praised Communist experimentation, it was also socialist goals which excited them. Feuer quotes Oswald Garrison Villard who, commenting in 1929 on the charge that Soviet dictatorship was like Mussolini's dictatorship, stated that there was "this difference: the Bolsheviks are working for the good of the masses of the working people." Feuer concludes that "American liberalism at this time did not believe in Acton's metaphysical law that evil means necessarily corrupt the end." In 1929, an American, whether liberal or radical, who defended the Soviet Union typically did so on pragmatic grounds of allowing experimentation, but always with the assumption that ultimately the specific ends were desirable and justified the means. The defense was both progressive and pragmatic.

A more comprehensive study of attitudes toward the Soviets than Feuer's survey of travelers is Peter Filene's canvas of business and labor opinion, as well as that of intellectuals, from revolution to diplomatic recognition. Even with a wider net the same pattern emerges. It is well known that Lincoln

Steffens consciously adopted a pose of watchful and admiring waiting, for he was "intrigued by the idea of change for the sake of change," and he was dedicated to "the pragmatic rule-of-the-result." But Filene's evidence reveals that Steffens was unusual only in the extent to which he expressed his pragmatic relativism. Many liberals as well as radicals made essentially the same argument. Paxton Hibben in 1925 "frankly declared that judging the U.S.S.R. by the standards of Western democracy was equivalent to criticizing a giraffe for not living in water." Roger Baldwin, director of the American Civil Liberties Union, wrote in 1927:

> The fairest test by which to judge the Soviet experiment in relation to "liberty" is not by Western standards of political or civil liberties, but by the effects of the dictatorship's controls and repression on its own avowed object of creating a "free and classless society," with the state abolished.

The progressive-pragmatic argument was absent in critics of the Communists, according to Filene's evidence. Intellectuals, labor union leaders and businessmen who found fault with the Soviets simply declared them to be immoral, although unsympathetic businessmen added the argument that Communism could not work. Interestingly, on those occasions when businessmen expressed temporary sympathy for the Soviets (stimulated by what they regarded as Lenin's surrender to capitalism in the New Economic Policy in 1920's), they fell into a relativistic and progressive line. Russia did after all have a different history from the West, said businessmen, and perhaps it needed time, American investment and technology in order to progress along American lines.

Frank Warren's study of liberals during the depression decade agrees with Lasch that most liberals did not learn the lesson which they should have during the Great War, namely, "that repression, even when it is couched in democratic and humanitarian terms, remains oppression." And Warren agrees with Feuer that the 1920's seem to have given many liberals an appreciation of the "instrumental method without buttressing democratic ends." Warren cites the 1935 statement of Walter Duranty concerning Soviet collectivization and socialization:

> Their cost in blood and tears and other terms of human suffering has been prodigious, but I am not prepared to say that it is unjustified. In a world where there is so much waste and muddle it may perhaps be true that any plan, however rigid, is better than no plan at all and that any altruistic end, however remote, may justify any means however cruel.

After giving many parallel examples of the progressive-pragmatic mentality at work in defense of the Soviet Union during the 1930's, Warren concludes that precisely because many liberals "believe Russia to be an experiment removed them from the need to evaluate it." But, Warren adds, since science itself was progressive, and economic development was too, it is not hard to see that "ultimate values were buried beneath the lava of progress." Again, the intellectual style of defense for the dictatorship can be characterized as progressive and pragmatic, an intellectual style not found in the "anti-communist" liberal critics of the Soviets discussed by Warren.

It is with some surprise that one finds the same pattern of argument in American reactions to Mussolini's Italy as to Communist Russia. John Diggins shows that sympathy for Mussolini came during the 1920's not only from such "conservatives" as Irving Babbit, George Santayana, Kenneth Roberts and Stark Young, but from Charles Beard, Horace Kallen, Herbert Schneider, Ida Tarbell, Herbert Croly and of course Lincoln Steffens. In discussing the response to Mussolini of those he calls "pragmatic Liberals," Diggins emphasizes the relativism which allowed some of them to view sympathetically dictatorial change without cutting the sympathy off with an unfavorable value judgment. Horace Kallen argued in 1927, in the *New Republic*, that the Fascists deserved the same suspension of judgment as the Soviets: "Each should have the freest opportunity once it has made a start, of demonstrating whether it be an exploitation of men by a special interest or a fruitful endeavor after the good life." A *New Republic* editorial entitled "An Apology for Fascism" was printed in the same issue and supported Kallen's plea for tolerance, invoking the familiar defense of experimentation. No more in the case of Italy than in that of the Soviet Union, however, was the pragmatic rationale unconnected to specific hopes for the future. Diggins concludes that what ultimately attracted American liberals was Mussolini's theoretical corporatism, which they optimistically viewed as scientific state planning. Diggins also characterizes intellectual critics of Mussolini's Italy in a way which parallels critics of Communist Russia. The argument of opponents was less experimental, less explicitly pragmatic and relativist and, in Diggins' words, it rang "with moral certitudes."

It is obvious from this review of some of the recent scholarship surveying American attitudes toward European dictatorships, that significant elements of the early twentieth-century climate of opinion continued into the 1920's and 1930's. Those Americans who were sympathetic to the dictators invoked the same progressive-pragmatic rationale which was frequently used to support domestic reform in the United States prior to (and after) World War I. The rationale was the same, but the dictatorships were new. The progressive-pragmatic mentality tried to understand and to "use" the dictatorships just as it attempted to work within the changing realities of American society. The progressive-pragmatic temper seems to have been more capable of assimilating new phenomena than in making judgments as to their value. From the pragmatic method came the willingness to absorb the unfamiliar; from the faith in progress came the willingness to think that the unfamiliar would become good. The evidence is abundant that the

Great War did not dispel, however much it threatened and reduced, this pattern of thought. The demise of the progressive-pragmatic outlook was postponed as long as events in the world could be absorbed without the destruction of hope, but the demise occurred when a pragmatic analysis and a relativistic suspension of judgment no longer were supported by faith in progress. The 1930's brought the beginning of the end, and laid intellectual foundations for what became the dominant postwar temper through at least the 1950's. The opinion gradually developed among Americans during the 1930's that the European dictatorships constituted evidence that the world could not be understood or coped with on the basis of the progressive-pragmatic outlook. Increasingly, as the decade advanced, the view was expressed that all the dictatorships, irrespective of the distinguishing features of each, shared in common evil characteristics which had to be resisted. What was increasingly attacked as evil was the total absorption of the individual into the state.

The story of the idea of totalitarianism in the United States is long and complex. During the 1920's there were many Americans who condemned dictatorships as immoral. They disagreed with a pragmatic defense of dictatorships but they did not usually develop a full counter-argument, probably because they viewed Stalin and Mussolini in the 1920's as merely the latest versions in the world's long history of autocrats. During the early 1930's, it became more common to make comparisons which stressed the similarities among Communist, Fascist and then Nazi forms of government. Such comparisons were destructive to claims of superiority on the part of any particular dictatorship, since the distinctive goals avowed by any one were canceled out by the means which all employed. The more these comparisons were made, the more controversial became the progressive-pragmatic plea of tolerance for the Soviet Union (which by the 1930's was the only dictatorship still commonly receiving the old defense).

As comparisons which likened the dictatorships to one another weakened the claims of any particular one, so did the increasingly made allegation that the dictatorships swallowed up the lives of individuals in an unprecedented and total manner. In 1934, as if a word sprung into the language to express a new mood, "totalitarian" started to be used more frequently to refer to the peculiar denial of individualism and aggrandizement of the state under the contemporary dictatorships. The timing of the word's appearance in the United States suggests the impetus which Hitler gave to the idea of totalitarianism, for it was most often applied to Nazi Germany and Fascist Italy in 1934 and 1935. Mussolini's Italy consciously and explicitly gave birth to the idea of totalitarianism, but it was Hitler's Germany which most effectively dramatized the idea in action for most Americans. Leland Stowe, an American correspondent in Germany, devoted a chapter of his book on the Nazis in 1934 to "The Totalitarian State," which he summed up by quoting a former friend who had become a Nazi:

> There are to be no more private Germans. Each is to attain significance only by his service to the State and to find complete self-fulfillment in this service. Thus, to express it in more emphatic terms, there are to be no more mere human beings in Germany, but only Germans.

Part of the meaning of this Nazi totalitarianism was immediately translated for Americans by the liberal press, which gave early coverage to the terror in Germany.

The significance of the common early definition of totalitarianism in terms of Germany and Italy, rather than Russia, in terms of Fascism and not Communism, is that it allowed those who sympathized with the Soviet Union to perpetuate the progressive-pragmatic defense. Thus, defining totalitarianism as Fascism, Norman Thomas was able to write in 1934:

> The concept of the totalitarian state is infinitely more dangerous to the future than the acceptance of a temporary dictatorship for a transitional period. There are in the latter corrective elements, a conscious desire for a new social order freed from the exploitation of a profit-making class, and an economic program which are totally lacking in Fascism. The tendency of life in Russia is up, and not down, which is more than can be said for Germany.

Here the idea of totalitarianism was invoked in such a way as to leave the progressive-pragmatic outlook intact. But though this was most common in 1934, the issue was joined immediately by some who argued that all the dictatorships were totalitarian. Emil Lengyel wrote in the same year:

> Stalin's Russia, Mussolini's Italy, and Hitler's Germany are "totalitarian" States, which means they have claims on men not only as political, but also as economic beings. Man's entire life is submerged in the "total" State, and his independent personality is replaced by a community consciousness ... Every will must be subordinated to that of the totalitarian State.

Those who agreed with Lengyel's definition of totalitarianism could declare that "the barbarity of Fascism and Nazism is being condemned and fought by the persons who have remained perfectly indifferent to the Golgotha of the Russian politicals." The nature of the debate was clear by 1934. Much of the history of American social thought during the rest of the decade involves the development of this debate.

If totalitarianism were defined synonymously only with Nazism and Fascism, it would not necessarily undermine the progressive-pragmatic view since hope could still be placed in Russia. But if the Soviet Union were totalitarian too, as Lengyel's definition had it, the implications were far-reaching. Instead of the familiar world conflict between progressive experimentation and the status quo, the true fight for a moral man had to be against Left as well as Right, on the assumption that both were totalitarian. The old dichotomy was dissolved. And if the true fight were to be against totalitarianism, a premium would be placed upon one's moral judgment of humane means rather than upon one's visions of ultimate ends. Protection of individual rights would take priority over redistribution of wealth. The reformer's sensibility would give way to the civil libertarian's sensibility. This was the logic, or at least the psychology, of the idea of totalitarianism, as Lengyel defined it. It was in fact a logic acted out by many, if not most, American intellectuals during the 1930's. The result was that by the end of 1939, after the Soviet purge trials and the Russo-German Pact, most Americans came to accept the Soviet Union, as well as Germany and Italy, as totalitarian. Until the United States entered the war in 1941 with Russia as an ally, and then again after the war's end in 1945, Lengyel's definition of totalitarianism was a commonplace.

The significance of the idea of totalitarianism, as it came to be defined by 1940, and again after the war, stemmed from its integral part in the new climate of opinion which was forming during the late 1930's and which emerged dominant after World War II. The American perception that totalitarianism was spreading throughout the world, and the new emphasis in American accounts of the 1940's upon the seeming willingness of people to "escape their freedom" into totalitarianism, provoked an embracement of traditional America as a free society by formerly dissident intellectuals. A corresponding American fear of revolution anywhere in the world became by the 1950's as revealing an index to the "conservative" postwar intellectual temper as the earlier pragmatic defense of revolutionary dictatorships had been to the progressive mentality. Consequently, it can be predicted that, as the dominant "conservative" postwar climate is increasingly attacked in the 1970's, the idea of totalitarianism will be increasingly reinterpreted, criticized or minimized.

Selected Additional Reading

Aaron, Daniel. *Writers on the Left*. (New York: Harcourt Brace, 1961.)

Aaron, Daniel, and Robert Bendiner, eds. *The Strenuous Decade*. (New York: Doubleday, 1970.)

Bell, Daniel, *Marxian Socialism in the United States*. (Princeton: Princeton, 1967.) (Originally published in Donald Drew Egbert, Stow Persons, eds., *Socialism and American Life*, 2 vols., [Princeton: Princeton, 1952].)

Chamberlin, William Henry. *The Confessions of an Individualist*. (New York: Macmillan, 1940.)

Chamberlin, William Henry. *The Evolution of a Conservative*. Chicago: Regnery, 1959.)
Filene, Peter. *Americans and the Soviet Experiment, 1917–1933*. (Cambridge, Mass.: Harvard, 1967.)
Goldman, Eric. *Rendezvous with Destiny*. (New York: Knopf, 1952.)
Hicks, Granville. *Part of the Truth*. (New York: Harcourt, 1965.)
Hofstadter, Richard. *The Age of Reform*. (New York: Knopf, 1957.)
Howe, Irving, and Lewis Coser. *The American Communist Party*. (New York: Praeger, 1957.)
Kempton, Murray. *Part of Our Time*. (New York: Simon and Schuster, 1955.)
Lasch, Christopher. *The New Radicalism in America*. (New York: Knopf, 1965.)
Leuchtenburg, William. *Franklin D. Roosevelt and the New Deal*. (New York: Harper and Row, 1963.)
Lyons, Eugene. *The Red Decade: The Stalinist Penetration of America*. (Indianapolis: Bobbs-Merrill, 1941.)
Salzman, Jack, and Barry Wallenstein, eds. *Years of Protest*. (New York: Pegasus, 1967.)
Schlesinger, Arthur M., Jr. *The Age of Roosevelt*, 3 vols. (Boston: Houghton Mifflin, 1957–1960.)
Susman, Warren I. "The Thirties," in *The Development of an American Culture*, Stanley Coben and Lorman Ratner, eds. (Englewood Cliffs, N.J.: Prentice-Hall, 1970.)
Swados, Harvey, ed. *The American Writer and the Great Depression*. (Indianapolis, Bobbs-Merrill, 1966.)
Viereck, Peter. *Conservatism Revisited and the New Conservatism*. (New York: Free Press, 1965.)
Viereck, Peter. *Shame and Glory of the Intellectuals*. (New York: G. Putnam Sons, 1965.)
Warren, Frank. *Liberals and Communism*. (Bloomington: Indiana, 1966.)

Section Five
The Search for Consensus, 1940–1960

DAVID W. MARCELL

Contents

Introduction

If the outbreak of the second European war in a generation in September, 1939, did not make obsolete the intellectual concerns of the 1930's, it nonetheless altered drastically the social and historical context in which the ideologies of the West competed. For the next two decades war and the threat of war became primary factors conditioning American social thought. Though sometimes indirect and subtle, the influence of possible holocaust, nuclear or otherwise, can be detected in most of the major intellectual debates and documents of the 1940's and 1950's. "Fortress America" no longer existed after Pearl Harbor, and the necessity of global involvement and defense produced new pressures on Americans. The question of national security became compelling in new ways, and, correspondingly, personal security also became a more complex matter. Moreover, by the end of the 1950's it had become apparent that the institutions and concentrations of power required for American national security themselves produced new and deep problems for democracy.

Although World War II created many new problems, it did solve—or defer—some old ones. The Depression, with its pervasive social, economic, and intellectual dimensions, melted away in the face of wartime imperatives. The Soviet Union, a source of tension and disconcertion for America even before its collectivist experiment, became a temporary ally in the crusade against the Fascism of the Axis. Thus, several of the issues which had helped define social thought in the 1930's were transformed by the exigencies of the war effort, and by the need for Americans to find a common intellectual basis for their opposition to Nazi and Japanese totalitarianism. This need threw many American intellectuals back upon the bulwark of traditional democratic ideals and values.

The alliance with the Soviet Union, however, was a temporary one, born of necessity, and as an Allied victory appeared imminent in 1945 it became clear that in the post-war world the confrontation between the United States and the Soviet Union would be definitive and of long duration. The Cold War perpetuated the wartime conditions of the early forties, and by the latter part of that decade the intellectual consequences of the prolonged military and diplomatic crisis were becoming evident.

Liberals who in the 1930's had regarded the Communist Party as merely the extreme, necessary cutting edge of liberalism, and who had thus lent the Party sympathy, support, and—in some cases—had even become members, now found that their association made them liable to charges of treason and disloyalty. The chickens of the Popular Front illusion were coming home to roost. Nor was the conservative reaction against the default of some of the liberals confined to the Republican Party: the Truman administration, yielding to a variety of nonpartisan pressures, led the way in purging "security risks" from government, often with only a cursory nod at the niceties of due process. By the early 1950's, spurred partly by the defeat of Nationalist China, the notorious espionage case of Alger Hiss, and the outbreak of hostilities in Korea, the American people were primed for the demagoguery of Senator Joseph McCarthy.

In many ways the McCarthy episode is a paradigm for the problems of post-war America. The fear, anxiety, and confusion which surrounded McCarthy's allegations and the public response to them revealed a growing uncertainty, both among the public at large and among the intelligentsia, about the durability of America's institutions and ideology and about the ability of democracy to withstand the effects of a protracted international crisis. From the vantage point of the present it seems clear that American security in the 1950's was hardly in doubt, but the nuclear capability on both sides of the Iron Curtain constituted, as the phrase went, a "balance of terror." With this prospect as background, liberals found it increasingly difficult to criticize America without giving aid and comfort to the Communists—which had seemed harmless enough in the 1930's—thus providing additional ammunition for the American Right. Consequently, during the 1950's, the middle ground upon which American pragmatic liberals had stood during the New Deal became seriously eroded. As a result, meaningful attention to serious public problems on the domestic front—housing, urban conditions, education, racial discrimination—was deferred to the 1960's and 1970's.

The Cold War, however, provided the primary impetus for two developments in American life and society which dominated and defined the decade of the 1950's: national abundance and the enormous consolidation of big business, big science, big government, and a gigantic and growing military establishment. With the Gross National Product soaring annually, employment levels reaching an all-time high, and job security becoming a reality for more and more Americans at all economic levels, ideological disputation seemed both dangerous and increasingly irrelevant to the needs of the decade. Partly in response to the trauma and intimidation of the McCarthy period, and partly in recognition of the institutionalization and consolidation of many facets of Ameriean life, intellectuals turned their attention to the nonideological dimensions of the American experience: to questions of personal identity and anxiety amid affluence; to the problem of conformity and public opinion; to the question of the American character and the uniqueness of American history; and to the peculiar agreement on questions of value which scholars of the 1950's viewed as defining American society past and present. Those intellectuals who criticized American life and the direction of its development—thinkers such as C. Wright Mills or David Riesman—were, to a great extent, voices crying in a wilderness of complacency, conformity, and anti-intellectualism. It was symptomatic of the decade that the epithet "egghead" was used to stigmatize Adlai Stevenson in his two somewhat cerebral campaigns against Dwight D. Eisenhower, who, by common agreement, was the antithesis of the "egghead."

Yet it was in the Eisenhower years that the long-deferred American commitment to equality for Negroes began to emerge. The treatment of black Americans was so transparently inconsistent with national ideals that, in a life or death struggle with the Communist bloc in which the nonwhite, underdeveloped nations played a crucial role, vast and drastic changes in American attitudes and practices were required. And the demand for these changes came largely from the black community itself, from a sector of the national community which, until the 1950's, had been intimidated and passive. By the end of the decade the sit-in movement and various successful economic boycotts on behalf of Negro equality had begun, and the demand for "Freedom Now" was beginning to be heard throughout the country. But despite such forward steps as the Supreme Court decision of May 17, 1954, the situation for most black Americans had not improved materially by 1960, and this failure would make inevitable a more militant posture among the black leadership in the 1960's.

The documents and commentaries which follow provide certain reflections on the dominant themes and problems of social thought in the 1940's and 1950's. They are not definitive; they are, I hope, suggestive.

The Democratic Inheritance

Carl Becker
The Affirmation of Traditional Democratic Values

(1940)

By June, 1940, many Americans had begun to realize that war with the Axis was imminent. The mobilization of the economy, however, was only one response to the crisis. At another level, intellectuals, long comfortable with the ideological freedom of philosophic relativism, began to look to their own arsenals in preparation for the forthcoming struggle with the absolutism of the Fascists. On what moral and ethical grounds could democracy be justified and upheld? And how could it be regarded as a system—and a philosophy—superior to totalitarian alternatives? These were questions which demanded an answer that was more than a reaffirmation of old clichés.

Carl Becker (1873–1945), formerly a President of the American Historical Association and Professor of History at Cornell University, responded to the challenge in the following essay. Becker fell back on certain axioms pertaining to the freedom of the individual to live and think according to the dictates of his conscience and his experience. Upon those axioms, "older and more universal than democracy," rested the faith and hope of democrats everywhere. In articulating this faith Becker expressed eloquently the tenets of the value consensus scholars and critics in the 1950's would find unifying American society and history.

Not so long ago one of my lively-minded colleagues invited me to provide democracy with an ideology. The need for one, he said, was urgent. He maintained that in the conflict between the democratic and the totalitarian states the great advantage of the latter was that they united their subjects by centering their activities on something beyond their personal interests, on a common ideal end which, however fantastic and unreal it might be, they could pursue with profound conviction. I reminded him that democracy

---

Carl Becker, "Some Generalities That Still Glitter," *The Yale Review,* XXIX (June 1940), pp. 649–67. Reprinted by permission of the publisher.

already had an ideology, and a very good one. To which he replied: "True enough, it has one, and in the great crusading days it was a good one because men were then willing to sacrifice themselves for it. But it has ceased to be effective because it has ceased to be a living faith. We accept it perfunctorily, and with reservations, which means that we only half believe in it after all. What is needed is a restatement of the democratic faith, such as you could make. Whether the statement be strictly true or not doesn't greatly matter. What matters is that it should include those points which the adherents of democracy can agree upon, and be formulated in such a way that it will sound real and convincing, so that we can go all out for it." My colleague, needless to say, is an Englishman . . .

We do accept democracy somewhat perfunctorily—less so now that Hitler has brought into strong relief its essential virtues, but still rather from habit than from profound conviction. Long familiarity with democracy as a going concern, by disclosing its glaring defects and discords, has bred in many quarters a half-cynical skepticism which is alternately directed against the democratic reality as something scarcely worth preserving, and against the ideal as something impossible to achieve. The result is that if we go all out for the reality we are in danger of being thought hypocritical, while if we go all out for the ideal we are sure to be thought naïve. We can therefore only accept democracy with reservations, and it is difficult indeed to go all out for reservations.

This is the normal price paid by all religious and social systems for success and long life. Having conquered the world, they are subdued to it. The ideological faiths that originally gave them intellectual coherence and moral support, being gradually assimilated to the worldly conventions, come to be accepted as a matter of course, without serious reservations perhaps, but at least without the disturbing zeal engendered by deep conviction. If then, under the stress of profound discords in the system, the ideology is subjected to skeptical criticism and analysis, it is likely to fade away into the realm of myth, leaving nothing but inertia or naked force to preserve the system from decay or destruction . . .

Democracy is the one system that cannot employ this method of self-preservation, since the cardinal principle of its ideology is that free criticism and analysis by all and sundry is the highest virtue. Democracy, if it be consistent, must welcome the critical examination, not only of its current institutions and policies but even of the fundamental assumptions on which it rests. Democracy is thus a stupendous gamble for the highest stakes. It offers long odds on the capacity of the human mind. It wagers all it has that the freest exercise of the human reason will never disprove the proposition that only by the freest exercise of the human reason can a tolerably just and rational society ever be established.

The play is still going on, the outcome of the wager is still uncertain, but the gamble seems now a more desperate one than it did a century ago. During the last hundred years, the assumptions of the democratic faith have been subjected to the freest possible and the most penetrating critical examination; and the result is to leave us somewhat doubtful, not perhaps of the capacity of the human mind at its best, but certainly of the capacity of the average human mind to perceive that which is true and to cleave to that which is good. Our doubt in this respect arises in part from the fact that our conception of human reason, of its capacity to devise a rational system of law and government, and of the part it plays in shaping the conduct of men, is in certain important respects different from that which inspired the early prophets and protagonists of democracy.

In the early nineteenth century, the adherents of democracy were apt to say, with an air of saying everything, that democracy is a government by laws and not a government by men. For them a government by men was one in which the people were subject to the irresponsible will of one man or a few, registered in decisions that need not be justified and could be changed at any time. A government by laws, on the contrary, was one in which the people were subject to rules known beforehand and not easily changed—rules having a general or universal validity because they derived, not from the irresponsible will of individuals, but from the collective reason impersonally applied to the particular or the general situation. For the men of that time a government by men was personal and arbitrary government; a government by laws was impersonal and rational government.

This clear-cut distinction was real and convincing to the men of that time because it was based upon a particular conception of reason and law. In the rarefied climate of opinion of the eighteenth-century Enlightenment, the universe could be seen as a delicately adjusted mechanism constructed by a benevolent universal intelligence. Man was part of the mechanism, but a part of it that had been endowed with a share of the universal intelligence. The individual reason was, so to speak, a bit of universal intelligence placed within the individual man to make manifest to him the universal reason implicit in things and events. The individual might, indeed, act contrary to reason, since he might be misled by insufficient knowledge, or corrupted by nonrational impulses—the will or the emotions serving passions and appetites. But "reason," in itself untouched by these impulses, was an instrument of precision always available, so that any man, when properly "informed" and "in his right mind," could always distinguish between his "best interests" and his "selfish interests," could always, that is to say, recognize the "truth" and subordinate his will and adjust his conduct to it if he would. Reason was, in short, a possession of man but something apart from him, a kind of impersonal spiritual compass, carefully insulated in a box set behind the eyes, to serve as an undeflectable and entirely reliable guide to correct thinking and right conduct . . .

This way of regarding man and the universe, so real and convincing to Rousseau and Volney, to Godwin and Shelley, to Mazzini, with qualifications even to Bentham and the Mills, is no longer possible for us. For good or ill, we can no longer think of the universe as having been constructed by a benevolent intelligence to be the safe and adequately endowed playground for the education of mankind. For good or ill, we must think of the world not as a creation but as a self-conditioned becoming. For good or ill, we must think of man as part of that becoming, an animal organism which has slowly emerged, without instructions or credentials, from a universe as unaware of him as of itself, and as indifferent to his fate as to its own. Unable any longer to regard man as the favorite child of God, obliged to see him only as part of an evolutionary process, we must assume that, like other animal organisms, he is what he successively becomes, and that his mind, like the rest of him, is at any moment what his biological and cultural inheritance and the conditions of time and place have made it . . .

With the universe thus divested of rational purpose, and the mind of man reduced to a biological character, ideas could no longer be properly understood apart from the conditions of time and place in which they appeared. Ideas, in the realm of law and government more especially, so far from being ideal forms laid away in heaven to be apprehended by pure contemplation, came to be regarded as in some sense weapons employed in the mundane conflict for attaining practical ends. To determine the truth of an idea in the world of logical concepts was less important than to estimate its function in the world of social relations; and to estimate its function, it was necessary to know what individual or group interests inspired it, what unexamined presuppositions in the prevailing climate of opinion provided it with intellectual credit, and what measure of success or failure it encountered in the competitive struggle for existence and survival . . . In the realm of law and government, ideas could best be regarded as ideologies, performing a necessary function in the particular social situation which gave birth to them, but inevitably losing much of their point and relevance as the situation was transformed.

In this climate of opinion, the cardinal doctrines of the democratic faith could be most conveniently apprehended as an ideology in relation to the conflicts of a bygone revolutionary age. They could be taken neither as true nor false, but either as "glittering generalities," incapable of realization, or as "bourgeois ideas," "cultural constructs" emerging from a capitalist economy because suited to the interests of a ruling class. It ceased to be self-evident that all men were endowed by their Creator with certain inalienable rights, although one could understand why the idea seemed to Jefferson and his compatriots a good one at the time. Far more self-evident was the conclusion that man, being the only creator, could be endowed with such rights only as he might from time to time win for himself in the competitive struggle for advantage and security. Democracy was what it turned out to be—something to be taken not as an ideal projection of immutable truths but as an imperfect and mutable going concern. As a going concern, it could be supported on its merits as desirable, but only with reservations which allowed for the certainty that the particular institutional forms through which it functioned would inevitably be transformed by the impact of novel social conditions . . .

In this connection, something must be credited to the incessant preoccupation with machines and the machine process, which confirmed common men in a native disposition to take a literal and pragmatic view of life. The hand of man is subdued to what it works in, and the mind admires what the hand can accomplish. Modern man is, therefore, enamored of mechanical force. Fascinated by the delicate precision and sheer power of the devices he has invented, he is disposed to use them for doing whatever by their aid can be done, in the confident expectation that what can be done with such clean efficiency must be worth doing. He finds it easier, and far more exhilarating, to extend his personality by driving seventy miles an hour than to deepen his understanding by mastering the "Critique of Practical Reason." And since he cares much for the machines, while they care nothing for him, he must adjust his activities and his thinking to their virtues and limitations . . . The attitude of the machine is insensibly communicated to the man who uses it. If he would use it at all, he must use it on its own terms. He, too, must dispense with wishful thinking and the moral imperative, must learn how to accommodate himself to the fact, to yield to the pressure of what is, of what can be done in the world, without wasting valuable time in wishing that it might be different from what it turns out to be.

This literal and pragmatic attitude towards life was admirably suited to survival in the accelerating tempo of a complicated technological society. The ruthless competition for profits and jobs, the organized technique required for success in advertising and high-powered salesmanship, the hectic struggle for survival or arrival in the business world, in political life, in the professions, even in scholarship and the arts, imposed upon men an ever more insistent demand to be efficient, to make good by delivering the goods, by approved methods if possible, but at all events to deliver the goods—or else! Not the right-thinking man but the man who had what it takes was likely to be preferred and awarded the prize. Under this pressure, the disposition would be to allow the man who had what it takes to take what he had, to think him good enough if he was good enough to get by with it. Confronted with the accomplished fact in almost any situation in life, the disposition would be to be satisfied with the casual judgment, "that's that," and go on from there. Protests against it on the ground that it ought not to be, that it contravened some established principle of law or justice or morality, could always be most simply disposed of by an abrupt and disconcerting "So what?" . . .

It does not matter that we cannot share the belief of an earlier generation in the easy triumph of the right-thinking man. We may still believe in his triumph. We may admit that mind is an integral part of the animal organism, and that the pronouncements of reason are subtly shaped by subconscious desire and emotion. We may admit it, and we should admit it gladly, since to know the limitations of reason is to increase its power in the long run. If we know (and we knew it long before Freud) that the wish is father to the thought, that the heart has reasons that reason knows not of, it was, after all, reason that revealed this secret to us, and the secret, once revealed, enables reason to avoid illusions that would otherwise vitiate its conclusions. The fallacy is to suppose that because truth is in some sense relative it cannot be distinguished from error, or that the margin of error cannot be progressively reduced. The fallacy is to suppose that reason cannot transcend its lowly animal origin, to suppose that because it is a function of the organism's total activity and can be and is employed in the service of purely egoistic and brutal impulses, it cannot serve purposes of a more humane and impersonal import . . .

To have faith in the dignity and worth of the individual man as an end in himself, to believe that it is better to be governed by persuasion than by coercion, to believe that fraternal good will is more worthy than a selfish and contentious spirit, to believe that in the long run all values are inseparable from the love of truth and the disinterested search for it, to believe that knowledge and the power it confers should be used to promote the welfare and happiness of all men rather than to serve the interests of those individuals and classes whom fortune and intelligence endow with temporary advantage—these are the values which are affirmed by the traditional democratic ideology. But they are older and more universal than democracy and do not depend upon it. They have a life of their own apart from any particular social system or type of civilization. They are the values which, since the time of Buddha and Confucius, Solomon and Zoroaster, Plato and Aristotle, Socrates and Jesus, men have commonly employed to measure the advance or the decline of civilization, the values they have celebrated in the saints and sages whom they have agreed to canonize. They are the values that readily lend themselves to rational justification, yet need no justification. No one ever yet found it necessary to justify a humane and friendly act by saying that it was really a form of brutality and oppression; but the resort to coercion in civil government, in war and revolution, in the exploitation of the poor or the liquidation of the rich, has always to be justified by saying that the apparent evil is an indirect means of achieving the greater or the ultimate good. Even the Hitlers and the Stalins, in order to win the support of their own people, find it necessary to do lip service to the humane values, thus paying the customary tribute of hypocrisy which virtue exacts from vice.

Whatever the limitations of reason may be, it is folly to renounce it, since it is the only guide we have—the only available means of enlarging the realm of scientific knowledge, the only means of discriminating the social value of the various uses to which such knowledge may be put. Whatever the limitations of reason may be, they are not so great that the civilized man cannot recognize the existence and the necessity of naked force and coercion in an imperfect social world, without attributing to them the creation of those humane and rational values which by their very nature affirm that naked force and coercion are at best necessary evils.

The case for democracy is that it accepts the rational and humane values as ends, and proposes as the means of realizing them the minimum of coercion and the maximum of voluntary assent. We may well abandon the cosmological temple in which the democratic ideology originally enshrined these values without renouncing the faith it was designed to celebrate. The essence of that faith is belief in the capacity of man, as a rational and humane creature, to achieve the good life by rational and humane means. Apart from this faith, there is no alternative for the modern man except cynicism or despair—or the resort to naked force, which is itself but masked despair or cynicism disguised. For even more obvious now than in the seventeenth century is the truth of Pascal's famous dictum: "Thought makes the whole dignity of man; therefore, endeavor to think well, that is the only morality." The chief virtue of democracy, and the sole reason for cherishing it, is that with all its faults it still provides the most favorable conditions for the maintenance of that dignity and the practice of that morality.

Robert Frost
Environment and the National Identity

(1942)

On December 5, 1941, two days before Pearl Harbor, the poet Robert Frost (1874–1963) read a short poem before a meeting of the Phi Beta Kappa chapter of William and Mary College in Williamsburg, Virginia. Published the following year, the poem remained relatively unacclaimed until John F. Kennedy's Presidential Inauguration in January, 1961, when, at the president-elect's invitation, Frost chose "The Gift Outright" to commemorate the occasion. The poem suggests, in a few brief lines, the complex process of the achievement of national identity and destiny, and the special relationship of the New World environment to American history.

The land was ours before we were the land's.
She was our land more than a hundred years

Before we were her people. She was ours
In Massachusetts, in Virginia,
But we were England's, still colonials,
Possessing what we still were unpossessed by,
Possessed by what we now no more possessed.
Something we were withholding made us weak
Until we found it was ourselves
We were withholding from our land of living,
And forthwith found salvation in surrender.
Such as we were we gave ourselves outright
(The deed of gift was many deeds of war)
To the land vaguely realizing westward,
But still unstoried, artless, unenhanced,
Such as she was, such as she would become.

William Faulkner
The Writer and the Human Spirit

(1950)

The awarding of a Nobel Prize for Literature in 1950 to the Southern novelist William Faulkner (1897–1962) came as a surprise to many Americans. Although by then the author of some twenty books, Faulkner's reputation in America (though not in Europe, especially France) was essentially that of a gifted but stylistically eccentric regionalist and celebrator of a culture which America had once, at great cost of fortune and spirit, rejected in bloody conflict. Faulkner's Acceptance Speech of November, 1950, however, was significant not only because it called attention to the deeper, universal implications of his writings, but also because, in its own right, it stood as a courageous affirmation of the human spirit. In attempting, as he once put it, "to tell the truth of man," Faulkner's writings, as well as his Nobel Speech, told a larger truth about Americans and the ideals they aspired to. Uttered in the face of the threat of nuclear annihilation which followed the outbreak of war in Korea in June, 1950, the Speech takes on additional importance.

I feel that this award was not made to me as a man but to my work—a life's work in the agony and sweat of the human spirit, not for glory (and least of all for profit), but to make out of the material of the human spirit something

---

Acceptance Speech, W. Faulkner, 1950, as published in *Nobel Lectures in Literature*, pp. 444–45,

which was not there before; so this award is only mine in trust. It will not be hard to find a dedication for the money part of it to commemorate with the purpose and the significance of its origin but I would like to do the same with the acclaim too by using this fine moment as a pinnacle from which I might be listened to by the young man or young woman, already dedicated to the same anguish and sweat, who will some day stand here where I am standing.

Our tragedy today is a general and universal physical fear so long sustained by now that we can even bear it. There are no longer problems of the spirit. There is only the question: When will I be blown up? Because of this, the young man or woman writing today has forgotten the problems of the human heart in conflict with itself which alone can make good writing because only that is worth writing about, worth the agony and the sweat.

He must learn them again, he must teach himself that the basest of all things is to be afraid, and teaching himself that, forget it forever leaving no room in his workshop for anything but the old verities and truths of the heart, the old universal truths lacking which any story is ephemeral and doomed—love and honor and pity and pride and compassion and sacrifice. Until he does so, he labors under a curse. He writes not of love but of lust, of defeats in which nobody loses anything of value, of victories without hope and, worst of all, without pity or compassion. His griefs grieve on no universal bones, leaving no scars. He writes not of the heart but of the gland.

Until he relearns these things, he will write as though he stood among and watched the end of man. I do not believe in the end of man. It is easy enough to say that man is immortal simply because he will endure: then when the last ding-dong of doom has clanged and faded from the last worthless rock hanging tideless in the last red and dying evening, that even then there will still be one more sound: that of his puny inexhaustible voice still talking. I believe more than this. I believe man will not merely endure, he will prevail. He is immortal, not because he, alone among creatures, has an inexhaustible voice but because he has a soul, a spirit, capable of compassion and sacrifice and endurance. The poet's, the writer's duty is to write about these things. It is his privilege to help man endure by lifting his heart, by reminding him of courage and honor and hope and pride and compassion and pity (and sacrifice which have been the glory of his past). The poet's voice need not merely be the record of man, it can be one of the props to help him endure and prevail.

Science and Society

Vannevar Bush
The Scientific Community and the Government

(1945)

The employment of a nuclear device to help bring World War II to an end ushered in the horrors and potential majesty of the nuclear age. Never before had man's technological capability been demonstrated so strikingly and starkly, nor had his potential for self-destruction been so terribly exercised. But apart from the dramatic effects of Hiroshima and Nagasaki, the nuclear age also meant to many the necessary continuance of the partnership of government and the scientific-industrial community on a scale that would eventually dwarf even the gigantic efforts of the wartime emergency. The war had brought science and government together; the postwar years confirmed and reinforced the union.

In his Report to the President in 1945, scientist Vannevar Bush (1890–) summed up the need for the continued and expanded partnership. Science, he argued, was a national resource, and it could continue to contribute to the national welfare only if its efforts were directly supported and encouraged by the government. His thesis in *Science—The Endless Frontier* served as a rallying point for the scientific community, and his arguments were a major factor in the creation of the National Science Foundation in 1950.

Scientific Progress is Essential

Science can be effective in the national welfare only as a member of a team, whether the conditions be peace or war. But without scientific progress no amount of achievement in other directions can insure our health, prosperity, and security as a nation in the modern world.

For the War Against Disease

We have taken great strides in the war against disease. The death rate for all diseases in the Army, including overseas forces, has been reduced from

Vannevar Bush, *Science—The Endless Frontier: A Report to the President* (Washington, D.C., 1945), pp. 1–30.

14.1 per thousand in the last war to 0.6 per thousand in this war. In the last 40 years life expectancy has increased from 49 to 65 years, largely as a consequence of the reduction in the death rates of infants and children. But we are far from the goal. The annual deaths from one or two diseases far exceed the total number of American lives lost in battle during this war. A large fraction of these deaths in our civilian population cut short the useful lives of our citizens. Approximately 7,000,000 persons in the United States are mentally ill and their care costs the public over $175,000,000 a year. Clearly much illness remains for which adequate means of prevention and cure are not yet known.

The responsibility for basic research in medicine and the underlying sciences, so essential to progress in the war against disease, falls primarily upon the medical schools and universities. Yet we find that the traditional sources of support for medical research in the medical schools and universities, largely endowment income, foundation grants, and private donations, are diminishing and there is no immediate prospect of a change in this trend. Meanwhile, the cost of medical research has been rising. If we are to maintain the progress in medicine which has marked the last 25 years, the Government should extend financial support to basic medical research in the medical schools and in universities.

For Our National Security

The bitter and dangerous battle against the U-boat was a battle of scientific techniques—and our margin of success was dangerously small. The new eyes which radar has supplied can sometimes be blinded by new scientific developments. V-2 was countered only by capture of the launching sites.

We cannot again rely on our allies to hold off the enemy while we struggle to catch up. There must be more—and more adequate—military research in peacetime. It is essential that the civilian scientists continue in peacetime some portion of those contributions to national security which they have made so effectively during the war. This can best be done through a civilian-controlled organization with close liaison with the Army and Navy, but with funds direct from Congress, and the clear power to initiate military research which will supplement and strengthen that carried on directly under the control of the Army and Navy.

And for the Public Welfare

One of our hopes is that after the war there will be full employment. To reach that goal the full creative and productive energies of the American people must be released. To create more jobs we must make new and better and cheaper products. We want plenty of new, vigorous enterprises. But new products and processes are not born fullgrown. They are founded on new principles and new conceptions which in turn result from basic scientific research. Basic scientific research is scientific capital. Moreover, we cannot any longer depend upon Europe as a major source of this scientific capital. Clearly, more and better scientific research is one essential to the achievement of our goal of full employment.

How do we increase this scientific capital? First, we must have plenty of men and women trained in science, for upon them depends both the creation of new knowledge and its application to practical purposes. Second, we must strengthen the centers of basic research which are principally the colleges, universities, and research institutes. These institutions provide the environment which is most conducive to the creation of new scientific knowledge and least under pressure for immediate, tangible results. With some notable exceptions, most research in industry and in Government involves application of existing scientific knowledge to practical problems. It is only the colleges, universities, and a few research institutes that devote most of their research efforts to expanding the frontiers of knowledge . . .

For science to serve as a powerful factor in our national welfare, applied research both in Government and in industry must be vigorous. To improve the quality of scientific research within the Government, steps should be taken to modify the procedures for recruiting, classifying, and compensating scientific personnel in order to reduce the present handicap of governmental scientific bureaus in competing with industry and the universities for top-grade scientific talent. To provide coordination of the common scientific activities of these governmental agencies as to policies and budgets, a permanent Science Advisory Board should be created to advise the executive and legislative branches of Government on these matters.

The most important ways in which the Government can promote industrial research are to increase the flow of new scientific knowledge through support of basic research, and to aid in the development of scientific talent. In addition, the Governments should provide suitable incentives to industry to conduct research, (*a*) by clarification of present uncertainties in the Internal Revenue Code in regard to the deductibility of research and development expenditures as current charges against net income, and (*b*) by strengthening the patent system so as to eliminate uncertainties which now bear heavily on small industries and so as to prevent abuses which reflect discredit upon a basically sound system. In addition, ways should be found to cause the benefits of basic research to reach industries which do not now utilize new scientific knowledge.

We Must Renew Our Scientific Talent

The responsibility for the creation of new scientific knowledge—and for most of its application—rests on that small body of men and women who understand the fundamental laws of nature and are skilled in the techniques of scientific research. We shall have rapid or slow advance on any scientific frontier depending on the number of highly qualified and trained scientists exploring it.

The deficit of science and technology students who, but for the war, would have received bachelor's degrees is about 150,000. It is estimated that the deficit of those obtaining advanced degrees in these fields will amount in 1955 to about 17,000—for it takes at least 6 years from college entry to achieve a doctor's degree or its equivalent in science or engineering. The real ceiling on our productivity of new scientific knowledge and its application in the war against disease, and the development of new products and new industries, is the number of trained scientists available.

The training of a scientist is a long and expensive process. Studies clearly show that there are talented individuals in every part of the population, but with few exceptions, those without the means of buying higher education go without it. If ability, and not the circumstance of family fortune, determines who shall receive higher education in science, then we shall be assured of constantly improving quality at every level of scientific activity. The Government should provide a reasonable number of undergraduate scholarships and graduate fellowships in order to develop scientific talent in American youth. The plans should be designed to attract into science only that proportion of youthful talent appropriate to the needs of science in relation to the other needs of the nation for high abilities . . .

A Program for Action

The Government should accept new responsibilities for promoting the flow of new scientific knowledge and the development of scientific talent in our youth. These responsibilities are the proper concern of the Government, for they vitally affect our health, our jobs, and our national security. It is in keeping also with basic United States policy that the Government should foster the opening of new frontiers and this is the modern way to do it. For many years the Government has wisely supported research in the agricultural colleges and the benefits have been great. The time has come when such support should be extended to other fields. . .

Therefore I recommend that a new agency for these purposes be established. Such an agency should be composed of persons of broad interest and experience, having an understanding of the peculiarities of scientific research and scientific education. It should have stability of funds so that long-range programs may be undertaken. It should recognize that freedom of inquiry must be preserved and should leave internal control of policy, personnel, and the method and scope of research to the institutions in which it is carried on. It should be fully responsible to the President and through him to the Congress for its program.

Early action on these recommendations is imperative if this nation is to meet the challenge of science in the crucial years ahead. On the wisdom with which we bring science to bear in the war against disease, in the creation of new industries, and in the strengthening of our Armed Forces depends in large measure our future as a nation. . .

. . . Nowhere in the Governmental structure receiving its funds from Congress is there an agency adapted to supplementing the support of basic research in the universities, in both medicine and the natural sciences; adapted to supporting research on new weapons for both Services*; or adapted to administering a program of science scholarships and fellowships.

A new agency should be established, therefore, by the Congress for the purpose. Such an agency, moreover, should be an independent agency devoted to the support of scientific research and the advanced scientific education alone. Industry learned many years ago that basic research cannot often be fruitfully conducted as an adjunct to or a subdivision of an operating agency or department. Operating agencies have immediate operating goals and are under constant pressure to produce in a tangible way, for that is the test of their value. None of these conditions is favorable to basic research. Research is the exploration of the unknown and is necessarily speculative. It is inhibited by conventional approaches, traditions, and standards. It cannot be satisfactorily conducted in an atmosphere where it is gauged and tested by operating or production standard. Basic scientific research should not, therefore, be placed under an operating agency whose paramount concern is anything other than research. Research will always suffer when put in competition with operations. The decision that there should be a new and independent agency was reached by each of the committees advising in these matters.

I am convinced that these new functions should be centered in one agency. Science is fundamentally a unitary thing. The number of independent agencies should be kept to a minimum. Much medical progress, for example, will come from fundamental advances in chemistry. Separation of the sciences in tight compartments, as would occur if more than one agency were involved, would retard and not advance scientific knowledge as a whole.

Five Fundamentals

There are certain basic principles which must underlie the program of Government support for scientific research and education if such support is to be effective and if it is to avoid impairing the very things we seek to foster. These principles are as follows:

1. Whatever the extent of support may be, there must be stability of funds over a period of years so that long-range programs may be undertaken.

2. The agency to administer such funds should be composed of citizens selected only on the basis of their interest in and capacity to promote the work of the agency. They should be persons of broad interest in and understanding of the peculiarities of scientific research and education.

**Ed. note*: At the time of writing the Air Force was still part of the Army.

3. The agency should promote research through contracts or grants to organizations outside the Federal Government. It should not operate any laboratories of its own.

4. Support of basic research in the public and private colleges, universities, and research institutes must leave the internal control of policy, personnel, and the method and scope of the research to the institutions themselves. This is of the utmost importance.

5. While assuring complete independence and freedom for the nature, scope, and methodology of research carried on in the institution receiving public funds, and while retaining discretion in the allocation of funds among such institutions, the Foundation proposed herein must be responsible to the President and the Congress. Only through such responsibility can we maintain the proper relationship between science and other aspects of a democratic system. The usual controls of audits, reports, budgeting, and the like, should, of course, apply to the administrative and fiscal operations of the Foundation, subject, however, to such adjustments in procedure as are necessary to meet the special requirements of research.

Basic research is a long-term process—it ceases to be basic if immediate results are expected on short-term support. Methods should therefore be found which will permit the agency to make commitments of funds from current appropriations for programs of five years duration or longer. Continuity and stability of the program and its support may be expected (*a*) from the growing realization by the Congress of the benefits to the public from scientific research, and, (*b*) from the conviction which will grow among those who conduct research under the auspices of the agency that good quality work will be followed by continuing support.

Military Research

As stated earlier in this report, military preparedness requires a permanent, independent, civilian-controlled organization, having close liaison with the Army and Navy, but with funds direct from Congress and the clear power to initiate military research which will supplement and strengthen that carried on directly under the control of the Army and Navy. As a temporary measure the National Academy of Sciences has established the Research Board for National Security at the request of the Secretary of War and the Secretary of the Navy. This is highly desirable in order that there may be no interruption in the relations between scientists and military men after the emergency wartime Office of Scientific Research and Development goes out of existence. The Congress is now considering legislation to provide funds for this Board by direct appropriation.

I believe that, as a permanent measure, it would be appropriate to add to the agency needed to perform the other functions recommended in this report the responsibilities for civilian-initiated and civilian-controlled military research. The function of such a civilian group would be primarily to conduct long-range scientific research on military problems—leaving to the Services research on the improvement of existing weapons.

Some research on military problems should be conducted, in time of peace as well as in war, by civilians independently of the military establishment. It is the primary responsibility of the Army and Navy to train the men, make available the weapons, and employ the strategy that will bring victory in combat. The Armed Services cannot be expected to be experts in all of the complicated fields which make it possible for a great nation to fight successfully in total war. There are certain kinds of research—such as research on the improvement of existing weapons—which can best be done within the military establishment. However, the job of long-range research involving application of the newest scientific discoveries to military needs should be the responsibility of those civilian scientists in the universities and in industry who are best trained to discharge it thoroughly and successfully. It is essential that both kinds of research go forward and that there be the closest liaison between the two groups.

Placing the civilian military research function in the proposed agency would bring it into close relationship with a broad program of basic research in both the natural sciences and medicine. A balance between military and other research could thus readily be maintained.

The establishment of the new agency, including a civilian military research group, should not be delayed by the existence of the Research Board for National Security, which is a temporary measure. Nor should the creation of the new agency be delayed by uncertainties in regard to the postwar organization of our military departments themselves. Clearly, the new agency, including a civilian military research group within it, can remain sufficiently flexible to adapt its operations to whatever may be the final organization of the military departments.

Norman Cousins
An Expression of Outrage

(1958)

While the partnership of science and government gave promise of massive federal support for research and progress, not all who viewed the results were comforted. The purpose of the partnership, it seemed to some observers, was intrinsically nationalistic and potentially predatory. Research in the military sphere received top priority, and, paradoxically, national security seemed to diminish with the growth of the nation's military and scientific capacity.

Norman Cousins, "Wanted: Two Billion Angry men," *Saturday Review*, 41 (February 1, 1958), p. 22.

The irony of this situation was not lost on Norman Cousins (1912–), editor of the *Saturday Review*. A consistent critic of America's military and scientific priorities, Cousins pointed out in the following editorial the tragedy and incongruity of nuclear nationalism. On behalf of the "world's people" Cousins protested against the warlike posture of the "national sovereignties."

There is no point in talking about the possibility of a war breaking out. The war is already being fought. It is being waged by national sovereignties against human life.

It is true that national sovereignties are arrayed against each other under conflicting ideological banners. But the consequence of this conflict will not be victory by one over the other. The consequence can only be a mass cheapening of life or its elimination from this planet.

Everything being done by the national sovereignties to advance their supposed security succeeds only in intensifying the peril to life on earth. The weapons they are making are an advanced form of the competition between the sovereignties. Should these weapons be used, the nations behind the sovereignties will be pulverized and the humans along with them. The hope of the statesmen, of course, is to create a balance of terror so that neither side will dare to attack. But the same hideous momentum that produced the weapons can lead to their use. Neither side will be made secure by the fact that the other side possesses the means of instantaneous, devastating attack. Neither side will feel under the obligation to wait until it is hit first. It is upon such a frail reed that the cause of life on earth is now made to rest.

It is wrong to say that nuclear explosives are being tested; they are being used. Every time one of the explosives is fired human beings are hurt. Just in the act of exploding a test nuclear bomb, life-destroying materials are put into the air. These explosions form no ordinary clouds; they are not dispersed by the winds; they retain their ability to poison and kill for more than two dozen years. With each bomb the canopy of poison above the earth grows heavier. Not long ago only one nation was involved in this kind of experimentation. Today, three nations are contributing to the general poisoning. Tomorrow, perhaps a half-dozen or more national sovereignties will insist on their right to add their own portions of poison to the sky.

There is no disagreement about one aspect of such general testing. All experts agree that at some point the burden of poison will become heavier than human life can sustain. The only disagreement has to do with when that point will be reached. Also, whether the amount of poison already in the air has caused widespread harm or only limited harm; in short, whether 10,000 persons will die this year of leukemia produced by the bomb poisons in the atmosphere or whether only one-fourth or one-fifth that number will die.

The men at the head of sovereign nations are helpless to deal with the onrushing peril. They are part of something unworkable as it concerns the making of world peace, for unfettered sovereignty today is an unworkable concept. It makes no difference how benign or well-intentioned are the men who represent the sovereignties. So long as their ultimate aim is to maintain the present station of a nation above law, the statesmen will work at opposite ends from what human life requires in order to be sustained on this planet.

In a very real sense, the statesmen are trying to deal with the problems of yesterday rather than the problems of today and tomorrow. It is true that the Second World War was brought on in large part because the free nations of the world were weak and disarmed. But if disarmament a generation ago was no answer, neither is an armaments race today the answer. If an arms race leads to war and if war leads to the liquidation of both freedom and life, then the arms race offers not military security but the prospect of mutual suicide.

Here the advocates of unfettered national sovereignty argue that they would rather take their chances with an arms race ending in mutual suicide than with the danger of being disarmed in the face of almost certain Communist world conquest. If these were the only alternatives then something might be said for the arms race. But these are not the only alternatives. Neither disarmament nor armament can create a peace. Real peace depends on the amount of support that can be mobilized in the world for transforming the United Nations into a body with the effective powers of world law.

So long as peace is pursued under present methods; so long as each nation is allowed to retain the right and the capacity to destroy millions of human beings; so long as nations are allowed to engage in the kind of acts which are forbidden inside their countries to individual citizens; so long as lawlessness is the normal way of life among nations—so long as these conditions prevail there can be no peace.

It is not true that only the totalitarian states are opposed to a world under law. The free nations have yet to make the specific proposals that go as far beyond sovereignty as is necessary to make world law work.

Meanwhile, what the world needs today are two billion angry men who will make it clear to their national leaders that the earth does not exist for the purpose of being a stage for the total destruction of man. Two billion angry men can insist that the world's resources be utilized for human good. They can demand that the nations stop using the sky as an open sewer for radioactive poisons, and that an end be put to the uncontrolled devices that pursue future generations by way of damaged genes. They can compel the nations to end the long age of the cave and begin a real civilization. A war is now being waged against the world's peoples and they have the need and duty to defend themselves.

C. Wright Mills
The Consequences of Consolidation

(1956)

Terror and the threat of nuclear extinction were not the only consequences of the amalgam of science, military, and government. The consolidation of these clusters of power, according to one social critic, produced a new phenomenon in America: an elite class of rulers whose status and privileged positions exempted them from popular review. Hidden behind the complexities and enormities of the sprawling public and private bureaucracies, this elite manipulated a power concentration unprecedented in human history and impervious to democratic processes.

Publication of *The Power Elite* in 1956 gave sociologist C. Wright Mills (1916–1962) undisputed primacy as analyst and critic of American society. *The Power Elite* was a shocking commentary on the social structure of America not only because of its deceptively dispassionate tone, but also because Mills explicitly disavowed the conspiratorial explanation so frequently implied by left-wing commentators. Taking a long-range historical view, Mills identified and documented the power elite's existence and, moreover, showed how the elite had evolved out of the very nature of middle-class capitalism, democracy, and the shattering historical events of the Twentieth Century. Though regarded as a radical in the 1950's, Mills offered an interpretation of American society that directly anticipated the theme of President Eisenhower's Farewell Address scarcely five years later.

The powers of ordinary men are circumscribed by the everyday worlds in which they live, yet even in these rounds of job, family, and neighborhood they often seem driven by forces they can neither understand nor govern. "Great changes" are beyond their control, but affect their conduct and outlook none the less. The very framework of modern society confines them to projects not their own, but from every side, such changes now press upon the men and women of the mass society, who accordingly feel that they are without purpose in an epoch in which they are without power.

But not all men are in this sense ordinary. As the means of information and of power are centralized, some men come to occupy positions in American society from which they can look down upon, so to speak, and by their decisions mightily affect, the everyday worlds of ordinary men and women. They are not made by their jobs; they set up and break down jobs for thousands of others; they are not confined by simple family responsibilities; they

---

can escape. They may live in many hotels and houses, but they are bound by no one community. They need not merely "meet the demands of the day and hour"; in some part, they create these demands, and cause others to meet them. Whether or not they profess their power, their technical and political experience of it far transcends that of the underlying population. What Jacob Burckhardt said of "great men," most Americans might well say of their elite: "They are all that we are not."

The power elite is composed of men whose positions enable them to transcend the ordinary environments of ordinary men and women; they are in positions to make decisions having major consequences. Whether they do or do not make such decisions is less important than the fact that they do occupy such pivotal positions: their failure to act, their failure to make decisions, is itself an act that is often of greater consequence than the decisions they do make. For they are in command of the major hierarchies and organizations of modern society. They rule the big corporations. They run the machinery of the state and claim its prerogatives. They direct the military establishment. They occupy the strategic command posts of the social structure, in which are now centered the effective means of the power and the wealth and the celebrity which they enjoy.

The power elite are not solitary rulers. Advisers and consultants, spokesmen and opinion-makers are often the captains of their higher thought and decision. Immediately below the elite are the professional politicians of the middle levels of power, in the Congress and in the pressure groups, as well as among the new and old upper classes of town and city and region. Mingling with them, in curious ways which we shall explore, are those professional celebrities who live by being continually displayed but are never, so long as they remain celebrities, displayed enough. If such celebrities are not at the head of any dominating hierarchy, they do often have the power to distract the attention of the public or afford sensations to the masses, or, more directly, to gain the ear of those who do occupy positions of direct power. More or less unattached, as critics of morality and technicians of power, as spokesmen of God and creators of mass sensibility, such celebrities and consultants are part of the immediate scene in which the drama of the elite is enacted. But that drama itself is centered in the command posts of the major institutional hierarchies . . .

Within American society, major national power now resides in the economic, the political, and the military domains. Other institutions seem off to the side of modern history, and, on occasion, duly subordinated to these. No family is as directly powerful in national affairs as any major corporations; no church is as directly powerful in the external biographies of young men in America today as the military establishment; no college is as powerful in the shaping of momentous events as the National Security Council. Religious, educational, and family institutions are not autonomous centers of national power; on the contrary, these decentralized areas are increasingly shaped by the big three, in which developments of decisive and immediate consequence now occur.

Families and churches and schools adapt to modern life; governments and armies and corporations shape it; and, as they do so, they turn these lesser institutions into means for their ends. Religious institutions provide chaplains to the armed forces where they are used as a means of increasing the effectiveness of its morale to kill. Schools select and train men for their jobs in corporations and their specialized tasks in the armed forces. The extended family has, of course, long been broken up by the industrial revolution, and now the son and the father are removed from the family, by compulsion if need be, whenever the army of the state sends out the call. And the symbols of all these lesser institutions are used to legitimate the power and the decisions of the big three.

The life-fate of the modern individual depends not only upon the family into which he was born or which he enters by marriage, but increasingly upon the corporation in which he spends the most alert hours of his best years; not only upon the school where he is educated as a child and adolescent, but also upon the state which touches him throughout his life; not only upon the church in which on occasion he hears the word of God, but also upon the army in which he is disciplined.

If the centralized state could not rely upon the inculcation of nationalist loyalties in public and private schools, its leaders would promptly seek to modify the decentralized educational system. If the bankruptcy rate among the top five hundred corporations were as high as the general divorce rate among the thirty-seven million married couples, there would be economic catastrophe on an international scale. If members of armies gave to them no more of their lives than do believers to the churches to which they belong, there would be a military crisis.

Within each of the big three, the typical institutional unit has become enlarged, has become administrative, and, in the power of its decisions, has become centralized. Behind these developments there is a fabulous technology, for as institutions, they have incorporated this technology and guide it, even as it shapes and paces their developments.

The economy—once a great scatter of small productive units in autonomous balance—has become dominated by two or three hundred giant corporations, administratively and politically interrelated, which together hold the keys to economic decisions.

The political order, once a decentralized set of several dozen states with a weak spinal cord, has become a centralized, executive establishment which has taken up into itself many powers previously scattered, and now enters into each and every cranny of the social structure.

The military order, once a slim establishment in a context of distrust fed by state militia, has become the largest and most expensive feature of government, and, although well versed in smiling public relations, now has all the grim and clumsy efficiency of a sprawling bureaucratic domain.

In each of these institutional areas, the means of power at the disposal of decision makers have increased enormously; their central executive powers have been enhanced; within each of them modern administrative routines have been elaborated and tightened up.

As each of these domains becomes enlarged and centralized, the consequences of its activities become greater, and its traffic with the others increases. The decisions of a handful of corporations bear upon military and political as well as upon economic developments around the world. The decisions of the military establishment rest upon and grievously affect political life as well as the very level of economic activity. The decisions made within the political domain determine economic activities and military programs. There is no longer, on the one hand, an economy, and, on the other hand, a political order containing a military establishment unimportant to politics and to money-making. There is a political economy linked, in a thousand ways, with military institutions and decisions. On each side of the world-split running through central Europe and around the Asiatic rimlands, there is an ever-increasing interlocking of economic, military, and political structures. If there is government intervention in the corporate economy, so is there corporate intervention in the governmental process. In the structural sense, this triangle of power is the source of the interlocking directorate that is most important for the historical structure of the present.

The fact of the interlocking is clearly revealed at each of the points of crisis of modern capitalist society—slump, war, and boom. In each, men of decision are led to an awareness of the interdependence of the major institutional orders. In the nineteenth century, when the scale of all institutions was smaller, their liberal integration was achieved in the automatic economy, by an autonomous play of market forces, and in the automatic political domain, by the bargain and the vote. It was then assumed that out of the imbalance and friction that followed the limited decisions then possible a new equilibrium would in due course emerge. That can no longer be assumed, and it is not assumed by the men at the top of the three dominant hierarchies.

For given the scope of their consequences, decisions—and indecisions—in any one of these ramify into the others, and hence top decisions tend either to become co-ordinated or to lead to a commanding indecision. It has always been like this. When numerous small entrepreneurs made up the economy, for example, many of them could fail and the consequences still remain local; political and military authorities did not intervene. But now, given political expectations and military commitments, can they afford to allow key units of the private corporate economy to break down in slump? Increasingly, they do intervene in economic affairs, and as they do so, the controlling decisions in each order are inspected by agents of the other two, and economic, military, and political structures are interlocked.

At the pinnacle of each of the three enlarged and centralized domains, there have arisen those higher circles which make up the economic, the political, and the military elites. At the top of the economy, among the corporate rich, there are the chief executives; at the top of the political order, the members of the political directorate; at the top of the military establishment, the elite of soldier-statesmen clustered in and around the Joint Chiefs of Staff and the upper echelon. As each of these domains has coincided with the others, as decisions tend to become total in their consequence, the leading men in each of the three domains of power—the warlords, the corporation chieftains, the political directorate—tend to come together, to form the power elite of America. . .

The elite who occupy the command posts may be seen as the possessers of power and wealth and celebrity; they may be seen as members of the upper stratum of a capitalistic society. They may also be defined in terms of psychological and moral criteria, as certain kinds of selected individuals. So defined, the elite, quite simply, are people of superior character and energy.

The humanist, for example, may conceive of the "elite" not as a social level or category, but as a scatter of those individuals who attempt to transcend themselves, and accordingly, are more noble, more efficient, made out of better stuff. It does not matter whether they are poor or rich, whether they hold high position or low, whether they are acclaimed or despised; they are elite because of the kind of individuals they are. The rest of the population is mass, which, according to this conception, sluggishly relaxes into uncomfortable mediocrity.

This is the sort of socially unlocated conception which some American writers with conservative yearnings have recently sought to develop. But most moral and psychological conceptions of the elite are much less sophisticated, concerning themselves not with individuals but with the stratum as a whole. Such ideas, in fact, always arise in a society in which some people possess more than do others of what there is to possess. People with advantages are loath to believe that they just happen to be people with advantages. They come readily to define themselves as inherently worthy of what they possess; they come to believe themselves "naturally" elite; and, in fact, to imagine their possessions and their privileges as natural extensions of their own elite selves. In this sense, the idea of the elite as composed of men and women having a finer moral character is an ideology of the elite as a privileged ruling stratum, and this is true whether the ideology is elitemade or made up for it by others.

In eras of equalitarian rhetoric, the more intelligent or the more articulate among the lower and middle classes, as well as guilty members of the upper, may come to entertain ideas of a counter-elite. In western society, as a matter of fact, there is a long tradition and varied images of the poor, the exploited, and the oppressed as the truly virtuous, the wise, and the blessed. Stemming from Christian tradition, this moral idea of a counter-elite, composed of essentially higher types condemned to a lowly station, may be and has been used by the underlying population to justify harsh criticism of ruling elites and to celebrate utopian images of a new elite to come.

The moral conception of the elite, however, is not always merely an ideology of the overprivileged or a counter-ideology of the underprivileged. It is often a fact: having controlled experiences and select privileges, many individuals of the upper stratum do come in due course to approximate the types of character they claim to embody. Even when we give up—as we must—the idea that the elite man or woman is born with an elite character, we need not dismiss the idea that their experiences and trainings develop in them characters of a specific type.

Nowadays we must qualify the idea of elite as composed of higher types of individuals, for the men who are selected for and shaped by the top positions have many spokesmen and advisers and ghosts and make-up men who modify their self-conceptions and create their public images, as well as shape many of their decisions. There is, of course, considerable variation among the elite in this respect, but as a general rule in America today, it would be naïve to interpret any major elite group merely in terms of its ostensible personnel. The American elite often seems less a collection of persons than of corporate entities, which are in great part created and spoken for as standard types of "personality." Even the most apparently free-lance celebrity is usually a sort of synthetic production turned out each week by a disciplined staff which systematically ponders the effect of the easy ad-libbed gags the celebrity "spontaneously" echoes.

Yet, in so far as the elite flourishes as a social class or as a set of men at the command posts, it will select and form certain types of personality, and reject others. The kind of moral and psychological beings men become is in large part determined by the values they experience and the institutional roles they are allowed and expected to play. From the biographer's point of view, a man of the upper classes is formed by his relations with others like himself in a series of small intimate groupings through which he passes and to which throughout his lifetime he may return. So conceived, the elite is a set of higher circles whose members are selected, trained and certified and permitted intimate access to those who command the impersonal institutional hierarchies of modern society. If there is any one key to the *psychological* idea of the elite, it is that they combine in their persons an awareness of impersonal decision-making with intimate sensibilities shared with one another. To understand the elite as a social class we must examine a whole series of smaller face-to-face milieux, the most obvious of which, historically, has been the upper-class family, but the most important of which today are the proper secondary school and the metropolitan club.

Affluence—and Anxiety

Dwight D. Eisenhower
Recent Economic Achievements

(1956)

In January, 1956, President Dwight D. Eisenhower (1890–1969) presented his Economic Report to the Congress. The Report contained, among other things, news that the United States was on the verge of achieving an unprecedented annual Gross National Product of 400 billion dollars; the Report also contained the administration's view of the reasons behind this growth. According to the President, America's economic growth should be ascribed to "the qualities of the American people"; and its continuance depended "far more on what individuals do for themselves than on what the Federal Government does or can do for them." The President's Letter of Transmittal of the Report to the Congress, which follows, stated also that the administration looked forward to a balanced budget and "the strengthening of competitive enterprise . . ." The President's letter represents what economist John K. Galbraith termed the "conventional wisdom" explaining the reasons behind America's economic successes.

Full employment, rising incomes, and a stable dollar have been cherished goals of our society. The practical attainment of these ideals during 1955 was the year's great economic achievement.

The past year has brought fresh witness to the basic strength and resiliency of our economy. We have broken through to new and higher ground, and have reached the threshold of a 400 billion dollar economy.

Whether we observe economic activity at the stage of production, or employment, or income disbursement, or consumer spending, we find evidence of progress and prosperity. The Nation's expanding income is being shared widely. Employment and wages are at record levels. Both investment and consumer spending are going forward at a good pace. Some groups of people have not, however, enjoyed a full measure of prosperity, and we must keep that fact before us as we build for the future.

Dwight D. Eisenhower, "Letter of Transmittal," *Economic Report of the President* (Washington, D.C., 1956), pp. iii–vi.

The Role of Government

The mainspring of our economy is to be found in the qualities of the American people. Given free institutions and a favorable physical environment, an expanding economy is the natural fruit of the enterprise of such a people.

Today, we believe as strongly in economic progress through free and competitive enterprise as our fathers did, and we resent as they did any unnecessary intrusion of Government into private affairs. But we have also come to believe that progress need not proceed as irregularly as in the past, and that the Federal Government has the capacity to moderate economic fluctuations without becoming a dominant factor in our economy.

Our governmental policies have concentrated on building an economic environment that favors an orderly expansion of private activities. The Federal Government has not sought to maintain good times by expanding our already huge governmental outlays or by permitting the value of money to depreciate.

The Administration has sought, in cooperation with the Congress, to discharge its responsibility through a series of closely related policies. *First*, by removing direct controls over prices and wages, which had outlived their usefulness. *Second*, by preserving an actively competitive environment and assisting new and small businesses. *Third*, by curtailing governmental activities that could be handled as well or better by private enterprise. *Fourth*, by restricting public expenditures, and yet adding to the country's defensive strength and its stock of public assets, especially highways, hospitals, and educational facilities. *Fifth*, by lightening the burden of taxes imposed on individuals and businesses. *Sixth*, by extending the ties of trade and investment with other nations of the Free World. *Seventh*, by tempering the impact of unemployment, old age, illness, and blighted neighborhoods on people, yet not impairing self-reliance. *Eighth*, by extending the automatic workings of our fiscal system that tend to offset or cushion changes in income arising from changes in economic activity. *Ninth*, by attacking fundamental causes of weakness in the farm situation. *Tenth*, by acting promptly and resolutely when either recessionary or inflationary influences in the general economy became evident.

To help keep our surging economy in a healthy condition the Government in 1955 held the tax line. The Federal Reserve System shifted from a policy of active credit ease to one of moderate restraint. These policies contributed in large degree to the achievement and maintenance of prosperity without price inflation.

Extending Prosperity

A period of general prosperity, such as we have recently been experiencing, presents a challenge to an intelligent citizenry. We must find ways and means of extending prosperity to the less flourishing sectors of our economy.

The position of farmers in our dynamic economy has aroused deep concern. It is imperative that we strengthen farm programs on the basis of a realistic appraisal of the present situation.

The persisting decline in farm prices and incomes reflects a continuing imbalance between farm output and its ultimate disposition. The imbalance and resulting huge surpluses are to be traced largely to the technological revolution in American agriculture, changing domestic demands for farm products, the expansion of agricultural production abroad, and the repeated extension of wartime price-support levels long after the end of World War II.

Many parts of our agricultural policy are working well and require only moderate changes. Together with the nine-point program built around the Soil Bank put forward in the recent Message on Agriculture, they constitute a many-sided attack on the ills that beset agriculture. There is no easy cure for persisting surplus conditions. The programs now recommended, if framed wisely and adopted promptly, will promote the welfare of farmers and the Nation.

The basic cause of low incomes is low productivity, irregular employment, or both. The Government can do a great deal to help people who have been left behind in the onrush of progress by undertaking special programs for raising their productivity.

One of the largest groups of low-income families is in rural areas, mostly on farms too small for efficient operation. The Rural Development Program is a soundly conceived approach to helping these farm families raise their productivity and thereby improve their economic status. Legislation is needed which will permit the program to be expanded in line with recommendations made last year.

To cope with chronic unemployment which has persisted in some communities, despite the attainment of practically full employment in the Nation at large, a new Area Assistance Program is recommended.

Vocational rehabilitation, widened coverage of the Federal Old-Age and Survivors Insurance Program, and housing needs of older people are fields in which advances should be made.

Relatively few people are as yet protected by insurance against catastrophic illness. The pooling of risks by private carriers, or if need be through a Federal program, would help meet this problem.

A joint Federal-State program for indemnifying flood victims on losses to real property, business inventories, and household effects should be authorized.

Building for Future Prosperity

Lasting prosperity of the Nation depends far more on what individuals do for themselves than on what the Federal Government does or can do for them. The rate of our economic advance in the years ahead will depend largely on our ability as a people to preserve an environment that rewards individual initiative and encourages enterprise, innovation, and investment.

Government can contribute to the strengthening of competitive enterprise through monetary, fiscal, and housekeeping policies that promote high and rising levels of economic activity; by helping small and medium-sized businesses overcome impediments to their expansion; and by vigorous measures for preventing monopolistic practices and combinations.

For the present fiscal year a balanced budget is in prospect. Once a budgetary surplus comes definitely into sight and economic conditions continue to be favorable, we should begin reducing our huge public debt. Such an act of fiscal integrity would signify with unmistakable clarity that our democracy is capable of self-discipline.

To help meet the pressing need for more schoolrooms, the Congress is urged to authorize a program of Federal aid for school construction which, over a five-year period, could be expected to stimulate the States and localities to sufficiently greater efforts to remove the accumulated shortages.

The country urgently needs a modernized interstate highway system to relieve existing congestion, to provide for the expected growth of motor vehicle traffic, to strengthen the Nation's defenses, to reduce the toll of human life exacted each year in highway accidents, and to promote economic development.

The development of consumer instalment credit has been highly beneficial to our economy. However, it sometimes accentuates movements in the buying of consumer durable goods. Although present conditions do not call for the use of any authority to regulate the terms of instalment credit, this is a good time for the Congress and the Executive Branch to study the problem.

Sound policies to promote the expansion of the international flow of goods, capital, enterprise, and technology will powerfully advance our national security and economic welfare, and help to build a stronger and more unified community of free nations.

Early passage of legislation authorizing membership of the United States in the Organization for Trade Cooperation and providing for further customs simplification is of high importance.

Conclusion

Foresight has helped our Nation make great strides in recent years toward a balanced and sustained prosperity. We have succeeded in expanding the scope of free enterprise, and yet increased the sense of security that people need in a highly industrialized age.

Taking recent developments all together, it is reasonable to expect that high levels of production, employment, and income will be broadly sustained during the coming year, and the underlying conditions will remain favorable to further economic growth.

Great opportunities lie ahead for American businessmen, consumers, workers, farmers, and investors. The recommendations of this Report should be helpful in the realization of these opportunities.

David M. Potter
Abundance and the American Character

(1954)

Regardless of the reasons behind the tremendous surge of the American economy in the post-war period, there was no doubt that most Americans were enjoying lives of unprecedented abundance in the 1950's. Contrary to Marx's prediction, America's middle class grew and prospered, and if an elite did reap disproportionate benefits from the economy's growth, there was no gainsaying that the middle class benefited too. Increasingly, "the American way of life" connoted wealth as well as freedom and democracy.

Historian David M. Potter (1910–), generalizing upon the effects of abundance upon American history, noted that abundance (and not "free land," as Frederick Jackson Turner had suggested in 1893) was the most important single influence shaping the development of American values, institutions and national character. Drawing upon economic, sociological, and psychological as well as historical data, Potter cogently set forth his conclusions in *People of Plenty* (1954). The book, which remains preeminent as a study of American character traits and their origins, reflects implicitly the climate of the 1950's.

Let us consider the situation of a six-month-old American infant, who is not yet aware that he is a citizen, a taxpayer, and a consumer.

This individual is, to all appearances, just a very young specimen of *Homo sapiens*, with certain needs for protection, care, shelter, and nourishment which may be regarded as the universal biological needs of human infancy rather than specific cultural needs. It would be difficult to prove that the culture has as yet differentiated him from other infants, and, though he is an American, few would argue that he has acquired an American character. Yet abundance and the circumstances arising from abundance have already dictated a whole range of basic conditions which, from his birth, are constantly at work upon this child and which will contribute in the most intimate and basic way to the formation of his character.

To begin with, abundance has already revolutionized the typical mode of his nourishment by providing for him to be fed upon cow's milk rather than upon his mother's milk, taken from the bottle rather than from the breast. Abundance contributes vitally to this transformation, because bottle feeding

---

David M. Potter, *People of Plenty: Economic Abundance and the American Character* (Chicago, 1954, 1963), pp. 193–208. Reprinted by permission of the publisher, the University of Chicago Press, and the author.

requires fairly elaborate facilities of refrigeration, heating, sterilization, and temperature control, which only an advanced technology can offer and only an economy of abundance can make widely available. I will not attempt here to resolve the debated question as to the psychological effects, for both mother and child, of bottle feeding as contrasted with breast feeding in infant nurture. But it is clear that the changeover to bottle feeding has encroached somewhat upon the intimacy of the bond between mother and child. The nature of this bond is, of course, one of the most crucial factors in the formation of character. Bottle feeding also must tend to emphasize the separateness of the infant as an individual, and thus it makes, for the first time, a point which the entire culture reiterates constantly throughout the life of the average American. In addition to the psychic influences which may be involved in the manner of taking the food, it is also a matter of capital importance that the bottle-fed baby is, on the whole, better nourished than the breast-fed infant and therefore likely to grow more rapidly, to be more vigorous, and to suffer fewer ailments, with whatever effects these physical conditions may have upon his personality.

It may be argued also that abundance has provided a characteristic mode of housing for the infant and that his mode further emphasizes his separateness as an individual. In societies of scarcity, dwelling units are few and hard to come by, with the result that high proportions of newly married young people make their homes in the parental ménage, thus forming part of an "extended" family, as it is called. Moreover, scarcity provides a low ratio of rooms to individuals, with the consequence that whole families may expect as a matter of course to have but one room for sleeping, where children will go to bed in intimate propinquity to their parents. But abundance prescribes a different regime. By making it economically possible for newly married couples to maintain separate households of their own, it has almost destroyed the extended family as an institution in America and has ordained that the child shall be reared in a "nuclear" family, so-called, where his only intimate associates are his parents and his siblings, with even the latter far fewer now than in families of the past. The housing arrangements of this new-style family are suggested by census data for 1950. In that year there were 45,983,000 dwelling units to accommodate the 38,310,000 families in the United States, and, though the median number of persons in the dwelling unit was 3.1, the median number of rooms in the dwelling unit was 4.6. Eighty-four percent of the dwelling units reported less than one person per room.[1] By providing the ordinary family with more than one

[1] Data from United States Department of Commerce, *Census of Housing: 1950*, Vol. I, Part I (Washington: Government Printing Office, 1953), p. xxx. For purposes of enumeration kitchens were counted as rooms, but bathrooms, hallways, and pantries were not. Many dwelling units were, of course, occupied by single persons or others not falling under the definition of a family, but the number of households—43,468,000 —was also less than the number of dwelling units.

room for sleeping, the economy thus produces a situation in which the child will sleep either in a room alone or in a room shared with his brothers or sisters. Even without allowing for the cases in which children may have separate rooms, these conditions mean that a very substantial percentage of children now sleep in a room alone, for, with the declining birth rate, we have reached a point at which an increasing proportion of families have one child or two children rather than the larger number which was at one time typical. For instance, in the most recent group of mothers who had completed their childbearing phase, according to the census, 19.5 percent had had one child and 23.4 had had two. Thus almost half of all families with offspring did not have more than two children throughout their duration. In the case of the first group, all the children were "only" children throughout their childhood, and in the second group half of the children were "only" children until the second child was born. To state this in another, and perhaps a more forcible, way, it has been shown that among American women who arrived at age thirty-four during the year 1949 and who had borne children up to that time, 26.7 percent had borne only one child, and 34.5 percent had borne only two.[2] If these tendencies persist, it would mean that, among families where there are children, hardly one in three will have more than two children.

The census has, of course, not got around to finding out how the new-style family, in its new-style dwelling unit, adjusts the life-practice to the space situation. But it is significant that America's most widely circulated book on the care of infants advises that "it is preferable that he [the infant] not sleep in his parents' room after he is about 12 months old," offers the opinion that "it is fine for each [child] to have a room of his own, if that's possible," and makes the sweeping assertion that "it's a sensible rule not to take a child into the parents' bed for any reason."[3] It seems clear beyond dispute that the household space provided by the economy of abundance has been used to emphasize the separateness, the apartness, if not the isolation, of the American child.

Not only the nourishment and housing, but also the clothing of the American infant are controlled by American abundance. For one of the most sweeping consequences of our abundance is that, in contrast to other peoples who keep their bodies warm primarily by wearing clothes, Americans

[2] Clyde V. Kiser, "Fertility Trends in the United States," *Journal of the American Statistical Association*, XLVII (1952), 31–33. Figures given by Kiser, based on research by P. K. Whelpton, also include childless women; but my concern here is with the sibling relationships of children and not with the fertility of women, and I have therefore based my statements upon the record of women who have borne children rather than upon women of childbearing age. My statement has no way of allowing for half-brothers and sisters born of different mothers or for differentiating the number of children who survive from the number born.

[3] Benjamin Spock, *The Pocket Book of Baby and Child Care* (New York: Pocket Books, Inc., 1946), pp. 96–97.

keep their bodies warm primarily by a far more expensive and even wasteful method: namely, by heating the buildings in which they are sheltered. Every American who has been abroad knows how much lighter is the clothing—especially the underclothing—of Americans than of people in countries like England and France, where the winters are far less severe than ours, and every American who can remember the conditions of a few decades ago knows how much lighter our clothing is than that of our grandparents. These changes have occurred because clothing is no longer the principal device for securing warmth. The oil furnace has not only displaced the open fireplace; it has also displaced the woolen undergarment and the vest.

This is a matter of considerable significance for adults but of far greater importance to infants, for adults discipline themselves to wear warm garments, submitting, for instance, to woolen underwear more or less voluntarily. But the infant knows no such discipline, and his garments or bedclothes must be kept upon him by forcible means. Hence primitive people, living in outdoor conditions, swaddle the child most rigorously, virtually binding him into his clothes, and breaking him to them almost as a horse is broken to the harness. Civilized peoples mitigate the rigor but still use huge pins or clips to frustrate the baby's efforts to kick off the blankets and free his limbs. In a state of nature, cold means confinement and warmth means freedom, so far as young humans are concerned. But abundance has given the American infant physical freedom by giving him physical warmth in cold weather.

In this connection it may be surmised that abundance has also given him a permissive system of toilet training. If our forebears imposed such training upon the child and we now wait for him to take the initiative in these matters himself, it is not wholly because the former held a grim Calvinistic doctrine of child-rearing that is philosophically contrary to ours. The fact was that the circumstances gave them little choice. A mother who was taking care of several babies, keeping them clean, making their clothes, washing their diapers in her own washtub, and doing this, as often as not, while another baby was on the way, had little choice but to hasten their fitness to toilet themselves. Today, on the contrary, the disposable diaper, the diaper service, and most of all the washing machine, not to mention the fact that one baby seldom presses upon the heels of another, make it far easier for the mother to indulge the child in a regime under which he will impose his own toilet controls in his own good time.

Thus the economy of plenty has influenced the feeding of the infant, his regime, and the physical setting within which he lives. These material conditions alone might be regarded as having some bearing upon the formation of his character, but the impact of abundance by no means ends at this point. In so far as it has an influence in determining what specific individuals shall initiate the infant into the ways of man and shall provide him with his formative impressions of the meaning of being a person, it must be regarded as even more vital. When it influences the nature of the relationships between these individuals and the infant, it must be recognized as reaching to the very essence of the process of character formation . . .

Abundance, then, has played a critical part in revolutionizing both the physical circumstances and the human associations which surround the American infant and child. These changes alone would warrant the hypothesis that abundance has profoundly affected the formation of character for such a child. But to extend this inquiry one step further, it may be worth while to consider how these altered conditions actually impinge upon the individual. Here, of course, is an almost unlimited field for investigation, and I shall only attempt to indicate certain crucial points at which abundance projects conditions that are basic in the life of the child.

One of these points concerns that cohesive force which holds the family together. The family is the one institution which touches all members of society most intimately, and it is perhaps the only social institution which touches young children directly. The sources from which the family draws its strength are, therefore, of basic importance. In the past, these sources were, it would seem, primarily economic. For agrarian society, marriage distinctively involved a division of labor. Where economic opportunity was narrowly restricted, the necessity for considering economic ways and means in connection with marriage led to the arrangement of matches by parents and to the institution of the dowry. The emotional bonds of affection, while always important, were not deemed paramount, and the ideal of romantic love played little or no part in the lives of ordinary people. Where it existed at all, it was as an upper-class luxury. (The very term "courtship" implies this upper-class orientation.) This must inevitably have meant that the partners in the majority of marriages demanded less from one another emotionally than do the partners of romantic love and that the emotional factor was less important to the stability of the marriage. Abundance, however, has played its part in changing this picture. On the American frontier, where capital for dowries was as rare as opportunity for prosperous marriage was plentiful, the dowry became obsolete. Later still, when abundance began to diminish the economic duties imposed upon the housewife, the function of marriage as a division of labor ceased to seem paramount, and the romantic or emotional factor assumed increasing importance. Abundance brought the luxury of romantic love within the reach of all, and, as it did so, emotional harmony became the principal criterion of success in a marriage, while lack of such harmony became a major threat to the existence of the marriage. The statistics of divorce give us a measure of the loss of durability in marriage, but they give us no measure of the factors of instability in the marriages which endure and no measure of the increased focus upon emotional satisfactions in such marriages. The children of enduring marriages, as well as the children of divorce, must inevitably feel the impact of this increased emphasis upon emotional factors, must inevitably sense the difference in the foundations of the institution which holds their universe in place.

In the rearing of a child, it would be difficult to imagine any factors more vital than the distinction between a permissive and an authoritarian regime or more vital than the age at which economic responsibility is imposed. In both these matters the modern American child lives under a very different dispensation from children in the past. We commonly think of these changes as results of our more enlightened or progressive or humanitarian ideas. We may even think of them as results of developments in the specific field of child psychology, as if the changes were simply a matter of our understanding these matters better than our grandparents. But the fact is that the authoritarian discipline of the child, within the authoritarian family, was but an aspect of the authoritarian social system that was linked with the economy of scarcity. Such a regime could never have been significantly relaxed within the family so long as it remained diagnostic in the society. Nor could it have remained unmodified within the family, once society began to abandon it in other spheres . . .

If abundance has fostered a more permissive regime for the child, amid circumstances of democratic equality within the family, it has no less certainly altered the entire process of imposing economic responsibility upon the child, hence the process of preparing the child for such responsibility. In the economy of scarcity, as I have remarked above, society could not afford to support any substantial quota of nonproductive members. Consequently, the child went to work when he was as yet young. He attended primary school for a much shorter school year than the child of today; only a minority attended high school; and only the favored few attended college. Even during the brief years of schooling, the child worked, in the home, on the farm, or even in the factory. But today the economy of abundance can afford to maintain a substantial proportion of the population in nonproductive status, and it assigns this role, sometimes against their will, to its younger and its elder members. It protracts the years of schooling, and it defers responsibilities for an unusually long span. It even enforces laws setting minimal ages for marrying. It extends the jurisdiction of juvenile courts to the eighteenth or the twentieth year of age.

Such exemption from economic responsibility might seem to imply a long and blissful youth free from strain for the child. But the delays in reaching economic maturity are not matched by comparable delays in other phases of growing up. On the contrary, there are many respects in which the child matures earlier. Physically, the child at the lower social level will actually arrive at adolescence a year or so younger than his counterpart a generation ago, because of improvement in standards of health and nutrition.[4] Culturally, the child is made aware of the allurements of sex at an earlier age, partly by his familiarity with the movies, television, and popular magazines,

[4] Alfred C. Kinsey *et al.*, *Sexual Behavior in the Human Male* (Philadelphia: W. B. Saunders Co., 1948), p. 397.

and partly by the practice of "dating" in the early teens. By the standards of his peer group, he is encouraged to demand expensive and mature recreations, similar to those of adults, at a fairly early age. By reason of the desire of his parents that he should excel in the mobility race and give proof during his youth of the qualities which will make him a winner in later life, he is exposed to the stimuli of competition before he leaves the nursery. Thus there is a kind of imbalance between the postponement of responsibility and the quickening of social maturity which may have contributed to make American adolescence a more difficult age than human biology alone would cause to be. Here, again, there are broad implications for the formation of character, and here, again, abundance is at work on both sides of the equation, for it contributes as much to the hastening of social maturity as it does to the prolongation of economic immaturity.

Some of these aspects of the rearing of children in the United States are as distinctively American, when compared with other countries, as any Yankee traits that have ever been attributed to the American people. In the multiplicity which always complicates social analysis, such aspects of child-rearing might be linked with a number of factors in American life. But one of the more evident and more significant links, it would seem certain, is with the factor of abundance. Such a tie is especially pertinent in this discussion, where the intention of the whole book has been to relate the study of character, as the historian would approach it, to the same subject as it is viewed by the behavioral scientist. In this chapter, especially, the attempt has been made to throw a bridge between the general historical force of economic abundance and the specific behavioral pattern of people's lives. Historical forces are too often considered only in their public and over-all effects, while private lives are interpreted without sufficient reference to the historical determinants which shape them. But no major force at work in society can possibly make itself felt at one of these levels without also having its impact at the other level. In view of this fact, the study of national character should not stand apart, as it has in the past, from the study of the process of character formation in the individual. In view of this fact, also, the effect of economic abundance is especially pertinent. For economic abundance is a factor whose presence and whose force may be clearly and precisely recognized in the most personal and intimate phases of the development of personality in the child. Yet, at the same time, the presence and the force of this factor are recognizable with equal certainty in the whole broad, general range of American experience, American ideals, and American institutions. At both levels, it has exercised a pervasive influence in the shaping of the American character.

Joseph R. McCarthy
Communists in the State Department

(1950)

In February, 1950, before a Republican Women's Club in Wheeling, West Virginia, the junior Senator from Wisconsin, Joseph R. McCarthy (1908–1957), read a speech in which he claimed to have the names of a number of Communists currently employed by the State Department in Washington. Though the charge was investigated and discredited, the speech put the Senator in the national limelight, where he stayed until 1954, when the Senate censured him for acting "contrary to Senatorial ethics and tending to bring the Senate into dishonor and disrepute, to obstruct the constitutional process of the Senate and to impair its dignity . . ."

In the four years between the initial speech, broadcast over radio station WWVA, and his formal censure, Senator McCarthy became one of the most powerful and controversial men in America. While his investigating committee failed to find any cases of Communist espionage in the government, his accusations of treason and disloyalty created a climate of repression and conformity in which a mere allegation might be tantamount to conviction. While his supporters claim McCarthy awakened the country to the threat of internal subversion, his critics maintain that McCarthy's demagoguery marked a low point in the history of civil liberties in America.

. . . Five years after a world war has been won, men's hearts should anticipate a long peace, and men's minds should be free from the heavy weight that comes with war. But this is not such a period—for this is not a period of peace. This is a time of the "cold war." This is a time when all the world is split into two vast, increasingly hostile camps—a time of a great armaments race . . .

At war's end we were physically the strongest nation on earth and, at least potentially, the most powerful intellectually and morally. Ours could have been the honor of being a beacon in the desert of destruction, a shining living proof that civilization was not yet ready to destroy itself. Unfortunately, we have failed miserably and tragically to arise to the opportunity.

The reason why we find ourselves in a position of impotency is not because our only powerful potential enemy has sent men to invade our shores, but rather because of the traitorous actions of those who have been treated so well by this Nation. It has not been the less fortunate or members

Joseph R. McCarthy, Speech at Wheeling, West Virginia, February 9, 1950. Reprinted in the *Congressional Record* (81st Congress, 2nd Session), pp. 1954 ff.

of minority groups who have been selling this Nation out, but rather those who have had all the benefits that the wealthiest nation on earth has had to offer—the finest homes, the finest college education, and the finest jobs in Government we can give.

This is glaringly true in the State Department. There the bright young men who are born with silver spoons in their mouths are the ones who have been the worst... In my opinion the State Department, which is one of the most important government departments, is thoroughly infested with Communists.

I have in my hand 57 cases of individuals who would appear to be either card-carrying members or certainly loyal to the Communist Party, but who nevertheless are still helping to shape our foreign policy.

One thing to remember in discussing the Communists in our Government is that we are not dealing with spies who get 30 pieces of silver to steal the blueprints of a new weapon. We are dealing with a far more sinister type of activity because it permits the enemy to guide and shape our policy...

This brings us down to the case of one Alger Hiss who is important not as an individual any more, but rather because he is so representative of a group in the State Department. It is unnecessary to go over the sordid events showing how he sold out the Nation which had given him so much. Those are rather fresh in all of our minds.

However, it should be remembered that the facts in regard to his connection with this international Communist spy ring were made known to the then Under Secretary of State Berle three days after Hitler and Stalin signed the Russo-German alliance pact. At that time one Whittaker Chambers—who was also part of the spy ring—apparently decided that with Russia on Hitler's side he could not longer betray our Nation to Russia. He gave Under Secretary of State Berle—and this is all a matter of record—practically all, if not more, of the facts upon which Hiss' conviction was based.

Under Secretary Berle promptly contacted Dean Acheson and received word in return that Acheson (and I quote) "could vouch for Hiss absolutely" —at which time the matter was dropped...

As you know, very recently the Secretary of State proclaimed his loyalty to a man guilty of what has always been considered as the most abominable of all crimes—of being a traitor to the people who gave him a position of great trust. The Secretary of State in attempting to justify his continued devotion to the man who sold out the Christian world to the atheistic world, referred to Christ's Sermon on the Mount as a justification and reason therefor, and the reaction of the American people to this would have made Abraham Lincoln happy.

When this pompous diplomat in striped pants, with a phony British accent, proclaimed to the American people that Christ on the Mount endorsed Communism, high treason, and betrayal of a sacred trust, the blasphemy was so great that it awakened the dormant indignation of the American people. He has lighted the spark which is resulting in a moral uprising and will end only when the whole sorry mess of twisted, warped thinkers are swept from the national scene so that we may have a new birth of national honesty and decency in Government.

Allen Ginsberg
Another View of America

(1956)

Reaction to economic abundance and intellectual conformity took diverse and varied forms. None was more interesting, however, than the advent of the Beat (for "beatitude") Generation of writers and poets such as Jack Kerouac, Lawrence Ferlinghetti, and Allen Ginsberg (1926–). Coupling the intuitive mysticism of the Eastern religious cults with a frenetic discharge of energy and movement that was distinctively American, the Beats vehemently denied the conformism and inhibitions of the dominant culture. Recalling the mood and much of the posture of the romantic intellectuals of the pre-Civil War decades, the Beat writers provided an illuminating dissent from middle-class values, one which anticipated the Hippie movement of the 1960's.

Central to the literature of the Beat Generation was Allen Ginsberg's *Howl* (1956), a collection of poems dedicated to his friend, Jack Kerouac. *Howl* expressed disgust and revulsion at the crass materialism and timid intellectualism of America. Filled with language and metaphors designed to shock the bourgeois, *Howl* served as a point of departure for numerous critics of American culture and values. "America," reprinted below, sums up Ginsberg's dissenting position.

America I've given you all and now I'm nothing.
America two dollars and twentyseven cents January 17, 1956.
I can't stand on my own mind.
America when will we end the human war?
Go fuck yourself with your atom bomb.
I don't feel good don't bother me.
I won't write my poem till I'm in my right mind.
America when will you be angelic?
When will you take off your clothes?
When will you look at yourself through the grave?
When will you be worthy of your million Trotskyites?

Allen Ginsberg, "America" from *Howl* (San Francisco, 1956), pp. 31–34.

America why are your libraries full of tears?
America when will you send your eggs to India?
I'm sick of your insane demands.
When can I go into the supermarket and buy what I need with my good looks?
America after all it is you and I who are perfect not the next world.
Your machinery is too much for me.
You made me want to be a saint.
There must be some other way to settle this argument.
Burroughs is in Tangiers I don't think he'll come back it's sinister.
Are you being sinister or is this some form of practical joke?
I'm trying to come to the point.
I refuse to give up my obsession.
America stop pushing I know what I'm doing.
America the plum blossoms are falling.
I haven't read the newspapers for months, everyday somebody goes on trial for murder.
America I feel sentimental about the Wobblies.
America I used to be a communist when I was a kid I'm not sorry.

I smoke marijuana every chance I get.
I sit in my house for days on end and stare at the roses in the closet.
When I go to Chinatown I get drunk and never get laid.
My mind is made up there's going to be trouble.
You should have seen me reading Marx.
My psychoanalyst thinks I'm perfectly right.
I won't say the Lord's Prayer.
I have mystical visions and cosmic vibrations.
America I still haven't told you what you did to Uncle Max after he came over from Russia.

I'm addressing you.
Are you going to let your emotional life be run by Time Magazine?
I'm obsessed by Time Magazine.
I read it every week.
Its cover stares at me every time I slink past the corner candystore.
I read it in the basement of the Berkeley Public Library.
It's always telling me about responsibility. Businessmen are serious. Movie producers are serious. Everybody's serious but me.
It occurs to me that I am America.
I am talking to myself again.

Asia is rising against me.
I haven't got a chinaman's chance.

I'd better consider my national resources.
My national resources consist of two joints of marijuana millions of genitals and unpublishable private literature that goes 1400 miles an hour and twentyfive-thousand mental institutions.
I say nothing about my prisons nor the millions of underprivileged who live in my flowerpots under the light of five hundred suns.
I have abolished the whorehouses of France, Tangiers is the next to go.
My ambition is to be President despite the fact that I'm a Catholic.

America how can I write a holy litany in your silly mood?
I will continue like Henry Ford my strophes are as individual as his automobiles more so they're all different sexes.
America I will sell you strophes $2500 apiece $500 down on your old strophe
America free Tom Mooney
America save the Spanish Loyalists
America Sacco & Vanzetti must not die
America I am the Scottsboro boys.
America when I was seven momma took me to Communist Cell meetings they sold us garbanzos a handful per ticket a ticket costs a nickel and the speeches were free everybody was angelic and sentimental about the workers it was all so sincere you have no idea what a good thing the party was in 1835 Scott Nearing was a grand old man a real mensch Mother Bloor made me cry I once saw Israel Amter plain. Everybody must have been a spy.
America you don't really want to go to war.
America it's them bad Russians.
Them Russians them Russians and them Chinamen. And them Russians.
The Russia wants to eat us alive. The Russia's power mad. She wants to take our cars from out our garages.
Her wants to grab Chicago. Her needs a Red Readers' Digest. Her wants our auto plants in Siberia. Him big bureaucracy running our fillingstations.

That no good. Ugh. Him make Indians learn read. Him need big black niggers. Hah. Her make us all work sixteen hours a day. Help.
America this is quite serious.
America this is the impression I get from looking in the television set.
America is this correct?
I'd better get right down to the job.
It's true I don't want to join the Army or turn lathes in precision parts factories, I'm nearsighted and psychopathic anyway.
America I'm putting my queer shoulder to the wheel.

Dwight D. Eisenhower
Wisdom, Peace, and Militarism

(1961)

The departure from public life of President Eisenhower in January, 1961, provided the occasion for one of the President's most important and memorable public addresses. While the existence of vast and burgeoning "military-industrial complex" had been recognized long before his retirement, Eisenhower's recognition of the problem in his Farewell Address gave it new urgency. As a professional military man himself, that Eisenhower should take cognizance of the situation as problematic, let alone make it the focus of his last public address, revealed how serious the situation of the "warfare state" had become. Indeed, it is largely because of President Eisenhower's final warning on the subject that the term "military-industrial complex" entered the national vocabulary, and that the relationship of the military to nominally private manufacturers caused such widespread concern in the 1960's. Eisenhower's Farewell Address stands with Washington's as a timely and statesmanlike pronouncement of what one citizen's experience had distilled into wisdom.

My fellow Americans, three days from now, after half a century in the service of our country, I shall lay down the responsibilities of office as, in traditional and solemn ceremony, the authority of the Presidency is vested in my successor.

This evening I come to you with a message of leavetaking and farewell, and to share a few final thoughts with you, my countrymen.

Like every other citizen, I wish the new President, and all who will labor with him, Godspeed. I pray that the coming years will be blessed with peace and prosperity for all.

Our people expect their President and the Congress to find essential agreement on issues of great moment, the wise resolution of which will better shape the future of the Nation.

My own relations with the Congress, which began on a remote and tenuous basis when, long ago, a Member of the Senate appointed me to West Point, have since ranged to the intimate during the war and immediate postwar period, and, finally, to the mutually interdependent during these past eight years.

In this final relationship, the Congress and the administration have, on most vital issues, cooperated well, to serve the national good rather than

Dwight D. Eisenhower, "Farewell Address," *Congressional Record* (February 16, 1961), pp. 2210–11.

mere partisanship, and so have assured that the business of the Nation should go forward. So, my official relationship with the Congress ends in a feeling, on my part, of gratitude that we have been able to do so much together.

We now stand ten years past the midpoint of a century that has witnessed four major wars among great nations. Three of these involved our own country. Despite these holocausts America is today the strongest, the most influential, and most productive nation in the world. Understandably proud of this preeminence, we yet realize that America's leadership and prestige depend, not merely upon our unmatched material progress, riches, and military strength, but on how we use our power in the interests of world peace and human betterment.

Throughout America's adventure in free government our basic purposes have been to keep the peace; to foster progress in human achievement, and to enhance liberty, dignity, and integrity among people and among nations. To strive for less would be unworthy of a free and religious people. Any future traceable to arrogance, or our lack of comprehension or readiness to sacrifice would inflict upon us grievous hurt both at home and abroad.

Progress toward these noble goals is persistently threatened by the conflict now engulfing the world. It commands our whole attention, absorbs our very being. We face a hostile ideology—global in scope, atheistic in character, ruthless in purpose, and insidious in method. Unhappily, the danger it poses promises to be of indefinite duration. To meet it successfully, there is called for, not so much the emotional and transitory sacrifices of crisis, but rather those which enable us to carry forward steadily, surely, and without complaint the burdens of a prolonged and complex struggle —with liberty the stake. Only thus shall we remain, despite every provocation, on our charted course toward permanent peace and human betterment.

Crises there will continue to be. In meeting them, whether foreign or domestic, great or small, there is a recurring temptation to feel costly action could become the miraculous solution to all current difficulties. A huge increase in newer elements of our defense; development of unrealistic programs to cure every ill in agriculture; a dramatic expansion in basic and applied research—these and many other possibilities, each possibly promising in itself, may be suggested as the only way to the road we wish to travel.

But each proposal must be weighed in the light of a broader consideration: The need to maintain balance in and among national programs—balance between the private and the public economy, balance between cost and hoped-for advantage—balance between the clearly necessary and the comfortably desirable; balance between our essential requirements as a nation and the duties imposed by the Nation upon the individual; balance between actions of the moment and the national welfare of the future. Good judgment seeks balance and progress; lack of it eventually finds imbalance and frustration.

The record of many decades stands as proof that our people and their Government have, in the main, understood these truths and have responded to them well, in the face of stress and threat. But threats, new in kind or degree, constantly arise. I mention two only.

A vital element in keeping the peace is our military establishment. Our arms must be mighty, ready for instant action, so that no potential aggressor may be tempted to risk his own destruction.

Our military organization today bears little relation to that known by any of my predecessors in peacetime, or indeed by the fighting men of World War II or Korea.

Until the latest of our world conflicts, the United States had no armaments industry. American makers of plowshares could, with time and as required, make swords as well. But now we can no longer risk emergency improvision of national defense; we have been compelled to create a permanent armaments industry of vast proportions.

Added to this, 3.5 million men and women are directly engaged in the defense establishment. We annually spend on military security more than the net income of all U.S. corporations.

This conjunction of an immense military establishment and a large arms industry is new in the American experience. The total influence—economic, political, even spiritual—is felt in every city, every state house, every office of the Federal Government.

We recognize the imperative need for this development. Yet we must not fail to comprehend its grave implications. Our toil, resources, and livelihood are all involved; so is the very structure of our society.

In the councils of government, we must guard against the acquisition of unwarranted influence, whether sought or unsought, by the military-industrial complex. The potential for the disastrous rise of misplaced power exists and will persist.

We must never let the weight of this combination endanger our liberties or democratic processes. We should take nothing for granted. Only an alert and knowledgeable citizenry can compel the proper meshing of the huge industrial and military machinery of defense without peaceful methods and goals, so that security and liberty may prosper together.

Akin to, and largely responsible for the sweeping changes in our industrial-military posture, has been the technological revolution during recent decades.

In this revolution, research has become central; it also becomes more formalized, complex, and costly. A steadily increasing share is conducted for, by, or at the direction of, the Federal Government.

Today, the solitary inventor, tinkering in his shop, has been overshadowed by task forces of scientists in laboratories and testing fields. In the same fashion, the free university, historically the fountainhead of free ideas and scientific discovery, has experienced a revolution in the conduct of research.

Partly because of the huge costs involved, a Government contract becomes virtually a substitute for intellectual curiosity. For every old blackboard there are now hundreds of new electronic computers.

The prospect of domination of the Nation's scholars by Federal employment, project allocations, and the power of money is ever present—and is gravely to be regarded.

Yet, in holding scientific research and discovery in respect, as we should, we must also be alert to the equal and opposite danger that public policy could itself become the captive of a scientific-technological elite.

It is the task of statesmanship to mold, to balance, and to integrate these and other forces, new, and old, within the principles of our democratic system—ever aiming toward the supreme goals of our free society.

Another factor in maintaining balance involves the element of time. As we peer into society's future, we—you and I, and our Government—must avoid the impulse to live only for today, plundering, for our own ease and convenience, the precious resources of tomorrow.

We cannot mortgage the material assets of our grandchildren without risking the loss also of their political and spiritual heritage. We want democracy to survive for all generations to come, not to become the insolvent phantom of tomorrow.

Down the long lane of the history yet to be written America knows that this world of ours, ever growing smaller, must avoid becoming a community of dreadful fear and hate, and be, instead, a proud consideration [*sic*] of mutual trust and respect.

Such a confederation must be one of equals. The weakest must come to the conference table with the same confidence as do we, protected as we are by our moral, economic, and military strength. That table, though scarred by many past frustrations, cannot be abandoned for the certain agony of the battlefield.

Disarmament with mutual honor and confidence, is a continuing imperative. Together we must learn how to compose differences, not with arms, but with intellect and decent purpose. Because this need is so sharp and apparent I confess that I lay down my official responsibilities in this field with a definite sense of disappointment.

As one who has witnessed the horror and lingering sadness of war—as one who knows that another war could utterly destroy this civilization which has been so slowly and painfully built over thousands of years—I wish I could say tonight that a lasting peace is in sight.

Happily, I can say that war has been avoided. Steady progress toward our ultimate goal has been made. But, so much remains to be done. As a private citizen, I shall never cease to do what little I can to help the world advance along that road.

So—in this my last good night to you as your President—I thank you for the many opportunities you have given me for public service in war and peace. I trust that in that service you find some things worthy; as for the rest of it, I know you will find ways to improve performance in the future.

You and I—my fellow citizens—need to be strong in our faith that all nations, under God, will reach the goal of peace with justice. May we be ever unswerving in devotion to principle, confident but humble with power, diligent in pursuit of the Nation's great goals.

To all the peoples of the world, I once more give expression to America's prayerful and continuing aspiration:

We pray that peoples of all faiths, all races, all nations, may have their great human needs satisfied; that those now denied opportunity shall come to enjoy it to the full; that all who yearn for freedom may experience its spiritual blessings; that those who have freedom will understand, also, its heavy responsibilities; that all who are insensitive to the needs of others will learn charity; that the scourges of poverty, disease, and ignorance will be made to disappear from the earth, and that, in the goodness of time, all peoples will come to live together in a peace guaranteed by the binding force of mutual respect and love.

What Happens to a Dream Deferred?

The United States Supreme Court
Separate and Unequal

(1954)

In the famous case of *Brown, et al.* v. *Board of Education of Topeka, et al.*, the Supreme Court unanimously ruled that racially separated systems of public education were unconstitutional. Reversing a half-century old position on segregation, the Court now declared that segregated school systems were intrinsically unequal, thus striking down the "separate but equal" doctrine which had stood since *Plessy* v. *Ferguson* in 1896. The Court based its ruling on the clause in the Fourteenth Amendment which guaranteed "equal protection" under the law to all citizens.

The May 17, 1954, decision (delivered by Chief Justice Warren) crystallized an issue which had been smouldering since 1863, when President Lincoln made public his Emancipation Proclamation ending slavery. Though there was widespread resistance to the implementation of the Court's ruling, in *Brown* v. *Topeka* the Federal government put itself on record as favoring integration as the solution to the race problem, and further, that the constitutional provisions for equality for all citizens should not be abridged.

These cases come to us from the States of Kansas, South Carolina, Virginia, and Delaware. They are premised on different facts and different local conditions, but a common legal question justifies their consideration together in this consolidated opinion.

In each of the cases, minors of the Negro race, through their legal representatives, seek the aid of the courts in obtaining admission to the public schools of their community on a nonsegregated basis. In each instance, they had been denied admission to schools attended by white children under laws requiring or permitting segregation according to race.

This segregation was alleged to deprive the plaintiffs of the equal protection of the laws under the Fourteenth Amendment. In each of the cases other

Brown, et al. v. *Board of Education of Topeka, et al.*, 347 U.S. 483 (1954).

than the Delaware case, a three-judge Federal District Court denied relief to the plaintiffs on the so-called "Separate but Equal" doctrine announced by this court in *Plessy* v. *Ferguson*, 163 U.S. 537.

Under that doctrine, equality of treatment is accorded when the races are provided substantially equal facilities, even though these facilities be separate. In the Delaware case, the Supreme Court of Delaware adhered to that doctrine, but ordered that the plaintiffs be admitted to the white schools because of their superiority to the Negro schools.

The plaintiffs contend that segregated public schools are not "equal" and cannot be made "equal," and that hence, they are deprived of the equal protection of the laws. Because of the obvious importance of the question presented, the Court took jurisdiction. Argument was heard in the 1952 term, and reargument was heard this term on certain questions propounded by the Court.

Postwar Sources Inconclusive

Reargument was largely devoted to the circumstances surrounding the adoption of the Fourteenth Amendment in 1868. It covered, exhaustively, consideration of the Amendment in Congress, ratification by the states, then existing practices in racial segregation, and the views of proponents and opponents of the Amendment.

This discussion and our own investigation convince us that, although these sources cast some light, it is not enough to resolve the problem with which we are faced.

At best, they are inconclusive. The most avid proponents of the postwar Amendments undoubtedly intended them to remove all legal distinctions among "all persons born or naturalized in the United States."

Their opponents, just as certainly, were antagonistic to both the letter and the spirit of the Amendments and wished them to have the most limited effect. What others in Congress and the State Legislature had in mind cannot be determined with any degree of certainty.

An additional reason for the inclusive nature of the Amendment's history, with respect to segregated schools, is the status of public education at that time. In the South, the movement toward free common schools, supported by general taxation, had not yet taken hold. Education of white children was largely in the hands of private groups. Education of Negroes was almost nonexistent, and practically all of the race was illiterate. In fact, any education of Negroes was forbidden by law in some states.

Today, in contrast, many Negroes have achieved outstanding success in the arts and sciences as well as in the business and professional world. It is true that public education has already advanced further in the North, but the effect of the Amendment on Northern States was generally ignored in the Congressional debates.

Even in the North, the conditions of public education did not approximate those existing today. The curriculum was usually rudimentary; ungraded schools were common in rural areas; the school term was but three months a year in many states; and compulsory school attendance was virtually unknown.

As a consequence, it is not surprising that there should be so little in the history of the Fourteenth Amendment relating to its intended effect on public education.

Half Century of Cases

In the first cases in this court construing the Fourteenth Amendment, decided shortly after its adoption, the court interpreted it as proscribing all state-imposed discriminations against the Negro race.

The doctrine of "Separate but Equal" did not make its appearance in this court until 1896 in the case of *Plessy* v. *Ferguson, supra*, involving not education but transportation.

American courts have since labored with the doctrine for over half a century. In this court, there have been six cases involving the "Separate but Equal" doctrine in the field of public education.

In *Cumming* v. *County Board of Education*, 175 U.S. 528, and *Gong Lum* v. *Rice*, 275 U.S. 78, the validity of the doctrine itself was not challenged. In most recent cases, all on the graduate school level, inequality was found in that specific benefits enjoyed by white students were denied to Negro students of the same educational qualifications. *Missouri ex rel. Gaines* v. *Canada*, 305 U.S. 337; *Sipuel* v. *Oklahoma*, 332 U.S. 331; *Sweatt* v. *Painter*, 339 U.S. 629; *McLaurin* v. *Oklahoma State Regents*, 339 U.S. 637.

In nine of these cases it was necessary to reexamine the doctrine to grant relief to the Negro plaintiff. And in *Sweatt* v. *Painter*, supra, the court expressly reserved decision on the question whether *Plessy* v. *Ferguson* should be held inapplicable to public education.

In the instant cases, that question is directly presented. Here, unlike *Sweatt* v. *Painter*, there are findings below that the Negro and white schools involved have been equalized, or are being equalized, with respect to buildings, curricula, qualifications and salaries of teachers, and other "tangible" factors.

Our decision, therefore, cannot turn on merely a comparison of these tangible factors in the Negro and white schools involved in each of the cases. We must look instead to the effect of segregation itself on public education.

In approaching this problem, we cannot turn the clock back to 1868, when the Amendment was adopted, or even to 1896, when *Plessy* v. *Ferguson* was written. We must consider public education in the light of its full development and its present place in American life throughout the nation. Only in this way can it be determined if segregation in public schools deprives these plaintiffs of the equal protection of the laws.

A Function of Government

Today, education is perhaps the most important function of state and local governments. Compulsory school attendance laws and the great expenditures for education both demonstrate our recognition of the importance of education to our democratic society. It is required in the performance of our most basic public responsibilities, even service in the armed forces. It is the very foundation of good citizenship.

Today, it is a principal instrument in awakening the child to cultural values, in preparing him for later professional training, and in helping him to adjust normally to his environment.

In these days, it is doubtful that any child may reasonably be expected to succeed in life if he is denied the opportunity of an education. Such an opportunity, where the state has undertaken to provide it, is a right which must be made available to all on equal terms.

We come then to the question presented: Does segregation of children in public schools solely on the basis of race, even though the physical facilities and other "tangible" factors may be equal, deprive the children of the minority group of equal educational opportunities? We believe that it does.

In *Sweatt* v. *Painter, supra*, in finding that a segregated law school for Negroes could not provide them equal educational opportunities, this court relied in large part on "those qualities which are incapable of objective measurement but which make for greatness in a law school."

In *McLaurin* v. *Oklahoma State Regents, supra*, the court, in requiring that a Negro admitted to a white graduate school be treated like all other students, again resorted to intangible considerations: ". . . his ability to study, engage in discussions and exchange views with other students, and, in general, to learn his profession."

Such considerations apply with added force to children in grade and high schools. To separate them from others of similar age and qualifications solely because of their race generates a feeling of inferiority as to their status in the community that may affect their hearts and minds in a way unlikely ever to be undone.

The effect of this separation on their educational opportunities was well stated by a finding in the Kansas case by a court which nevertheless felt compelled to rule against the Negro plaintiffs:

> "Segregation of white and colored children in public schools has a detrimental effect upon the colored children. The impact is greater when it has the sanction of the law; for the policy of separating the races is usually interpreted as denoting the inferiority of the Negro group.
>
> "A sense of inferiority affects the motivation of a child to learn. Segregation with the sanction of law, therefore, has a tendency to retard the educational and mental development of Negro children and to deprive them of some of the benefits they would receive in a racially integrated school system."

Whatever may have been the extent of psychological knowledge at the time of *Plessy* v. *Ferguson*, this finding is amply supported by modern authority. Any language in *Plessy* v. *Ferguson* contrary to this finding is rejected.

We conclude that in the field of public education the doctrine of "Separate but Equal" has no place. Separate educational facilities are inherently unequal. Therefore, we hold that the plaintiffs and others similarly situated for whom the actions have been brought are, by reason of the segregation complained of, deprived of the equal protection of the laws guaranteed by the Fourteenth Amendment. This disposition makes unnecessary any discussion whether such segregation also violates the Due Process Clause of the Fourteenth Amendment.

"Separate but Equal" Denied

Because these are class actions, because of the wide applicability of this decision, and because of the great variety of local conditions, the formulation of decrees in these cases presents problems of considerable complexity. On reargument, the consideration of appropriate relief was necessarily subordinated to the primary question—the constitutionality of segregation in public education.

We have now announced that such segregation is a denial of the equal protection of the laws. In order that we may have the full assistance of the parties in formulating decrees, the cases will be restored to the docket, and the parties are requested to present further argument on Questions 4 and 5 previously propounded by the court for the reargument this term.

The Attorney General of the United States is again invited to participate. The Attorneys General of the states requiring or permitting segregation in public education will also be permitted to appear as *amici curiae* upon request to do so by September 15, 1954, and submission of briefs by October 1, 1954.

James Reston
Sociology and the Law

(1954)

Reaction to the May 17 Supreme Court decision was instantaneous and electric. Liberals cheered the reversal of the Court's position on integrated schooling, while racial (and legal) conservatives condemned the Court's

---

James Reston, "A Sociological Decision," *The New York Times*, Tuesday, May 18, 1954.

failure to follow the precedent of *Plessy* v. *Ferguson.* Ignoring the various civil rights decisions which since World War II had been leading up to the May 17 ruling, critics of the Court argued that its decision was based on sentiment and not on law.

Though a supporter of the decision, James Reston (1909–) of *The New York Times* agreed that the Court had relied more heavily on sociological and psychological data than on legal precedent in justifying its ruling. In pointing up the highlights of the decision, Reston related the Court's position to earlier "Brandeis type" judgments and to the contemporary requirements of a democracy.

The Supreme Court not only upheld Justice John M. Harlan's famous dictum that "the Constitution is colorblind" today but also based its decision on the primacy of the general welfare.

At a time when the Executive and Legislative Branches of the Government were involved in a major conflict over their respective powers, the principal court of the land managed to agree unanimously on what heretofore had been one of the most controversial questions of the century.

In ruling out racial segregation in the nation's public schools, it rejected history, philosophy, and custom as the major basis for its decision and accepted instead Justice Benjamin N. Cardoza's test of contemporary social justice.

Relying more on the social scientists than on legal precedents—a procedure often in controversy in the past—the court insisted on equality of the mind and heart rather than on equal school facilities:

> "To separate them [Negro children] from others of similar age and qualifications solely because of their race," Chief Justice Earl Warren said for the court, "generates a feeling of inferiority as to their status in the community that may affect their hearts and minds in a way unlikely ever to be undone."

The court's opinion read more like an expert paper on sociology than a Supreme Court opinion. It sustained the argument of experts in education, sociology, psychology, psychiatry, and anthropology in the Gebhart case, namely, that even with equal school buildings, segregated Negro children received a substantially inferior education.

Two arguments seemed to impress the court: the testimony in the South Carolina, Kansas, and Delaware cases on the effects of segregation on the Negro students in those states; and the testimony of social scientists on the effects of discrimination on personality development.

In the South Carolina case, witnesses testified that compulsory racial segregation in the public schools of that state injured Negro students by:

Impairing their ability to learn.

Deterring the development of their personalities.

Depriving them of equal status in the school community.

Destroying their self-respect.

Denying them full opportunity for democratic social development.

Subjecting them to the prejudices of others.

Stamping them with a badge of inferiority.

The argument in the South Carolina case which the court sustained was this:

> In a democracy, citizens from every group, no matter what their social or economic status or their religious or ethnic origins, are expected to participate widely in the making of important public decisions.
>
> The public school, even more than the family, the church, business institutions, has become an effective agency for giving to all people that broad background of attitudes and skills required to function effectively as participants in a democracy.

Thus, this argument continues, "education" comprehends the entire process of developing and training the mental, physical, and moral powers and capacities of human beings and these capacities cannot be developed properly, even in the finest of school buildings, if the students are segregated from the majority of the law.

The appellants in the case presented to the court a brief by what they described as a "consensus of social scientists with respect to the issue . . ." This "Brandeis-type" brief seems to contain the major arguments on this key question of the detrimental effects of segregation in the schools.

The report argued that segregation damaged not only the minority Negro students in the segregated schools but the majority group students as well. It made these points about the effects on Negro children:

> Negro children observing that they are kept apart from the white children who are better treated, "often react with feelings of inferiority and a sense of personal humiliation."
>
> Some Negro children—usually of the lower socio-economic classes—"may react by overt aggressions and hostility directed toward their own group or members of the dominant group."
>
> Middle-class and upper-class minority group children are "likely to react to their racial frustrations and conflicts by withdrawal and submissive behavior."
>
> "Minority group children of all social and economic classes," the report said, "often react with a generally defeatist attitude and a lowering of personal ambitions.

"This, for example, is reflected in a lowering of pupil morale and a depression of the educational aspiration level among minority group children in segregated schools.

"In producing such effects, segregated schools impair the ability of the child to profit from the educational opportunities provided him."

The report to the court also noted that white children, under these circumstances, were hurt because they were encouraged to think of whole groups of people as inferior. This, it was contended, set up conflicts in the white child's mind because he was taught principles of equality that were not applied to the Negro children.

The report also made these points:

> The child who is compelled to attend a segregated school may be able to cope with ordinary expressions of prejudice by regarding the prejudiced person as evil or misguided; but he cannot readily cope with symbols of authority, the full force of the authority of the state—the school or the school board, in this instance—in the same manner.
>
> Segregation leads to a blockage in the communications and interaction between the two groups. Such blockages tend to increase mutual suspicion, distrust and hostility.
>
> Segregation not only perpetuates rigid stereotypes and reinforces negative attitudes toward members of the other group, but also leads to the development of a social climate within which violent breaks of racial tensions are likely to occur.

Thus the court today added one more illustration to Justice Cardoza's power of prophecy:

> When the social needs demand one settlement rather than another, . . . there are times when we must bend symmetry, ignore history, and sacrifice custom in the pursuit of other and larger ends.
>
> From history and philosophy and custom, we pass, therefore, to the force which in our day and generation is becoming the greatest of them all, the power of social justice which finds its outlet and expression in the method of sociology . . .
>
> The final cause of law is the welfare of society . . .

Martin Luther King
On Love and Freedom

(1963)

During the late 1950's Negro Americans began to press resolutely for the full extension of their rights as citizens. First, a series of economic boycotts and sit-ins were used to pressure Southern whites into abandoning segregated public facilities. Negro leaders soon recognized, however, that the key to full citizenship lay in the use of political power through exercise of the right to vote. Thus by the early 1960's the attention of the civil rights leaders shifted to the issue of voter registration.

In Birmingham, Alabama, in the spring of 1963, attempts to register Negro voters were met by official harassment and police brutality. Reverend Martin Luther King (1929–1968), who had emerged as the leader of the civil rights movement in the 1950's, was jailed, and his conduct was criticized by a number of his fellow clergymen. Dr. King replied in the following letter, which reveals not only his own views but the reasons behind the increasing militancy of Black Americans in the late 1950's and early 1960's.

My Dear Fellow Clergymen:

While confined here in the Birmingham city jail I came across your recent statement calling my present activities "unwise and untimely." Seldom do I pause to answer criticism of my work and ideas. If I sought to answer all the criticisms that cross my desk, my secretaries would have little time for anything other than such correspondence in the course of the day, and I would have no time for constructive work. But since I feel that you are men of genuine good will and that your criticisms are sincerely set forth, I want to try to answer your statement in what I hope will be patient and reasonable terms. . . .

You deplore the demonstrations taking place in Birmingham. But your statement, I am sorry to say, fails to express a similar concern for the conditions that brought about the demonstrations. I am sure that none of you would want to rest content with the superficial kind of social analysis that deals merely with effects and does not grapple with underlying causes. It is unfortunate that demonstrations are taking place in Birmingham, but it is even more unfortunate that the city's white power structure left the Negro community with no alternative.

In any nonviolent campaign there are four basic steps; collection of the facts to determine whether injustices exist, negotations, self-purification and direct action. We have gone through all these steps in Birmingham. There can be no gainsaying the fact that racial injustice engulfs this community. Birmingham is probably the most thoroughly segregated city in the United States. Its ugly record of police brutality is widely known. Its unjust treatment of Negroes in the courts is a notorious reality. There have been more unsolved bombings of Negro homes and churches in Birmingham than in any other city in the nation. These are the hard, brutal facts of the case. On the basis of these conditions Negro leaders sought to negotiate with the city fathers. But the latter consistently refused to engage in good-faith negotiation . . .

You may well ask, "Why direct action? Why sit-ins, marches, etc.? Isn't negotiation a better path?" You are quite right in calling for negotiation. Indeed, this is the very purpose of direct action. Nonviolent direct action seeks to foster such a tension that a community which has constantly refused to negotiate is forced to confront the issue. It seeks so to dramatize the issue that it can no longer be ignored. My citing the creation of tension as part of the work of the nonviolent resister may sound rather shocking. But I readily acknowledge that I am not afraid of the word "tension." I have earnestly opposed violent tension, but there is a type of constructive, nonviolent tension which is necessary for growth. Just as Socrates felt that it was necessary to create a tension in the mind so that individuals could shake off the bondage of myths and half-truths and rise to the realm of creative analysis and objective appraisal, so must we see the need for nonviolent gadflies to create the kind of tension in society that will help men rise from the dark depths of prejudice and racism to the majestic heights of understanding and brotherhood.

The purpose of our direct action program is to create a situation so crisis-packed that it will inevitably open the door to negotiation. I therefore concur with you in your call for negotiation. Too long has our beloved southland been bogged down in a tragic effort to live in monologue rather than dialogue.

You express a great deal of anxiety over our willingness to break laws. This is certainly a legitimate concern. Since we so diligently urge people to obey the Supreme Court's decision of 1954 outlawing segregation in the public schools, at first glance it may seem rather paradoxical for us consciously to break laws. One may well ask, "How can you advocate breaking some laws and obeying others?" The answer lies in the fact that there are two types of laws; just and unjust. I agree with St. Augustine that "an unjust law is no law at all."

Now what is the difference between the two? How does one determine whether a law is just or unjust? A just law is a man-made code that squares with the moral law or the law of God. An unjust law is a code that is out of harmony with the moral law. To put it in the terms of St. Thomas Aquinas, an unjust law is a human law that is not rooted in eternal law and natural law, any law that uplifts human personality is just. Any law that degrades human personality is unjust. All segregation statutes are unjust because segregation distorts the soul and damages the personality. It gives the segregator a false sense of superiority and the segregated a false sense of inferiority. Segregation, to use the terminology of the Jewish philosopher Martin Buber, substitutes an "I-it" relationship for an "I-thou" relationship and ends up relegating persons to the status of things. Hence segregation is not only politically, economically and sociologically unsound, it is sinful. Paul Tillich has said that sin is separation. Is not segregation an existential expression of man's tragic separation, his awful estrangement, his terrible sinfulness? Thus it is that I can urge men to disobey segregation ordinances, for such ordinances are morally wrong. . .

I must make two honest confessions to you, my Christian and Jewish brothers. First, I must confess that over the past few years I have been gravely disappointed with the white moderate. I have almost reached the regrettable conclusion that the Negro's great stumbling block in his stride toward freedom is not the White Citizen's Counciler or the Ku Klux Klanner but the white moderate who is more devoted to "order" than to justice; who prefers a negative peace which is the absence of tension to a positive peace which is the presence of justice; who constantly says "I agree with you in the goal you seek, but I cannot agree with your methods"; who paternalistically believes he can set the timetable for another man's freedom; who lives by a mythical concept of time and who constantly advises the Negro to wait for a "more convenient season." Shallow understanding from people of good will is more frustrating than absolute misunderstanding from people of ill will. Lukewarm acceptance is much more bewildering than outright rejection.

I had hoped that the white moderate would understand that law and order exist for the purpose of establishing justice and that when they fail in this purpose they block social progress. I had hoped that the white moderate would understand that the present tension in the south is a necessary phase of the transition from an obnoxious negative peace, in which the Negro passively accepted his unjust plight, to a substantive and positive peace, in which all men will respect the dignity and worth of human personality. Actually, we who engage in nonviolent direct action are not the creators of tension. We merely bring to the surface the hidden tension that is already alive. We bring it out in the open where it can be seen and dealt with. Like a boil that can never be cured so long as it is covered up but must be opened with all its pus-flowing ugliness to the natural medicines of air and light, injustice must be exposed, with all the tension its exposure creates, to the light of human conscience and the air of national opinion before it can be cured. . .

Oppressed people cannot remain oppressed forever. The yearning for freedom eventually manifests itself, and that is what has happened to the

American Negro. Something within has reminded him of his birthright of freedom, and something without has reminded him that it can be gained. Consciously or unconsciously, he has been caught up by the *Zeitgeist*, and with his black brothers of Africa and his brown and yellow brothers of Asia, South America and the Caribbean, the U.S. Negro is moving with a sense of great urgency toward the promised land of racial justice. If one recognizes this vital urge that has engulfed the Negro community, he should readily understand why public demonstrations are taking place. The Negro has many pent-up resentments and latent frustrations, and he must release them. So let him march; let him make prayer pilgrimages to the city hall; let him go on freedom rides—and try to understand why he must do so. If his repressed emotions are not released in nonviolent ways, they will seek expression through violence; this is not a threat but a fact of history. I have not said to my people, "Get rid of your discontent." Rather, I have tried to say that this normal and healthy discontent can be channeled into the creative outlet of nonviolent direct action. And now this approach is being termed extremist.

But though I was initially disappointed as being categorized as an extremist, as I continued to think about the matter I gradually gained a measure of satisfaction from the label. Was not Jesus an extremist for love "Love your enemies, bless them that curse you, do good to them that hate you, and pray for them which despitefully use you, and persecute you." Was not Amos an extremist for justice "Let justice roll down like waters and righteousness like an everflowing stream." Was not Paul an extremist for the Christian gospel "I bear in my body the marks of the Lord Jesus." Was not Martin Luther an extremist "Here I stand; I can do no other so help me God." And John Bunyan "I will stay in jail to the end of my days before I make a butchery of my conscience." And Abraham Lincoln "This nation cannot survive half slave and half free." And Thomas Jefferson "We hold these truths to be self-evident, that all men are created equal . . ." So the question is not whether we will be extremists but what kind of extremists we will be. Will we be extremists for hate or for love? Will we be extremists for the preservation of injustice or for the extension of justice? Perhaps the south, the nation and the world are in dire need of creative extremists.

I had hoped that the white moderate would see this need. Perhaps I was too optimistic; perhaps I expected too much. I suppose I should have realized that few members of the oppressor race can understand the deep groans and passionate yearnings of the oppressed race, and still fewer have the vision to see that injustice must be rooted out by strong, persistent and determined action. I am thankful, however, that some of our white brothers have grasped the meaning of this social revolution and committed themselves to it. They are still all too few in quantity, but they are big in quality. Some—such as Ralph McGill, Lillian Smith, Harry Golden and James McBride Dabbs—have written about our struggle in eloquent and prophetic terms.

Others have marched with us down nameless streets of the south. They have languished in filthy, roach-infested jails, suffering the abuse and brutality of policemen who view them as "dirty nigger lovers." Unlike so many of their moderate brothers and sisters, they have recognized the urgency of the moment and sensed the need for powerful "action" antidotes to combat the disease of segregation . . .

Before closing I feel impelled to mention one other point in your statement that has troubled me profoundly. You warmly commended the Birmingham police force for keeping "order" and "preventing violence." I doubt that you would have so warmly commended the police force if you had seen its angry dogs sinking their teeth into six unarmed, nonviolent Negroes. I doubt that you would so quickly commend the policemen if you were to observe their ugly and inhuman treatment of Negroes here in the city jail; if you were to watch them push and curse old Negro women and young Negro girls; if you were to see them slap and kick old Negro men and young boys; if you were to observe them, as they did on two occasions, refuse to give us food because we wanted to sing our grace together. I cannot join you in your praise of the Birmingham police department.

It is true that the police have exercised discipline in handling the demonstrators. In this sense they have conducted themselves rather "nonviolently" in public. But for what purpose? To preserve the evil system of segregation. Over the past few years I have consistently preached that nonviolence demands that the means we use must be as pure as the ends we seek. I have tried to make clear that it is wrong to use immoral means to attain moral ends. But now I must affirm that it is just as wrong, or perhaps even more so, to use moral means to preserve immoral ends. Perhaps Mr. Connor and his policemen have been rather nonviolent in public, as was Chief Pritchett in Albany, Georgia, but they have used the moral means of nonviolence to maintain the immoral end of racial injustice. As T. S. Eliot has said, there is no greater treason than to do the right deed for the wrong reason . . .

If I have said anything in this letter that overstates the truth and indicates an unreasonable impatience, I beg you to forgive me. If I have said anything that *under*states the truth and indicates my having a patience that allows me to settle for anything less than brotherhood, I beg God to forgive me.

I hope this letter finds you strong in the faith. I also hope that circumstances will soon make it possible for me to meet each of you, not as an integrationist or a civil rights leader but as a fellow clergyman and a Christian brother. Let us all hope that the dark clouds of racial prejudice will soon pass away and the deep fog of misunderstanding will be lifted from our fear-drenched communities and in some not too distant tomorrow the radiant stars of love and brotherhood will shine over our great nation with all their scintillating beauty.

Beyond Ideology?

Daniel Bell
The Exhaustion of Utopia

(1960)

As the 1950's drew to a close, many observers felt that the traditional categories of intellectual and political life were losing their relationship to the experiences of men in society. Left and right, liberal and conservative, radical and reactionary—all seemed mere rhetorical devices unequal to the technological and cybernetic realities of 1960. At least there was a discernible tendency among Americans to resist these designations in considering the options which history and society held out to them. As President John F. Kennedy put it in a speech at Yale University in 1962, "Today these old sweeping issues have largely disappeared. The central problems of our times are more subtle and less simple. They relate not to basic clashes of philosophy or ideology, but to ways and means of reaching common goals—to research for sophisticated solutions to complex and obstinate issues . . ."

Sociologist Daniel Bell (1919–   ), in a collection of essays entitled *The End of Ideology* (1960), drew attention to his thesis by subtitling his collection "On the Exhaustion of Political Ideas in the Fifties." The exhaustion, Bell argued, was embracing all of the West, and was directly related to the historical trauma of the preceding decades. His Epilogue to the collection, reprinted here, stands as a revealing contrast to Carl Becker's essay which began this section.

Ideology is the conversion of ideas into social levers. Without irony, Max Lerner once entitled a book "Ideas Are Weapons." This is the language of ideology. It is more. It is the commitment to the consequences of ideas. When Vissarion Belinsky, the father of Russian criticism, first read Hegel and became convinced of the philosophical correctness of the formula "what is, is what ought to be," he became a supporter of the Russian autocracy.

Daniel Bell, "The End of Ideology in the West: An Epilogue," *The End of Ideology* (New York, 1960), pp. 400–407. Reprinted by permission of the publisher. The Free Press of Glencoe, Inc.

But when it was shown to him that Hegel's thought contained the contrary tendency, that dialectically the "is" evolves into a different form, he became a revolutionary overnight. "Belinsky's conversion," comments Rufus W. Mathewson, Jr., "illustrates an attitude toward ideas which is both passionate and myopic, which responds to them on the basis of their immediate relevances alone, and inevitably reduces them to tools."

What gives ideology its force is its passion. Abstract philosophical inquiry has always sought to eliminate passion, and the person, to rationalize all ideas. For the ideologue, truth arises in action, and meaning is given to experience by the "transforming moment." He comes alive not in contemplation, but in "the deed." One might say, in fact, that the most important, latent, function of ideology is to tap emotion. Other than religion (and war and nationalism), there have been few forms of channelizing emotional energy. Religion symbolized, drained away, dispersed emotional energy from the world onto the litany, the sacraments, the edifices, the arts. Ideology fuses these energies and channels them into politics.

But religion, at its most effective, was more. It was a way for people to cope with the problem of death. The fear of death—forceful and inevitable—and more, the fear of violent death, shatters the glittering, imposing, momentary dream of man's power. The fear of death, as Hobbes pointed out, is the source of conscience; the effort to avoid violent death is the source of law. When it was possible to believe, really believe, in heaven and hell, then some of the fear of death could be tempered or controlled; without such belief, there is only the total annihilation of the self.

It may well be that with the decline in religious *faith* in the last century and more, this fear of death as total annihilation, unconsciously expressed, has probably increased. One may hypothesize, in fact, that here is a cause of the breakthrough of the irrational, which is such a marked feature of the changed moral temper of our time. Fanaticism, violence, and cruelty are not, of course, unique in human history. But there was a time when such frenzies and mass emotions could be displaced, symbolized, drained away, and dispersed through religious devotion and practice. Now there is only this life, and the assertion of self becomes possible—for some even necessary—in the domination over others. One can challenge death by emphasizing the omnipotence of a movement (as in the "inevitable" victory of communism), or overcome death (as did the "immortality" of Captain Ahab) by bending others to one's will. Both paths are taken, but politics, because it can institutionalize power, in the way that religion once did, becomes the ready avenue for domination. The modern effort to transform the world chiefly or solely through politics (as distinguished from a religious transformation of the self) has meant that all other institutional ways of mobilizing emotional energy would necessarily atrophy. In effect, sect and church became party and social movement.

A social movement can rouse people when it can do three things: simplify ideas, establish a claim to truth, and, in the union of the two, demand a commitment to action. Thus, not only does ideology transform ideas, it transforms people as well. The nineteenth-century ideologies, by emphasizing inevitability and by infusing passion into their followers, could compete with religion. By identifying inevitability with progress, they linked up with the positive values of science. But more important, these ideologies were linked, too, with the rising class of intellectuals, which was seeking to assert a place in society.

The differences between the intellectual and the scholar, without being invidious, are important to understand. The scholar has a bounded field of knowledge, a tradition, and seeks to find his place in it, adding to the accumulated, tested knowledge of the past as to a mosaic. The scholar, *qua* scholar, is less involved with his "self." The intellectual begins with *his* experience, *his* individual perceptions of the world, *his* privileges and deprivations, and judges the world by these sensibilities. Since his own status is of high value, his judgments of the society reflect the treatment accorded him. In a business civilization, the intellectual felt that the wrong values were being honored, and rejected the society. Thus there was a "built-in" compulsion for the free-floating intellectual to become political. The ideologies, therefore, which emerged from the nineteenth century had the force of the intellectuals behind them. They embarked upon what William James called "the faith ladder," which in its vision of the future cannot distinguish possibilities from probabilities, and converts the latter into certainties.

Today, these ideologies are exhausted. The events behind this important sociological change are complex and varied. Such calamities as the Moscow Trials, the Nazi-Soviet pact, the concentration camps, the suppression of the Hungarian workers, form one chain; such social changes as the modification of capitalism, the rise of the Welfare State, another. In philosophy, one can trace the decline of simplistic, rationalistic beliefs and the emergence of new stoic-theological images of man, e.g. Freud, Tillich, Jaspers, etc. This is not to say that such ideologies as communism in France and Italy do not have a political weight, or a driving momentum from other sources. But out of all this history, one simple fact emerges: for the radical intelligentsia, the old ideologies have lost their "truth" and their power to persuade.

Few serious minds believe any longer that one can set down "blueprints" and through "social engineering" bring about a new utopia of social harmony. At the same time, the older "counter-beliefs" have lost their intellectual force as well. Few "classic" liberals insist that the State should play no role in the economy, and few serious conservatives, at least in England and on the Continent, believe that the Welfare State is "the road to serfdom." In the Western world, therefore, there is today a rough consensus among intellectuals on political issues: the acceptance of a Welfare State; the desirability of decentralized power; a system of mixed economy and of political pluralism. In that sense, too, the ideological age has ended.

Thus one finds, at the end of the fifties, a disconcerting caesura. In the West, among the intellectuals, the old passions are spent. The new generation, with no meaningful memory of these old debates, and no secure tradition to build upon, finds itself seeking new purposes within a framework of political society that has rejected, intellectually speaking, the old apocalyptic and chiliastic visions. In the search for a "cause," there is a deep, desperate, almost pathetic anger. The theme runs through a remarkable book, *Convictions*, by a dozen of the sharpest young Left Wing intellectuals in Britain. They cannot define the content of the "cause" they seek, but the yearning is clear. In the U.S. too there is a restless search for a new intellectual radicalism. Richard Chase, in his thoughtful assessment of American society, *The Democratic Vista*, insists that the greatness of nineteenth-century America for the rest of the world consisted in its radical vision of man (such a vision as Whitman's), and calls for a new radical criticism today. But the problem is that the old politico-economic radicalism (pre-occupied with such matters as the socialization of industry) has lost its meaning, while the stultifying aspects of contemporary culture (e.g., television) cannot be redressed in political terms. At the same time, American culture has almost completely accepted the avant-garde, particularly in art, and the older academic styles have been driven out completely. The irony, further, for those who seek "causes" is that the workers, whose grievances were once the driving energy for social change, are more satisfied with the society than the intellectuals. The workers have not achieved utopia, but their expectations were less than those of the intellectuals, and the gains correspondingly larger.

The young intellectual is unhappy because the "middle way" is for the middle-aged, not for him; it is without passion and is deadening. Ideology, which by its nature is an all-or-none affair, and temperamentally the thing he wants, is intellectually devitalized, and few issues can be formulated any more, intellectually, in ideological terms. The emotional energies—and needs—exist, and the question of how one mobilizes these energies is a difficult one. Politics offers little excitement. Some of the younger intellectuals have found an outlet in science or university pursuits, but often at the expense of narrowing their talent into mere technique; others have sought self-expression in the arts, but in the wasteland the lack of content has meant, too, the lack of the necessary tension that creates new forms and styles.

Whether the intellectuals in the West can find passions outside of politics is moot. Unfortunately, social reform does not have any unifying appeal, nor does it give a younger generation the outlet for "self-expression" and "self-definition" that it wants. The trajectory of enthusiasm has curved East, where, in the new ecstasies for economic utopia, the "future" is all that counts.

The end of ideology is not—should not be—the end of utopia as well. If anything, one can begin anew the discussion of utopia only by being aware of the trap of ideology. The point is that ideologists are "terrible simplifiers." Ideology makes it unnecessary for people to confront individual issues on their individual merits. One simply turns to the ideological vending machine, and out comes the prepared formulae. And when these beliefs are suffused by apocalyptic fervor, ideas become weapons, and with dreadful results.

There is now, more than ever, some need for utopia, in the sense that men need—as they have always needed—some vision of their potential, some manner of fusing passion with intelligence. Yet the ladder to the City of Heaven can no longer be a "faith ladder," but an empirical one: a utopia has to specify *where* one wants to go, *how* to get there, the costs of the enterprise, and some realization of, and justification for the determination of *who* is to pay.

The end of ideology closes the book, intellectually speaking, on an era, the one of easy "left" formulae for social change. But to close the book is not to turn one's back upon it. This is all the more important now when a "new Left," with few memories of the past, is emerging. This "new Left" has passion and energy, but little definition of the future. Its outriders exult that it is "on the move." But where it is going, what it means by Socialism, how to guard against bureaucratization, what one means by democratic planning or workers' control—any of the questions that require hard thought, are only answered by bravura phrases . . .

The problems which confront us at home and in the world are resistant to the old terms of ideological debate between "left" and "right," and if "ideology" by now, and with good reason, is an irretrievably fallen word, it is not necessary that "utopia" suffer the same fate. But it will if those who now call loudest for new utopias begin to justify degrading *means* in the name of some Utopian or revolutionary *end*, and forget the simple lessons that if the old debates are meaningless, some old verities are not—the verities of free speech, free press, the right of opposition and of free inquiry.

And if the intellectual history of the past hundred years has any meaning—and lesson—it is to reassert Jefferson's wisdom (aimed at removing the dead hand of the past, but which can serve as a warning against the heavy hand of the future as well), that "the present belongs to the living." This is the wisdom that revolutionists, old and new, who are sensitive to the fate of their fellow men, rediscover in every generation.

Selected Additional Reading

Fiedler, Leslie. *An End to Innocence.* (Boston: Beacon Press, 1952.)
Galbraith, John K. *The Affluent Society.* (New York: New American Library, 1958.)

Goldman, Eric. *The Crucial Decade and After.* (New York: Random House, 1960.)

Kirk, Russell. *The Conservative Mind.* (Chicago: Henry Regnery, 1953.)

Krutch, Joseph Wood. *The Measure of Man.* (New York: Grossett and Dunlap, 1953.)

Latham, Earl. *The Communist Controversy in Washington*, (Cambridge, Mass.: Harvard University Press, 1966.)

Lewis, Anthony. *Portrait of A Decade.* (New York: Bantam, 1965.)

Lubell, Samuel. *The Future of American Politics.* (New York: Doubleday, 1951.)

MacDonald, Dwight. *Memoirs of a Revolutionist.* (New York: Meridian, 1957.)

McGiffert, Michael, ed. *The Character of Americans.* (Homewood, Ill.: Dorsey, 1964, 1970.)

Mills, C. Wright. *Power, Politics and People.* (New York: Ballantine Books, 1963.)

Niebuhr, Reinhold. *The Children of Light and the Children of Darkness.* (New York: Scribner's, 1944.)

Niebuhr, Reinhold. *The Irony of American History.* (New York: Scribner's, 1952.)

Riesman, David, *et al. The Lonely Crowd: A Study of the Changing American Character.* (New Haven: Yale Press, 1950.)

Rosenberg Bernard, and D. M. White, eds. *Mass Culture.* (Glencoe, Ill., Free Press, 1958.)

Rovere, Richard. *Senator Joe McCarthy.* (New York: Harcourt Brace, 1959.)

Stone, I. F. *The Haunted Fifties.* (New York: Random House, 1963.)

Trilling, Lionel. *The Liberal Imagination.* (New York: Doubleday, 1950.)

Vierek, Peter. *Shame and Glory of the Intellectuals.* (New York: G. Putnam Sons, 1965.)

White, Morton. *Social Thought in America: The Revolt Against Formalism.* (Boston: Beacon, 1957.)

Whyte, William H. *The Organization Man.* (New York: Simon and Schuster, 1956.)

Section Six
The New Radicalism: Persons, Places, and Mission

RONALD BERMAN

Contents

The Mission: The Movement and Liberal America

Introduction

These essays span the persons, the milieu, and the mission of the new radicalism. The first section concerns the people and their style of life, their attitudes toward sexual freedom, the use of drugs, even the mannerisms of ordinary conduct. The next section deals with the habitat of the new left, the university. The last has to do with the radical view of culture.

Kenneth Keniston has rightly cautioned us in his *Young Radicals* against the presumption of a single identity for the New Left. He distinguishes two kinds of new radical, the *activist* and the *alienated.* The former believes in the possibility of political and social action. He is convinced that demonstrations and confrontations do in fact have a public effect. He is committed to those forms of action—among them the sit-in, the protest, and the march—which mobilize support for his views. The alienated radical is fundamentally different because he has withdrawn from the life of action. Convinced that no meaningful public change is possible in this corrupt society, he is intent only on his own private forms of experience. It is the alienated radical who makes a fetish of drugs or obscenity, who worships at the shrine of mysticism or primitivism. His bizarre manners and morals symbolically express total disaffection with the values of culture. Granted this difference, it remains true that the sympathies of the New Left do have a common center. The Movement as a whole may legitimately be described as one centered in the universities, dedicated to changing human nature itself, and motivated by the desire to replace a culture which it views as essentially totalitarian.

In considering the life style of the new radicalism it is important to remember that personal freedom, no matter how excessive others may find it, is the highest good for both activist and alienated. This is how the matter is put in one of the recent Free Press publications:

> Our culture, our art, the music, newspapers, books, posters, our clothing, our homes, the way we walk and talk, the way our hair grows, the way we

smoke dope and fuck and eat and sleep—it is all one message, and the message is FREEDOM!

In our political tradition freedom is valued highly enough to make its defense sound reasonable. There are, however, three major problems inherent in the New Left view of freedom. If it is not to be anarchy, then it must have some form. If it is to be democratic, then the freedom of one individual must not conflict with that of another. And, if it is finally going to be practicable, it must have some limit. Regrettably, the New Left has not come near a solution to any of these problems. It might even be noted that freedom on the left has declined paradoxically into its opposite: liberty for the few has often in practice meant compulsion for the many. And it is on the New Left that the doctrine of elitism has most recently made its appearance. Convinced that there is no real opportunity for their beliefs to be persuasive, the members of New Left have often and publicly asserted that ideas contrary to theirs ought to be suppressed. In this it resembles the tyrannies of the Left that have to our misfortune arisen since the First World War.

The second group of materials concerns the university. Since the new radicalism is largely a student movement it is only natural to find that movement at work within its own milieu. And, since it is a movement dominated by intellectuals or would-be intellectuals, the university microcosm is the most logical place in which to enact ideas. One notes that there are other reasons for the concentration of the new radicalism on the campus. For one thing, no other part of the culture is so vulnerable. There are singularly few penalties for action on the campus, actions which, in other aspects of life, would result in ostracism, legal penalties, and economic disaster. The university, it was once said, is a place where ideas have no consequences. Since faculty tend to be overwhelmingly liberal the radical movement has benefited from a sympathetic audience within the campus framework. Since administrators have proved to be so fearful of criticism from either the public or the student body, they have not been especially competent in dealing with confrontations. And, since the traditions of the university are what they are, the New Left may expect to find less opposition on the campus and within the academic community than elsewhere.

It should be added in all fairness that the university invites criticism as well. As we can see from some of the following pieces, the New Left is concerned with better education. No one can argue with the desire to make teaching better or even more interesting than it now is. The argument arises not from the motives but from the expressions and the actions which embody the dogma. Violence on the campus proceeds from the assumption that anything is justified in the guerilla warfare the radical conducts against his opposition. Common sense makes it pretty clear, however, that the riot is the last resort of those whose ideas lack the power to convince. It is the very opposite of a solution.

New Left dogma asserts that the university is the agency which changes individuals into supporters of "the system." The concrete issues are these: scholarly objectivity is attacked as a pretext which prevents the true, radical solution to problems from being known; conformity to the codes of intellectual life is interpreted as a *de facto* if not *de juro* form of support for things as they are; a curriculum centered on such things as Shakespeare or the study of higher mathematics is of very little use for changing class consciousness. In general, it may be said that for the New Left the university is "objectively" fascist: an institution in which the values of our culture are passed on from one guilty generation to another.

Those values are the subject of the third section, which deals with the mission of the New Left. Using the weapons of philosophy the new radicals have been engaged in proving the hypothesis of western decadence. Their ideas derive in general from the twentieth-century Marxist philosophers. If their general view comes from Lenin or Mao Tse-tung, their specific ideas have been inspired by such men as C. Wright Mills and Herbert Marcuse. It is an article of philosophic faith of the New Left that the culture of the United States is in reality a form of fascism. In spite of our liberal ideals, they argue, a totalitarian war is being carried on in Vietnam; rigid sanctions are imposed upon personal freedom; minorities are subjected to intolerable degradation. In these arguments they prefer to be neither historical nor comparative. They do not judge this nation in terms of any other historical reality. They do not compare the injustices which are generally acknowledged to exist here with those that are actually the product of national policy elsewhere. The brutalities which are a fact of life behind the Iron Curtain are all too easily made equivalent with those things in our national life that both the public and the government are honorably concerned about reforming. The horrendous treatment of minorities in the Third World is all too often overlooked, and our own failings are made the measure of human fallibility. The word "fascist" has had an unfortunate resurrection in this decade, for it has been applied to anything that those on the New Left happen to dislike. The unspoken premise, however, ought to be revealed. Our country is accused of fascism not because it resembles Nazi Germany but because, given our political structure, it is difficult for radicalism to influence the electorate. In short, an elitist group, powerfully and uncritically convinced of its destiny, sees in whatever opposes it, no matter how democratic that opposition may be, evidence of totalitarianism.

Persons: Life Styles and Influences

This section opens with an essay by Paul Goodman celebrating the new radical life-style. Written in 1964, it praises precisely those qualities of personal and intellectual dissent which reveal the energy of new ideas. The rest of the section is in effect a commentary on this early hopefulness. By the time we reach the piece on "The White Panthers" it can be seen that the life-style of the New Left is no longer conceived of as a corrective to the monotony of American life, but as a revolutionary challenge to middle-class ethics. It plainly intimates a destructive attack upon the politics which support those ethics. Leslie A. Fiedler, who considers himself a post-modern, which is to say part of the *avant garde* left, reveals in his essay a sympathy toward this style of life. The essays of Will Herberg, a conservative associated with the *National Review*, and Irving Howe, a member of the Old Left, dwell on the dangers the new life-style offers to a real program of radical reform.

Paul Goodman
Crisis and New Spirit

(1964)

To assess [the young radicals], we must be quite clear about the ideas that *in fact* possess these young people and determine their style of thinking. Here is a thumbnail sketch:

> . . . the youth have been . . . strongly influenced by their "own" writers, by the Beats and by college magazines, like *Big Table, i.e., The Black Mountain Review* . . . Behind such writing, of course, have been Henry Miller, Genêt,

From *Utopian Essays and Practical Proposals*, Paul Goodman.

and so forth, who have taught acceptance of one's experience as it is, whatever it is, without regard for official values or conventional norms. Besides, the young people have read dismayed accounts of the "American" scene and self-dismay at sharing in it, *e.g.*, in Salinger and Nathanael West. And they avidly read the magazines that are cynical about this "American" scene but exploit it, like *Esquire* and *Playboy* . . .

But further, in the past couple of years, superseding the Beats, there has spread a Hipster literature. This also accepts the scene as unchangeable, but tries to avoid the polarizing choice by asserting: "Cultivate your own experience at the expense of the only society there is. Be cool. Play roles." This stance is the same as that taken by Thrasymachus in the beginning of the *Republic* and seems to be highly immoral. But, in fact, hipsterism—like Mailer, its chief philosopher—is a desperate complex of moral indignation, pretty acute self-awareness, painful moral confusion, and tantrums and violence. It is the ideology of an underprivileged group struggling for fulfillment. *In an important sense, youth is always such an underprivileged group,* and must take to such ideas.

This, I submit, is the actuality of the intellectual climate of the students who now come to the study of academic ethics. The classical, Biblical, chivalric, and humanistic ideals that used to nourish us well are not in fact comprehensible to these young. Modern history has been too catastrophic. Our society is at present too base. We must not hope to inculcate complete and universal principles of action; these arouse only suspicion. Also, let us be frank, most teachers do not know them with enough confidence, do not *live* them with enough confidence, to be able to prove them.

In this context, among the academic philosophies, it is European and Oriental existentialism and American pragmatism that, in my opinion, prove to be relevant and are actually influential. And this is a good thing. The students grasp them because they are believable to them; and the lesson they teach is that in the absurd situation of a dehumanized society, it is possible to act and cope. This is what Camus was saying. That is, far from being demoralizing, causing anxiety and making life problematic, these philosophies, especially in combination, begin to recover morality for those who *are* anxious and baffled. By their existentialism they learn words to affirm themselves as and where they are, to be authentic and not have to play roles or satisfy standards that are empty to them, and to dissipate corporate "images" and political ideologies. In the version of Martin Buber, existentialism gives them a firm relation to their fellows in a face-to-face community. And in the existentialist aspects of Zen and Tao, which are the aspects that influence them, they learn to notice the possibilities in the present moment, so they no longer feel trapped.

Paul Jacobs and Saul Landau
The New Radicals

(1966)

The Movement is much more than anti-Vietnam marches, civil rights demonstrations, and student sit-ins. To be in The Movement is to search for a psychic community, in which one's own identity can be defined, social and personal relationships based on love can be established and can grow, unfettered by the cramping pressures of the careers and life styles so characteristic of America today.

The Movement rejects the careers and life styles of the American liberal, too, for to The Movement it is the liberal way of life and frame of mind that represent the evil of America. Those in The Movement feel that modern American liberals have substituted empty rhetoric for significant content, obscured the principles of justice by administrative bureaucracy, sacrificed human values for efficiency, and hypocritically justified a brutal attempt to establish American hegemony over the world with sterile anti-Communism. The Movement sees the liberals righteously proclaiming faith in American democracy from their comfortable suburban homes or offices, while the United States Air Force drops napalm on villages and poisons the rice paddies.

So, those in The Movement see not only the openly authoritarian or totalitarian society as an enemy but the administered, bureaucratic, dehumanized, rhetorical-liberal one as well. They reject liberal authority. They were stirred, momentarily, by President Kennedy's call for a commitment to freedom, but were so disappointed by his actions in Cuba and Vietnam that they turned on him with bitterness. And the Johnson Administration's foreign policy reinforces their view that America flouts, in action, the traditions of freedom and justifies the use of military instruments associated with the Nazis.

The new movement is also a revolt against the postwar "over-developed society," with its large bureaucracies in government, corporations, trade unions, and universities. To those in The Movement the new technologies of automation and cybernation, with their computers and memory-bank machines, are instruments of alienation, depersonalizing human relations to a frightening degree... Even worse, the decision-making over which the governed no longer have control extends far beyond politics: in the technological order every aspect of the people's lives is under the control of administrators far removed from responsibility to the governed. And the

---

elders of those in The Movement have exchanged their decision-making right for the comforts of American affluence. . .

In their personal life style, their aesthetic sense, many in The Movement reject affluence and its associated symbols. The ambition to escape from poverty is no spur to action in their lives, for many are children of America's post-Depression *nouveau* middle class. Their parents are the once-poor scholars who head rich academic institutes; the ex-union organizers who run their own large businesses; the former slum dwellers who develop segregated real-estate tracts; the families once on the W.P.A. who live in suburbia—all those who have made it. But their parents' desire to own, to accumulate, to achieve the status and prestige which go with material wealth, are meaningless goals to the children. . .

In some measure, too, the modes of extreme personal behavior adopted by this group—their permissive view of marijuana or hallucinogenics like LSD, their matter-of-fact acceptance of sexual freedom and their habitual profanity—are part of their search for identity. That search assumes a rejection of everything connected with their old identity and of the technological, bureaucratic values they see as dominant in American life. It is also possible that their difficulties in finding personal meaning in the routine politics of the civil rights struggle and their anguish in seeing the country carry out a foreign policy they believe to be totally bad force these young people into seeking meaning in experiences. They think the ivory-towered men of ideas have cheated them, lied to them, and that action and spontaneous experience will show them truth.

Above all, those in The Movement now restlessly seek to find a new politics and a new ideology that will permit them to link existential humanism with morally acceptable modes of achieving radical social change.

Paul Jacobs and Saul Landau
An Interview

(1966)

A twenty-two-year-old man, now working in the S.D.S. National Office. He graduated from a high-ranking Eastern college in 1964, is unmarried. He comes from a middle-class Jewish background; both of his parents were members of the Socialist Party in the 1930's.

I did some political work for A.D.A. types when I was in high school; it wasn't until I got to college that I became deeply involved. After I saw the H.U.A.C. movie *Operation Abolition* I became really angry. It's hard to describe the strong identification I had with the students in that movie. It also showed me that the student movement was important, and I became active in the anti-H.U.A.C. campaign . . .

I guess there was a gradual radicalization that took place from reading, talking, getting involved later in the peace movement and anti-H.U.A.C. I went to the S.D.S. convention and I remember being very impressed by Tom Hayden, Al Haber, and Robb Burlage.

The Power Elite and the books and magazines of the English New Left made big impressions on me; and so did *Communitas*. But when I heard Goodman speak, I was turned off. I read the *Correspondent* and I guess it made me a peacenik. I was moved by Edgar Snow's *Red Star Over China*. I read a little Marx, but only through courses, from Lewis Feuer's anthology; and a little Fromm, Camus, Sartre, after graduating. I spent most of my time at college in meetings. I guess some of the liberal faculty members influenced us. I had an emotional reaction to *Grapes of Wrath* and *Man's Fate*. More recently, *Catch-22* and *One Flew Over the Cuckoo's Nest* have really moved me. And movies—I mentioned *Operation Abolition*—like *He Who Must Die* and *Come Back, Africa* affect me deeply.

It's funny you ask about sex. In S.D.S. fucking is a statement of community, and there's a lot of inter-fucking, but it's not casual. Sex comes out of a relationship and is used to build a relationship stronger. I'm not thinking of marriage, but I'm not promiscuous. There isn't much promiscuity, and from the people I know in S.D.S. sex is usually linked to love . . .

Again, pot isn't important except in a few chapters. There isn't any pot at S.D.S. parties, and only in one or two chapters do S.D.S. people turn on and call the rest of us square.

S.D.S. has a serious role: to make a New Left movement with a radical politics and analysis—to build a new society.

We don't have many working-class contacts . . .

J. Simmons and B. Winograd
Tripping Out

(1969)

A trip can be any happening that turns-on a participant and bathes him in the raw sensuous-emotional experiencing of the living world which lies behind our concocted word-screens. To trip is to be transported out of the ordinary and into some subjective state where you are directly connected with an unfolding present. Our workaday distinction between the individual and the other objects is blurred and the person is divested of his paper identity badges.

Tripping out is the most definitive and the most controversial thing that happeners are doing. Put simply, tripping involves the cultivation of direct experience, unmolested by poses and running interpretations. The trip is a subjective experiencing which combines the intense and the extraordinary, and this direct experience can be anything from the taste of an orange to a joust with the shadows in your mind. The ultimate in tripping is to reach a state of awareness so heightened and unmediated that it overwhelms and temporarily supplants one's ordinary conceptions and perceptions of one's self and the world. This state of sensory, mental, and emotional amaze is called "blowing your mind" in hip circles, but it has been called other things in other days. For some, at least this is a beneficial experience resulting in self-insight, a realization of customarily obscured immensities, and an acceptance—in the existential sense—of the ongoing moment. But beyond, or rather before, any of these benefits, there is the fact of the trip one is taking as a pleasure and an end in itself. There is a feeling among many of the contemporary trippers that insight and self-integration can only be won after you have existentially learned the nature of pleasure and experience . . .

It's a rule that no one is ever brought around to the apartment unless they're cool and each of the seven people here tonight is up on something. Everyone is known to Ron and Pauline (who rent the place) except Gordon, and Jeff brought him so he's okay. Ron and Pauline have been living together now for several months and they have become quite domestic. They're up on acid tonight.

Joints are being passed around from hand to hand as they're listening to Sandy Bull's something else rendering of the love theme from Black Orpheus. A fellow is stretched out on the floor with his head cushioned in a girl's lap. They aren't lovers; each of them has something going elsewhere. Maybe they will be sometime in the future, maybe not.

J. Simmons and B. Winograd, *It's Happening*, 1969, pp. 32–42. Reprinted by permission of the publisher, Brandon House Paperbacks.

There are good surrealist reproductions on the otherwise drab walls and a pile of science fiction paperbacks and Marvel Comics on the floor. A board and bricks bookcase supports the stereo and a hundred or so volumes including many of the titles from "Great Books" lists, along with the works of Goodman, Miller, Hesse, Watts and Genêt. Many of them were stolen from libraries and bookstores.

The record changes to Bob Dylan's "Mr. Tambourine Man" and Pauline becomes lost in the music. There's almost no talking; everyone seems to be on his own trip tonight. But there's a subtle atmosphere of warmness, that some would call psychic, about the place now and the people feel free. Gordon moves about the room looking at the pictures and out the windows at the life below. He picks up Heinlein's *Stranger In A Strange Land* and begins reading.

Ron is the veteran and even though he is bathing in the reverberating colors of his own acid high he brings himself down periodically to check and see that the others are all right. They say that he once sat by a girl who had flipped out of her skull for three straight days and nights and talked her down to where she again remembered who she was and was able to go out into the streets without being picked up by the Nabs. She had had a history of family hassles and psychiatric care and so most everyone had warned her not to take LSD. But maybe she had been right to go ahead anyway because she'd been less hung up since. Every once in awhile she still dropped by the apartment, her visits dramatizing her feeling that *this*, the apartment and the people in it, was a significant part of her life. Some would say that she had died and been reborn here; others would be more pedantic and say that the place had been an important phase in her development . . .

Most happeners seem to take for granted the inherent worth and value of tripping. There is a strong, but usually vague, faith that people are in some way the better for having tripped and most trippers fret only about the substance or intensity of their own voyages compared with others, or the rigid mentalities of straights. Those with a lingering allegiance to the Protestant Ethic (and this is probably the majority) feel that tripping is a healthful antidote to workaday pressures and an aid to personal balance and growth. Those who are preoccupied with psychoanalytic and existential hangups feel that drug-assisted tripping out is a means without equal for learning about and living with oneself and the world. Lovers say that tripping together is a more certain way of achieving that merging of spirit which can transmute the world into a magic garden and mere existence into LIFE. Those of an artistic bent say that tripping is a wondrous way of enhancing their sensitivity and creativity. Others (and this includes only a minority, contrary to the hysterical claims from many newsmen and officials) tell you that riding motorcycles, dancing, doing a sex thing, or even bopping behind drugs is something else.

J. Simmons and B. Winograd
The Psychedelic Drug Scene

(1969)

Dear Dad:
Dope ... potacidspeedmetheshitboojointtrippedfreakfiend ... Timothy Leary is not a Lady Wrestler. And. Geronimo wasn't George Washington's nephew. And that's not half of it, like you said. Flip Out. It all runs together; indivisible, etc. etc. etc. from—if you can take it—the world in which we live. Real. World. REAL WORLD. Our world, not yours. The world of everything, dream dance escape thought and blood. A machine has cranked us out. And our father doesn't know how to stop it, much less fix it. I know it scares you but it scares me too. It's not a NEW thing (how could you call A World thousands of years old, new?) but it is (could it be a hidden, old, familiar with a new ring?). Yes. The Psychedelic World was what you called it—bringing to your mind a different picture than mine. "What is it all about?", you and others like and unlike you ask of me and of others. Well, one thing, it is *all* about; *all* around ever under and behind you and me. I'd like to show you this world, this world neither of us knows but the one in which I lovingly live. It's hold grows tighter each day. My World capturing yet freeing me from That World. You say it's a vice closing in on my rational processes; a delicious piece of sticky fly-paper drawing me until I'm stuck UPrightdownsideOUT. Your World. That World. Ohhh, yes!I know it unlike I know anything else. But I don't like it. *Let* me not like it. It doesn't scare me, for life has been cast naked in That World. We've seen its bared skin marred scarred tarred and feathered. My World. The Next World? Standing before me and scaring me and making me wonder about whether I *really* know and care about the what and why of my doing and activities in This World. You've locked us out of That World (presuming rather presumptuously that we had a wish to get in) with loving sternness and killing terms. There's a LOVE in MY WORLD for the new exciting land that was always far off the map in fifth grade geography. Things aren't always knowable and certain and stifling. To walk through it is its essence, so, Dad, let's TAKE A TRIP.

Stripped of any of its other meanings, the drug scene, or drug scenes if you prefer, is just what the young girl writing the above letter indicated. The drug scene is the central plaza of happening America. It is the main ring, the granite cornerstone with a bronze plaque, the center of the what's happening universe. It is the crossroads for conflicting ideologies. "That World" versus

---

J. Simmons and B. Winograd, *It's Happening*, 1969, pp. 85–90. Reprinted by permission of the publisher, Brandon House Paperbacks.

"My World." It is here, in the drug scene, that generational change in America most vividly thrusts itself forward; declaring that yesterday's rights and wrongs about things people should do are not the right do's and don'ts for the children who'll be tomorrow's fathers and mothers . . .

The world of drugs, though, isn't ideal. Its shortcomings—the burned deals, the oregano-weighted grass, the petty brotherly thievery—are the mirrored reflections of the larger society. They are not the same specific faults, but the similarities are too striking to pass by without a look and a wonder. Yet, even though it is at least a partial reflection of the other side, the drug world is a domain, an empire all its own. There are rules about this and rules about that. Lock the door; hide the stuff; pull the drapes; dim the lights. There are roles to play. The educator and chief missionary; the keeper of the goods and services; the dealer and his "dynamite." It keeps itself and its growth under a surprising degree of control, aware that drugs are a legal, if not a moral crime. It's a subculture of deviants, say the academicians playing with the typecasting function society has bestowed upon behavioral scientists; the deviants who structure their own world with special roles, rules, beliefs, and expectations. Just like the big world, but only a corrupted microcosm struggling to keep alive . . .

Kenneth Keniston
Young Radicals

(1968)

. . . It seems to me useful to suggest that student dissenters generally fall somewhere along a continuum that runs between two ideal types—first, the political activist or protester, and second, the withdrawn, culturally alienated student.

The Activist—The defining characteristic of the "new" activist is his participation in a student demonstration or group activity that concerns itself with some matter of general political, social, or ethical principle. Characteristically, the activist feels that some injustice has been done, and attempts to "take a stand," "demonstrate," or in some fashion express his convictions. The specific issues in question range from protest against a paternalistic college administration's actions to disagreement with American Vietnam policies, from indignation at the exploitation of the poor to anger at the

---

From *Young Radicals: Notes on Committed Youth*, pp. 300–304, 329–30, by Kenneth Keniston,

firing of a devoted teacher, from opposition to the Selective Service laws which exempt him but not the poor, to—most important—outrage at the deprivation of the civil rights of other Americans.

The initial concern of the protester is almost always immediate, *ad hoc*, and local . . . Whatever the issue, the protester rarely demonstrates because his *own* interests are jeopardized, but rather because he perceives injustices being done to *others* less fortunate than himself. For example, one of the apparent paradoxes about protests against current draft policies is that the protesting students are selectively drawn from the subgroup *most* likely to receive student deferments for graduate work . . .

If one runs down the list of "causes" taken up by student activists, in rare cases are demonstrations directed at improving the lot of the protesters themselves; identification with the oppressed is a more important motivating factor than an actual sense of immediate personal oppression . . .

Clearly, many current American political institutions like *de facto* segregation are opposed; clearly, too, most students of the New Left reject careerism and familism as personal values. In this sense, we might think of the activist as (politically) "alienated." But his label seems to me more misleading than illuminating, for it overlooks the more basic *commitment* of most student activists to other ancient, traditional, and creedal American values like free speech, citizen's participation in decision-making, equal opportunity and justice. Insofar as the activist rejects all or part of "the power structure," it is because current political realities fall so far short of the ideals he sees as central to the American creed. And insofar as he repudiates careerism and familism, it is because of his implicit allegiance to other human goals he sees, once again, as more crucial to American life. Thus, to emphasize the "alienation" of activists is to neglect their more basic allegiance to creedal American ideals.

One of these ideals is, of course, a belief in the desirability of political and social action. Sustained in good measure by the successes of the student civil rights movement, the protester is usually convinced that demonstrations are effective in mobilizing public opinion, bringing moral or political pressure to bear, demonstrating the existence of his opinions, or, at times, in "bringing the machine to a halt." In this sense, then, despite his criticisms of existing political practices and social institutions, he is a political optimist . . .

The Culturally Alienated—In contrast to the politically optimistic, active, and socially concerned protester, the culturally alienated student is far too pessimistic and too firmly opposed to "the System" to wish to demonstrate his disapproval in any organized public way. His demonstrations of dissent are private: through non-conformity of behavior, ideology, and dress, through personal experimentation and, above all, through efforts to intensify his own subjective experience, he shows his distaste and disinterest in politics and society. The activist attempts to change the world around him, but the alienated student is convinced that meaningful change of the social and political world is impossible; instead, he considers "dropping out" the only real option.

Alienated students tend to be drawn from the same general social strata and colleges as protesters. But psychologically and ideologically, their backgrounds are often very different. Alienated students are more likely to be disturbed psychologically; and although they are often highly talented and artistically gifted, they are less committed to academic values and intellectual achievement than are protesters. The alienated student's real campus is the school of the absurd, and he has more affinity for pessimistic existentialist ontology than for traditional American activism. Furthermore, such students usually find it psychologically and ideologically impossible to take part in organized group activities for any length of time, particularly when they are expected to assume responsibilities for leadership. Thus, on the rare occasions when they become involved in demonstrations, they usually prefer peripheral roles, avoid responsibilities, and are considered a nuisance by serious activists . . .

In many colleges, alienated students often constitute a kind of hidden underground, disorganized and shifting in membership, in which students can temporarily or permanently withdraw from the ordinary pressures of college life. The alienated are especially attracted to the hallucinogenic drugs like marijuana, mescaline, and LSD, precisely because these agents combine withdrawal from ordinary social life with the promise of greatly intensified subjectivity and perception. To the confirmed "acid-head," what matters is intense, drug-assisted perception; the rest—including politics, social action and student demonstrations—is usually seen as "role-playing."

The recent and much-publicized emergence of "hippie" subcultures in several major cities and increasingly on the campuses of many selective and progressive colleges illustrates the overwhelmingly apolitical stance of alienated youth. For although hippies oppose war and believe in interracial living, few have been willing or able to engage in anything beyond occasional peace marches or apolitical "human be-ins." Indeed, the hippie's emphasis on immediacy, "love," and "turning-on," together with his basic rejection of the traditional values of American life, inoculates him against involvement in long-range activist endeavors like education or community organization, and even against the sustained effort needed to plan and execute demonstrations or marches. For the alienated hippie, American society is beyond redemption (or not worth trying to redeem); but the activist no matter how intense his rejection of specific American policies and practices, retains a conviction that his society can and should be changed.

For alienated students, distrust extends far beyond a low view of human nature; they also believe that intimacy ends in disillusion, that attachment to a group entails the loss of individuality, and that all appearances are untrustworthy. Nor can American culture be trusted: it is mechanical, boring, trashy, cheap, conformist, and dull. Any kind of positive commitment is viewed negatively.

In addition, most alienated students are native existentialists. Few of them, when they began the research study, had read existentialist philosophers; yet they had often spontaneously arrived at a view of the world close to that of the most pessimistic existentialists like Sartre. From middle adolescence on, alienated students had become increasingly aware of the darkness, isolation, and meaninglessness of life. The universe itself is dead, lacking in structure, inherently unpredictable and random. Individual life, too, is devoid of purpose and preordained form. Consequently, any meaning or truth that an individual finds is inevitably subjective and solipsistic. Morality, too, is seen as egocentric, arbitrary, and individualistic. Given the unpredictability of the future, long-range ethical idealism is impossible; the present becomes overwhelmingly important . . .

Another distinctive outlook of these students is a profound pessimism about, and distaste for, politics and political action. One student, asked about world affairs, wrote, "I leave speculations about world affairs to our politicians . . . political activity is like the games children play . . . whatever happens will not affect my thinking." Another, discussing atomic warfare, notes, "Since the race is doomed to die someday, I can't see that it makes much difference." And still another, predicting a nuclear war "very eventually," says, "I'll let it bother me then." These are not, then, students who believe in the efficacy or value of political action.

Much of the explicit philosophy of these students is negative. They are, like Nietzsche (one of their favorite writers), philosophers with hammers, whose favorite intellectual sport is exposing the hypocrisy of others. They distrust all Positive Thinking and therefore find it almost impossible to agree with any questionnaire statement that clearly expresses an affirmative view. But despite the negative cast of their *explicit* views, the alienated share an *implicit* positive search in a common direction. Implicitly their philosophies emphasize the positive value of passion and feeling, the search for awareness, contact, intensity, the cultivation of responsiveness, the importance of solitude, and the need somehow to express their experience of life. Their positive values are therefore "expressive" or aesthetic, in that their main focus is the present, their main source is the self, and their main aim is the development of awareness, responsiveness, and sentience. Rejecting the traditional American values of success, self-control, and achievement, they maintain that passion, feeling, and awareness are the truest forces at man's disposal. For most of them, the primary objective in life is to attain and maintain openness to experience, contact with the world and spontaneity of feeling. Anything that might fetter or restrain their responsiveness and openness is opposed: the goal, as one student puts it, is "circumscribing my life as little as possible."

Lawrence Lipton
Life Styles

(1968)

At the Pentagon demonstration new life style trips were created because of the interaction of people and experiences the college kids went through and the politicos went through. But that was a minor part of it, because the main focus was on the Pentagon trip. The main focus in Chicago is going to be on creating those experiences for people which will turn their head around, which will get them to stop thinking about things ten thousand miles away in Vietnam, and start thinking about themselves, start thinking about going BACK to St. Louis, BACK to Kansas City, going back to all the small towns, and going BACK to Birmingham, Alabama, and Jackson, Miss., and Miami and Boston and everywhere. Going back to where they are and build a family there that's not incestuous again, but that opens out reaches out and absorbs, absorbs, absorbs. There was a big debate about three, four years ago, with Staughton Lynd and Bayard Rustin. People were talking about: the Achilles Heel of Parallelism is economics, you do a parallel thing, but how does it survive? It's fuckin' simple how it survives: You live simply, people got to read "Walden." Simplicity. You got to make your own clothes; if somebody digs making clothes all day long, they create a surplus that everybody can share. Let the people who dig farming farm. Let everybody get into the idea of just doing it, of BEING responsible, sharing and helping one another along. You try and balance each other out, like the Hopi way—there's a very key concept to that—rather than complete.

This year is going to be the life or death of America, I think.
Yippees, are they the Free Men?

The Death of Hippie, which was ritualized in a symbolical funeral procession and cremation last year in San Francisco, was hailed by the "mourners" as the birth of Free Man. Free Man is a label that so many others had striven to pin on themselves throughout history that any reasonable man could be forgiven a twinge of skepticism when the event took place. The kindest thing one could do was wait and see, telling himself, Free Man is as Free Man does—not what he says or promises or proclaims. I think we see in Youth International Party (Yippee) the beginning of what may well be the Free Man. And the initial confrontation with the Establishment, on any significant scale, may well be the Democratic Party convention in Chicago next August. Here may be the alternative, a parapolitical alternative, to the utterly discredited promises of political solutions. The Cultural Revo-

---

Lawrence Lipton, "Radio Free America," *Los Angeles Free Press* (March 1, 1968), p. 4.

lution, which began with the Beat Generation, proliferated into the Hippie movement and is now coming of age in the Youth International Party, "a clear alternative," Jerry Rubin calls it, "an underground, an opposition," a true revolutionary action group for the qualitative social change which is now exploding into reality.

Daniel Walker
Life Styles

(1968)

By early January, plans for the Festival of Life had progressed rapidly, and underground newspapers carried articles promoting the event.

The following example is from the *New York Free Press*:

> We've got to get crazy. Craziest motherfuckers they ever seen in this country. Cause that's the only way we're gonna beat them. So fucking crazy that they can't understand it at ALL. They know something's up, something's going on down there, something's happening, some change coming on in this country, just like Dylan says, "There's something happening but you don't know what it is, do you, Mr. Jones?"
>
> We won't tell 'em what it is. What do you want to tell them for? Don't tell 'em shit. NEVER.
>
> . . . That's the problem you have when you focus in on an issue, when you make a demand. They can deal with a demand.
>
> We put a finger up their ass and tell them, "I ain't telling you what I want," then they got a problem.

Rights in Conflict: A Report Submitted by Daniel Walker, Director of the Chicago Study Team, to the National Commission on the Causes and Prevention of Violence (New York, 1968), p. 32.

John Sinclair
The White Panthers

(1969)

First I must say that this statement, like all statements, is bullshit without an active program to back it up. We have a program which is on-going and total and which must not be confused with anything that is said or written about it.

Our program is cultural revolution through a total assault on the culture, which makes use of every tool, every energy and every medium we can get our collective hands on. We take our program with us everywhere we go and use any means necessary to expose people to it.

Our culture, our art, the music, newspapers, books, posters, our clothing, our homes, the way we walk and talk, the way our hair grows, the way we smoke dope and fuck and eat and sleep—it is all one message, and the message is, FREEDOM!

We are free mother country madmen in charge of our own lives and we are taking this freedom to the peoples of America in the streets, in ballrooms and teen-clubs, in their front rooms watching TV, in their bedrooms reading the Fifth Estate or the Sun or jacking off or smoking secret dope, in their schools where we come and talk to them or make our music in their weird gymnasiums—they love it—we represent the only contemporary life-style in America for its kids and it should be known that these kids are READY!

They're ready to move but they don't know how, and all we do is show them that they can get away with it. BE FREE, goddammint, and fuck all them old dudes, is what we tell them, and they can see that we mean it. The only influence we have, the only thing that touches them, is that we are for real. We are FREE, we are a bunch of arrogant motherfuckers and we don't give a damn for any cop or any phonyass authority control-addict creep who wants to put us down. I heard Stokely Carmichael in 1966 call for "20 million arrogant black men" as America's salvation, and there are a lot of arrogant black motherfuckers in the streets today—for the first time in America there are a generation of visionary maniac white mother country dope fiend rock and roll freaks who are ready to get down and kick out the jams—ALL THE JAMS—break everything loose and free everybody from their very real and imaginary prisons—even the chumps and punks and honkies who are always fucking with us. We demand total freedom for everybody! . . .

WE ARE THE SOLUTION. We have no "problems." Everything is

John Sinclair, "Introduction to the White Panthers," *San Diego Free Press* (February 18–March 14, 1969), p. 8. Reprinted with permission of the author.

free for everybody. Money sucks. Leaders suck. Underwear sucks. School sucks. The white honkie culture that has been handed to us on a silver platter is meaningless to us! We don't want it! Fuck God in the ass. Fuck your woman until she can't stand up. Fuck everybody you can get your hands on.

Our program of rock and roll, dope, and fucking in the streets is a program of total freedom for everyone. And we are totally committed to carrying out our program. We breathe revolution . . .

We have no illusions. Knowing the power of symbols in the abstract world of Americans we have taken the White Panther as our mark to symbolize in our strength and arrogance and to demonstrate our commitment to the program of the Black Panther Party as well as to our own—indeed, the two programs are the same.

The actions of the Black Panthers in America have inspired us and given us strength, as has the music of black America, and we are moving to reflect that strength in our daily acitivity just as our music contains and extends the power and feeling of the black magic music that originally informed our bodies and told us that we could be free.

Leslie A. Fiedler
The New Mutants

(1965)

. . . The new irrationalists . . . deny all the apostles of reason, Freud as well as Socrates; and if they seem to exempt Marx, this is because they know less about him, have heard him evoked less often by the teachers they are driven to deny. Not only do they reject the Socratic adage that the unexamined life is not worth living, since for them precisely the unexamined life is the only one worth enduring at all. But they also abjure the Freudian one: "Where id was, ego shall be," since for them the true rallying cry is, "Let id prevail over ego, impulse over order," or—in negative terms—"Freud is a fink!" . . .

I am thinking, of course, of the recent demonstrations at Berkeley and elsewhere, whose ostensible causes were civil rights or freedom of speech or Vietnam, but whose not so secret slogan was all the time: *The Professor is a Fink!* And what an array of bad anti-academic novels, I cannot help remind myself, written by disgruntled professors, created the mythology out of which that slogan grew. Each generation of students is invented by the generation of teachers just before them; but how different they are in dream

Leslie A. Fiedler, "The New Mutants," *Partisan Review* (Fall 1965), pp. 510–21. Reprinted with permission of the publisher and the author.

and fact—as different as self-hatred and its reflection in another. How different the professors in Jeremy Larner's *Drive, He Said* from those even in Randall Jarrell's *Pictures from an Institution* or Mary McCarthy's *Groves of Academe* . . .

Universities have long rivaled the churches in their devotion to institutionalizing hypocrisy; and more recently they have outstripped television itself (which most professors affect to despise even more than they despise organized religion) in the institutionalization of boredom.

But what the students were protesting in large part, I have come to believe, was the very notion of man which the universities sought to impose upon them: that bourgeois-Protestant version of Humanism, with its view of man as justified by rationality, work, duty, vocation, maturity, success; and its concomitant understanding of childhood and adolescence as a temporarily privileged time of preparation for assuming those burdens. The new irrationalists, however, are prepared to advocate prolonging adolescence to the grave, and are ready to dispense with school as an outlived excuse for leisure. To them work is as obsolete as reason, a vestige (already dispensable for large numbers) of an economically marginal, pre-automated world; and the obsolescence of the two adds up to the obsolescence of everything our society understands by maturity.

Nor is it in the name of an older more valid Humanistic view of man that the new irrationalists would reject the WASP version; Rabelais is as alien to them as Benjamin Franklin. Disinterested scholarship, reflection, the life of reason, a respect for tradition stir (however dimly and confusedly) chiefly their contempt; and the Abbey of Theleme would seem as sterile to them as Robinson Crusoe's Island. To the classroom, the library, the laboratory, the office conference and the meeting of scholars, they prefer the demonstration, the sit-in, the riot: the mindless unity of an impassioned crowd (with guitars beating out the rhythm in the background), whose immediate cause is felt rather than thought out, whose ultimate cause is itself . . .

Indeed, they regard Christianity, quite as the Black Muslim (with whom they have certain affinities) do, as a white ideology: merely one more method—along with Humanism, technology, Marxism—of imposing "White" or Western values on the colored rest of the world. To the new barbarian, however, that would-be post-Humanist (who is in most cases the white offspring of Christian forebears) his whiteness is likely to seem if not a stigma and symbol of shame, at least the outward sign of his exclusion from all that his Christian Humanist ancestors rejected in themselves and projected mythologically upon the colored man. For such reasons, his religion, when it becomes explicit, claims to be derived from Tibet or Japan or the ceremonies of the Plains Indians, or is composed out of the non-Christian sub-mythology that has grown up among Negro jazz musicians and in the civil rights movement. When the new barbarian speaks of "soul," for instance, he means not "soul" as in Heaven, but as in "soul music" or even "soul food."

It is all part of the attempt of the generation under twenty-five, not exclusively in its most sensitive members but especially in them, to become Negro, even as they attempt to become poor or pre-rational. About this particular form of psychic assimilation I have written sufficiently in the past (summing up what I had been long saying in our improbable novels of passion and our even more improbable love songs).

The young to whom I have been referring, the mythologically representative minority (who, by a process that infuriates the mythologically inert majority out of which they come, "stand for" their times), live in a community in which what used to be called the "Sexual Revolution," the Freudian-Laurentian revolt of their grandparents and parents, has triumphed as imperfectly and unsatisfactorily as all revolutions always triumph. They confront, therefore, the necessity of determining not only what meanings "love" can have in their new world, but—even more disturbingly—what significance, if any, "male" and"female" now possess. For a while, they (or at least their literary spokesmen recruited from the generation just before them) seemed content to celebrate a kind of *reductio* or *exaltatio ad absurdum* of their parents' once revolutionary sexual goals: The Reichian-inspired Cult of the Orgasm.

Young men and women eager to be delivered of traditional ideologies of love find especially congenial the belief that not union or relationship (much less offspring) but physical release is the end of the sexual act; and that, therefore, it is a matter of indifference with whom or by what method ones pursues the therapeutic climax, so long as that climax is total and repeated frequently. And Wilhelm Reich happily detaches this belief from the vestiges of Freudian rationalism, setting it instead in a context of Science Fiction and witchcraft; but his emphasis upon "full genitality," upon growing up and away from infantile pleasures, strikes the young as a disguised plea for the "maturity" they have learned to despise. In a time when the duties associated with adulthood promise to become irrelevant, there seems little reason for denying oneself the joys of babyhood—even if these are associated with such regressive fantasies as escaping it all in the arms of little sister (in the Gospel according to J. D. Salinger) or flirting with the possibility of getting into bed with papa (in the Gospel according to Norman Mailer). . .

What is at stake from Burroughs to Bellow, Ginsberg to Albee, Salinger to Gregory Corso is a more personal transformation: a radical metamorphosis of the Western male—utterly unforeseen in the decades before us, but visible now in every high school and college classroom, as well as on the paperback racks in airports and supermarkets. All around us, young males are beginning to retrieve for themselves the cavalier role once piously and class-consciously surrendered to women: *that of being beautiful and being loved.* Here once more the example to the Negro—the feckless and adorned Negro male with the blood of Cavaliers in his veins—has served as a model. And what else is left to young men, in any case, after the devaluation of the grim duties they had arrogated to themselves in place of the pursuit of loveliness?

All of us who are middle-aged and were Marxists, which is to say, who once numbered ourselves among the last assured Puritans, have surely noticed in ourselves a vestigial roundhead rage at the new hair styles of the advanced or—if you please—delinquent young. Watching young men titivate their locks (the comb, the pocket mirror and the bobby pin having replaced the jack-knife, catcher's mitt and brass knuckles), we feel the same baffled resentment that stirs in us when we realize that they have rejected work. A job and unequivocal maleness—these are two sides of the same Calvinist coin, which in the future buys nothing.

Few of us, however, have really understood how the Beatle hairdo is part of a syndrome, of which high heels, jeans tight over the buttocks, etc., are other aspects, symptomatic of a larger retreat from masculine aggressiveness to female allure—in literature and the arts to the style called "camp." And fewer still have realized how that style, though the invention of homosexuals, is now the possession of basically heterosexual males as well, a strategy in their campaign to establish a new relationship not only with women but with their own masculinity. In the course of that campaign, they have embraced certain kinds of gesture and garb, certain accents and tones traditionally associated with females or female impersonators; which is why we have been observing recently (in life as well as fiction and verse) young boys, quite unequivocally male, playing all the traditional roles of women, the vamp, the coquette, the whore, the icy tease, the pure young virgin.

Not only oldsters, who had envisioned and despaired of quite another future, are bewildered by this turn of events, but young girls, too, seem scarcely to know what is happening—looking on with that new, schizoid stare which itself has become a hallmark of our times. And the crop-headed jocks, those crew-cut athletes who represent an obsolescent masculine style based on quite other values, have tended to strike back blindly; beating the hell out of some poor kid whose hair is too long or whose pants are too tight—quite as they once beat up young Communists for revealing that their politics had become obsolete. Even heterosexual writers, however, have been slow to catch up, the revolution in sensibility running ahead of that in expression; and they have perforce permitted homosexuals to speak for them (Burroughs and Genêt and Baldwin and Ginsberg and Albee and a score of others), even to invent the forms in which the future will have to speak.

Will Herberg
Who Are the Hippies?

(1967)

The sociology of the hippies is not yet well understood or sufficiently investigated. But what we do know suggests that they are largely young, though many approaching middle age may be found among them; mostly of good middle-class families, and with some education. They say they cannot stand the constraints, the conventionalities, and the hypocrisies of our society, and so they have determined to secede and establish their own "joy" society in the midst of ours, but inwardly dissociated from it. They are inner *expatriates*, going off to live their authentic lives, not to Paris or the South Seas, but to the sidewalks, parks, and beaches of our big cities . . .

The deepest truth about the hippie style of life seems to be that the hippies are compulsive "enjoyers." They totally reject, in word and in fact, the idea of work, production, achievement; for them, the right kind of life is the life of enjoyment, bliss, even ecstasy. They *wallow* in life, so to speak: wallow in nature, wallow in "love," wallow in wallowing. Their ideal, quite literally, is a pure and unadulterated *self-indulgence*, a self-indulgence on a strange primitivistic level. In their utter absorption in enjoyment, and horrified rejection of work and production, they are—strange as it may seem—distantly related to David Riesman's "other-directed" suburbanite, who, too, views the older work-conscious, production-minded ethos with marked distaste, and strains for "gracious living" and the "civilized" enjoyment of the "finer things of life." But the suburbanite's enjoyment is anxiously "civilized" and conventional; the hippie's enjoyment is perhaps as anxiously "wild" and primitivistic. Yet there is a connection.

The keynote of the hippies' life of bliss is *love*. Theirs is indeed an orgiastic love-mystique. The term "love" appears everywhere, in everything the hippies have anything to do with, on their banners, on their persons, on their scanty possessions. Their articulate expressions are always about love; their gatherings are "love-ins"; their chants are "Buddhist love-songs" (of doubtful provenance). They meet every situation with proclamations of love . . .

Yet, paradoxically, though their style of life is orgiastic wallowing, and wallowing in love, the hippies exhibit a rather low level of sexual vitality. They are essentially epicene. In appearance and in dress, the men and women look very much alike: the men make no effort to exhibit an aggressive masculinity, nor the women a passionate feminine lure. The hippies themselves say that, in

---

Will Herberg, "Who Are the Hippies?" *National Review* (August 8, 1967), pp. 844–46, 872. Reprinted with permission of the publisher.

their usage, love does not mean sex; there is, naturally, a good deal of sexual activity among them, but they almost never bring sex into their hippie style of life. This, I think, is a point of considerable significance in an attempt to understand hippiedom.

The hippies have their drug problem. Many come with, or acquire, serious narcotic addictions; the hippies in San Francisco have established their own clinic to deal with the worst of these cases. But their attitude to LSD is quite different. Remember that their whole mode of life is wallowing in "experience," and LSD comes to them as a most promising agent—to deepen "experience," to widen it, to extend it, as a way toward the life of higher ecstasy. Marijuana and LSD are said to be rampant among the hippies, as part of their cultic way. In this, of course, they resemble other "far-out" groups in this country, by whom these drugs have also been adopted as "consciousness-extending," "life-enhancing," "ecstasy-inducing." The inducement of ecstasy and esctatic visions has indeed been the function of a number of drugs (mescal, hashish) employed by religious cults in the past, which the hippie cult rather curiously resembles, though in a loose way.

The hippies, with their cult of love, are naturally almost all pacifists, and many are also Vietniks. But political agitation, even well-defined political ideology, is remote from their anti-activist style of life, and they do not make much of an appearance in today's so-called protest movements.

So far, what do we have? We have a picture of a kind of primitivistic sect of uncertain size, loosely organized, devoted to a life of orgiastic enjoyment of nature, of "experience," of love, love, love . . . with no interest in any of the usual public preoccupations of Left groups. All this information is measurably true, and it does serve to fill out the hippie image. But somehow, we feel that we are missing something, that we have not yet got the hippie in proper focus.

Perhaps a proper focus may be obtained if we try to see the hippie phenomenon in longer perspective. There was once, perhaps as far back as the beginning of the second century, a small Christian sect known as the "Adamites." It was their conviction that, in becoming Christians, they had been restored to the sinless purity of before the Fall, in fact, to Adam's primitive innocence in Paradise. (The sect was also known as the Paradisals.) They advocated a thoroughgoing antinomianism and anarchism, the community of goods, vegetarianism, sexual promiscuity, and nudity, as obviously belonging to the paradisal state they were enjoying.

Now let us examine some of the better-defined positions of the Adamite-Paradisals:

1. *A sense of primal innocence*, without "knowledge of good and evil."

2. *Antinomianism*, rejection, in principle, if not always in practice, of all restrictive law imposed from the "outside."

3. *Hostility to all authority*, as infringing upon their paradisal freedom.

4. *Pacifism*, since there can be no hurt in Paradise.

5. *Sexual freedom*, and no sense of shame, like Adam and Eve in Paradise.

6. *Community of goods.*

7. *Free-floating fantasy-thinking:* impatience with critical thinking as the product of man's fall.

8. *Emotional self-indulgence:* resentment at demands for inner restraint and emotional self-discipline.

9. *A comprehensive cult of love*, as appropriate to the sinless life in Paradise . . .

. . . the hippies rejoice in a sense of primal innocence: they are the "children of love," embracing all mankind, indeed, all being, in love; incapable of doing hurt to man, beast, or nature. They resent all coercion and authority; they affirm pacifism, sexual freedom, and freedom from shame; they have a vague "leftist" leaning toward socialism. But, above all, it is in their orgiastic wallowing in enjoyment and love that they recall the Adamites; for the Adamites, despite Scripture which tells us that Adam and Eve were put into Paradise to "keep and to tend it," in other words to work and cultivate it, always insisted that Paradise was for "bliss and joy." . . .

Love, for them, is an orgiastic feeling in which they wallow in self-indulgence. This kind of love is corrupting both to the cultist and those upon whom it is lavished. Love, in any true sense, does not arise spontaneously as dumb feeling, to lose itself in a turbid morass of love mystique. Love is concern and commitment in its ultimate dimension. Not he loves his neighbor who sings love chants and invites the "experience of love," but he who understands how to share his neighbor's hopes and concerns, and to support his neighbor by helping to erect personal and social protections for his neighbor against the sinful self-aggrandizement of men in society. Love as feeling without doing rots and spoils; and surely it would be hard to find anything so rancid as the love-unction of the hippie love mongers.

And now we come to the final point. It is not innocent to pretend to an innocence impossible for man; unacknowledged sinfulness is a deadly poison, ruinous to the individual and to society both. For unacknowledged sinfulness means a refusal to see oneself in realistic perspective; it means a loss of the sense of ambiguity in life, of its hopes and possibilities, indeed, but also of its perversions and frustrations. The hippies, with their paradisal naiveté, would encourage this illusion of primal innocence in us and in mankind, an illusion so appealing that we are forever falling into it even without encouragement . . .

Irving Howe
New Styles in Leftism

(1965)

Cultural Style

The "new leftist" appears, at times, as a figure embodying a style of speech, dress, work and culture. Often, especially if white, the son of the middle class—and sometimes the son of middle class parents nursing radical memories—he asserts his rebellion against the deceit and hollowness of American society. Very good; there is plenty to rebel against. But in the course of his rebellion he tends to reject not merely the middle class ethos but a good many other things he too hastily associates with it: the intellectual heritage of the West, the tradition of liberalism at its most serious, the commitment to democracy as an indispensable part of civilized life. He tends to think of style as the very substance of his revolt, and while he may, on one side of himself, engage in valuable activities in behalf of civil rights, student freedom, etc., he nevertheless tacitly accepts the "givenness" of American society, has little hope or expectation of changing it, and thereby, in effect, settles for a mode of personal differentiation.

Primarily that means the wish to shock, the wish to assault the sensibilities of a world he cannot overcome. If he cannot change it, then at least he can outrage it. He searches in the limited repertoire of sensation and shock: for sick comics who will say "fuck" in nightclubs; for drugs that will vault him beyond the perimeters of the suburbs; for varieties, perversities, and publicities of sex so as perhaps to create an inner, private revolution that will accompany—or replace?—the outer, public revolution.

But "the new leftist" is frequently trapped in a symbiotic relationship with the very middle class he rejects, dependent upon it for his self-definition: quite as the professional anti-Communist of a few years ago was caught up with the Communist party which, had it not existed, he would have had to invent—as indeed at times he did invent. So that for all its humor and charm, the style of the "new leftist" tends to become a rigid anti-style, dependent for its survival on the enemy it is supposed to panic. To *épater le bourgeois*—in this case, perhaps, to *épater le père*—is to acquiesce in a basic assumption of at least the more sophisticated segments of the middle class: that values can be inferred from, or are resident in, the externals of dress, appearance, furnishings and hairdo's . . .

Let me specify a few more of the characteristic attitudes among the "new leftists":

Irving Howe, "New Styles in 'Leftism,'" *Dissent* (Summer 1965), pp. 308–19. Reprinted with permission of the publisher and author.

1. *An extreme, sometimes unwarranted, hostility toward liberalism.* They see liberalism only in its current versions, institutional, corporate and debased; but avoiding history, they know very little about the elements of the liberal tradition which should remain valuable for any democratic socialist. For the "new leftists," as I have here delimited them, liberalism means Clark Kerr, not John Dewey; Max Lerner, not John Stuart Mill; Pat Brown, not George Norris. And thereby they would cut off the resurgent American radicalism from what is, or should be, one of its sustaining sources: the tradition that has yielded us a heritage of civil freedoms, disinterested speculation, humane tolerance.

2. *An impatience with the problems that concerned an older generation of radicals.* Here the generational conflict breaks out with strong feelings on both sides, the older people feeling threatened in whatever they have been able to salvage from past experiences, the younger people feeling the need to shake off dogma and create their own terms of action . . .

The issue of totalitarianism is neither academic nor merely historical; no one can seriously engage in politics without clearly and publicly defining his attitude toward it. I deliberately say "attitude" rather than "analysis," for while there can be a great many legitimate differences of analytic stress and nuance among democratic socialists in discussing the totalitarian society, morally there should be only a candid and sustained opposition to it.

3. *A vicarious indulgence in violence, often merely theoretic and thereby all the more irresponsible.* Not being a pacifist, I believe there may be times when violence is unavoidable; being a man of the twentieth century, I believe that a recognition of its necessity must come only after the most prolonged consideration, as an utterly last resort. To "advise" the Negro movement to adopt a policy encouraging or sanctioning violence, to sneer at Martin Luther King for his principled refusal of violence, is to take upon oneself a heavy responsibility—and if, as usually happens, taken lightly, it becomes sheer irresponsibility.

It is to be insensitive to the fact that the nonviolent strategy has arisen from Negro experience. It is to ignore the notable achievements that strategy has already brought. It is to evade the hard truth expressed by the Rev. Abernathy: "The whites have the guns." And it is to dismiss the striking moral advantage that nonviolence has yielded the Negro movement, as well as the turmoil, anxiety and pain—perhaps even fundamental reconsideration—it has caused among whites in the North and the South . . .

4. *An unconsidered enmity toward something vaguely called the Establishment.* As the term "Establishment" was first used in England, it had the value of describing—which is to say, delimiting—a precise social group; as it has come to be used in the United States, it tends to be a term of all-purpose put-down. In England it refers to a caste of intellectuals with an Oxbridge

education, closely related in values to the ruling class, and setting the cultural standards which largely dominate both the London literary world and the two leading universities.

Is there an Establishment in this, or any cognate, sense in the United States? Perhaps. There may now be in the process of formation, for the first time, such an intellectual caste; but if so, precise discrimination of analysis and clear boundaries of specification would be required as to what it signifies and how it operates. As the term is currently employed, however, it is difficult to know who, besides those merrily using it as a thunderbolt of opprobrium, is *not* in the Establishment. And a reference that includes almost everyone tells us almost nothing.

5. *An equally unreflective belief in "the decline of the West"*—apparently without the knowledge that, more seriously held, this belief has itself been deeply ingrained in Western thought, frequently in the thought of reactionaries opposed to modern rationality, democracy and sensibility.

The notion is so loose and baggy, it means little. Can it, however, be broken down? If war is a symptom of this decline, then it holds for the East as well. If totalitarianism is a sign, then it is not confined to the West. If economics is a criterion, then we must acknowledge, Marxist predictions aside, that there has been an astonishing recovery in Western Europe. If we turn to culture, then we must recognize that in the West there has just come to an end one of the greatest periods in human culture—that period of "modernism" represented by figures like Joyce, Stravinsky, Picasso. If improving the life of the workers is to count, then the West can say something in its own behalf. And if personal freedom matters, then, for all its grave imperfections, the West remains virtually alone as a place of hope . . .

But is it not really childish to talk about "the West" as if it were some indivisible whole we must either accept or reject without amendment? There are innumerable strands in the Western tradition, and our task is to nourish those which encourage dignity and freedom. But to envisage some global apocalypse that will end in the destruction of the West, is a sad fantasy, a token of surrender before the struggles of the moment.

6. *A crude, unqualified anti-Americanism, drawing from every possible source, even if one contradicts another: the aristocratic bias of Eliot and Ortega, Communist propaganda, the speculations of Tocqueville, the ressentiment of post-war Europe, etc.*

7. *An increasing identification with that sector of the "third world" in which "radical" nationalism and Communist authoritarianism merge.* Consider this remarkable fact: In the past decade there have occurred major changes in the Communist world, and many of the intellectuals in Russia and eastern Europe have reexamined their assumptions, often coming to the conclusion, masked only by the need for caution, that democratic values are primary

in any serious effort at socialist reconstruction. Yet at the very same time most of the "new leftists" have identified not with the "revisionists" in Poland or Djilas in Yugoslavia—or even Tito. They identify with the harder, more violent, more dictatorial segments of the Communist world . . .

The Place: The New Left and the Universities

The violence on the American campus in 1968 and 1969 was preceded by a great deal of theorizing on the part of the new left as to the nature of our universities. It was largely concluded that the university was the propaganda arm of the culture—a place in which all of the decadent values of our culture were instilled into the younger generation. That conclusion has been the foundation for the guerrilla warfare of the left on the campus. The commentary discusses this assumption, and offers some alternative ideas.

Studies on the Left, Objectivity

(1959)

In academic circles, the term "objectivity" is generally used to indicate the dispassion, the non-partisanship with which the "true scholar" approaches his work. It is also frequently used to indicate the prevalent, or "majority" view. For example, there are not very many students who will stand up for their "subjective" evaluation of another scholar's work in opposition to the supposedly objective judgment inherent in the fact that the man has been given a professorship at a prominent Ivy League university, and a great deal of praise by established scholars. Many, perhaps most, students will distrust their own subjective opinion in the face of all this objective data, and they may even state that there is no other standard of evaluation. In other words, they have made the subtle and all-important equation between quality on the one hand, and acceptability or market value on the other, and are well on

"The Radicalism of Disclosure," Editorial. *Studies on the Left* (Fall 1959), pp. 2–4.

their way to a bright academic future. The objectivity here assumed is reducible to the weight of authority, the viewpoint of those who are in position to enforce standards, the value judgments of the not so metaphorical marketplace of ideas.

Similarly, the use of the term to indicate scholarly dispassion is, at bottom, a way of justifying acceptance (either active or passive) of the status quo. When a man is digging up facts to support traditional and accepted interpretations, or when he has no interest in the significance of these facts for larger theoretical questions, he may, without too much difficulty, prevent himself from becoming impassioned. When he is turning out an obviously marketable piece showing that the American Constitution is the best guarantee of freedom that man will ever come up with, that the causes of some historical event are so complex that they are beyond discovery, or that some poet had an aversion to dogs, he may understandably remain unimpassioned. But this does not necessarily mean that he is any less biased than his neighbor, although it might very well mean that he cares less. On the other hand, when a scholar arrives at a radical or unconventional interpretation, he may very well become excited by what he is doing. For the act of contradiction involves emotions more tumultuous than those aroused by the state of acceptance. Scholarly dispassion is the true medium of the scholar satisfied with (or browbeaten by) things as they are.

As graduate students anticipating academic careers, we feel a very personal stake in academic life, and we feel that, as radicals, we are hampered in our work by the intrusion of prevailing standards of scholarship, which set up a screen between ourselves and our product, an automatic censoring device which trims and deflates and confines our work, under the pretext of what is supposed to be "objective scholarship," until we no longer know it as our own. Like little boys writing poems in the style of Terence, we learn the traditional, acceptable genres in our fields, and then develop the skills necessary to produce similar work, until slowly, subtly, but surely, we come to look upon our work, not as the expression of our union with man and society, but merely as our means of livelihood and security—a product for sale, neither our possession nor our creation. And the closer we come to taking our places as working people in the profession, the harder it is to remember who we are, what we have to say, and why we got into the intellectual racket in the first place.

But when we think back, we recall that at some point in our education we thought that life was interesting and challenging, and that we wanted to know more about it. We wanted to understand the phenomena which excited us: the functioning of the galaxy; the role of men in history; the creative process. And we wanted to know how we could participate creatively in life. We wanted to learn the origins of racism so that we could help to stamp it out; we wanted to know why people suffer, so that we could help to make suffering less in our time. We were not very dispassionate about our work then, because it is not easy to be dispassionate about racism, or the creative process, or the galaxy, about war and peace, and the fate of man. We did not think, at that time, that history is dull, and the search for knowledge, drudgery.

Nor do we think so yet. There is work for the radical scholar, the thinker who is committed to the investigation of the origins, purposes and limitations of institutions and concepts, as well as for the conservative or liberal scholar who is committed to their efficient maintenance and improvement. There is room in scholarship for the application of reason to the *reconstruction* of society, as well as to legalistic interpretation and reform. There is a place for the scholar who looks upon traditional formulations, theories, structures, even "facts" with a habitually critical attitude stemming from his distaste for things as they are, and from his distrust of the analyses of those who are committed to the maintenance of the status quo.

There is a place for him because, if he is a scholar as well as a malcontent, an honest researcher as well as a radical, his very partisanship, bias—call it what you will—gives him a kind of objectivity. Because he stands opposed to established institutions and conventional conceptions, the radical scholar possesses an unconcern for their safety or preservation which enables him to carry inquiry along paths where the so-called "objective" conservative or liberal scholar would not care to tread . . .

The Port Huron Statement
The University and Social Change

(1962)

. . . The civil rights, peace, and student movements are too poor and socially slighted, and the labor movement too quiescent, to be counted with enthusiasm. From where else can power and vision be summoned? We believe that the universities are an overlooked seat of influence.

First, the university is located in a permanent position of social influence. Its educational function makes it indispensable and automatically makes it a crucial institution in the formation of social attitudes. Second, in an unbelievably complicated world, it is the central institution for organizing, evaluating, and transmitting knowledge. Third, the extent to which academic resources presently are used to buttress immoral social practice is revealed first, by the extent to which defense contracts make the universities engineers

---

Students for a Democratic Society, *The Port Huron Statement* (1962), pp. 61–63.

of the arms race. Too, the use of modern social science as a manipulative tool reveals itself in the "human relations" consultants to the modern corporations, who introduce trivial sops to give laborers feelings of "participation" or "belonging," while actually deluding them in order to further exploit their labor. And, of course, the use of motivational research is already infamous as a manipulative aspect of American politics. But these social uses of the universities' resources also demonstrate the unchangeable reliance by men of power on the men and storehouses of knowledge: this makes the university functionally tied to society in new ways, revealing new potentialities, new levers for change. Fourth, the university is the only mainstream institution that is open to participation by individuals of nearly any viewpoint.

These, at least, are facts, no matter how dull the teaching, how paternalistic the rules, how irrelevant the research that goes on. Social relevance, the accessibility to knowledge, and internal openness—these together make the university a potential base and agency in a movement of social change . . .

1. Any new left in America must be, in large measure, a left with real intellectual skills, committed to deliberativeness, honesty, and reflection as working tools. The university permits the political life to be an adjunct to the academic one, and action to be informed by reason.

2. A new left must be distributed in significant social roles throughout the country. The universities are distributed in such a manner.

3. A new left must consist of younger people who matured in the post-war world, and must be directed to the recruitment of younger people. The university is an obvious beginning point.

4. A new left must include liberals and socialists, the former for their relevance, the latter for their sense of thoroughgoing reforms in the system. The university is a more sensible place than a political party for these two traditions to begin to discuss their differences and look for political synthesis.

5. A new left must start controversy across the land, if national policies and national apathy are to be reversed. The ideal university is a community of controversy, within itself and in its effects on communities beyond.

6. A new left must transform modern complexity into issues that can be understood and felt close-up by every human being. It must give form to the feelings of helplessness and indifference, so that people may see the political, social, and economic sources of their private troubles and organize to change society. In a time of supposed prosperity, moral complacency, and political manipulation, a new left cannot rely on only aching stomachs to be the engine force of social reform. The case for change, for alternatives that will involve uncomfortable personal efforts, must be argued as never before. The university is a relevant place for all of these activities.

But we need not indulge in illusions: The university system cannot complete a movement of ordinary people making demands for a better life. From its schools and colleges across the nation, a militant left might awaken its allies, and by beginning the process towards peace, civil rights, and labor struggles, reinsert theory and idealism where too often reign confusion and political barter. The power of students and faculty united is not only potential; it has shown its actuality in the South, and in the reform movements of the North.

To turn these possibilities into realities will involve national efforts at university reform by an alliance of students and faculty. They must wrest control of the educational process from the administrative bureaucracy. They must make fraternal and functional contact with allies in labor, civil rights, and other liberal forces outside the campus. They must import major public issues into the curriculum... They must make debate and controversy, not dull pedantic cant, the common style for educational life. They must consciously build a base for their assault upon the loci of power...

Paul Potter
The Intellectual and Social Change

(1964)

All paths in the university seem to turn ultimately back upon the university and back upon the established order within it. The academic pecking order; the establishment of professional organizations and the criteria of excellence they set forth—all of these were turned back upon the bureaucratic organization of the university, upon the isolation of the intellectual, or upon his faithful service to the Establishment and to the status quo. This left those intellectuals who wished to play a dissenting role in a peculiarly exposed position. There was not a place for them to go. There was no home for them. The university, which was supposed to provide their home, was not willing to play that role. The agencies in which they might work, in which they were welcomed, were not agencies that wanted critical dissent; they were agencies that wanted expert advice in carrying out the already established programs. And this was a pattern, I think, which dominated the post-war era. There are exceptions to that. In some sense I make this position an archetype more than it may have been. But let me give a few specific examples of how the intellectuals were exposed.

Paul Potter, "The Intellectual and Social Change," from *The New Student Left*, Mitchell Cohen and Dennis Hale, eds., pp. 16–18. Reprinted by permission of the Beacon Press,

I think the whole debate on civil liberties that raged in the post-war era and especially in the 1950's is a good example of this exposure. It was a debate that was divorced from any analysis of the problems of the society at large. It was a fraudulent debate. It was a debate which could only have been a significant debate in a society that was actually threatened by anarchy or by imminent revolution. It was not a real debate and yet the intellectuals participated in it with vigor because it seemed to be the only way of extricating themselves from the squeeze that they were in.

Another example would be the ADA and its development—the amalgamation presumably of labor and intellectuals into a vital political force, an amalgamation which in its very effectiveness led to the co-option of more intellectuals into the power structure, rather than the freeing of the intellectuals from the burdens of an oppressive university system.

A final example of the impetus of the intellectual in the universities, was (and is) beautifully illustrated by faculty politics—the most petty, mundane, bureaucratically centered system of politics that I can imagine. It is not a set of political activities that has as its basis the idea of liberating the university from the society. It is a set of politics which is organized around personal advancement, prestige, centers of influence and power within the university—not within society.

But I think there has been a change, and the change is what I want to talk about most of all. For the first time, there are alternatives to the intellectual other than service to the Establishment or isolation from society, and those alternatives are being enunciated and proclaimed and implemented by social movements in the society. For the first time there is a base of power outside the university to which the intellectual can turn—which he can utilize in freeing himself from the strictures of the university system, in defending himself from the exposed position which he held in society until 1955 or later.

This, essentially, is another place to go. It is a home. It is not the home that that any of us predicted. The home that we've been looking for is in the university, and the home the intellectual is finding is in social movements, political action, and agitation.

Out of this comes a new view, a new view that is expressed by an increasing number of intellectuals and students. . . They no longer think of the university as a Gestalt—as a possibility of a new synthesis, of a deep and beautiful image shimmering in the far-distant future. They think of the university very concretely as a mechanism thay can utilize, that they can manipulate to gain certain ends which they consider important. . .

Intellectual want direct power. They no longer want to deal with power as an abstract symbol of the classroom and of lectures. They want to utilize power for social ends. . .

Mario Savio
An End to History

(1966)

Last summer I went to Mississippi to join the struggle there for civil rights. This fall I am engaged in another phase of the same struggle, this time in Berkeley. The two battlefields may seem quite different to some observers, but this is not the case. The same rights are at stake in both places—the right to participate as citizens in democratic society and the right to due process of law. Further, it is a struggle against the same enemy. In Mississippi an autocratic and powerful minority rules, through organized violence, to suppress the vast, virtually powerless, majority. In California, the privileged minority manipulates the University bureaucracy to suppress the students' political expression. That "respectable" bureaucracy masks the financial plutocrats; that impersonal bureaucracy is the efficient enemy in a "Brave New World."

In our free speech fight at the University of California, we have come up against what may emerge as the greatest problem of our nation—depersonalized, unresponsive bureaucracy. We have encountered the organized status quo in Mississippi, but it is the same in Berkeley. Here we find it impossible usually to meet with anyone but secretaries. Beyond that, we find functionaries who cannot make policy but can only hide behind the rules. We have discovered total lack of response on the part of the policy makers. To grasp a situation which is truly Kafkaesque, it is necessary to understand the bureaucratic mentality. And we have learned quite a bit about it this fall, more outside the classroom than in.

As bureaucrat, an administrator believes that nothing new happens. He occupies an ahistorical point of view. In September, to get the attention of this bureaucracy which had issued arbitrary edicts suppressing student political expression and refused to discuss its action, we held a sit-in on the campus. We sat around a police car and kept it immobilized for over thirty-two hours. At last, the administrative bureaucracy agreed to negotiate. But instead, on the following Monday, we discovered that a committee had been appointed, in accordance with usual regulations, to resolve the dispute. Our attempt to convince any of the administrators that an event had occurred, that something new had happened, failed. They saw this simply as something to be handled by normal university procedures.

The same is true of all bureaucracies. They begin as tools, means to certain legitimate goals, and they end up feeding their own existence. The conception

Mario Savio, "An End to History." *The New Radicals*, ed. Paul Jacobs and Saul Landau, 1966, pp. 230–34. Reprinted by permission of the publisher, Knopf-Random House.

that bureaucrats have is that history has in fact come to an end. No events can occur now that the Second World War is over which can change American society substantially. We proceed by standard procedures as we are.

The most crucial problems facing the United States today are the problem of automation and the problem of racial injustice. Most people who will be put out of jobs by machines will not accept an end to events, this historical plateau, as the point beyond which no change occurs. Negroes will not accept an end to history here. All of us must refuse to accept history's final judgment that in America there is no place in society for people whose skins are dark. On campus, students are not about to accept it as a fact that the university has ceased evolving and is in its final state of perfection, that students and faculty are respectively raw material and employees, or that the University is to be autocratically run by unresponsive bureaucrats.

Here is the real contradiction: the bureaucrats hold history as ended. As a result significant parts of the population both on campus and off are dispossessed, and these dispossessed are not about to accept this ahistorical point of view. It is out of this that the conflict has occurred with the university bureaucracy and will continue to occur until that bureaucracy becomes responsive or until it is clear the university cannot function. . .

The university is the place where people begin seriously to question the conditions of their existence and raise the issue of whether they can be committed to the society they have been born into. After a long period of apathy during the fifties, students have begun not only to question but, having arrived at answers, to act on those answers. This is part of a growing understanding among many people in America that history has not ended, that a better society is possible, and that it is worth dying for.

This free speech fight points up a fascinating aspect of contemporary campus life. Students are permitted to talk all they want so long as their speech has no consequences.

One conception of the university, suggested by a classical Christian formulation, is that it be in the world but not of the world. The conception of Clark Kerr, by contrast, is that the university is part and parcel of this particular stage in the history of American society; it stands to serve the need of American industry; it is a factory that turns out a certain product needed by industry or government. Because speech does often have consequences which might alter this perversion of higher education, the university must put itself in a position of censorship. It can permit two kinds of speech: speech which encourages continuation of the status quo, and speech which advocates changes in it so radical as to be irrelevant in the foreseeable future. Someone may advocate radical change in all aspects of American society, and this I am sure he can do with impunity. But if someone advocates sit-ins to bring about changes in discriminatory hiring practices, this can not be permitted because it goes against the status quo of which the university is a part. And this is how the fight began here.

The administration of the Berkeley campus has admitted that external, extra-legal groups have pressured the university not to permit students on campus to organize picket lines, not to permit on campus any speech with consequences. And the bureaucracy went along. Speech with consequences, speech in the area of civil rights, speech which some might regard as illegal, must stop.

Many students here at the university, many people in society, are wandering aimlessly about. Strangers in their own lives, there is no place for them. They are people who have not learned to compromise, who for example have come to the university to learn to question, to grow, to learn—all the standard things that sound like clichés because no one takes them seriously. And they find at one point or other that for them to become part of society, to become lawyers, ministers, businessmen, people in government, that very often they must compromise those principles which were most dear to them. They must suppress the most creative impulses that they have; this is a prior condition for being part of the system. The university is well structured, well tooled, to turn out people with all the sharp edges worn off, the well-rounded person. The university is well equipped to produce that sort of person, and this means that the best among the people who enter must for four years wander aimlessly much of the time questioning why they are on campus at all, doubting whether there is any point in what they are doing, and looking toward a very bleak existence afterward in a game in which all of the rules have been made up, which one cannot really amend . . .

Steve Weissman
Freedom and the University

(1966)

A Free University, like the free society upon which its long-term success depends, is at present only a distant vision. But that vision—based upon the belief that even students have a right to shape the environment in which they live and work—is our most powerful weapon for the subversion of the multiversity. For most students accept the vision of the multiversity. Though alienated, they do not comprehend the source of their alienation. They accept the authoritarian and conformist patterns of the multiversity as

Steve Weissman, "Freedom and the University." *The New Radicals*, ed. Paul Jacobs and Saul Landau, 1966, pp. 234–37. Reprinted by permission of the publisher, Knopf-Random House.

natural, inevitable. What right have they to do more than gripe over even the most demeaning and absurd regulation? Are they not being *given* an education? If they don't like it where they are, are they not *free* to be given that education at the multiversity of their choice? Democracy? Most students would be honored to serve on some sandbox administration committee: they wouldn't even realize that their decision-making power was complete only if they made the "right' decisions.

On campus as off, the belief in human dignity, freedom, democracy, and participation in decision-making is in a sorry state. Our first tasks are thus educational:

1. The Campus Freedom Party. Throughout the country, and especially in the South, activists are organizing political parties to run candidates for student government offices. In most cases, however, they are not running to win, or even with the assumption that putting a good man in a crummy office would change the way in which their university does business. Rather they are running educational campaigns, calling the sandbox by its name, and building constituencies for the abolition of the most obnoxious *in loco parentis* rules, for elimination of compulsory R.O.T.C., to protest the university keeping books for the draft board, for unlimited free speech and political activity, for an end to discriminatory admissions, housing, and hiring, to protest university purchases from and investments in discriminatory corporations, for co-op book stores, and for the idea of eventual student-faculty government. With these platforms student activists raise the vision of student democracy ("rather than student government"), pressure those who do get elected to accept minimal programs leading to that vision, and develop a nucleus to lead action when a direct provocation occurs. After the elections, the parties (or S.D.S. groups which sponsor them) attempt to engage their voters in a year-round multi-issue program of radical self-education, work in civil rights or with the poor, anti-war activity, educational reform, and participation in planning the next campaign.
2. Free Student Unions. One step beyond the political party is the student union. The union focuses not on twice-a-year elections, but on year-round collective bargaining with the administration. It also institutionalizes conflict, the sanction of a student strike, and the notion that students should govern themselves through a mass-participation organization. Berkeley's F.S.U. has so far had only limited success, partially because of the let down after F.S.M., partially because of the Vietnam protest. Perhaps F.S.U. would now be stronger and more "legitimate" if it had been started during—not after—the free speech controversy. Also, F.S.U. faces a continuing need to expand on the idea of time locals. Union members are organized on smaller units on the basis of their willingness to meet at a certain time, for example there is an 11 A.M. Thursday local. But most union members are not active in time locals, and there is an increasing desire to organize at least some of the

time locals on the basis of common political and educational interests and ideologies.

3. On-campus direct action and demonstrations. Student activists should make quite clear that they do not expect any great changes to come about through voting: the Regents and the administration, even most of the faculty, think it their right to direct the lives of students. If we are serious about controlling our lives and education, then we must constantly affirm the right to revolt when we are affected by rules and practices over which we have no say.

Compliance with rules should always be received as an unpleasant necessity, never as an obligation. When direct provocations arise, student activists are then prepared to organize massive non-compliance with the regulations in question (like the setting up of the prohibited political tables at Berkeley or sleep-outs against dorm curfews) or against the administration itself. Or, when possible, they can initiate guerrilla campaigns of demonstration, pickets, and sit-ins to call attention to and build opposition against particular injustices.

4. Organizing around ideas. Radical activists must continually counterpose their vision of the university and of human society to the liberal ideology which underlies most courses in history, political science, economics, sociology, philosophy and literature. Professors might have all the answers, but to what questions? Moreover, the conventional academic view of human nature and the possibilities of change is probably more pessimistic than that of the activist. One of our most important organizing jobs is to clarify in papers, in classes, and in public forums the bias behind the conventional wisdom and to make explicit our own values. Equally important is the need, especially for graduate students, to define areas of radical research, to go beyond refining established revelation, to pose alternatives to the presently accepted reality. The Vietnam protest offers many such opportunities, as do discussions of the War on Poverty, automation, urban problems, and the social responsibility of scientists . . .

Bradley Cleaveland
A Letter to Undergraduates

(1964)

Are you aware that the most salient characteristic of the "multiversity" is massive production of specialized excellence? *Specialized Excellence.* It will be some time before machines will displace the super-trades; thus massive

---

Bradley Cleaveland, "A Letter to Undergraduates," *Slate Supplement to the General Catalog*, A Journal of Educational Criticism, I, No. 4, Sept. 1964 (University of California, Berkeley). Reprinted by permission of the publisher.

training centers are necessary. But why do we insist upon calling them educational centers rather than training centers?

> *The multiversity is not an educational center, but a highly efficient industry: it produces bombs, other war machines, a few token "peaceful" machines, and enormous numbers of safe, highly skilled, and respectable automatons to meet the immediate needs of business and government.*

We all know that this is necessary to some extent for the maintenance of "American know-how"; otherwise the system would collapse and anarchy would reign, etc. But the forbidden fruit is to ask the devastating question WHY? WHY ONLY *know-how*? Or is it that we wish to produce the largest population of highly skilled idiots ever known to man? We may safely say that graduate schools should perform the function of training for specialized excellence . . . but even then not exclusively. And if you will recall, we are discussing the matter of undergraduate freedom to learn. What has occurred when undergraduate education is eradicated; whether it be for the excuse of "too many students," or "exploding knowledge," or in the name of political expedience during the "Cold War"?

> *When this occurs in public universities the result is abandonment of the American Democratic experiment in which the radical proposition of education for all is the central axiom.*

Dear undergraduate, your "learning" has come to an impasse. Below the level of formal responsibility (the Regents, president, and chancellors), the Academic Senate (the faculty) itself is guilty of a massive and disastrous default. It is said that the Regents have given to the faculty the power and responsibility to deal with your learning. To put it mildly, the Academic Senate has turned that power and responsibility into a sham, an unused fiction. If this be true, then who is responsible for seeing to it that the faculty do something? We can cancel out President Kerr: he has already admitted publicly that he is incompetent to attend to the matter of undergraduate learning. That takes us back up the bureaucratic ladder again . . . do you know what the phrase "The Regents of the University of California" means? Following is the meaning of that phrase:

> Edward Carter: Chairman of the Board of Regents, Director, Broadway-Hale Retail Stores, Northrup Aircraft, Pacific Tel & Tel, and First Western Bank; Dorothy Chandler: Director, L.A. *Times*, and wife of Norman Chandler of the Southern California News Publishing empire; William Coblentz: corporation lawyer, San Francisco; Frederick Dutton: U.S. Assistant Secretary of State; Mrs. William Randolph Hearst: ("housewife"), of the Hearst national newspaper empire; Mrs. Edward Heller: ("housewife"), widow and heir to Edward Heller, Director, Permanente Cement, Wells Fargo Bank, Schwabacher & Fry partner, and Pacific Intermountain Express; William E. Forbes: Southern California Music Com-

pany; Lawrence Kennedy: attorney, Redding, California, (just prior to Mr. Kennedy's appointment as a Regent, it was strongly urged that it might be appropriate to appoint an *educator* to the Board of Regents); Donald H. McLaughlin: ("mining geologist"), Director, Homestake Mining Company, one of the largest gold mining operations in the world, recent interests in uranium mining, Director, Western Airlines, American Trust, and a Peruvian copper-mining operation; Samuel Mosher: Director, Signal Gas & Oil, and Long Beach Oil Development Company, which was accused publicly a few months ago, by Lieutenant Governor Glenn Anderson, of trying to wrest public control of a recently discovered state owned oil field off Long Beach with a projected worth of over 3 billion . . . enough to shake up the world market and give California Petroleum men a virtual monopoly; Edwin Pauley: Director, Pauley Oil, Western Airlines; William Matson Roth: U.S. Special Deputy for Trade Relations, Director, National Life Insurance, Matson Shipping, Honolulu Oil, Pacific Intermountain Express; Norton Simon: Director, Hunt Foods, McCalls, Wesson Oil & Snowdrift, and also "land developer"; Phillip Boyd: former mayor of Palm Springs, Director, Deep Canyon Properties, Security National Bank; John Canaday: Vice President, Lockheed Aircraft, Director, Corporate Public Relations, Lockheed Aircraft; and Regent number sixteen on our list is the one and only representative of organized labor (the most reactionary element in labor at that): Cornelius Haggerty: President, Construction and Building Trades Council, AFL-CIO.

In these men you find substantial ownership and control of the vital raw materials and service industries in the West: communications, the press, television, air and surface transportation, fuel, and finance; virtually enough power to make or break five governors and ten university presidents. The board members are appointed for terms of sixteen years by the governor. There are also ex-officio members, *one of whom is an educator*: Clark Kerr. I would like to ask you to think for a moment about the "public" character of these men. In the first place, who even knows them? . . . except a few of us who are aware that they are "famous" or "very wealthy men." What do they do? *and why? for whose interest?*

Dear undergraduate, there is perhaps no other set of questions, in the political realm, of greater importance for you. Let us return for a moment to the matter of who is responsible for your freedom to learn. As I said a moment ago, the Regents have delegated power and responsibility to the Academic Senates of the eight campuses. Let us just call the Academic Senate the "faculty," which is the automatic membership of the Senate. At any rate, there is something terribly wrong here. If we assume that the faculty is incompetent to effect the necessary changes, then it would seem of the greatest urgency that the Regents themselves do something to correct the situation. If the Regents do not act, then we must conclude that they are (1) satisfied; or (2) incompetent; or (3) both. Two things are certain: (1) as corporate men of power, the Regents are getting precisely what they most desire—enormous numbers of highly skilled graduates to fill the corporate structure and to keep it running smoothly; (2) *it is debatable* from their own point of view, whether the Regents would find it practical to "educate" these skilled people as well as to *train* them. Why? To put the answer very crudely: the Regents, who run private corporations, just as the politicians who run public corporations, desire highly skilled, but politically and economically *dumb* "personnel." The politicians have, of course, even made laws to that effect . . . in the form of such legislation as the Hatch Act, which forbids partisan politics in government bureaucracies. Consequently, if the faculty refuses to face the problem of educating undergraduates, but instead is encouraged, and agrees, to make only piecemeal reform which only slightly lessens pressures in some areas while making them more severe in other areas, the Regents might be said to be very happy with such a course of action . . . in fact that is what they are doing. The course/grade/unit system will probably be "adjusted," and the bread and circus will become more intense and dazzling: note the priority in the university building program . . . first you build the student-union complex, then an auditorium which will be the "largest this side of the Mississippi," and "sometime in the future" will come an undergraduate library. But why do private and public corporate men act this way?

From time immemorial, men of power have considered it wise to keep their constituents at a level of ignorance whereby the process of ruling them is most easily accomplished.

Or are we to entertain the possibility that the Regents have upset the applecart of history? Have they become revolutionaries? It is true that they recently removed the ban on Communist speakers on campus. Of course, they resisted for fifteen years . . . since the McCarthy era. And during the McCarthy era they were able to force the Academic Senate into adopting a loyalty oath. If you can forgive the faculty of a university for *that*, you can forgive them for *anything*. Many professors did not forgive the Senate, however, and resigned. The spine of this faculty, close to forty professors, left in disgust, left scars behind which will never heal. Moreover, what the hell difference does it make whether you hear a Communist every year or so. Most of you would laugh at him . . . like laughing at a movement which involves the entire world! If any one of you wisely decided to study a Communist speaker's proposals, to think about them, to read about them seriously, you not only would find it *impossible from the standpoint of time*, but you would also be considered a heretic by your fellow "students." It is probably accurate to say that the removal of the speaker ban on Communists was a great contribution on the symbolic level . . . like a Charter Day ceremony. Politically, it was very wise.

Speaking of politics, what relation exists between the university and the U.S. Government? Aside from providing trained personnel for public corporations (agencies, bureaus, etc.) as in private ones, is there as direct a relation between the university and government as between the university and the Regents? Yes, it seems that the university, or shall we call a spade a spade—the Regents—it seems that the Regents are snuggled up pretty tightly to the seats of power in Washington (though it is difficult to tell who-hugs-whom the hardest in Washington):

> Item—from the *Cal Reporter*, May 13, 1963: "According to the Financial Report of 1961–62, the U.S. Government spent about 227 millions on Special Projects. These included 150 millions for Lawrence Radiation Laboratory (U.C.), 76 millions for Los Alamos Radiation Lab (U.C.). The income for the entire University (eight campuses) excluding these special projects was 250 millions."

Let us summarize for a moment. Your learning opportunities are limited to "getting ahead," or acquiring a skill to do so. You are obstructed from the realities of the twentieth-century world-in-revolution. You are left with the conclusion that the Regents are conducting a major love affair with the U.S. Government, both of whom are not particularly anxious to see you "get smart" for fear that you might become radical student politicos. In conducting this love affair with the government, the Regents have left the matter of "educating" the infant-undergraduate to the adolescent faculty, knowing that they cannot do the job properly. The major implication in all of this is that if you wish to remain infants then you can . . . but if you wish to deny your infantile character then you must realize that you can't talk to your adolescent baby-sitters, the faculty, about your corrupt daddies, the Regents. The reason is simple: the baby-sitters are afraid of their daddies. No . . . if you really want to do something then you must stand up straight, like the young men and women you really are, and begin to *speak* what you feel, to speak loudly, strongly, and to say your highest ideals, your deepest dreams, to pull out all of the stops, to let go and to tell the world . . . *speak to the world and tell them that you want to live!!!*

Have I sufficiently taken care of your objections? If not, chances are that what remains is *fear*, and that is *your* problem. If I have taken care of your objections, then you might be asking, *how do you start a rebellion on the campus?* . . .

Ronald Berman
The University

(1968)

In response to objectivity it was proposed by *Studies on the Left* that a radical scholarship be instituted. This would be objective *because* of its "partisanship" and "bias." The character of this scholarship would be fixed by its orientation: opposed firmly to "established institutions." This approach was to be formulated in another important sense, involving not only conclusions but attitudes. It was a theme often repeated in the essay that excitement and passion were in themselves at least as valuable as method. That false distinctions were being made seemed not to be noticed; the stance of attack is no more productive of truth than that of defense. As for passion, in the realm of scholarship it is much the same as in that of sex. The contemplation of ideas—and it is surely unnecessary to invoke piously the great philosophies—may properly be thought of as generating its own excitement. Intellectual excitement, in fact, is radically unlike the feeling that arouses groups and supplies effervescence to ideologies. In any event, this position taken early in the decade has furnished the new left with one of its *points d'appui* on university education. It was not entirely the structure of administration which inhibited the learning of radicals but the nature of curriculum and inquiry. And it was essentially the role of intellectuals which estranged students on the new left. When some of the defenders of the Berkeley riots wrote about the "yearnings and commitments of the present generation of students" they referred, in existential shorthand, to the central criticism of objectivity by the new left. In brief, what is taught at the university has no relationship to what is real. Objectivity is a mode that deals with dead issues of history. It involves no political imperatives. The passions of "yearning" and the politics of "commitment" demand another mode entirely.

The passions which are so often referred to and which have a kind of moral status of their own take as their object a more visionary university than now exists. New left writing often describes the ideal university as a place in which these passions ought to be cultivated. The student movement, according to *The New Radicals*, is in search of "a psychic community, in which one's own identity can be defined, social and personal relationships based on love can be established." Much the same point is made by the S.D.S. *Port Huron Statement*, in which the present university system is intensely criticized for failing to capture the private energies of students. It is a theme often stated. Some of this thought can be traced to the existential philosophers, some to the justified

---

Ronald Berman, *America in the Sixties* (New York: Macmillan, 1968), pp. 148–56. Reprinted, without footnotes, with permission of the publisher.

disappointment of students in oversized, over-endowed, over centralized learning. A certain amount can be traced to the work of Paul Goodman, whose *Community of Scholars* furnished a utopian model of personal relationships. The important distinction for Goodman was that between a "community of scholarship" and "a community for living."

Goodman and his followers on the new left believe that the university exists for more than intellectual reasons. In this they would appear to be perfectly justified. It is in certain corollaries that dissent may be produced. The passion which is so valued as an attitude loses its integrity as an action: one of the most common defenses of the student demonstration is that its use of force is a sign of sincerity. It is defended as a mode of passionate argument, and one of the less hopeful consequences of Berkeley was the theory that such demonstrations be accepted as normative. As a theory it demands qualification: as an action it is simply the violent suppression of opposition views. Finally, that passion which is so abstractly expressed and that community which is so intensely defended have forms of being which appear to be removed from the life of intellect. It ought to be pointed out that "passion" and "community" have rather heavily sexual referents in new left educational theory. As one member of S.D.S. put it, "In S.D.S. fucking is a statement of community, and there's a lot of inter-fucking, but it's not casual. Sex comes out of a relationship and is used to build a relationship stronger." This may be pleasing or displeasing according to one's morality; it can only be irrelevant to the university. . .

The existential failure of the university is frequently linked to its social function, ostensibly the continuance of liberal oligarchy. For the new left the university is part of the power structure, that part which acculturates and propagandizes. A good deal of published theory on this subject has appeared, Bradley Cleaveland's "Education, Revolutions, and Citadels," John Weiss' "The University as Corporation," James Bauerlein's "The Social Function of the University," Mark Shechner's "Cold War and the University of California." It is the burden of these pieces that the university—specifically the University of California—has the dual function of producing human material for the economy and inculcating a Cold War mentality.

Perhaps the most famous of these essays is Bradley Cleaveland's "A Letter to Undergraduates," which appeared on the Berkeley campus a short time before the demonstrations began. If there is an official version of new left thought on university education it is this essay, which throughout the movement, has been the subject of admiration and a certain amount of spoliation. Cleaveland builds from a premise now familiar in new left thought: The world is in the process of a revolution which transcends merely national interests and which makes the antiquated idea of scholarly detachment a political danger. The institutions of the university are in fact political and corrupt. Fraternities and sororities, for example, are simply undemocratic distractions which serve to keep the student mind off reality. As for the structure of the system, the ceremonies and rituals of the university are silent forms of persuasion. They sanctify the oppresssion of intelligence by authority. The use of grades entails a Pavlovian system of rewards and punishments—those who fail constitute by their independence a danger to authority while those who do not fail learn that success in this culture is attained by hypocrisy. The extra-curricular life of lectures and arts, recreation and debates is simply a new form of bread and circuses. The heart of the matter is that "the multiversity is not an educational center, but a highly efficient industry: it produces bombs, other war machines, a few token 'peaceful' machines, and enormous numbers of safe, highly skilled, and respectable automatons to meet the immediate needs of business and government."

Once the conspiracy theory has been broached, an enormous amount of conjecture may be released. If the university is in fact a silent partner of the cold war it acts directly in the service of capitalism. Cleaveland's list of the corporate attachments of the Board of Regents has become famous. He lists the directorships and stockholdings in such a way as to intimate that the corporations benefit directly from the operation of the university. The function of the university and the desires of the Regents are one: "as corporate men of power, the Regents are getting precisely what they most desire—enormous numbers of highly skilled graduates to fill the corporate structure and to keep it running smoothly." This is surely no place in which to indulge in defense of the Regents—it might simply be noted that they fulfill the traditional role of the American trustee, which is to attract money to the university and make it responsive to the community of private taxation upon which it depends. It is possible that the new left at Berkeley has been driven to see corporations as the enemy because they offer a more precise target than the real opposition, which is the middle class of California.

The accusation that the university is the intellectual arm of the state appears with regularity. One view holds that the university is the instrument of "the military-industrial establishment." Generally, the university serves as one of the resources of this complex; specifically, it trains an intellectual elite for purposes best revealed in *Brave New World.* A second view declares that the corporations "reproduce in the heart of the University itself their own goals and values." In order to accomplish this the administration models its own structure after that of holding companies. On top is the final authority of the Chairman of the Board; at the base a mass of students and faculty with no rights "except those they can extort by the threat of direct action." A third view claims that the universities no longer distinguish truth from national defense because their values derive in fact from the Pentagon. Behind these statements lies the microcosm theory, which adapts for the new left the now moribund idea of the ivory tower. For most of the twentieth century the universities have been criticized because of their distance from social realities. It has been public sentiment that a university education disqualified one for knowledge of, let alone success in, the actual world. The new left agrees that the university deals with mythology rather than reality. It emphatically disagrees with the notion that education prevents social success.

As seen by the new left the universities act as the agency of the culture in shaping our ideas of democracy, capitalism, and nationalism. If the universities were once lost in the past they are now the slaves of the present; ideological microcosms of the outer society. The new student left views the American university as we would once have viewed the Prussian university. There have been two positions. The first of these holds that the influx of federal funds and the emphasis on technology have made the universities direct agencies of the state. It is no longer the power of taxation which has the power to destroy but the power of donation. An enormous amount of university financing is dependent on federal aid; as a consequence there are vast programs of research, building and training which are directly related to the needs of the state. Insofar as a great deal of this relates to military needs, the new left, in its pacifist aspect, is much disturbed. Particularly at Berkeley the anomaly of the largest system of federal research cohabiting with the largest single group of left intelligentsia has made itself exquisitely plain. The second position, unlike the first, seems not to have a basis in fact, it is that the university offers an apologetic in its teaching for the totalitarian liberal state. Both positions are expressed in the important F.S.M. document, "We want a University." Here is a sense of the economic entente: "Current federal and private support programs for the university have been compared to classic examples of imperialism and neocolonialism. The government has invested in underdeveloped, capital-starved institutions, and imposed a pattern of growth and development upon them." Here is a sense of the ideological entente: "the main concern of the university should not be [as it now is] passing along the morality of the middle class, nor the morality of the white man, nor even the morality of the potpourri we call 'western society'."

The suspicion with which the new left regards federal influence on the schools can only be shared by critics of whatever persuasion. On this particular issue the bulletins of the F.S.M. have some resemblance to those of the *National Review*. The neutral critic will share the feeling of the new left toward educational gigantism. He will be less inclined to believe that the university and the corporate liberal oligarchy are in cahoots. He will give absolutely no credence to the theory that the university intentionally prevents radicalism from seeking truth. As for the charge that the university represents western thought—he is likely to approve highly of that. Since the days of the Platonic Academy the university has been identical with western thought. Since the medieval foundations of learning it has been concerned profoundly with morality. Purely as a consequence of American custom and fiscal practice it has been responsive to the middle class. If there is a particular weakness in new left educational theory it is that dialogue is conducted in ignorance of this.

What is most objectionable to the neutral critic is that moral voluptuousness permitted itself by the new left. No one who has taught a term at any college much to the left of Bob Jones can fail to be aware of the almost crippling liberty of the campus. The odd thing is that "participatory" democracy, far from being found within the enclaves of radicalism, is the gratifying, maddening possession of most faculties. As a matter of form, all ranks of the University of California (from Assistant Professor up) have equal voting rights. As a matter of practice most academic discussions attempt a consensus rather than depend on a strict majority vote. As for the teaching process itself, the intellectual freedom allowed is proverbial, and there are watchdog committees which exist for the sole purpose of extending that freedom. One notes at this point that the idea of academic freedom for the new left has more than intellectual connotations.

Before considering this as it developed from the Berkeley experience it remains to adduce the matter of power. I have noted . . . the intense disappointment of intellectuals in their public role; the student left shares this very nearly by definition. The single most obvious thing that may be said is that the cultural impotence of intellectuals has been translated into a new and factitious idiom. The relative inefficacy of ideas has caused the new left to assert that actual power is being denied them. In other words, *the fact that intellectuals have little social influence is ascribed not to the nature of thought but to the structure of university policies.* This has led to some tragicomic statements, notably that of the *Port Huron Statement:* "With administrators ordering the institution, and faculty the curriculum, the student learns by his isolation to accept elite rule within the university, which prepares him to accept later forms of minority control." What this really means is that no one can be conscious of truth unless he is in administrative charge of the institution which studies it. It is not necessary to go deeply into the matter of elite rule, except to note that it is demanded by any organization, and by the nature of professional standards. What matters more essentially is the translation of power, which first referred to the condition of intellectuals and then to their influence.

One of the most illuminating statements on this issue was made by Paul Potter of S.D.S. in 1964. He then wrote that "Intellectuals want direct power. They do no longer want to deal with power as an abstract symbol of the classroom and of lectures. They want to utilize power for social ends." The confusion between the power of ideas and actions is quintessential. A corollary of this might read, "ideas themselves, having no social power, may not be trusted to the ponderous mechanism of historical dispersion. The power that should be sought by intellectuals is of another order: the direct exercise of ideologies in a political context." When Potter added that the new radicals "think of the university very concretely as a mechanism they can utilize, that they can manipulate to gain certain ends," he expressed the strategy of Berkeley.

Steven Kelman
Beyond New Leftism

(1969)

American students created two momentous political events last year: the primary victory of Eugene McCarthy in New Hampshire, and the anti-war demonstrations in Chicago. Yet despite these two surges, the student movement, now almost a decade old, is in a state of internal disintegration and flux. This is true of both its moderate and militant wings. Indeed, the outward differences between the liberal students of the McCarthy crusade and those of the S.D.S.-style New Left have tended to obscure the fact that in both movements the causes of confusion are similar.

It is one sign of the disintegration of liberalism as an ideology on the campus today that campus liberals have virtually abandoned any attempt to offer an alternative political analysis to that of the New Left. What drove a young activist last year into S.D.S. rather than into McCarthy movement was fundamentally a different perception of his role. Members of S.D.S. view themselves as part of the wretched of the earth, whereas Young Democrats see themselves as future directors of the Bureau of Housing and Urban Development. When asked to justify their membership in the Young Democrats rather than in S.D.S., they will almost inevitably refer, not to any serious political differences, but to the possibility of being "more effective." Campus liberalism today is above all a movement for "respectable" students, future-oriented and careful about understanding anything which might endanger their records or careers. Liberal college students could put out long hours and sleep on hard floors for "clean Gene," secure in the knowledge that they were signing their names to nothing that might eventually make its way to the F.B.I. In this respect the atmosphere of the early 1950's is still widely prevalent on campus.

Capitalizing on their opponents' weaknesses, S.D.S. in turn constantly attacked the McCarthy movement last year for "working within the system" and for being simpleminded in its political analysis. In reply, the McCarthy people, instead of dissecting the terms foisted on them by S.D.S., baldly answered back that they were proud to be working within the system.

Now, when S.D.S. members talk about "the system" they are referring to a political structure which they believe to be thoroughly undemocratic and elite-controlled. Thus, however much one may disagree with their premises about the nature of American society, the New Left's terrorist-confrontation

---

Steven Kelman, "Beyond New Leftism," *Commentary* (February 1969), pp. 67–71. Reprinted by permission of the publisher and author.

approach at least, has a certain primitive logical consistency, since by definition one cannot change a "totalitarian" system by any sort of democratic means. But when campus liberals adopt the S.D.S. term "the system," the expression emerges bastardized, if not unrecognizable. Far from being a focus for social criticism, it exists as a vague presence alternately to be paid allegiance to or turned away from. For S.D.S. "the system" simply is undemocratic; for liberals, America is democratic but its people, albeit democratically, are making the wrong decisions. The Harvard *Crimson*, for instance, reported last March that a volunteer at the end of the McCarthy campaign in New Hampshire had "lost his faith in the system." ("Losing one's faith" in something is the most frequent trauma of the liberal student activist.) Actually, he had lost his faith not in "the system" but in individual Americans, for it developed that he felt that the people he had come in contact with during the campaign were stupid. Such is the level of the crisis of campus liberalism.

Lacking strong intellectual moorings, the liberal, hesitant about committing himself to Marxism-Leninism, which is both dogmatic and a danger to his future, and yet continually frustrated by the difficulties of producing the changes in policies that he wants—especially an end to the war in Vietnam—is reduced to a proud fuzziness. In this state he is susceptible to the tactics and the ideology both of the Right and of the extreme Left. The most convincing argument which impels some liberal activists into radical movements like The Resistance goes something like: "We wrote letters, we marched, we petitioned, we worked for McCarthy. But the war still went on." I have heard this argument put forth literally tens of times, and *never* heard a liberal respond: "But did we ever convince a majority of Americans that our views are right?" The system in which these liberals so easily lose faith is democracy itself.

Both campus liberalism and S.D.S. style radicalism today draw on similar social currents and intellectual modes in the university. Today's generation of student political activists, both liberals and radicals, has grown up in a climate of unprecedented social and political isolation from the American people. Radicals in the '30's usually came from families suffering directly from the same Depression which affected most other Americans. Thus the imperative, for example, to participate in trade-union organizing came not only from the Marxist liturgy but also from the facts of life. By contrast, the affluent middle-class position of most activists today has led to a merger of traditional middle-class prejudices against the "boob-ocracy" with the more sophisticated political notions of the elitist wing of the intellectual Left. While activist students lose their optimistic faith in American society as they grow up, they retain their hostility toward most non-middle-class whites. A sign, reading simply "Dumb Power," held by a heckler at a Wallace rally in Boston, indicates well the component of snobbism in student political consciousness. This was expressed in civil-rights activism in the South and in protests against the war in Vietnam, the two great student causes of the '60's, both of which offered the opportunity to compare one's beliefs favorably with those of ignorant rednecks or longshoremen.

Such attitudes toward "the people" are bound to produce a very insecure belief in democracy and democratic social change. The young may hold on to the ideology of democracy longer than they hold on to their faith in the American political system, but an intellectual faith in democracy cannot survive forever in the face of a gut feeling that the people are consistently wrong.

Members of S.D.S. extricate themselves from this dilemma by developing an alternative ideology. They postulate, paying the debt to their childhood, the fundamental goodness of people. In fact, they argue that if the people are informed of the facts, they will *always* make the decisions that S.D.S. thinks they should make. If they appear never to make the right judgments, it must be because of manipulation and "false consciousness." To S.D.S., there can never be legitimate disagreements, only different levels of consciousness. In the short run, before the destruction of the system which fosters false consciousness, one need not be concerned about "bourgeois democratic" methods or "bourgeois civil liberties." (That S.D.S. has resurrected these hoary terms is but another indication that, today, there is little "new" about the "New" Left.)

The liberal activist, however, unable to relate to any other forces in the society (except, perhaps, as a nostalgic nod to yesteryear, the Negroes) adopts the 1960's variant of the Puritan ethic, according to which political success is a function, not of winning mass support, but of hard work and "commitment." It was this doctrine which led to the massive outpouring of effort into the McCarthy campaign.

The elitist "liberalism" that often lurked under the innocent facade of some of McCarthy's followers—the converse of the elitist "radicalism" which dominates S.D.S.—descends from the opportunistic liberalism of the 1950's. If one believes, with the new liberals, that the mass of the American people are inherently conservative, ignorant, and mesmerized by an alleged private affluence, one looks to the educated or to those, like the blacks, whose minority status has given them a unique existential experience, as the only agents for social change.

If, on the other hand, like S.D.S., one rejects the possibility of change coming from within American society, one turns romantically to Ho, Ché, and the peasant masses of the Third World. It was just such a denial of the potential of an authentic, majoritarian movement of social change in America, a denial now shared by both groups of student elitists, that served as the intellectual pretext for so many ex-radicals and liberals to justify their participation in the "American celebration" during the Eisenhower years. It is all too possible that, if the war ends, the Nixon era may cause the elitism of the intelligentsia to show its other face—the self-satisfied and often conservative meliorism of the 1950's.

The simple fact for those concerned about social progress is that liberalism is in serious intellectual crisis, and this intellectual crisis relates directly to its political crisis. One can only hope for—and work toward—the development of a trend within the student movement that will reject the middle-class snobbery which has separated intellectual protests from the mundane and often inarticulate desires for change that are a part of the feelings of a majority of the American people. A principled commitment and willingness to defend democracy is viable in the long run only if combined with a political strategy that has realistic chances of obtaining majority support for the types of programs one wants. It is precisely the lack of such a strategy for gaining a democratic majority which has made sincere campus liberal activists so unfortunately subject to influence from elitism and anti-democratic New Left conceptions. The present contemptuous dismissal of the trade-union movement, a force without which any progressive majority is simply numerically impossible, is a good example of this loss of perspective . . .

The "new" student liberalism has accepted and propagated the opinion that union rank-and-file members are largely reactionaries and even "honkies." It has blamed rioting and crime in the Negro community on a generalized "white racism" or, more specifically, on the police, rather than on real-estate interests, low-wage employers, and political conservatives whose policies have been responsible for ghetto conditions in the first place. It permits those who went to high school in the suburbs or to prep school in New England to sneer "racist" at low-income urban whites who are rightly concerned with crime, living conditions, or keeping their jobs—and to cop out on the more difficult task of providing alternative answers to these problems from those presented by the Nixons and Wallaces. It leads student liberals frequently to make statements like, "The unions are *the* most reactionary force in this country," only to retreat embarrassedly when reminded of the role of corporate business.

If students who are drawn to the democratic framework still hope to accomplish anything of lasting value they will have to put forward not only alternative tactics to those of the New Left, but an alternative political philosophy and social morality as well. At present, however, the moral critique of the "new" student liberalism is radical, but its social analysis and political strategy are not.

Nevertheless, some significant beginnings have been made toward re-establishing a principled and intelligent democratic-Left current within the student movement. First, there are the youth workers from the Kennedy campaign—the insurgent movement within the Democratic party which had the most blue-collar and black support—who have formed the Kennedy Action Corps. Given the possibility of a 1972 Presidential bid by Edward Kennedy, this group may have something more than the memory of R.F.K. to keep it alive. It could serve as a political bridge between the campuses and the "forgotten Americans."

Second, there is the New Democratic Coalition, an alliance of some of the younger leaders of both the Kennedy and McCarthy campaigns, which could be another center for democratic radicalism. Here, too, much depends on the way in which the group resolves the different approaches to domestic politics reflected in its leadership. Its Executive Committee, for example, includes Michael Harrington, national chairman of the Socialist party, and David Hoeh, leader of the McCarthy New Hampshire delegation to the Democratic Convention and subsequently an unsuccessful Congressional candidate.

Harrington is a major proponent of the "coalition" strategy for social progress. He calls for an alliance of Negroes, labor, the poor and middle-class liberals and democratic radicals to press for massive federal social spending, democratic planning, and a democratic foreign policy. Harrington is also one of the most effective proponents of the view that middle-class liberals and radicals must develop a creative relationship with organized labor.

Hoeh, while no doubt sharing many of Harrington's ultimate goals, has a fundamentally different view on how to achieve them. He too favors working within the Democratic party. But in an article in the *New Republic* last October he indicated that he placed fundamental reliance on the liberal middle class, and that he included in his "new coalition," without the mildest reservation, what he called "giant business." The only part of the working class honored with admission was what he referred to as "progressive labor."

Third, as a result of the current confusion among liberal students and the Marxist-Leninist dogmatism of the New Left, democratic socialism, which many older Americans may think of as only one of the more appealing leftist doctrines of a completely bygone era, is now undergoing a campus revival. While it is true that democratic socialist ideas have influenced several youth organizations, their main vehicle of expression has been the Young People's Socialist League, the youth affiliate of the Socialist party of the late Norman Thomas. Three years ago Y.P.S.L. was revived by a group of young people, many of whom were disaffected veterans of S.D.S. The mentors of Y.P.S.L. have been Michael Harrington, Irving Howe, and other intellectuals grouped around the League for Industrial Democracy and *Dissent* magazine; trade unionists coming out of the socialist movement, among them Albert Shanker of the American Federation of Teachers and Walter Reuther of the U.A.W.; and civil-rights activists like A. Philip Randolph, Bayard Rustin, and Tom Kahn.

The socialists have not been caught in the bind of some moderate opponents of the New Left, who appear to be pleading for gradualism and compromise as the alternatives to enthusiasm and radical change. In the explosive atmosphere which exists on many American campuses, pleas for gradualism have become synonymous with defense of the status quo. This is not an entirely invalid view, for as Harrington argues in *Toward a Democratic Left*, the new technology has created social conditions which require that man must either master technology, or be mastered by it. To procrastinate is to lend oneself to the worst. The real question is not whether there will be change, but what character the change will take. Will it develop into new forms of oppression, or will it be democratic and creative?

The student democratic socialists acknowledge the necessity for radical change, but they insist that this change—as well as the society they want to develop—be democratic. Hence their opposition to S.D.S., and the very different tactics which they have adopted. Their activities are directed toward overcoming the hostilities that prevent various disadvantaged groups from uniting around common concerns so as to be able to build a majoritarian coalition that can rebuild the Democratic party; and toward defending the ideals of free discussion and democracy. The Harvard chapter of Y.P.S.L., for example, of which the present author is a former chairman, has been involved in supporting striking Harvard printers and in organizing the boycott of California grapes in support of Cesar Chavez's farm workers' union. It issued a critique of "Economics 1," Harvard's largest course, which succeeded in bringing important changes to its reading list. Without sit-ins or confrontations, but merely by publicizing a document which even its opponents admitted was "well-researched and well-written," Y.P.S.L. accomplished what no previous "student power" efforts for curriculum change ever had. On the issue of the status of military-training programs on campus, such as academic credit, Y.P.S.L. called for a student referendum. S.D.S. opposed the referendum, and demanded the unilateral right, through confrontation, to determine not only that R.O.T.C. be deprived of its special privileges, but furthermore, that it should be expelled from campus on the grounds that no student has the right to participate in it.

The turning point for Y.P.S.L. at Harvard was the sit-in staged by S.D.S.'s psychodrama politics at its presence of a recruiter from the Dow Chemical Company on campus. The Dow Affair represented S.D.S.'s psychodrama politics at its worst. Originally S.D.S. had voted against a sit-in. But a small group of members decided to ignore the majority's decision, sat in, and demanded that the Dow recruiter sign a statement saying that Dow would never come back to Harvard. At that point, the mass of S.D.S. members, ever willing to subordinate political judgment to the excitement of getting in on the action—and above all never willing to be "out-radicalized" by others—joined in.

The sit-in, coming at a time of heightened opposition to the war and widespread frustration (the Young Democrats had endorsed a "Dump Johnson" drive, but the McCarthy movement had not yet been launched), was an electrifying event on campus. But support for the sit-in was surprisingly low, and of those outside S.D.S. who joined it, many later became guilt-ridden and felt that, in a fit of emotion, they had let themselves be "had" into supporting a totalitarian position. Furthermore, and just as importantly, many students were annoyed by the abdication of student liberal leaders. The *Crimson* supported the sit-in, saying that Dow had no right to be on campus, and the Young Democrats, who were split, finally voted only a mild disapproval of the sit-in, after voting down a stronger condemnation.

At this point, Y.P.S.L., still relatively unknown on campus, came out with a statement and petition supporting "the rights of free speech and free recruitment on campus," and warning that on the precedent of S.D.S. tactics, rightist students could also keep out those they disliked. At the same time the petition asked for clemency for the protestors and called upon the faculty to take a position on the war. University administrators, who were under great pressure from alumni and others to expel some of the leaders of the sit-in, based their case for leniency largely on this petition, which had over 1200 signatures. It was with this statement—which mixed a pro-civil liberties position with a strong anti-war stand—that Y.P.S.L. established for itself an independent role on campus.

The modest successes of Y.P.S.L. at Harvard and elsewhere indicate that there is an unexploited potential constituency on other campuses as well. Up to now, the mood has been set largely by S.D.S., whose politics offered an easy outlet for the alienated young in the form of such political gestures as yelling "pig," "liberating" a university building, or following Che's life style. Meanwhile, campus liberals, suspended uneasily between confrontations and careerism, have simply given up the fight. The lesson of the Dow Affair at Harvard seems to be that many students will seize upon a thoughtful alternative to the New Left's political actions once the opportunity is offered.

Indeed, despite the fact that their posture is less frenetic—and therefore less appealing—than that of New Leftists, democratic radicals may be heading for a brighter future than might at first glance appear. (It is interesting to note that at Harvard this year both S.D.S. and campus liberalism are in a state of drastic decline, while Y.P.S.L. is growing. S.D.S has been attracting about half the number of people to its meetings, as compared with the previous year, and the Young Democrats' membership is less than a third of what it was two years ago.) McCarthy's failure seems to have burned out many of the students who were all too briefly lit up by the message of his campaign. Many are reverting to "revolutionary pessimism"—radicalism about what needs to be done, but conservatism about the chances of accomplishing it. At the same time, S.D.S. is threatened, not only by serious ideological divisions, especially with the Maoists, but, what is worse, by sociopaths like those who form the "Motherfucker" faction. This group has eliminated whatever political content might originally have existed in the New Left by denying the possibility of individual sanity in a corrupt society, and resorting to mental terrorism. "The future of our struggle is the future of crime in the streets," their leader has proclaimed. To protest the war, the "Motherfuckers" throw cow's blood and urine indiscriminately at passing cars. They disrupt S.D.S.'s own meetings, surely a case of the chickens coming home to roost. Those in the S.D.S. leadership who are politically serious and committed, despair at the problem of such *enragés*. But, at least for the present, there is little they can do about it.

The experience of Y.P.S.L. at Harvard indicates that the kind of approach offered by democratic socialists could find widespread acceptance among students who are capable of steering an intelligent course between protestors and politicos. This is the course that will have to be followed by any radical democratic movement that hopes to have a future in America, and those committed to building such a movement may yet find new and unexpected allies among the young.

Stephen Donadio
Columbia: An Interview

(1968)

I'd like to ask what your reaction is to this exchange between Nat Hentoff and Herbert Marcuse at the Theatre for Ideas. "Hentoff: 'We've been talking about new institutions, new structures, as the only way to get fundamental change. What would that mean to you, Mr. Marcuse, in terms of the university, in terms of Columbia?' Marcuse: 'I was afraid of that, because I now finally reveal myself as a fink. I have never suggested or advocated or supported destroying the established universities and building new anti-institutions instead. I have always said that no matter how radical the demands of the students, and no matter how justified, they should be pressed within the existing universities and attained within the existing universities. I believe—and this is where the finkdom comes in—that American universities, at least quite a few of them, today are still enclaves of relatively critical thought and relatively free thought. So we do not have to think of replacing them by new institutions. But this is one of the very rare cases in which I think you can achieve what you want to achieve within the existing institutions.'"

Rudd: For a man who deals in analyzing a society where criticism is a non-entity and where there are strict limits and controls on thought, Professor Marcuse seems to have a blind spot when it comes to the controls and limits on thought in the university, which are tremendous. If anything, our

Stephen Donadio, "Columbia: Seven Interviews," *Partisan Review* (Summer 1968), pp. 354–92. Interview with Mark Rudd and Lewis Cole, p. 375.

student movement opens up alternatives, because it reveals to people the existence of ideology within the university, which Professor Marcuse seems to ignore when he says that the University is the center of "relatively" open, free, critical thought. The "relatively" part sounds like "a temporary partial bombing halt."

Cole: And say it is a center for relatively critical thought: the university is also a center for counter-insurgency research, for implementing imperialist policies throughout the world. And these two functions exist hand in hand, so that it finally becomes a question of whether you're going to let the critical thought factory and the murder factory be in the same building.

Rudd: Lew makes the assumption that the two functions can and do exist simultaneously within the university, critical thought and war production. The alternative assumption is, I think, more true: that is, that the university exists in order to produce manpower for use here in the United States. In order to have the proper manpower, it has to train people in the proper ideas; and the proper ideas are basically bourgeois ideology.

Cole: There are individual classes where that might not be so, and everybody always got very hung up on this when we'd be talking to the college faculty and they'd say, "Well, that isn't so in *my* class, certainly!" But a university is an *institution*, it operates as an institution, and the question is what that institution is doing as a whole. This critical thought that Marcuse talks about—he's talking about it in a complete vacuum. What's the purpose of having critical thought if it's going to be used by a society for co-opting?

The Mission: The Movement and Liberal America

If reforms are to be made, in the present New Left view, the culture as we know it will have to be completely destroyed and rebuilt. This section presents some views on the nature of that assumption. The New Left believes that liberalism is its principal enemy since it diverts the energies of the left from a confrontation with political power. It reserves its anger for the "establishment"—those writers, teachers and professional men of liberal persuasion who have come to terms with the culture they live in. These men, the new radicals argue, should in fact be leading the cause of revolution.

It has indeed been argued that liberal American society is functionally repressive. Herbert Marcuse has argued in *One-Dimensional Man* that society makes all dissent quite useless because it is able to absorb and negate that dissent effortlessly. In his view it is our very prosperity and stability which is a danger. One may wish to disagree with the idea that we are "totalitarian" because we are able to tolerate pluralities of thought. And one must disagree with Marcuse's thesis that such toleration itself is evil. With this idea radicalism has come full circle: it attacks society for being free and praises itself for being intolerant.

C. Wright Mills
The New Left

(1963)

It is no exaggeration to say that since the end of World War II in Britain and the United States smug conservatives, tired liberals and disillusioned radicals have carried on a weary discourse in which issues are blurred and potential debate muted; the sickness of complacency has prevailed, the bi-partisan banality flourished. There is no need . . . to explain again why all this has come about among "people in general" in the N.A.T.O. countries; but it may be worthwhile to examine one style of cultural work that is in effect an intellectual celebration of apathy.

Many intellectual fashions, of course, do just that; they stand in the way of a release of the imagination—about the cold war, the Soviet bloc, the politics of peace, about any new beginnings at home and abroad. But the fashion I have in mind is the weariness of many N.A.T.O. intellectuals with what they call "ideology," and their proclamation of "the end of ideology." So far as I know, this began in the mid-fifties, mainly in intellectual circles more or less associated with the Congress for Cultural Freedom and the magazine *Encounter*. Reports of the Milan Conference of 1955 heralded it; since then, many cultural gossips have taken it up as a posture and an unexamined slogan. Does it amount to anything?

Its common denominator is not liberalism as a political philosophy, but the liberal rhetoric, become formal and sophisticated and used as an uncriticised weapon with which to attack Marxism. In the approved style, various of the elements of this rhetoric appear simply as snobbish assumptions. Its sophistication is one of tone rather than of ideas: in it, the *New Yorker* style of reportage has become politically triumphant. The disclosure of fact—set forth in a bright-faced or in a dead-pan manner—is the rule. The facts are duly weighed, carefully balanced, always hedged. Their power to outrage, their power truly to enlighten in a political way, their power to aid decision, even their power to clarify some situation—all that is blunted or destroyed.

So reasoning collapses into reasonableness. By the more naive and snobbish celebrants of complacency, arguments and facts of a displeasing kind are simply ignored; by the more knowing they are duly recognized, but

C. Wright Mills, "The New Left," *Power, Politics and People: the Collected Essays of C. Wright Mills*, edited by Irving Louis Horowitz, 1963, pp. 247–48, 251–59.

they are neither connected with one another nor related to any general view. Acknowledged in a scattered way, they are never put together: to do so is to risk being called, curiously enough, "one-sided."

This refusal to relate isolated facts and fragmentary comment with the changing institutions of society makes it impossible to understand the structural realities which these facts might reveal; the longer-run trends of which they might be tokens. In brief, fact and idea are isolated, so the real questions are not even raised, analysis of the meanings of fact not even begun.

Practitioners of the no-more-ideology school do of course smuggle in general ideas under the guise of reportage, by intellectual gossip, and by their selection of the notions they handle. Ultimately, the-end-of-ideology is based upon a disillusionment with any real commitment to socialism in any recognizable form. *That* is the only "ideology" that has really ended for these writers. But with its ending, *all* ideology, they think, has ended. *That* ideology they talk about; their own ideological assumptions, they do not.

Underneath this style of observation and comment there is the assumption that in the West there are no more real issues or even problems of great seriousness. The mixed economy plus the welfare state plus prosperity—that is the formula. U.S. capitalism will continue to be workable; the welfare state will continue along the road to ever greater justice. In the meantime, things everywhere are very complex, let us not be careless, there are great risks . . .

This posture—one of "false consciousness" if there ever was one—stands in the way, I think, of considering with any chances of success what may be happening in the world.

* * * * *

. . . who is it that is getting fed up? Who is it that is getting disgusted with what Marx called "all the old crap"? Who is it that is thinking and acting in radical ways? All over the world—in the bloc, outside the bloc and in between—the answer's the same: it is the young intelligentsia.

I cannot resist copying out for you, with a few changes, some materials I've just prepared for a 1960 paperback edition of a book of mine on war:

"In the spring and early summer of 1960—more of the returns from the American decision and default are coming in. In Turkey, after student riots, a military junta takes over the state, of late run by Communist-Container Menderes. In South Korea too, students and others knock over the corrrupt American-puppet regime of Syngman Rhee. In Cuba, a genuinely left-wing revolution begins full-scale economic reorganization—without the domination of U.S. corporations. Average age of its leaders: about 30—and certainly a revolution without any Labor As Agency. On Taiwan, the eight million Taiwanese under the American-imposed dictatorship of Chiang Kai-shek, with his two million Chinese grow increasingly restive. On Okinawa—a

U.S. military base—the people get their first chance since World War II ended to demonstrate against U.S. seizure of their island: and some students take that chance, snake-dancing and chanting angrily to the visiting President: "Go home, go home—take away your missiles." (Don't worry, 12,000 U.S. troops easily handled the generally grateful crowds; also the President was "spirited out the rear end of the United States compound"—and so by helicopter to the airport). In Great Britain, from Aldermaston to London, young—but you were there. In Japan, weeks of student rioting succeed in rejecting the President's visit, jeopardize a new treaty with the U.S.A., displace the big-business, pro-American Prime Minister, Kishi. And even in our own pleasant Southland, Negro and white students are—but let us keep that quiet: it really *is* disgraceful.

"That is by no means the complete list; that was yesterday; see today's newspaper. Tomorrow, in varying degree, the returns will be more evident. Will they be evident enough? They will have to be very obvious to attract real American attention: sweet complaints and the voice of reason—these are not enough. In the slum countries of the world today, what are they saying? The rich Americans, they pay attention only to violence—and to money. You don't care what they say, American? Good for you. Still, they may insist; things are no longer under the old control; you're not getting it straight, American: your country—it would seem—may well become the target of a world hatred of the like of which the easy-going Americans have never dreamed. Neutralists and Pacifists and Unilateralists and that confusing variety of Leftists around the world—all those tens of millions of people, of course they are misguided, absolutely controlled by small conspiratorial groups of trouble-makers, under direct orders straight from Moscow and Peking. Diabolically omnipotent, it is *they* who create all this messy unrest. It is *they* who have given the tens of millions the absurd idea that they shouldn't want to remain, or to become, the seat of American nuclear bases—those gay little outposts of American civilization. So now they don't want U-2's on their territory; so now they want to contract out of the American military machine; they want to be neutral among the crazy big antagonists. And they don't want their own societies to be militarized.

"But take heart, American: you won't have time to get really bored with your friends abroad: they won't be your friends much longer. You don't need *them*; it will all go away; don't let them confuse you."

Add to that: In the Soviet bloc, who is it that has been breaking out of apathy? It has been students and young professors and writers; it has been the young intelligentsia of Poland and Hungary, and of Russia too. Never mind that they've not won; never mind that there are other social and moral types among them. First of all, it has been these types. But the point is clear—isn't it?

That's why we've got to study these new generations of intellectuals around the world as real live agencies of historic change. Forget Victorian

Marxism except whenever you need it; and read Lenin again (be careful)—Rosa Luxemburg, too.

"But it's just some kind of moral upsurge, isn't it?" Correct. But under it: no apathy. Much of it is direct non-violent action, and it seems to be working, here and there. Now we must learn from their practice and work out with them new forms of action.

"But it's all so ambiguous. Turkey, for instance. Cuba, for instance." Of course it is; history-making is always ambiguous; wait a bit; in the meantime, *help* them to focus their moral upsurge in less ambiguous political ways; work out with them the ideologies, the strategies, the theories that will help them consolidate their efforts: new theories of structural changes of and by human societies in our epoch.

"But it's utopian, after all, isn't it?" No—not in the sense you mean. Whatever else it may be, it's not that: tell it to the students of Japan.

Isn't all this, isn't it something of what we are trying to mean by the phrase, "The New Left?" Let the old men ask sourly, "Out of Apathy—into what?" The Age of Complacency is ending. Let the old women complain wisely about "the end of ideology." We are beginning to move again.

Carl Oglesby
Liberalism and the Corporate State

(1966)

Seven months ago at the April March on Washington, Paul Potter, then President of Students for a Democratic Society, stood in approximately this spot and said that we must name the system that creates and sustains the war in Vietnam—name it, describe it, analyze it, understand it, and change it.

Today I will try to name it—to suggest an analysis which, to be quite frank, may disturb some of you—and to suggest what changing it may require of us.

We are here again to protest against a growing war. Since it is a very bad war, we acquire the habit of thinking that it must be caused by very bad men. But we only conceal reality, I think, to denounce on such grounds the menacing coalition of industrial and military power, or the brutality of the blitzkrieg we are waging against Vietnam, or the ominous signs around us that heresy may soon no longer be permitted. We must simply observe, and quite plainly say, that this coalition, this blitzkrieg, and this demand for

Carl Oglesby, "Liberalism and the Corporate State," *Monthly Review*, Vol. 17, No. 8 (January 1966), pp. 21–29. Reprinted by permission of Monthly Review, Inc.

acquiescence are creatures, all of them, of a government that since 1932 has considered itself to be fundamentally *liberal.*

The original commitment in Vietnam was made by President Truman, a mainstream liberal. It was seconded by President Eisenhower, a moderate liberal. It was intensified by the late President Kennedy, a flaming liberal. Think of the men who now engineer that war—those who study the maps, give the commands, push the buttons, and tally the dead: Bundy, McNamara, Rusk, Lodge, Goldberg, the President himself.

They are not moral monsters.

They are all honorable men.

They are all liberals . . .

The . . . facts of recent history describe one main aspect of the estate of Western liberalism. Where is our American humanism here? What went wrong?

Let's stare our situation coldly in the face. All of us are born to the colossus of history, our American corporate system—in many ways, an awesome organism. There is one fact that describes it: with about five percent of the world's people, we consume about half the world's goods. We take a richness that is in good part not our own, and we put it in our pockets, our garages, our split-levels, our bellies, and our futures.

On the *face* of it, it is a crime that so few should have so much at the expense of so many. Where is the moral imagination so abused as to call this just? Perhaps many of us feel a bit uneasy in our sleep. We are not, after all, a cruel people. And perhaps we don't really need this super-dominance that deforms others. But what can we do? The investments are made. The financial ties are established. The plants abroad are built. Our system *exists.* One is swept up into it. How intolerable—to be born moral, but addicted to a stolen and maybe surplus luxury. Our goodness threatens to become counterfeit before our eyes—unless we change. But change threatens us with uncertainty—at least.

Our problem, then, is to justify this system and give its theft another name—to make kind and moral what is neither, to perform some alchemy with language that will make this injustice seem to be a most magnanimous gift.

A hard problem. But the Western democracies, in the heyday of their colonial expansionism, produced a hero worthy of the task.

Its name was free enterprise, and its partner was an *illiberal liberalism* that said to the poor and the dispossessed: What we acquire of your resources we repay in civilization. The white man's burden. But this was too poetic. So a much more hard-headed theory was produced. This theory said that colonial status is in fact a *boon* to the colonized. We give them technology and bring them into modern times.

But this deceived no one but ourselves. We were delighted with this new theory. The poor saw in it merely an admission that their claims were irrefutable. They stood up to us, without gratitude. We were shocked—but also confused, for the poor seemed again to be right. How long is it going to be the case, we wondered, that the poor will be right and the rich will be wrong?

Liberalism faced a crisis. In the face of the collapse of the European empires, how could it continue to hold together our twin need for richness and righteousness? How can we continue to sack the ports of Asia and still dream of Jesus?

The challenge was met with a most ingenious solution: the ideology of anti-Communism. This was the bind: we cannot call revolution bad, because we started that way ourselves, and because it is all too easy to see why the dispossessed should rebel. So we will call revolution *Communism*. And we will reserve for ourselves the right to say what Communism means. We take note of revolution's enormities, wrenching them where necessary from their historical context and often exaggerating them, and say: Behold, Communism is a bloodbath. We take note of those reactionaries who stole the revolution, and say: Behold, Communism is a betrayal of the people. We take note of the revolution's need to consolidate itself, and say: Behold, Communism is a tyranny.

It has been all these things, and it will be these things again, and we will never be at a loss for those tales of atrocity that comfort us so in our self-righteousness. Nuns will be raped and bureaucrats will be disemboweled. Indeed, revolution is a *fury*. For it is a letting loose of outrages pent up sometimes over centuries. But the more brutal and longer-lasting the suppression of this energy, all the more ferocious will be its explosive release.

Far from helping Americans deal with this truth, the anti-Communist ideology merely tries to disguise it so that things may stay the way they are. Thus, it depicts our presence in other lands not as a coercion, but a protection. It allows us even to say that the napalm in Vietnam is only another aspect of our humanitarian love—like those exorcisms in the Middle Ages that so often killed the patient. So we say to the Vietnamese peasant, the Cuban intellectual, the Peruvian worker: "You are better dead than red. If it hurts or if you don't understand why—sorry about that."

This is the action of *corporate liberalism*. It performs for the corporate state a function quite like what the Church once performed for the feudal state. It seeks to justify its burdens and protect it from change. As the Church exaggerated this office in the Inquisition, so with liberalism in the McCarthy time—which, if it was a reactionary phenomenon, was still made possible by our anti-Communist corporate liberalism.

Let me then speak directly to humanist liberals. If my facts are wrong, I will soon be corrected. But if they are right, then you may face a crisis of conscience. Corporatism or humanism; which? For it has come to that. Will you let your dreams be used? Will you be grudging apologists for the corporate state? Or will you help try to change it . . .

Thomas Hayden
Letter to the New (Young) Left

(1966)

In a publication such as *The Activist*, written and read by a community sharing some degree of consensus regarding political values, it should not be necessary to labor in detail over the several challenges confronting the peoples of the world, and especially confronting those who claim to be of the Left. However, in part:

Internationally, the growing power and even higher expectations of the "underdeveloped" nations; the numerous issues directly relating to man's nuclear arsenal; the population problem; the influence of the Cold War conflict on seemingly every private and public facet of the common life; the polarizing effects of the Cold War; the disintegration of easily-grasped categories like "democratic," "undemocratic," "neutral"; the evolution from Stalinism to ? in Russia; the hazy and threatening future of China; the movement of power away from the West in the United Nations; the development of outer space; the coming of new communications systems . . .

Domestically, the failures of the welfare state to deal with the hard facts of poverty in America; the drift of decision-making power away from directly representative, legislative or executive institutions into corporate and military hands neither checked by nor responsible to the courted "public"; the persistence of a racism that mocks our principles and corrupts everyday life; the encroachment upon our civil liberties seen in the intellectually-masked "balancing" theory of the five Supreme Court judges as well as in the naked paranoia of our most rabid Communist-phobes; the resurgence of a leaderless McCarthyism raising the flag and fist in every city across the land; the near-total absence of left position in an incredibly conservative Congress; the growing dominance of the military over formerly civilian decisions; the decline of already-meager social welfare legislation in the face of larger defense appropriations; the squandering and continuous—though somewhat checked—exploiting of our natural resources; the ugliness and ill-planned nature of our cities; the development of a technology great in its potential . . .

Educationally, the endless repressions of free speech and thought, the stifling paternalism that infects the student's whole perception of what is real and possible and enforces a parent-child relationship until the youth is

Thomas Hayden, "A Letter to the New (Young) Left," from *The New Student Left*, Mitchell Cohen and Dennis Hale, eds., pp. 2–4. Reprinted by permission of the Beacon Press,

suddenly transplanted into "the world"; the sterility of the student government and the general student community; curriculums conspicuously anachronistic in the fields of Africa, Asia, and Latin America; whole new areas of study in astronomy and nuclear physics . . .

The problems are immense. We of the Left, however, find no rest in theory, and little hope in leadership. Liberal philosophy has dealt inadequately with the twentieth century. Marx, especially Marx the humanist, has much to tell us but his conceptual tools are outmoded and his final vision implausible. The revolutionary leaders of the rising nations have been mostly non-ideological, either forced to be so or preferring (as is the case of Guevara) to forge their political views in the heat and exigencies of revolution and the present. The American intellectuals? C. Wright Mills is appealing and dynamic in his expression of theory in the grand manner, but his pessimism yields us no formulas, no path out of the dark, and his polemicism sometimes offends the critical sense. The others? There is, I find, an inhibiting, dangerous conservative temperament behind the facade of liberal realism which is so current: Niebuhr in theology; Kornhauser, Lipset, and Bell in political science and sociology; the neo-Freudians in psychology; Hofstadter in history; Schlesinger and others of the A.D.A. mind in the Democratic Party. Their themes purport to be different but always the same impressions emerge: Man is inherently incapable of building a good society; man's passionate causes are nothing more than dangerous psychic sprees (the issues of this period too complex and sensitive to be colored by emotionalism or moral conviction); ideals have little place in politics—we should instead design effective, responsible programs which will produce the most that is realistically possible . . . Here and there, from the pages of *Dissent* or from isolated radicals and scholars, including Mills himself, come cries: No! You false liberals are suffering from the failure of your youthful dreams; you are eviscerating the great optimistic tradition of liberalism from the Enlightenment to the twentieth century; you are justifying disinterest in morality; you are eliminating emotion, dissent, outrage and, yes, the wellsprings of life itself.

John Gerassi
A Letter

(1968)

The teacher may like to see a change, but does not need it. On the contrary, he is really wary of changes lest they destroy his career, his sinecure, his rationale, his whole life-style. His objection to the system is that it is eating away at his authority . . . His concern is "to restore society to health." What health? What garden of Eden? It is not just the restoration of the "legitimacy of the national government," that liberals seek, but their own. Their world is meaningless without authority and they correctly understand that their authority is destroyed in a world based on collective humanism rather than on competition . . .

To others, who would not reject the system, a grade could mean telling the student how well he is doing, *not* in relation to *others*, but in relation to himself and his own potential. I tried an experiment this year: I told students they would all receive A's and then asked them to do what they wanted—for themselves—whatever the course inspired them to really want to say. The result was revealing. Some didn't do anything, true. But never before have I received such solid, thoughtful, meaningful work from not only registered students, but also auditors. Most illuminating, however, was the amount of work I received that was the product of a collective—including a twenty-page poem about Nicaraguan rebel "General of the People" Sandino, written by six students working together. Does it matter whether or not it was good? . . .

To the future of mankind, what will matter will be the attitude of such students who can relate and correlate their egos *to try to create together*—that is if they are allowed to continue.

The American System cannot let them. For what would happen if such an attitude spread? Sooner or later workers would manage General Motors together, the distinction between foreman and lineman—a distinction imposed not by respect but by authority—would disappear, and then before you know it, there would be no academic department chairmen, no associate professors with tenure, holding literally life-power over instructors. No grades, no authority—except the authority willingly delegated because of respect earned not through knowledge and "objective" competitive accomplishments, but through the use of that knowledge in warmth and human consideration.

John Gerassi, "Trouble at San Francisco State: An Exchange," *The New York Review of Books* (April 11, 1968), p. 45. Reprinted with permission from *The New York Review of Books*.

That is why the liberal, ingrained, faculty-ized academician has no choice but to defend the System as it is. He is no different than the conservative ingrained àcademician. He belongs to the same class, the sub-power-class.

Thus did liberals and social democrats, who have always talked of individual human values, inevitably betray these values when their own authority and that of their class were at stake. German social democrats voted for rearmament. Léon Blum stopped arms shipment to Spain. Guy Mollet shouted (February 9, 1956): "France will fight in Algeria and she will stay." Two years later François Mitterand, now revered by American intellectuals as the greatest leader of France's non-communist Left, added: "Algeria is France. From Flandres to the Congo, only one law, only one nation, only one parliament. That is the constitution and that is our will. The only negotiation is war." A true inspiration to L.B.J.

And here at home, American liberal intellectuals objected (usually privately) to Joe McCarthy's tactics, not his goals. (Today they tell activists, as Henry Steele Commager points out in his eloquent *New Republic* article of February 24, 1968: "I may agree with you, but I disagree profoundly with the manner in which you say it.") They heralded Diem. They praised the Alliance for Progress. Until Johnson took away its liberal rhetoric, they considered the Peace Corps "one of the most hopeful creations of the twentieth century." They let America execute the Rosenbergs. They, the Liberals, the Harrimans, the Kennans, then the Schlesingers and Hilsmans, invented and propagated the whole Cold War. And now they will vote for Robert Kennedy—and make impotent speeches when the police of Oakland, Detroit, Carolina, and Newark unleash their systematic "final solution" to the black problem. Why? Because to do anything more than march, sit-in, and talk might challenge the whole "legitimacy"—and their own hard-earned authority.

And when their consciences cannot stand it anymore, when they can no longer claim that Vietnam, Detroit, Santo Domingo, Guatemala, the Congo, Brazil, etc., were inevitable but understandable mistakes of American "pluralism," then, like Camus, their hero, perhaps a great writer but surely not a great man, they will withdraw even more into their search for the pure cause, putting down the activists' mistakes (for all men who act *do* make mistakes) by concentrating their efforts on discrediting them—to placate their own frustrated consciences.

Finally, when the New Left will condemn them for supporting the whole System, with its legal machinery, its "free" press, its "right to dissent," and, yes its educational apparatus, all designed, as Carl Davidson said, "to sustain the dominant order, containing potential forces for change within its pre-established, ultimately castrating, confines," they will shout "romanticism" (heresy)—and resort to smears.

Academic liberals are the scholastics of the modern era, and like their medieval colleagues, the consequence of their actions in life is to keep God omnipotent. They only difference is that today God is Imperial America.

Ronald Berman
The Totalitarian Liberal State

(1968)

On the new left there are three interpretations of liberalism: corporate liberalism, conservative liberalism, and fascist liberalism. The further left one proceeds the more choric these interpretations appear. The last, with its attendant vocabulary, is of particular interest. Those who subscribe to it view liberalism as a conspiracy imposed by the old left and its former enemies. They are therefore hostile to the idea of political dialectic, and have little use for activists like Bayard Rustin and Michael Harrington who are willing to make their radicalism programmatic. It is customary for them to begin—and terminate—argument with the declaration that current American history is a recapitulation of the history of the Third Reich. At the same time they are themselves passionately attached to totalitarian democracy of the "direct" or "*de facto*" kind, especially as it operates in such iconic cases as that of Cuba. Perhaps a brief review of the concept of fascist liberalism will be useful, if only for the sense it may generate of new left historicism. The subject is of course qualified by the irony that liberalism, in its crusade against the ogres of the right, furnished the semantic of fascism to those who now attack it.

There is some orchestration to the use of the fascist liberalism concept. It is sometimes put in the form of a metaphor and sometimes in that of elaborated argument. Yet it is at all times an expressive attitude and belongs to the realm of feeling. Here are some indications of the shaping of a new political vocabulary;

> The most hated government in the world today is the government of our country. In the remotest corner of the earth, the initials U.S.A., which once stood for hope, have replaced the crooked cross of Nazi Germany as the symbol of tyranny and death.[1]

> Vietnam is the Guernica, the Rotterdam, and the Lidice of the 1960's. Johnson to most of the world recalls Hitler, invoking "national honor" and anti-Communism to rationalize mass murder.[2]

> It is doubtful if the non-Jewish people of Germany were as well informed

---

Ronald Berman, *America in the Sixties* (New York: Macmillan, 1968), pp. 110–13. Reprinted with permission of the publisher.

[1] From the constitution of the Progressive Labor Party. Quoted in *The New Radicals*, by Paul Jacobs and Saul Landau (New York, 1966), p. 188.

[2] "A Statement From Leaders of the Vietnam Day Committee," Norman Mailer, *et al., We Accuse* (Berkeley, 1965), p. 158. Used by permission of the publisher, Diablo Press.

> of the Nazi cruelties as the American people are of these obscenities in Vietnam. But like the Germans, whom we have been condemning for twenty-five years, we prefer not to dwell too long on such unpleasantnesses—nor to face up to the pattern they form when joined to American actions in Latin America and the Congo. The worst crimes of the Nazis took place under a crude fascist government and in the midst of the dislocations of a losing war. . . . Ours are being carried out against a background of domestic security.[3]

There is a certain casualness about accuracy, but surely the important thing is the symbolic function of language as opposed to its historical use. When Norman Mailer implies that "Adolf Hitler's motives" are ours[4] and when M. S. Arnoni likens "intellectuals from the State Department" to "Eichmann's cold efficiency"[5] a new political habit is evidently in gestation.

Those who practice this historicism are or would be intellectuals. They are students, professors, writers, and bureaucrats of activism. Since they are men of a certain knowledgeability the question of their intentions seems to frame itself in strategic terms. One tends to reject the merely polemical—some theoretical purpose seems to be served by current insistence that liberalism is a form of fascism. One rejects also purely unself-conscious belief, which is not likely given the intellectual equipment of, say, Staughton Lynd. An example may be helpful. In *Studies on the Left* Warren Susman of Rutgers wrote of liberalism as economic fascism—although, to be sure, it was ready to assume political character:

> Let us face what now exists: A corporate state in serious economic trouble. Politically, it is clearly and simply a dictatorship, generally benevolent although afraid it might lose its power if it becomes too benevolent (cf., civil rights)—but a dictatorship clearly and distinctly. . . . This is as complete a dictatorship as ever existed in history. Hitler had no more power than John F. Kennedy—in fact he had less. So John F. Kennedy takes the Sudetenland (Cuba)—what will he want next?[6]

Ernst Nolte, in his history of fascism, has written of opinions like these that they form a category outside of mere history of ideas.[7] They are metaphors and intuitions: "A lie which the intellect sees for what it is but which is at one with the deeper motivations of life." Nolte refers to the famous article

[3] "Liberalism in the Pursuit of Extremism," *Liberation* (February, 1965), 3. Used by permission.

[4] *We Accuse*, p. 10.

[5] *Ibid.*, p. 65.

[6] Warren Susman. "The Radicalism of Exposure," *Studies on the Left*, III (1962–1963), pp. 72–73. Used by permission.

[7] Ernst Nolte, *Three Faces of Fascism* (New York, 1966), pp. 57–58.

of Maurras on the suicide of Colonel Henry, an article which cannot be said so much to have resisted fact as to have transcended it. By the time Maurras had done, Henry was seen to have been executed by the Dreyfusards. This kind of lie is not strictly speaking propaganda: Like the legend of the stab in the back of the German army, it signifies what is really an intuitive agreement among those who subscribe to it. It is so resistant to demonstration as to have its improbability assert the limits of faith.

It is in fact an article of faith at present that the liberalism of the Sixties is a form of fascism. When the matter was brought to consciousness, as in the imbroglio over the statements of the Vietnam Day Committee, the result was to *satisfy* the true believers of the superiority of metaphor. The V.D.C. movement, like other elements of the left, has been engaged in the discovery of its own ideology. In the course of this it has hesitated between the alternatives of metaphorical and literal belief—in the case of fascist liberalism between the kind of habit of mind displayed by Susman and a more intelligent if less honorable equivocation. The latter may be seen in this defense of the V.D.C.: "Yes, one can compare Hitler and Johnson—or Stalin and Johnson. The comparisons are unfair—comparisons always are. We make them partly because language fails us." . . . [8]

Midge Decter
Anti-Americanism

(1968)

. . . partly fairly, partly not, all the issues that had roused a spirit of opposition—mainly war and poverty and equality for Negroes, but not only these—were fused into one; and in that fusion much of the opposition—enough of it to leave an ineradicable imprint on the entire culture of this decade—was funneled into a single piously articulated attitude of anti-Americanism.

It is this attitude, and not adherence to any particular school or schools of radical political ideology, that earns one admittance to that precinct of the intellectual community called the New Left. It is this attitude, and not the chronological accident of one's birth date, that entitles one to claim membership in that exclusive and intimidating generation Under Thirty. It is this attitude, and not a commitment to the free adventure of the mind, that now

[8] "Comment by David McReynolds," *Liberation* (November 1965), p. 29. Used by permission.

accredits one as a truly free spirit beyond the taint of having sold one's soul for pleasure or profit.

Thus we have, within twenty short years, come full circle. The word "evil" hangs heavy in the language of intellectual discussion just as it came to do in the years after World War II. Then it was applied to the Soviet Union, now to the United States, but the refusal to countenance political complexity that it bespeaks remains the same. Now, as then, dissent from the prevailing currents of fashionable opinion is adjudged to constitute moral failure and places the dissenter beyond the pale of argument. It is astonishing—and more than astonishing—appalling—to realize that the developments of two decades, in a rapidly changing world, have not deterred many of America's most intelligent, most serious, most talented people from their appointed round.

With all due respect, then, to the trials and frustrations of the 'sixties, the response of the intellectual community to those trials and frustrations has been both disastrous in itself and a depressing omen for the future.

At precisely a time when the values for which this community believes itself to stand—the enlargement of intellectual possibility and the devotion to standards of excellence—are being most threatened from the outside, it has responded only in kind, by threatening them further from the inside.

When a historian like Staughton Lynd proclaims Hanoi to be the mode for the achievement of freedom by small nations, he is perverting both the use of his intellectual discipline and his mandate as a thinking man.

When the organizers of a movement to withhold federal income tax in protest against the war draw up a statement which identifies the United States with Nazi Germany, they are, while pretending to appeal to the moral sense, perverting that sense.

When Susan Sontag, wishing to express her horror at the fruits of modern technology, launches an attack upon the Faustian spirit of the whole of Western Civilization ending with the observation that "the white race . . . [is] the cancer of humanity," she undermines the very ground on which she herself is entitled to speak or write.

When Andrew Kopkind, a highly talented young journalist, finds in the fascist tactics wielded by a group of Negroes at a conference of radicals a necessary—finally even a hopeful—experience, he reveals a carelessness toward the virtues of freedom that a writer may indulge in only at his peril.

When Robert Brustein, dean of the Yale drama school, indiscriminately and in a tone of deepest self-gratulation lends his sponsorship to any and all works of art whose intention is subversive, he is in fact subverting nothing so much as that artistic integrity to which he professes devotion.

The examples could multiply. They abound in the liberal weeklies, in the highly influential *New York Review of Books*, in some of the quarterlies, and are to be heard from the platform of every forum, symposium, teach-in, and round table on peace.

What is sorriest about this present climate is that it witnesses another betrayal for which yet another high price is sure to be exacted—in disillusionment and bitterness and violent reaction. An intellectual temper which has not the patience to sort out the illegitimate from the legitimate cannot long sustain itself. We learned this from the 'fifties; it will be this decade's lesson, too. The 'seventies will very likely bring a turning back—a turning back from the value of all social passion as well as from the futility of violence. And may we not expect that the disillusion of tomorrow will become the hard, cold, oppressive philosophy of day after tomorrow?

Theodore Draper
The Ghost of Social Fascism

(1969)

Why should anyone today want to bother with such a relic of the past as "the theory of social-fascism"? One reason is that it once bothered us so much; another is that it may be bothering us again.

Historically, the so-called theory of social-fascism and the practice based on it constituted one of the chief factors contributing to the victory of German fascism in January 1933. Yet this theory has not been given any careful study, and the existing material deals most inadequately with what is still a terribly painful and appalling subject. I hope in what follows to fill out some part of the story, if only in outline, and thus to make it more intelligible both to those old enough to have lived through that dark time and to those young enough to have heard of it without quite knowing what it was all about.

But I would be less than candid if I did not confess that I was moved to look back at social fascism because it is no longer of merely historical interest. In its original incarnation, it helped to bring about such a vast and shattering catastrophe that it once seemed such ideas could never again be revived on a large and dangerous scale. Yet this is exactly what has been happening. The term itself has not come back into general use, but the thinking behind it again has its devotees.

A new revolutionary generation has raised questions that are not altogether new. Who is the "main enemy"? Are "reformists" more dangerous than "reactionaries"? Is liberal democracy nothing but a "mask" for bourgeois

---

Theodore Draper, "The Ghost of Social Fascism," *Commentary* (February 1969), pp. 29, 38–40. Reprinted without footnotes, from *Commentary*, by permission of the publisher and the author.

dictatorship or even some form of totalitarianism? Is it necessary to provoke violent confrontations in order to unmask this type of liberalism? If a revolutionary minority strives to destroy a democratic, even a "bourgeois-democratic," order, is it necessarily going to be the main beneficiary—or even avoid the fate of the democratic order it has helped to pull down?

Answers to such questions made the difference between life and death for millions of people a few decades ago. In what follows, I have tried to restudy and reconstruct the earlier experience as a historical phenomenon that deserves to be better known for its own sake and that presents us with some large and difficult problems of special interest today.

Most students of Communist history associate the theory of social-fascism with Stalin and Stalinism. There is good reason for this, but the theory itself had deeper roots.

The first seeds of the theory of social-fascism were sown as far back as 1922–24—and not by Stalin. The term itself was reminiscent of other uncomplimentary terms—"social-patriots," "social-chauvinists," "social-imperialists," and "social traitors"—used by Lenin during the First World War to denote those Social-Democrats who wished to fight for the defense, rather than the defeat, of their own countries. These older terms provided a precedent for an analogous use of the word "social" in connection with the postwar phenomenon of "fascism." . . .

Unlikely as it may seem to those who did not live through it, the theory of social-fascism lived on after Hitler took power.

For this purpose, I have made up a little anthology that takes the subject into 1934. The various items require little comment, and I have merely grouped them under appropriate subject headings. All of these quotations have been taken from the most authoritative Communist sources and spokesmen for a period of over a year after January 1933 . . .

The Usefulness of Fascism

"The establishment of an *open fascist dictatorship, by destroying all the democratic illusions among the masses and liberating them from the influence of Social-Democracy, accelerates the rate of Germany's development* toward proletarian revolution."

"The bourgeoisie is compelled to abandon the democratic façade and to put the naked dictatorship of violence in the foreground. This development makes it easier for those carrying out a correct, united front, anti-fascist policy to overcome the illusions, which have been fostered by Social-Democracy for decades, with regard to the role of the State, and with regard to economic democracy and the policy of the 'lesser evil.'"

"Even fascist demagogy can now have a two-fold effect. It can, in spite of the fascists, help us to free the masses of the toilers from the illusions of parliamentary democracy and peaceful evolution . . ."

"The rapid fascisation of the capitalist governments naturally confronts us with added difficulties, but the bitterness of class antagonisms and the complete bankruptcy of the Second and Amsterdam [trade union] Internationals offer us *tremendous new possibilities*" (italics in original).

"The present wave of fascism is not a sign of the strength, *but a sign of the weakness and instability of the whole capitalist system* . . . Germany was and remains the weakest link in the chain of imperialist states . . . That is why the proletarian revolution is nearer in Germany than in any other country."

"Fascism does not only make the struggle of the working class more difficult; it also accelerates the processes of the maturing of the revolutionary crisis."

"The Social-Democracy proves once again that it is inseparably allied with capitalism, that it still remains the chief buttress of the bourgeoisie, even when the latter go over to measures of open violence, including repressive measures against Social-Democracy."

"If the fascists are persecuting Social-Democracy as a party, they are beating it as a faithful dog that has fallen sick. They are beating it because they know that it is incapable of resistance, that, when it is beaten, it will come forward all the quicker to the service of the bourgeois dictatorship, even in the open fascist form."

"The complete exclusion of the social-fascists from the state apparatus, and the brutal suppression of even Social-Democratic organizations and their press, does not in any way alter the fact that Social-Democracy is now, as before, the chief support of the capitalist dictatorship."

"History now offers a real possibility of liquidating the mass influence of the Social-Democratic party, which is responsible for the victory of fascism and which is the main support of the bourgeoisie, and the possibility of establishing the unity of the labor movement."

"Social-Democracy continues to play the role of the main social prop of the bourgeoisie also in the countries of open fascist dictatorship."

"In spite of all their disagreements, the fascists and social-fascists are, and remain, twins, as Comrade Stalin remarked . . . There are no disagreements between the fascists and the social-fascists as far as the necessity for the further fascisation of the bourgeois dictatorship is concerned. The Social-Democrats are in favor of fascisation, provided the parliamentary form is preserved."

"Even after the prohibition of its organization, Social-Democracy remains the main social prop of the bourgeoisie . . . The present situation [December 1933] in the German labor movement offers us the possibility of destroying the mass influence of the SPG [Social-Democratic party of Germany] and of reestablishing the unity of the labor movement on a revolutionary basis."

"Every revolutionary must know that the path toward the annihilation of fascism, the path to the proletarian revolution and to its victory can only be the path that leads via the organizational and ideological abolition of the influence of Social-Democracy."

"It is, therefore, necessary above all *to make a clear stand in regard to Social-Democracy, and first and foremost in regard to 'Left' Social-Democracy, this most dangerous foe of Communism* (italics in original)."

"We must destroy the Social-Democratic influence on the working masses and we must not tolerate any vacillations in our ranks in the struggle against the Social-Democracy as the chief social support of the bourgeoisie."

I hope the reader has not skipped too quickly over this collection of seemingly quaint, musty quotations. Not so long ago, men paid for them with their lives, Communists and Social-Democrats alike. In March 1933 the "mask" was finally torn from the Weimar constitution. A newly elected Reichstag voted, 441 to 94, to give Hitler dictatorial powers. All 94 negative votes were cast by Social-Democrats (the remaining 27 Social-Democratic deputies and all 81 Communists could not vote, being already in exile, in hiding, or under arrest). The Communist party was officially outlawed on March 31; the trade unions were smashed in May; the Social-Democratic party was banned on June 22. Thereafter, Hitler made no distinction between Communists and Social-Democrats: he took their lives, cast them into concentration camps or, if they were lucky, drove them into exile, impartially.

Yet the theory of social-fascism survived many more months. It was finally discarded in 1934 in order to make way for the Popular Front line adopted the following year. At the Seventh World Congress in July-August 1935, speakers admitted that it had been a mistake to hold the view that the Müller government had worked for fascisation and that the Brüning government was already a "government of fascist dictatorship," to have underrated the Nazi movement on the assumption that it could not take power, to have concentrated the main fire against Social-Democracy instead of the growing menace of fascism. These *mea culpas* quietly interred the theory of social-fascism which then became so embarrassing that the Communist movement has gone to extraordinary lengths to expunge it from the historical record. There is almost nothing in its entire history that the Communist movement is more ashamed of and so unwilling to defend.

But this was no ordinary aberration, and it demands far more study and reflection than it has received. Hitler's accession to power in January 1933 was the decisive dividing line, the crucial turning point, of the inter-war years. It led directly to World War II, from which our most oppressive and intractable international problems still derive. The responsibility for Hitler's victory was undoubtedly widespread. I know of no party, no economic interest, no secular or religious group, and no foreign country, including our own, which can escape some measure of culpability. But of all of them, the theory and practice of social-fascism was the most devastating, the most unnecessary, and the most self-destructive.

The problem it raises is: What are the limits, if any, of criticism and opposition in a democratic or, if you will, a "bourgeois-democratic" society—even from a revolutionary standpoint?

It was one thing to criticize the Social-Democrats for banning the 1929 May Day street demonstrations or the Brüning regime for governing so highhandedly. There was a sense, I believe, in which it could be reasonably argued that such policies undermined or endangered the Republic and made it more vulnerable to Hitlerism. But it was quite another thing to charge that these policies proved the Social-Democrats and the Brüning regime were themselves "introducing fascism" or "masked" forms of fascism. This type of criticism could only aim at bringing the democratic house down on all alike, including its revolutionary critics.

Such critics could not be interested in whether wrong policies undermined or endangered the Republic; they were themselves doing all in their power to undermine and endanger the Republic. Indeed, they assumed that the Republic was a greater enemy than anything that could follow it. They were chiefly concerned with drawing a line of blood between themselves and all others to the "right" of them, including the most "left-wing" of the Social-Democrats. This line made sense only on the assumption that the Communists were going to seize power themselves. In this case they knew that they were going to suppress Social Democrats as well as Nazis, as the Russian Bolsheviks had suppressed Social-Democrats as well as Tsarists. The theory of social-fascism was a rationalization of Communist dictatorship in the guise of rationalizing everyone else into a variety of fascism.

The Communists gained ground in Germany from 1928 to 1932. But they never came close to winning a majority of the German working class, let alone a majority of the German people. In order to make their bid for power, they opened a chasm between themselves and the rest of the German working class and most of the German people, which, once they realized that their bid had failed, they could not close. They tried vainly in the last half of 1932 to tinker with the practical implications of the theory of social-fascism, but it was always too little and too late. Then they paid as heavily as or even more heavily than those whom they had once defiled as "social-fascists" and whose cooperation they were ultimately forced to seek.

By 1935, the German Communist leader, Wilhelm Pieck, had to avow that "we Communists fight with might and main for every scrap of democratic liberty," and the new head of the Communist International, Georgi Dimitrov, gave assurances that "in the capitalist countries we defend and shall continue to defend every inch of bourgeois-democratic liberties which are being attacked by fascism and bourgeois reaction, because the interests of the class struggle of the proletariat so dictate." Whatever these words were worth for the future, they were a pitiless commentary on the Communist past. An official obituary was never written for the theory of social-fascism; it was buried silently, furtively, and shamefully, as if its very name would dishonor those who might utter it.

This was how the original theory of social-fascism came to an end. It amounts to a case history of an extraordinary political aberration. And this is precisely what is so important and fascinating about it. Other movements, other revolutionary movements, have shown an amazing devotion to fanciful and self-defeating ideas. But these traits have usually marked relatively small movements which harmed themselves more than anyone else. There is hardly a comparable example in this century of a great movement—and the Communist movement may well be the greatest historical phenomenon specifically of the 20th century—in the grip of a political pathology capable of causing such havoc to itself and to so many others on such a monstrous scale. So extreme a divorce between ideology and reality deserves far more attention than it has received. It may be especially commended to the attention of those who are flirting with a new anti-liberal version of the theory of social-fascism.

Irving Howe
Intellectuals

(1968)

There is a rising younger generation of intellectuals: ambitious, self-assured, at ease with prosperity while conspicuously alienated, unmarred by the traumas of the totalitarian age, bored with memories of defeat, and attracted to the idea of power. This generation matters, thus far, not so much for its leading figures and their meager accomplishments, but for the political-cultural style—what I shall call the new sensibility—it thrusts into absolute opposition both to the New York writers and to other groups. It claims not to seek penetration into, or accommodation with, our cultural and academic institutions; it fancies the prospect of a harsh generational fight; and given the premise with which it begins—that everything touched by older men reeks of betrayal—its claims and fancies have a sort of propriety. It proposes a revolution, I would call it a counterrevolution, in sensibility. Though linked to New Left politics, it goes beyond any politics, making itself felt, like a spreading blot of anti-intellectualism, in every area of intellectual life. Not yet fully cohered, this new cultural group cannot yet be fully defined, nor is it possible fully to describe its projected sensibility, since it declares itself through a refusal of both coherence and definition.

Irving Howe, "The New York Intellectuals," *Commentary* (October 1968), pp. 44–46. Reprinted from *Commentary*, by permission of the publisher and the author.

There is no need to discuss once more the strengths and weaknesses of the New Left, its moral energies and intellectual muddles. Nor need we be concerned with the tactical issues separating New Left politics from that of older left-wing intellectuals. Were nothing else at stake than, say, "coalition politics," the differences would be both temporary and tolerable. But in reality a deeper divergence of outlook has begun to show itself. The new intellectual style, insofar as it approximates a politics, mixes sentiments of anarchism with apologies for authoritarianism; bubbling hopes for "participatory democracy" with manipulative elitism; unqualified populist majoritarianism with the reign of the cadres.

A confrontation of intellectual outlooks is unavoidable. And a central issue is certain to be the problem of liberalism, not liberalism as one or another version of current politics, nor even as a theory of power, but liberalism as a cast of mind, a structure of norms by means of which to humanize public life. For those of us who have lived through the age of totalitarianism and experienced the debacle of socialism, this conflict over liberal values is extremely painful. We have paid heavily for the lesson that democracy, even "bourgeois democracy," is a precious human achievement, one that, far from being simply a mode of mass manipulation, has been wrested through decades of struggle by the labor, socialist, and liberal movements. To protect the values of liberal democracy, often against those who call themselves liberals, is an elementary task for the intellectuals as a social group.

Yet what I have just been saying, axiomatic as it may seem, has in the last few years aroused opposition, skepticism, open contempt among professors, students, and intellectuals. On the very crudest, though by no means unpopular, level, we find a vulgarization of an already vulgar Marxism. The notion that we live in a society that can be described as "liberal fascism" (a theoretic contribution from certain SDS leaders) isn't one that serious people can take seriously; but the fact that it is circulated in the academic community signifies a counterrevolution of the mind: a refusal of nuance and observation, a willed return to the kind of political primitivism which used to declare the distinctions of bourgeois rule—democratic, authoritarian, totalitarian—as slight in importance.

For the talk about "liberal fascism" men like Norman Mailer must bear a heavy responsibility, insofar as they have recklessly employed the term "totalitarian" as a descriptive for present day American society. Having lived through the ghastliness of the Stalinist theory of "social fascism" (the granddaddy of "liberal fascism") I cannot suppose any literate person really accepts this kind of nonsense, yet I know that people can find it politically expedient to pretend that they do. It is, in Ernest Nolte's phrase, "a lie which the intellect sees for what it is but which is [felt to be] at one with the deeper motivations of life."

There are sophisticated equivalents. One of these points to the failings and crises of democracy, concluding that the content of decision has been increasingly separated from the forms of decision-making. Another emphasizes the manipulation of the masses by communication media and declares them brainwashed victims incapable of rational choice and acquiescing in their own subjugation. A third decries the bureaucratic entanglements of the political process and favors some version, usually more sentiment than scheme, for direct plebiscitory rule. With varying intelligence, all point to acknowledged problems of democratic society; and there could be no urgent objection were these criticisms not linked with the premise that the troubles of democracy can be overcome by undercutting or bypassing representative institutions. Thus, it is quite true that the masses are manipulated, but to make that the crux of a political analysis is to lead into the notion that elections are mere "formalities" and majorities mere tokens of the inauthentic; what is needed, instead, is Marcuse's "educational dictatorship" (in which, I hope, at least some of the New York intellectuals would require the most prolonged reeducation). And in a similar vein, all proposals for obligatory or pressured "participation," apart from violating the democratic right not to participate, have a way of discounting those representative institutions and limitations upon power which can alone provide a degree of safeguard for liberal norms.

Perhaps the most sophisticated and currently popular of anti-democratic notions is that advanced by Herbert Marcuse: his contempt for tolerance on the ground that it is a veil for subjection, a rationale for maintaining the status quo, and his consequent readiness to suppress "regressive" elements of the population lest they impede social "liberation." About these theories, which succeed in salvaging the worst of Leninism, Henry David Aiken has neatly remarked: "Whether garden-variety liberties can survive the ministrations of such 'liberating tolerance' is not a question that greatly interests Marcuse." Indeed not.

Such theories are no mere academic indulgence or sectarian irrelevance; they have been put to significant use on the American campus as rationalizations for schemes to break up meetings of political opponents and as the justification for imaginary *coups d'état* by tiny minorities of enraged intellectuals. How depressing that "men of the Left," themselves so often victims of repression, should attack the values of tolerance and freedom.

Selected Additional Reading

Listed below are some books covering the modern radical movement. The reader should note, however, that not all the information he is likely to need can be found in books alone. There are two other kinds of publication covering this subject. One of these consists of the established journals of the left: *Commentary*, *Dissent*, *Liberation*, *Nation*, *New Politics*, *New Republic*, *The New*

York Review of Books, Partisan Review. The other consists of more ephemeral publications, appearing from time to time and place to place. Some of these are limited to college campuses; others will serve the radical *arrondissements* of our larger cities. Some representative titles are *Alternatives, The Berkeley Barb, Free Press* (a title shared by underground newspapers in Los Angeles, New York, San Francisco, San Diego and other cities), *Rat, Ramparts, Realist, Studies on the Left.*

Aaron, Daniel. *Writers on the Left.* Harcourt Brace (New York, 1961).

Altbach, Philip. *Student Politics and Higher Education in the United States: A Select Bibliography.* Harvard U. Center for Int. Affairs (Cambridge, 1967).

Aron, Raymond. *The Opium of the Intellectuals.* Norton (New York, 1962).

The Atlantic, editors of. *The Troubled Campus.* Little Brown (Boston, 1966).

Berger, Peter L. and Richard J. Neuhaus. *Movement and Revolution.* Doubleday (Garden City. N.Y. 1970).

Chomsky, Noam. "Resistance," *New York Review of Books* (December 7, 1967).

Coles, Robert. *Children of Crisis.* Little Brown (Boston, 1967).

Draper, Hal. *Berkeley: The New Student Revolt.* Grove (New York, 1965).

Finn, James. *Protest: Pacifism and Politics.* Random House (New York, 1968).

Hoffman, Abbie. *Revolution for the Hell of It.* Dial (New York, 1968).

Howe, Irving. *The Radical Papers.* Doubleday (New York, 1966).

Keniston, Kenneth. *The Uncommitted.* Harcourt Brace (New York, 1965).

Kunen, James Simon. *The Strawberry Statement.* Random House (New York, 1969).

Lasch, Christopher. *The New Radicalism in America.* Knopf (New York, 1965).

Long, Priscilla, ed. *The New Left.* Porter Sargent (Boston, 1969).

Luce, Phillip Abbott. *The New Left.* McKay (New York, 1966).

Marcuse, Herbert. *A Critique of Pure Tolerance.* Beacon (Boston, 1966).

Marcuse, Herbert, *An Essay on Liberation.* Beacon (Boston, 1969).

Martin, David. *Pacifism.* Schocken (New York, 1966).

Partisan Review, editors of. "The New Radicalism," (Winter 1965–Winter 1966).

Quinn, Edward and Paul Dolan. *The Sense of the 60's.* Free Press (New York, 1968).

Rader, Dotson. *I Ain't Marchin' Anymore.* Paperback Library (New York, 1969).

Roszak, Theodore. *The Making of a Counter Culture.* Doubleday (Garden City, N.Y., 1969).

Rubin, Jerry. *Do It!.* Simon and Schuster (New York, 1970).

Vietnam Day Committee. *We Accuse.* Diablo (Berkeley, 1965).

Walker, Daniel. *Rights in Conflict.* Dutton (New York, 1969).

ABCDE798765432